The Waite Group's C Programming
Using Turbo C®++

Second Edition

The Waite Group's

PROGRAMMING USING TURBO C®++

SECOND EDITION

Robert Lafore

SAMS
PUBLISHING

A Division of Prentice Hall Computer Publishing
201 West 103rd Street, Indianapolis, IN 46290

This book is dedicated to Mitch Waite.

From The Waite Group, Inc.

Editorial Director: *Scott Calamar*
Managing Editor: *John Crudo*
Technical Editors: *Harry Henderson, Joel Powell*

From Sams Publishing

Publisher: *Richard K. Swadley*
Acquisitions Manager: *Jordan Gold*
Development Editor: *Scott Palmer*
Editors: *Don MacLaren and Andy Saff*
Cover Designer: *Kathy Hanley*
Production: *Ayrika Bryant, Rich Evers, Mitzi Foster Gianakos, Dennis Clay Hager, Stephanie McComb, Angela M. Pozdol, Ryan Rader, and Dennis Wesner*
Indexers: *John Sleeva and Suzanne Snyder*

Overview

Contents

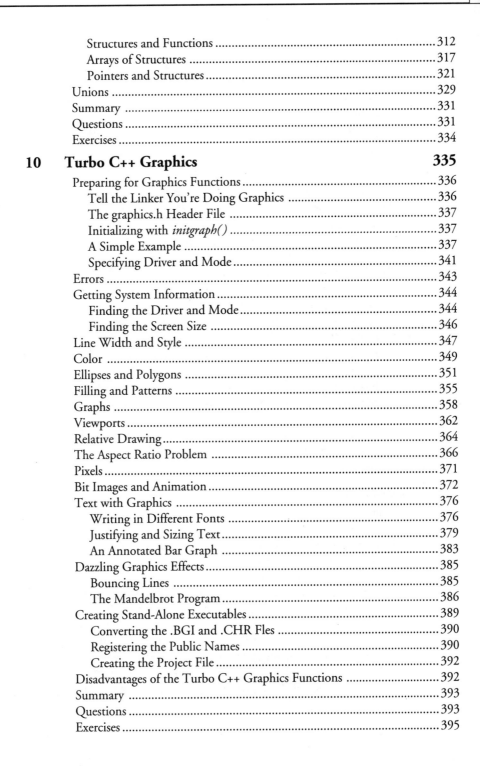

Foreword to the First Edition

by Ray Duncan

In just a decade, C has made the transition from an obscure Bell Laboratories house language to the programming language of choice for professionals. C has been used successfully for every type of programming problem imaginable—from operating systems to spreadsheets to expert systems—and efficient compilers are available for machines ranging in power from the Apple to the Cray. On the new wave of the windowing, graphics-intensive 68000-based personal computers such as the Macintosh, Amiga, and Atari, C is the *de facto* standard for serious developers.

Why has C met with such success when other languages, born in the same time-frame and designed with similar objectives, have gained only limited acceptance or have faded from view altogether? C's intimate association with UNIX—and the penetration into academia that was made possible by Bell Laboratory's broadminded licensing plans for universities—must be partly responsible, but the largest measure of C's success seems to be based on purely practical considerations: the portability of the compiler; the standard library concept; a powerful and varied repertoire of operators; a spare, elegant syntax; ready access to the hardware when needed; and the ease with which applications can be optimized by hand-coding isolated procedures.

The increasing dominance of C for both systems and applications programming has created a tremendous market for C books. I must confess that I am a compulsive buyer of computer books of every sort: an addiction based on curiosity, on a desire to learn from the approaches and styles of other authors, and on a continual search for excellent new books to recommend to readers of my column in *Dr. Dobb's Journal.* While indulging this pleasant but somewhat expensive habit over the last few years, I have built up quite a collection of C tutorials and reference works, but I have found nearly all of the introductory C books to be unsatisfying. The authors have difficulty discussing C without blurring the issues with UNIX-specific details, or they succumb to a fascination with clever C tricks, or they simply progress so quickly from elementary concepts to lengthy, complex example programs that they leave the reader behind.

When Mitchell Waite asked me if I would like to review Robert Lafore's manuscript for this book, I was surprised but gratified. I have long considered Robert's *Assembly*

Language Primer for the IBM PC and XT (New American Library, 1985) to set the standard of quality in its category, and I hoped that his C primer would be equally well organized, lucid, and complete. I certainly was not disappointed! I believe the book you are holding in your hands is the most accessible book on C that has yet been published. The material is presented in Robert's usual clear, forthright style, and the pace is steady but not intimidating. Best of all, the example programs are short but interesting, clearly demonstrate the concepts under discussion, and they are relevant to everyday programming problems on the IBM PC—you don't need to speak UNIX or buy your own VAX to reap their benefits.

Ray Duncan is a software developer and columnist for *Dr. Dobb's Journal* and the author of many computer books.

About the Author

Robert Lafore has been involved in the computer industry since 1965, when he learned assembly language on the DEC PDP-5, whose 4K of main memory was considered luxurious. He holds degrees in mathematics and electrical engineering; founded Interactive Fiction, a computer game company; and has served as managing editor of The Waite Group. Mr. Lafore is author of the best-selling *Assembly Language Primer for the IBM PC and XT, Microsoft C Programming for the PC, Object-Oriented Programming in Turbo C++,* and *Lafore's Window's Programming Made Easy,* among other titles. Mr. Lafore has also been a petroleum engineer in Southeast Asia, a systems analyst at the Lawrence Berkeley Laboratory, and has sailed his own boat to the South Pacific.

Preface

The first edition of this book was well received by readers, selling over 200,000 copies since its debut in 1987. Revisions over the years have kept it more or less up to date, (incorporating, for example, the transition from Kernighan and Ritchie C to ANSI C). However, despite these efforts, the book was beginning to show its age, and the author and publisher recognized that it was time for a complete housecleaning. Thus, the appearance of this Second Edition. Here are some highlights:

- All the example programs have been rewritten to compile with no errors or warnings with the latest version of the Turbo C++ compiler.

- A new chapter includes a working software application: an address-book database program that allows the user to store and retrieve names, addresses, and phone numbers. This program uses a modern Graphic User Interface (GUI).

- The second half of the book has been reorganized to give a more progressive presentation from general-to-specific and from easy-to-more-advanced material.

- Hardware-oriented sections have been collected from various places and combined into Chapter 15, "Hardware-Oriented C."

- A new chapter on the important subject of memory management has been created by combining considerable new material with existing text.

Of course, we've also endeavored to retain throughout the easy-to-read style that made the first edition so popular.

Acknowledgments for the Second Edition

My thanks to John Crudo and Scott Calamar of the Waite Group for their support and patience in the preparation of this new edition, to Harry Henderson for his usual eagle-eyed editing job, and to Joel Powell for his expertise in the technical edit.

Acknowledgments for the First Edition

I'd like to thank Mitchell Waite of The Waite Group for his dedicated and painstaking editing (complete with humorous asides and subliminal suggestions) and Harry Chesley, co-author of *Supercharging C* (Addison-Wesley), for his expert advice.

I am also indebted to the following individuals at Sams: Jim Hill for having the faith to buy this book idea, Damon Davis for publishing it, Jim Rounds for nursing it into the system, and Wendy Ford and Don Herrington for overseeing its production.

I would also like to thank Doug Adams for his technical edit, Bruce Webster of Byte magazine, Ray Duncan, and Herbert Schildt for reviewing the final manuscript, Harry Henderson for checking the final manuscript, and Don MacLaren of BooksCraft for his painstaking and skilled copy editing. In addition, thanks to Allen Holub for his editing of the revised edition.

Introduction

This book has two interconnected goals: to teach the C programming language and to show how C can be used to write applications for PC computers. That is, we not only explain C, but show how it's used in a real-world programming environment.

Borland's Turbo C++ for DOS (or the similar Borland C++) compiler provides the best platform yet devised for learning C. Its Integrated Development Environment (IDE) combines all the features needed to develop a C program—editor, compiler, linker, debugger, and help system—into a single, easy-to-use screen display. This enables you to develop programs far more simply and conveniently than you can using the traditional command-line compiler system. Turbo C++ is also very fast and surprisingly inexpensive.

Incidentally, don't be confused by the product name. Borland calls it *Turbo C++,* but it is really an extension of the old Turbo C, with C++ capabilities added. You can use this product (or Borland C++) for either C or C++ programming. In this book we use it for C. You don't need to know anything about C++.

With this book and Turbo C++ (or Borland C++), you'll be taking a fast and efficient path to mastery of the C language and the ability to write applications for PC computers.

What's Different About This Book?

Many introductory books on C present the language in a theoretical context, ignoring the machine the language is running on. This book takes a different approach: it teaches C in the context of PC (MS-DOS based) computers. There are several advantages to this approach.

First, focusing on a specific computer platform makes learning the language easier and more interesting. For example, graphics programming isn't standardized across platforms, so a generic C text can't use graphics. Programming examples must therefore concentrate on simple text-based interaction. In the PC world, on the other hand, we can make use of such features as graphics characters, program control of the cursor, and bit-mapped color graphics—capabilities that can enliven program examples and demonstrations.

Also, as we move to more complex aspects of the language, we can explain Turbo C++ constructs that might otherwise seem theoretical and mysterious—such as pointers and unions—by relating them to actual applications on the IBM hardware.

Finally, if your goal is to write programs specifically for PC computers, learning C in the PC environment—with examples that address specific aspects of PC hardware—will give you a head start in creating your own applications.

Learn by Doing

This book uses a hands-on approach. We believe that trying things out yourself is one of the best ways to learn, so examples are presented in the form of complete working programs, which can be typed and executed (or loaded from the accompanying disk). In general, we show what the output from the examples looks like, so you can be sure your program is functioning correctly. Very short examples are used at the beginning of the book, working toward longer and more sophisticated programs toward the end.

Illustrations and Exercises

We have also tried to make this a very visual book. Many programming concepts are best explained with pictures, so wherever possible we use figures to support the text.

Each chapter ends with a set of questions to test your general understanding of the material covered and programming exercises to ensure that you understand how to put the concepts to work. Answers to both questions and exercises are provided in the back of the book.

Why Use C?

The C programming language has become the overwhelming choice of serious program-mers. Why? C is unique among programming languages in that it provides the conve-nience of a higher level language such as BASIC or Pascal, but at the same time allows much closer control of a computer's hardware and peripherals, as assembly language does. Most operations performed on the PC in assembly language can be accomplished—usually far more conveniently—in C. This is probably the principal reason for C's popularity on the PC.

C has other advantages, however. The better C compilers can now generate amazingly fast code. This code is so efficient that it's often difficult to produce significant speed increases by rewriting it in assembly language. C is also a well structured language: its syntax makes it easy to write programs that are modular and therefore easy to understand and maintain. The C language includes many features that are specifically designed to help create large or complex programs. Finally, C is portable: it is easier to convert a C program to run on a different machine than it is to convert programs written in most other languages.

C and C++

The C++ language is a superset of C: it adds object-oriented capabilities to the C language. C++ is most useful for large programming projects involving many programmers and many thousands of lines of code. Smaller programs are often easier to write in C. Also, C++ requires many new and difficult programming concepts. Unless you have a specific need for an object-oriented language, we suggest you stick with C, as this book does.

What You Should Know Before You Read This Book

No prior programming experience is necessary for you to use this book. C probably isn't quite as easy to learn as BASIC, but there's no reason a student can't plunge directly into C as a first programming language. Of course if you're already familiar with BASIC, Pascal, or some other language, that won't hurt.

You should be familiar with the MS-DOS operating system. You should be able to list directories and create, execute, copy, and erase files. You should also be familiar with tree-structured directories and how to move about in them.

What Equipment You Need to Use This Book

You can use this book with a variety of different hardware and software configurations. Here's what you'll need.

Hardware

You'll need a computer that runs the MS-DOS operating system. It should have at least an 80286 processor, but the more advanced the processor, the faster your programs will compile. You also need a hard (fixed) disk drive and a floppy drive. You must have a full 640K of conventional memory, plus at least 1MB of extended memory. (Practically, this means your computer must have 2MB or more of RAM.)

You can use a character-only monochrome display for most of the book; the exceptions being Chapter 10, "Turbo C++ Graphics," and part of Chapter 15, "Hardware-Oriented C," which deal with graphics. However, you'll be happier with a VGA color system. The graphics examples are written for VGA (and the Turbo C IDE looks better in color anyway).

A mouse is convenient (and fun) for operating Turbo C's IDE, which features pull-down menus, resizable windows, and other features of a typical graphics user interface. However, you can do everything from the keyboard if you don't have a mouse.

Although it isn't absolutely essential, you'll probably want a printer to generate program listings and record program output.

Software

You should use the MS-DOS operating system with a version number of 3.31 or greater. Of course, later versions are preferable.

If you're using Windows, you'll be interested to know that Turbo C++ works in Windows' MS-DOS compatibility box. All the example programs in this book also run in the DOS box.

You'll need one of two Borland compilers. The most usual choice is called *Turbo C++ for DOS*. It's widely available at computer stores and can also be ordered directly from Borland International, P.O Box 660001, Scotts Valley, CA 95067. (You can also use the older *Turbo C* product, Version 2.0 or greater.)

Another Borland product, Borland C++, is very similar to Turbo C++. Borland C++ may be sold separately, or bundled with Borland C++ and Application Frameworks, which contains a complete Windows development system. In either case, Borland C++ is considerably more expensive than Turbo C++, but if you already own it, you'll find it will work in almost exactly the same way as Turbo C++. We'll note the minor exceptions as we go along.

Turbo C++ (or Borland C++) is all you need to develop anything from a one-line program to a serious application with thousands of lines of code. There is no longer any necessity for a separate program editor or a separate debugger.

ANSI-Standard C

C was created by Dennis Ritchie at Bell Laboratories in the early 1970s. (C's predecessor was a language called *B*). In 1978, Brian Kernighan and Dennis Ritchie published a book, *The C Programming Language,* which for many years served as an effective definition of C.

In 1989, a new version of the language emerged from the American National Standards Institute: ANSI-standard C. This version includes many features (such as type `void` and function prototyping) that weren't present in the "traditional" Kernighan and Richie C. The Turbo C++ compiler, and this book, conform to the new ANSI-standard C, except where Turbo C++ provides useful additions to the standard.

Typographical Conventions

In the text sections of this book (as opposed to program listings), all C-language keywords—such as `if`, `while`, and `switch`—are shown in a special monospace font to better distinguish them from the ordinary English-language usage of these words. Likewise, all C functions, including user-written functions and library functions such as `printf()` and `gets()`, are in mono, as are variable names.

When string constants such as `"Good morning"` and `"Fatal error"` are used in the text, they're set off by double quotes, just as they're in the C language itself. Character constants are set off by single quotes, again following the convention of the C language: `'a'` and `'b'` are characters.

Operators, which often consist of a single character such as (+) and (/), are often surrounded by parentheses for clarity. Keyboard keys, such as Ctrl key, Del key, and Z key, are capitalized as they are on the keyboard and followed by the word *key*.

Program names aren't in bold, but include their file extensions, such as .c in myprog.c and .obj in myprog.obj.

Good Luck, Lieutenant

This book covers a lot of ground—from simple one-line programs to complex graphics and database applications. Our intention is to make the exploration of this territory as easy and as interesting as possible, starting slowly and working up gradually to more challenging concepts. We hope we've succeeded and that you have as much fun reading this book as we had writing it.

The Turbo C++ Development System

- Setting up the Turbo C++ System
- Program creation in the IDE
- Writing a simple C program
- The structure of C programs
- The `printf()` function

This chapter launches you on your C programming career. It has two goals. First, we discuss how to set up the Turbo C++ development system, the directories and files used by the system, and how you use Turbo C++ to create programs. Second, we present your first C program. From this program you'll learn about the organization of C programs in general and about the printf() function in particular.

Note that almost every reference in the text to Turbo C++ applies equally well to Borland C++. We'll point out the few places where Borland C++ behaves differently.

Setting Up the Turbo C++ Development System

In this section, we briefly introduce the components of the Turbo C++ development system and make some suggestions for setting it up so that you can compile the example programs in this book.

The Integrated Development System (IDE)

Turbo C++ features an integrated development environment (IDE). (It's also referred to as the Programmer's Platform.) The IDE is a screen display with windows and pull-down menus. The program listing, its output, error messages, and other information are displayed in separate windows. You use menu selections (or key combinations) to invoke all the operations necessary to develop your program, including editing, compiling, linking, and program execution. You can even debug your program within the IDE. An on-line help facility is available through menu selections. You can choose options (such as compiler optimization and memory model) from menus; gone are the days of trying to remember obscure command-line switches.

All this operates very smoothly and rapidly. It's also surprisingly easy to learn. In fact, the IDE provides an almost ideal environment for learning C; it's the system used in this book.

The Install Program

All the components of the Turbo C++ development system are loaded into one directory, called TC, on your hard disk. (If you're using Borland C++, they're placed in BORLANDC.) This directory is divided into several subdirectories, some of which contain a great many files. Fortunately, the creation of this directory structure and the loading of the files from the distribution disks are completely automated by an install program.

Before you start to set up your system, you should back up the distribution diskettes with the DISKCOPY utility. Use the backups to load the system.

Setting up the system is easy. Put disk 1 into the A: drive (or whatever drive the disks fit) and enter

```
C>a:install
```

You'll be asked to approve various default values already supplied by the INSTALL program. These cover such things as the names of the directories where the system will be installed and what memory models you want to use. The screens are largely self-explanatory, and a status line at the bottom of the screen tells you what keys to press. If you accept the default values, you won't have much thinking to do. However, you may want to consider some options.

Directories

Unless you tell the INSTALL program otherwise, it puts all the subdirectories and files in a directory called TC (or BORLANDC). If you don't like this name, or already have a directory called TC, you must type new pathnames in the appropriate places. Don't change the names of the subdirectories, like BIN, INCLUDE, LIB, and so on.

Optional Components

In Turbo C++, you'll be allowed to select which of various components you want to install. These are

IDE	Integrated development environment
CMD	Command-line compiler
LIB	Normal C library
CLASS	C++ class library
BGI	Borland graphics interface
HELP	Help files
EXMPL	Example programs

You'll need the IDE, LIB, BGI, and HELP options. You don't need CMD, the command-line compiler, which is used only in special situations. Because we're working in the C language and not C++, you don't need CLASS, the C++ class library. For this book, you don't need the example programs, although you might want to look at them anyway. You can save disk space by not installing the options you don't need.

In Borland C++, a great many more options are available. We'll assume, if you've bought this more expensive product, that you need capabilities in addition to the DOS compiler. For this book, however, the minimum you must select from the install screen are IDE and BGI. The other elements you need are installed automatically.

Memory Models

There are five memory models: Small, Medium, Compact, Large, and Huge. In the Small model, your program can have up to 64K of code and 64K of data storage. In the Medium model, the program code can exceed this 64K limit, but the data is still restricted to 64K. Other models offer different arrangements of memory space.

Chapter 14, "Application Example," explores memory models more thoroughly. At this point, what you need to know is that each memory model requires a separate library file, and each library file takes up space on your hard disk. All the programs in this book can be compiled with the Small memory model. If you want to save disk space, you should tell INSTALL that you don't need the other memory models. Change the default Yes answers to No for all but the Small options (it's actually called *Small/Tiny*, because it includes the special-purpose Tiny memory model).

When you've set the options to your satisfaction, select the Start Installation option. INSTALL will create the necessary directories and unpack and install the appropriate files. You'll be asked periodically to place the various disks in the source drive.

The AUTOEXEC.BAT and CONFIG.SYS Files

After all the files have been loaded, you'll need to modify the PATH command in your AUTOEXEC.BAT file so that Turbo C++'s executable files are available from any directory. These files are in the \TC\BIN directory, so the command should look something like this:

```
PATH=C:\TC\BIN
```

For Borland C++, this would be

```
PATH=C:\BORLANDC\BIN
```

The CONFIG.SYS file should be modified to include the line FILES=20. Don't forget to reboot after changing the CONFIG.SYS file.

Files Used in C Program Development

Now that you've installed your system, you may be eager to start programming. First, however, let's examine the results of the installation process. If you're used to a simple language such as Pascal or BASIC, you may be surprised by the sheer number of files that came with the Turbo C++ system. At this point, it's difficult to understand exactly what all these files do, but you might like to have a rough idea before plunging into your first C program.

Executable Files

Executable files are stored in the subdirectory BIN. The most important executable is TC.EXE (or BC.EXE if you're using Borland C++). Executing this program places the IDE on your screen and provides all the development tools you need. However, there are many other files.

Various files that begin with the letters DPMI are used by Turbo C++ for memory management. Ordinarily, you don't need to worry about them.

The BIN directory also contains utility programs you can use in special situations. Here are some of them:

GREP	Searches for strings in groups of files
TOUCH	Updates file date and time
TLIB	Library file manager
UNZIP	Unpacks .ZIP (compressed) files
THELP	Popup utility to access help file

None of these is essential for program development. The IDE invoked by the TC.EXE (or BC.EXE) file does everything you need.

Library and Runtime Files

Various files are combined with your program during linking. These files contain routines for a wide variety of purposes. There are library files, runtime object files, and math library files. They are all stored in the LIB directory.

Library Files

Library files are groups of precompiled routines for performing specific tasks. For example, if a programmer uses a function such as `printf()` (which is described later in this chapter) to display text on the screen, the code to create the display is contained in a library file. A library file has a unique characteristic: only those parts of it that are necessary will be linked to a program, not the whole file. If this weren't true, every program would be enormous.

C is especially rich in the number and variety of its library routines. Many processes which in other languages are built into the definition of the language (such as input/ output statements) are handled in C by library functions.

As was mentioned earlier, each memory model has one library file. The files are called cs.lib, cc.lib, cl.lib, cm.lib, and ch.lib. The cs.lib file is used with the Small and Tiny models, cc.lib is used with the Compact model, cl.lib is used with the Large model, and so on. The INSTALL program installs one library file in LIB for each memory model you specify. If you request only the Small model, only cs.lib will be installed.

Another library file, graphics.lib, is linked with your program if you use the Turbo C++ graphics library functions (which are covered in Chapter 10, "Turbo C++ Graphics").

Math Libraries

If you're going to use floating point arithmetic in your programs (as many examples in this book do), you'll need another library file. Each memory model has one such file, named maths.lib, mathc.lib, and so on. As with library files, the IDE selects the correct floating point file for your program, depending on the memory model you specify.

For floating point math you'll also need either fp87.lib or emu.lib. The first of these files is used if you have a math coprocessor chip (such as an 8087 or 80287) installed in your computer. The second is used if you don't have a math coprocessor and must "emulate" its function in software.

Runtime Object Files

In addition to needing library files, each program must be linked with a *runtime* library object file. Again, each memory model has such a file, with names like c0s.obj, c0c.obj, and so on. These files contain the code to perform various functions after your program is running, such as interpreting command-line arguments (discussed in Chapter 8, "Keyboard and Cursor").

Header Files

The subdirectory called INCLUDE contains *header files.* These files (also called *include* files) are text files, like the ones you generate with a word processor or the Turbo C++ Editor. Header files can be combined with your program before it is compiled, in the same way that a typist can insert a standard heading in a business letter. Each header file has a .h file extension.

Header files serve several purposes. You can place statements in your program listing that aren't program code but are instead messages to the compiler. These messages, called *compiler directives,* can tell the compiler such things as the definitions of words or phrases used in your program. Some useful compiler directives have been grouped together in header files, which can be included in the source code of your program before it goes to the compiler.

Header files also contain *prototypes* for the library functions. Prototypes provide a way to avoid program errors. Chapter 5, "Functions," covers header files and prototypes in more detail.

Programmer-Generated Files

You can place the programs that you write in any subdirectory you choose; for instance, a subdirectory called TCPROGS. Whatever subdirectory you are in when you invoke TC is usually where the source files you type, the executable file created by the system, and any other files generated by the system are placed.

Files and More Files

Why does C use so many different files? Dividing the various aspects of the language into separate files gives the language more flexibility. By keeping the input/output routines in separate library files, for instance, it's easier to rewrite C to work on a different computer: all that needs to be changed are the files containing input/output functions; the language itself remains the same.

The multiplicity of different library files also means that the routines used with a particular program can be custom tailored to that program's needs: if you don't need the huge memory model, for example, you don't need to use the larger and slower routines that go with it. You can add routines for floating point math or file I/O if you need them; if you don't, they don't take up space in your finished program.

Finally, being able to divide the source code into separate files makes large programs easier to organize, as we'll see in later chapters.

Try not to feel overwhelmed by the complexity of the development system. As you learn more about C, the purposes of the various files will become clearer.

Using the Integrated Development Environment

This section shows how to use the IDE to write, compile, link, and run a simple C program. Later we'll examine in detail the syntax of the program itself.

Invoking the IDE

Change to the subdirectory where you want to develop your program. To activate the IDE, all you need to do is type tc at the DOS prompt.

```
C>tc
```

or if you're using Borland C++,

```
C>bc
```

That's all there is to it. The IDE screen, which initially displays only a menu bar at the top of the screen and a status line below, will appear.

The menu bar displays the menu names File, Edit, Search, Run, and so forth. The status line tells you what various function keys will do.

Using Menus

When you first invoke the IDE, the menu bar will be active. If it isn't, you can make it active by pressing the F10 function key. When it's active, one name on the menu bar is highlighted. To select different menus, move the highlight left and right with the cursor (arrow) keys.

To cause a highlighted menu to drop down so that you can see its contents, press the down cursor key. Another approach to viewing a menu is to press the Alt key and the first letter of the menu name. Thus, to activate the Search menu, you would press the Alt and S keys. If you have a mouse, you can view the contents of a menu simply by clicking the desired menu name. (*Click* means to move the mouse pointer to the desired location and briefly press the left mouse button.) To move up and down the menu, use the up and down cursor keys. To close a menu and return to the menu bar, press the Esc key.

As you move through the items on a menu, the status line changes to provide a description of the selected item. To activate a particular selection, press the Enter key while it is highlighted, or click it with the mouse. The action specified will be carried out.

Opening an Edit Window with File/New

To type your first program, you'll need to open an Edit window. To do this, activate the File menu by clicking the word *File* with the mouse, or by moving the menu-bar high-light to it and pressing the Enter key. Select New from this menu, either by clicking New with the mouse or by moving the highlight down the menu with the cursor key and pressing the Enter key. (Selecting New from the File menu in this way is often abbreviated as *File/New*.)

You'll see a *window* appear on the screen. It's colored differently than the screen background and has a double-lined border, as shown in Figure 1.1.

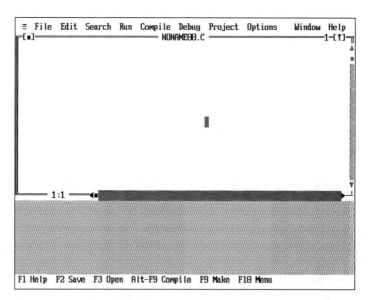

Figure 1.1. The IDE screen with edit window.

You can expand this window to fill the screen by clicking the arrow in the upper-right corner, or by selecting Zoom from the Window menu. If the listing is too large to fit in the window, you can scroll the window contents with the up and down cursor keys. To return to the menu bar from the window, press the F10 key again. Now exit to DOS by selecting Quit from the File menu.

Opening an Edit Window from the Command Line

We've seen one way to open an edit window for a new program. Another approach is to supply the name of the file to be opened on the command line when TC is first invoked. In our case, we want to create a file called oneline.c, so at the DOS prompt, we type

```
C>tc oneline.c
```

This causes the IDE to be displayed on the screen as before. However, the Edit window will be automatically opened and given the name ONELINE.C.

The oneline.c program doesn't exist yet, so this window will be empty. Later, a file called oneline.c will be created. (If this file existed already, it would be opened, and its contents displayed in the Edit window.)

Now, with a blank Edit window awaiting us, we're ready to type our first program.

Writing a Program

The Edit window should be active, with the cursor flashing at the upper-right corner. Type the program oneline.c, as follows:

```
void main(void)
   {
   printf("I charge thee, speak!");
   }
```

Type as you would on a typewriter. Characters will appear where the cursor is positioned. Press the Enter key to move the cursor to the beginning of the next line. Use the cursor keys to reposition the cursor anywhere on the screen. If you make a mistake, use the Backspace key to delete the character to the left of the cursor, or the Del key to delete the character under the cursor. You can delete an entire program line by positioning the cursor on it and pressing the Ctrl Y key combination.

We won't go into further detail here on using the Turbo Editor. We've explained enough here to get you started typing simple programs. Appendix E, "The Turbo C++ Editor," describes additional Editor features, and Borland's Turbo C++ documentation covers the Editor and other IDE features in detail. For quick reference, select Contents from the Help menu, and then select Editor Commands by double-clicking the appropriate heading. You'll see a list of categories, such as Block commands, Cursor Movement commands, and so on. Double-click again to see a list of editor commands.

Be careful to enter the program exactly as shown, paying attention to the parentheses after the word main, to the braces (not brackets) above and below the printf() statement, and to the semicolon at the end of this statement. At this point, don't worry about what the program does (although you can probably guess this), or why it's written the way it is. We'll show how to get it running first, and then go back and explain its syntax.

Saving the Program

After you've typed the source file for the program, you should save it on your disk. To do this, select Save from the File menu. You can accomplish the same effect simply by pressing the F2 function key. Many actions can be activated by using either the menu system or the function keys. The function keys are harder to learn but faster once you know them.

If you invoked TC with the name oneline.c on the command line, then the file you're typing has already been given this name, as you can see at the top of the Edit window. In this case, the file will be saved to disk immediately when you select File/Save.

On the other hand, if you opened the Edit window by selecting File/New, then the file will have the temporary name NONAME00.C. When you select File/Save, a dialog box will appear. (A dialog box is a temporary window where you enter additional information.) At the top of this dialog box is a field called Save Editor File As. Type the name oneline.c and press the Enter key. The file will be saved under this name.

Saving the source file isn't necessary before compiling and running your program, but it's a good idea. There's always a small chance that executing the program will crash the system; if your source file isn't saved, it's gone forever.

Making an .exe File

After you've written the source file for your program, you need to turn it into an executable file. This is called *making* the .exe file. Let's examine what this means in a general sense before we see how to carry out the task.

Compiling

The version of the program you typed is understandable to human beings (at least if they know C). However, it isn't understandable to the microprocessor in your computer. A program that is to be executed by the microprocessor must be in the form of a *machine language* file. Thus there must be two versions of the program: the one you type into the edit window, which is called the *source file,* and the machine-language version, which is called the *executable* (or sometimes *binary* file).

The *compiler,* which is a part of the IDE, translates this source code into another file, consisting of machine language.

Linking

The process would be conceptually simple if compiling were the end of the story, and you simply executed this new compiler-generated file to run your program. However, there's another step in most compiled languages, including Turbo C++: a process called *linking*.

Linking is necessary for several reasons. First, your program may (and in fact almost certainly will) need to be combined with various library routines. As we noted, these are functions that perform tasks such as input/output. Library routines are stored in files with the .lib extension. Second, you may not want to compile all of your program at the same time. Larger C programs commonly consist of several separate files, some of which may already be compiled. The linker combines these files into a single executable file.

Like the compiler, the linker is built into Turbo C++'s IDE.

> The text editor produces .c source files, which go to the compiler, which produces .obj object files, which go to the linker, which produces .exe executable files.

The compiler generates an intermediate kind of file called an object file. The linker then links all the necessary object files together to produce a final, executable program. The relationship of the compilation process to the linking process is shown schematically in Figure 1.2.

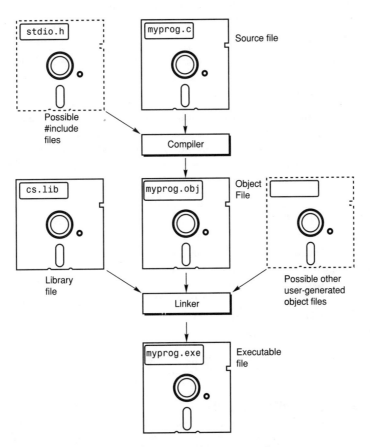

Figure 1.2. Relationship of compiler and linker.

In Turbo C++ (and most other versions of C), the source file you type is given the .c file extension (as in myprog.c). The intermediate object files are automatically given the extension .obj by the compiler (myprog.obj), and the executable program files are given the extension .exe by the linker (myprog.exe). The operating system recognizes files with the extension .exe as executable files, so you can run them directly, like other application programs.

Setting the Output and Source Directories

Before you actually generate .OBJ and .EXE files, you need to tell Turbo C++ where to put these files. This should be the directory where you created your .C source file. Select Directories from the Options menu. You'll see a window with four fields called Include Directories, Library Directories, Output Directory, and Source Directory. The Include Directories field should already be set to C:\TC\INCLUDE, and Library Directories should be set to C:\TC\LIB. You need to set the Output directory field to C:\TCPROGS or whichever directory you're using to hold your program files. This is where the compiler will put your .OBJ file and where the linker will put the .EXE file.

Compiling and Linking in the IDE

In the Turbo C++ IDE, compiling and linking can be performed together in one step. There are two ways to do this: you can select Make EXE File from the Compile menu, or you can press the F9 key.

A great many things happen when you initiate the Make process. As you learned earlier, the compiler first transforms your source file, oneline.c, into an object file, oneline.obj. The linker then combines this file with various other files and parts of files. The resulting file is called oneline.exe. However, the IDE doesn't apply this process blindly.

The Turbo C++ Project Feature

Before compiling and linking a file, a part of the IDE called Project checks the time and date on the file you're compiling. (This data is stored in each file.) Why is this a good idea? In complex programs, with many source files, checking the time and date of file creation can avoid unnecessary compilation of source files. Chapter 13, "Advanced Topics," discusses this, and the other capabilities of Project/Make, in greater detail. For now, the important thing to know is that pressing the F9 key causes the program in the Edit window to be compiled and linked.

If you want, you can perform compiling and linking separately by selecting first Compile and then Link from the Compile menu.

Screen Display for Compiling and Linking

While compiling is taking place, you'll see a window appear in the middle of the screen with the legend Compiling at the top. This window contains a variety of information: the name of the file being compiled, the number of lines compiled, the number of warnings, the number of errors, and the available memory. If your program was written correctly, this window will hardly be on the screen long enough to see, because Turbo C++ compiles so quickly. If you've made a typing mistake, however, you'll have plenty of time to examine this window. In the "Correcting Syntax Errors" section, we'll explore the possibility that you made a typing error.

While linking is taking place, a different window appears. It looks much the same as the Compiling window but with the legend Linking at the top. If you look closely you'll see file names flash by in the Linking field. These are files, such as emu.lib, maths.lib, c0s.obj, and cs.lib, that are being linked with the oneline.obj file. When the linking process terminates, the screen appears as shown in Figure 1.3 (if no mistakes were made when you wrote your program).

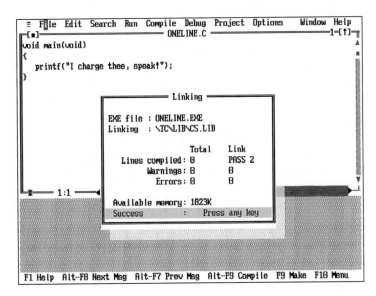

Figure 1.3. A successful link.

Executing a Program

If there were no errors in the compiling or linking process, you're now ready to run the program. You can do this from the IDE by selecting Run from the Run menu, or by pressing the Ctrl F9 key combination.

When you run the program you'll see the screen flicker briefly. The program has written a message to the screen but not to the IDE screen. To see the program's output, select User Screen from the Window menu, or press the Alt F5 key combination. You'll see the normal DOS screen, which should look like this:

```
C>tc
I charge thee, speak!
```

The first line is what you typed to invoke TC. The second line is the output from the program. Pressing any key takes you back to the IDE screen.

Sometimes you may find the output from one program appearing on the same line of the output screen as output from another program or from DOS. To avoid visual confusion, you can guarantee that output starts on a new line by selecting DOS Shell from the File menu before running your program. At the resulting DOS prompt, type exit to return to the IDE. Program output then starts on the line below exit. To start with a completely clean slate, as it were, you can clear the screen by typing cls before exiting back to the IDE.

Correcting Syntax Errors

It is quite likely that your first attempt to compile a program won't be successful. If you have made an error typing your program, the compiler will recognize this and let you know about it in the Compiler window. You'll see that the number of errors isn't listed as 0, and the word Errors appears instead of the word Success in the bottom of the window.

When this happens, press any key to remove the compiler window. You'll see the Edit window with your program, with one line and one character in the line highlighted in different colors. Another window, called the Message window, will appear at the bottom of the screen. It will contain one or more error messages, one of which will be highlighted.

For example, suppose you left out the closing quotes after the phrase I charge thee, speak! in the oneline.c program. In the Edit window the opening quote will be highlighted, and in the message window, which appears at the bottom of the screen, the phrase Error: Unterminated string or character constant in function main is highlighted. This situation is shown in Figure 1.4.

One error often confuses the compiler into thinking there are other errors as well, and that's true in this case. Because the string is never terminated, the compiler assumes all the rest of the program is part of the string. It therefore displays two other error messsages: Error: Function call missing) in function main and Compound statement missing. (See Figure 1.4.)

To correct the error, you must edit the program. You activate the Edit window by pressing the F6 key. The cursor is conveniently situated on the line containing the error. Now the appropriate correction can be made to the program; in this case, the missing quote is inserted.

If more than one error needs to be corrected, you can repeatedly move back and forth between the Error window and the Edit window by pressing the F6 key. To view each error in turn, use the cursor keys to move the highlight in the Message window.

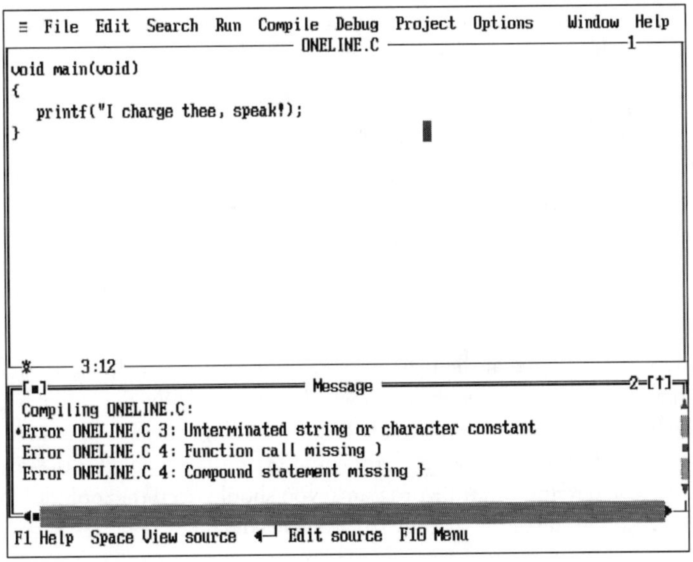

```
 ≡  File  Edit  Search  Run  Compile  Debug  Project  Options      Window  Help
──────────────────────────── ONELINE.C ─────────────────────1───
void main(void)
{
   printf("I charge thee, speak!);
}



┌─*──── 3:12 ─────────────────────────────────────────────────────
┌[■]─────────────────────────── Message ═══════════════════════2=[↑]┐
Compiling ONELINE.C:
•Error ONELINE.C 3: Unterminated string or character constant
 Error ONELINE.C 4: Function call missing )
 Error ONELINE.C 4: Compound statement missing }

└─◄■──────────────────────────────────────────────────────────────►┘
F1 Help  Space View source  ◄─┘ Edit source  F10 Menu
```

Figure 1.4. Compiler error.

The linker displays errors in much the same way that the compiler does but for different reasons. For example, if you misspell `printf()` as `printx()`, your program will compile correctly, but the linker will signal an error, because it won't be able to find a `printx()` function to link to your program.

When all the errors are corrected, press the F2 key to save the source file, and then press the F9 key to compile and link again (or you can make the corresponding menu selections to carry out these actions).

The ease with which errors can be identified and corrected is one of Turbo C++'s most pleasing features. In the process of learning C you're likely to have more than one opportunity to try out this process.

Correcting Logical Errors

When you start writing more complex programs, you'll often find that a program compiles and links without errors but nevertheless fails to operate as intended. In such situations you'll probably want to use Turbo C++'s debugger features to analyze what's going on. You can single step through a program, watch variables change as each statement is executed, and perform other activities to help you analyze your program's aberrant behavior.

Appendix F, "The Turbo C++ Debugger," introduces Turbo C++'s debugging features. You probably don't need to know the details of debugging now, but you might want to skim through this appendix so that you'll have an idea what features are available. Then you can put them to use when you need them.

Exiting the IDE

After you make the Edit window active, you can close it in three different ways. You can click the small square in the upper-left corner, you can select Close from the Window menu, or you can press the Alt F3 key combination.

To exit from the IDE, select Quit from the File menu, or press the Alt X key combination. This takes you back to DOS.

From DOS you can see that the files oneline.c, oneline.bak, oneline.obj, and oneline.exe have been created. The .bak file, which is a backup for the .c file, is created automatically by the editor. This backup file can be useful if the original of your source file becomes corrupted. For simple programs, the .obj file can be erased after the .exe file is created. (When you develop multifile programs, you should keep the .obj files to facilitate the Make process, as we'll see in Chapter 13, "Advanced Topics.")

You can execute your .exe file directly from DOS by typing the file's name at the DOS prompt.

```
C>oneline
```

You should see the same output phrase as before. Because most programs eventually run as stand-alone applications, this is the most realistic way to view your program's output. However, during program development, it isn't as convenient as executing from within the IDE.

Now that you understand the mechanics of creating a working Turbo C++ program, let's look at the syntax of the program itself.

The Basic Structure of C Programs

When they first encounter a C program, most people find it as complicated as an algebra equation. It seems densely packed with obscure symbols and long program lines and they think, "Uh oh, I'll never be able to understand this." However, most of this apparent complexity is illusion. A program written in C is really not much more difficult to understand than one written in any other language, once you've gotten used to the syntax. Learning C, as is true with any language, is largely a matter of practice. The more you look at C programs, the less complex they appear, until at some point you wonder why you ever thought they looked complicated.

In the balance of this chapter, and the ones that follow, we'll introduce you to C in a carefully graded progression so that each example is as simple as possible. We want to avoid the situation where you're suddenly confronted with a program so complicated that it looks like the chalkboard scribblings of a mad scientist. If the examples seem *too* simple, don't worry; they won't stay that way long.

Let's investigate the various elements of oneline.c.

```
void main(void)
   {
   printf("I charge thee, speak!");
   }
```

Function Definition

First, note the name *main*. All C programs are divided into units called *functions*. A function is similar to a subroutine in BASIC or a function in Pascal. We'll have more to say about functions in Chapter 5, "Functions"; for now, note that main() is a function. Every C program consists of one or more functions; this program has only one. No matter how many functions there are in a C program, main() is the one to which control is passed from the operating system when the program is run; it's the first function executed.

The word void preceding main specifies that the function main() won't return a value. The second void, in parentheses, specifies that the function takes no arguments. We won't worry about either of these issues until Chapter 5.

C programs consist of functions. The main() function is the first one to which control is passed when the program is executed.

Thus our program begins the way all C functions do: with a name, followed by parentheses. This signals the compiler that a function is being defined.

Delimiters

Following the function definition are braces which signal the beginning and end of the body of the function. The opening brace ({) indicates that a block of code that forms a distinct unit is about to begin. The closing brace (}) terminates the block of code. Braces in C perform a function similar to BEGIN and END statements in Pascal. In our program there is only one statement between the braces: the one beginning with printf.

Braces are also used to delimit blocks of code in situations other than functions; they're used in loops and decision-making statements, for example. We'll find out more about that in the next few chapters.

Although these elements may seem straightforward, we'll bet that at some point in your programming career you'll (1) forget the parentheses after main or (2) forget one or both of the braces that delimit the program.

Statement Terminator

The line in our program that begins with the word `printf` is an example of a *statement*. A statement in C is terminated with a semicolon. Note that a semicolon doesn't *separate* statements, as it does in Pascal. Also note (especially if you're a BASIC programmer) that the semicolon terminates the line, not the carriage return you type afterwards. C pays no attention to carriage returns in your program listing. In fact, the C compiler pays no attention to any of the so-called *whitespace* characters: the carriage return (newline), the space, and the tab. You can put as many or as few whitespace characters in your program as you like; they're invisible to the compiler.

While we're on the subject of semicolons, we'll make another bet: at some point you'll forget to use one at the end of a C statement.

Figure 1.5 shows the points of program structure we've discussed so far.

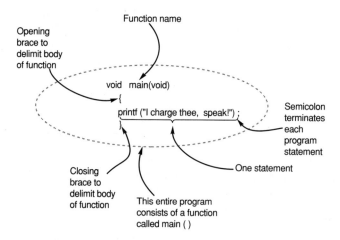

Figure 1.5. Structure of a simple C program.

Program Style, Round One

Because you can put as many whitespace characters as you want in your program, it is almost a universal practice to use these characters to make the program easier to read. This is done by conforming more or less to the style guidelines used by Kernighan and Ritchie in *The C Programming Language* (see the Bibliography), as we did in our example. It would also be perfectly permissible to write the oneline.c program as

```
void main(void){printf("I charge thee, speak!");}
```

The compiler wouldn't know the difference. However, stretching the code out vertically makes for a more comprehensible program, and aligning matching braces makes it easier to ensure that each opening brace has a closing brace.

The whitespace characters (space, tab, newline) are invisible to the compiler.

Indentation of blocks of code enclosed in braces is an important aspect of making C programs readable. In this example the program line and the braces are indented three spaces (our standard indent throughout this book). Indenting isn't critical in this short example, but when there are many sets of nested braces in a program, indentation becomes increasingly important.

The *printf()* Function

The program line

```
printf("I charge thee, speak!");
```

causes the phrase in quotes to be printed on-screen. The word `printf` is actually a function name, just as `main` is a function name. Because `printf` is a function, it is followed by parentheses. In this case, the parentheses contain the phrase to be printed, surrounded by quotes. This phrase is a function *argument*—information passed from `main()` to the function `printf()`. We won't dwell too much on arguments and the formal aspects of functions at this point; we'll save that for Chapter 5, "Functions." Note however that when we mention function names such as `printf()` and `main()` in the text we'll usually include the parentheses following the name just to make it clear that we're talking about a function and not a variable or something else.

`"I charge thee, speak!"` is an example of a *string* of characters. In C, string constants such as this are surrounded by quotes; this is how the compiler recognizes a string. We'll be using strings as we go along, and we'll dig into their complexities in Chapter 6, "Arrays and Strings."

Notice that we have used the function `printf()` in our program. That is, we have called it just as we would call a subroutine in BASIC or a procedure in Pascal, but there is no code for this function in our program. Where is `printf()` stored? It's in the cs.lib library file. When compiling the program, the compiler realizes that `printf()` isn't a function included in the oneline.c source file, so it leaves a message to that effect for the linker. The linker looks in cs.lib (because we're using the small memory model), finds the section of this file containing `printf()`, and causes this section to be linked with our `oneline.c` program. A similar process is followed for all C library functions.

One other aspect of our sample C program deserves mention: except for some letters in the string in quotes, it's written entirely in lowercase. Unlike some programming languages, C distinguishes between uppercase and lowercase letters. Thus the functions `PRINTF()` and `Printf()` aren't the same as the function `printf()`. Some programmers follow the convention of keeping pretty much everything in lowercase (except constants, which we'll look at later) for ease of typing. Other programmers, however, use both lowercase and uppercase when naming functions and variables.

> C distinguishes between uppercase and lowercase.

Exploring the *printf()* Function

The `printf()` function is actually a powerful and versatile output function. We're going to spend the remainder of this chapter exploring it. The `printf()` function is important because it is the workhorse output statement in C.

Printing Numbers

The `printf()` function uses a unique format for printing constants and variables. For a hint of its power let's look at another example

```
void main(void)
    {
    printf("This is the number two: %d", 2);
    }
```

Invoke the IDE and a new file called printwo.c. Type this program and link and compile it as described earlier. Can you guess what message will be printed when you run it? Here's the output:

```
This is the number two: 2
```

Why was the digit 2 printed, and what effect does the %d have? The function `printf()` can be given more than one argument. In the oneline.c example we gave it only one: the string "I charge thee, speak!" Now we're giving it two: a string ("This is the number two: %d") on the left and a value (the number 2) on the right. These two arguments are separated by a comma. The `printf()` function takes the value on the right of the comma and plugs it into the string on the left. Where does it plug it in? Where it finds a *format specifier* such as %d.

Format Specifiers

The format specifier tells `printf()` where to put a value into the string and what format to use in printing the value. In this example, the %d tells `printf()` to print the value 2 as a decimal integer. Other specifiers could be used for the number 2. For instance, %f would cause the 2 to be printed as a floating point number, and %x would print it as a hexadecimal number. We'll explore these possibilities later.

Why not simply put the number 2 into the original string?

```
printf("This is the number two: 2");
```

In this example it wouldn't make any difference in what is printed, because 2 is a constant. However, as we'll see in Chapter 2, "C Building Blocks," variables can also be used in the `printf()` function, giving it the capability of changing what it prints while the program is running.

Printing Strings

Using format specifiers we can print string constants as well as numbers. Here's an example that shows both a string and a number being printed together:

```
void main(void)
    {
    printf("%s is %d million miles\nfrom the sun.", "Venus", 67);
    }
```

Type this program (call it venus.c), compile, link, and execute it. The output will be

```
Venus is 67 million miles
from the sun.
```

The `printf()` function has replaced the %s symbol with the string `"Venus"` and the %d symbol with the number 67, as shown in Figure 1.6.

(A) The constants on the right are plugged in, in order, to the format specifiers in the string on the left.

```
printf("%s is %d million miles\n from the sun.","venus!",67);
```

(B) The resulting string is displayed on the monitor.

Figure 1.6. The printf() function.

This example also includes a new symbol, the \n. In C this means *newline* and stands for a single character that, when inserted in a string, has the effect of a carriage return and linefeed: that is, following a \n character, printing is resumed at the beginning of the next line. (The newline character is stored in memory as a single character—a linefeed—but it has the effect of both a carriage return and linefeed.)

Printing Characters

In our final example in this chapter we'll show how `printf()` can be used to print a single character.

You might think that a character is simply a string with only one character in it, but this isn't the case in C; characters and strings are distinct entities. Here's a program, called sayjay.c, that prints a character and a string:

```
void main(void)
    {
    printf("\nThe letter %c is ", 'j');
    printf("pronounced %s.", "jay");
    }
```

Here we've made two different program lines, each with a `printf()` function. The output of this program will be

```
The letter j is pronounced jay.
```

In this program `'j'` is a character and `"jay"` is a string. Notice that `'j'` is surrounded by single quotes (actually apostrophes), and `"jay"` is surrounded by double quotes. This is how the compiler tells the difference between a character and a string.

Also note that even though the output is printed by two separate program lines, it doesn't consist of two lines of text. That's because `printf()` doesn't automatically print a newline character at the end of a line; if you want one, you must explicitly insert it. The initial newline (`\n`) character ensures that the output will start at the beginning of a line.

Syntax Highlighting

You may have noticed (if you're fortunate enough to be using a color monitor) that the different elements of the program are shown in different colors. Function names are green, strings are red, characters are magenta, symbols (like parentheses and braces) are yellow, and so on. This makes the program easier to read and helps you avoid typing mistakes. For instance, if you forget the closing quotes for a string (as we discussed in the oneline.c program), parts of the program that shouldn't be part of the string, like the closing parenthesis and the semicolon at the end of the statement, will appear in string color instead of symbol color. Be on the lookout for this sort of thing. It's like having someone looking over your shoulder, saying "Don't forget the closing quotes!"

You can change the colors of various syntax elements if you like. Select Environment from the Options menu, select Colors from the submenu, and then click Edit Window in the resulting Group list. Select the syntax element from the Item list on the right and select colors from the color boxes. You shouldn't need to do this unless you find particular items hard to read.

Warning Levels

We've already discussed compiler errors, which occur when the compiler knows you've made a mistake. An error means "You've really blown it. I have no idea how to compile your source code." Besides errors, the compiler may also generate warnings. A warning is less severe than an error. It means something like "I think I know what you mean, but you might want to check it again," or maybe, "Are you sure you want to do this?"

Default: Selected Warnings

There are several dozen situations where Turbo C++ can issue warnings. However, by default, Turbo C++ gives you warnings for only about two-thirds of these questionable situations. We've been using these default settings until now. However, the remaining one-third of the situations also indicate something not quite right about your program. Especially when you're learning C, it makes sense to get as much help from the compiler as you can. We therefore recommend turning on all the warnings. The example programs in this book should all compile with no warnings.

To turn on all the warnings, select Compiler from the Options menu and select Messages from the resulting submenu. Select Display from the sub-submenu. You'll see a dialog box called Compiler Messages. In this box are three radio buttons in a group called Display Warnings. These buttons are labeled All, Selected, and None. By default the Selected button is checked (that is, there's a dot beside it). This provides warnings for selected situations. To turn on all the warnings, click the All radio button, as shown in Figure 1.7. Then click OK to make the dialog box go away.

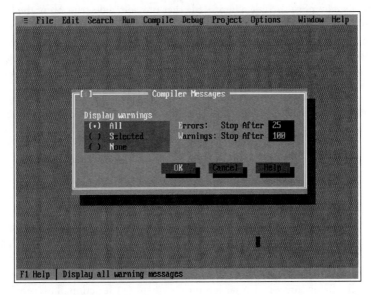

Figure 1.7. The Compiler Messages dialog box.

Saving the Settings

When you make a change in the Options menu, you usually want to save this new setting so that the next time you start Turbo C++, you'll get the same setting without having to go through the whole process again. You should do this with the warning messages option you just set. Select Save from the Options menu and click OK.

Testing the New Settings

Now that you've set the compiler to display more warning messages, let's see what happens when we compile a program. Load oneline.c and select Compile from the Compile menu. (If you select Make and your source file hasn't been changed since the last time you compiled, Turbo C++ will simply tell you it's "Up To Date" without compiling it.)

Wow! What's this? The Compiling box reports two warnings! If we press any key or click the mouse, we'll see the Message box at the bottom of the window. It says

```
Warning ONELINE.C 3: No declaration for function 'printf'
Warning ONELINE.C 3: Call to function 'printf' with no prototype
```

What do these messages mean? How do we make them go away?

Including a Header File in Your Program

Although they run just fine, C purists would complain that the example programs we've seen thus far in this chapter are incomplete. As we've just seen, the compiler agrees that something is wrong. Here's what the purists say, "Every time you use a library function, like printf(), you must include a header file that provides a description of the function. The compiler can use this description to tell whether you're using the function correctly." (We'll learn more about this when we discuss functions in Chapter 5, "Functions.") This function description is called a declaration or a prototype. Thus both the warning messages shown previously mean the same thing: our program is missing a function declaration.

How do you include the function declaration in your program so that the warning messages can be eliminated? Here's a new program, oneline2.c, that does this:

```
#include <stdio.h>

void main(void)
    {
    printf("I charge thee, speak!");
    }
```

The first line is an instruction to the compiler that says, "Take the file stdio.h and place it here." This file is pasted into the oneline2.c file, just as you would use a word processor to paste one section of text into another. The file stdio.h is called an *include* file or a *header* file. It contains the declaration for the printf() function. This provides the information the compiler was complaining about, so with this added line, oneline2.c compiles without warnings.

All this discussion about function declarations, instructions to the compiler, and including other files in your source file probably seems rather mysterious and unnecessarily complicated. Fortunately, at this point you don't need to understand too much about it. For now, here's what you should remember: for every library function, such as `printf()`, that you use in your program, you need to include the appropriate header file at the beginning of your program. For `printf()`, the file is stdio.h. Actually, many common I/O functions use this same header file, so it will be a familiar feature in our example programs.

Summary

In this chapter, you've learned how to set up the Turbo C++ IDE to create, compile, link, and run C programs. To this end, you've learned about the organization of the various files provided with Turbo C++. You've learned what simple C programs look like and that even the main part of a C program is a function. You know some of the potential of the `printf()` function, including how to print number, character, and string constants. You know how to use format specifiers and the purpose of the newline character. At this point, you should be able to write one- or two-line C programs that print various phrases on the screen.

In Chapter 2, "C Building Blocks," we'll continue our exploration of the `printf()` function, and we'll look at other input and output functions. We'll also examine two other important C building blocks: variables and operators.

Questions

1. A source file and an executable file have the extensions

    a. .c and .obj
    b. .c and .exe
    c. .obj and .exe
    d. .bak and .obj

2. After the source file for a C program has been written, it must be c_____, l_____, and e_____.

3. The library files that come with the C programming system contain

    a. Functions that perform input and output
    b. A text editor for program development
    c. Functions for advanced math and other purposes
    d. The compiler and linker

4. The executable files that come with the C programming system include a program to a_____ the different phases of the compilation process.

5. What is the purpose of the parentheses following the word `main` in a C program?

6. The braces that surround the code in a C program

    a. Delimit a section of code
    b. Show what code goes in a particular function
    c. Separate the code from the constants
    d. Separate the source file from the object file

7. True or false: a carriage return must be used at the end of every C program statement.

8. What's wrong with the following C program?

```
void main
(
print"Oh, woe and suffering!"
)
```

9. What two sorts of things can go in the parentheses following the function `printf()`?

10. What is the output of the following program?

```
void main(void)
    {
    printf("%s\n%s\n%s", "one", "two", "three");
    }
```

Exercises

1. Write a two-statement program that will generate the following output:

```
Mr. Green is 42,
Mr. Brown is 48.
```

Use string constants to represent the names and integer constants to represent the ages.

2. Write a program that will print the phrase `a, b, and c are all letters`. Use character constants to represent the letters.

C Building Blocks

- Variable types
- The printf() output function
- The scanf() and getche() input functions
- Special characters
- Arithmetic operators
- Relational operators
- Comments

Before you can begin to write interesting programs in C, you need to know at least some fundamentals of the language. In this chapter, we present a selection of these basic building blocks.

Three important aspects of any language are the way it stores data, how it accomplishes input and output, and the operators it uses to transform and combine data. These are the three kinds of building blocks we'll discuss in this chapter. Of course, in a single chapter we can't present every aspect of each of these topics; much will remain to be said in later chapters. However, what we cover here will be enough to get you off the ground.

In the following chapters we'll put these building blocks to use exploring the control statements of the language: loops, decisions, and functions.

Variables

Variables may be the most fundamental aspect of any computer language. A variable is a space in the computer's memory set aside for a certain kind of data and given a name for easy reference. *Is an address*   *int x = 7*

Variables are used so that the same space in memory can hold different values at different times. For instance, suppose you're writing a program to calculate someone's paycheck. You'll need to store at least the hourly rate and the hours worked. If you want to do the calculation for more than one employee, you'll need to use the same program and the same spaces in memory to store similar data for additional employees. A variable is a space in memory that plays the same role many times but may contain a different value each time.

What different kinds of variables does the language recognize? How is this data stored? How do you tell the computer what sort of data you want to store? These are the questions we'll be exploring in this section.

Constants and Variables

y = x + 7

In Chapter 1, we showed how the printf() function can be used to print constant numbers, strings, and characters. For example, this statement

```
printf("This is the number two: %d", 2);
```

from the program printtwo.c, printed the constant 2, plugging it into the format specifier, %d. This produced the output

```
This is the number two: 2
```

Of course this isn't very useful, because we more easily could have written the statement

```
printf("This is the number two: 2");
```

to achieve the same result. The power of the printf() function—indeed, the power of

computer languages in general—comes from the ability to use variables, which can hold
many different values, in program statements. Let's rewrite the printwo.c program to use a
variable instead of a constant.

```
#include <stdio.h>

void main(void)
    {
    int num;
    num = 2;
    printf("\nThis is the number two: %d", num);
    }
```

(handwritten annotations: int num; = tells compiler to allocate space/address; num = 2; escape character (character return to start of line & line feed))

This program, which we'll call var.c, gives the same output as before, but it has
achieved it in quite a different way. It creates a variable, num, assigns it the value 2, and
then prints the value contained in the variable.

This program contains several new elements. In the first program statement,

```
int num;
```

a variable is defined: it is given a name and a type (type int, which we'll examine soon).

In the second statement,

```
num = 2;
```

the variable is assigned a value. The assignment operator (=) is used for this purpose. This
operator has the same function as the (=) operator in BASIC or the (:=) operator in Pascal.
(We'll have more to say about assignment operators in the last section of this chapter.)

In the third statement of the program, the variable name, num, is used as one of the
arguments of the printf() statement, replacing the constant 2 used in the example in
Chapter 1.

Variable Definitions

The statement

```
int num;
```

is an example of a *variable definition*. If you're a Pascal programmer, you're familiar with
this sort of statement; BASIC may or may not use variable definitions. The definition
consists of the *type* name, int, followed by the name of the variable, num. In a C program
all variables must be defined. If you have more than one variable of the same type, you can
define them all with one type name, separating the variable names with commas.

```
int apples, oranges, cherries;
```

Defining a variable tells the compiler the *name* of the variable and the *type* of variable.
Specifying the name at the beginning of the program enables the compiler to recognize the

variable as "approved" when you use it later in the program. This is helpful if you commit the common error of misspelling a variable name deep within your program; the compiler will flag the error, whereas BASIC would simply assume you meant a different variable. Defining variables also helps you organize your program; collecting the variables together at the beginning of the program helps you grasp the overall logic and organization of your program.

> All variables must be defined to specify their name and type and set aside storage.

When you define a variable, the compiler sets aside an appropriate amount of memory to store that variable. In the present case we've specified an integer variable, so the compiler will set aside two bytes of memory. This is large enough to hold numbers from –32,768 to 32,767. Actually, the amount of memory used for an integer (and other variable types) isn't defined as part of the C language; it is dependent on the particular computer system and compiler being used. However, Turbo C++ operates with two-byte integers, so we'll assume that's the case here.

Figure 2.1 shows how an integer looks in memory.

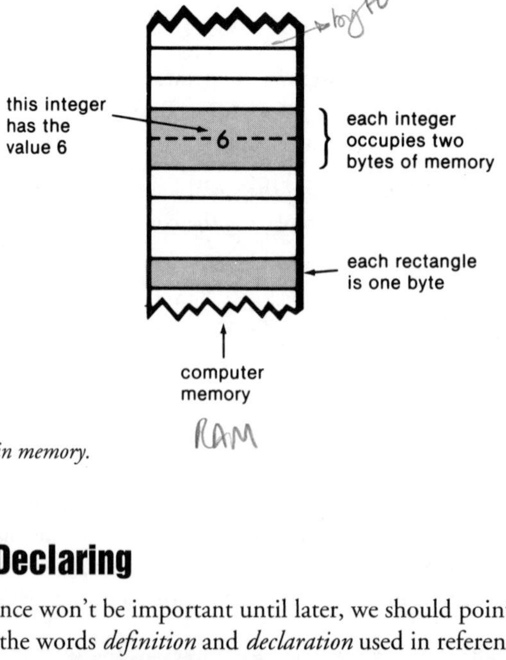

Figure 2.1. An integer in memory.

Defining and Declaring

Although the difference won't be important until later, we should point out a subtle distinction between the words *definition* and *declaration* used in reference to variables. We've been discussing variable *definitions,* which specify the name and type of a variable and also set aside memory space for the variable. A variable *declaration,* by contrast, specifies the variable's name and data type but doesn't set aside any memory for the variable. Variable declarations are important in multifile programs, where a variable that is defined in one file must be referred to in a second file. The second file uses a declaration for this purpose, as we'll see in Chapter 13, "Advanced Topics."

The Turbo C++ documentation prefers to call definitions *defining declarations* and to call declarations *referencing declarations.* In most cases the word *declaration* is used for both meanings. We prefer the more consistent approach of distinguishing between the meanings, as is done by Kernighan and Ritchie (see Bibliography) and by other compiler vendors.

Variable Types

There are, of course, other types of variables besides integers, which is the only type we've seen so far. We'll summarize them here and then give examples of the uses of the more common types.

Most variable types are numeric, but there is one that isn't: the *character* type. You've already met character constants; you know that they consist of a letter or other character surrounded by single quotes. A character variable is a one-byte space in memory in which the character constants, such as 'a' or 'X', can be stored. The type name for a character is char. Thus, to declare two character variables, called ch1 and ch2, you would use the statement

```
char ch1, ch2;
```

There are also several different kinds of numerical variables. We'll look at them briefly now. Later we'll learn more about them when we use them in actual programs.

You already know about integers (type int). For situations when the normal integer is too small, the *long integer* (type long or long int can be used. It occupies *four* bytes of memory and can hold integers from –2,147,483,648 to 2,147,483,647. This is a useful data type for numbers like the purchase price of a home in Marin County, California.

There are also two kinds of *floating point* variables. Floating point numbers are used to represent values that are *measured,* like the length of a room (which might have a value of 145.25 inches) as opposed to integers, which are used to represent values that are *counted,* like the number of rooms in a house. Floating point variables can be very large or small. One floating point variable, type float, occupies four bytes and can hold numbers from about 10^{38} to 10^{-38} with between six and seven digits of precision. (Precision means how many digits can actually be used in the number; if you attempt to store a number with too many digits, such as 2.12345678, in a floating point variable, only six digits will be retained: 2.12345.)

A *double-precision* floating point variable, type double, occupies eight bytes and can hold numbers from about 10^{308} to 10^{-308} with about 15 digits of precision. (The slight vagueness in specifying these limits of precision arises from the fact that variables are actually stored in the computer in binary, which doesn't represent an integral number of decimal digits.) There is also a larger long double type. It occupies 10 bytes and holds numbers from 10^{-4932} to 10^{4932} with 19-digit precision.

Figure 2.2 shows some of these variable types as they would look in the computer's memory.

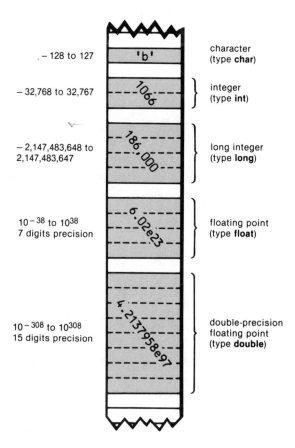

−128 to 127	'b'	character (type **char**)
−32,768 to 32,767	1066	integer (type **int**)
−2,147,483,648 to 2,147,483,647	186,000	long integer (type **long**)
10^{-38} to 10^{38} 7 digits precision	6.02e23	floating point (type **float**)
10^{-308} to 10^{308} 15 digits precision	4.2137958e97	double-precision floating point (type **double**)

Figure 2.2. Variable types in memory.

Another variable type, short, is often used in C programs on other computers, where it has a different size from type int. (On 32-bit operating systems, for example, it is half the size of an integer.) However, in Turbo C++, type short is a two-byte integer just like type int and therefore is seldom used.

The character type and the integer types also have unsigned versions (type unsigned char, unsigned int, and unsigned long) which change the range of numbers the type can hold. For instance, the unsigned int type holds numbers from 0 to 65,535, rather than from –32,768 to 32,767 as the regular int type does. These unsigned types can be useful in special circumstances but aren't used as often as the signed versions.

You may be wondering why we haven't mentioned a string type. The reason is simple: there is no string variable type in C. Instead, strings are represented by arrays of characters. We've shown some examples of string constants already. For string variables, we'll have to wait until Chapter 6, "Arrays and Strings."

Let's look at a program that uses character, floating point, and integer variables. We'll call this program event.c.

```
#include <stdio.h>

void main(void)
    {
    int event;
    char heat;
    float time;

    event = 5;
    heat = 'C';
    time = 27.25;
    printf("\nThe winning time in head %c", heat);
    printf(" of event %d was %f.", event, time);
    }
```

Here's the output of this program:

```
The winning time in heat C of event 5 was 27.250000.
```

This program uses three common variable types: int, char, and float. You'll notice that we've used a new format specifier, %f, to print the floating point number. We'll discuss this and other format specifiers soon, in the section on input/output. For now, remember that %f is used to print floating point numbers the same way that %d is used to print integers and %c is used to print characters.

Floating Point Variables

Floating point numbers are different from integers in that they're stored in memory in two parts, rather than one. These two parts are called the *mantissa* and the *exponent*. The mantissa is the value of the number, and the exponent is the power to which it is raised.

Scientists and engineers use a similar technique for representing numbers: it's called *exponential notation*. For example, in exponential notation the number 12,345 would be represented as 1.2345e4, where the number 4, following the e, is the exponent—the power of 10 to which the number will be raised—and 1.2345 is the value of the number. The exponent can also be negative: .0098765 is represented in exponential notation as 9.8765e–3. The idea in exponential notation is to transform every number, no matter how large or how small, into a value with only one digit to the left of the decimal point, followed by the appropriate power of 10. In effect, the exponent represents how many places you need to move the decimal point to transform the number into this standard form.

Exponential notation permits the storage of far larger and far smaller numbers than is possible with integer data types. However, arithmetic and other operations are performed more slowly on floating point numbers, so an integer variable is preferable unless the larger capacity of floating point numbers is necessary.

In Turbo C++, a floating point number of type `float` is stored in four bytes: one for the exponent, and three for the value of the number, as shown in Figure 2.3.

The format isn't actually quite the same as the exponential notation used by humans, because the value of the number and the exponent are stored in the computer's memory in binary rather than decimal. However, the effect is the same. The one-byte exponent is large enough to hold exponents between 38 and −38. For instance, the number 123,456,000,000,000,000,000,000,000,000,000,000,000.0 (which has 38 digits following the 1) is close to the largest number that can be stored; it would be represented in exponential notation as 1.23456e38.

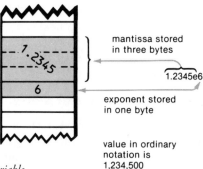

Figure 2.3. Floating point variable.

Because only three bytes are available for holding the value of the number, only six or seven digits of precision are available in floating point variables. Thus, you can write numbers like 4345345.8476583746123, but the computer will store only 4.345345e6.

Just because a floating point variable is stored in the computer in exponential notation doesn't mean it must print that way or that you need to type it using exponential notation. In the event.c program shown earlier, the %f format specifier causes the number to be printed in the normal way with a decimal point. However, as we'll see in the next section, you can force `printf()` to print in exponential notation or even to make a choice between decimal and exponential.

Initializing Variables

It's possible to combine a variable definition with an assignment operator so that a variable is given a value at the same time it's defined. For example, the event.c program could be rewritten, producing event2.c.

```c
#include <stdio.h>

void main(void)
   {
   int event = 5;
   char heat = 'C';
   float time = 27.25;

   printf("\nThe winning time in heat %c", heat);
   printf(" of event %d was %f.", event, time);
   }
```

The output is just the same, but we've saved some program lines and simplified the program. This is a commonly used approach.

Input/Output

It's all very well to store data in the computer and make calculations with it, but you also need to be able to input new data into the computer and print the results of your calculations. In this section we'll continue our examination of the output function `printf()`, and we'll introduce two input functions: `scanf()`, a versatile function that can handle many different kinds of input, and `getche()`, a specialized input function that tells your program which character you've typed, the instant you type it.

The *printf()* Function

We've been using `printf()` up to now without too much explanation of all its possibilities. Let's take a closer look.

Format Specifiers

As we've seen, a format specifier (such as %d or %c) is used to control what format will be used by `printf()` to print a particular variable. In general, you want to match the format specifier to the type of variable you're printing. We've already used four of the format specifiers available with `printf()`: %d to print integers, %c to print characters, %s to print strings, and %f to print floating point numbers. Although these are by far the most commonly used, there are others as well. Here's a list of the format specifiers for `printf()`:

%c	Single character
%s	String
%d	Signed decimal integer

continues

%f	Floating point (decimal notation)
%e	Floating point (exponential notation)
%g	Floating point (%f or %e, whichever is shorter)
%u	Unsigned decimal integer
%x	Unsigned hexadecimal integer (uses abcdef)
%o	Unsigned octal integer
l	Prefix used with %d, %u, %x, %o to specify long integer (for example %ld)

Field-Width Specifiers

The printf() function gives the programmer considerable power to format the printed output. Let's see how this is done.

In our event.c program the floating point variable time was printed with six digits to the right of the decimal, even though only two of these digits were significant.

```
The winning time in heat C of event 5 was 27.250000.
```

It would be nice to be able to suppress these extra zeros, and printf() includes a way to do just that. We'll rewrite the event.c program, inserting the string .2 (period 2) between the % character and the f in the second printf() statement.

```c
#include <stdio.h>

void main(void)
    {
    int event = 5;
    char heat = 'C';
    float time = 27.25;

    printf("\nThe winning time in heat %c", heat);
    printf(" of event %d was %.2f.", event, time);
    }
```

Here's the output of this program, which is called event3.c:

```
The winning time in heat C of event 5 was 27.25.
```

As you can see, a number *following* the decimal point in the field-width specifier controls how many characters will be printed following the decimal point.

A digit *preceding* the decimal point in the field-width specifier controls the width of the space to be used to contain the number when it is printed. Think of this field width as an imaginary box containing the number. An example (with integer values) is shown in Figure 2.4.

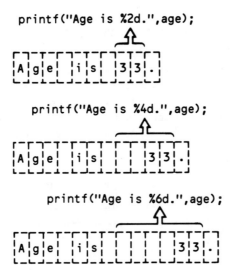

Figure 2.4. Field-width specifier.

Specifying the field width can be useful in creating tables of figures, as the following program, field.c, demonstrates.

```c
#include <stdio.h>

void main(void)
    {
    printf("\n");
    printf("%.1f %.1f %.1f\n", 3.0, 12.5, 523.3);
    printf("%.1f %.1f %.1f", 300.0, 1200.5, 5300.3);
    }
```

Here's the output:

```
3.0 12.5 523.3
300.0 1200.5 5300.3
```

Even though we used spaces in the format strings to separate the numbers (the spaces in the format string are simply printed as spaces in the output) and specified only one decimal place with the .1 string, the numbers don't line up and so are hard to read. However, if we insert the number 8 before the decimal place in each field-width specification we can put each number in a box eight characters wide. Here's the modified program, field2.c:

```c
#include <stdio.h>

void main(void)
    {
    printf("\n");
```

```
printf("%8.1f%8.1f%8.1f\n", 3.0, 12.5, 523.3);
printf("%8.1f%8.1f%8.1f", 300.0, 1200.5, 5300.3);
}
```

We should acknowledge the cluttered appearance of the `printf()` statements. Instant legibility isn't one of C's strong points (at least not until you've been programming in it for a while). Although you know the purpose of all the elements in these statements, your eye may have trouble unraveling them. It may help to draw lines between the individual format specifiers to clarify what's happening. Figure 2.5 shows this format string dissected.

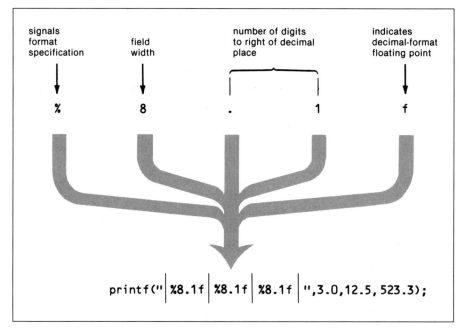

Figure 2.5. `printf()` *format string.*

> The format specifier in printf() determines the interpretation of a variable's type, the width of the field, the number of decimal places printed, and the justification.

Here's the output of the program, showing that, although the format specifiers may be hard to read, the output is a model of organization:

```
  3.0    12.5    523.3
300.0  1200.5  5300.3
```

A minus sign preceding the field-width specifier will put the output on the left side of the field instead of the right. For instance, let's insert minus signs in the field-width specifiers in the preceding program to create field3.c.

```c
#include <stdio.h>

void main(void)
    {
    printf("\n");
    printf("%-8.1f%-8.1f%-8.1f\n", 3.0, 12.5, 523.3);
    printf("%-8.1f%-8.1f%-8.1f", 300.0, 1200.5, 5300.3);
    }
```

— left justify not right justify

The output will be lined up on the *left* side of the fields, like this:

```
3.0     12.5    523.3
300.0   1200.5  52300.3
```

This format may be useful in certain circumstances, especially when printing strings.

The various uses of the format specifier are summarized in Appendix A, "Reference."

Escape Sequences

We saw in Chapter 1 how the newline character, \n, when inserted in a printf() format string, would print the carriage return-linefeed combination. The newline character is an example of something called an *escape sequence,* so called because the backslash symbol (\) is considered an *escape character:* it causes an escape from the normal interpretation of a string so that the next character is recognized as having a special meaning. Here's an example called tabtest.c that uses the newline character and a new escape sequence, \t, which means *tab.*

```c
#include <stdio.h>

void main(void)
    {
    printf("\nEach\tword\tis\ntabbed\tover\tonce");
    }
```

tab 8 times

represents a special character

Here's the output:

```
Each    word    is
tabbed  over    once
```

Turbo C++ tabs over eight characters when it encounters the \t character; this is another useful technique for lining up columns of output. The \n character causes a new line to begin following is.

The tab and newline are probably the most often used escape sequences, but there are others as well. The following list shows the common escape sequences.

\n	Newline
\t	Tab

continues

\b	Backspace
\r	Carriage return
\f	Formfeed
\'	Single quote
\"	Double quote
\\	Backslash
\xdd	ASCII code in hexadecimal notation (each d represents a digit)
\ddd	ASCII code in octal notation (each d represents a digit)

The first few of these escape sequences are more or less self-explanatory. The newline, which we've already seen, has the effect of both a carriage return and linefeed. Tab moves over to the next eight-space-wide field. Backspace moves the cursor one space left. Formfeed advances to the top of the next page on the printer.

Characters that are ordinarily used as delimiters—the single quote, double quote, and the backslash itself—can be printed by preceding them with the backslash. Thus, the statement

```
printf("Dick told Spot, \"Let's go!\"\n");
```

will print

```
Dick told Spot, "Let's go!"
```

Printing Graphics Characters

What's the purpose of those last two escape sequences, \xdd and \ddd?

As you probably know, every character (letters, digits, punctuation, and so forth) is represented in the computer by a number. True ASCII (an acronym for American Standard Code for Information Interchange) codes run from 0 to 127 (decimal). These cover the upper- and lowercase letters, digits from 0 to 9, punctuation, and control characters such as linefeed and backspace.

PC computers use an additional 128 characters, with codes running from 128 to 255. These codes were instituted by IBM and consist of foreign-language symbols and graphics characters. IBM has also defined a few characters below ASCII code 32 to be graphics characters. The entire set of IBM character codes is listed in Appendix D, "ASCII Chart."

We've already seen how to print ordinary ASCII characters on the screen using characters or strings in printf(). We also know how to print certain special characters with a backslash escape sequence, but graphics and other nonstandard characters require a different approach. They must be printed by sending the backslash and the number representing their character code.

(Actually another approach to printing graphics characters is to insert them directly into a string. To do this, hold down the Alt key, type the ASCII code for the character as three decimal digits on the numeric keypad (not the numbers on the top row of the keyboard), and release the Alt key. However, seeing the actual character in the listing gives no clue about how to type it, and some printers don't handle graphics characters, so we'll stick with the numerical approach.)

In C, the number representing a character must be specified in either octal or hexadecimal notation. Traditionally, octal has been used in UNIX-based systems. However, the rest of the PC world, including all operating system and assembly language programming, speaks hexadecimal; that's what we'll do in this book. There is no way to use decimal numbers as part of escape sequences—evidence of C's genesis in the world of systems programmers, who tend to think in terms of octal or hexadecimal, rather than decimal. (If you aren't familiar with the hexadecimal system, consult Appendix B, "Hexadecimal Numbering.")

Let's look at a program, charbox.c, that prints a simple graphics character, a small rectangle.

```c
#include <stdio.h>

void main(void)
   {
   printf("\nHere is the character: \xDB");
   }
```

The output of this program is shown in Figure 2.6.

Here is the character: ■

Figure 2.6. Printing a graphics character.

We've used the hexadecimal number DB (219 in decimal), which represents a solid rectangle.

Here's another example of the use of graphics characters:

```c
#include <stdio.h>

void main(void)
   {
   printf("\n");
   printf("\xC9\xCD\xBB\n");
   printf("\xC8\xCD\xBC\n");
   }
```

This program, called box6char.c, prints nothing but graphics characters. It displays a box on the screen, as shown in Figure 2.7.

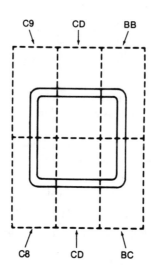

Figure 2.7. Box made with graphics characters.

> Graphics characters are printed using their hex code in an escape sequence, such as \xB0.

These graphics characters are specific to the PC world, so programs using them can't be ported to UNIX or other systems without modification. However, graphics characters offer an easy way to create graphics-like images on the PC screen. Programs using this form of graphics can be run on any PC system, even those without real graphics capabilities, making this the most universal form of graphics in the PC world. While not as versatile as color graphics, graphics characters can be used in many applications where simple graphics are required. One example is the Turbo C++ IDE itself.

We'll use other examples of graphics characters in programming examples in later chapters.

The *scanf()* Function

You already know about C's most-used *output* statements, printf(). In this section we're going to introduce an important *input* function, scanf(). C has a bewilderingly large collection of input and output functions, but printf() and scanf() are the most versatile in that they can handle all of the different variables and control their formatting.

Here's a program that uses scanf(). You can give it the filename age.c:

```
#include <stdio.h>

void main(void)
    {
    float years, days;

    printf("\nPlease type your age in years: ");
    scanf("%f", &years);
    days = years * 365;
    printf("You are %.1f days old.", days);
    }
```

Like printf(), scanf() requires the header file stdio.h, so no additional header file is required for this function.

Besides scanf(), this program introduces two new symbols: the arithmetic operator for multiplication (*) and the address operator, represented by the ampersand (&). We'll talk about both of these later in the chapter. For the moment, simply note the surprising fact that scanf() requires the use of an ampersand before the variable name.

A typical interaction between the program and a precocious youngster might look like this:

```
Please type your age in years: 2
You are 730.0 days old.
```

Because we're using floating point, we can also input decimal fractions.

```
Please type your age in years: 48.5
You are 17702.5 days old.
```

As you can see, the format for scanf() looks very much like that for printf(). As in printf(), the argument on the left is a string that contains format specifiers. In this case there is only one: %f. On the right is the variable name, &years.

The format specifiers for scanf() are similar to those for printf(), but there are a few differences. Table 2.1 shows them side-by-side for comparison.

Table 2.1. Format specifiers for printf() and scanf().

Format	printf()	scanf()
Single character	%c	%c
String	%s	%s
Signed decimal integer	%d	%d
Floating point (decimal notation)	%f	%f or %e
Floating point (exponential notation)	%e	%f or %e

continues   **43**

Table 2.1. continued

Format	printf()	scanf()
Floating point (%f or %e, whichever is shorter)	%g	
Unsigned decimal integer	%u	%u
Unsigned hexadecimal integer	%x	%x
Unsigned octal integer	%o	%o

As we noted earlier, the first four type characters are the most commonly used.

In `scanf()` (unlike the `printf()` function) %e can be used in place of %f; they have the same effect. You can type your input using either exponential or decimal notation; either format is accepted by both %e and %f. The %g specifier, which allows `printf()` to choose exponential or decimal notation, whichever is shorter, isn't necessary with `scanf()`, because the user makes the decision.

The l prefix is used before d, o, u, and x to specify type `long int`. Before e and f, it specifies type `double`. The L prefix before e and f specifies type `long double`.

The `scanf()` function can accept input to several variables at once. To demonstrate this, let's revise our event.c program to use input from the user, rather than assigning values to the variables within the program. This is event4.c:

```
#include <stdio.h>

void main(void)
    {
    int event;
    char heat;
    float time;

    printf("\nType event number, heat letter, and time: ");
    scanf("%d %c %f", &event, &heat, &time);
    printf("The winning time in heat %c", heat);
    printf(" of event %d was %.2f.", event, time);
    }
```

Here's the output:

```
Type event number, heat letter, and time: 4 B 36.34
The winning time in heat B of event 4 was 36.34.
```

How does `scanf()` know when we've finished typing one value and started another? Let's look at the process. As we type our three input values, 4, `'B'`, and 36.34, we separate them by spaces. The scanf() function matches each space we type with a corresponding space between the conversion type characters in the scanf() format string "%d %c %f". If we had tried to separate the values with another character—a dash or comma, for example—this wouldn't have matched the space in the format string. The space we type serves as a delimiter because it matches the space in the format string. This process is shown in Figure 2.8.

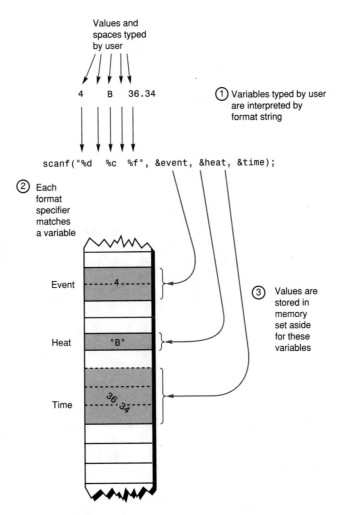

Figure 2.8. Using scanf() *with multiple inputs.*

Actually, we can use any whitespace character (space, newline, or tab) as a delimiter when we type our input values; each will match the space in the format string. Here's a sample using the Return key:

45

```
Type event number, heat letter, and time:
7
A
49.2
The winning time in heat A of event 7 was 49.20.
```

Here's an example using the Tab key:

```
Type event number, heat letter, and time: 3     A       14.7
The winning time in heat A of event 3 was 14.70.
```

There are other, more complex ways of handling the formatting of input to scanf(), but we won't be concerned about them now.

The Address Operator (&)

The scanf() function in the age.c and event4.c programs used a new symbol: the ampersand (&) preceding the variable names used as arguments.

```
scanf("%f", &years);
scanf("%d %c %f", &event, &heat, &time);
```

What is its purpose? It would seem more reasonable to use the name of the variable without the ampersand, as we did in printf() statements in the same programs. However (for reasons that will become clear later), the C compiler requires the arguments to scanf() to be the *addresses* of variables, rather than the variables themselves. This peculiarity of scanf() is one of C's least user-friendly characteristics; it is close to certain you'll forget the ampersands before the variables in scanf() at least once. However, the idea of *addresses* is the key to one of C's most powerful and interesting capabilities, so let's explore it further.

The memory of your computer is divided into bytes, and these bytes are numbered, from 0 to the upper limit of your memory (655,359, if you have 640K of memory). These numbers are called the *addresses* of the bytes. Every variable occupies a certain location in memory, and its address is that of the first byte it occupies. Figure 2.9 shows an integer with a value of 2 at address 1366.

Suppose we have defined an integer variable, num, in a program and assigned it the value 2. If the program later refers to the name of the variable, num, the compiler will give the *value* stored in that variable, or 2. However, if you refer to the name of the variable preceded by the ampersand, &num, the compiler will give the *address* where num is stored, or 1366.

Here's a program, addrtest.c, that demonstrates this operation:

```
#include <stdio.h>

void main(void)
    {
    int num;
```

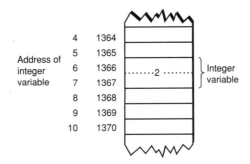

Figure 2.9. Address of variable.

```
num=2;
printf("\nValue=%d, address=%u", num, &num);
}
```

Here's the output:

```
Value=2, address=1366
```

On our particular computer, the address where the variable num is stored is 1366. In another computer it would almost certainly be different, because of variations in the size of the operating system and other factors. In any case, knowing where a variable is stored will turn out to be very important in C programming, as we'll learn when we get to the chapter on pointers.

In the meantime, all you need to remember about the address operator is that in using scanf() you need to precede variable names with the ampersand (except in the case of strings, which we're coming to soon).

The *getche()* Function

get character echo appears on screen.
getche()
getche = does not appear on screen.

For some situations, the scanf() function has one glaring weakness: you need to press the Return key before the function will digest what you've typed. We often want a function, however, that will read a single character the instant it's typed, without waiting for Return. For instance, in a game we might want a spaceship to move each time we pressed one of the cursor-control (arrow) keys; it would be awkward to press the Return key each time we pressed an arrow key.

We can use the getche() function for this purpose. The get means it gets something from the outside world; in other words, it's an input function. The ch means it gets a character, and the e means it echoes the character to the screen when you type it. (There is a similar function, getch(), which doesn't echo the typed character to the screen.) Another function, getchar(), is better known to programmers working on UNIX systems, but in Turbo C++ getchar is *buffered,* which means it doesn't pass the character typed by the user to the program until the user presses the Return key.

Here's a simple program, gettest.c, that uses getche(). The getche() function requires a different header file, conio.h, so we must include that as well.

```
#include <stdio.h>
#include <conio.h>

void main(void)
   {
   char ch;

   printf("\nType any character: ");
   ch = getche();
   printf("\nThe character you typed was %c.", ch );
   }
```

(handwritten margin note: 1 byte long / 2 bytes = ? / 4 bytes = ?)

Here's a sample interaction:

```
Type any character: T
The character you typed was T.
```

If you run this program, you'll notice that the phrase The character you typed was is printed immediately when you press any character key; you don't have to press the Return key.

Another point to notice is that the function itself takes on or *returns* the value of the character typed. It's almost as if the function were a variable that assigned itself a value; the function becomes the character typed. This is considerably different from the technique used in scanf(), where the value returned was placed in a variable that was one of scanf()'s arguments. Figure 2.10 shows the operation of the getche() function..

There is a downside to using getche(); if you make a mistake, you can't backspace to correct it, because as soon as you type a character, it's gobbled up by your program.

We'll see how useful getche() can be in the next chapter, when we learn such skills as how to count characters in phrases typed by the user.

There is more to say about input/output, and we'll be returning to the topic throughout the book.

Operators

Operators are words or symbols that cause a program to do something to variables. For instance, the arithmetic operators (+) and (–) cause a program to add or subtract two numbers. There are many different kinds of operators; to list them all here would be to invite debilitating ennui. Instead we'll mention the most common: arithmetic and relational operators and the less well-known (to non-C programmers) increment/decrement operators and arithmetic assignment operators. (Operators are summarized in Appendix A, "Reference.")

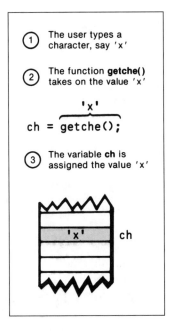

Figure 2.10. Operation of `getche()`

Arithmetic Operators

In the age.c program we used the multiplication operator (*) to multiply two numbers together. C uses the four arithmetic operators that are common in most programming languages and one, the remainder operator, which isn't so common.

+	Addition
-	Subtraction
*	Multiplication
/	Division
%	Remainder

[handwritten annotations:]
$a = x \% y$
$a = 1$
—
$a = x \mathbin{/} y$
$= 2$

$x = 7, y = 3$

$\begin{array}{r} 2 \\ 3\overline{)7} \\ -6 \\ \hline 1 \end{array}$

Here's a program, ftoc.c, that uses several arithmetic operators. It converts temperatures in Fahrenheit to centigrade.

```c
#include <stdio.h>

void main(void)
    {
    int ftemp, ctemp;

    printf("\nEnter temperature in degrees Fahrenheit: ");
    scanf("%d", &ftemp);
```

```
ctemp = (ftemp-32) * 5 / 9;
printf("Temperature in degrees centigrade is %d", ctemp);
}
```

Here's a sample interaction with the program:

```
Enter temperature in degrees Fahrenheit: 32
Temperature in degrees centigrade is 0
```

Here's another:

```
Enter temperature in degrees Fahrenheit: 70
Temperature in degrees centigrade is 21
```

This program uses the standard formula for converting degrees Fahrenheit into degrees centigrade: subtract 32 from the Fahrenheit temperature and multiply the result by five-ninths.

```
ctemp = (ftemp-32) * 5 / 9;
```

There are several things to note about this statement. First, you'll see that we've surrounded some of the operators, the (*) and the (/), with spaces but haven't used spaces around the minus sign. The moral here is that the C compiler doesn't care whether you use spaces surrounding your operators or not, so you're free to arrange your expressions however they look best to you. If you don't like the way the spaces are arranged in the example, you can arrange them another way when you type the program.

Operator Precedence

The second point to notice about the ftemp.c program is that we've used parentheses around (ftemp–32). For those of you who remember your algebra the reason will be clear; we want the 32 subtracted from `ftemp` *before* we multiply it by 5 and divide by 9. Because multiplication and division are normally carried out before addition and subtraction, we use parentheses to ensure that the subtraction is carried out first.

The fact that (*) and (/) are evaluated before (+) and (–) is an example of *precedence;* we say that (*) and (/) have a higher precedence than (+) and (–). We'll be returning to this idea of precedence when we discuss different kinds of operators.

The Remainder Operator

The remainder operator (sometimes called the *modulo* operator) may be unfamiliar to you; it is used to find the remainder when one number is divided by another. For example, in the statement below, the variable `answer` will be assigned the value 3, because that's the remainder when 13 is divided by 5.

```
answer = 13 % 5;
```

We'll find uses for all the arithmetic operators as we go along, but the remainder operator is useful in unexpected ways.

Expressions Versus Variables

Where can you use expressions containing arithmetic operators? We've already shown examples of their use in assignment statements, such as

```
days = years * 365;
```

It's also possible to include expressions involving arithmetic operators (and other kinds of operators as well) directly into `printf()` and other kinds of statements. For example, the following usage is just fine:

```
#include <stdio.h>

void main(void)
    {
    int num = 2;

    printf("\nNumber plus four is %d.", num + 4);
    }
```

When this program, called exptest.c, is executed, the following phrase will be printed:

```
Number plus four is 6.
```

Instead of a constant or a variable, `printf()` has printed out the value of the expression

```
num + 4
```

An *expression* is simply a combination of constants, variables, and operators that can be evaluated to yield a value. Because the variable `number` has the value 2, the expression evaluates to 6, and that's what is printed, so you can use an expression almost anyplace you can use a variable. This is done more often in C than it is in most languages; we'll see examples as we go along.

> An entire expression can be used almost anyplace a variable can be used.

While we're on the subject of arithmetic operators, we should mention two kinds of operators that you may not have encountered before in other languages: arithmetic assignment operators and increment/decrement operators. Both are widely used in C and both help to give C source listings their distinctive appearance.

Arithmetic Assignment Operators

If you compare a C program with a program with a similar purpose written in another language, you may well find that the C source file is shorter. One reason for this is that C has several operators that can compress often-used programming statements. Consider the following statement:

```
total = total + number;
```

Here the value in `number` is added to the value in `total`, and the result is placed in `total`. In C, this statement can be rewritten

```
total += number;
```

The effect is exactly the same, but the expression is more compact, as shown in Figure 2.11.

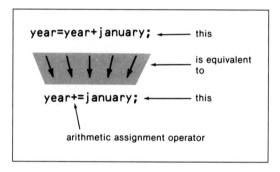

Figure 2.11. The arithmetic assignment operator.

Here's a program, assign.c, that makes use of this *plus-equal operator.*

```
#include <stdio.h>

void main(void)
    {
    int total = 0;
    int count = 10;

    printf("\nTotal=%d\n", total);
    total += count;
    printf("Total=%d\n", total);
    total += count;
    printf("Total=%d\n", total);
    }
```

Here's the output, showing the results of repeatedly adding the value of `count`, which is 10, to `total`.

```
Total=0
Total=10
Total=20
```

All the arithmetic operators listed earlier can be combined with the equal sign in the same way.

+=	Addition assignment
-=	Subtraction assignment
*=	Multiplication assignment
/=	Division assignment
%=	Remainder assignment

There are assignment versions of some other operators as well, such as logical operators and bitwise operators, which we'll encounter later.

The Increment Operator

C uses another operator that isn't common in other languages: the increment operator. Consider the following program, incop.c:

```c
#include <stdio.h>

void main(void)
    {
    int num=0;

    printf("\n");
    printf("Number=%d\n", num);
    printf("Number=%d\n", num++);
    printf("Number=%d\n", num);
    }
```

(handwritten annotations: uses # before adding 1 ; uses # after adding 1 ; ++num 0 1 1)

Here's the output:

```
Number=0
Number=0
Number=1
```

How did the variable num get to be 1? As you can guess by examination of the program, the (++) operator had the effect of incrementing num; that is, adding 1 to it. The first printf() statement printed the original value of num, which was 0. The second printf() statement also printed the original value of num; then, *after* num was printed, the (++) operator incremented it. Thus the third printf() statement printed the incremented value. The effect of num(++) is exactly the same as that of the statement

```c
num = num + 1;
```

However, num (++) is far more compact to write, as shown in Figure 2.12. It also may compile into more efficient code.

Let's rewrite the program, making a subtle change and producing incop2.c.

```c
#include <stdio.h>

void main(void)
    {
    int num=0;
```

float sal[50];

sal++

50+4=54

int = +2

so

int grade [50]

52 grades++

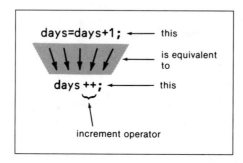

Figure 2.12. The increment operator.

```
printf("\n");
printf("Number=%d\n", num);
printf("Number=%d\n", ++num);
printf("Number=%d\n", num);
}
```

What did we do? We moved the (++) operator to the beginning of the num variable. Let's see what effect this has on the output.

```
Number=0
Number=1
Number=1
```

Now the variable num in the second printf() statement is incremented *before* it is printed.

Because there's an increment operator you can guess there will be a decrement operator as well. Let's modify our program again, using (--) the decrement operator and producing decop.c.

```
#include <stdio.h>

void main(void)
    {
    int num=0;

    printf("\n");
    printf("Number=%d\n", num);
    printf("Number=%d\n", num--);
    printf("Number=%d\n", num);
    }
```

Now instead of being incremented, the num variable is decremented: reduced by 1.

```
Number=0
Number=0
Number=-1
```

The effect is just the same as executing the statement

```
num = num - 1;
```

> The (++) and (- -) operators can increment and decrement a variable without the need for a separate program statement.

The ability to increment (or decrement) a variable deep within an expression and to control whether it will be incremented before or after it is used, is one of the features that makes a single line of code so powerful in C. We'll see many examples of these operators as we go along.

Relational Operators

In the next two chapters we'll be dealing with loops and decisions. These constructs require the program to ask questions about the relationship between variables. Is a certain variable greater than 100? If so, stop looping. Is the character the user just typed equal to a space? If so, increment the count of the number of words.

Relational operators are the vocabulary the program uses to ask questions about variables. Let's look at an example of a relational operator, in this case the *less-than* (<) operator. This program is called lessthan.c:

[handwritten: IF hours = 40   40 stored @ memory location "hours"]

```
#include <stdio.h>

void main(void)
    {
    int age;

    age = 15;
    printf("\nIs age less than 21? %d", age < 21 );
    age = 30;
    printf("\nIs age less than 21? %d", age < 21 );
    }
```

The output from this program looks like this:

```
Is age less than 21? 1
Is age less than 21? 0
```
[handwritten: True / false]

in this program the printf() statements take the whole expression

```
age < 21
```

and print its value. What is its value? That depends on the value of the variable age. When age is 15, which *is* less than 21, a 1 is printed. When age is 30, which isn't less than 21, a 0 is printed. It would seem that 1 stands for true, and 0 stands for false. This turns out to be the case. In C, true is represented by the integer 1, and false is represented by the integer 0. In some languages, such as Pascal, true and false values are represented by a special variable type called *Boolean.* In C, there is no such data type, so true and false values are represented by integers. The operation of the relational expression is shown in Figure 2.13.

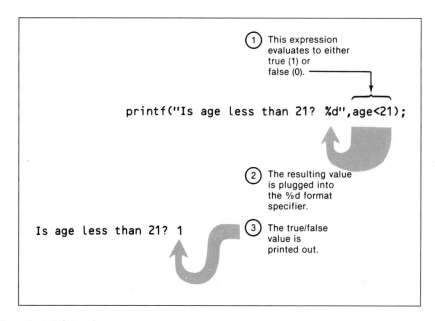

Figure 2.13. Relational expression in a `printf()` statement.

The relational operators in C look much like those in other languages. There are six of them.

<	Less than
>	Greater than
<=	Less than or equal to
>=	Greater than or equal to
==	Equal to
!=	Not equal to

Note that the relational operator *equal to* is represented by *two* equal signs. A common mistake is to use a single equal sign as a relational operator. For reasons that we'll learn later, the compiler doesn't notice that this is an error, so it can be a particularly frustrating bug to track down.

Here's an example using the equal-to (==) operator (sometimes called the *equal-equal* operator).

```
#include <stdio.h>
```

```
void main(void)
   {
   int speed;

   speed = 75;
   printf("\nIs speed equal to 55? %d", speed == 55 );
   speed = 55;
   printf("\nIs speed equal to 55? %d", speed == 55 );
   }
```

Here's the output of the equalto.c program:

```
Is speed equal to 55? 0
Is speed equal to 55? 1
```

Note again how the expression

```
speed == 55
```

evaluates to either a false (0) or a true (1) value.

An interesting point to notice about true and false values is that, although C will generate a 1 when it means true and a 0 when it means false, it will recognize *any* non-zero value as true. That is, there are a lot of integers that C thinks of as true, but only one—0—it thinks of as false. We'll make use of this fact in later programs.

Precedence, Round II

What will be printed if you execute the following program? Remember that true is the integer 1 and false is the integer 0. These values can be used just like any other integer values, as shown by the prec.c program.

```
#include <stdio.h>

void main(void)
   {
   printf("\nAnswer is %d", 2+1 < 4 );
   }
```

If you guessed *Answer is 1,* you're right. First 2+1 is evaluated to yield 3, then this is compared with 4. It's less, so the expression

```
2+1 < 4
```

is true. True is 1 so that's what's printed.

Now watch closely: we're going to try something a little tricky. What will this program, prec2.c, print?

```
#include <stdio.h>

void main(void)
   {
   printf("\nAnswer is %d", 1<2 + 4 );
   }
```

Did you guess *Answer is 5?* If so, you probably decided that 1<2 would evaluate to true, or 1, and 1 added to 4 would give 5. Sorry, this is plausible but incorrect. We misled you with the use of spaces in the expression 1<2 + 4. Here's how we should have written it:

```
1 < 2+4
```

There are two lessons here. First, as we mentioned before, the compiler doesn't care where you put spaces; both forms of the expression compile into the same program. Second, arithmetic operators have a *higher precedence* than relational operators. That is, in the absence of parentheses, the arithmetic operators are evaluated *before* the relational operators. In the expression above, the arithmetic operator (+) is evaluated first, yielding a value of 6 from the expression 2+4. Then the relational operator (<) is evaluated. Because 1 is less than 6, the value of the entire expression is true. Thus, the output of this program will be

```
Answer is 1
```

> Arithmetic operators have a higher precedence—that is, are evaluated before—relational operators.

All operators in C are ranked according to their precedence. We haven't encountered many of these operators yet, so we won't pursue the subject of precedence further here. It will, however, arise from time to time as we learn more about C. Precedence is a more important issue in C than it is in some languages because of the complexity of the expressions that are routinely created. Appendix A, "Reference," includes a table showing the precedence of all the C operators.

Comments

It's helpful to be able to put comments into the source code file that can be read by humans but are invisible to the compiler. Modern C compilers recognize two kinds of comments: the new slash-slash comment and the old slash-star comment.

New Style Comments

Here's a revision of our age program, with comments added. It's called agecom.c.

```
// agecom.c
// calculates age in days
#include <stdio.h>

void main(void)
    {
    float years, days;
```

```
printf("\nPlease type your age in years: "); // print prompt
scanf("%f", &years);            // get age in years from user
days = years * 365;              // calculate age in days
printf("You are %.1f days old.\n", days);    // print result
}
```

A comment begins with the two-character symbol slash- slash (//) and continues until the end of the line.

In this example we've used two full-line comments to name the program and to say what it does. We've also placed comments on the lines with the program code. The only problem with comments that share lines with code is that it's easy to run out of space. C's long program statements, and the fact that they're indented, combine to reduce the number of character spaces available on a line.

Although a lot of comments probably aren't necessary in this program, it is usually the case that programmers use too few comments rather than too many. Comments should be added anyplace there's a possibility of confusion. We'll refrain from repeating the standard lecture on how an adequate number of comments can save hours of misery and suffering when you later try to figure out what the program does.

Note that the double-slash comment is an exception to the rule that the compiler ignores whitespace characters; in this case the newline character at the end of the line signals the end of the comment.

The double-slash comment style is comparatively new to C. It first appeared in C++ and was later adopted by C compiler writers. It isn't, strictly speaking, ANSI C. However, it's so much easier to use than the old style of comment that it's receiving almost universal acceptance.

Old Style Comments

The old style C comment looks like this:

```
/* this is a comment */
```

Here the slash-star symbol (/*) begins the comment, and the star-slash symbol (*/) ends it. The end of the line doesn't end the comment, so the ending symbol is absolutely necessary.

The old-fashioned comment style is useful for multiline comments, because you don't need a symbol at the beginning of each line. The comment continues until the */ symbol.

```
/*
This is
a multiline
comment
*/
```

It's easy to make errors with the old-style comment symbols, and the results of such errors can be particularly baffling to debug. For instance, if you forget the close-comment symbol (*/) at the end of a comment, the compiler will assume that your entire program from then on is a comment. It won't compile this code, and it also won't issue any error messages, or at least any messages that relate specifically to comments. Tracking down this sort of bug can be a major inconvenience, so if you use the old-style comments, be careful that every begin-comment symbol is matched with a close-comment symbol. It's also hard to type the old-style comment, with its combination of upper- and lowercase characters. We'll use the new style in our program examples.

Summary

In this chapter we've introduced some of the more fundamental parts of C: variables, input/output, and operators.

You've learned that there are six major variable types in C: character, integer, long integer, floating point, double-precision floating point, and long double-precision floating point. You've learned how to declare and initialize variables and how to use them in assignment and other kinds of statements.

Concerning input/output functions, you've learned about format and field-width specifiers in the printf() function, about escape sequences, and about how to print graphics characters. You've been introduced to the scanf() and getche() input functions, seen how scanf() is good for a variety of input and can handle multiple variables, and learned how getche() returns any character typed.

We've covered two major categories of operators, arithmetic operators and relational operators, and mentioned two less important but very "C-like" operators, the arithmetic assignment statement and the increment/decrement operator. We've also discussed comments and operator precedence.

With these fundamentals under your belt, you should be ready to wade into the next few chapters, where we discuss program structures such as loops, decisions, and functions.

Questions

1. Declaring variables is advantageous because it

    a. Helps organize the program
    b. Helps the compiler work efficiently
    c. Avoids errors from misspelled variable names
    d. Simplifies the writing of very short programs

2. The five major data types in C are

   c_____

   i_____

   f_____

   l_____

   d_____

3. Which of these C statements is correct?

   a. int a
   b. float b
   c. double float c
   d. unsigned char d

4. True or false: two variables can be declared in one statement.

5. Type `float` occupies _____ times as many bytes of memory as type `char`.

6. Type `int` can accommodate numbers from _____ to _____.

7. Which of the following is an example of initializing a variable?

   a. num=2
   b. int num
   c. num < 2
   d. int num=2

8. True or false: type `long` variables can hold numbers only twice as big as type `int` variables.

9. Floating point variables are used instead of integers to

   a. Avoid being too specific about what value a number has
   b. Make possible the use of large numbers
   c. Permit the use of decimal points in numbers
   d. Conceal the true value of the numbers

10. What do the escape sequences \x41 and \xE0 print?

11. Express the following numbers in exponential notation:

    a. 1,000,000
    b. 0.000,001
    c. 199.95
    d. −888.88

12. Express the following numbers in decimal notation:

    a. 1.5e6

    b. 1.5e–6

    c. 7.6543e3

    d. –7.6543e–3

13. What's wrong with this program?

```
// q2-13.c
// calculates age in days
#include <stdio.h>

void main(void)
   {
   float years, days;

   printf("\nPlease type your age in years: "); // print prompt
   scanf("%f", years);                          // get input
   days = years * 365;                          // find answer
   printf("You are %.1f days old.\n", days);    // print answer
   }
```

14. A field-width specifier in a `printf()` function:

    a. Controls the margins of the program listing

    b. Specifies the maximum value of a number

    c. Controls the size of type used to print numbers

    d. Specifies how many character positions will be used for a number

15. True or false: a function can have a value.

16. Which of the following are arithmetic operators?

    a. +

    b. &

    c. %

    d. <

17. Rewrite the following statement using the increment operator:
`number = number + 1;`

18. Rewrite the following statement using arithmetic assignment statement: `usa = usa + calif;`

19. What is the meaning of the characters \t and \r?

20. The function `scanf()` reads

    a. A single character
    b. Characters and strings
    c. Any possible number
    d. Any possible variable type

21. True or false: you need to press the Return key after typing a character in order for `getche()` to read it.

22. A relational operator is used to

    a. Combine values
    b. Compare values
    c. Distinguish different types of variables
    d. Change variables to logical values

23. Are the following expressions true or false?

    a. 1 > 2
    b. 'a' < 'b' T
    c. 1 = = 2 F
    d. '2' = = '2' T

24. Precedence determines which operator:

    a. Is most important
    b. Is used first
    c. Is fastest
    d. Operates on the largest numbers

25. Is the following a correctly formed comment?

    ```
    /* This is a
    /* comment which
    /* extends over several lines
    */
    ```

Exercises

1. Modify the age.c program to print the age in minutes instead of days.

2. Write a program that prints the square of a number the user types. (The square is the number times itself.) Use floating point.

3. Rewrite the box.c program so that it draws a similar box, but one that is four characters wide and four characters tall.

Std directives
    #include
    #define

editor command #include that says go to disk pack & get <stdio.h>
file & attach to my file. Sdio.h has defns of printf ex & put it
there & tells computer what to do @ those pts.

    printf ("Hello");
     To the std output device   put Hello
    Printf (prn, "Hello");
             print to   printer Hello

    printf (pfile, "Hello");
              print to file
together {int age
        {scanf ("%d", &age)

Together {char nam [20];   \array name
         {scanf ("%s", name);

Loops

- for loop
- while loop
- do while loop
- Nested loops
- Values of functions and assignment expressions
- break and continue statements

In the last chapter, we introduced variables, input/output functions, and operators. With these programming elements we wrote programs that were almost useful: converting from Fahrenheit to centigrade, for example. However, the programs were limited because, when executed, they always performed the same series of actions, in the same way, exactly once.

Almost always, if something is worth doing, it's worth doing more than once. You can probably think of several examples of this from real life, such as going to the movies and eating a good dinner. Programming is the same; we frequently need to perform an action over and over, often with variations in the details each time. The mechanism that meets this need is the *loop,* and loops are the subject of this chapter.

There are three major loop structures in C: the for loop, the while loop, and a cousin of the while loop called the do loop (or do while loop). We'll discuss each of these in turn. We're going to start with the for loop because it has close analogies in both BASIC and Pascal, whereas—at least in old-style BASIC—there is no equivalent to the while loop. Also, the for loop is conceptually easy to understand, although the details can get complicated. This is true because all its elements are stated explicitly at the beginning of the loop. In the other loops, the elements are scattered throughout the program.

The *for* Loop

It is often the case in programming that you want to do something a fixed number of times. Perhaps you want to calculate the paychecks for 120 employees or print the squares of all the numbers from 1 to 50. The for loop is ideally suited for such cases.

Let's look at a simple example of a for loop:

```
// forloop.c
// prints numbers from 0 to 9
#include <stdio.h>    // for printf()

void main(void)
    {
    int count;

    for (count=0; count<10; count++)   // from 0 to 9
       printf("\ncount=%d", count);    // print value of count
    }
```

Type the program (forloop.c) and compile it. When executed, it will generate the following output:

```
count=0
count=1
count=2
count=3
count=4
count=5
count=6
count=7
```

```
count=8
count=9
```

This program's role in life is to execute a `printf()` statement 10 times. The `printf()` function prints the phrase count= followed by the value of the variable count. Let's see how the `for` loop causes this to happen.

Structure of the *for* Loop

The parentheses following the keyword `for` contain what we'll call the *loop expression.* This loop expression is divided by semicolons into three separate expressions: the *initialize expression,* the *test expression,* and the *increment expression.*

Expression	Name	Purpose
count=0	Initialize expression	Initializes loop variable
count<10	Test expression	Tests loop variable
count++	Increment expression	Increments loop variable

Figure 3.1 shows the structure of the `for` loop.

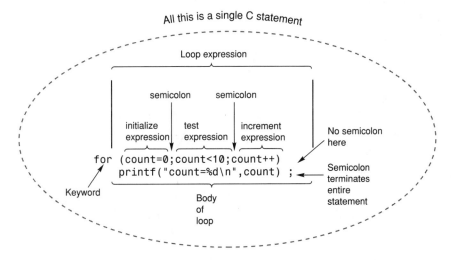

Figure 3.1. Structure of the for *loop.*

The variable count occupies a key role in this `for` loop. In conjunction with the three parts of the loop expression, count is used to control the operation of the loop. Specifically, it keeps track of how many times we've been through the loop.

Let's look in more detail at the three parts of the loop expression and how they operate on the variable count.

The Initialize Expression

The initialize expression, count=0, initializes the count variable. The initialize expression is always executed as soon as the loop is entered. We can start at any number; in this case we initialize count to 0. However, loops are often started at 1 or some other number.

The Test Expression

The second expression, count<10, tests each time through the loop to see if count is less than 10. To do this, it makes use of the relational operator for less-than (<). If the test expression is true (count is less than 10), the body of the loop (the printf() statement) will be executed. If the expression becomes false (count is 10 or more), the loop will be terminated and control will pass to the statements following the loop (in this case, there aren't any, so the entire program terminates).

The Increment Expression

The third expression, count++, increments the variable count each time the loop is executed. To do this, it uses the increment operator (++), described in the last chapter.

The loop variable in a for loop doesn't have to be increased by 1 each time through the loop. It can also be decreased by 1, as we'll see later on in this chapter, or changed by some other number, using an expression such as

```
count = count + 3
```

In other words, practically any expression can be used for the increment expression.

The Body of the *for* Loop

Following the keyword for and the loop expression is the body of the loop: that is, the statement (or statements) that will be executed each time round the loop. In our example, there is only one statement.

```
printf("count=%d\n", count);
```

Note that this statement is terminated with a semicolon, whereas the for with the loop expression is not. That's because the entire combination of the for keyword, the loop expression, and the statement constituting the body of the loop are considered to be a single C statement.

In a for loop, don't place a semicolon between the loop expression and the body of the loop, because the keyword for and the loop expression don't constitute a complete C statement.

Operation of the *for* Loop

Let's follow the operation of the loop, as depicted in Figure 3.2. First the initialization expression is executed, then the test condition is examined. If the test expression is false to begin with, the body of the loop won't be executed at all. If the condition is true, the body of the loop is executed and, following that, the increment expression is executed. This is why the first number printed by our program is 0 and not 1; printing takes place before count is incremented by the (++) operator. Finally the loop recycles and the test expression is queried again. This will continue until the test expression becomes false—count becomes 10—at which time the loop will end.

We should note here that C permits an unusual degree of flexibility in the writing of the for loop. For instance, if separated by commas, more than one expression can be used for the initialize expression and for the increment expression so that several variables can be initialized or incremented at once. Also, none of the three expressions actually needs to refer to the loop variable; a loop variable isn't even essential. In many cases, the for loop is used roughly as we've shown it in the example, but we'll see an instance of multiple initialization in the next example.

Multiple Statements in Loops

The preceding example used only a single statement in the body of the loop. Two (or more) statements can also be used, as shown in the following program:

```
// forloop2.c
// prints numbers from 0 to 9, keeps running total
#include <stdio.h>                    // for printf()

void main(void)
   {
   int count, total;

   for (count=0, total=0; count<10; count++)
      {
      total = total + count;          // add count to total
      printf("\ncount=%d, total=%d", count, total);
      }
   }
```

Type the program in (call it forloop2.c) and compile it. This program not only prints the numbers from 0 to 9, it also prints a running total.

```
count=0, total=0
count=1, total=1
count=2, total=3
count=3, total=6
count=4, total=10
count=5, total=15
count=6, total=21
count=7, total=28
```

```
count=8, total=36
count=9, total=45
```

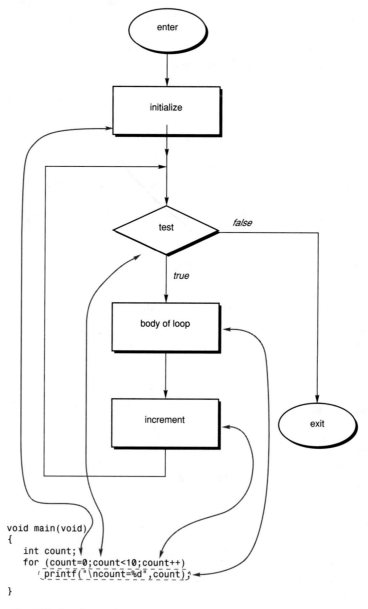

```
void main(void)
{
    int count;
    for (count=0;count<10;count++)
        printf("\ncount=%d",count);
}
```

Figure 3.2. Operation of the `for` *loop.*

Truly, a performance to make any power user envious.

The most important new feature of this program is the use of braces ({ and }) to encapsulate the two statements that form the body of the loop.

```
{
total = total + count;
printf("count=%d, total=%d\n", count, total);
}
```

There are two points to remember about this multistatement loop body. The first is that the whole package—the opening brace, the statements, and the closing brace—is treated as a single C statement, with the semicolon understood. This is often called a *compound statement* or *block*. Thus, you don't need to type a semicolon after the last brace. The second point is that each statement within the block is also a C statement and must be terminated with a semicolon in the usual way. Figure 3.3 shows the operation of the for loop with multiple statements in the loop body. This figure is similar to that for the single-statement loop body; we've included it here partly to facilitate comparison with the operation of the while loop in the next section.

Note that we could have used the (+=) arithmetic assignment operator to add the value of count to the value of total in the expression

```
total += count;
```

As we saw in Chapter 2, this is equivalent to

```
total = total + count;
```

Loop Style Note

Many C programmers, including the venerable Kernighan and Ritchie (referred to in Chapter 1, "The Turbo C++ Development System,") handle braces in a somewhat different way than we've shown above. They put the opening brace on the same line as the loop expression.

```
for (count=0, total=0; count<10; count++) {
   total = total + count;
   printf("count=%d, total=%d\n", count, total);
}
```

This has the advantage of saving a line in the listing. However, the compiler doesn't care which way you choose, and we feel that aligning the matching braces vertically makes it easier to ensure that each opening brace is matched by a closing brace and helps to clarify the structure of the program. Both approaches are common. For ease of learning we'll use the braces-on-separate-lines approach.

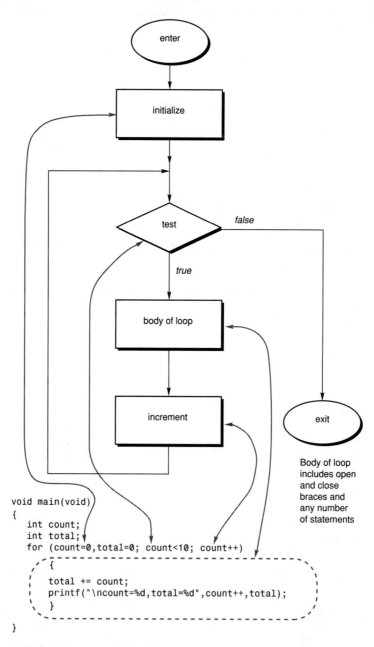

Figure 3.3. Multiple statements in the for *loop.*

Multiple Initializations in the *for* Loop

Another subtlety we've introduced into the forloop2.c program is that the initialization expression in the for loop contains two statements, separated by a comma: count=0 and total=0. As we mentioned, this is perfectly legal syntax.

```
for (count=0, total=0; count<10; count++)
```

In this particular program we didn't really need to put the initialization of total within the loop; we could also have said

```
total = 0;
for (count=0; count<10; count++)
```

but we wanted to show how two (or more) statements can be used in the initialization expression, and we saved a line of code—a desirable end in the eyes of most C programmers.

As we noted, multiple statements can also be used in this way in the increment expression; that is, you can increment two or more variables at the same time. However, only one expression is allowed in the test expression, because a single condition must determine when the loop terminates.

The use of multiple statements in the initialization expression also demonstrates why semicolons are used to separate the three kinds of expressions in the for loop. If commas had been used (as commas are used to separate the arguments of a function, for example), they couldn't also have been used to separate multiple statements in the initialization expression without confusing the compiler. The comma is sometimes called the *sequential evaluation operator,* because it separates a list of similar items that will be evaluated in turn. Items separated by commas are evaluated from left to right.

An ASCII Table Program

Here's a program that uses a for loop to print a table of ASCII codes. As you learned in Chapter 2, in the PC family, each of the numbers from 0 to 255 represents a separate character. From 0 to 31 are control codes (such as the carriage return, tab, and linefeed) and some graphics characters; from 32 to 127 are the usual printing characters; and from 128 to 255 are graphics and foreign language characters.

```
// asctab.c
// prints table of ASCII characters
#include <stdio.h>              // for printf()

void main(void)
   {
   int n;

   printf("\n");
   for (n = 32; n < 256; n++)   // codes from 32 to 255
      printf ("%3d=%c\t", n, n); // print as number
   }                            // and as character
```

A section of the output is shown below:

```
41=)   42=*  43=+  44=,   45=-  46=.  47=/  48=0  49=1  50=2
51=3   52=4  53=5  54=6   55=7  56=8  57=9  58=:  59=;  60=<
61==   62=>  63=?  64=@   65=A  66=B  67=C  68=D  69=E  70=F
71=G   72=H  73=I  74=J   75=K  76=L  77=M  78=N  79=O  80=P
81=Q   82=R  83=S  84=T   85=U  86=V  87=W  88=X  89=Y  90=Z
91=]   92=\  93=]  94=^   95=_  96='  97=a  98=b  99=c  100=d
101=e 102=f 103=g 104=h 105=i 106=j 107=k 108=l 109=m 110=n
111=o 112=p 113=q 114=r 115=s 116=t 117=u 118=v 119=w 120=x
```

This program uses the tab character (\t) in the printf() statement. This causes the next item printed to start eight spaces from the start of the last item. In other words, it divides the screen into columns eight characters wide. On an 80-column screen then, we have room for 10 items. (In the listing above the columns are actually only six spaces wide; we compressed it so that the printout would fit on the page.) The printf() function also uses a field-width specifier of 3 so that each number is printed in a box three characters wide, even if it has only two digits.

The *printf()* Function as a Conversion Device

The printf() statement in our asctab.c program is performing a complex task with a minimum of fuss: printing both the character and its ASCII code. In most languages, this would require a separate conversion function to change the number n into the character whose ASCII value is n.

In C, we can use the same variable, n, for both number and character; only the format specifier changes: %c prints the character, while %d prints the number.

```
printf ("%3d=%c\t", n, n);
```

> Format specifiers can interpret the same variable in different ways.

What's actually stored in the computer's memory is an integer, n, as specified in the type declaration statement. The %d format specifier prints the decimal representation of n, while the %c format specifier prints the character whose ASCII code is n.

Drawing a Line with a Graphics Character

In Chapter 2 we introduced a graphics character representing a rectangle (ASCII code DB hexadecimal). Let's use this character and a for loop to draw a line across the screen. Here's the program:

```
// line.c
// draws a solid line using rectangular graphics character
#include <stdio.h>        // for printf()
```

```
void main(void)
   {
   int cols;

   printf("\n");
   for (cols=1; cols<40; cols++)
      printf("%c", '\xDB');
   }
```

Each time through the loop another rectangle is printed, creating a solid line of rectangles. The process is shown in Figure 3.4.

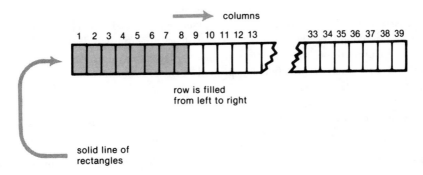

Figure 3.4. Operation of the line.c program.

✳ Nested *for* Loops

It is possible to nest one `for` loop inside another. To demonstrate this structure, we'll concoct a program that prints the multiplication table.

```
// multab.c
// generates the multiplication table
#include <stdio.h>          // for printf()

void main(void)
   {
   int cols, rows;

   for(rows=1; rows < 13; rows++)        // outer loop
      {
      printf("\n");
      for(cols=1; cols < 13; cols++)     // inner loop
         printf( "%3d ", cols*rows );
      }
   }
```
→ going to run 12 times

When you run this program, you'll get the following output:

```
 1   2   3   4   5   6   7   8   9  10  11  12
```

```
 2   4   6   8  10  12  14  16  18  20  22  24
 3   6   9  12  15  18  21  24  27  30  33  36
 4   8  12  16  20  24  28  32  36  40  44  48
 5  10  15  20  25  30  35  40  45  50  55  60
 6  12  18  24  30  36  42  48  54  60  66  72
 7  14  21  28  35  42  49  56  63  70  77  84
 8  16  24  32  40  48  56  64  72  80  88  96
 9  18  27  36  45  54  63  72  81  90  99 108
10  20  30  40  50  60  70  80  90 100 110 120
11  22  33  44  55  66  77  88  99 110 121 132
12  24  36  48  60  72  84  96 108 120 132 144
```

In this program the inner loop steps through 12 columns, from 1 to 12, while the outer loop steps through 12 rows. For each row, the inner loop is cycled through once; then a newline is printed in preparation for the next row. Each time through the inner loop— that is, at each intersection of a column and a row—the product of the row number (rows) and the column number (cols) is printed by the printf function. For instance, if the variable cols was 8, meaning we're on the eighth column, and rows was 4, meaning we're on the fourth row, then the program multiplies 8 by 4 and prints the product at the intersection of this row and column. Since we used the less-than operator (<), the loop variables cols and rows never reach the limit of 13; the loops both terminate at 12.

To ensure that the columns line up, we use a field-width specifier of 3 in the printf() function.

Indentation and Nesting

As you can see, the body of the outer for loop is indented, and the body of the inner for loop (in this case a single line) is further indented. These multiple indentations make the program easier to read and understand. Although invisible to the compiler, some form of indentation is employed by almost all C programmers for nested loops.

The actual multiplication of cols times rows takes place inside the printf() function.

```
printf("%3d ", cols * rows );
```

We could have used another variable, say product (which would need to be defined) and written the inner loop as

```
{
product = rows * cols;
printf ("%3d ", product );
}
```

However, as we've noted, C programmers usually try to telescope statements in order to achieve compactness and eliminate unnecessary variables.

The fill.c Program

Here's another example of the nested `for` loop construction. This one looks like the multiplication table example, but instead it fills a box-shaped area of the screen with a solid color. It's actually an extension of the line.c program: fill.c repeatedly prints lines of rectangles to create a solid area. Here's the listing:

```c
// fill.c
// fills square area on screen
#include <stdio.h>          // for printf()

void main(void)
    {
    int cols, rows;

    for (rows=1; rows<=22; rows++)        // from row to row
        {
        printf("\n");
        for (cols=1; cols<=40; cols++)  // from column to column
            printf("\xDB");
        }
    }
```

going to run 22 times

As in the multab.c program, fill.c uses an outer `for` loop to control the rows and an inner `for` loop to control the columns. That is, the inner loop cycles through the columns to write a single row of rectangles, then the outer loop increments to go on to the next row. Figure 3.5 shows what the output of the program looks like while the program is in progress.

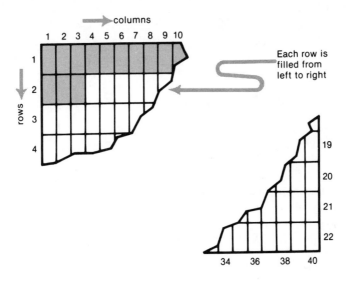

Figure 3.5. Output of the fill.c program.

We've used a new relational operator in this program, the (<=) operator, meaning *less than or equal to*. This means that the numbers used in the test expressions in the for loops, 22 and 40, are actually reached by the variables, as shown in Figure 3.5. In earlier programs the variables stopped one short of these limits, because the less-than (<) operator was used.

Notice also that because '\xDB' is a character, and a character can be part of a string, we've put '\xDB' directly into the printf() format string, making it a one-character string. We could have written

```
printf("%c", '\xDB');
```

as we did in the line.c program, but the representation used in fill.c is simpler.

The *while* Loop

The second kind of loop structure available in C is the while loop. Although at first glance this structure seems to be simpler than the for loop, it actually uses the same elements, but they're distributed throughout the program.

Let's try to compare, as directly as possible, the operation of the for loop and the while loop. The following program uses a while loop to reproduce the operation of our earlier forloop2.c program, which printed the numbers from 0 to 9 and gave a running total.

```c
// wloop.c
// prints numbers from 0 to 9, keeps running total
#include <stdio.h>              // for printf()

void main(void)
    {
    int count = 0;              // initialize variables
    int total = 0;

    while ( count < 10 )        // loop while count < 10
        {
        total = total + count;
        printf("\ncount=%d, total=%d", count++, total);
        }
    }
```

As before, this program produces the following:

```
count=0, total=0
count=1, total=1
count=2, total=3
count=3, total=6
count=4, total=10
count=5, total=15
count=6, total=21
```

```
count=7, total=28
count=8, total=36
count=9, total=45
```

Certainly the expression in parentheses following the keyword while is simpler than the three-part expression in the for loop. It dispenses with the initialization and increment expressions, retaining only the test expression

```
count < 10;
```

The resulting structure is shown in Figure 3.6

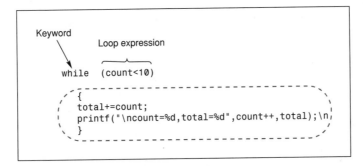

Figure 3.6. Structure of the while loop.

If the expressions that initialize and increment the counting variable aren't in the while loop expression itself, where did they go?

The initialization step is now included in a variable definition.

```
int count = 0;
```

The incrementing of the count variable can be seen in the printf() statement, which includes, instead of the variable count you might expect, the expression count++ instead. This means that, as soon as count is printed, it is incremented.

Notice how easily we were able to increment the variable. In most other languages we would have needed a separate statement

```
count = count + 1;
```

following the printf() statement; in C the expression

```
count++
```

has the same effect.

The operation of the while loop is shown in Figure 3.7.

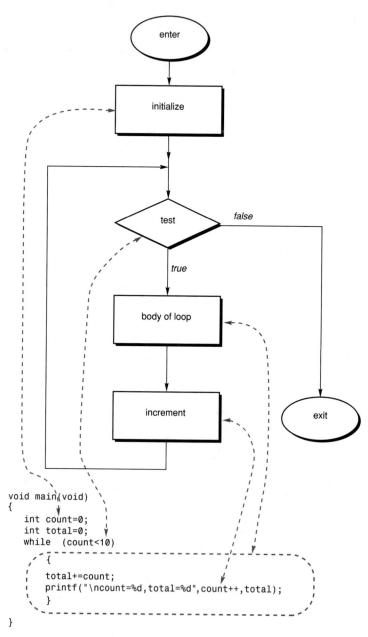

Figure 3.7. Operation of the while loop.

The loop variable count is initialized outside the loop in the declaration int count=0. When the loop is first entered, the condition count<10 is tested. If it's false, the loop terminates. If it's true, the body of the loop is executed. The increment expression is buried in the body of the loop. When the printf() statement that forms the loop body has finished printing, count is incremented by the (++) operator.

The Unexpected Condition

In situations where the number of iterations in a loop are known in advance, as they are in the wloop.c example, while loops are actually less appropriate. In this case the for loop is a more natural choice, because we can use its explicit initialize, test, and increment expressions to control the loop. When then is the while loop the appropriate choice?

The while loop shines in situations where a loop may be terminated unexpectedly by conditions developing within the loop. As an example, consider the following program:

```
// charcnt.c
// counts characters in a phrase typed in
#include <stdio.h>                    // for printf()
#include <conio.h>                    // for getche()

void main(void)
    {
    int count=0;

    printf("\nEnter a phrase:\n");    // prompt user
    while ( getche() != '\r' )        // get one char at a time
        count++;                      // count each one
    printf("\nCharacter count is %d", count);  // display total
    }
```

This program invites you to type a phrase. As you enter each character it keeps a count of how many characters you've typed, and when you press the Return key, it prints the total. Here's how it looks in operation:

```
Enter a phrase:
cat
Character count is 3

Enter a phrase:
Knowledge rests not upon truth alone, but also upon error.
Character count is 58
```

(This last phrase is from Carl Jung, and considering that it was written before the invention of computers, it is surprisingly applicable to the art of programming.)

> while loops are more appropriate than for loops when the condition that terminates the loop occurs unexpectedly.

Why is the `while` loop more appropriate in charcnt.c than a `for` loop? The loop in this program terminates when the character typed at the keyboard is the Return character. There's no need for a loop variable, because we don't have to keep track of where we are in the loop, and thus we have no need to initialize or increment expressions, because there is no loop variable to initialize or increment. Thus the `while` loop, consisting only of the test expression, is the appropriate choice.

Let's look more closely at the loop expression in the `while` loop.

```
( getche() != '\r' )
```

This incorporates the function `getche()`, which, as we saw in Chapter 2, returns the value of a character the instant the character is typed. As you also learned, this function takes on, or returns, the value of the character typed, so the function can be treated like a variable and compared with other variables or constants. In this program we compare it with the constant '\r', the carriage return character that `getche()` will return when the user presses the Return key. The evaluation of the loop expression is shown in Figure 3.8.

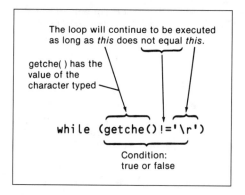

Figure 3.8. A function has a value.

Since we use the not-equal operator (`!=`), the `while` loop will continue to be executed as long as it doesn't encounter a '\r'. When it does encounter it, the loop will terminate and the total number of characters typed will be printed.

Using Functions as Elements in Expressions

Putting the `getche()` function into the `while` loop expression certainly makes for unusual looking syntax (at least that's how it strikes non-C programmers). Do we really need to do this? Doesn't it complicate things unnecessarily? As Will Rogers said when someone complained of the evils of old age, consider the alternative. We'll rewrite the program to use an explicit variable, ch, in the `while` expression, instead of the `getche()` function.

```
// charcnt2.c
// counts characters in a phrase typed in
```

```
#include <stdio.h>                    // for printf()
#include <conio.h>                    // for getche()

void main(void)
   {
   int count = -1;
   char ch = 'a';                     // make sure it's not 'r'

   printf("\nEnter a phrase:\n");     // prompt user
   while ( ch != '\r' )               // quit if [Enter] pressed
      {
      ch = getche();                  // get character
      count++;                        // count it
      }
   printf("\nCharacter count is %d", count);
   }
```

Now the while loop expression is simplified, but look at the effect of this change on the
rest of the program. We now have an extra variable ch. We need to initialize ch to avoid
the possibility (remote though it may be) that it would start out with the value '\r'. We
have an extra statement in the body of the while loop. Also, count must be initialized to
an odd-looking –1 value because the program now checks which character is read after the
loop is entered instead of before. Altogether, it appears that including the getche()
function in the while expression is a good idea. It's also a very popular sort of construction in C.

ASCII Revisited

Here's a situation where it makes sense to use a separate ch variable, because we need it
later in the program.

```
// ascii.c
// finds ASCII code of a character
#include <stdio.h>          // for printf()
#include <conio.h>          // for getche()

void main(void)
   {
   char ch = 'a';           // ensure it's not '\r'

   while ( ch != '\r' )     // quit on '\r'
      {
      printf("\nType a character:");
      ch=getche();
      printf("\nThe code for %c is %d.\n", ch, ch);
      }
   }
```

This program asks the user to type a character and then prints the ASCII code for the
character. It will do this over and over. It's sort of a shorthand version of the asctab.c
program shown earlier, but it's more useful when you only want to check the ASCII codes

for one or two keyboard characters without looking at the entire table. Here's some sample output:

```
Type a character: a
The code for a is 97.

Type a character: b
The code for b is 98.

Type a character: A
The code for A is 65.
```

We can't put getche() in the while loop test expression because we want to print a prompt to the user before invoking it. Because the getche() function is no longer included in the loop test expression, it has become part of an assignment statement.

```
ch = getche();
```

The printf() function, as in the asctab.c program, prints both the character version of ch and the numeric version, using the %c and %d format specifiers. Note that we can print a numerical value of ch even though at the start of the program it was declared a variable of type char. This demonstrates a useful feature of C: Character variables can be interpreted as either characters or numerical values (with a range of –128 to 127). Pressing the Enter key terminates the program.

Nested *while* Loops

Just as for loops can be nested, so can while loops. The following program shows a while loop nested within a for loop.

```
// guess.c
// lets you guess a letter
#include <stdio.h>        // for printf()
#include <conio.h>        // for getche()

void main(void)
    {
    int j;
    char ch;

    for(j=0; j<5; j++ )                     // play game five times
        {
        printf("\nType in a letter from 'a' to 'e':\n");
        while ( (ch=getche()) != 'd' )   // get char; is it 'd'?
            {                             // loop if not 'd'
            printf("\nSorry, %c is incorrect.\n", ch);
            printf("Try again.\n");
            }
        printf("\nThat's it!\n");         // exit loop; it's 'd'
        }
    printf("Good bye!\n");                // played five times
    }
```

This program lets you guess a lowercase letter from 'a' to 'e' and tells you if you're right or wrong. The outer for loop lets you play the game exactly five times. The inner while loop determines whether your guess is correct. If not, it loops again, asking you to try again. When you do guess correctly (which should take you no more than five tries, if you're on your toes) the inner loop terminates. The correct answer is always 'd' (unless you modify the program).

Here's a sample interaction:

```
Type in a letter from 'a' to 'e':
a
Sorry, a is incorrect.

Try again.
c
Sorry, c is incorrect.

Try again.
d
That's it!
```

As in the nested for loop example, each of the loops is indented to help clarify the operation of the program.

Assignment Expressions as Values

The most radical aspect of the guess.c program is the use in the inner while loop test expression of a complete assignment expression as a value.

```
while ( (ch=getche()) != 'd' )
```

In the charcnt.c program we saw that a function could be used as if it were a variable; here the idea is carried to even greater lengths. How is this loop expression interpreted? First the function getche() must return a value. Say it's the character 'a'. This value is then assigned to the character variable ch. Finally, the entire assignment expression

```
ch=getche()
```

takes on the value of ch, which is 'a'. This value can then be compared with the character 'd' on the right side of the not equal relational operator (!=). Figure 3.9 shows this process. The use of assignment expressions as values is a common idiom in C.

Precedence: Assignment Versus Relational Operators

Note that there is an extra set of parentheses around the assignment expression in the test expression of the inner while loop discussed above.

```
while ( (ch=getche()) != 'd' )
```

If the parentheses weren't there, the compiler would interpret the EXPRESSION like this:

```
while ( ch = (getche() != 'd') )
```

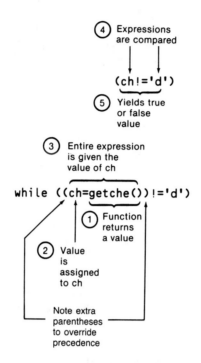

Figure 3.9. An assignment expression has a value.

This of course isn't what we want at all, because ch will now be set equal to the results of a true/false expression. The reason we need the parentheses is that the precedence of the relational operator (!=) is greater than that of the assignment operator (=). (This is shown in the table of operator precedence in Appendix A, "Reference.") Unless parentheses tell the compiler otherwise, the relational operator (!=) will be evaluated first. By inserting the parentheses, we ensure that the expression is evaluated correctly.

A Mathematical *while* Loop

Before we leave the subject of while loops, let's look at one more example. This one calculates the factorial of a number. As you no doubt remember from Mr. Klemmer's high-school math class, the factorial of a number (really an integer) is the number multiplied by all the numbers smaller than itself. Thus the factorial of 4 is 4*3*2*1, or 24.

Here's the listing:

```
// factor.c
// finds factorial of number typed in
#include <stdio.h>              // for scanf(), printf()
```

```
void main(void)
    {
    int number=1;              //  can't be 0 when we start
    long answer;

    while ( number != 0 )      //  user types 0 to terminate
        {
        printf("\nEnter a number: ");
        scanf("%d", &number);
        answer = 1;
        while ( number > 1 )     //  multiply 'number' times
            answer = answer * number--;
        printf("Factorial is: %ld\n", answer);
        }
    }
```

Here's a sample of interaction with the program:

```
Type number: 3
Factorial is: 6

Type number: 4
Factorial is: 24

Type number: 7
Factorial is: 5040

Type number: 12
Factorial is: 479001600
```

This program uses an outer while loop to recycle until a 0 value is entered. The inner loop uses the decrement operator to reduce the variable number—which starts out at the value typed by the user—by 1 each time through the loop. When number reaches 1, the loop terminates.

A new wrinkle in this program is the use of long integers. Because factorials grow so rapidly, even an initial value of 8 would have exceeded an integer variable's capacity of 32,767. Long integers provide an improvement in that they can hold numbers up to 2,147,483,647, as you learned in Chapter 2, "C Building Blocks." To accommodate long integers, we have used the variable type long in the declaration statement for answer and the format specifier ld in the printf() function. This works for values up to 12. If you want, you can extend the range of the program further by using type double.

Using *while* Loops and *for* Loops

Now that we know how to write two different kinds of loops, how do we decide which one to use in a given situation?

Generally speaking, if at the time you enter the loop you already know how many times you want to execute it, you're probably better off with the for loop. If, on the other hand, the conditions for terminating the loop are imposed by the outside world, such as the user typing a certain character, then you're better off with the `while` loop.

We'll use numerous examples of both kinds of loops throughout this book.

The *do while* Loop

The last of the three loops in C is the `do while` or do loop. This loop is very similar to the `while` loop. The difference is that in the do loop the test condition is evaluated after the loop is executed, rather than before.

Here's our familiar program, which prints the numbers from 0 to 9 and a running total, revised to use a do loop:

```
// doloop.c
// prints numbers from 0 to 9, keeps running total
#include <stdio.h>          // for printf()

void main(void)
    {
    int count = 0;
    int total = 0;

    do
        {
        total = total + count;
        printf("\ncount=%d, total=%d", count++, total);
        }
    while ( count < 10 );
    }
```

The output is the same as in previous versions of the program.

```
C>doloop
count=0, total=0
count=1, total=1
count=2, total=3
count=3, total=6
count=4, total=10
count=5, total=15
count=6, total=21
count=7, total=28
count=8, total=36
count=9, total=45
```

The do loop, unlike the other loops we've examined, has two keywords: `do` and `while`. The do keyword marks the beginning of the loop; it has no other function. The `while` keyword marks the end of the loop and contains the loop expression, as shown in Figure 3.10.

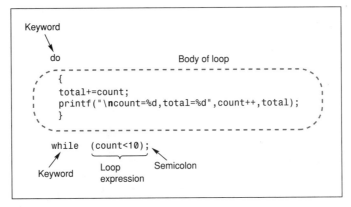

Figure 3.10. Structure of the do *loop.*

An important detail to note is that this loop, unlike the for and while loops, is terminated with a semicolon; that is, the test condition in the parentheses following while ends with a semicolon.

The operation of the do loop is sort of an upside-down version of the while loop. The body of the loop is first executed, then the test condition is checked. If the test condition is true, the loop is repeated; if it is false, the loop terminates, as can be seen in Figure 3.11. The important point to notice is that the body of the loop will always be executed at least once, because the test condition isn't checked until the end of the loop.

Pascal programmers might want to note that the do loop is similar to the repeat until loop in Pascal, except that it continues to loop as long as the test condition is true, while repeat until loops until the test condition is true.

When would you use a do loop? Any time you want to be sure the loop body is executed at least once. This situation is less common than that where the loop might not be executed at all, so the do loop is used less often than the while loop. When in doubt, use the while loop; the operation of the program is clearer if the test condition is set forth at the beginning of the loop. If you find yourself writing a lot of do loops, you might want to try restructuring your program to turn some of them into whiles.

Revised Guessing Game

Here's an example of a situation that calls for a do loop. Suppose we want to revise our guess-the-letter game so that instead of assuming you want to play a fixed number of times, it asks whether you want to play again after each game. To achieve this effect, we can rewrite the program as follows:

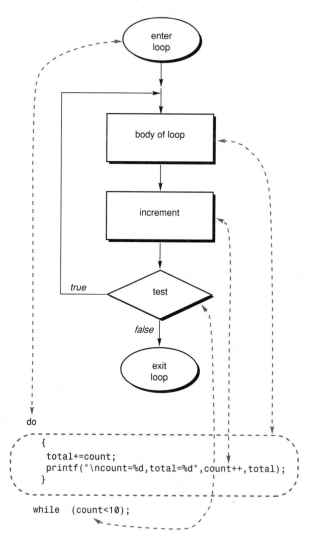

Figure 3.11. Operation of the do loop

```
// guessdo.c
// lets you guess a letter
// uses do loop to ask if new game wanted
#include <stdio.h>        // for printf()
#include <conio.h>        // for getche()

void main(void)
    {
    char ch;
```

```
    do
        {
        printf("\n\nType in a digit from 'a' to 'e':\n");
        while( (ch=getche()) != 'c' )  // get char; is it 'c'?
            {                          // not 'c'
            printf("\nSorry, %c is incorrect.\n", ch);
            printf("Try again.\n");
            }
        printf("\nThat's it!\n");      // loop exit; it's 'c'
        printf("\nPlay again? (Type 'y' or 'n'): ");
        }
    while ( getche() == 'y');          // loop until input not 'y'
    printf("\nThanks for playing!");   // exit do loop
    }
```

Here's a sample session with the guessdo.c program:

```
Type in a digit from 'a' to 'e':
b
Sorry, b is incorrect.
Try again.
c
That's it!

Play again? (Type 'y' or 'n'): y

Type in a digit from 'a' to 'e':
d
Sorry, d is incorrect.
Try again.
c
That's it!

Play again? (Type 'y' or 'n'): n
Thanks for playing!
```

Notice that the body of the do loop will always be executed once. If you called up the program in the first place, we can assume that you want at least one game. After the first game, we ask if you want to continue. It is this situation, in which something must be done once before we ask if it should be done again, that is properly implemented with a do loop.

> The do loop is useful when the body of a loop will always be executed at least once.

The *break* and *continue* Statements

To round out our discussion of loops we should mention that C has two statements which can be used with any of the loops described previously: break and continue.

The break statement bails you out of a loop as soon as it's executed. It's often used when an unexpected condition occurs; one that the loop test condition isn't looking for. We'll see examples of this statement later.

The continue statement is inserted in the body of the loop and when executed, takes you back to the beginning of the loop, bypassing any statements not yet executed. continue is a bit suspect in that it can make a program difficult to read and debug by confusing the normal flow of operations in the loop, so it is avoided by C programmers whenever possible.

Summary

This chapter has focused on the three C loops: for, while, and do while. You've learned how to create these and use them in a variety of situations. You've also learned how to nest one loop inside another and how to use variables, functions, and assignment statements with relational operators in the loop expression. In short, you're ready to do things again and again.

Questions

1. The three parts of the loop expression in a for loop are the i _____ expression, the t _____ expression, the i _____ expression.

2. A single-statement for loop is terminated with a
   a. Right bracket
   b. Right brace
   c. Comma
   d. Semicolon

3. A _____ is used to separate the three parts of the loop expression in a for loop.

4. A multiple-statement while loop is terminated with a
   a. Right bracket
   b. Right brace
   c. Comma
   d. Semicolon

5. Multiple increment expressions in a for loop expression are separated by _____.

6. A `while` loop is more appropriate than a `for` loop when

    a. The terminating condition occurs unexpectedly
    b. The body of the loop will be executed at least once
    c. The program will be executed at least once
    d. The number of times the loop will be executed is known before the loop is executed

7. True or false: the initialize expression and increment expression are contained in the loop expression in a `while` loop.

8. An expression contains relational operators, assignment operators, and arithmetic operators. In the absence of parentheses, they will be evaluated in the following order

    a. Assignment, relational, arithmetic
    b. Arithmetic, relational, assignment
    c. Relational, arithmetic, assignment
    d. Assignment, arithmetic, relational

9. The more deeply a loop is nested, the more _____ it should be indented.

10. An assignment statement itself can have a _____, just like a variable.

11. The advantage of putting complete assignment statements inside loop expressions is

    a. To avoid awkward program constructions
    b. To simplify the flow of control in the program
    c. To reduce the number of program statements
    d. To clarify the operation of the program

12. True or false: in almost every case where a variable can be used, an increment or decrement operator can be added to the variable.

13. A `do while` loop is useful when

    a. The body of the loop will never be executed
    b. The body of the loop will be executed at least once
    c. The body of the loop may never be executed
    d. The body of the executed loop was found by the butler

14. The `break` statement is used to exit from which part of a loop?

    a. Beginning
    b. Middle
    c. End
    d. None of the above

15. True or false: a `continue` statement causes an exit from a loop.

Exercises

1-20 & # squared.

⚹ 1. Write a program that prints the squares of all the numbers from 1 to 20. (Perhaps you can adapt a similar exercise from the last chapter.)

⚹ 2. Rewrite the charcnt.c program so that it counts characters until a period (.) is typed rather than the Return character.

3. Write a program that repeatedly calculates how many characters separate two letters typed by the user until it is terminated with the Return character. For instance, there are two characters ('b' and 'c') between 'a' and 'd'. Take advantage of the fact that the arithmetic operators work on character variables just as well as they do on numbers.

Decisions

- The `if` statement
- The `if-else` statement
- The `else-if` construct
- The `switch` statement
- The conditional operator

We all need to be able to alter our actions in the face of changing circumstances. If the forecast is for rain, then I'll take my raincoat. If the freeway is under construction, then I'll take the back road. If, when I propose, she says yes, I'll buy her a ring; if she says no, I'll start dating Gladys.

Computer languages, too, must be able to perform different sets of actions depending on the circumstances. C has three major decision-making structures: the if statement, the if-else statement, and the switch statement. A fourth, somewhat less important structure, is the conditional operator. In this chapter, we'll explore these four ways a C program can react to changing circumstances.

The *if* Statement

Like most languages, C uses the keyword if to introduce the basic decision-making statement. Here's a simple example:

```
// testif.c
// demonstrates if statement
#include <stdio.h>      // for printf()
#include <conio.h>      // for getche()

void main(void)
    {
    char ch;

    printf("\nType a character: ");
    ch = getche();
    if ( ch == 'y' )
        printf("\nYou typed y.");
    }
```

You can no doubt guess what will happen when this program is executed:

```
Type a character: y
You typed y.
```

If you type y, the program will print You typed y. If you type some other character, such as n, the program doesn't do anything.

Figure 4.1 shows the structure of the if statement. This structure is surprisingly similar to that of the while statement described in Chapter 3. The keyword is followed by parentheses, which contain a conditional expression using a relational operator. Following this, there is the body of the statement, consisting of either a single statement terminated by a semicolon, or (as we'll see shortly) multiple statements enclosed by braces. In fact, the only difference between the structure of the if statement and that of the while is that the words if and while are different.

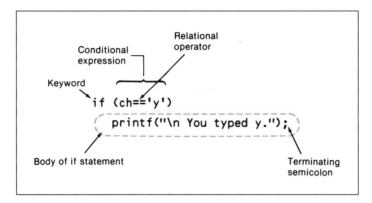

Figure 4.1. Structure of the if *statement.*

Notice too that there is no then keyword following the conditional expression, as there is in Pascal and usually is in BASIC.

There is no then keyword in C.

The if statement is similar to the while statement in operation as well as format. In both cases the statements making up the body of the statement won't be executed at all if the condition is false. However, in the while statement, if the condition is true, the statement (or statements) in the body of the loop will be executed over and over until the condition becomes else; whereas in the if statement they will be executed only once. Figure 4.2 shows the operation of the if statement.

A Word-Counting Program

In the last chapter we included a program, charcnt.c, which counted the number of characters in a phrase typed by the user. Here's a slightly more complex program that counts not only the number of characters but the number of words as well.

```c
// wordcnt.c
// counts characters and words in a phrase typed in
#include <stdio.h>     // for printf()
#include <conio.h>     // for getche()

void main(void)
    {
    int charcnt=0;
    int wordcnt=0;
    char ch;
```

```
printf("\nEnter a phrase:\n");
while ( (ch=getche()) != '\r' )    // quit on [Enter]
   {
   charcnt++;                       // count character
   if ( ch == ' ' )                // if space,
      wordcnt++;                    // count word
   }
printf("\nCharacter count is %d", charcnt);
printf("\nWord count is %d", wordcnt+1);
}
```

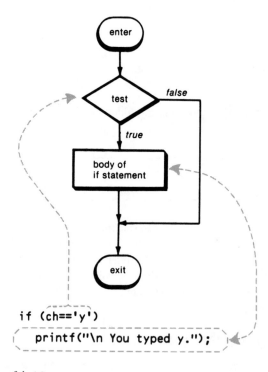

Figure 4.2. Operation of the if statement.

This program figures how many words there are by counting the number of spaces. (It could be fooled by multiple spaces between words, but we'll ignore that possibility.) Here's some sample interaction with the program:

```
Enter a phrase:
cat and dog
Character count is 11
Word count is 3

Enter a phrase:
This sentence actually uses nine words and sixty-five characters.
```

```
Character count is 65
Word count is 9
```

A tip of the hat to Douglas Hofstadter and his book *Metamagical Themas* (Basic Books, 1985) for the second phrase, which is the sort of example that is hard to type correctly the first time. (Don't use the Backspace key!) *counts that as a character.*

This program is similar to the charcnt.c program. The major addition is the if statement.

```
if ( ch == ' ' )
   wordcnt++;
```

This statement causes the variable wordcnt to be incremented every time a space is detected in the input stream. There will always be one more word than there are spaces between them (assuming no multiple spaces), so we add 1 to the variable wordcnt before printing it. (We could also have used ++wordcnt.)

Multiple Statements with *if*

As in the case of the various loop statements, the body of the if statement may consist of either a single statement terminated by a semicolon (as shown in the example above) or by a number of statements enclosed in braces. Here's an example of such a compound statement:

```
// testif2.c
// demonstrates multiple statements following if
#include <stdio.h>    // for printf()
#include <conio.h>    // for getche()

void main(void)
   {
   char ch;

   printf("\nType in a character: ");
   ch = getche();
   if ( ch == 'y' )
      {
      printf("\nYou typed y.");
      printf("\nNot some other character.");
      }
   }
```

In both testif.c programs we could have embedded the getche() function in the if expression, as we did in similar situations with the while loop in Chapter 3.

```
if ( getche() == 'y' )
```

This is more C-like, but we thought using it would make what the if statement was doing a bit less clear. However, in this next example, which is a program that reads two characters from the keyboard, we'll use this more compact construction.

Nested *if* Statements

Like the loop statements of the last chapter, if statements can be nested. Here's a simple example:

```
// nestif.c
// demonstrates nested if statements
#include <stdio.h>    // for printf()
#include <conio.h>    // for getche()

void main(void)
    {
    printf("\nType characters:\n");
    if ( getche() == 'n' )
        if ( getche() == 'o' )
            printf("\nYou typed no.");
    }
```

Nesting here means that one if statement is part of the body of another if statement. In the example above, the inner if statement won't be reached unless the outer one is true, and the printf() statement won't be executed unless both if statements are true, as the following interaction with the program shows:

```
Type character:
x                        ←A non-'n' to start with terminates the program

Type character:
nx                       ←A non-'o' as the second letter does likewise

Type character:
no                       ←Only 'n' followed by 'o' gets to the printf()
```

The operation of nested if statements is shown in Figure 4.3.

The *if-else* Statement

The if statement by itself will execute a single statement, or a group of statements, when the test expression is true. It does nothing when it is false. Can we execute a group of statements if and only if the test expression is *not* true? Of course. This is the purpose of the else statement, which is demonstrated in the following example:

```
// testelse.c
// demonstrates if-else statement
#include <stdio.h>    // for printf()
#include <conio.h>    // for getche()

void main(void)
```

multiple statements

```
{
char ch;
printf("\nType character:\n");
ch = getche();
if ( ch == 'y' )
    printf("\nYou typed y.");
else
    printf("\nYou didn't type y.");
}
```

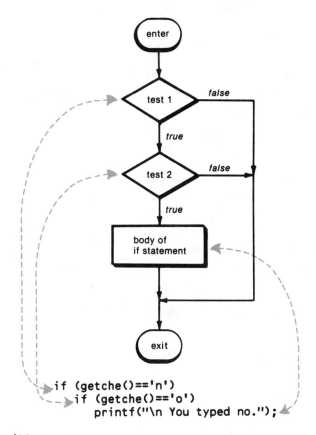

Figure 4.3. Nested if *statements.*

Typing y elicits one response, while typing anything else elicits a different response.

```
Type character:
y
You typed y.

Type character:
n
You didn't type y.
```

Figure 4.4 shows the structure of the if-else statement and Figure 4.5 flowcharts its operation.

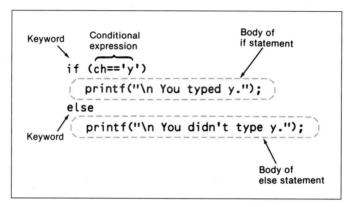

Figure 4.4. Structure of the if-else *statement.*

Notice that the else is indented to line up with the if. This is a formatting convention, which, if consistently followed, will enable you to better understand the operation of your program.

For clarity, each else should be indented the same amount as its matching if.

Character Graphics and the Checkerboard

As an example of the if-else statement at work, consider the following program, which prints a checkerboard on the monochrome screen.

```
// checker.c
// draws a checkerboard on the screen
#include <stdio.h>              // for printf()

void main(void)
    {
    int x, y;

    printf("\n");               // new line
    for (y=1; y<9; y++)         // stepping down
        {
        for (x=1; x<9; x++)     // stepping across
            if ( (x+y) % 2 == 0 )  // even numbered square?
                printf("\xDB\xDB");  // print filled square
            else
```

handwritten annotations: x=8 is the highest, y=8, rows, columns, |xDB|xDB xDB|xDB blank spaces

```
    printf(" ");            // print blank square
  printf("\n");             // new line
  }
}
```

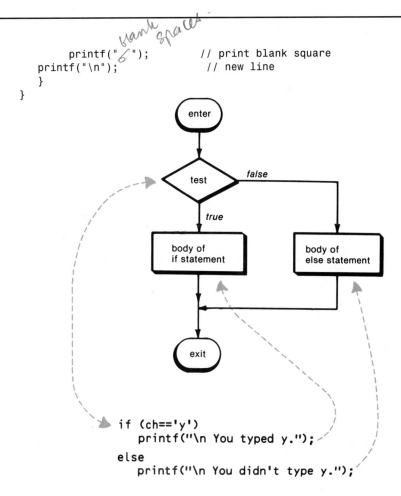

```
if (ch=='y')
    printf("\n You typed y.");
else
    printf("\n You didn't type y.");
```

Figure 4.5. Operation of the if-else *statement.*

Try out the program so that you can see what it does. Figure 4.6 shows roughly what you'll see.

This program is similar to those in Chapter 3 that drew a line and a rectangle in that it uses the graphics character \xDB and nested loops to scan part of the screen. Here, however, the if-else construction gives the program the power to alter its operation, depending on which part of the screen it's about to write on.

How does this program work? The outer for loop (the variable y) moves down the screen one row at a time. That is, y marks what row we're on, starting at y=1 for the top row and moving down to y=8. The inner loop (the variable x) moves across the screen one column at a time. That is, x marks what column we're on, starting at x=1 for the leftmost column and moving across until x=8.

Actually, each of the columns pointed to by x is two characters wide. This glitch in the program is necessary because the characters on the PC screen are about twice as high as they are wide, so to create a correctly proportioned checkerboard each square must consist of two characters side-by-side: either two spaces or two solid rectangles. The purpose of the two `printf()` functions is just this: one prints two spaces, the other prints two solid rectangles using the \xDB character.

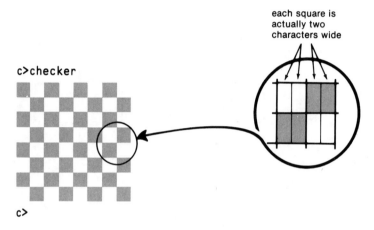

Figure 4.6. Output of the checker.c program.

Getting Even with the Remainder Operator

How does the program decide when to print a square and when not to? In effect, the program numbers the squares and then colors only the even-numbered squares, leaving the odd-numbered squares blank. It determines whether a square is odd or even in the statement

```
if ( (x+y) % 2 == 0 )
```

Each square is numbered, as shown in Figure 4.7. The number is obtained by adding the x and y coordinates of the square: x+y.

These numbers aren't unique (more than one square has the same number) but they do exhibit the desired alternation between odd and even.

How then does the statement shown above reveal when a number is odd and when it is even? The remainder operator (%), which we mentioned in Chapter 2, "C Building Blocks," is used for this purpose. With a divisor of two, the remainder will be 0 if the dividend is even and 1 if the dividend is odd. The if-else statement can then determine whether to print two colored rectangles or two spaces for a given square (that is, for a particular value of x and y).

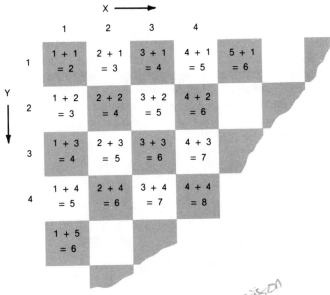

Figure 4.7. Numbering squares on the checkerboard.

Drawing Lines

For another example of character graphics and the if-else statement, let's look at a pair of programs that draw lines on the monochrome screen. Actually, *line* may be too strong a word; it's really more of a diagonal staircase pattern.

Here's the first program:

```
// lines.c
// prints diagonal line on screen
#include <stdio.h>                    // for printf()

void main(void)
    {
    int x, y;

    printf("\n");                     // new line
    for (y=1; y<24; y++)              // step down the screen
        {
        for (x=1; x<24; x++)         // step across the screen
            if ( x == y )            // are we on diagonal?
                printf("\xDB");       // yes, draw dark rectangle
            else
                printf("\xB0");       // no, draw light rectangle
```

```
    printf("\n");                    // next line
    }
  }
```

This program is similar to the checkerboard program, except that instead of printing on even-numbered squares, it prints wherever the x coordinate and the y coordinate are equal. This will create a diagonal line extending from the upper-left corner of the screen, where x=1 and y=1, down to the bottom of the screen, where x=23 and y=23.

Where the line isn't drawn, the background is filled in with a light gray. For this purpose the program uses another graphics character, \B0. This is the same size as the solid rectangle created by \DB but consists of a pattern of tiny dots, creating a gray effect. Part of the output of the program is shown in Figure 4.8.

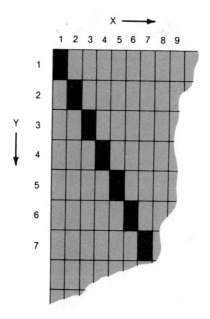

Figure 4.8. Output of the lines.c program.

In this program we haven't attempted to compensate for the aspect ratio of the characters on the screen as we did in the checkerboard program. As a consequence, each of the rectangles making up the line is twice as high as it is wide, and the line, which should appear to be at a 45-degree angle, actually slopes downward more steeply than that.

Nested *if-else* Statements

It is perfectly possible to nest an entire if-else construct within either the body of an if statement or the body of an else statement. The latter construction, shown in the following example, is quite common.

```
// lines2.c
// prints two diagonal lines on screen
#include <stdio.h>              // for printf()

void main(void)
   {
   int x, y;

   printf("\n");               // new line
   for (y=1; y<24; y++)        // step down the screen
      {
      for (x=1; x<24; x++)     // step across the screen
         if ( x == y )         // NW-SE diagonal?
            printf("\xDB");     // print solid color
         else
            if ( x == 24 - y ) // SW-NE diagonal?
               printf("\xDB");  // print solid color
            else
               printf("\xB0");  // print gray
      printf("\n");            // next line
      }
   }
```

(handwritten margin notes: "does only" "what's in braces")

This program is similar to the last one, except that it draws two lines on the screen, as shown in Figure 4.9. The first line is the same as in the last program. The second line goes in the opposite direction, from upper-right to lower-left. Thus the two lines create a dark X shape in the middle of a gray rectangle.

Note how the second if-else construction, which draws the second line, is nested inside the first else statement. If the test expression in the first if statement is false, then the test expression in the second if statement is checked. If it is false as well, the final else statement is executed. The process is shown in Figure 4.10.

You can see in the listing that each time a structure is nested in another structure, it is also indented for clarity. This is similar to the way nested loops are indented.

There are several alternatives to this nested if-else structure. One involves a format change, one involves a new C statement, switch; and the third involves logical operators. We'll look at this last alternative in a moment. First, however, let's examine a possible pitfall in the use of nested if-else statements.

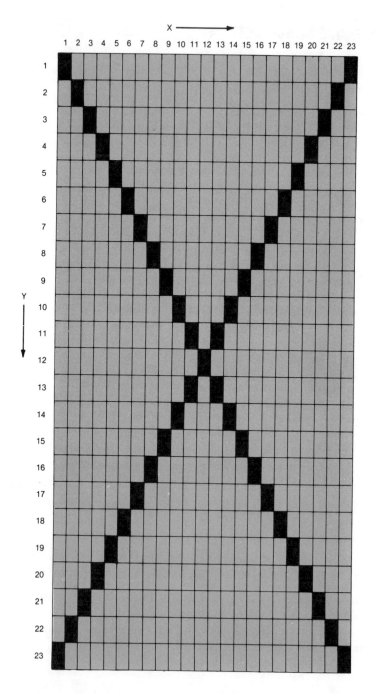

Figure 4.9. Output of the lines2.c program.

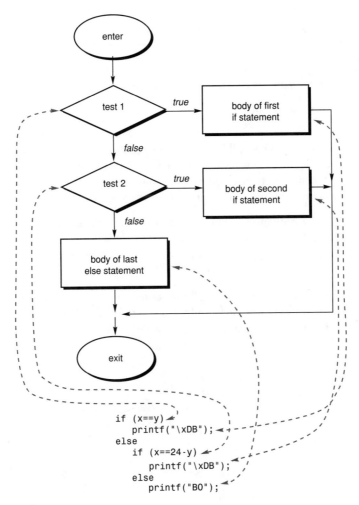

Figure 4.10. Nested if-else *statements.*

Which *if* Gets the *else*?

Consider the following program, which looks as if it would respond with an appropriate comment when the user types the temperature (in degrees Fahrenheit).

```
// temper.c
// makes remark about temperature
#include <stdio.h>     // for printf()

void main(void)
   {
   int temp;
```

```
        printf("\nPlease type in the temperature: ");
        scanf("%d", &temp);
        if ( temp < 80 )
            if ( temp > 60 )
                printf("Nice day!");
        else
            printf("Sure is hot!");
        }
```

[handwritten margin note: goes with this — unless there be a brace]

[handwritten note pointing to first if]

Suppose temp is 32. What will be printed when this program is executed? Would you guess nothing at all? That seems reasonable: the first if condition (temp < 80) will be true, so the second if condition (temp > 60) will be evaluated. It will be false, so it looks as if the program will exit from the entire nested if-else construct.

However, we have attempted to mislead you by altering the indentation. You may have been fooled, but the compiler won't be. Here's what happens:

```
Please type in the temperature: 32
Sure is hot!
```

The problem is that the else is actually associated with the if immediately preceding it, not the first if, as the indentation would lead you to believe. The rule is that an else is associated with the last if that doesn't have its own else. Here's a modified version of the program which will operate correctly:

```
// temper2.c
// makes remark about temperature
#include <stdio.h>      // for printf()

void main(void)
    {
    int temp;

    printf("\nPlease type in the temperature: ");
    scanf("%d", &temp);
    if ( temp < 80 )
        if ( temp > 60 )
            printf("Nice day!");
        else
            printf("Sure is chilly!");
    else
        printf("Sure is hot!");
    }
```

[handwritten note: then do all this but if temp >80, it will drop out]

Here the inner else is paired with the inner if, and the outer else is paired with the outer if. The indentation in this case isn't misleading.

> An else is associated with the last if that doesn't have its own else.

If you want to ensure that an else goes with an earlier if than the one it would ordinarily be matched with, you can use braces to surround the intervening if structure. Surrounding the if with braces makes it invisible to the else, which then matches up with the earliest nonbraced if. We've modified the example to show how this looks (note that this program doesn't print anything if the temperature is colder than 60).

```
//   temper3.c
//   makes remark about temperature
#include <stdio.h>     // for printf()

void main(void)
   {
   int temp;

   printf("\nPlease type in the temperature: ");
   scanf("%d", &temp);
   if ( temp < 80 )
      {                          // these braces make
      if ( temp > 60 )          // this "if"
         printf("Nice day!");   // invisible
      }                          // to
   else                          // this else
      printf("Sure is hot!");
   }
```

Logical Operators

We can simplify the lines2.c program from earlier in this chapter by using an operator we haven't yet encountered: the logical operator. Logical operators are a powerful way to condense and clarify complicated if-else structures (and other constructions as well). Let's see what effect a logical operator, in this case the OR operator, represented by two vertical bars (¦¦), will have on the program. Then we'll explore logical operators in general.

```
// lines3.c
// prints two diagonal lines on screen
#include <stdio.h>              // for printf()

void main(void)
   {
   int x, y;

   printf("\n");
   for (y=1; y<24; y++)
      {
      for (x=1; x<24; x++)
         if ( x==y ¦¦ x==24-y )   // if either condition
            printf("\xDB");       // is true, print solid box
         else                     // otherwise
```

for each row print 23 columns

```
        printf("\xB0");        // print gray box
    printf("\n");
    }
}
```

This program yields the same output as the previous example—a pair of crossed diagonal lines—but does so in a more elegant way. The logical OR operator (| |) means if either the expression on the right side of the operator (x==24-y), or the expression on the left (x==y) is true, then the entire expression (x==y | | x==24-y) is true.

Note that the logical operator (| |) performs an inclusive OR. That is, if either the expression on one side of the operator, or the expression on the other, or both expressions are true, then the entire expression is true. (An exclusive OR, by contrast, would provide a false result if the expressions on both sides were true; C doesn't have an exclusive OR operator.)

There are three logical (sometimes called *Boolean*) operators in C:

		Logical OR
&&	Logical AND
!	Logical NOT

Here's a program that uses the logical AND operator (&&):

```
// digitcnt.c
// counts characters and numerical digits in a phrase
#include <stdio.h>     // for printf()
#include <conio.h>     // for getche()

void main(void)
    {
    int charcnt=0;
    int digitcnt=0;
    char ch;

    printf("\nEnter a phrase:\n");
    while ( (ch=getche()) != '\r' )     // quit on [Enter]
        {
        charcnt++;                       // count character
        if ( ch > 47 && ch < 58 )        // if digit,
            digitcnt++;                  // count it
        }
    printf("\nCharacter count is %d", charcnt);
    printf("\nDigit count is %d", digitcnt);
    }
```

This program is a modification of our earlier charcnt.c and wordcnt.c programs. In addition to counting the characters in a phrase, it also counts any of the numeric digits 0 through 9 which are part of the phrase. Here's an example:

```
C>digitcnt
Enter a phrase:
He packed 4 socks, 12 shirts, and 1,000 hopes for the future.
```

```
Character count is 61
Digit count is 7
```

The key to this program is the logical AND operator (&&). This operator says: if both the expression on the left (ch>47) and the expression on the right (ch<58) are true, then the entire expression (ch>47 && ch<58) is true. This will only be true if ch is between 48 and 57; these are the ASCII codes for the digits from 0 to 9.

There are several things to note about these logical operators. Most obviously, they're composed of double symbols: (¦¦) and (&&). Don't use the single symbols: (¦) and (&). These single symbols also have a meaning (they're bitwise operators, which we'll examine later), but it isn't the meaning we want at the moment.

Perhaps it isn't so obvious, though, that the logical operators have a lower precedence than the relational operators, such as (==). It's for this reason that we don't need to use parentheses around the relational expressions x == y, ch > 47, and so on. The relational operators are evaluated first, then the logical operators. (We'll summarize operator precedence in a moment.)

> Logical operators have lower precedence than relational operators.

Although we don't make use of the fact here, you should know that logical operators are always evaluated from left to right. Thus, if you have a condition such as

```
if ( a<b && b<c )
```

you know that (a<b) will be evaluated first. Also, in this case, C is smart enough to know that if the condition to the left of the && is false, then there's no point in evaluating the rest of the expression, because the result will be false anyway.

The third logical operator is the NOT operator, represented by the exclamation point (!) and sometimes called the *bang* operator. This operator reverses the logical value of the expression it operates on; it makes a true expression false and a false expression true.

The NOT operator is a unary operator: that is, it takes only one operand. In this way it's similar to the negative sign in arithmetic: the (–) in –5 also takes only one operand.

Here's an example of the NOT operator applied to a relational expression.

```
!(x < 5)
```

This means "not x less than five." In other words, if x is less than 5, the expression will be false, because (x < 5) is true. We could express the same condition as (x >= 5).

The NOT operator is often used to reverse the logical value of a single variable, as in the expression

```
if( !flag )
```

This is more concise than the equivalent

```
if( flag==0 )
```

Operator Precedence, Revisited

Because we've now added the logical operators to the list of operators we know how to use, it is probably time to review all of these operators and their precedence. Table 4.1 summarizes the operators we've seen so far. The higher an operator is in the table, the higher its precedence. (A more complete precedence table can be found in Appendix A, "Reference.")

Table 4.1. Operator order of precedence.

Operators	Type
! -	Unary: logical NOT, arithmetic minus.
* / %	Arithmetic (multiplicative).
+ -	Arithmetic (additive).
< > <= >=	Relational (inequality).
== !=	Relational (equality).
&& ||	Logical AND and OR.
= += -= *= /= %=	Assignment

Unary operators—those which act on only one value—have the highest priority. Then come arithmetic operators; here multiplication and division have higher precedence than addition and subtraction. Similarly, those relational operators that test for inequality have a higher precedence than those that test for equality. Next come the logical operators and finally the assignment operators. As you know, parentheses can be used to override any of these precedence relations.

The *else-if* Construct

We've seen how if-else statements can be nested. Let's look at a more complex example of this arrangement:

```
// calc.c
// four-function calculator
#include <stdio.h>     // for printf(), scanf()

void main(void)
    {
    float num1=1.0, num2=1.0;
```

```
    char op;

    while ( !(num1==0.0 && num2==0.0) )
       {
       printf("\n\nEnter number, operator, number\n");
       scanf("%f %c %f", &num1, &op, &num2);
       if ( op == '+')
          printf(" = %f", num1 + num2);
       else
          if (op == '-')
             printf(" = %f", num1 - num2);
          else
             if (op == '*')
                printf(" = %f", num1 * num2);
             else
                if (op == '/')
                   printf(" = %f", num1 / num2);
       }  // end while
    }  // end main()
```

This program gives your computer, for which you spent thousands of dollars, all the raw power of a four-function pocket calculator. You first type a number, then an operator—which can be any of the arithmetic operators (+), (–), (*), or (/)—and finally a second number. The program then prints the answer.

Entering zero values for both numbers terminates the program (no matter what value you use for the operator). This is handled by the logical expression in the `while` statement. Notice the use of the logical NOT operator (!). When both num1 and num2 are zero, then the expression

```
!(num1==0.0 && num2==0.0)
```

is false, so the loop terminates. This expression is equivalent to

```
num1 !=0.0 || num2 != 0.0
```

If either variable is non-zero, the loop continues.

Here we've used `scanf()` to read in the first number, the operator and the second number in a single statement. As we discussed in Chapter 2, "C Building Blocks," the white spaces between the variables in the format string in the `scanf()` statement permit you to separate the variables you type with any sort of whitespace characters: spaces, tabs, or newlines. Actually, it's not even necessary to type any whitespace character in this example. `scanf()` will know you've finished typing the first number when it sees a non-numeric character, and it will then wait for the second number. Here are examples of different approaches used with the calc.c program:

```
Enter number, operator, number
3 + 3                                      ← Separated by spaces
 = 6.000000
```

```
Enter number, operator, number
1                                              ← Separated by newlines
/
3
 = 0.333333
Enter number, operator, number
1000*1000                                      ← No separation
 = 1000000.000000
Enter number, operator, number
1000000/3
 = 333333.333333
```

Structurally, the important point to notice about this program is how the if-else constructs are nested. Because there are so many, the nesting and the resulting indentation gets quite deep, making the program difficult to read. There's another way to write, and think about, this situation. This involves the creation of a sort of imaginary construct called *else-if.* We reformat the program but not in a way the compiler will notice.

calc2.c
```c
// four-function calculator
#include <stdio.h>     // for printf()

void main(void)
    {
    float num1=1.0, num2=1.0;
    char op;

    while ( !(num1==0.0 && num2==0.0) )
        {
        printf("\n\nEnter number, operator, number\n");
        scanf("%f %c %f", &num1, &op, &num2);
        if ( op == '+')
            printf(" = %f", num1 + num2);
        else if (op == '-')
            printf(" = %f", num1 - num2);
        else if (op == '*')
            printf(" = %f", num1 * num2);
        else if (op == '/')
            printf(" = %f", num1 / num2);
        } // end while
    } // end main()
```

This operates exactly as before, but we've rearranged the whitespace to make the program easier to read. By simply deleting spaces and the newline, each if is moved up next to the preceding else, thus making a new construction: else-if. We think of else-if as meaning, "if the test expression that follows is true, execute the statement in the body of the else-if (in this case a printf() statement) and go to the end of the entire else-if chain; otherwise, go to the next else-if statement in the chain." Figure 4.11 shows this process in a flowchart.

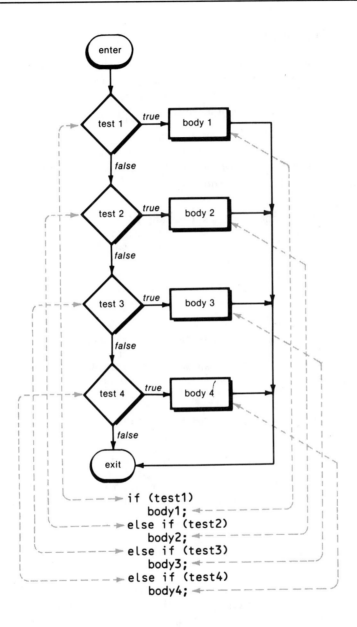

Figure 4.11. The else-if *construct.*

The else-if construction is a reformatting of nested if-else statements.

The *break* Statement

In the next section we'll look at the switch statement, which provides an alternative to the else-if construct. However, the switch statement relies on another statement, break, so we'll digress briefly to see how break is used to escape from a loop; then we'll go on to explore the role it plays in the switch statement.

We'll demonstrate break with a guessing game program. In this game the user picks a number between 1 and 99 and the program tries to guess what it is. The user replies to the computer's guesses by saying whether the guess is higher or lower than the number the computer is thinking of. Here's the listing:

```c
// numguess.c
// program guesses number user is thinking of
#include <stdio.h>                   // for printf()
#include <conio.h>                   // for getche()

void main(void)
    {
    float guess, incr;
    char ch;

    printf("\nThink of a number between 1 and 99, and\n");
    printf("I'll guess what it is.  Type 'e' for equals,\n");
    printf("'g'for greater than, and 'l' for less than.\n");
    incr = guess = 50;              // two assignments at once
    while ( incr > 1.0 )           // while not close enough
        {
        printf("\nIs your number greater or less than %.0f?\n",
                                                        guess);
        incr = incr / 2;
        if ( (ch=getche()) == 'e' )  // if guessed it already
            break;                   // escape from loop
        else if (ch == 'g')          // if guess too low
            guess = guess + incr;    //    try higher
        else                         // if guess too high
            guess = guess - incr;    //    try lower
        }
    printf("\nThe number is %.0f.  Am I not clever?", guess);
    }
```

The strategy employed by numguess.c is to ask questions that cut in half the range in which the number might lie. Thus the program first asks if the number is greater or less than 50. If the number is greater than 50, the program asks if the number is greater or less than 75, while if it's less than 50 the program asks if it's greater or less than 25. The process continues until the program deduces the number. Here's a sample interaction, with the user thinking of the number 62:

```
Think of a number between 1 and 99,
and I'll guess what it is. Type 'e' for equals,
'g' for greater than, and 'l' for less than.
```

```
Is your number greater or less than 50?
g
Is your number greater or less than 75?
l
Is your number greater or less than 63?
l
Is your number greater or less than 56?
g
Is your number greater or less than 59?
g
Is number greater or less than 61?
g
The number is 62. Am I not clever?
```

The test expression in the while loop waits for the variable incr (for increment)—which is added to or subtracted from guess and then divided by 2 each time through the loop—to become 1. At that point the program knows that the number has been guessed, so it prints the guess. However, there is the possibility the program will actually print the number the user is thinking of when it's trying to narrow down the range; it might ask if the number is greater or less than 75, for example, when in fact the user is thinking of 75. At this point, the honorable user will type e. Now the program knows it can stop trying to guess the number, so it needs to get out of the loop right away. The break statement is used for this purpose.

Break is often useful when a condition suddenly occurs that makes it necessary to leave a loop before the loop expression becomes false. As we'll see next, it is also essential in the switch statement.

Several other points about numguess.c should be noted. First, the following statement is written on two lines:

```
printf("\nIs your number greater or less than %.0f?\n",
                                              guess);
```

This linebreak was necessary because the one line exceeded the width of the page. The C compiler doesn't mind if you break a line in the middle this way, as long as you don't break it in the middle of a string.

Second, in the statement

```
incr = guess = 50;
```

we've assigned two variables a value using only one statement. This is possible because an assignment statement itself has a value (as we mentioned in Chapter 3). In this case, the statement

```
guess = 50;
```

takes on the value 50, and the variable incr can then be set equal to this value.

The *switch* Statement

Now that we know how the break statement works, we're ready to move on to switch. The switch statement is similar to the else-if construct but has more flexibility and a clearer format. It is analogous to the case statement in Pascal and the selectcase statement in the newer versions of BASIC. Let's rewrite our calc2.c program to use switch.

```c
// calc3.c
// four-function calculator
#include <stdio.h>                    // for printf()
#include <conio.h>                    // for getche()

void main(void)
   {
   float num1=1.0, num2=1.0;
   char op;

   while ( !(num1==0.0 && num2==0.0) )
      {
      printf("\n\nEnter number, operator, number\n");
      scanf("%f %c %f", &num1, &op, &num2);
      switch ( op )
         {
         case '+':
            printf(" = %f", num1 + num2);
            break;
         case '-':
            printf(" = %f", num1 - num2);
            break;
         case '*':
            printf(" = %f", num1 * num2);
            break;
         case '/':
            printf(" = %f", num1 / num2);
            break;
         default:
            printf("Unknown operator");
         }  // end switch
      }  // end while
   }  // end main()
```

Structurally, the statement starts out with the keyword switch, followed by parentheses containing an integer or character variable which we'll call the *switch variable* (although it can also be an expression, like a+b). The structure of the switch statement is shown in Figure 4.12.

Following each of the case keywords is an integer or character constant. (It can be a constant expression, like 'a' + 2, but it must evaluate to a constant; variables aren't allowed here.) This constant is terminated with a colon (not a semicolon). There can be one or more statements following each case keyword. These statements need not be

enclosed by braces, although the entire body of the switch statement—all the cases—is
enclosed in braces.

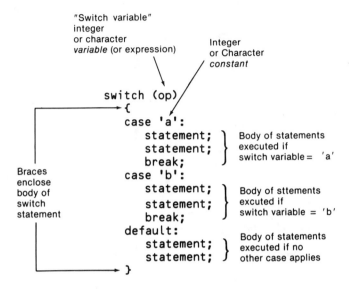

Figure 4.12. The structure of the switch *statement.*

When the switch is entered, the switch variable should already have been set to some
value, probably the value of one of the integer or character constants that follow the case
keywords. If so, control is immediately transferred to the body of statements following this
particular case keyword. The operation of the switch statement in the calc3.c program is
shown in Figure 4.13.

If the switch variable does not match any of the case constants, control goes to the
keyword default, which is usually at the end of the switch statement. Using the default
keyword can be a great convenience; it acts as a sort of master else statement, saying in
effect, "If none of the above, then do this." (If there is no default keyword, the whole
switch statement simply terminates when there is no match.) In the example above, if the
user has typed a character that isn't one of the four for which there is a case constant,
then control will pass to the statements following the default keyword. Here's how that
possibility looks in operation when an illegal operator symbol is typed:

Type number, operator, number

```
2 q 2
Unknown operator
```

The break statements are necessary to terminate the switch statement when the body
of statements in a particular case has been executed. As it did in the numguess.c example
earlier, the break statement has the effect of immediately taking the program out of the
structure it finds itself in: a loop in numguess.c and a switch here.

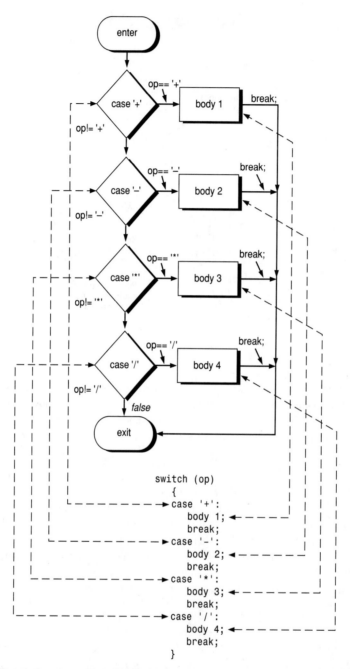

Figure 4.13. Operation of the switch statement.

> If no break statement is used following a case, control will fall through to the next case.

Without the break, the program will execute not only the statements for a particular case but all the statements for the following cases as well. (This is unlike the operation of the Pascal and BASIC case statement.) Needing to write all the breaks may sound like an inconvenience, but it actually makes for a more flexible construction, as shown in the following variation of the calc3.c program:

```c
// calc4.c
// four-function calculator
#include <stdio.h>                       // for printf()

void main(void)
    {
    float num1=1.0, num2=1.0;
    char op;

    while ( !(num1==0.0 && num2==0.0) )
        {
        printf("\n\nEnter number, operator, number\n");
        scanf("%f %c %f", &num1, &op, &num2);
        switch ( op )
            {
            case '+':
                printf(" = %f", num1 + num2);
                break;
            case '-':
                printf(" = %f", num1 - num2);
                break;
            case '*':
            case 'x':
                printf(" = %f", num1 * num2);
                break;
            case '/':
            case '\\':
                printf(" = %f", num1 / num2);
                break;
            default:
                printf("Unknown operator");
            } // end switch
        } // end while
    } // end main()
```

This program tries to be a little more friendly to the user by dealing with the instances when the user types an 'x' instead of a * to mean multiply, or a '\' instead of a '/' to mean divide. Because control falls right through one case to the case below in the absence of a break statement, this construction makes it easy for several values of the switch variable to execute the same body of code.

Note that, because the backslash is already the escape character, we must type \ \ to indicate the backslash itself.

Here's what happens when you type the new operators:

```
C>calc4

Type number, operator, number
2 \ 3
 = 0.666667

Type number, operator, number
10 x 10
 = 100.000000
```

The Conditional Operator

We'll finish off this chapter with a brief look at one of C's stranger constructions, a decision-making operator called the *conditional operator*. It consists of two symbols used on three different expressions, and thus it has the distinction of being the only ternary operator in C. (Ternary operators work on three variables, as opposed to the more common binary operators, such as (+), which operate on two expressions, and unary operators, such as (!), which operate on only one.) The conditional operator has the form

```
condition ? expression1 : expression2.
```

The conditional operator consists of both the question mark and the colon. `condition` is a logical expression that evaluates to either True or False, while `expression1` and `expression2` are either values or expressions that evaluate to values.

Here's how it works. `condition` is evaluated. If it's true, the entire conditional expression takes on the value of `expression1`. If it's false, the conditional expression takes on the value of `expression2`. Note that the entire conditional expression—the three expressions and two operators—takes on a value and can therefore be used in an assignment statement.

Here's an example:

```
max = (num1 > num2)  ?  num1 : num2;
```

The purpose of this statement is to assign to the variable max the value of either num1 or num2, whichever is larger. First the condition (num1>num2) is evaluated. If it's true, the entire conditional expression takes on the value of num1; this value is then assigned to max. If (num1>num2) is false, the conditional expression takes on the value of num2, and this value is assigned to max. This operation is shown in Figure 4.14.

This expression is equivalent to the `if`-`else` statement:

```
if (num1 < num2)
    max = num2;
else
    max = num1;
```

It is more compact, however, than the `if`-`else`; because the entire statement takes on a value, two separate assignment statements aren't needed. This operator can be used very elegantly in the right sort of situation.

Here's another example:

```
abs = (num < 0) ? -num : num;
```

This statement evaluates to the absolute value of num, which is simply num if num is greater than zero, but –num if num is less than zero.

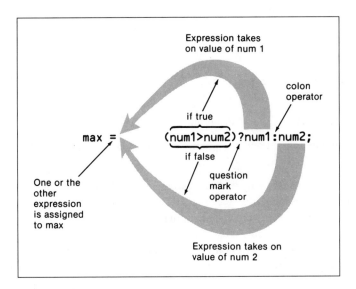

Figure 4.14. The conditional operator.

Summary

You now know a good deal about the major elements of decision-making in C. You've learned about the three major decision-making statements—`if`, `if`-`else`, and `switch`. You've seen how `if` statements and `if`-`else` statements can be nested and how a series of `if`-`else` statements can be transformed into the `else`-`if` construction. You've learned the elements of the `switch` statement: the switch variable, switch constants, and the `case` and `default` keywords. You've also learned about the three logical operators—NOT (!), OR

(¦¦), and AND (&&)—and about the break statement, which causes an immediate exit from a loop or switch structure. Finally, you learned about the conditional operator, which returns one or the other of two values, depending on whether a condition is true or false.

Questions

1. In a simple if statement with no else, what happens if the condition following the if is false?

   a. The program searches for the last else in the program
   b. Nothing
   c. Control "falls through" to the statement following the if
   d. The body of the if statement is executed

2. Is the following a correct C program?

```
void main(void)
{
if ( getche() == 'a' ) then
    printf("\nYou typed a.");
}
```

3. True or false: nesting one if inside another should be avoided for clarity.

4. The main difference in operation between an if statement and a while statement is

   a. The conditional expression following the keyword is evaluated differently
   b. The while loop body is always executed, the if loop body only if the condition is true
   c. The body of the while statement may be executed many times, the body of the if statement only once
   d. The conditional expression is evaluated before the while loop body is executed but after the if loop body

5. The statements following else in an if-else construction are executed when

   a. The conditional expression following if is false
   b. The conditional expression following if is true
   c. The conditional expression following else is false
   d. The conditional expression following else is true

6. Is this C program correct?

```
void main(void)
{
if(getch()=='a') printf("It's an a"); else printf("It's not");
}
```

7. True or false: the compiler interprets else-if differently than it does an equivalent if-else.

8. The statements following a particular else-if in an else-if ladder are executed when

   a. The conditional expression following the else-if is true and all previous conditions are true
   b. The conditional expression following the else-if is true and all previous conditions are false
   c. The conditional expression following the else-if is false and all previous conditions are true
   d. The conditional expression following the else-if is false and all previous conditions are false

9. Which if in a program does an else pair up with?

   a. The last if with the same indentation as the else
   b. The last if not matched with its own else
   c. The last if not enclosed in braces
   d. The last if not enclosed in braces and not matched with its own else

10. The advantage of a switch statement over an else-if construction is

    a. A default condition can be used in the switch
    b. The switch is easier to understand
    c. Several different statements can be executed for each case in a switch
    d. Several different conditions can cause one set of statements to be executed in a switch

11. Is this a correct switch statement?

```
switch(num)
    {
    case 1;
        printf("Num is 1");
    case 2;
        printf("Num is 2");
    default;
        printf("Num is neither 1 nor 2");
    }
```

12. True or false: a break statement must be used following the statements for each case in a switch statement.

13. Is this a correct `switch` statement?

```
switch (temp)
    {
    case temp<60:
        printf("It's really cold!");
        break;
    case temp<80:
        printf("What charming weather!");
        break;
    default:
        printf("Sure is hot!);
    }
```

14. The purpose of the conditional operator is to

    a. Select the highest of two values
    b. Select the more equal of two values
    c. Select one of two values alternately
    d. Select one of two values depending on a condition

15. If num is –42, what is the value of this conditional expression?

```
( num < 0 ) ? 0 : num*num;
```

Exercises

1. Write a program that will ask the user how fast he or she drives, and then print what response a police officer would make to the following speed ranges: >75, >55, >45, <45. Use nested `if-else` statements.

2. Modify the checker.c program to draw a checkerboard where each square, instead of being one row high and two columns wide, is three rows high and six columns wide.

3. Modify the lines2.c program to draw four lines, the first two the same as in lines2.c, the third a vertical line passing through the center of the rectangle (where the first two lines cross), and the fourth a horizontal line passing through the center of the rectangle. The effect is something like a British flag. Use logical operators.

Functions

- Functions
- Returning a value from a function
- Sending values to a function
- Arguments
- External variables
- Preprocessor directives

No one can perform all of life's tasks personally. You may ask a repair person to fix your TV set, hire someone to mow your lawn, or rely on a store to provide fresh vegetables rather than growing your own. A computer program (except for a very simple one) is in much the same situation; it can't handle every task alone. Instead, it calls on other program-like entities—called *functions* in C—to carry out specific tasks. In this chapter, we'll explore the topic of functions. We'll look at a variety of ways functions are used, starting with the simplest case and working up to examples that demonstrate some of the power and versatility of functions in C.

At the end of the chapter, we'll explore another area of C that ties into the idea of functions in several ways: that of *preprocessor directives*.

What Do Functions Do?

[handwritten: funct'n procedure in COBOL but its like a diff prog]

As we noted in Chapter 1, "The Turbo C++ Development System," a function in C serves a similar purpose to a subroutine in BASIC and to functions or procedures in Pascal. Let's examine in more detail why a function is used.

Avoiding Unnecessary Repetition of Code

Probably the original reason functions (or subroutines, as they were first known) were invented was to avoid having to write the same code over and over. Suppose you have a section of code in your program that calculates the square root of a number. If, later in the program, you want to calculate the square root of a different number, you don't want to have to write the same instructions all over again. Instead, in effect, you want to jump to the section of code that calculates square roots and then jump back again to the normal program flow when you're done. In this way, a single section of code can be used many times in the same program. The saving of code is depicted in Figure 5.1.

Program Organization

This is all the early subroutines did. However, over the years it was found that using the subroutine idea made it easier to organize programs and keep track of what they were doing. If the operation of a program could be divided into separate activities and each activity placed in a separate subroutine, each subroutine could be written and checked out more or less independently. Separating the code into modular functions also made programs easier to design and understand.

Independence

As this idea took hold, it became clear that there was an advantage in making subroutines as independent from the main program and from one another as possible. For instance, subroutines were invented that had their own "private" variables—that is, variables that couldn't be accessed from the main program or the other subroutines. This meant that a programmer didn't need to worry about accidentally using the same variable names in different subroutines; the variables in each subroutine were protected from inadvertent tampering by other subroutines. Thus, it was easier to write large and complex programs. Pascal, BASIC, and most other modern programming languages make use of this independence, and C does too, as we'll find out soon.

[handwritten: location needs to be stored in a register.]

[handwritten: ALU - Arithmetic logic unit + comparing unit]

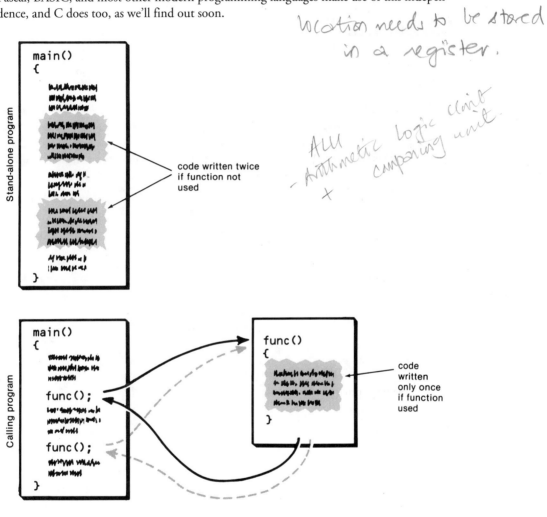

Figure 5.1. Code savings using functions.

C Functions and Pascal Procedures and Functions

For Pascal programmers, we should mention at this point a difference between C and Pascal that might cause some initial confusion. In Pascal, functions and procedures are two separate entities. A function in that language returns a value, whereas a procedure carries out a task or returns data via arguments. In C these two constructs are combined: a C function can return data via arguments and can also return a value. We'll note other differences between C and Pascal as we go along.

Simple Functions

As we noted, using a function is in some ways like hiring someone to perform a specific job for you. Sometimes the interaction with such a person is very simple; sometimes it's more complex. Let's start with a simple case.

Suppose you have a task which is always performed in exactly the same way—mowing your lawn, say. When you want it done, you get on the phone to the lawn person and say, "It's time, do it now." You don't need to give instructions, because that task is all the person does. You don't need to be told when the job is done. You assume the lawn will be mowed in the usual way, the person does it, and that's that.

Let's look at a simple C function that operates in the same way. Actually, we'll be looking at two things: a program that "calls" or activates the function (just as you call the lawn person on the phone) and the function itself. Here's the program:

```c
// textbox.c
// puts box around text
#include <conio.h>              // for printf()
void line(void);                // prototype for line()

void main(void)
    {
    printf("\n");
    line();                                     // draw line
    printf("\xDB TITUS ANDRONICUS \xDB\n");   // message
    line();                                     // 2nd line
    }


// line() — this is function definition
// draws solid line on screen
void line(void)                 // function declaration
    {
    int j;                      // counter

    for (j=1; j<=20; j++)       // print block 20 times
        printf("\xDB");         // solid block
    printf("\n");               // print carriage return
    }
```

This program draws a box around the words TITUS ANDRONICUS (one of the lesser known Roman emperors). Figure 5.2 shows what the output looks like.

To achieve this effect we've first drawn a line of rectangles across the screen (using the graphics character /xDB), then printed the emperor's name—preceded and ended by a rectangle to form the ends of the box—and finally drawn another line. However, instead of writing the code to draw the line twice, we made it into a function, called line().

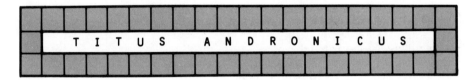

Figure 5.2. Output of textbox.c.

The Structure of Functions

The textbox.c program looks almost like two little programs, but actually each of these "programs" is a function. As we mentioned in Chapter 1, "The Turbo C++ Development System," main() is a function, so it's not surprising that line(), which is also a function, looks like it. The only thing special about main() is that it is always executed first. It doesn't even matter if main() is the first function in the listing; you can place other functions before it and main() will still be executed first.

In this example, main() calls the function line(). *Calls* means "to cause to be executed." To draw the two lines of boxes, main() calls line() twice.

There are three program elements involved in using a function: the function definition, the call to the function, and the function prototype. Let's look at each of these in turn.

The Function Definition

The function itself is referred to as the function definition. The definition starts with a line that includes the function name, among other elements.

```
void line(void)    // note: no semicolon
```

This line is the declarator (a name only a lexicographer could love). The first void means that line() doesn't return anything, and the second means that it takes no arguments. We'll examine return values and arguments later in the chapter.

Note that the declarator doesn't end with a semicolon. It isn't a program statement, whose execution causes something to happen. Rather, it tells the compiler that a function is being defined.

The function definition continues with the body of the function: the program statements that do the work. Figure 5.3 shows the declarator and the function body that make up the function definition.

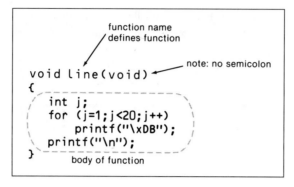

Figure 5.3. Function definition.

The body of the function is enclosed in braces.

Calling the Function

As with the C library functions we've seen, such as `printf()` and `getche()`, our user-written function `line()` is called from `main()` simply by using its name, including the parentheses following the name. The parentheses let the compiler know that you're referring to a function and not to a variable or something else. Calling a function like this is a C statement, so it ends with a semicolon.

```
line();    // function call -- note semicolon
```

This function call causes control to be transferred to the code in the definition of `line()`. This function draws its row of squares on the screen, and then returns to `main()`, to the statement immediately following the function call.

Function Prototype (Declaration)

There's a third function-related element in the textbox.c example. This is a line before the beginning of `main()`:

```
void line(void);    // function prototype -- note semicolon
```

This looks very much like the declarator line at the start of the function definition, except that it ends with a semicolon. What is its purpose?

You've already seen many examples of variables in C programs. All the variables were defined by name and data type before they were used. A function is declared in a similar way at the beginning of a program before it is called. The function declaration (or prototype—the terms mean the same thing) tells the compiler the name of the function, the data type the function returns (if any) and the number and data types of the function's arguments (if any). In our example, the function returns nothing and takes no arguments; hence the two `void`s.

Notice that the prototype is written before the `main()` function. This causes the prototype to be visible to all the functions in a file. You'll learn more about this when we discuss external variables later in this chapter.

The key thing to remember about the prototype is that the data type of the return value must agree with that of the declarator in the function definition, and the number of arguments and their data types must agree with those in the function definition. In this case, both the return value and the arguments are `void`, but you'll soon see examples of other data types. If the data types don't agree, you'll get unhappy messages from the compiler.

> A prototype declares a function
> A function call executes a function
> A function definition is the function itself

Local Variables

The variable `j` used in the `line()` function is known only to `line()`; it is invisible to the `main()` function. If we added this statement to `main()` (without declaring a variable `j` there):

```
printf("%d", j);
```

we would get a compiler error because `main()` wouldn't know anything about this variable. We could declare another variable, also called `j`, in the `main()` function; it would be a completely separate variable, known to `main()` but not to `line()`. This is a key point in the writing of C functions: variables defined in a function are unknown outside the function. The question of which functions know about a variable and which don't is called the *visibility* of the variable. A local variable will be visible to the function it is defined in, but not to others.

A local variable used in this way in a function is known in C as an *automatic* variable, because it is automatically created when a function is called and destroyed when the function returns. The length of time a variable lasts is called its *lifetime*. We'll have more to say about visibility and lifetime in Chapter 12, "Memory," when we discuss storage types.

A Sound Example

Let's reinforce our understanding of functions with another example. This one uses the special character `'/x7'`, which is called BELL in the standard ASCII code. On the PC, printing this character, instead of ringing a bell, causes a beeping sound. Here's the program:

```
// beeptest.c
// tests the twobeep function
```

```
#include <stdio.h>          // for printf()
#include <conio.h>          // for getche()

void twobeep(void);         // function prototype

void main(void)
   {
   twobeep();                    // function call
   printf("\nType any character: ");
   getche();                     // wait for keypress
   twobeep();                    // function call
   }

// twobeep() function definition
// beeps the speaker twice
void twobeep(void)             // function declarator
   {
   long j;

   printf("\x7");                // first beep
   for (j=1; j< 1000000L ; j++)  // delay
      ;                          // (null statement)
   printf("\x7");                // second beep
   }
```

This program first calls a subroutine, twobeep(), which does just what its name says: it sounds two beeps separated by a short silent interval. Then the program asks you to strike a key; when you do, it sounds the two beeps again.

Note how the delay is constructed: A for loop is set up to cycle 1,000,000 times. However, there is no body of program statements in this loop. Instead, there is a statement consisting of only the semicolon. This constitutes a null statement: a statement with nothing in it. It's only role is to terminate the for loop. If you're using a slower computer with an 8088 or 80286 microprocessor, you may want to decrease the delay by making the constant smaller: 100,000 or even 10,000.

Note that constants which exceed the range of type int (32,767 to –32,768) must be type long. The compiler wants you to verify that it's your intention to use this type by appending an uppercase L to the constant, 1000000L. If you forget the L, you'll get a warning message.

Functions that Return a Value

Let's look at a slightly more complicated kind of function: one that returns a value. An analogy can be made here with hiring someone to find out something for you. In a way, you do this when you dial 767–8900 to find out what time it is. You make the call, the person (or computer) on the other end of the line gives you the time, and that's that. You don't need to tell them what you want; that's understood when you call that number. No information flows from you to the phone company, but some flows from it back to you.

A function that uses no arguments but returns a value performs a similar role. You call the function, it gets a certain piece of information and returns it to you. The function getche() operates in just this way; you call it—without giving it any information—and it returns the value of the first character typed on the keyboard.

Suppose we wanted a function that returned a character as getche() does but that also automatically translated any uppercase characters into lowercase. Such a function, with a calling program that uses a switch statement to create a rudimentary menu program, follows:

[handwritten note: unresolved external reference — reference did not have anything on it / not right address.]

```c
// getlow.c
// tests getlc function
#include <stdio.h>     // for printf()
#include <stdio.h>     // for getche()
char getlc(void);      // function prototype

void main(void)
   {
   char chlc;          // char returned

   printf("\nType 'a' for first selection, 'b' for second: ");
   chlc = getlc();     // get converted character
   switch (chlc)       // print msg, depending on char
      {
      case 'a':
         printf("\nYou typed an 'a'.");
         break;
      case 'b':
         printf("\nYou typed a 'b'.");
         break;
      default:
         printf("\nYou chose a non-existent selection.");
      }  // end switch
   }  // end main()

// getlc
// returns character
// converts to lowercase if in uppercase
char getlc(void)
   {
   char ch;                // char from keyboard

   ch = getche();          // get character
   if ( ch>64 && ch<91 )   // if it's uppercase,
      ch = ch + 32;        // add 32 to convert to lower
   return (ch);            // return character to caller
   }
```

Our new function, getlc() (for *get lowercase*), returns a value of type char. The return type is no longer void as in previous examples. Notice that both the prototype and the declarator in the function definition begin with char to reflect this fact. The getlc() function is called from the main program with the statement

```
chlc = getlc();
```

Just as in the case of getche(), the function itself appears to "take on the value" it is returning. It can thus be used as if it were a variable in an assignment statement, and the value returned (a lowercase character) will be assigned to the variable chlc, which is then used in the switch statement to determine which message will be printed. Here are examples of output from the program:

```
Type 'a' for first selection, 'b' for second: a
You typed an 'a'.

Type 'a' for first selection, 'b' for second: A
You typed an 'a'.

Type 'a' for first selection, 'b' for second: c
You chose a nonexistent selection.
```

Notice how the capital A typed by the user is successfully converted to lowercase. (We should mention that Turbo C includes library functions for case conversion: toupper() and tolower().)

The *return* Statement

In the textbox.c and beeptest.c programs shown earlier, the functions returned (jumped back to) the calling program when they encountered the final closing brace (}) which defined the end of the function. No separate "return" statement was necessary.

This approach is fine if the function isn't going to return a value to the calling program. In the case of our menu.c program, however, we want to return the value of the character read from the keyboard. In fact, we want to return one of two possible values: the character itself, if it is in lowercase already, or a modified version of the character, if it is in uppercase, so we use the if statement to check if ch is in uppercase (uppercase letters run from ASCII 65 to 90). If so, we add 32 (the difference between ASCII's A = 65 and a = 97) to ch. Finally, we return to the calling program with the new value of the character, by placing the variable name between the parentheses following return.

The return statement has two purposes. First, executing it immediately transfers control from the function back to the calling program. Second, whatever is inside the parentheses following return is returned as a value to the calling program.

Figure 5.4 shows a function returning a value to the calling program.

The return statement need not be at the end of the function. It can occur anywhere in the function; as soon as it's encountered, control will return to the calling program. For instance, we could have rewritten the getlc() function like this:

```
// getlc()
// returns character
```

```
// converts to lowercase if in uppercase
char getlc(void)
    {
    char ch;                // char from keyboard

    ch = getche();          // get character
    if ( ch>64 && ch<91 )   // if it's uppercase,
        return(ch + 32);    // add 32 to convert to lower
    else
        return (ch);        // return character to caller
    }
```

Here different `return` statements will be used depending on whether ch is uppercase or not.

The `return` statement can also be used without a value following it. When this is the case, no value is returned to the calling program.

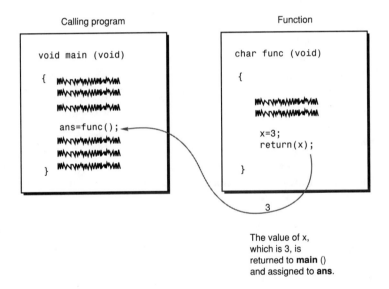

Figure 5.4. Function returning a value.

Returning Type *int*

Here's another example of a function that returns a value, this time of type `int`. This example, called `getmins()`, gets a time in hours and minutes from the user. The main program uses this function to calculate the difference in seconds between two times:

```
// intimes.c
// calculates difference between two times
#include <stdio.h>         // for printf(), scanf()
int getmins(void);         // func prototype
```

```
void main(void)
    {
    int mins1, mins2;                        // minutes

    printf("\nEnter first time (form 3:22): ");
    mins1 = getmins();                       // get minutes
    printf("Enter second (later) time: ");
    mins2 = getmins();                       // get minutes
                                             // find difference
    printf("Difference is %d minutes.", mins2-mins1 );
    }

// getmins()
// gets time in hours:minutes format
// returns time in minutes
int getmins(void)
    {
    int hours, minutes;

    scanf("%d:%d", &hours, &minutes);        // get user input
    return ( hours*60 + minutes );           // convert to minutes
    }
```

Essentially, what the function getmins does is accept a time in hours and minutes from the user and convert it into minutes by multiplying the hours by 60 and adding the minutes. There is one new wrinkle in the use of the scanf() function, however.

New Wrinkle in *scanf()*

If you're very attentive you may have noticed something new in the scanf() statement: there is a colon between the two format specifiers, %d and %d, rather than a space as in the past.

```
scanf("%d:%d", &hours, &minutes);
```

This has the effect of requiring the user to type a colon between the two numbers for the two %d's, rather than permitting only whitespace characters (space, tab, newline). Thus, the user can type the time in standard hours and minutes format, using a colon to separate them. Here's a sample session with intimes.c:

```
Enter first time (form 3:22): 6:00
Enter second (later) time: 7:45
Difference is 105 minutes.
```

You may notice that scanf() isn't a very forgiving function; if you type anything but a colon, scanf() will terminate immediately without waiting for the minutes to be typed and without giving you any warning that it's doing so. A truly user-friendly program would add some code to give better feedback to the user.

Returning Type *float*

Here's an example in which a function returns type `float`. In this program, the `main()` function asks the user for the radius of a sphere, and then calls a function named `area()` to get the radius from the user and calculate the area of the sphere. The `area()` function returns the area of the sphere in the form of a floating point value, which `main()` then prints.

```
// sphere.c
// calculates area of a sphere
#include <stdio.h>     // for printf(), scanf()
float area(void);      // prototype

void main(void)
    {
    float  answer;

    printf("\nEnter radius of sphere: ");
    answer = area();
    printf("Area of sphere is %.2f",  answer);
    }

// area()
// gets radius from user, returns area of sphere
float  area(void)
    {
    float rad;

    scanf("%f", &rad);
    return( 4 * 3.14159 * rad * rad );
    }
```

Let's take a look at a sample of interaction with the sphere.c program:

```
Enter radius of sphere: 10
Area of sphere is 1256.64

Enter radius of sphere: 4000
Area of sphere is 201061760.00
```

The last example calculates the approximate surface area of the earth: a little over 200 million square miles. With so much space available, it's surprising people are willing to pay such high prices for land in Manhattan.

Prototypes and Return Values

In the programs getlow.c, intimes.c, and sphere.c, we've shown functions that return three different kinds of return values: type `char`, type `int`, and type `float`. Notice that in each case the prototype for the function reflects this return type:

```
char getlc(void);      // prototype in getlow.c

int getmins(void);     // prototype in intimes.c

float area(void);      // prototype in sphere.c
```

If you try to assign the return value of a function to a variable of the wrong type, the compiler will issue a warning. For example, if in the sphere.c program, you mistakenly defined the variable answer to be of type int instead of float, when the compiler got to the line

```
answer = area();
```

it would see that the value of a function that's supposed to return type float was being assigned to a variable of type int and issue this warning:

```
Warning SPHERE.C 11: Call to function 'area' with no prototype.
```

It's not really that there isn't a prototype but that you're using the function in a way not supported by the prototype. The compiler thinks maybe you mean another function that doesn't have a prototype. In any case, the use of prototypes is an important way to keep errors from creeping into your program.

Limitation of *return*

Before we move on to other things, you should be aware of a key limitation in the use of the return statement: you can only use it to return one value. If you want your function to return two or more values to the calling program, you need another mechanism. In the following sections we'll see how, using arguments, it's possible to pass more than one piece of information to a function. However, getting more than one piece of information back will be a topic for Chapter 7, "Pointers," because it requires a knowledge of the concepts of addresses and pointers.

Using a return statement, only one value can be returned by a function.

Using Arguments to Pass Data to a Function

So far the functions we've used haven't been very flexible. We call them and they do what they're designed to do, either returning a value or not. Like our lawn person who always mows the grass exactly the same way, we can't influence them in the way they carry out their tasks. It would be nice to have a little more control over what functions do, in the same way it would be nice to be able to tell the lawn person, "Just do the front yard today, we're having a barbecue out back."

The mechanism used to convey information to a function is the *argument.* You've already used arguments in `printf()` and `scanf()` functions; the format strings and the values used inside the parentheses in these functions are arguments.

Here's an example of a program in which a single argument is passed to a user-written function:

```
// bargraph.c
// draws bargraph, demonstrates function arguments
#include <stdio.h>          // for printf()
void bar(int);              // function prototype

void main(void)
    {
    printf("\n");
    printf("Terry\t");       // print name
    bar(27);                 // draw line 27 chars long
    printf("Chris\t");       // print name
    bar(41);                 // draw line 41 chars long
    printf("Reggie\t");      // and so on
    bar(34);
    printf("Cindy\t");
    bar(22);
    printf("Harold\t");
    bar(15);
    }

// bar()
// function draws horizontal bar, 'score' characters long
void bar(int score)         // function declarator
    {
    int j;

    for(j=1; j<=score; j++)  // draw 'score' number of
        printf("\xCD");      //     double-line characters
    printf("\n");            // newline at end of bar
    }
```

This program generates a bargraph of names and bars representing, say, the scores in a spelling test. The output of the program is shown in Figure 5.5.

In this program the purpose of the function bar() is to draw a horizontal line, made up of the double-line graphics character ('\xCD') on the screen. For each person (Terry, Chris, etc.), the main program prints the name and then calls the function, using as an argument the score received by that person on the test.

Structure of a Function Call with Arguments

There are a number of things to notice about this program. First, in the main program, the number we want to pass to the function bar() is included in the parentheses following bar in the function call.

```
bar(27);
```

We could have used a variable name instead of the constant 27; we'll see an example of this shortly.

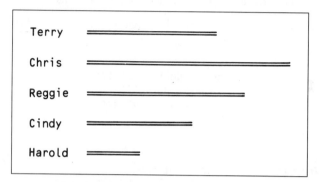

```
Terry   ══════════════
Chris   ═══════════════════
Reggie  ═════════════════
Cindy   ═══════════
Harold  ══════
```

Figure 5.5. Output of the bargraph.c program.

In the function definition, a variable name score is placed in the parentheses following bar.

```
void bar(int score)
```

This ensures that the value included between parentheses in the main program is assigned to the variable between parentheses in the function definition. This is shown schematically in Figure 5.6. Notice that the data type of score is also specified in the function definition. This constitutes a definition of the argument variable, setting aside memory space for it in the function.

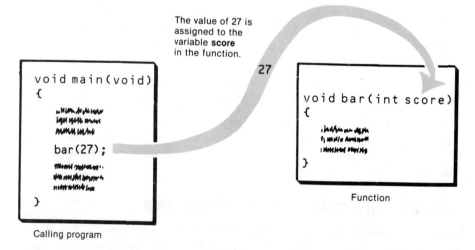

Figure 5.6. Passing a value to a function.

The structure of a function with an argument is shown in Figure 5.7.

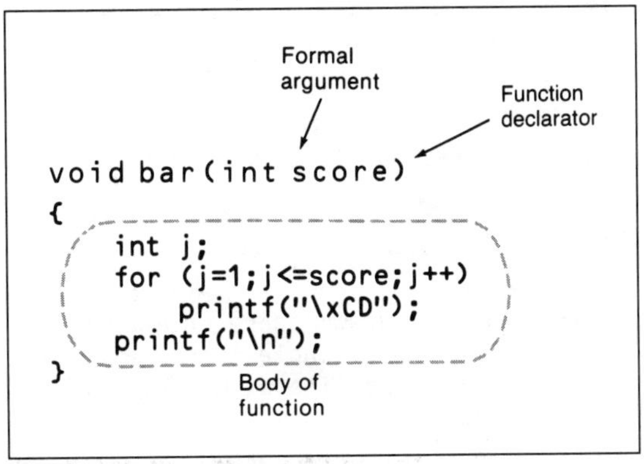

Figure 5.7. Function definition with argument.

Note that the prototype for the function,

```
void bar(int);
```

specifies the data type of the argument: type int. The compiler checks this type against the type of the argument you actually use when calling the function. In bargraph.c, we use arguments like 27, 41, and so on. These are type int, so the compiler is happy. If, however, we had used an argument of type float or type char, the compiler would have issued a warning. Again, this is an important error-checking mechanism that helps save you from yourself.

Passing Variables as Arguments

In the example above we passed constants (such as the number 27) as an argument to the function bar(). We also can use a variable in the calling program, as this variation on the bargraph.c program demonstrates:

```
// bargr2.c
// draws bargraph, demonstrates function arguments
#include <stdio.h>              // for printf(), scanf()
void bar(int inscore);         // function prototype
                               //    with identifier

void main(void)
    {
    int inscore=1;

    printf("\n");
    while ( inscore != 0 )     // exit on zero score
        {
```

```
        printf("Score=");           // prompt the user
        scanf("%d", &inscore);      // get score from user
        bar(inscore);               // draw line
        }
    }

// bar
// function to draw horizontal bar
void bar(int score)
    {
    int j;

    for(j=1; j<=score; j++)     // draw 'score' number of
        printf("\xCD");         //     double-line character
    printf("\n");               // newline at end of bar
    }
```

In this program the function bar() is the same as before. However, the main program has been modified to accept scores from the keyboard. Figure 5.8 shows a sample of interaction with the program. Entering 0 terminates it.

Because the scores we pass to bar() are no longer known in advance, we must use a variable to pass them to the bar() function. We do this in the statement

```
bar(inscore);
```

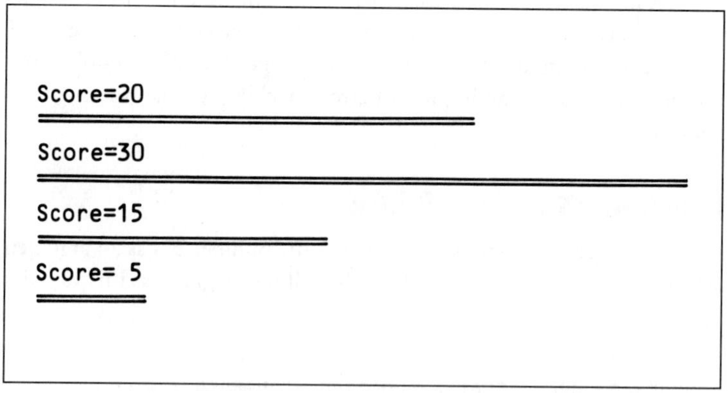

```
Score=20
════════════════════════════════

Score=30
══════════════════════════════════════════════════

Score=15
════════════════════════

Score= 5
════════
```

Figure 5.8. Output of the bargr2.c program.

Now, whatever value the user types is recorded by scanf() and assigned to the variable inscore. When bar() is called, this is the value passed to it as an argument. Figure 5.9 shows this process.

Different names have been assigned to the arguments in the calling and called functions: inscore in the calling program and score in the function. Actually, we could have used the same name for both variables; because they're in different functions, the compiler would still consider them to be separate variables.

Note that the argument in the calling program is referred to as the *actual argument,* while the argument in the called function is the *formal argument.* In this case, the variable inscore in the calling program is the actual argument, and the variable score in the function is the formal argument. Knowing these terms won't help you program better, but it may impress people at parties.

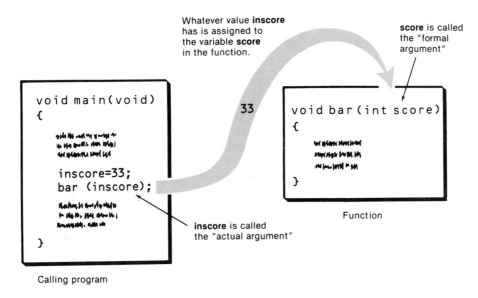

Figure 5.9. Variable used as argument.

Passing Multiple Arguments

We can pass as many arguments as we like to a function. Here's an example of a program that passes two arguments to a function, rectang(), whose purpose is to draw variously sized rectangles on the screen. The two arguments are the length and width of the rectangle, where each rectangle represents a room in a house.

```
// roomplot.c
// tests the rectang() function
#include <stdio.h>              // for printf()
void rectang(int, int);        // function prototype

void main(void)
    {
    printf("\nLiving room\n");  // print room name
    rectang(22,12);            // draw room
    printf("\nCloset\n");      // etc.
```

147

```
   rectang(4,4);
   printf("\nKitchen\n");
   rectang(16,16);
   printf("\nBathroom\n");
   rectang(6,8);
   printf("\nBedroom\n");
   rectang(12,12);
   }  // end main()

// rectang()
// draws rectangle of length, width
// length goes across screen, width goes up-and-down
void rectang(int length, int width)
   {
   int j, k;

   length /= 2;                        // horizontal scale factor
   width /= 4;                         // vertical scale factor
   for (j=1; j<=width; j++)            // number of lines
      {
      printf("\t\t");                 // tab over
      for (k=1; k<=length; k++)       // line of rectangles
         printf("\xDB");              // print one rectangle
      printf("\n");                   // next line
      }
   }  // end rectang()
```

This program prints the name of a room and then draws a rectangle representing the dimensions of the room. A sample of the output from the program is shown in Figure 5.10.

The operation of the function is very much like that of the rectangle-drawing program in Chapter 3, "Loops." Our new wrinkle here is the use of scale factors. These are necessary so that the room dimensions can be expressed in feet. The function divides the length (the horizontal dimension on the screen) by 2 and the width (the vertical dimension) by 4. This makes it possible for a series of typical rooms to fit on the screen and also compensates for the fact that a character on the screen is twice as high as it is long. To make a square room look square, we must divide its vertical dimension by twice as much as its horizontal dimension. The division operation for the scale factors is carried out using an assignment operator. As we saw in Chapter 2, "C Building Blocks," the statement

```
length /= 2;
```

is equivalent to

```
length = length / 2;
```

The process of passing two arguments is similar to passing one. The value of the first actual argument in the calling program is assigned to the first formal argument in the function, and the value of the second actual argument is assigned to the second formal argument, as shown in Figure 5.11.

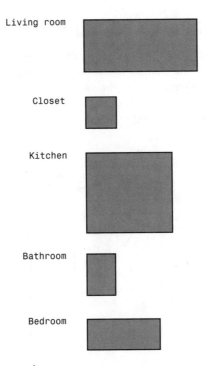

Living room

Closet

Kitchen

Bathroom

Bedroom

Figure 5.10. Output of the roomplot.c program.

```
void main(void)                    void rectang(int length, int width)
{                                  {
    ▨▨▨,▨▨▨~▨,▨▨▨            ▨▨ ▨▨ ▨▨▨ ▨▨,▨▨ |▨
    ▨▨ ▨▨,▨▨▨▨▨▨▨            |▨▨ ▨▨▨ ▨▨|▨▨▨~▨▨▨
                                       | ▨,▨▨▨▨ ▨▨|▨▨▨ ▨
    rectang(22,12);               ▨, .▨▨▨▨▨▨▨ |▨

    ▨▨,▨, ▨,▨▨▨▨,▨▨
    ▨▨ ▨,▨▨▨▨▨▨ ▨ ▨
}                                  }
```

Calling program   Function

The first actual argument is assigned
to the first formal argument; the
second actual argument is assigned
to the second formal argument.

Figure 5.11. Multiple arguments passed to function.

Of course, three or more arguments could be used in the same way.

Using More Than One Function

You can use as many functions as you like in a program, and any of the functions can call any of the other functions. There is an important difference here between C and Pascal. In Pascal, a function (or a procedure), call it Alpha, can be defined inside another function, Beta, so that it isn't visible to other functions, like Gamma, that aren't in Beta. In C, however, all functions are visible to all other functions. This situation is shown in Figure 5.12.

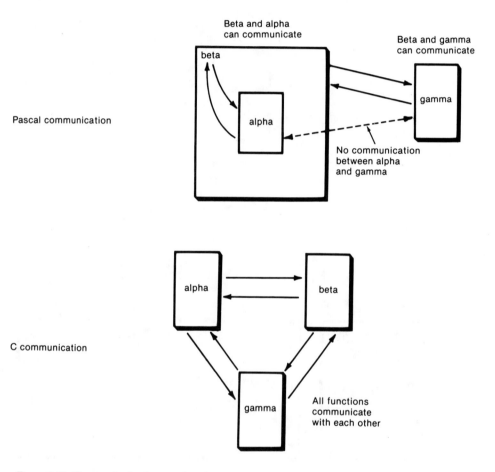

Figure 5.12. Communication between functions.

In this respect, C is more like BASIC, where it is impossible to nest or "hide" one subroutine inside another.

In C, all functions, including main(), have equal status and are visible to all other functions.

Which approach is better? Being able to nest functions, as in Pascal, does provide some added flexibility in certain situations—you could use the same function name for two different functions, for example, which might be advantageous in large programs. However, the C approach—all functions are equal—is conceptually easier and usually doesn't result in any inconvenience to the programmer.

Let's look at a program involving several functions. This program calculates the sum of the squares of two integers typed by the user. The program actually uses three functions as well as main(). The first function does the actual calculation, while main() simply gets the numbers from the user and prints the result. The second function returns the square of a number (the number multiplied by itself), and the third function returns the sum of two numbers.

```c
// multifun.c
// tests sumsqr() function
#include <stdio.h>              // for printf(), scanf()
int sumsqr(int, int);          // function prototypes
int sqr(int);
int sum(int, int);

void main(void)
    {
    int num1, num2;            // user-supplied values

    printf("\nEnter two numbers: ");  // gets two numbers,
    scanf("%d %d", &num1, &num2);     // prints sum of squares
    printf("Sum of the squares is %d", sumsqr(num1,num2) );
    }

// sumsqr function
// returns sum of squares of two arguments
int sumsqr(int j,int k)
    {
    return( sum( sqr(j), sqr(k) ) );
    }

// sqr function
// returns square of argument
int sqr(int z)
    {
    return(z * z);
    }

// sum function
// returns sum of two arguments
```

```
int sum(int x, int y)
   {
   return(x + y);
   }
```

Notice that none of the functions is nested inside any other. In Pascal, we could have placed, for instance, the sum() and sqr() functions inside the sumsqr() function. In C, all the functions are visible to all other functions. The main program, for instance, could call sum() or sqr() directly if it needed to.

Another point to note is that functions can appear in any order in the program listing. They can be arranged alphabetically, in the order in which they're called, by functional group, or any other way the programmer wishes. Arranging the functions in an order that makes them easier to refer to can be a real advantage for the programmer, especially in larger programs with dozens of functions. Note too that the main() function doesn't need to be the first one in the program, although it usually is.

External Variables

So far, the variables we have used in our example programs have been confined to the functions using them; that is, they have been *visible* or accessible only to the function in which they were defined. Such variables, which are declared inside a particular function and used only there, are called *local* (or *automatic*) variables. While local variables are preferred for most purposes, it is sometimes desirable to use a variable known to (that is, visible to) all the functions in a program, rather than just one. This is true when many different functions must read or modify a variable, making it clumsy or impractical to communicate the value of the variable from function to function using arguments and return values. In this case, we use an *external* variable (sometimes called a *global* variable).

Here's an example of a program that uses an external variable:

```
// extern.c
// tests use of external variables
#include <stdio.h>                    // for printf()
void oddeven(void);                   // function prototypes
void negative(void);

int keynumb;                          // external variable

void main(void)
   {
   printf("\nEnter keynumb: ");
   scanf("%d", &keynumb);
   oddeven();                         // function call
   negative();                        // function call
   }

// oddeven()
// checks if keynumb is odd or even
```

```
void oddeven(void)
   {
   if ( keynumb % 2 )               // reference external var
      printf("Keynumb is odd.\n");
   else
      printf("Keynumb is even.\n");
   }

// negative()
// checks if keynumb is negative
void negative(void)
   {
   if ( keynumb < 0 )               // reference external var
      printf("Keynumb is negative.\n");
   else
      printf("Keynumb is positive.\n");
   }
```

In this program, main() and two other functions, oddeven() and negative(), all have access to the variable keynumb. To achieve this new global status for keynumb, it was necessary to declare it outside of all of the functions, including main(). Thus it appears before the definition of main().

Here's a sample interaction with the program:

```
Enter keynumb: -21
Keynumb is odd.
Keynumb is negative.

Enter keynumb: 44
Keynumb is even.
Keynumb is positive.
```

As you can see, main() is able to place a value in the variable keynumb, and both oddeven() and negative() are able to read the value of the variable.

We should point out the dangers of indiscriminate use of external variables. It may seem tempting to simplify things by making *all* variables external; BASIC programmers in particular tend to fall victim to this practice. However, there are several reasons why it isn't a good idea. First, external variables aren't protected from accidental alteration by functions that have no business modifying them. Second, as we'll see in Chapter 12, "Memory," external variables use memory less efficiently than local variables. The rule is that variables should be local unless there's a very good reason to make them external.

Static Variables

There's another class of variable we should mention at this point: *static variables*. Static variables are used only in certain specialized situations, but it's useful to know they exist.

To understand why we need static variables, you should know that the regular local (automatic) variables that we've been using all along only exist while the function using them is executing. For example, in the roomplot.c program earlier in this chapter, the variables i and j, which are local variables in the function rectang(), are created when rectang() is called by main() and destroyed when rectang() returns. (Technically this is handled by pushing local variables on the stack when calling a function and popping them off when the function returns, but you don't need to worry about these details.)

However, sometimes you want a function to remember something between calls to it. That is, if a local variable in the function is left with a value when the function returns, you would like to find the same value there when you call the function again. Unfortunately, local variables can't do this, because they not only lose their values, but cease to exist altogether when the function returns.

An external variable could solve this problem, because external variables keep their values for the life of the program, not being associated with any function; but sometimes you don't want to incur the disadvantages of an external variable (such as having it be visible to every function in the program).

This is where static variables come in. A static variable is defined within a function like a local variable and is visible within the function. However, it keeps its value between calls to the function.

Here's an example of a static variable in use. Suppose you want a function that remembers how many times it has been called. (No, this isn't too likely, but it illustrates the point.) Using a static variable makes this possible.

```c
// staticd.c
// demonstrates static variables
#include <stdio.h>       // for printf()
int func(void);          // prototype

void main(void)
   {
   int  j;

   for(j=0; j<4; j++)
      printf("\nYou've called me %d times", func() );
   }

int func(void)
   {
   static int k;

    return(++k);
   }
```

The static variable k in the function func() keeps its value between calls and so remembers how many times it has been called. The main() program calls it four times.

Here's the output:

```
You've called me 1 times
You've called me 2 times
You've called me 3 times
You've called me 4 times
```

There is more to be said about the twin questions of visibility and lifetime: which functions can access a variable and how long the variable lasts. These questions relate to another important topic: C's capability of combining separately compiled object files together at link time into a single executable program. We'll return to these topics in later chapters.

Prototype Versus Classical K and R

When Kernighan and Ritchie defined the C language in their 1978 book (see the bibliography), they didn't include function prototypes. Prototypes are a refinement introduced by the recent ANSI standard and should be used in all new programs. However, many existing programs were written using the older K and R approach, so you may need to be familiar with it. Comparing the prototype system with the classical K and R approach also helps clarify the advantages of prototypes.

Examples of the Two Approaches

Let's look at two versions of a single program. The first uses the prototype approach.

```
// proto.c
// program uses prototyping
#include <stdio.h>              // for printf()
void func(int);                 // function prototype

void main(void)                 // return and args for main()
   {
   int actarg = 1234;

   func(actarg);                // function call
   }

// func()
// function prints out value of argument
void func(int formarg)          // function declarator
   {                            //    includes arg declarations
   printf("\nArgument is %d", formarg);
   }
```

There should be no surprises here. The main() function passes a value to func(), which prints it.

Now let's look at the K and R approach without prototypes.

```
// noproto.c
// program doesn't use prototyping
#include <stdio.h>                       // for printf()
                                         // no prototype for func
main()                                   // no return or args
    {
    int actarg = 1234;
    func(actarg);                        // function call
    }

// func()
// function prints out value of argument
func(formarg)                            // function declarator
int formarg;                             // declare argument
    {
    printf("\nArgument  is %d", formarg);
    }
```

Although it uses the obsolete format, this program will still compile and run in Turbo C++. The ANSI standard, to which Turbo C++ adheres, allows the old-style approach so that older source files can be compiled. Turbo C++ does generate warning messages to let you know if you're not ANSI compatible.

There are two major differences between nonproto.c and proto.c. First, as its name implies, noproto.c doesn't use a prototype for the function. This works, provided that the function returns a value of type int. If the function returns any other type, such as float, then it must have a prototype. However, the prototype need not include the data types of the arguments. To be ANSI compatible, the prototype must include the data types of the arguments.

The second major difference is that the function declarator and the definition of the function parameters are on separate lines. This has the same effect as the single-line ANSI approach, but it's not so intuitive, and it doesn't match the format of the prototype (if there is one).

Advantages of Prototyping

Why were prototypes adopted for the ANSI standard? As we've seen, their major advantage is that the data types of a function's arguments are clearly specified at the beginning of a program. A common error in K and R programs was to call a function using the wrong data type for an argument; int, for example, instead of long. This could lead to program failure that was difficult to debug, because there was no warning from the compiler. When a prototype is used, however, the compiler knows what data types to expect as arguments for the function and is always able to flag a mismatch as an error. Also—as in declaring variables—the prototype clarifies for the programmer and anyone else looking at the listing what each function is and what its arguments should be.

The ANSI standard introduced type void for functions that didn't return anything. Previously, a function that didn't return anything was considered to be type int by default, an inconsistent and potentially confusing approach. This is why Turbo C++ generates warning messages for noproto.c: in the absence of prototypes, it assumes main() and func() are type int but sees that they don't return a value of this (or any) type.

ANSI also introduced void as meaning that the function takes no arguments, thus removing another potential source of confusion.

Argument Names in the Declarator

ANSI C makes another service available to the programmer. Argument names can be used in the prototype as a reminder of what the function arguments are. So far we've shown prototypes without these names. For instance, in the roomplot.c example, the prototype is

```
void rectang(int, int);
```

This conforms to ANSI C, in that it tells the compiler the data types of the arguments. However, a human being reading the source code may be confused as to which argument is which, because they both have the same data type. This can be inconvenient, especially when the prototypes and the functions are in different files, and the function itself may not be readily accessible. To clarify the situation, the prototype can be changed to

```
void rectang(int length, int width);
```

Not only is this clearer, it also matches exactly the declarator in the function definition. You may want to use this approach all the time; you certainly should use it in multifile programs with functions taking multiple arguments of the same data type.

What About *main()*?

Although prototypes are specified for all functions, we don't use one for main(). You can do this if you want, but because main() is a special case, the prototype is understood to exist. Turbo C doesn't generate error messages if you neglect a prototype for main().

You can also leave out the void used to specify the arguments to main() without eliciting any error messages. In subsequent programs, however, we'll use arguments to main(), so inserting the void makes it clear that we didn't just forget the arguments; we're deliberately not using them.

Preprocessor Directives

At this point, we'll shift gears a little and explore a topic which at first glance might not seem to have much to do with functions: the use of *preprocessor directives*. We mentioned the directive #include earlier; here we'll focus on another directive, #define, and also explore #include a little further. Various other directives will appear from time to time as we go along.

Preprocessor directives form what can almost be considered a language within the language of C. This is a capability that doesn't exist in many other higher-level languages (although there are similar features in assembly language).

To understand preprocessor directives, let's first review what a compiler does. When you write a line of program code

```
num = 44;
```

you're asking the compiler to translate this code into machine-language instructions that can be executed by the microprocessor chip in the computer. Thus, most of your listing consists of instructions to the microprocessor. Preprocessor directives, on the other hand, are instructions *to the compiler itself.* Rather than being translated into machine language, they're operated on directly by the compiler before the compilation process even begins; hence the name preprocessor.

> Normal program statements are instructions to the microprocessor; preprocessor directives are instructions to the compiler.

Preprocessor directives always start with a number sign (#). The directives can be placed anywhere in a program but are most often used at the beginning of a file, before main( ), or before the beginning of particular functions.

The *#define* Directive

The simplest use for the #define directive is to assign names (DAYS_YEAR or PI, for instance) to constants (such as 365 or 3.14159). As an example, let's modify the sphere.c program from earlier in the chapter. In its original incarnation, the constant 3.14159 appeared in this program in the area( ) function in the line

```
return( 4 * 3.14159 * rad * rad );
```

We'll also change the area( ) function so that it has nothing to do but calculate the area; the radius is obtained from the user in main( ) and passed to area( ) as an argument. Here's the modified program:

```
// sphere2.c
// calculates area of a sphere
#include <stdio.h>
#define PI 3.14159                    // #define directive
float area(float);

void main(void)
    {
    float radius;
```

```
    printf("\nEnter radius of sphere: ");
    scanf("%f", &radius);
    printf("Area of sphere is %.2f", area(radius) );
    }
// area()
// returns area of sphere
float area(float rad)
    {
    return( 4 * PI * rad * rad );  // use of identifier
    }
```

In this new version, the preprocessor first looks for all program lines beginning with the number sign (#). When it sees the #define directive, it goes through the entire program, and at every place it finds PI, it substitutes the phrase 3.14159. This is a mechanical process: simply the substituting of one group of characters, 3.14159, for another, PI. It's very much like a word processor's "global search and replace." Figure 5.13 shows the structure of the #define directive.

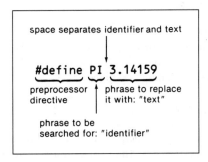

Figure 5.13. Structure of the #define *directive.*

The phrase on the left (PI), which will be searched for, is called the *identifier*. The phrase on the right (3.14159), which will be substituted for it, is called the *text*. A space separates the identifier from the text. By convention, the identifier (in this case, PI) is written in all caps. This makes it easy when looking at the listing to tell which parts of the program will be altered by #define directives.

Why Use *#define?*

Perhaps you wonder what we've gained by substituting PI for 3.14159 in our program. Hopefully, we've made the program easier to read. Although such a common constant as 3.14159 is easily recognized, there are many instances where a constant doesn't reveal its purpose so readily. For example, we'll see later that 72 is the extended code for the Up Arrow keyboard key. Which would be more meaningful to you in a program listing, the number 72 or a constant like UP_ARROW?

There is another, perhaps more important reason for using the #define directive in this way. Suppose a constant like 3.14159 appears many times in your program. Further suppose that you later decide you want an extra digit of precision; you need to change all instances of 3.14159 to 3.141592. Ordinarily, you would need to go through the program and manually change each occurrence of the constant. However, if you have defined 3.14159 to be PI in a #define directive, you need to make only one change, in the #define directive itself.

```
#define PI 3.141592
```

The change will be made automatically to all occurrences of PI before compilation begins.

The *const* Modifier

The new ANSI standard C defines a modifier, const, that can be used to achieve almost the same effect as #define when creating constants. Here's how it looks:

```
const float PI = 3.141592;
```

This statement creates a variable of type float and gives it the value 3.141592, similar to a normal function declaration. However, the const tells the compiler not to permit any changes to the variable. If you try to modify PI, therefore you'll get an error message from the compiler. This approach is gaining in popularity.

Macros

The #define directive is actually considerably more powerful than we have shown so far. This additional power comes from #define's ability to use arguments. Before we tackle this, let's look at one more example of #define without an argument to make the transition clearer. In this example we show that #define can be used, not only for constants, but to substitute for any phrase we like. Suppose your program needs to print the message Error at several places in the program. You use the directive

```
#define ERROR printf("\nError.\n");
```

Then if you have a program statement such as

```
if (input > 640)
    ERROR
```

it will be expanded into

```
if (input > 640)
    printf("\nError.\n");
```

by the preprocessor before compilation begins. The moral here is that an identifier defined by #define can be used as an entire C statement.

Now let's look at an example of #define with an argument. If you've ever thought that the printf() function makes you go to a lot of trouble just to print a number, consider this alternative:

```
// macroprn.c
// demonstrates macros, using printf() statements
#include <stdio.h>                    // for printf()

#define PR(n) printf("%.2f\n", n);   // macro definition

void main(void)
   {
   float num1 = 27.25;
   float num2;

   printf("\n");
   num2 = 1.0 / 3.0;
   PR(num1);                          // calls to macro
   PR(num2);
   }
```

Here's the output of the program:

```
C>macroprn
27.25
0.33
```

You can see that our abbreviated version of the printf() statement, PR(n), actually prints the two numbers.

In this program, whenever the preprocessor sees the phrase PR(n) it expands it into the C statement

```
printf("%.2f\n",n);
```

> A #define directive can take arguments, much as a function does.

However, that's not all it does. In the #define directive, the n in the identifier PR(n) is an argument that matches the n in the printf() statement in the text. The statement PR(num1) in the program causes the variable num1 to be substituted for n. Thus, the phrase PR(num1) is equivalent to

```
printf("%.2f\n", num1);
```

Figure 5.14 shows how this process works.

A #define directive that uses arguments in this way is called a *macro*. Macros have some of the characteristics of functions, as will be made clearer in the next example.

Syntax note: Whenever you use a #define directive, you shouldn't use any spaces in the identifier. For instance,

```
#define PR (n) printf("%.2f\n",n);
```

wouldn't work, because the space between PR and (n) would be interpreted as the end of the identifier.

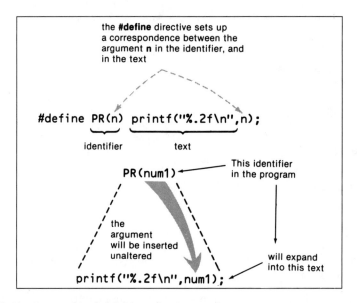

the **#define** directive sets up a correspondence between the argument **n** in the identifier, and in the text

```
#define PR(n) printf("%.2f\n",n);
```

identifier   text

PR(num1)   This identifier in the program

the argument will be inserted unaltered

will expand into this text

```
printf("%.2f\n",num1);
```

Figure 5.14. Arguments used in the #define directive.

Macros and Functions

Macros and functions can actually perform many of the same tasks. For instance, let's modify our sphere2.c program from earlier in the chapter to use a macro, instead of the function area(), to do the actual calculation of the area of a sphere. Here's the revised program:

```
// sphereM.c
// calculates area of a sphere
// uses a macro
#include <stdio.h>                // for printf(), scanf()
#define PI 3.14159                // definition of PI
#define AREA(X) (4 * PI * X * X)  // macro for area of sphere

void main(void)
    {
    float radius;
```

```
    printf("\nEnter radius of sphere: ");
    scanf("%f", &radius);
    printf( "Area of sphere is %.2f", AREA(radius) );
    }
```

Here the preprocessor will substitute the text

```
(4 * 3.14159 * radius * radius)
```

for the identifier AREA(radius). Note that we've used an identifier within an identifier: AREA(radius) is expanded, and the PI within it is changed to 3.14159.

Use of Parentheses in Macros

Liberal use of parentheses in a macro can save considerable grief. Why? Suppose your program contains the following lines:

```
#define SUM(x,y) x + y
- - - - -
ans = 10 * SUM(3,4)
```

What value will ans be given when you run the program? You might think 3 would be added to 4, giving 7, and that result, when multiplied by 10, would yield 70. Wrong. Look at the expansion of the assignment statement. SUM(3,4) turns into simply 3 + 4. Thus, the entire statement becomes

```
ans = 10 * 3 + 4
```

Multiplication has a higher precedence than addition, so the result will be 30 + 4, or 34. This is different enough from the correct answer of 70 to suggest that we have a problem. The solution is to put parentheses around the entire text part of the #define directive.

```
#define SUM(x,y) (x + y)
```

Now the assignment statement is expanded into

```
ans = 10 * (3 + 4)
```

which yields the correct result.

Even enclosing the entire text in parentheses, however, doesn't solve all possible problems. Consider a macro that does multiplication.

```
#define PRODUCT(x,y) (x * y)
- - - - -
ans = PRODUCT(2+3,4)
```

Here the programmer was rash enough to use an expression, 2+3, as an argument for the macro. One might hope that this would yield an answer of 20 (2+3 is 5, multiplied by 4). However, look what happens in the expansion:

```
ans = (2+3*4).
```

The multiplication will be done first, so we'll have 2 + 12, or 14. Here, the solution is to enclose each argument in parentheses. For clarity, we didn't do this in the examples above, but we should have. Suppose in the sphereM.c program we had used an expression such as rad+3 as an argument to the AREA(radius) macro. It would have been expanded to (4 * PI * rad + 3 * rad + 3) or (4*PI*rad + 3*rad + 3), which is no way to calculate the area of a sphere of radius rad+3.

> For safety's sake, put parentheses around the entire text of any define directive that uses arguments and also around each of the arguments.

Thus, to be sure your macros will do what you want, enclose the entire text expression in parentheses and each variable in the text expression, as well.

When to Use Macros

Macros can often be used more conveniently than functions, as our example above demonstrates. Of course, the task to be carried out by the macro shouldn't be too complex, as macros are essentially single statements. Assuming a fairly simple task, however, when should you use a macro and when a function?

Each time a macro is invoked, the code it generates is actually inserted in the executable file for the program. This leads to multiple copies of the same code. The code for a function, however, only appears once, so using a function is more efficient in terms of memory size. On the other hand, no time is wasted calling a macro; whereas, when you call a function, the program has to arrange for the arguments to be transferred to the function and jump to the function's code. A function, therefore, takes less memory but is slower to execute, while a macro is faster but uses more memory. You have to decide which approach suits your particular program better.

> A macro generates more code but executes more quickly than a function.

Excessive use of macros can also make a program difficult to read, because it requires constant reference back and forth between the #define directives at the beginning of the program and the identifiers in the program body. Deciding when to use a macro and when not to is largely a matter of style.

The *#include* Directive Revisited

As we've seen, the #include directive causes a file to be inserted into your source file, much as a word processor inserts a block of text into a document.

Header Files and Prototypes

In Chapter 1, "The Turbo C++ Development System," we showed how to use `#include` to insert header files into a program to provide the function declarations necessary for the library functions used in that program. Now that you've learned about function declarations (prototypes), you can understand why the header file is necessary. In the header file stdio.h, for example, you'll find the following prototypes:

```
int _Cdecl printf(const char *__format, ...);
```

and

```
int _Cdecl scanf(const char *__format, ...);
```

You can discover these yourself by using the IDE editor to open the file \tc\include\stdio.h and search for `printf()` and `scanf()`. We don't need to understand all of the intricacies of these declarations to recognize them as prototypes. Similarly, the conio.h file contains the prototype

```
int _Cdecl getche(void);
```

You could look up these prototypes and type them into your program by hand, but it's much easier to simply `#include` the appropriate header file. Header files contain prototypes for many related functions and also any constant definition used with these functions. Thus a few `#include` directives at the beginning of your program provide the compiler with a great deal of information and save a lot of research and typing.

Other Uses for *#include*

There are other uses for `#include` besides inserting header files for library functions. For example, suppose you write a lot of math-oriented programs that repeatedly refer to formulas for calculating areas of different shapes. You could place all these formulas, as macros, in a single separate source file. Then, instead of having to retype all the macros every time you wrote a program that used them, you could insert them into the .c source file using the `#include` directive.

Such a separate source file might look like this:

```
#define PI 3.14159
#define AREA_CIRCLE(radius) (PI*radius*radius)
#define AREA_SQUARE(length,width) (length*width)
#define AREA_TRIANGLE(base,height) (base*height/2)
#define AREA_ELLIPSE(radius1,radius2) (PI*radius1*radius2)
#define AREA_TRAPEZOID(height,side1,side2) (height*(side1+side2)/2)
```

This isn't something you would want to type over and over again if you could avoid it. Instead, you type it once with your editor and save it as a file. You might call the file areas.h. The .h extension is commonly used for *header* files.

When you write your source file for a program that needs to use these formulas, you simply include the directive

```
#include "areas.h"
```

at the beginning of your program. All the statements shown above will be added to your program as if you had typed them. (If you do this you should also change the Source Directories field in the Options/Directories menu selection to reflect the directory containing your header file.)

Formats for *#include*

You may wonder why we used quotes around the file areas.h in the previous example. There are actually two ways to write #include statements. The variation in format tells the preprocessor where to look for the file you want included.

The variation shown above

```
#include "areas.h"
```

shows the filename surrounded by quotes. This causes the preprocessor to start searching for the areas.h file in the directory containing the current source file. If it doesn't find it there, it will look in other directories.

The other approach, which most of the examples so far have used to include header files for library functions, is to use angle brackets.

```
#include <stdio.h>
```

This format causes the preprocessor to start searching in the standard include directory. In Turbo C++, this is \tc\include\ (as specified by the Include Directories field in the Options/Directories menu selection). Your program will work if you use quotes instead of angle braces or vice versa, but because the compiler will waste time looking in the wrong directory first, your program won't compile quite so quickly.

Summary

In this chapter you've learned how to use functions: how to write them, how to use them to return values, and how to send them information using arguments. You've learned that a function commonly uses local variables which are visible only within the function itself and not to other functions. You've learned, too, to use external variables, which are visible to all functions. Finally you've learned about the preprocessor directives #define, which can be used to give names to constants or even whole C statements, creating a function-like capability, and #include, which causes one source file to be included in another.

Questions

1. Which of these are valid reasons for using functions?

    a. They use less memory than repeating the same code
    b. They run faster
    c. They keep different program activities separate
    d. They keep variables safe from other parts of the program

2. True or false: a function can still be useful even if you can't pass it any information and can't get any information back from it.

3. Is this a correct call to the function abs(), which takes one argument?

    ```
    ans = abs(num)
    ```

4. True or false: to return from a function you must use the keyword return.

5. True or false: you can return as many data items as you like from a function to the calling program, using the keyword return().

6. Is this a correctly written function?

    ```
    abs(num);
        {
        int num;
        if ( num<0 )
            num = -num;
        return(num);
        }
    ```

7. Which of the following are differences between Pascal and C?

    a. Pascal uses functions and procedures, C only functions
    b. There is no way to return from a Pascal function as there is in C
    c. Functions can be nested in Pascal but not in C
    d. Pascal functions are all of type int

8. True or false: the variables commonly used in C functions are accessible to all other functions.

9. Which of the following are valid reasons for using arguments in functions?

    a. To tell the function where to locate itself in memory
    b. To convey information to the function that it can operate on
    c. To return information from the function to the calling program
    d. To specify the type of the function

10. Which of the following can be passed to a function via arguments?

    a. Constants
    b. Variables (with values)
    c. Preprocessor directives
    d. Expressions (that evaluate to a value)
    e. Functions (that return values)

11. Is the following a correctly structured program?

```
void main(void)
    {
    int three=3;
    type(three);
    }
void type(float num)
    {
    printf("%f",num);
    }
```

12. Which of the following is true?

    a. C functions are all equal
    b. C functions can be nested within each other
    c. C functions are arranged in a strict hierarchy
    d. C functions can only be called from `main()`

13. External variables can be accessed by _____ function(s) in a program.

14. An external variable is defined

    a. In `main()` only
    b. In the first function that uses it
    c. In any function that uses it
    d. Outside of any function

15. An external variable can be referenced

    a. In `main()` only
    b. In the first function that uses it
    c. In any function that uses it
    d. Outside of any function

16. What is a preprocessor directive?

    a. A message from the compiler to the programmer
    b. A message to the linker from the compiler
    c. A message from the programmer to the compiler
    d. A message from the programmer to the microprocessor

17. The #define directive causes one phrase to be _____ for another.

18. Is this a correctly formed #define statement?

    ```
    #define CM PER INCH 2.54
    ```

19. In this #define directive, which is the identifier and which is the text?

    ```
    #define EXP 2.71828
    ```

20. What is a macro?

    a. A #define directive that acts like a function
    b. A #define directive that takes arguments
    c. A #define directive that returns a value
    d. A #define directive that simulates scanf()

21. A variable shouldn't be used to store values that never change because

    a. The program will run more slowly
    b. The program will be harder to understand
    c. There is no such data type
    d. The value of the "constant" might be altered

22. Will the following code correctly calculate postage that is equal to a fixed rate times the sum of the combined girth and height of a parcel?

    ```
    #define SUM3(length,width,height) length + width + height
    - - -
    postage = rate * SUM3(l,w,h)
    ```

23. The #include directive causes one source file to be _____ in another.

24. A header file is

    a. A file which must precede all source code files
    b. A source code file
    c. A file that can be #included in other source code files
    d. A source code file containing various definitions and macros

25. Standard header files can be found in the _____ directory.

Exercises

1. Write a program that prints the larger of two numbers entered from the keyboard. Use a function to do the actual comparison of the two numbers. Pass the two numbers to the function as arguments and have the function return the answer with `return`.

2. Rewrite the intimes.c program from this chapter so that instead of working only with hours and minutes, it works with hours, minutes, and seconds. Call this program times.c

3. Rewrite the times.c program from exercise 2 to use a macro instead of a function. Getting the data from the user must take place in the main program, but the conversion from hours-minutes-seconds to seconds should take place in the macro.

```
{ int row, x, y;
    print("key in the figure you want");
    scanf("%d", &row);
    for (x=1; x<= row; x++)
    { for y=1; y<=x; y++
        print("x");
        print("\n");
    }
}
```

```
*
* *
* * *
* * * *
* * * * *
```

Arrays and Strings

- Arrays
- Initializing arrays
- Multidimensional arrays
- Arrays as function arguments
- Strings
- String functions

You might wonder why we have placed the topics of arrays and strings together in one chapter. The answer is simple: strings are arrays: arrays of type char. Thus to understand strings we need to understand arrays. In this chapter we'll cover arrays first and then move on to strings.

We should note that, in many C books and courses, arrays and strings are taught at the same time as pointers. We feel it is clearer to introduce these topics separately. Pointers will be a new concept for many readers, and it seems unfortunate to complicate the discussion of arrays and strings, which aren't that different from their counterparts in other languages, by introducing pointers at the same time. We'll get to pointers soon enough; they're the subject of Chapter 7, "Pointers."

Arrays

If you have a collection of similar data elements, you may find it inconvenient to give each one a unique variable name. For instance, suppose you wanted to find the average temperature for a particular week. If each day's temperature had a unique variable name, you would end up reading in each value separately,

```
printf("Enter Sunday temperature: ");
scanf("%d", &suntmp);
printf("Enter Monday temperature: ");
scanf("%d", &montmp);
- - - - -
```

and so on, for each day of the week, with an expression for the average such as this:

```
(suntmp + montmp + tuestmp + wedtmp + thutmp + fritmp + sattmp)/7
```

This is an altogether unwieldy business, especially if you want to average the temperatures for a month or a year.

Clearly we need a convenient way to refer to such collections of similar data elements. The array fills the bill. It provides a way to refer to individual items in a collection by using the same variable name but differing subscripts, or index numbers. Let's see how we'd solve our problem of averaging the temperatures for a week using arrays.

```
// temp.c
// averages one week's temperatures
#include <stdio.h>                    // for printf(), scanf()

void main(void)
    {
    int temper[7];                    // array definition
    int day, sum;

    printf("\nEnter 7 temperatures\n");
    for (day=0; day<7; day++)         // put temps in array
        {
```

```
        printf("Enter temperature for day %d: ", day);
        scanf("%d", &temper[day]);
        }
    sum = 0;                            // calculate average
    for (day=0; day<7; day++)
        sum += temper[day];
    printf("Average is %d.", sum/7);
    }
```

This program reads in seven temperatures, stores them in an array, shown symbolically in Figure 6.1, and then to calculate an average temperature, reads them back out of the array, adding them together and dividing by 7.

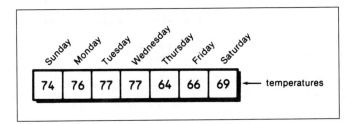

Figure 6.1. Symbolic representation of an array.

Here's a sample run:

```
Enter temperature for day 0: 74
Enter temperature for day 1: 76
Enter temperature for day 2: 77
Enter temperature for day 3: 77
Enter temperature for day 4: 64
Enter temperature for day 5: 66
Enter temperature for day 6: 69
Average is 71.
```

(Meteorology buffs will notice that temperatures rose slowly during the first part of this particular week in August and that a cold front passed through on Wednesday night.)

There's a lot of new material in this program, so let's take it apart slowly.

Array Definition

An array is a collection of variables of a certain type, placed contiguously in memory. Like other variables, the array needs to be defined, so the compiler will know what kind of array, and how large an array, we want. We do that in the example above with the line

```
int temper[7];
```

(handwritten margin notes: "how many variables of int with be in the array" / "int temper [7];" / "type of variable" / "name of variable" / "int with be" / "of variable")

Here the int specifies the type of variable, just as it does with simple variables, and the word temper is the name of the variable. The [7], however, is new. This number tells how many variables of type int will be in our array. (Each of the separate variables in the array is called an *element*.) The brackets tell the compiler that we're dealing with an array. Figure 6.2 is a schematic representation of what the array looks like.

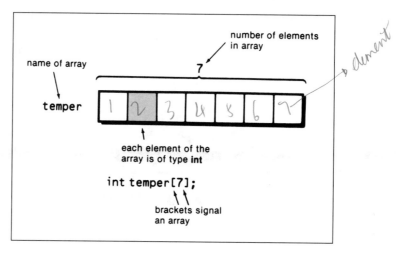

Figure 6.2. Array definition.

Referring to Individual Elements of the Array

Once the array has been established, we need a way to refer to its individual elements. This is done with subscripts, the numbers in brackets following the array name. Note, however, that this number has a different meaning when referring to an array element than it does when defining the array, when the number in brackets is the size of the array. When referring to an array element, this number specifies the element's position in the array. All the array elements are numbered, starting at 0. The element of the array with the number 2 would be referred to as

⁎ temper[2] *(handwritten: —3rd element of array.)*

Note that, because the numbering starts with 0, this isn't the second element of the array but the third. Thus, the last array element is one less than the size of the array. This arrangement is shown in Figure 6.3.

In our program we're using an integer variable, day, as a subscript to refer to the various elements of the array. This variable can take on any value we want and so can point to the different array elements in turn. This ability to use variables as subscripts is what makes arrays so useful.

```
temper[day]
```

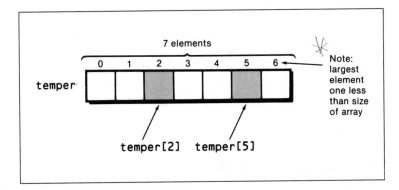

Figure 6.3. Array references.

Entering Data into the Array

Here's the section of code that places data into the array:

```
for (day=0; day<7; day++)      // put temps in array
   {
   printf("Enter temperature for day %d: ", day);
   scanf("%d", &temper[day]);
   }
```

The for loop causes the process of asking for and receiving a temperature from the user to be repeated seven times. The first time through the loop, day has the value 0, so the scanf() statement will cause the value typed to be stored in array element temper[0], the first element of the array. This process will be repeated until day becomes 6. That is the last time through the loop, which is a good thing, because there is no array element temper[7].

> The first element in an array is numbered 0, so the last element is 1 less than the size of the array.

This is a common idiom in C for dealing with arrays: a for loop that starts with 0 and goes up to, but doesn't include (note the less-than sign), the size of the array.

In the scanf() statement, we've used the address operator (&) on the element of the &temper[day] array, just as we've used it earlier on other variables (&num, for example) to

175

be read in by the scanf() function. In so doing, we're passing the address of this particular array element to the function, rather than its value; this is what scanf() requires.

Reading Data from the Array

The balance of the program reads the data back out of the array and uses it to calculate an average. The for loop is much the same, but now the body of the loop causes each day's temperature to be added to a running total called sum. When all the temperatures have been added up, the result is divided by 7, the number of data items.

```
sum = 0;                        // calculate average
for (day=0; day<7; day++)
   sum += temper[day];
printf("Average is %d.", sum/7);
```

Using Different Variable Types

Although the example above used an array of type int, an array can be of any variable type. As an example, let's rewrite temp.c to be of type float.

```
// fltemp.c
// averages one week's temperatures
#include <stdio.h>                    // for printf(), scanf()

void main(void)
   {
   float temper[7];              // array definition
   float sum;
   int day;

   printf("\nEnter 7 temperatures\n");
   for(day =0; day<7; day++)          // put temps in array
      {
      printf("Enter temperature for day %d: ", day);
      scanf("%f", &temper[day]);
      }

   sum = 0;                     // calculate average
    for(day=0; day<7; day++)
      sum += temper[day];
   printf("Average is %.1f", sum/7.0);
   }
```

This program operates in much the same way as temp.c, except that now it can accept numbers with decimal fractions as input and so can calculate a more precise average. Here's a sample run:

```
Enter temperature for day 0: 80.5
Enter temperature for day 1: 78.2
Enter temperature for day 2: 67.4
Enter temperature for day 3: 71.4
```

```
Enter temperature for day 4: 74.6
Enter temperature for day 5: 78.3
Enter temperature for day 6: 80.1
Average is 75.8
```

We had a cooling trend in the middle of the week, with ideal beach temperatures on the weekends.

We've changed the array (and the variable sum) to type `float`, and we've altered the format specifiers in the `scanf()` and `printf()` statements accordingly.

Reading in an Unknown Number of Elements

So far we've worked with a fixed amount of input, requiring a data item for each of the days of the week. What if we don't know in advance how many items will be entered into the array? Here's a program that will accept any number of temperatures—up to 40—and average them:

```c
// fltemp2.c
// averages arbitrary number of temperatures
#include <stdio.h>                    // for printf(), scanf()

void main(void)
    {
    float temper[40];                 // array definition
    float sum=0.0;
    int num, day=0;

    printf("\n(Enter 0 to quit)\n");
    do                                // put temps in array
        {
        printf("Enter temperature for day %d: ", day);
        scanf("%f", &temper[day]);
        }
    while ( temper[day++] > 0 );

    num = day-1;                      // number of temps entered
    for (day=0; day<num; day++)       // calculate average
        sum += temper[day];
    printf("Average is %.1f", sum/num);
    }
```

[handwritten annotation: &temper [0] = temper sub zero is a variable]

Here's a run in which only three temperatures are entered:

```
Enter temperature for day 0: 71.3
Enter temperature for day 1: 80.9
Enter temperature for day 2: 89.2
Enter temperature for day 3: 0
Average is 80.5
```

As you can see, we've replaced the for loop with a do while loop. This loop repeatedly asks the user to enter a temperature and stores the responses in the array temper, until a temperature of 0 or less is entered. (Clearly this isn't a program for cold climates.) When the last item has been typed, the variable day will have reached a value 1 greater than the total number of items entered. This is true because it counts the 0 (or negative number), which the user entered to terminate the input. Thus to find the number of items entered, num, we subtract 1 from day. The variable num is then used as the limit in the second for loop, which adds up the temperatures, and it's also used as the divisor of the resulting sum.

There's another change in the program as well. We've used a #define directive to give the identifier LIM the value of 40.

```
#define LIM 40
```

We then used LIM in the array definition. Using a #defined value as an array size is common in C. Later, if we wish to change the size, all we need do is change the 40 in the #define statement, and the change will be reflected anywhere this value appears. In this particular program, the number is only used once, but we'll soon see examples in which the array dimension occurs repeatedly in the program, making the use of the #define directive a real convenience.

Bounds Checking

We've made the size of the array to be 40 in the #define directive. This is large enough to hold one month's temperatures, with some left over, but suppose a user decided to enter two months worth of data? As it turns out, there probably would be Big Trouble. The reason is that in C there is no check to see if the subscript used for an array exceeds the size of the array. Data entered with too large a subscript will simply be placed in memory outside the array: probably on top of other data or the program itself. This will lead to unpredictable results, to say the least, and there will be no error message from the compiler to warn you that it's happening.

> C doesn't warn you when an array subscript exceeds the size of the array.

The solution, if there's the slightest reason to believe the user might enter too many items, is to check for this possibility in the program. For instance, we could modify the do-while loop as follows:

```
do
    {
    if ( day >= LIM )               // beyond array end?
        {
        printf("Buffer full.\n");
        day++;                      // won't be incremented later
        break;                      // exit loop
        }
    printf("Enter temperature for day %d: ", day);
```

```
      scanf("%f", &temper[day]);
      }
while ( temper[day++] > 0 );
```

Now if the loop is entered with day equal to 40, which is 1 past the end of the buffer at 39, the message `Buffer full` will be printed and the `break` statement will take us out of the loop to the second part of the program. (We need to increment day because the `while` statement won't be executed.) Here's a run showing the last few lines before the user oversteps the bounds:

```
Enter temperature for day 38: 73.4
Enter temperature for day 39: 62.2
Buffer full.
Average is 75.1
```

As you can see, the temperature for day 39 is accepted, but then the program realizes that one more item would be one too many, prints the message, and breaks out of the loop.

Initializing Arrays

So far, we've shown arrays that started life with nothing in them. Suppose we want to compile our program with specific values already fixed in the array? This is analogous to initializing a simple variable.

```
int george = 45;
```

Here's a program demonstrating the initializing of an array. The program makes change; you type a price in cents, and the program tells you how many half-dollars, quarters, dimes, nickels, and pennies it takes to make up this amount.

```
// change.c
// program to make change
#include <stdio.h>            // for printf(), scanf()
#define LIM 5                 // size of array

void main(void)
   {
   int table[LIM] = { 50, 25, 10, 5, 1 };
   int dex, amount, quantity;

   printf("\nEnter amount in cents (form 367): ");
   scanf("%d", &amount);
   for (dex=0; dex<LIM; dex++)
      {
      quantity = amount / table[dex];
      printf("Value of coin=%2d, ", table[dex] );
      printf("number of coins=%2d\n", quantity );
      amount = amount % table[dex];
      }
   }
```

Here's a sample run:

```
Enter amount in cents (form 367): 143
Value of coin=50, number of coins= 2
Value of coin=25, number of coins= 1
Value of coin=10, number of coins= 1
Value of coin= 5, number of coins= 1
Value of coin= 1, number of coins= 3
```

The program has figured out that $1.43 is two half-dollars, one quarter, one dime, one nickel, and three pennies. This is smarter than some checkout people.

The program works by taking the value of the largest coin, 50, and dividing it into the amount typed (the variable amount). It prints the answer, which is the number of half-dollars necessary, and then it performs the same division but this time with the remainder operator (%). This remainder, in turn, is used as the new amount, which is divided by the next smallest size of coin, 25. The process is repeated five times, once for each coin.

The array is used to hold the values, expressed in cents, of the various coins. Here's the statement that initializes the array to these values:

```
int table[LIM] = { 50, 25, 10, 5, 1 };
```

The list of values is enclosed by braces, and the values are separated by commas. The values are assigned in turn to the elements of the array so that table[0] is 50, table[1] is 25, and so on, up to table[4], which is 1.

Array Size and Initialization

The change.c program used the value LIM (which was #defined as 5) in the array declaration.

```
int table[ LIM] = { 50, 25, 10, 5, 1 };
```

We could simply omit this number, however, leaving an empty pair of brackets following table.

```
int table[] = { 50, 25, 10, 5, 1 };
```

How can we get away with this? The answer is that if no number is supplied for the size of the array, the compiler will kindly count the number of items in the initialization list and fix that as the array size.

What happens if a number is supplied, but it doesn't agree with the actual number of items on the list? If the number is larger than the number of items, the extra spaces in the array will be filled in with zeros. If the number is too small, the compiler will complain (as well it might; where could it put the leftover values?).

Array Contents and Initialization

You also should know what the initial values of array elements will be if they aren't initialized explicitly. In other words, if we execute an array declaration inside the function, like this:

```
main()
    {
    int array[10];
    - - - - -
```

and then, without putting anything into the array, we say

```
printf("Array element 3 has the value %d", array[3]);
```

what value will be printed? Would you guess 0? That's close, but not right. In fact, what you'll get is a garbage number, whatever value was sitting in that particular part of memory before the function was called and the array declared. At least that's true in the case of the automatic variable declaration shown. However, if the array was declared as an external or static variable, it will be initialized to 0.

The lesson is that if you want your array initialized to all zeros, but don't want to do it yourself, make sure it's external or static.

More Than One Dimension

So far we've looked at arrays with only one dimension—that is, only one subscript. It's also possible for arrays to have two or more dimensions. This permits them to emulate or *model* multidimensional objects, such as graph paper with rows and columns or the computer display screen itself.

Modeling Rows and Columns

Here's a sample program that records not only one list of data as our previous programs have, but two lists side-by-side. This program stores the travel expenses for a number of secret agents who are known only by their code numbers.

```
// travel.c
// stores list of secret agents' travel expenses
#include <stdio.h>      // for printf(), scanf()
#define ROWS 10         // number of rows in array
#define COLUMNS 2       // number of columns in array

void main(void)
    {
    float agents [ROWS] [COLUMNS];
    float number, expenses;
    int index=0, outdex;

    printf("\nEnter 3-digit agent numbers,\n");
    printf("then travel expenses (007 1642.50)\n");
```

```
    printf("Enter 0 0 to quit.\n");

    do                          // get list of agents and expenses
       {
       printf("Agent's number and expenses: ");
       scanf( "%f %f", &number, &expenses );
       agents[index][0] = number;
       agents[index][1] = expenses;
       }
    while ( agents[index++][0] != 0 );

    for (outdex=0; outdex<index-1; outdex++)   // print list
       {
       printf("Agent %03.0f ", agents[outdex][0] );
       printf("spent %7.2f.\n", agents[outdex][1] );
       }
    }  // end travel
```

There are two parts to the program: a do-while loop, which gets the data from the user and stores it in the two-dimensional array table[][], and a for loop, which prints the contents of the array. Here's a sample run:

```
Enter 3-digit agent numbers,
then travel expense (007 1642.50)
Enter 0 0 to quit.
Agent's number and expenses: 101 2331.50
Agent's number and expenses: 007 8640
Agent's number and expenses: 901 123.25
Agent's number and expenses: 904 500.6
Agent's number and expenses: 0 0
Agent 101 spent 2331.50.
Agent 007 spent 8640.00.
Agent 901 spent  123.25.
Agent 904 spent  500.60.
```

The do-while loop is similar to that in the fltemp3.c program that obtained the temperature from the user. However, instead of getting only one piece of data each time through the loop, we get two; placing them in the variables agents[index][0] and agents[index][1] with the scanf() statement.

```
scanf( "%f %f", &agents[index][0], &agents[index][1] );
```

The first subscript is the row number, which changes for each agent. The second subscript tells which of two columns we're talking about: the one on the left, which contains the agent numbers, or the one on the right, which lists expenses for a particular month. Each subscript goes in its own set of brackets following the variable name. The array arrangement is shown in Figure 6.4.

Notice that the entire array is of type float. We've tried to disguise this by not printing decimal places with the agent numbers, but in reality, the agent numbers are of type float just as the expenses are. We chose float because we wanted to use dollars and cents for the expenses. The ideal arrangement would be to have the agent numbers be of type int and the expenses of type float, but arrays must be of a single data type. This is an important limitation of arrays. In Chapter 9, "Structures," we'll see how something called a *structure* will permit the use of multiple types in an array.

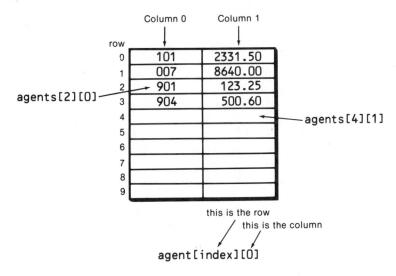

Figure 6.4. Array used in travel.c program.

Floating Point Weirdness

Incidentally, sometimes when you try to use a floating point variable in an I/O function such as scanf(), you'll get the runtime error message

```
Floating points formats not linked
```

This means that the compiler wasn't expecting to use floating point variables and is surprised to see them in the function. If this happens, Borland suggests putting the following statements anywhere in your source file:

```
extern void _floatconvert();
#pragam extref _floatconvert
```

This may be necessary, for example, in the travel.c and highex.c programs in this chapter.

Modeling the Display Screen

Here's a program that plots a two-dimensional grid on the screen. Initially, the grid is filled with dots (periods), but after the grid is drawn, the program cycles through a loop and asks the user for a pair of coordinates. When the user types the two coordinates (separated by a comma), the program draws a gray box at the corresponding location on the screen.

Using this program provides a visual way to understand how a two-dimensional coordinate system works. Try typing pairs of numbers. Where will 0,0 be plotted? How about 5,0? Or 0,5? Remember that the horizontal or x-coordinate is typed first, and then the vertical or y-coordinate. Here's the listing:

```c
// plot.c
// plots coordinates on screen
#include <stdio.h>                    //  for printf(), etc.
#define HEIGHT 5
#define WIDTH 10

void main(void)
   {
   char matrix [HEIGHT] [WIDTH];
   int  x,y;

   for(y=0; y<HEIGHT; y++)            // fill matrix with periods
     for(x=0; x<WIDTH; x++)
       matrix[y][x] = '.';
   printf("\nEnter coordinates in form x,y (4,2).\n");
   printf("Use negative numbers to quit.\n");

   while ( x >= 0 )                   // until neg coordinates
      {
      for(y=0; y<HEIGHT; y++)         // print matrix
        {
        for(x=0; x<WIDTH; x++)
           printf("%c ", matrix[y][x] );
        printf("\n\n");
        }
      printf("Coordinates: ");
      scanf("%d,%d", &x, &y);         // get coordinates
      matrix[y][x]='\xB1';            // put gray box there
      }  // end while
   }  // end plot
```

Figure 6.5 shows a sample of interaction with the program. The user has previously entered the coordinates 2,1; on this turn, the coordinates are 5,2. The program has plotted both pairs on the screen.

Remember that the results of typing coordinates that exceed the bounds of the array can be disastrous. Don't type an x-coordinate greater than 9 or a y-coordinate greater than 4. (You probably will anyway. The worst that can happen is a system crash.) Alternatively, you could modify the program to trap out-of-bounds entries, as we showed earlier; for simplicity, we haven't done this here.

Initializing Two-Dimensional Arrays

We've learned how to initialize a one-dimensional array. What about two dimensions? As an example, we'll modify the plot.c program to play the game of battleship. In this game, one player (the computer) has concealed a number of ships at different locations in a

10-by-5 grid. The other player (the human) by typing coordinates tries to find the ships. If the human guesses right, a hit is scored, and the coordinates on the grid are marked with a solid rectangle. If the human guesses wrong, the coordinates are marked with a light gray rectangle, making it easier to remember what areas have already been tested.

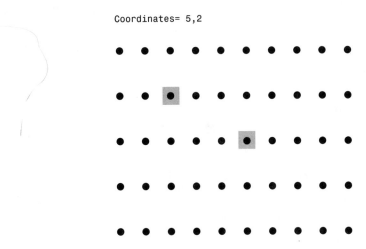

Coordinates= 5,2

Figure 6.5. Output of the plot.c program.

There are five ships concealed in the grid: one battleship 4 units long, two cruisers 3 units long, and two destroyers 2 units long. They're all placed either horizontally or vertically (not diagonally). In the program a ship will be represented by the number 1 and coordinates where there is no ship by the number 0.

We put the ships into the array by initializing the array when we write the program. Note that even though this is a character array (to save memory space), we use numbers as values.

```
// bship.c
// plays battleship game
#include <stdio.h>      // for printf() and scanf()
#define HEIGHT 5        // dimensions of playing area
#define WIDTH 10


void main(void)
   {
   char enemy [HEIGHT] [WIDTH] =  // ship deployment
     { { 0, 0, 0, 0, 0, 0, 0, 0, 0, 0 },
       { 0, 1, 1, 1, 1, 0, 0, 1, 0, 1 },
       { 0, 0, 0, 0, 0, 0, 0, 1, 0, 1 },
       { 1, 0, 0, 0, 0, 0, 0, 1, 0, 0 },
       { 1, 0, 1, 1, 1, 0, 0, 0, 0, 0 }  };
```

```
char friend [HEIGHT] [WIDTH];
int x,y;

for(y=0; y<HEIGHT; y++)          // fill array with periods
  for(x=0; x<WIDTH; x++)
    friend[y][x] = '.';
printf("Enter coordinates in form x,y (4,2).\n");
printf("Use negative numbers to quit.\n");

while ( x >= 0 )                 // until neg coordinates
  {
  for(y=0; y<HEIGHT; y++)        // print array
    {
    for(x=0; x<WIDTH; x++)
      printf("%c ", friend[y][x] );
    printf("\n\n");
    }
    printf("Coordinates: ");
  scanf("%d,%d", &x, &y);        // get coordinates
  if ( enemy[y][x]==1 )          // if it's a hit
     friend[y][x]='\xDB';        // put solid box there
  else                           // otherwise
     friend[y][x]='\xB1';        // gray box
  } // end while
} // end bship
```

The ships are located in the array initialization at the start of the program. You should be able to see the battleship on the left, oriented horizontally, in the second row down. A sample run is shown in Figure 6.6.

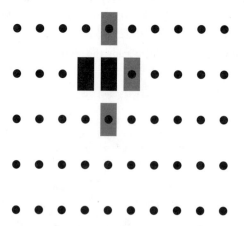

Figure 6.6. Output of the bship.c program.

06TCP06

[handwritten: Initialize array to 8
int nums[4] = {8, 8, 8, 8};
int num[4] = (8);
8 8 8 8
8 9 0 0 8]

The player in Figure 6.6 tried 4,0, which was a miss and then 4,1, which was a hit. Then, thinking the ship might be located vertically, the user tried 4,2 to no avail. Trying 5,1 proved that the ship didn't extend to the right. The next choice, 3,1, was a hit, so now the user will see how big a ship it is by going further left. The other ships still lurk in the darkness, waiting to be discovered.

(It would be fun to modify the program so that two people could compete, but that would take us too far afield.)

Notice the format used to initialize the array—an outer set of braces and then 5 inner sets of braces, each with 10 members separated by commas. The inner sets of braces are separated from each other by commas as well.

We can conclude that lists go in braces and that the elements of the list are separated by commas, whether the members of the list are composed of numbers or other lists.

> The values used to initialize an array are separated by commas and surrounded by braces.

Initializing Three-Dimensional Arrays

We aren't going to show a programming example that uses a three-dimensional array. However, an example of initializing a three-dimensional array will consolidate your understanding of subscripts. *[handwritten: [ ][ ][ ] = 6 in 4th bracket]*

```
int threed[3][2][4] =
   {    {  { 1, 2, 3, 4 },
          { 5, 6, 7, 8 },  },
        {  { 7, 9, 3, 2 },
          { 4, 6, 8, 3 },  },
        {  { 7, 2, 6, 3 },
          { 0, 1, 9, 4 }   }   };
```
[handwritten annotations: 0 1 2 on left; grp, row, element]

This is an array of arrays of arrays. The outer array has three elements, each of which is a two-dimensional array of two elements, each of which is a one-dimensional array of four numbers.

Quick now, how would you address the array element holding the only 0 in this definition? The first subscript is [2], because it's in the third group of three two-dimensional arrays; the second subscript is [1], because it's in the second of two one-dimensional arrays; and the third subscript is [0], because it's the first element in the one-dimensional array of numbers. We could say, therefore, that the expression

```
threed[2][1][0] == 0
```

is true.

Arrays as Arguments

We've seen examples of passing various kinds of variables as arguments to functions. Is it possible also to pass an array to a function? The answer is, "Sort of." Let's see what this means.

Here's a program that uses a function called max() to find the element with the largest value in an array:

```
// maxnum.c
// tells largest number in array typed in
#include <stdio.h>            // for printf(), scanf()
#define MAXSIZE 20            // size of array
int max(int[], int);          // function prototype

void main(void)
    {
    int  list[MAXSIZE];
    int size = 0;             // start at element [0]
    int num;                  // temp storage

    printf("\nEnter numbers, 0 to exit\n");
    do                        // get list of numbers
        {
        printf("Enter number: ");
        scanf("%d", &list[size]);
        }
    while ( list[size++] != 0 );  // exit loop on 0
    num = max(list,size-1);       // get largest number
    printf("Largest number is %d", num);   // print it
    }

// max()
// returns largest number in array
int max(int list[], int size)
    {
    int dex, max;
    max = list[0];                // assume 1st element largest
    for (dex=1; dex<size; dex++)  // check remaining elements
        if ( max < list[dex] )    // if one bigger,
            max = list[dex];      //   make it the largest
    return(max);
    }
```

The user types a set of numbers (no more than 20) and the program prints the largest one. Here's a sample run:

```
Enter numbers, 0 to exit
Enter number: 42
Enter number: 1
Enter number: 64
Enter number: 33
Enter number: 27
```

```
Enter number: 0
Largest number is 64
```

The first part of this program should look familiar. It's our usual do-while loop for reading a list of numbers. The only new element here is the statement

```
num = max(list,size-1);
```

This is the call to the function max(), which returns the largest number. There are two arguments to the function: the first is the array list, the second is the variable size.

The critical thing to notice here is how we pass the array to the function: we use the name of the array all by itself. We've seen array elements that look like list[index], before, but what does the array name mean without any brackets? It turns out that the array name used alone is equivalent to the address of the array. Actually, it's equivalent to the address of the first element in the array, which is the same thing.

Thinking about addresses and values can become confusing, so let's recapitulate what we know about the addresses of simple variables. Let's imagine an integer variable num with a value of 27. Perhaps it has been initialized like this:

```
int num = 27;
```

Figure 6.7 shows how this variable looks in memory.

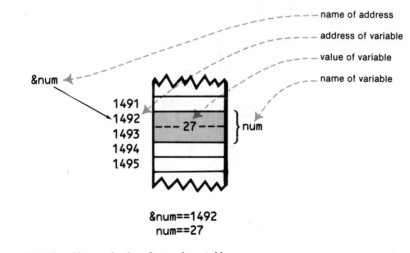

Figure 6.7. The address and value of a simple variable.

There are four things to know about the variable: its name (num), its value (27), its address (which happens to be 1492, although this will vary from program to program and system to system), and—watch closely—the name of the address, which is &num.

Now let's see what a similar representation looks like for an array.

> An array is referred to by its address, which is represented by the name of the array, used without subscripts.

Figure 6.8 shows the array `list[]`, which in this instance is located in memory starting at address 1500. Note the value of a typical element in the array (64), the name of this element (`list[2]`), the address of the array (1500), and the name of this address (`list`). Why isn't the address of the array called something like `&list`? This would be consistent with the way the addresses of variables are named, but it would leave the word `list`, which isn't used to name anything else about the variable, going begging. Thus, `list` refers to an address if `list` is an array but would refer to a value if `list` were a simple variable.

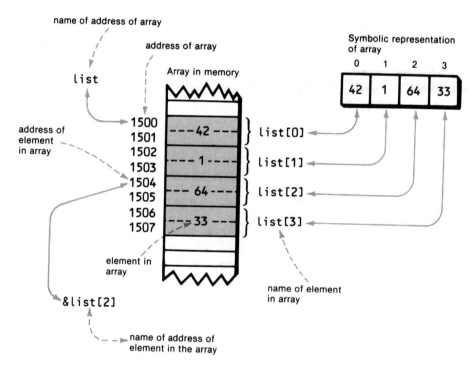

Figure 6.8. The address and elements of an array.

Incidentally, can you think of another way to represent the address `list`? How about this?

  `&list[0]`

Because `list[0]` is the first element of the array, it will have the same address as the array itself, and because `&` is the address operator, `&list[0]` gives the address of the first element of the array. In other words,

```
list == &list[0]
```

An understanding of addresses will become increasingly important as we move in the next chapter to the study of pointers, because addresses are closely related to pointers.

To summarize, to tell the compiler we want to talk about the address of an array, we use the name of the array, with no brackets following it. Thus (to return to the maxnum.c program), our call to the function `max()` passes the address of the array, represented by the word `list`, to the function.

Addresses of Things Versus Things

It's important to realize that passing the address of something isn't the same thing as passing that something. When a simple variable name is used as an argument passed to a function, the function takes the value corresponding to this variable name and installs it as a new variable in a new memory location created by the function for that purpose.

What happens when the address of an array is passed to a function as an argument? Does the function create another array and move the values into it from the array in the calling program? No. Because arrays can be very large, the designers of C determined that it would be better to have only one copy of an array no matter how many functions wanted to access it. Instead of passing the values in the array, therefore, only the address of the array is passed. The function then uses the address to access the original array. This process is shown in Figure 6.9.

Thus, in the `max()` function, when we reference elements of the array, as in the statement `max = list2[dex];` references to the array `list2[]` are actually references to the array `list[]`. We can give the array any name we want in the function, but all we're doing is telling the function where the original array, `list[]`, is. There is no array `list2[]`; this is simply the way the function refers to the array `list[]`.

> Passing an array name to a function doesn't create a new copy of the array.

Sorting an Array

Before we go on to strings, let's look at a function that sorts the values in an array. Sorting is an important task in many applications, particularly database programs in which a user wants to rearrange a list of items in numerical or alphabetical order. Here's the listing:

```
// sortnum.c
// sorts numbers typed to array
#include <stdio.h>              // for printf(), scanf()
#define MAXSIZE 20              // size of buffer
void sort(int[], int);         // prototype

void main(void)
   {
   int list[MAXSIZE];          // buffer for numbers
   int size = 0;               // size 0 before input
   int dex;                    // index to array

   printf("\nEnter numbers, 0 to exit\n");
   do                          // get list of numbers
   {
```

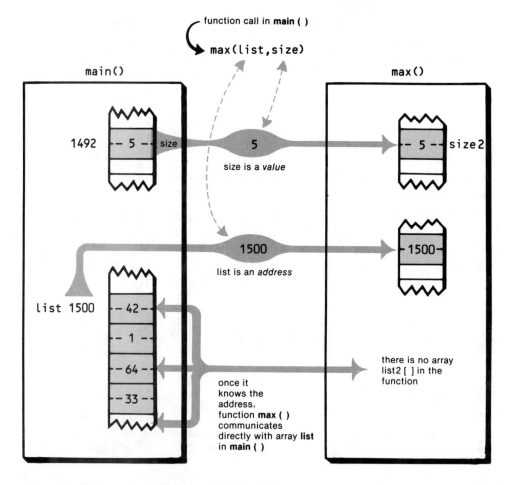

Figure 6.9. Passing a value and an array address to a function.

```
      printf("Enter number: ");
      scanf("%d", &list[size]);
      }
   while ( list[size++] != 0 );   // exit loop on 0
   sort(list,--size);             // sort numbers
   for (dex=0; dex<size; dex++)   // print sorted list
      printf("%d\n", list[dex]);
   } // end main()
// sort()
// sorts array of integers
void sort(int list[], int size)
   {
   int out, in, temp;

   for (out=0; out<size-1; out++)     // for each element
      for (in=out+1; in<size; in++)   // look at those lower
         if (list[out] > list[in])    // if element greater than
            {                         //   any lower down,
            temp = list[in];          // swap them
            list[in] = list[out];
            list[out] = temp;
            }
   } // end sort()
```

Here's an example of the program at work:

```
Enter numbers, 0 to exit
Enter number: 46
Enter number: 25
Enter number: 73
Enter number: 58
Enter number: 33
Enter number: 18
Enter number: 0
18
25
33
46
58
73
```

The program first asks for a list of numbers (as you can see from the array definition, you shouldn't type more than 20). As the user types the numbers, they're placed in the array list[]. Once the user terminates the list by typing 0 (which isn't placed on the list), the program calls the sort() function, which sorts the values in the list.

The overall structure of the program is similar to that of maxnum.c. It first gets a series of numbers from the user and puts them in an array, list[]. Then it calls the sort() function, and finally it prints the contents of the newly sorted array.

In this program we've used the same name, list[], for the array in the function as we did in the calling program. A different name could be used to refer to the array; either way, it's the same array.

The Bubble Sort

The sorting process used in the sort() function may require a word of explanation. The function starts off thinking about the first array variable, list[0]. The goal is to place the smallest item on the list in this variable, so the function goes through all the remaining items on the list, from list[1] to list[size-1], comparing each one with the first item. Whenever it finds one that is smaller than the first item, it swaps them. This will put the smallest item in list[0].

Once the smallest item is dealt with, the function wants to put the next smallest item in list[1], so it goes through all the remaining items, from list[2] on, comparing them with list[1]. Whenever it finds one that is smaller, it swaps them. This will end up with list[1] containing the second smallest item. This process is continued until the entire list is sorted. This approach is called the *bubble sort,* because the smaller values bubble up through the list. Figure 6.10 shows how it works. (We should note that the bubble sort, while easy to program, is less efficient than many other sorting algorithms.)

The outer loop, with the variable out, determines which element of the array will be used as the basis of comparison (as list[0] is the first time through the loop). The inner loop, with the variable out, steps through the remaining items, comparing each one with the first (from list[1] to the end of the list, the first time through). When the comparision of two items shows they're out of order, they're swapped.

The swapping process requires us to put the value of the first variable, list[in], in a temporary location; put the second value, list(out), in the first variable; and finally, return the temporary value (originally from list[in] to list[out]).

Remember that all this swapping and rearranging of values takes place in the original array, list[], in the calling program. The sort() function finds out where the array is (from the address passed to it) and manipulates it by "remote control," without having to drag all the values from the array into the function.

Two-Dimensional Arrays as Arguments

We've seen how to pass a one-dimensional array as an argument, but what about a two-dimensional array? As an example, we'll blend our travel.c program, which recorded the travel expenses for a list of secret agents, and our maxnum.c program, which figured out the largest element in an array. The resulting program will print the agent number and the amount spent by the agent with the highest travel expenses.

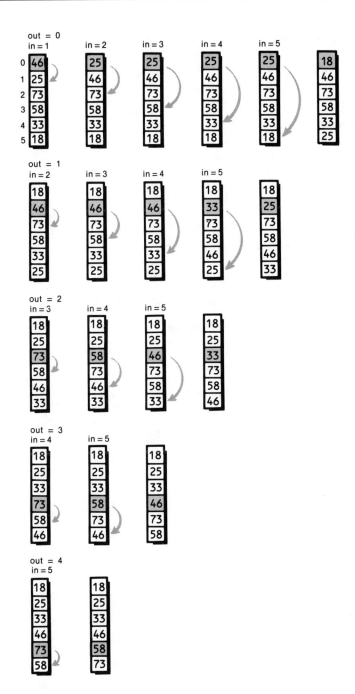

Figure 6.10. Bubble sort.

Here's the program listing:

```c
// highex.c
// stores list of secret agents' travel expenses and
// reports number of agent with highest expenses
#include <stdio.h>     // for printf(), scanf()
#define ROWS 10        // number of rows in array
#define COLUMNS 2      // number of columns in array
int  maxex(float[][COLUMNS], int);  // prototype

void main(void)
    {
    float agents[ROWS][COLUMNS];
    float number, expenses;
    int index=0;

    printf("\nEnter 3-digit agent numbers,\n");
    printf("then travel expenses (007 1642.50)\n");
    printf("Enter 0 0 to quit.\n");

    do                     // get list of agents and expenses
       {
       printf("Agent's number and expenses: ");
       scanf( "%f %f", &number, &expenses);
       agents[index][0] = number;
       agents[index][1] = expenses;
       }
    while ( agents[index++][0] != 0.0 );
    index--;               // restore to size of array

    index = maxex(agents, index);    // find agent's index
    printf("Agent with highest expenses: %03.0f. ",
                                    agents[index][0] );
    printf("Amount: %.2f.", agents[index][1] );
    }  // end main()

// maxex()
// returns array index to largest  amount in column 1
int  maxex(float list[][COLUMNS], int size)
    {
    int dex, maxdex;
    float max;
    max = list[0][1];           // assume 1st element largest
    maxdex = 0;                 // save its index
    for (dex=1; dex<size; dex++) // check remaining elements
       if ( max < list[dex][1] ) // if one bigger,
          {
          max = list[dex][1];    // make it the largest
          maxdex = dex;          // save its index
          }
    return(maxdex);             // return index
    }  // end maxex()
```

Here's a sample run. Now we've typed a list of agent numbers and expenses, and the program has figured out the agent with the highest expenses and printed the number and the amount.

```
Enter 3-digit agent numbers,
then travel expenses (007 1642.50)
Enter 0 0 to quit.
Agent's number and expenses: 901 645.25
Agent's number and expenses: 801 784.50
Agent's number and expenses: 302 112.95
Agent's number and expenses: 007 9456.99
Agent's number and expenses: 405 298.60
Agent's number and expenses: 006 5019.00
Agent's number and expenses: 0 0
Agent with highest expenses: 007. Amount: 9456.99.
```

In many ways, accessing a two-dimensional array from a function is similar to accessing an array of one dimension, but there is at least one surprise.

The method of passing the address of the array to the function is identical no matter how many dimensions the array has, because all we pass is the address of the array (in this case, agents).

```
index = maxex(agents, index);
```

However, the declaration of the array in the function may look a bit mysterious.

```
float list[][COLUMNS];
```

We don't need to tell the function how many rows there are. Why not? Because the function isn't setting aside space in memory for the array. All it needs to know is that the array has two columns; this permits it to reference accurately any array variable. For instance, to find the space in memory where agents[3][1] is stored, the function multiplies the row index (3) by the number of elements per row (COLUMNS, which is 2), and then adds the column index (which is 1). The result is 3 * 2 + 1 = 7, as shown in Figure 6.11.

We've had to modify the function max() from our earlier program in order to return the row index of the agent in question, rather than a numerical quantity as before. This involves saving the index whenever we save a new maximum.

At this point you should be starting to feel comfortable with arrays. You know how to define arrays of differing sizes and dimensions, how to initialize arrays, how to refer to particular array elements, and how to pass an array to a function. With this under your belt, you should be ready to handle strings, which are simply a special kind of array.

Strings

Strings are the form of data used in programming languages for storing and manipulating text, such as words, names, and sentences. In C, a string isn't a formal data type as it is in some languages (for example, Pascal and BASIC). Instead, it is an array of type char. When you think about it, this makes a good deal of sense; a string is a series of characters, and that's just what an array of type char is. Most languages actually treat strings as arrays of characters but conceal this fact from the programmer to varying degrees. BASIC, for example, never lets on that strings are arrays, but Pascal, although treating strings as a separate data type, does permit you to reference individual string characters as array members.

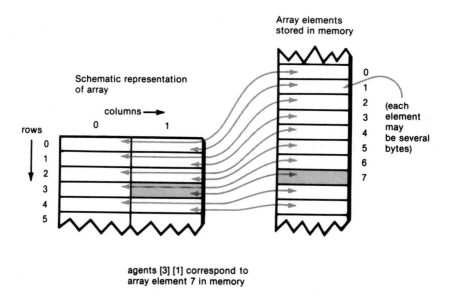

Figure 6.11. Two-dimensional array stored in memory.

String Constants

We've already seen examples of strings, as in the statement

```
printf("%s", "Greetings!");
```

"Greetings!" is a string constant. That means the string itself is stored somewhere in memory, but it can't be changed (just as your program can't change the 3 in the expression x = 3;). Figure 6.12 shows what this string constant looks like stored in memory.

Each character occupies one byte of memory, and the last character of the string is the character \0. What character is that? It looks like two characters, but it's actually an escape sequence, like \n. It's called the *null character,* and it stands for a character with a numerical value of 0 (zero). Note that this isn't the same as the character 0.

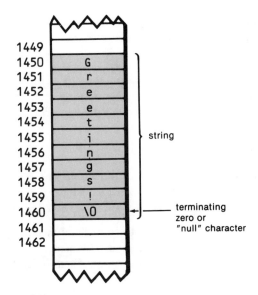

Figure 6.12. String constant stored in memory.

> All strings must end with a null character, /0, which has a numerical value of 0.

The terminating null (\0) is important, because it is the only way functions that work with the string can know where the end of the string is. In fact, a string not terminated by a \0 character isn't really a string at all but merely a collection of characters.

String Variables

We've looked at a string constant; now let's see what a string variable looks like. Here's an example program that reads in a string from the keyboard, using scanf(), and prints it as part of a longer phrase:

```c
// ezstring.c
// reads string from keyboard and prints it
#include <stdio.h>          // for printf(), scanf()

void main(void)
   {
   char fname[15];                    // array to hold name

   printf("\nEnter your name: ");
   scanf("%s", fname);                // get name from user
   printf("Greetings, %s.", fname);   // display name
   }
```

Here's a sample run:

```
Enter your name: Hieronymous
Greetings, Hieronymous.
```

Before a string can be read into a program, some space in the computer's memory must be set aside for it. This shouldn't be too surprising; after all, memory must also be set aside before a simple variable can be stored in a program. For instance, before we can successfully execute the line

```
scanf("%d", &num);
```

we need to declare the variable num, causing the compiler to set aside an appropriately sized chunk of memory to store the value the user enters.

The situation is similar for strings, except that, because there is going to be a series of characters arriving, a series of bytes must be set aside for them. In ezstring.c, we've declared an array of 15 characters. This should be enough for names 15 characters long, right? Well, not quite. Don't forget the terminating null character \0. When scanf() gets the name from the keyboard, it automatically includes the \0 when it stores the string in memory; thus, if your array is 15 characters long, you can only store strings of 14 characters.

The operation of ezstring.c is shown in Figure 6.13.

The warning applied to arrays in general applies to strings: don't overflow the array that holds the string. If the user of ezstring.c typed a name of more than 14 characters, the additional characters would be written over other data or the program itself. Perhaps a better choice for the array definition would have been

```
char fname[81]
```

This would permit a name to go all the way across the screen: 80 characters. Hardly anyone's name is that long!

You may have noticed something odd about the scanf() statement in the ezstring.c program. That's right; there's no address operator (&) preceding the name of the string we're going to print.

```
scanf("%s", fname);
```

This is because fname is an address. We need to preface numerical and character variables with the & to change values into addresses, but fname is already the name of an array, and therefore, it's an address and doesn't need the &.

Because a string name is an address, no address operator need precede it in a scanf() function.

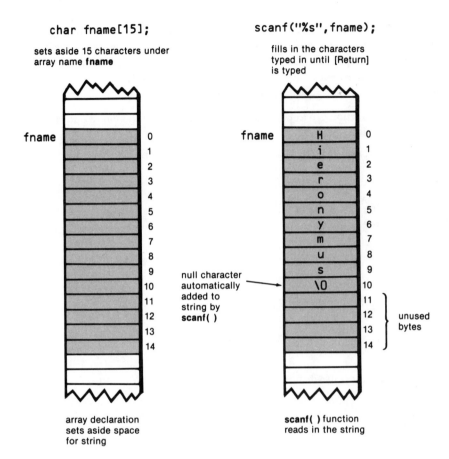

Figure 6.13. String placed in memory by scanf().

The String I/O Functions *gets()* and *puts()*

There are many C functions whose purpose is to manipulate strings. One of the most common is used to input a string from the keyboard. Why is it needed? Because our old friend the scanf() function has some limitations when it comes to handling strings. For example, consider the following trial run with the ezstring.c program:

```
Enter your name: Genghis Khan
Greetings, Genghis.
```

The program has suddenly adopted an informal style, dropping the last name (something it might be unwise to do unless you knew Genghis very well). Where did the second word of our string go? Remember that scanf() uses any whitespace character to terminate entry of a variable. The result is that there is no way to enter a multiword string into a single array using scanf() (at least without a lot of trouble).

201

The solution to this problem is to use another C library function: gets(). The purpose of gets() is, as you may have guessed, to GET a String from the keyboard. It isn't as versatile an input function as scanf(); it specializes in doing one thing: reading strings. It is terminated only when the Return key is pressed, so spaces and tabs are perfectly acceptable as part of the input string.

The gets() function is part of a matching pair; there is a function to output strings as well: puts() (for PUT String).

Here's a revised version of our ezstring.c program that makes use of both these functions:

```
// getput.c
// reads string and prints string using gets() and puts()
#include <stdio.h>                    // for gets(), puts()

void main(void)
    {
     char fname[81];

     puts("\nEnter your name: ");
     gets(fname);                     // get name from user
     puts("Greetings, ");
     puts(fname);                     // display name
    }
```

Let's see what happens when our favorite Mongol warrior tries this new version of the program.

```
Enter your name:
Genghis Khan
Greetings,
Genghis Khan
```

Now the program remembers the entire name and there's less chance of Genghis being offended. The gets() function has done just what we wanted.

The puts() function is a special-purpose output function specializing in strings. Unlike printf(), it can only output one string at a time and, like gets(), it has no ability to format a string before printing it. The syntax of puts() is simpler than printf(), however, so it's the function to use when you want to output a single string.

Avoid Mixing scanf() and gets()

We should note that you may run into trouble if you use a mixture of scanf() and gets() functions for input. The problem is that scanf() has a number of peculiarities, and one of them is that a newline character may be left unread in the keyboard buffer after scanf() returns. For example, if we execute the following statements

```
scanf("%d", &age);      // user enters 21
gets(name);             // user enters "Smith"
```

the user will type a number, press the Return key and wait for scanf() to digest the number. The number will be read and removed from the buffer all right, but often (depending on the compiler) the newline character will be left in the buffer. If so, then the gets() will read the newline and think the user has entered a string with no characters but the newline. In effect, the gets() function won't be executed.

> The scanf() function can cause problems when used with gets().

One way out of this dilemma is to forget about scanf() altogether and use gets() to read numbers as well as strings. You can do this by reading the number in the form of a string like "21" and then using a conversion function to convert the string to a numerical value. The atoi() function (which stands for *ASCII to Integer*) takes a string as an argument and returns an integer with the same numerical value. If the string is "21", the function returns the number *21*. The atof() function performs a similar conversion for floating point numbers.

Here's an example program that shows how gets() can be used for a variety of input types. (It's a modified version of the event4.c program from Chapter 2, "C Building Blocks.")

```
// atox.c
// demonstrates reading numbers with gets()
#include <stdio.h>        // for printf(), gets()
#include <stdlib.h>       // for atoi(), atof()

void main(void)
    {
    char string[81];       // utility string
    int event;
    char heat;
    float  time;
    char name[81];

    printf("\n\nEnter the event number (1, 2, etc.): ");
    gets(string);
    event = atoi(string);              // convert to integer
    printf("Enter the heat letter (A, B, etc.):  ");
    gets(string);
    heat = string[0];                  // convert to character
    printf("Enter the winning time (48.85): ");
    gets(string);
    time = atof(string);               // convert to float
    printf("Enter winner's name: ");
    gets(name);                        // no conversion
```

```
printf("\nThe winner of heat %c of event %d, ", heat, event);
printf("\nin a time of %f seconds, was %s", time, name);
}
```

Here's an example of interaction with the program:

```
Enter the event number (1, 2, etc.): 7
Enter the head letter (A, B, etc.): B
Enter the winning time (48.85): 54.47
Enter the winner's name: Johnson

The winner of heat B of event 7,
in a time of 54.470000 seconds, was Johnson
```

We've used a homemade approach to the string-to-character conversion: we take the first character from the string typed (which should be the only character in the string if the user follows instructions).

There are other conversion functions. Use atol() to convert a string to type long, itoa() to convert an integer to a string, ltoa() to convert type long to a string, fcvt() to convert type double to a string, and so forth.

Initializing Strings

Just as arrays can be initialized, so also can strings. Because a string is an array of characters, we can initialize one in exactly that way, as the following example demonstrates:

```
char feline[] = { 'c', 'a', 't', '\0' };
```

However, C concedes that strings are a special kind of character array by providing a shortcut.

```
char feline[] = "cat";
```

As you can see, this is considerably easier to write (and read); but it means the same thing to the compiler. Notice that although the individual characters were surrounded by single quotes, the string is surrounded by double quotes. Notice too that we don't need to insert the null character \0. Using the string format causes this to happen automatically.

Let's look at a variation on the last program, making use of an initialized string.

```
// strinit.c
// reads string and prints string, shows string initialization
#include <stdio.h>        // for puts() and gets()

void main(void)
    {
    char salute[] = "Greetings,";   // initialized string
    char fname[81];                 // uninitialized string

    puts("\nEnter your name: ");
    gets(fname);                     // get name from user
```

```
puts(salute);
puts(fname);                        // display name
}
```

The output will be exactly the same as before (assuming the same name is typed). However, "Greetings" is no longer printed as a string constant in the puts() function; instead, it's included in the array declaration. The puts() function can then print it using the array address as an argument. Here's a sample run with strinit.c:

```
Enter your name:
Cato the Elder
Greetings,
Cato the Elder
```

We see that our initialization process works just fine. However, the format of the output could be improved. It would have been nicer if the name was on the same line as the salutation.

```
Greetings, Cato the Elder
```

What's happened is that as the puts() function prints the string automatically replaces the null character at the end of the string with a newline character, so all strings printed by puts() end with a newline. Therefore, sometimes puts() isn't the ideal choice for outputting strings, and printf() must be used instead.

Examining a String

We've told you how a string looks in memory, but you shouldn't take our word for it; you can write a program to investigate this for yourself. The following program examines each memory location occupied by a string and prints what it finds there. In the process, it demonstrates a new C library function, strlen().

```
// strexam.c
// looks at string in memory
#include <stdio.h>   // for gets(), printf()
#include <string.h>  // for strlen()

void main(void)
   {
   char fname[81];                  // string buffer
   int dex;                         // loop index
   int length;                      // length of string

   puts("Enter your name: ");
   gets(fname);                     // get name
   length = strlen(fname);          // find length of name
   for (dex=0; dex<length+4; dex++) // display each letter
      printf("Addr=%5u char='%c'=%3u\n",
             &fname[dex], fname[dex], fname[dex] );
   }
```

Here's an example of the output:

```
Enter your name:
Plato
Addr= 3486 char='P'= 80
Addr= 3487 char='l'=108
Addr= 3488 char='a'= 97
Addr= 3489 char='t'=116
Addr= 3490 char='o'=111
Addr= 3491 char=' '=  0
Addr= 3492 char='<'= 60
Addr= 3493 char='#'= 35
Addr= 3494 char='u'=117
```

To show what happens after the end of the string, we've printed four characters beyond the end of the string that was typed. First there's the terminating null character, which prints as a space but has the value 0. Then there are garbage characters, which have whatever values were in memory before this part of memory was declared to be an array. If we had declared a static or external array, these spaces would all have been 0 instead of garbage characters.

We've used the address operator (&) to get the address of each of the characters that make up the string.

```
&name[dex]
```

We've also used our old trick of printing the characters in two different formats: once as a character and once as a number. The last new thing in this program is the use of the new string function, strlen(). We use the value returned by this function to tell us how many characters to print from the for loop.

```
length = strlen(name);
```

String Functions

In keeping with its philosophy of using a small language kernel and adding library functions to achieve greater power, C has no special string-handling operators. In BASIC you can assign a value to a string with an equal sign, and in Pascal you can compare two strings with a less-than sign. In C, however, which thinks of strings as arrays, there are no such string operators.

However, C does have a large set of useful string-handling library functions. We've used one of the most common, the strlen() function, in the strexam.c program. This function returns the length of the string whose address is given to it as an argument. Thus in our program, the expression

```
strlen(name)
```

will return the value 5 if the string name has the value Plato. (As you can see, strlen() doesn't count the terminating null character.)

An Array of Strings

Earlier in the chapter we saw several examples of two-dimensional arrays. Let's look now at a similar phenomenon, one dealing with strings: an array of strings. Because a string is itself an array, an array of strings is really an array of arrays, or a two-dimensional array .

Our example program asks you to type your name. When you do, it checks your name against a master list to see whether you're worthy of entry to the palace (or perhaps it's only an "in" restaurant on the Upper East Side). Here's the listing:

```c
// compare.c
// compares word typed with words in program
#include <stdio.h>        // for printf(), gets()
#include <string.h>       // for strcmp()
#define MAX 5             // number of strings
#define LEN 40            // maximum length of string

void main(void)
    {
    int dex;                 // loop index
    int enter=0;             // flag: set to 1 if entry OK
    char name[ 40];          // storage for name typed by user
    char list[MAX][LEN] =    // array of strings
                { "Katrina",
                  "Nigel",
                  "Alistair",
                  "Francesca",
                  "Gustav"     };
    printf("\nEnter your name: ");
    gets(name);                          // get name
    for (dex=0; dex<MAX; dex++)          // go thru list
       if( strcmp(&list[dex][0],name)==0 )  // if match
          {
          enter = 1;                     // set flag
          break;                         // leave loop
          }
    if ( enter == 1 )                    // if flag set
       printf("You may enter, oh honored one."); // one response
    else                                 // otherwise
       printf("Guards! Remove this person!");   // different one
    } // end main()
```

There are two possible outcomes when you interact with this program. Either your name is on the list

```
Enter your name:  Gustav
You may enter, oh honored one.
```

or it isn't.

```
Enter your name: Robert
Guards! Remove this person!
```

Notice how our array of strings is initialized. Because a phrase in quotes is already a one-dimensional array, we don't need to use braces around each name as we did for two-dimensional character arrays. We do need braces around all the strings, however, because this is an array of strings. As before, the individual elements of the array—strings in this case—are separated by commas.

The order of the subscripts in the array declaration is important. The first subscript, MAX, gives the number of items in the array, while the second subscript, LEN, gives the length of each string in the array. Having a fixed length array for each string, no matter how long it actually is, can lead to a considerable waste of space. (In Chapter 7, "Pointers," we'll show how to avoid this problem.)

We've used another string function, strcmp(), in this program, in the expression

```
strcmp( &list[dex][0], name ) == 0
```

The strcmp() function compares two strings and returns an integer value based on the comparison. If we assume that string1 is on the left side within the parentheses and string2 is on the right,

```
strcmp(string1, string2)
```

the value returned will have the following meanings:

Returned Value	Meaning
less than zero	string1 less than string2
zero	string1 identical to string2
greater than zero	string1 greater than string2

In this context, *less than* and *greater than* mean that if you put string1 and string2 in alphabetical order, the one that appeared first (closer to the As) would be considered less than those following. However, we don't make use of the less-than and greater-than capabilities of the function in this program. Here we only need to know when the strings are identical, which is true when the function returns a value of 0.

Another wrinkle in this program is the use of a *flag* to remember whether there has been a match. The flag, a variable that remembers a condition for a short time, is called enter, and it is set to 1 (true) if any of the names match and remains 0 if there are no matches at the end of the loop. The if-else statement then queries the flag to find out what to print.

Deleting Characters

It's often useful to be able to delete a character from the middle of a string (if you're writing a word processing program or text editor, for example). There are no library functions to do this in Turbo C, so we'll develop a routine to perform this function.

Here's a program that demonstrates `strdel()`, our homemade STRing DELete function:

```
// delete.c
// deletes a character from a string
#include <stdio.h>              // for printf(), etc.
#include <string.h>             // for strcpy()
void strdel(char str[], int n);  // prototype

void main(void)
   {
   char  string[81];           // buffer for string
   int position;               // position of character

   printf("\nEnter string, then enter position\n");
   gets(string);               // get string
   scanf("%d", &position);     // get character
   strdel(string,position);    // delete character
   puts(string);               // print new string
   }

// strdel()
// deletes character from string
void strdel(char str[], int n)  // buffer, size of buffer
   {
   strcpy(&str[n], &str[n+1] );  // move 2nd part of string
   }                             // one space to left
```

This program asks for a string and for the position in the string of the character to be deleted (remember that the first character is 0). Then the program calls the `strdel()` function to delete the character at that position. Here's a sample interaction:

```
Enter string, then enter position
cart
2
cat
```

The program has deleted character number 2, r, from the string `"cart"`.

The `strdel()` function works by moving one space to the left all characters that are to the right of the character being deleted. This is shown in Figure 6.14.

To move the characters, the function makes use of the `strcpy` library function. This function simply copies one string to another. For instance, if a program included the following statements

```
char buffer[10];
- - - - -
strcpy(buffer, "Dante");
```

the string `"Dante"` would be placed in the array `buffer[]`. The string would include the terminating null, which means that six characters in all would be copied.

If you're a BASIC programmer, you may be wondering why we can't achieve the same effect more simply by saying

```
buffer = "Dante";        // illegal construction
```

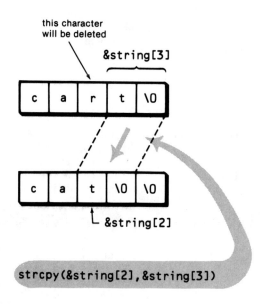

Figure 6.14. Operation of the strdel() function.

We can't do this because C treats strings far more like arrays than BASIC does. Because it is impossible to set one array equal to another with an assignment statement, it is also impossible to set one string equal to another in this way. A function must be used instead.

Now let's look closely at which string is being copied and where it's being copied to. Two arguments are needed by the strcpy() function: the string to be copied is the second argument, and the place it will be copied to is the first argument.

We want to move one space to the left the string following the character being deleted. In the cart-to-cat example, the string we want to copy has only two characters: t and the null character \0. What is the name of this string? How do we represent it as an argument to strcpy()? Remember that we identify an array by the address where it begins. The same is true of strings. In this case, the string we want to move begins at the letter t. What's the address of this character? It's &string[3], which is also the address of the string we want to move, so this is the second argument we give strcpy().

Now we want to move this string one character to the left. That means putting it at the address of the r, which is the character we want to delete. The address of the r is

`&string[2]`, because the `r` is in position 2 in the string.

Thus, assuming that `n` has the value 2, the statement

```
strcpy(&str[n], &str[n+1] );
```

will copy the string `"t\0"` to position `&str[2]`, blotting out the character 'r' as it does so.

Other String and Memory Manipulation Functions

The Turbo C compiler comes with many more string functions than we've shown here. The `strcat()` function concatenates (joins) two strings, the `strchr()` function finds a specified character in a string, the `strstr()` function finds a string within another string, and so on. Conversion routines manipulate strings. For instance, the `toupper()` function changes the characters in a string to all uppercase, and `tolower()` to all lowercase.

Other functions are subtle variations on those already mentioned. For example, `stricmp()` compares two strings without regard to case, and `strncmp()` compares only the first n characters of one string with another. Using some of these string operations requires an understanding of pointers, which will be our topic in the next chapter.

We should note that there are also functions that manipulate sequences of bytes in memory that aren't (or aren't necessarily) strings. For example, the `memcpy()` function copies bytes from one area of memory to another. However, it takes the number of bytes to copy as an argument rather than looking for the terminating NULL as the string functions do.

```
memcpy(dest_address, src_address, number_of_bytes);
```

Another memory manipulation function is `memcmp()`, for comparing two areas of memory.

Summary

In this chapter, we've learned how to handle arrays in a variety of forms. We've learned how to declare arrays, how to access their elements, and how to give them initial values when the program is compiled. We've covered one- and two-dimensional arrays and even taken a peek at initializing a three-dimensional array. We've learned that the addresses of arrays can be passed to functions so that functions can access the elements of the array.

Next, we looked at strings, which are simply arrays of type `char`. We've seen how to initialize strings and how to use two new I/O functions: `gets()` and `puts()`. We've also examined a trio of string functions: `strlen()`, which returns the length of a string; `strcmp()`, which compares two strings; and `strcpy()`, which copies one string into the space occupied by another.

Questions

1. An array is a collection of variables of

   a. Different data types scattered throughout memory
   b. The same data type scattered throughout memory
   c. The same data type placed next to each other in memory
   d. Different data types placed next to each other in memory

2. Why is a string like an array?

   a. They're both character arrays
   b. An array is a kind of string
   c. They both access functions the same way
   d. A string is a kind of array

3. An array definition specifies the t_____, n_____, and s_____ of the array.

4. Is this a correct array definition?

   ```
   int num(25);
   ```

5. Which element of the array does this expression reference?

   ```
   num[4]
   ```

6. What's the difference between the 3s in these two expressions?

   ```
   int num[3];
   num[3] = 5;
   ```

   a. First is particular element, second is type
   b. First is size, second is particular element
   c. First is particular element, second is array size
   d. Both specify array elements

7. What does this combination of statements do?

   ```
   #define LIM 50
   char collect[LIM];
   ```

   a. Makes LIM a subscript
   b. Makes LIM a variable of type char
   c. Makes collect[] an array of type LIM
   d. Makes collect[] an array of size LIM

8. If an array has been defined this way,

   ```
   float prices[MAX];
   ```

   is the following a good way to read values into all the elements of the array?

   ```
   for(j=0; j<=MAX; j++)
      scanf("%f", prices[j]);
   ```

9. Is this a correct way to initialize a one-dimensional array?

   ```
   int array = { 1, 2, 3, 4 };
   ```

10. What will happen if you try to put so many variables into an array when you initialize it that the size of the array is exceeded?

    a. Nothing
    b. Possible system malfunction
    c. Error message from the compiler
    d. Other data may be overwritten

11. What will happen if you put too few elements in an array when you initialize it?

    a. Nothing
    b. Possible system malfunction
    c. Error message from the compiler
    d. Unused elements will be filled with 0s or garbage

12. True or False: If you want to initialize an array it must be a static array or an external array.

13. What will happen if you assign a value to an element of an array whose subscript exceeds the size of the array?

    a. The element will be set to 0
    b. Nothing, it's done all the time
    c. Other data may be overwritten
    d. Possible system malfunction

14. Can you initialize a two-dimensional array this way?

    ```
    int array[3][3] = {  { 1, 2, 3 },
                         { 4, 5, 6 },
                         { 7, 8, 9 }  };
    ```

15. In the array in question 14, what is the name of the array variable with the value 4?

16. If an array had been defined like this:

    ```
    int array[12];
    ```

    the word array represents the a _____ of the array.

17. If you don't initialize a `static` array, what will the elements be set to?

    a. 0
    b. An undetermined value
    c. A floating point number
    d. The character constant \0

18. When you pass an array as an argument to a function, what is actually passed?

    a. The address of the array
    b. The values of the elements in the array
    c. The address of the first element in the array
    d. The number of elements in the array

19. True or false: a function operates on an integer array passed to it as an argument by placing the values of that array into a separate place in memory known only to the function.

20. A string is

    a. A list of characters
    b. A collection of characters
    c. An array of characters
    d. An exaltation of characters

21. "A" is a _____ but 'A' is a _____.

22. What is the following expression?

    `"Mesopotamia\n"`

    a. A string variable
    b. A string array
    c. A string constant
    d. A string of characters

23. A string is terminated by a _____ character, which is written _____.

24. The function _____ is designed specifically to read in one string from the keyboard.

25. If you have defined a string like this:

    `char name[10];`

    and you type a string into this array, the string can consist of a maximum of _____ characters.

26. True or false: the function `puts()` always adds a \n to the end of the string it is printing.

27. Which is more appropriate for reading in a multiword string?

    a. `gets()`
    b. `printf()`
    c. `scanf()`
    d. `puts()`

28. Assuming the following initialization:

```
char string[] = "Blacksmith";
```

how would you refer to the string `"smith"` (the last five letters of the string)?

29. What subtle format problem does this statement exhibit?

```
name = "George";
```

30. What expression would you use to find the length of the string `name`?

Exercises

1. Modify the temp.c program so that it not only accepts seven temperatures and calculates the average, but also prints the temperatures that have been read.

2. Modify the fltemp2.c program to use a `while` loop instead of a `do-while` loop.

 3. Write a function, and a program to test it, that will insert a character anywhere in a string. The call to the function should have the form

```
strins(string, character, position);
```

Before writing this function, ask yourself which end of the string `strcpy()` starts copying from.

Pointers

- Pointers
- Returning multiple values from functions
- Pointers and arrays
- Pointer arithmetic
- Pointers and strings
- Double indirection
- Pointers to arrays

Pointers are regarded by most people as one of the most difficult topics in C. There are several reasons for this. First, the concept behind pointers—indirection—may be a new one for many programmers, because it isn't commonly used in such languages as BASIC or Pascal. Second, the symbols used for pointer notation in C aren't as clear as they might be; for example, the same symbol is used for two different but related purposes, as we'll see.

Conceptually, however, pointers aren't really that obscure, and with a little practice the symbols start to make a sort of sense. In other words, pointers may be difficult, but they aren't *too* difficult. Our goal in this chapter is to demystify pointers, to explain as clearly as possible what they're for and how they work. To this end we start slowly, in an attempt to ensure that the groundwork is laid carefully, before we go on to use pointers in more advanced situations.

Pointer Overview

Before we show programming examples that demonstrate the use of pointers, we're going to discuss generally what pointers are and why they're used.

What Is a Pointer?

A pointer provides a way of accessing a variable (or a more complex kind of data, such as an array) without referring to the variable directly. The mechanism used for this is the address of the variable. In effect, the address acts as an intermediary between the variable and the program accessing it. There is a somewhat analogous mechanism in the spy business, in which an agent in the field might leave reports in a special place (a post office box or a hollow tree) and have no direct contact with the other members of the network. Thus if captured, there is very little information the agent can be forced to reveal about the organization. We can say that the agent has only indirect access to those for whom the information is intended.

In a similar way, a program statement can refer to a variable indirectly, using the address of the variable as a sort of post office box or hollow tree for the passing of information.

Why Are Pointers Used?

Pointers are used in situations when passing actual values is difficult or undesirable. (It's seldom the case that an enemy program will force a function to reveal the names of variables in the calling program!) Some reasons to use pointers are

1. To return more than one value from a function

2. To pass arrays and strings more conveniently from one function to another

3. To manipulate arrays more easily by moving pointers to them (or to parts of them), instead of moving the arrays themselves

4. To create complex data structures, such as linked lists and binary trees, where one data structure must contain references to other data structures

5. To communicate information about memory, as in the function `malloc()`, which returns the location of free memory by using a pointer.

We'll explore some of these uses for pointers in this chapter. We'll save the use of pointers with structures, linked lists, and `malloc()` for Chapter 12, "Memory."

Another reason sometimes given for using pointers is that pointer notation compiles into faster or more efficient code than, for example, array notation. It isn't clear that this is actually a major factor for modern compilers; probably many programmers become enamored of pointer notation and grasp at any excuse to use it.

You've Already Used Pointers

If you think that reason 2—passing arrays more conveniently from one function to another—sounds familiar, that's because it is; in Chapter 6 you used pointers to pass arrays and strings to functions. Instead of passing the array itself, you passed the address of the array. This address is an example of a pointer constant. There are also pointer variables; it's the interplay between pointer constants and pointer variables that gives pointers such power. We'll see further examples of pointers used with arrays later in this chapter.

> A pointer constant is an address; a pointer variable is a place to store addresses.

Returning Data from Functions

We're going to start our examination of pointers by finding out how functions can return multiple values to the program that called them. You've already seen that it's possible to pass many values to a function and return a single value from it, but what happens when you want to return more than one value from a function to the calling program? Because there is no mechanism built into functions to do this, we must rely on pointers. Of the many ways pointers can be used, this is perhaps the simplest; at the same time, it is a technique that accomplishes an essential task. There are many situations in which a function must communicate more than one value to the calling program.

Review: Passing Values to a Function

Before we show how this works, let's review what happens when we pass values *to* a function. (You've already seen examples of such functions in Chapter 5—the function that adds two numbers, for example.) Here's a very simple program that passes two values, the integers 4 and 7, to a function called `gets2()`:

```
// values.c
// tests function which accepts two values
#include <stdio.h>              // for printf()
void gets2(int, int);          // prototype

void main(void)
   {
   int x=4, y=7;               // initialize variables

   gets2(x, y);                // pass vars to function
   }

// gets2()
// prints out values of two arguments
void gets2(int xx, int yy)
   {
   printf("\nFirst is %d, second is %d", xx, yy);
   }
```

This isn't an enormously useful function: it simply prints the two values passed to it. However, it demonstrates an important point: the function receives the two values from the calling program and stores them—or rather, stores duplicates of them—in its own private memory space. In fact, it can even give these values different names, known only to the function: in this case, xx and yy instead of x and y. Figure 7.1 shows how this looks. The function then can operate on the new variables, xx and yy, without affecting the original x and y in the calling program.

Passing Addresses to a Function

Now let's look at the reverse situation: passing two values from the function back to the calling program. How do we do this? A two-step process is used. First, the calling program, instead of passing values to the function, passes it addresses. These addresses are where the calling program wants the function to place the data it generates; in other words, they're the addresses of the variables in the calling program where we want to store the returned values. Here's the program:

```
// passback.c
// tests function that returns two values
#include <stdio.h>          // for printf()
void rets2(int *, int *);   // prototype

void main(void)
   {
   int x, y;                // variables

   rets2( &x, &y );         // get values from function
   printf("\nFirst is %d, second is %d", x, y);
   }
```

(handwritten annotations at top of page)

Void insert (char *);
insert (name)
(address name)
int x, y;
prompt (&x, &y);
name of an array is an address, but if variable declared in a table so get an address, but if an array used in a table address get only if by brackets

```
// rets2()
// returns two numbers
void rets2(int *px, int *py)
    {
    *px = 3;                    // set contents of px to 3
    *py = 5;                    // set contents of py to 5
    }
```

Here's what happens when you run the program:

```
First is 3, second is 5.
```

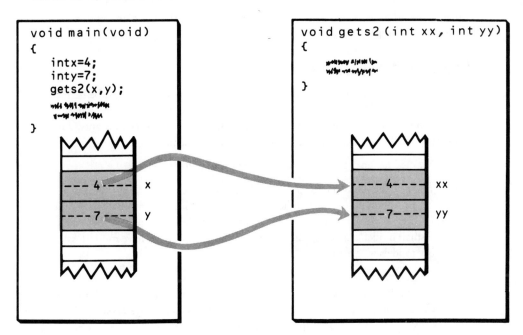

```
void main(void)                        void gets2 (int xx, int yy)
{                                      {
    intx=4;
    inty=7;
    gets2(x,y);
                                       }
```

x   4   xx
y   7   yy

Values are passed to function
and duplicated in the function's;
memory space.

Figure 7.1. Values duplicated in function's memory.

This program again doesn't do anything very useful. The calling program, main(), calls the rets2() function, which supplies two values, 3 and 5, to the calling program. The calling program then prints the values. But while it may not be useful, the program is crammed with new ideas. Let's take it apart step-by-step.

First, notice that the calling program itself never gives any values to the variables x and y. Yet when the program is run, these variables have values; they're printed by the calling

221

program, as we can see from the output. We can infer that the rets2() function must somehow have supplied these values to the calling program.

The calling program told rets2() where to put the values by passing it addresses. It did this using the address operator &. The expression

```
rets2( &x, &y );
```

causes the addresses of x and y to be passed to the function and stored in the function's private memory space. These addresses have been given names by the function: px and py. That's how the function can refer to them, just as if they were any other kind of variables (of course we could have used any names we wanted here, like the more descriptive but longer ptr_to_x and ptr_to_y).

Defining Pointer Variables

As with any variables, the places set aside for these addresses, px and py, must be defined so that the compiler will know how large a memory space to allot for them and what names we want to give them. Because we're storing addresses, or pointer constants, you might expect a whole new data type here, something along the lines of

```
ptr px, py;      // not exactly how pointers are defined
```

where ptr might be the data type for pointers. After all, addresses are all the same size, and we want to set aside enough memory to hold an address. Ordinarily, two bytes will hold an address. (When memory models other than "small" are used, this may not be true; however, the small model is used for all programs in this book. We'll have more to say about memory models in Chapter 12, "Memory.")

Defining a pointer variable does in fact set aside two bytes of memory, but there is an added complexity. For reasons which we'll explain later, the compiler needs to know, not only that we're defining a pointer, but also to *which kind of data item the pointer points*. In other words, every time we set aside space to store the address of a variable, we need to tell the compiler the data type of the variable. This information must be communicated to the compiler, along with the fact that we're defining a pointer. Let's make a second guess at what such a definition might look like

```
int_ptr px, py;   // still not how pointers are defined
```

where int_ptr is the data type for pointers that point to integer variables. We're getting closer. However, C is a concise language, so instead of using the word *ptr*, C uses the asterisk (*). The asterisk is used differently from the words representing simple data types (for example, int and float); it is used immediately before each variable, rather than being used once at the beginning of the definition. Thus, the real definition for two integer pointers is

```
int *px, *py;      // correct definition of two pointers
```

The definition sets aside two bytes in which to store the address of an integer variable and gives this storage space the name px. It also sets aside another two bytes in which to store the address of another integer variable and gives this space the name py. The asterisks tell the compiler that these variables will contain addresses (not values), and the int tells it that the addresses will point to integer variables. Note that the definition itself doesn't say anything about what will be placed in these variables.

The format of this definition is shown in Figure 7.2.

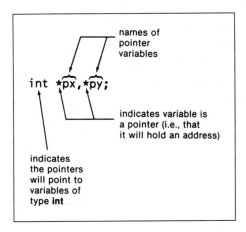

Figure 7.2. Format of pointer declaration.

(Note that the asterisk as it's used here is a unary operator: it operates on only one variable (such as px in *px). Thus, the compiler can't confuse it with the same symbol used for multiplication, which is a binary operator, operating on two variables.)

The concise nature of this definition format is one of the causes of confusion about pointers, so we'll reiterate what's happening: for each variable name (px and py in this case) the definition causes the compiler to set aside a two-byte space in memory into which an address can be placed, as shown in Figure 7.3.

In addition, the compiler is aware of the type of variable the address refers to; in this case, integers.

Supplying Values to Pointer Variables

Now, when the function is called by the calling program with the statement

```
rets2( &x, &y );
```

the two addresses provided by the calling program, &x and &y, are placed in the spaces provided by the definition in the function. Thus, control is passed to the function, but also these two addresses (which, in this case, might be 1310 and 1312) are placed in the space set aside for px and py. This process is shown in Figure 7.4.

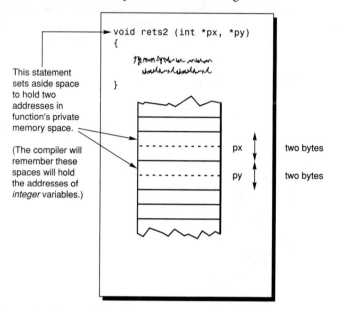

Figure 7.3. Operation of pointer declaration.

07TCP03

Let's examine this process carefully to make sure we've got the terms straight. We can say that px and py are pointer *variables* and that the addresses 1310 and 1312 are pointer *constants.* Figure 7.5 shows a close-up view of these variables being assigned these constant values.

The Indirection Operator

The function now knows the addresses of the variables into which the calling program wants values placed. The big question is, how does the function access these variables? (To return to our spy analogy: how does the spy go about leaving a message in the hollow tree?)

Think about this question for a moment, because in the answer lies the key to what pointers really are. If the function knew the names for x and y (if they were external variables, for example), it could simply say

```
x = 3;
y = 5;
```

The function doesn't know the names of the variables; all it knows are the addresses where these variables are stored. We want a new kind of operator, something like `variable_pointed_to_by` so that we can make such assignment statements as

```
variable_pointed_to_by_px = 3;    // not really how it's done
variable_pointed_to_by_py = 5;
```

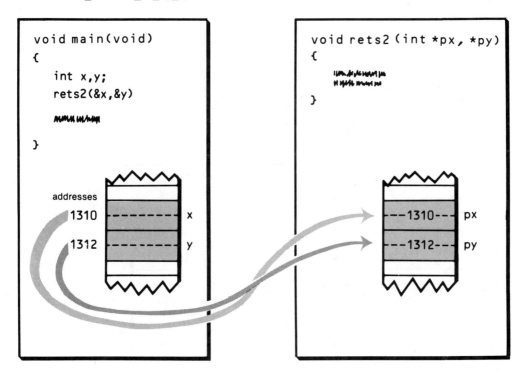

Addresses are passed to
function, and stored
in the function's memory
space.

Figure 7.4. Addresses stored in function's memory.

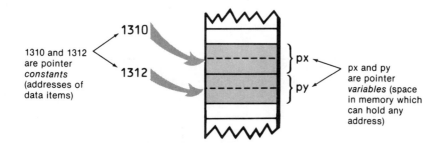

Figure 7.5. Pointer constants placed in pointer variables.

As you might expect, C uses a much more concise format for this operator. Here's how pointers are actually used:

```
*px = 3;
*py = 5;
```

It's our old friend the asterisk again. However—and herein lies the source of much confusion—it's used in a slightly different way than it is in pointer definitions. In a definition it means *pointer data type,* just as int means *integer data type.* Here it means something else: *variable pointed to by,* so the first statement translates into "assign the variable pointed to by px the value of 3," and the second, "assign the variable pointed to by py the value 5." Figure 7.6 shows the effect.

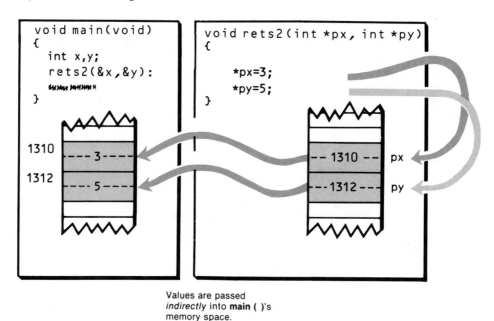

Values are passed *indirectly* into **main ( )**'s memory space.

Figure 7.6. Values returned to calling program.

In a definition the (*) symbol means *pointer type;* in other statements it means *variable pointed to by.*

The function has indirectly passed the values 3 and 5 to the variables x and y. It's indirect because the function didn't know the names of the variables, so it used their addresses (which were stored in the function, having been passed to it from the calling program), along with the indirection operator (*), to achieve the same effect. Figure 7.7 shows the structure of an assignment statement using the indirection operator.

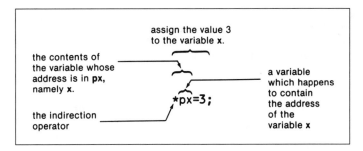

Figure 7.7. The indirection operator.

We can conclude that the main() program has one way of accessing the variables x and y, while rets2() has another. main() calls them x and y, while rets2() calls them *px and *py. This situation is depicted somewhat fancifully in Figure 7.8.

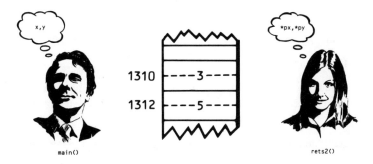

Figure 7.8. Different perspectives.

Finally, we know how a function can return values to the calling program.

Going Both Ways

Once a function knows the addresses of variables in the calling program, it not only can place values in these variables, it can also take values out. That is, pointers can be used not only to pass values from a function to the calling program but also to pass them from the program to the function. Of course, we've seen in earlier chapters that values can be passed directly to a function, but once pointers are being used to go one way, they can easily be used to go the other.

Consider the following function, which adds a constant to two values in the calling program. The function reads the value from the calling program's address space, adds the constant to it, and returns the result to the same spot.

```
// addtotwo.c
// tests function that adds constant to two values
#include <stdio.h>                 // for printf()
void addcon(int *px, int *py);    // prototype

void main(void)
    {
    int x=4, y=7;                  // initialize variables

    addcon(&x, &y);                // add 10 to both variables
    printf("\nFirst is %d, second is %d", x, y);
    }

// addcon()
// adds constant to values in calling program
void addcon(int *px, int *py)
    {
    *px = *px + 10;                // add 10 to contents of px
    *py = *py + 10;                // add 10 to contents of py
    }
```

When the program is run, it prints

```
First is 14, second is 17.
```

Here the values 4 and 7 are stored in the variables x and y in the calling program. The calling program passes the addresses of these variables to the function addcon(), which adds the constant 10 to them.

This program looks much like passback.c, except for the assignment statements in the function.

```
*px = *px + 10;
*py = *py + 10;
```

Here the indirection operator has been used on both sides of the equal sign. The first statement means that we get the contents of the variable pointed to by px (this is x, whose value is 4), add 10 to it and return the result to the same place (the variable pointed to by px—which is still x but whose value will now be 14). In a similar way the second statement will cause the variable y to end up being 17.

In other words, we can use the symbol *px, where px is a variable containing the address of x, almost exactly as we could have used the variable x itself, had it been accessible to us.

Pointers Without Functions

Our examples so far have dealt with pointers that store addresses passed to functions. This is a common use for pointers and an easy one to implement, but it may tend to obscure some of the operation of pointers. The reason for this is that the function-call mechanism itself takes over the task of assigning an address to the pointer variable. That is, when we call a function with the statement

```
addcon(&x, &y);
```

then the function `addcon()`, which starts with the declarator

```
void addcon(int *px, int *py)
```

will automatically assign the addresses of x and y to the pointer variables px and py.

Let's look at an example in which we need to perform this assignment "by hand" in the program itself, rather than using a call to a function to do it for us.

The following program carries out the same task as did the addtotwo.c program. However, instead of calling a function to add a constant to the two variables, it does so directly in the program.

```
// addin.c
// shows use of pointers within program
// uses scaling factors
#include <stdio.h>                    // for printf()

void main(void)
    {
    int x=4, y=7;
    int *px, *py;                     // pointer variables

    printf("\nx is %d, y is %d\n", x, y);
    px = &x;                          // put addresses of numbers
    py = &y;                          //    in pointers
    *px = *px + 10;                   // add constant to contents
    *py = *py + 10;                   //    of pointers
    printf("x is %d, y is %d\n", x, y);
    }
```

[handwritten margin note: contains address]

We use a `printf()` statement to print the values of x and y, then add 10 to them, then use another `printf()` statement to print the new values. Here's the output:

```
x is 4, y is 7.
x is 14, y is 17.
```

Of course all this could have been handled much more easily with the statements

```
x = x + 10;
y = y + 10;
```

However, directly assigning values to the variables wouldn't reveal nearly as much about pointers. (Actually, as battle-scarred C programmers, we should be using

```
x += 10;
y += 10;
```

but this tends to obscure the details of the operation for those not entirely comfortable with arithmetic assignment statements.)

The new elements in the program are the assignment statements

```
px = &x;
py = &y;
```

These statements take the addresses of the variables x and y and put them in the pointer variables px and py. This is what the function call addcon(&x, &y) did automatically in the addtotwo.c program. The statements

```
*px = *px + 10;
*py = *py + 10;
```

work just as they did in addtotwo.c; in fact, the output of the program is identical. The operation of the program is shown in Figure 7.9.

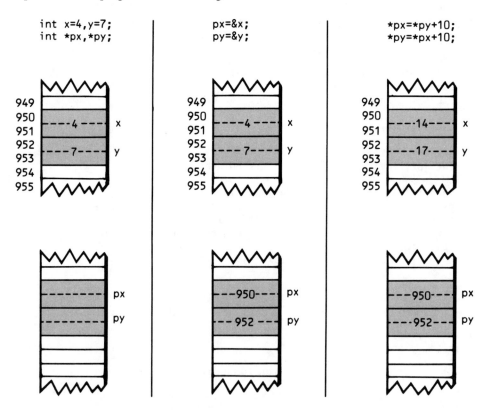

Figure 7.9. Operation of the addin.c program.

An important lesson can be learned by imagining what would happen if the statements px = &x and py = &y were left out of the program. Would it still work? No, because then there would be no address or at least not a correct address in the variables px and py. The references to *px and *py would refer not to x and y, but to whatever was located in the addresses that happened to be in px and py. Because these addresses could point to the program itself, or to the operating system, disaster could swiftly follow.

The moral is, make sure you assign a pointer variable an appropriate address before you use it.

---

*ptr is the contents of the address in ptr
&var is the address of var

Pointers and Arrays

In Chapter 6 we explored arrays and saw examples of array notation: how to reference array elements with such statements as table[x][y]. As it turns out, this array notation is really nothing more than a thinly disguised form of pointer notation. In fact, the compiler translates array notation into pointer notation when compiling, because the internal architecture of the microprocessor understands pointers but doesn't understand arrays.

To make clearer the relationship between pointers and arrays, let's look at a simple program, expressed first in array notation and then in pointer notation.

Here's the array version:

```
// array.c
// prints out values from array
#include <stdio.h>      // for printf()

void main(void)
    {
    int nums[] = { 92, 81, 70, 69, 58 };
    int dex;   — index

    printf("\n");
    for (dex=0; dex<5; dex++)
       printf("\n%d", nums[dex] );
    }
```

Here is the output. It shouldn't come as a surprise to anyone.

```
92
81
70
69
58
```

This is a straightforward program. Array notation is used to access individual elements of the array in the expression nums[dex].

Now let's see how this program would look using pointer notation.

```
// parray.c
// uses pointers to print out values from array
#include <stdio.h>        // for printf()

void main(void)
    {
    int nums[] = { 92, 81, 70, 69, 58 };
    int dex;

    printf("\n");
    for (dex=0; dex<5; dex++)
        printf("\n%d", *(nums+dex) );
    }
```

This version is identical to the first, except for the expression *(nums+dex). What does it mean? Its effect is exactly the same as that of nums[dex] in the earlier example; in other words, it accesses that element of the array nums whose subscript is contained in the variable dex. (Thus, if dex is 3, we'll get element nums[3], which is 69.)

How do we interpret *(nums+dex)? First, as we know, nums is the address of the array. Now if we add, say, the number 3 to this address, what will we get? In other words, if dex is 3, what is nums+dex? Would you guess the result would be an address three bytes from the start of the array? If so, you haven't counted on the extreme cleverness of the designers of C.

After all, what we want isn't an address three bytes from the start of the array, but the address of the third element in the array. If each element of the array is an integer, it takes up two bytes, so we want to look at the address six bytes from the start of the array. As shown in Figure 7.10, if the array nums starts at 1400, then when dex is 3 we want nums+dex to have the value 1406—which is the address of nums[3]—not the value 1403 (which is the second half of nums[1] and meaningless).

In other words, if we say nums+3, we don't mean three bytes, we mean three elements of the array: three integers if it's an integer array, three floating point numbers if it's a floating point array, and so on.

That's exactly what the C compiler delivers. It looks at the context of the plus sign, and if we're adding 3 to a pointer, it doesn't add 3, it adds 3 times however many bytes each element of the array occupies. How does it know how many bytes per element? In this case, because we're adding something to an address at the start of an array, nums[], it looks at the array declaration, finds out it's an array of type int, and because there are two bytes per integer, multiplies by 2.

Now that you know this, you should be able to figure out the meaning of the expression

*(nums+dex)

If dex is 3, this expression means *the contents of element 3 of the array nums[*. This value is 69. Thus, as we've noted, *(nums+dex) is the same thing as nums[dex]. Both of them are ways of referring to the contents of an array element.

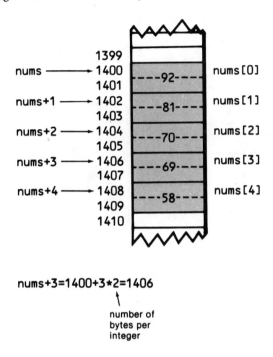

Figure 7.10. Pointer addition.

*(array+index) is the same as array[index]

There are also two ways to refer to the *address* of an array element. We can say nums+dex in pointer notation, and &nums[dex] in array notation. These relationships are shown in Figure 7.11.

What do we gain by using pointer notation as opposed to array notation? Probably not very much in this context. However, pointer notation is commonly used with arrays in this way, so it's good to be familiar with it. More important, similar notation is used in many other instances where array notation wouldn't work at all, as we'll see directly.

Return of the Killer Averages

As another example of the equivalence of array and pointer notation, we're going to translate the temperature-averaging program fltemp2.c from Chapter 6 into pointer notation. We'll use this program and a variant of it to demonstrate some important aspects of pointer variables and constants. You might want to refer back to fltemp2.c before looking at this modified version:

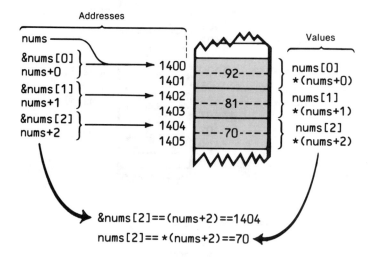

Figure 7.11. Addresses and values.

```
// ptrtemp.c
// averages arbitrary number of temperatures
// uses pointer notation
#include <stdio.h>              // for printf(), scanf()

void main(void)
   {
   float temper[40];            // array definition
   float sum = 0.0;
   int num, day = 0;

   printf("\n");
   do                           // put temps in array
      {
      printf("Enter temperature for day %d: ", day);
      scanf("%f", temper+day);
      }
   while ( *(temper+day++) > 0 ); // quit on 0
```

```
num = day-1;                        // number of temps entered
for (day=0; day<num; day++)         // calculate average
   sum += *(temper+day);
printf("Average is %.1f", sum/num);
}
```

This works as it did in Chapter 5, "Functions"; you type an arbitrary number of temperatures, and the program prints the average. We've modified three different expressions in this program, with the goal of changing the address &temper[day] into temper+day and the value stored there from temper[day] into *(temper+day). Here are the three lines affected:

```
scanf("%f", temper+day);
- - - -
while ( *(temper+day++) > 0 );
- - - -
sum += *(temper+day);
```

What we've done here is perform almost a literal translation from array notation to pointer notation. However, such a literal translation doesn't yield the most efficient or elegant programming.

Pointer Constants and Pointer Variables

Is there any way to simplify these three unwieldy expressions? In each, we're using the expression temper+day as a way to reference individual items of the array by varying the value of day. Could we get rid of day by using the increment operator on the address itself, instead of using the variable day? For example, can we use an expression like this?

```
while ( *(temper++) > 0 );   // can't do this
```
cause temper is defined as a constant

The answer is no, and the reason is that temper is a pointer *constant*. It isn't a variable. It is the address of the array temper, and this value won't change while the program is running. The linker has decided where this array will go—say address 810—and that's where it will stay. Trying to increment this address has no meaning; it's like saying

```
x = 3++;   // can't do this either
```

Because you can't increment a constant, the compiler will flag this as an error.

You can't change the value of a pointer constant, only of a pointer variable.

We've run into a problem. It would be nice to use a statement as clear as *(temper++), but we can't increment a constant. However, we can increment variables. This is one of the real strengths of the C language: the ability to use pointer variables. Let's rewrite the program to make use of such variables.

```
// ptrtemp2.c
// averages arbitrary number of temperatures
// uses pointer variables
#include <stdio.h>                     // for printf(), scanf()

void main(void)
   {
   float temper[40];                   // array definition
   float sum=0.0;
   int num, day=0;
   float *ptr;                         // pointer variable

   printf("\n");
   ptr = temper;                       // set pointer to array
   do                                  // put temps in array
      {
      printf("Enter temperature for day %d: ", day++);
      scanf("%f", ptr);
      }
   while ( *(ptr++) > 0 );

   ptr = temper;                       // reset pointer to array
   num = day-1;                        // number of temps entered
   for (day=0; day<num; day++)         // calculate average
      sum += *(ptr++);
   printf("Average is %.1f", sum/num);
   }
```

The strategy here is to place the address `temper` (say it's 810) into a pointer variable called `ptr`. Now we can refer to `ptr` in much the same way we refer to `temper`. We can use `ptr` as an address that will point to an array element, and we can use `*ptr` as the contents of that address. Moreover, because `ptr` is a variable, we don't need to add something to it to point to each element of the array in turn; all we need to do is increment it.

```
ptr++
```

We set `ptr` equal to the address `temper` before we enter the loop to read in the temperatures, and we reset it again before we enter the loop to average them. Then in both these loops we increment `ptr` with the ++ operator so that it points to each array element in turn. (Because `ptr` points to an array of type `float`, the ++ operator causes it to be incremented by four bytes.) The process is shown in Figure 7.12.

By using pointer variables we have simplified the program and made it run faster, because only one variable, `ptr`, must be referenced each time through the loop, instead of both `temper` and `day`.

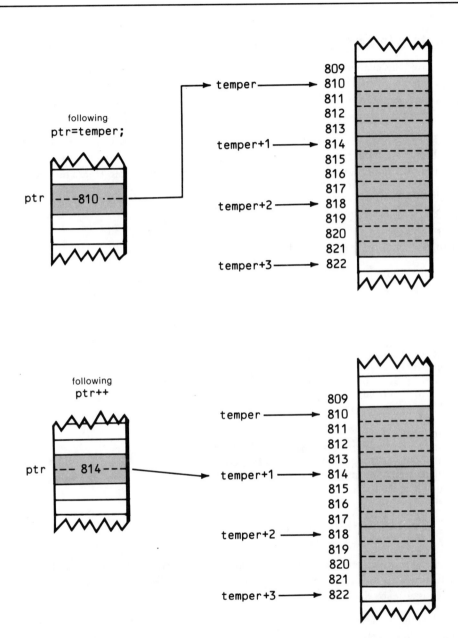

Figure 7.12. Incrementing a pointer variable.

Pointers to Arrays in Functions

We started this chapter by learning how pointers can be used for communication among functions, and then we examined how pointers can be used to reference array elements. Let's combine these two techniques to see how a function can use pointers to access elements of an array whose address is passed to the function as an argument.

As an example, we'll modify our program addtotwo.c, which adds a constant to two variables in the calling program, to add a constant to all the elements in an array. This is a function that might actually prove useful in a variety of circumstances. Here's the listing:

```
// addarray.c
// tests function to add constant to array values
#include <stdio.h>              // for printf()
#define SIZE 5                  // size of array
void addcon (int *, int, int);  // prototype

void main(void)
   {
   int array[SIZE] = { 3, 5, 7, 9, 11 };
   int konst = 10;              // constant to be added
   int j;

   addcon(array, SIZE, konst);   // call funct to add consts
   printf("\n");
   for (j=0; j<SIZE; j++)         // print out array
      printf("%d   ", *(array+j) );
   }

// addcon()
// adds constant to each element of array
void addcon(int *ptr, int size, int con)
// arguments: array, array size, constant
   {
   int k;
   for(k=0; k<size; k++)          // add const to each element
      *(ptr+k) = *(ptr+k) + con;
   }
```

Here the calling program supplies the address of the array, array; the size of the array, SIZE (which is #defined to be 5); and the constant to be added to each element, konst (which is assigned the value 10).

The function assigns the address of the array to the pointer ptr, the size to the variable num, and the constant to the variable con. Then a simple loop serves to add the constant to each element of the array.

The output of this program shows the new contents of the array to verify that the function has done its work. Here's what it looks like:

```
13   15   17   19   21
```

Pointers and Strings

Let's turn now to the relationship of pointers and strings. Because strings are arrays and arrays are closely connected with pointers, you might expect that strings and pointers are closely related, and this is correct.

String Functions and Pointers

Many of the C library functions that work with strings do so by using pointers. As an example, let's look at a string function that returns a pointer. The function is strchr(), which returns a pointer to the first occurrence of a particular character in a string. If we say

```
ptr = strchr(str, 'x');
```

then the pointer variable ptr will be assigned the address of the first occurrence of the character 'x' in the string str. Note that this isn't the position in the string, which runs from 0 to the end of the string, but the address, which runs from 2343—or wherever the string happens to start—to the end of the string.

Here is the function strchr() used in a simple program that allows the user to type a sentence and a character to be searched for. The program then prints the address of the start of the string, the address of the character, and the character's position relative to the start of the string (0 if it's the first character, 1 if it's the second, and so forth). This relative position is simply the difference between the two addresses.

```
// search.c
// searches string for a given character
#include <stdio.h>      // for printf()
#include <conio.h>      // for getche()

void main(void)
    {
    char ch, line[81], *ptr, *strchr();

    puts("Enter the sentence to be searched: ");
    gets(line);
    printf("Enter character to search for: ");
    ch = getche();

    ptr = strchr(line,ch);    // return pointer to char
    printf("\nString starts at address %u.\n", line);
    printf("First occurrence of char is address %u.\n", ptr);
    printf("This is position %d (starting from 0)", ptr-line);
    }
```

Here's a sample run:

```
Enter the sentence to be searched:
```

```
The quick brown fox jumped over the lazy dog.
Enter character to search for: x
String starts at address 3610.
First occurrence of character is address 3628.
This is character position 18.
```

In the declaration statement, we've set aside a pointer variable, ptr, to hold the address returned by strchr(). Because this is the address of a character, ptr is of type char*. Once the function has returned this address, we can print it and use it to calculate the position of the character in the string: the value ptr-line.

Are you wondering what the expression *strchr() is doing in the declaration statement? The strchr() function returns a pointer to a character, so it must be declared to be of this type. We could have left this declaration out if we had included the preprocessor statement

```
#include <string.h>
```

at the beginning of the program. This would work just as well (and is generally the preferred approach), because the header file string.h contains prototypes for the string handling functions. However, we've used this variation to keep you on your toes.

Strings Initialized as Pointers

We showed an example of initializing a string as an array in the program strinit.c in Chapter 6. Our next example shows how this program can be modified so that the string is initialized as a pointer. Here's the listing:

```
// strinit.c
// shows string initialization
// uses pointers
#include <stdio.h>       // for gets() and puts()

void main(void)
    {
    char *salute = "Greetings,";
    char name[81];

    puts("Enter your name: ");
    gets(name);
    puts(salute);
    puts(name);
    }
```

Here, to initialize the string, we've used the statement

```
char *salute = "Greetings,";
```

instead of

```
char salute[] = "Greetings,";
```

These two forms appear to have much the same effect in the program. Is there a difference? Yes, but it's quite a subtle one. The array version of this statement sets aside an array with enough bytes (in this case 10) to hold the word, plus one byte for the \0 (null) character. The address of the first character of the array is given the name of the array, in this case, salute. In the pointer version, an array is set aside in the same way, but a pointer variable is also set aside; it is this pointer that is given the name salute. Figure 7.13 shows how this looks.

In the array style of initialization, salute is a pointer constant, an address which can't be changed. In the pointer style, salute is a pointer variable, which can be changed. For instance, the expression

```
puts(++salute);
```

would print the string starting with the second character in the string:

```
reetings,
```

The added flexibility of the pointer approach can often be used to advantage, as we'll see shortly.

Initializing an Array of Pointers to Strings

There's another difference between initializing a string as an array or as a pointer. This difference is most easily seen when we talk about an array of strings (or if we use pointers, an array of pointers to strings).

In Chapter 6 we showed how to initialize an array of strings in the program compare.c. In the following example we'll modify this program so that the strings are initialized as pointers.

```
// comparep.c
// compares word typed in with words in program
// uses pointers
#include <stdio.h>          // for printf(), gets()
#include <string.h>         // for strcmp()
#define MAX 5               // number of strings

void main(void)
    {
    int dex;
    int enter=0;
    char name[40];
    char *list[MAX] =       // array of pointers to strings
             {  "Katrina",
```

```
                    "Nigel",
                    "Alistair",
                    "Francesca",
                    "Gustav"      };

    printf("Enter your name: ");        // get name
    gets(name);
    for (dex=0; dex<MAX; dex++)         // go thru list
        if( strcmp(list[dex],name)==0 ) // if match
            {
            enter = 1;                  // set flag
            break;                      // exit the loop
            }
    if ( enter == 1 )                   // if flag set
        printf("You may enter, oh honored one."); // one response
    else                                // otherwise
        printf("Guards! Remove this person!");   // different one
    }
```

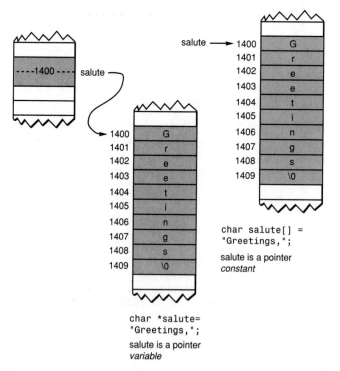

Figure 7.13. String array versus string pointer.

What does the expression char *list[MAX] mean? Such complex expressions are generally deciphered from right to left, as shown in Figure 7.14, this one means an array of pointers to characters.

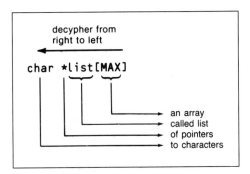

Figure 7.14. Declaration of array of pointers.

In the array version of this program, the strings were stored in a rectangular array with 5 rows and 10 columns. In the new version, the strings are stored contiguously in memory; they don't form an array, so there is no wasted space between them. However, an array of pointers to these strings has been created. Figure 7.15 shows the differences between these two approaches.

As you can see, the pointer version takes up less space in memory; it ends at 1039, while the array version ends at 1049. Thus, one reason to initialize strings as pointers is to use memory more efficiently. Another reason is to obtain greater flexibility in the manipulation of the strings in the array, as the next example will show.

> Initializing a group of strings using pointer notation uses less memory than initializing them as a two-dimensional array.

Lvalue and Rvalue

Occasionally, when experimenting with pointers and strings, you may receive error messages from the compiler that use the term *lvalue*, as in "lvalue required." What does this mean?

Essentially, an lvalue is a variable, as opposed to an *rvalue* which is a constant. The terms arose from the left-right positions in a typical assignment statement.

```
var = 3;
```

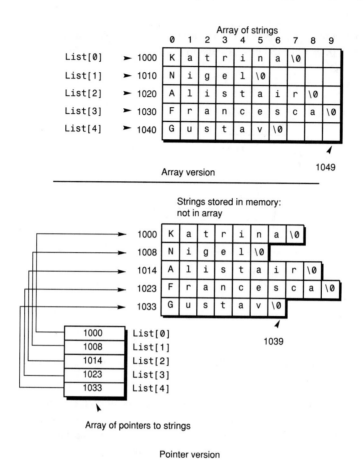

Figure 7.15. Array of strings versus array of pointers.

An expression that can appear on the left side of an assignment statement is a variable and is called an *lvalue*. An expression that must remain on the right side of the equal sign because it is a constant is called an *rvalue*. If you attempt to use a constant on the left side of the equal sign in the assignment statement, the compiler will flag it as an error.

Manipulating Pointers to Strings

As you know, when an array is passed as an argument to a function, it isn't actually the array that is passed but only its address. The array itself doesn't move. The same is true of strings: when we pass a string to a function, we're passing only its address. This ability to reference strings by addresses can be very helpful when we want to manipulate a group of strings. In the following example we'll sort an array of strings, using an approach similar to that of the sortnum.c program in Chapter 6. However, we won't move the strings themselves around in the array; instead, we'll sort an array of pointers to the strings.

This program accepts a series of names typed by the user, places them in an array, and sorts the pointers to the array so that, in effect, the names are rearranged into alphabetical order. Then, the resulting sorted list is printed. Here's the program:

```c
// sortstr.c
// sorts list of names typed in to array
#include <stdio.h>              // for printf(), etc.
#include <string.h>             // for strlen(), etc.

#define MAXNUM 30               // maximum number of names
#define MAXLEN 81               // maximum length of names

void main(void)
   {
   char name[MAXNUM][MAXLEN];   // array of strings
   char *ptr[MAXNUM];           // array of pntrs to strings
   char *temp;                  // extra pointer
   int count = 0;               // how many names
   int in, out;                 // sorting indexes

   printf("\n");
   while ( count < MAXNUM )     // get names
      {
      printf("Name %d: ", count+1);
      gets(name[count]);
      if ( strlen(name[count])==0 )
         break;                 // quit if no name
      ptr[count++] = name[count]; // each ptr points to name
      }
                               // sort the pointers
   for (out=0; out<count-1; out++)   // for each string
      for (in=out+1; in<count; in++) // look at those smaller
         if ( strcmp(ptr[out],ptr[in]) > 0 )  // compare
            {                             // if any smaller,
            temp = ptr[in];               // swap pointers
            ptr[in] = ptr[out];
            ptr[out] = temp;
            }

   printf("\nSorted list: \n");
   for (out=0; out<count; out++) // print sorted list
      printf("Name %d: %s\n", out+1, ptr[out]);
   }
```

A sample run:

```
Name 1: Thomas
Name 2: Cummings
Name 3: Sandburg
```
←Typed by user

```
Name 4: Masefield
Name 5: Shelley
Name 6: Auden
Name 7:

Sorted list:
Name 1: Auden
Name 2: Cummings
Name 3: Masefield
Name 4: Sandburg
Name 5: Shelley
Name 6: Thomas
```

← Printed by program

This program uses both an array of strings and an array of pointers. The pointers occupy the array declared by the expression

```
char *ptr[MAXNUM];
```

The strings occupy a two-dimensional array.

```
char name[MAXNUM][MAXKEN];
```

Because we don't know in advance how long they'll be, we must use a rectangular array to hold the strings that are typed (rather than initializing them as pointers to strings). We use rows 81 characters long; these will hold names extending across the entire screen.

As the strings are read in, the statement

```
ptr[count++] = name[count];
```

assigns the address of each string, which is stored in the array name[ ][ ], to an element of the pointer array ptr[ ]. Note that count is incremented on the left side of the equal sign, because this side is evaluated after the right side, and we don't want to change count until the assignment has been completed.

Next the array of pointers is sorted, and finally the strings are printed in alphabetical order, using the array of pointers as a reference. Figure 7.16 shows how the pointers look before and after sorting. The array name[ ][ ] itself remains unchanged; only the pointers to the elements of the array have been rearranged.

There is a subtle aspect to this program that may have escaped your notice. Let's take a closer look.

Parts of Arrays Are Arrays

The C language embodies an unusual but powerful capability: it can treat parts of arrays as arrays. More specifically, each row of a two-dimensional array can be thought of as a one-dimensional array. This can be very useful if one wishes to rearrange the rows of a two-dimensional array, as we just did in the sortstr.c example.

Do you see anything unusual about the following statement from sortstr.c?

```
ptr[count++] = name[count];
```

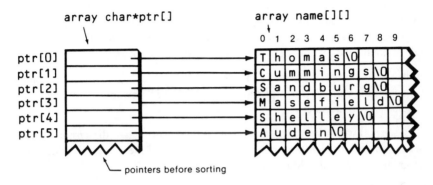

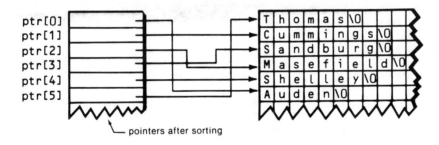

Figure 7.16. Sorting pointers to strings.

That's right: although the array name[][] is a two-dimensional array, we use only one subscript when we refer to it in this statement: name[count]. What does name[count] mean, if name[][] is a two-dimensional array?

Remember that we can think of a two-dimensional array as an array of arrays. In this case, the definition

```
char name[MAXNUM][MAXLEN];
```

can be thought of as setting up a one-dimensional array of MAXNUM elements, each of which is a one-dimensional array MAXLEN characters long. In other words, we have a one-dimensional array of MAXNUM strings. We refer to the elements of a one-dimensional array with a single subscript, as in name[count], where count can range up to MAXNUM. More specifically, name[0] is the address of the first string in the array, name[1] is the address of the second string, and so forth. Thus the expression name[count] makes sense and simplifies the coding of the program.

Double Indirection: Pointers to Pointers

The ability of the C language to treat part of an array as an array is actually a disguised version of another C topic, double indirection, or pointers that point to pointers. Being able to reference a pointer with a pointer gives C enormous power and flexibility in creating complex arrangements of data. As a hint of what's involved, let's look at an example of double indirection, derived from a two-dimensional array.

In the sortstr.c program, we dealt with parts of arrays as strings. This was in some ways easier than dealing with parts of arrays as arrays, which we'll now look at in a two-dimensional array of numbers.

We'll start off with a simple program that takes an existing two-dimensional array, adds a constant to each element, and prints the result. We'll use normal array notation for this program, so it should hold no surprises.

```
// double.c
// shows use of 2-dimensional arrays
#include <stdio.h>              // for printf()
#define ROWS 4
#define COLS 5

void main(void)
   {
   int table[ROWS][COLS] =      // array of arrays
            { { 13, 15, 17, 19, 21 },
              { 20, 22, 24, 26, 28 },
              { 31, 33, 35, 37, 39 },
              { 40, 42, 44, 46, 48 }  };
   int j, k;

   for(j=0; j<ROWS; j++)        // add constant to each element
      for(k=0; k<COLS; k++)
        table[j][k] = table[j][k] + 10;

   printf("\n");
   for(j=0; j<ROWS; j++)        // print out array
      {
      for (k=0; k<COLS; k++)
        printf("%d ", table[j][k] );
      printf("\n");
      }
   }  // end main()
```

Because the program adds a constant 10 to each element, the output looks like this:

```
23 25 27 29 31
30 32 34 36 38
41 43 45 47 49
50 52 54 56 58
```

Now, suppose we rewrite this program to use pointer notation instead of array notation. The question is, how do we write the expression table[j][k] in pointer notation? To do this, we make use of the fact that a two-dimensional array is an array of one-dimensional arrays, as shown in Figure 7.17.

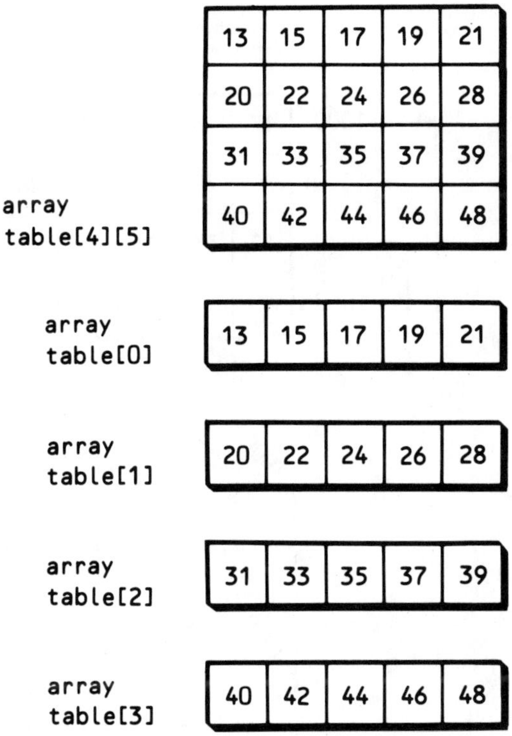

array
table[4][5]

13	15	17	19	21
20	22	24	26	28
31	33	35	37	39
40	42	44	46	48

array
table[0]

| 13 | 15 | 17 | 19 | 21 |

array
table[1]

| 20 | 22 | 24 | 26 | 28 |

array
table[2]

| 31 | 33 | 35 | 37 | 39 |

array
table[3]

| 40 | 42 | 44 | 46 | 48 |

Figure 7.17. Each row of an array is an array.

Let's figure out how to use pointers to refer to the fourth element in the third row of the array, or table[2][3], which is 37 (before the 10 is added).

First, the address of the entire array is table. Let's assume the array starts at address 1000 in memory, so table==1000. It's an integer array, so each element takes two bytes. There are five elements in each row, so each row takes 10 bytes. Thus each row starts 10 bytes further along than the last one. Because each row is a one-dimensional array, each of these one-dimensional arrays starts 10 bytes further along than the last one, as shown in the top part of Figure 7.18.

The compiler knows how many columns there are in the array, because we specified this in the array declaration, so it knows how to interpret the expression table+1: it takes the address of table (1000) and adds the number of bytes in a row (5 columns times 2 bytes per column, equaling 10 bytes). Thus `table+1` is interpreted as the address 1010. This is the address of the second one-dimensional array in the array, `table+2` is the address of the third such array, and so on. We're looking for an item in the third row, whose address is `table+2`, or 1020.

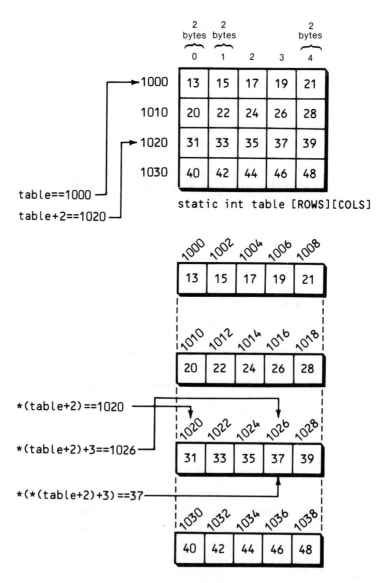

Figure 7.18. Pointing to element in two-dimensional array.

Now, how do we refer to the individual elements of a row? We've mentioned before that the address of an array is the same as the address of the first element in the array. For example, in the one-dimensional array `list[SIZE]`, `list` is the same as `&list[0]`. Again referring to Figure 7.18, we've already determined that the address of the array formed by the third row of `table[][]` is `table[2]`, or `table+2` in pointer notation. The address of the first element of this array is `&table[2][0]`, or `*(table+2)` in pointer notation. Both pointer expressions, `table+2` and `*(table+2)`, refer to the contents of the same address, 1020. Why use two different expressions for the same thing? The difference between `*(table+2)` and `table+2` is in the units of measurement. If you add 1 to `table+2` you get `table+3`, or the address of the fourth row of `table[][]`; you've added 10 bytes. If you add 1 to `*(table+2)`, however, you get the address of the next element in the row; you've added 2 bytes.

> An element of a two-dimensional array can be referenced with a pointer to a pointer.

Therefore, the address of the fourth element is `*(table+2)+3`. Finally, the *contents* of that element is `*(*(table+2)+3)`, which is 37. This expression is a pointer to a pointer.

In other words,

```
table[j][k] == *(*(table+j)+k)
```

We've figured out how to translate two-dimensional array notation into pointer notation. Now we can rewrite our program, incorporating this new notation.

```
// double2.c
// shows use of pointers on 2-dimensional arrays
#include <stdio.h>            // for printf()
#define ROWS 4
#define COLS 5

void main(void)
   {
   int table[ROWS][COLS] =   // array of arrays
           { { 13, 15, 17, 19, 21 },
             { 20, 22, 24, 26, 28 },
             { 31, 33, 35, 37, 39 },
             { 40, 42, 44, 46, 48 }  };
   int j, k;

   for(j=0; j<ROWS; j++)      // add constant to each element
      for(k=0; k<COLS; k++)
        *(*(table+j)+k) = *(*(table+j)+k) + 10;

   printf("\n");
   for(j=0; j<ROWS; j++)      // print out array
      {
```

```
        for (k=0; k<COLS; k++)
            printf("%d ", *(*(table+j)+k) );
        printf("\n");
        }
    }  // end main()
```

This version of the program will work just the same as the old one did.

The Rocketship Program

Let's look at a slightly more ambitious example that incorporates double indirection. This program models a very crude rocketship taking off. As a spectacular graphics display, the program leaves something to be desired (especially because we haven't learned how to clear the screen between pictures), but it does demonstrate how to manipulate array elements using pointers.

The program consists of a large loop. To cycle once through the loop, press any key. Each time through the loop, the program draws a line, representing the ground, consisting of five double lines (graphics character \xCD). It then draws the rocketship, defined in the program as four elements of a character array: a main body (\DB), a nose cone, and two engines (\x1E). After drawing the rocket, the rows of the array that contain the rocket are, in effect, rotated; each row moves up one character, and the top row is placed on the bottom. (Actually we don't rotate the array itself, as we'll see in a moment.) Then the array is printed again. The effect is of the rocketship rising from the ground, as shown in Figure 7.19.

Here's the listing for the program:

```
// move.c
// moves image on screen
#include <stdio.h>     // for printf()
#include <conio.h>     // for getche()
#define ROWS 10        // dimensions of image
#define COLS 5         //    to be rotated
#define HEIGHT 25      // height of screen in rows

void main(void)
    {
    int count, j, k;
    char *ptr[ROWS];                        // pointers to rows
    char *temp;                             // pointer storage
    char pict[ROWS][COLS] =                 // rocketship
            {   { 0,      0,      0,      0,      0      },
                { 0,      0,      0,      0,      0      },
                { 0,      0,      0,      0,      0      },
                { 0,      0,      0,      0,      0      },
                { 0,      0,      0,      0,      0      },
                { 0,      0,      0,      0,      0      },
                { 0,      0,      0,      0,      0      },
                { 0,      0,      0,      0,      0      },
```

```
                    { 0,      0,       '\x1E', 0,      0       },
                    { 0,             '\x1E', '\xDB', '\x1E', 0       }  };

   char gnd[] =                          // ground line
         { '\xCD', '\xCD', '\xCD', '\xCD', '\xCD', 0 };

   for(count=0; count<ROWS; count++)     // set up pointers
      *(ptr+count) = *(pict+count);

   for(count=0; count<ROWS-1; count++)
      {
      for(j=0; j<HEIGHT; j++)            // print blank lines
         printf("%c", '\n');
      for(j=0; j<ROWS; j++)              // print rocket
         {
         for(k=0; k<COLS; k++)
            printf("%c", *(*(ptr+j)+k) );
         printf("%c", '\n' );
         }
      printf("%s\n", gnd);               // print ground

      temp = *ptr;                       // save top row
      for(j=0; j<ROWS-1; j++)            // rotate pointers
         *(ptr+j) = *(ptr+j+1);          //    upward
      *(ptr+ROWS-1) = temp;              // top row to bottom
      getch();                           // wait for keypress
      }  // end for(count)
   }  // end move
```

Here's how the program works. We declare an array of pointers to characters.

```
char *ptr[ROWS];
```

In each of the elements of this array, we place the address of one row of the array pict[][] using the loop.

```
for(count=0; count<ROWS; count++)
   *(ptr+count) = *(pict+count);
```

We print the elements of the array as individual characters using two nested loops, a process we used in Chapter 6. In this case, however, we use pointer notation to refer to individual elements of the array, in the expression

```
printf("%c", *(*(ptr+j)+k) );
```

Notice that we don't actually refer to the array pict[][] itself but rather to the array of pointers, ptr[], that point to it.

To make the rocket appear to rise off the ground line, we in effect move the elements in each row of the array pict[][], upward one row at a time. If we actually moved all the array elements we would need to move all 50 characters in memory, and this would be time-consuming. Instead of moving the rows of the array, we simply move the pointers that point to these rows. There are only 10 pointers, so this is a much faster operation than moving 50 characters. (If we were trying to move an object wider than five characters, the speed advantage would be greater still.)

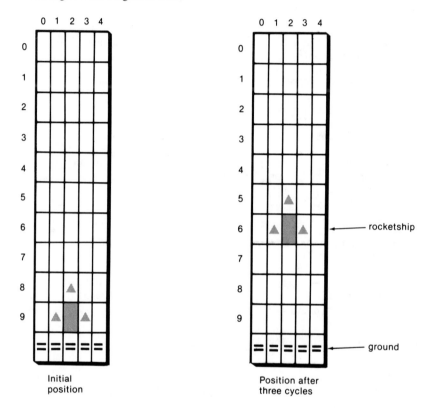

Figure 7.19. Rocketship rising from the ground.

The pointers are rotated in the array `ptr[]`: each element moves up one location, and the top element goes to the bottom. We store the top row, `ptr[0]`, in the pointer variable `temp`, then use a loop to move the contents of each row to the row whose subscript is one less than where it came from, and finally we insert the top element, stored in `temp`, back into the bottom row. (This is like the technique employed for sorting strings earlier in this chapter.) Figure 7.20 shows the pointers after three cycles through the loop; each pointer has moved up three rows in the array `*pict[ROWS]`.

Now when we print the array, we'll see that the rocket appears to have risen one character from the ground line each time through the loop. Actually, the array `pict[][]` remains unaltered, with the rocket still in the lowest position. However, by printing the rows of the array in a different order, the rocket appears to move.

Our method of clearing the screen is to print enough newlines to scroll the picture off the top. We'll see a better way to clear the screen in the next chapter.

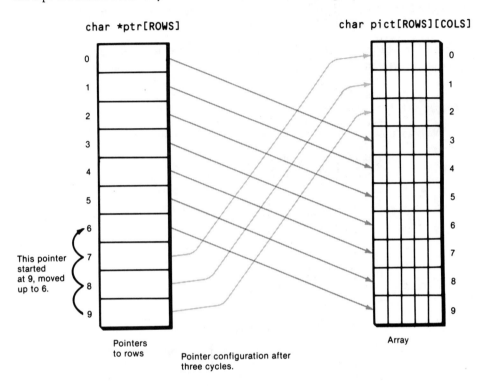

Figure 7.20. Rocketship pointer configuration.

Summary

This chapter has introduced the subject of pointers and has covered some of the less complex ways pointers can be used. We've seen how to declare pointer variables with such statements as int *ptr2; and we've learned how to refer to the values pointed to by pointers, using such expressions as *ptr2 (the asterisk having a different meaning in the two cases). We've used pointers to return multiple values from a function to the calling program and to permit a function to modify values contained in the calling program, with the use of expressions like *ptrx=*ptr+10.

The second major topic we covered in the chapter was the relationship of pointers to arrays. We saw how to reference individual array elements using pointer notation and how to perform arithmetic on pointers. We've seen that pointer variables can be modified but that pointer constants—the addresses of data structures—can't.

We've investigated the use of pointers with strings, seeing how some string library functions return pointers, and we've explored the uses that can be made of such functions. We've also learned how to initialize strings using pointers instead of arrays and the benefits of this approach.

Finally we've learned how to use pointer notation to refer to the elements of a two-dimensional array, and we've seen how this relates to the idea of a pointer to a pointer.

Questions

1. Why are pointers sometimes found to be difficult to understand?

   a. They point to data beyond our control.
   b. They use the same symbol to refer to two different things.
   c. The idea of indirection isn't used in some languages.
   d. They require a knowledge of quantum mechanics.

2. Which of these are reasons for using pointers?

   a. To manipulate parts of arrays
   b. To refer to key words such as `loop` and `if`
   c. To return more than one value from a function
   d. To refer to particular programs more conveniently

3. True or false: the address of an array is a pointer constant.

4. True or false: passing the addresses of arrays to functions is beyond the scope of this book.

5. True or false: passing a value to a function places the address of that value in the function's private memory space.

6. For a function to return more than one value, it must first be passed the addresses of the variables to be returned. This is because

   a. The function must always contain the same amount of numbers, whether addresses or values.
   b. The addresses are actually a code that is deciphered into values by the function.
   c. The function needs to know where to find library routines.
   d. The function needs to know where to put the values it returns.

7. If we call a function with the statement blotch(&white,&black), what purpose do &white and &black serve?

    a. They're integer values we're passing to the function.
    b. They're the addresses of the function and the calling program.
    c. They're the addresses of the variables where we want values returned or modified in the calling program.
    d. They're the addresses of library routines needed by the function.

8. To return more than one value from a function, we must pass the function the _____ of the values we want returned; then, in the function, we must first _____ pointers to hold these values, and finally we access the values using _____.

9. Which is the correct way to define a pointer?

    a. int_ptr x;
    b. int *ptr;
    c. *int ptr;
    d. *x;

10. Which are correct ways to refer to the variable ch, assuming the address of ch has been assigned to the pointer fingerch?

    a. *fingerch;
    b. int *fingerch;
    c. *finger;
    d. ch
    e. *ch

11. In the expression float *fptr; what has type float?

    a. The variable fptr
    b. The address of fptr
    c. The variable pointed to by fptr
    d. None of the above

12. Assuming that the address of the variable var has been assigned to the pointer variable pointvar, write an expression that doesn't use var and that will divide var by 10.

13. Assuming that the address of vox has been assigned to the pointer variable invox, which of the following expressions are correct?

    a. vox == &invox
    b. vox == *invox
    c. invox == *vox
    d. invox == &vox

14. When a function is called using &x as a parameter, where is the value of &x placed?

15. What statement must be added to the following program to make it work correctly?

```
void main(void)
    {
    int j, *ptrj;
    *ptrj = 3;
    }
```

16. Assuming we want to read in a value for x and the address of x has been assigned to ptrx, does this statement look all right?

```
scanf("%d", *ptrx);
```

17. Assuming that spread[] is a one-dimensional array of type int, which of the following refers to the value of the third element in the array?

    a. *(spread+2)
    b. *(spread+4)
    c. spread+4
    d. spread+2

18. Suppose an array has been defined as

```
int arr[3];
```

Can you use the expression arr++?

19. What will the following program do when executed?

```
void main(void)
    {
    int arr[] = { 4, 5, 6 };
    int j;
    for(j=0; j<3; j++)
        printf("%d   ", *(arr+j) );
    }
```

20. In the preceding program, the plus sign in the expression arr+j means to add j times _____ bytes, to arr.

21. What will the following program do when executed?

```
void main(void)
    {
    int arr[] = { 4, 5, 6 };
    int j;
    for(j=0; j<3; j++)
        printf("%d   ", arr+j );
    }
```

22. What will the following program do when executed?

```
void main(void)
   {
   int arr[] = { 4, 5, 6 };
   int j, *ptr;
   ptr = arr;
   for(j=0; j<3; j++)
      printf("%d  ", *ptr++ );
   }
```

23. Are the following statements equivalent?

```
char errmsg[] = "Error!";
char *errmsg = "Error!";
```

24. One difference between using array notation to define a group of strings and using pointer notation is that in array notation each string occupies _____ of memory, but when pointer notation is used each string occupies _____ of memory.

25. Given the declaration

```
char s7[] = "I come not to bury Caesar";
```

what will the following statements cause to be printed?

```
printf("%s", s7 );
printf("%s", &s7[0] );
printf("%s", s7+11 );
```

26. When you define a string using pointer notation and the string is 10 characters long, _____ bytes are set aside in memory. (Note: this isn't as easy as it looks.)

27. True or false: every column of a two-dimensional array can be considered to be another two-dimensional array.

28. Given the following array definition:

```
int arr7[2][3] = {  { 10, 11, 12 },
                    { 13, 14, 15 }  };
```

refer to the element occupied by the number 14 in array notation and then in pointer notation.

29. If you want to exchange two rows in a two-dimensional array, the fastest way is to

    a. Exchange the elements of the two rows
    b. Exchange the addresses of each element in the two rows
    c. Set the address of one row equal to the address of the other, and vice versa
    d. Store the addresses of the rows in an array of pointers and exchange the pointers

30. How do you refer to `arr7[x][y]` using pointer notation?

Exercises

In the following exercises, use pointer notation wherever possible.

1. Write a function, and a program to test it, that will place a zero in each of three variables in the calling program.

2. Write a function, and a program to test it, that will place a zero in each element of an array passed to it from the calling program.

3. Write a function, and a program to test it, that will change a string to the null string. The string is defined in the calling program.

Keyboard and Cursor

- Extended keyboard codes
- Turbo C++ text-window functions
- Command-line arguments
- Redirection of input and output

In this chapter we're going to change our focus from the C language itself to C's interaction with the PC computer. This doesn't mean that we've covered everything there is to know about C; we'll take up other important aspects of the language in later chapters. You now know enough, however, to begin exploring some of the features of the PC computer family and putting C to work in real-world situations.

We'll cover a variety of topics in this chapter, all connected by their focus on characters: those typed on the keyboard and those displayed on the screen. First we'll discuss extended character codes, which enable a program to read the function keys, cursor control keys, and special key combinations. Then we'll investigate the Turbo C++ text-window functions, which permit sophisticated manipulation of text on the screen. Almost all applications programs—word processors, database programs, and even games—need to make use of these capabilities to provide a more sophisticated level of interaction with the user.

At the end of the chapter we'll explain command-line arguments: arguments typed on the command line when you call your program from DOS. We'll also discuss redirection, which can be used to give even simple programs the ability to read and write files. As we go along, we'll discuss a variety of new C library functions.

Extended Keyboard Codes

We've already seen that the keyboard generates the usual ASCII codes for letters, numbers, and punctuation. Such keys all generate one-byte ASCII codes.

However, there are a great many keys and key combinations not represented by this one-byte character set. For instance, the function keys, F1 to F12, aren't represented, nor are the cursor control keys on the numeric keypad. How does a program determine when these keys are being pressed?

The PC provides a second set of 256 keys and key combinations by using an *extended code*. This code consists of two bytes; the first byte is 0 and the second byte is a number indicating the particular key or key combination. When a key that isn't in the normal character set—the F1 key, for example—is pressed, it first sends a 0 to the keyboard buffer and then the specific code. (The keyboard buffer is a temporary storage area where characters typed at the keyboard are stored until they're read by a program.) A program that expects to read extended codes checks for a character with the value 0. If it finds one, it knows the next character will be an extended code, with a completely different interpretation than the normal ASCII code.

> Extended keyboard codes use two characters, the first of which has an ASCII value of 0.

Because no character is represented by 0 in the normal ASCII character set, there is no confusion when this character is received; it always indicates an extended code will follow. Figure 8.1 shows the format of the extended code.

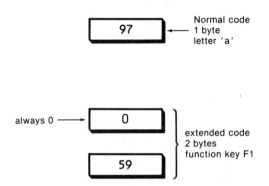

Figure 8.1. Normal and extended codes.

Exploring the Extended Codes

Here's a program that enables us to explore these extended keyboard codes:

```
// kbdtest.c
// prints code of keyboard key
#include <stdio.h>                    // for printf()
#include <conio.h>                    // for getch()

void main(void)
   {
   unsigned char key, key2;

   printf("\nPress any key\n");
   while ( (key=getch()) != '\r' )   // read keyboard
     if( key == 0 )                   // if extended code,
       {
         key2 = getch();              // read second code
         printf("%3d %3d\n", key, key2);
       }
       else
           printf("%3d\n", key);      // not extended code
   }  // end main()
```

This program prints the code for any key pressed: either the normal one-byte ASCII character code or the two-byte extended code. We don't want to echo the character typed, because there is no printable equivalent for the extended codes, so we use the function getch(), which works just like getche(), except that the character isn't printed on the screen.

In the while test expression, the program reads the first code. If it's 0, the program knows it's dealing with an extended code, so it reads the second part of the code, using getch() again, and prints the numerical value of both parts. If the first part isn't 0, the program concludes that it is simply a normal character and prints its value. Note that type unsigned char is needed to hold values greater than 127. Press the Enter key to exit the program.

Here's a sample run:

```
0   59
97
0   75
```

The first code shown here results from pressing the F1 function key, the second is simply a lowercase 'a', and the third is the Left Arrow (on the number 4 of the numeric keypad). Typing in this program and experimenting with it will provide a variety of insights about the extended codes available.

Table 8.1 shows the extended codes that can be obtained by typing a single key. The table shows the second byte of the code; the first byte is always 0. Many more codes can be accessed by using the Alt, Ctrl, or Shift keys in combination with another key, as shown in Table 8.2. These two-key codes are used less often than the single-key variety, but they do provide an amazing variety of choices for programs that need them.

Table 8.1. One-key extended codes.

Second Byte (Decimal)	Key that Generates Extended Code
59	F1
60	F2
61	F3
62	F4
63	F5
64	F6
65	F7
66	F8
67	F9
68	F10
133	F11
134	F12

Second Byte (Decimal)	Key that Generates Extended Code
71	Home
72	Up Arrow
73	PgUp
75	Left Arrow
77	Right Arrow
79	End
80	Down Arrow
81	PgDn
82	Ins
83	Del

Table 8.2. Two-key extended codes.

Second Byte (Decimal)	Keys that Generate Extended Code
15	Shift Tab
16 to 25	Alt Q, W, E, R, T, Y, U, I, O, P
30 to 38	Alt A, S, D, F, G, H, J, K, L
44 to 50	Alt Z, X, C, V, B, N, M
84 to 93	Shift F1 to F10
135, 136	Shift F11, F12
94 to 103	Ctrl F1 to F10
137, 138	Ctrl F11, F12
104 to 113	Alt F1 to F10
139, 140	Alt F11, F12
114	Ctrl PrtSc (start and stop printer echo)
115	Ctrl Left Arrow
116	Ctrl Right Arrow

continues

Table 8.2. continued

Second Byte (Decimal)	Keys that Generate Extended Code
117	Ctrl End
118	Ctrl PgDn
119	Ctrl Home
120 to 131	Alt 1, 2, 3, 4, 5, 6, 7, 8, 9, 0, –, =
132	Ctrl PgUp

Interpreting the Extended Codes

A common approach to writing C functions to interpret the extended codes is to use the switch statement, as we do in the following demonstration:

```c
// extend.c
// tests extended codes
#include <stdio.h>              // for printf()
#include <conio.h>             // for getch()

void main(void)
    {
    unsigned char key, key2;

    while( (key=getch()) != '\r' )    // read keyboard
        if( key == 0 )                // if extended code,
            {
            key2 = getch();          // read second code
            switch(key2)
                {
                case 59:
                    printf("\nFunction key 1"); break;
                case 60:
                    printf("\nFunction key 2"); break;
                case 75:
                    printf("\nLeft arrow"); break;
                case 77:
                    printf("\nRight arrow"); break;
                default:
                    printf("\nSome other extended code");
                }  // end switch
            }  // end if
        else
            printf("\nNormal code: %3d=%c", key, key);
    }  // end main()
```

This program is similar to kbdtest.c, but it uses `switch` to analyze and print interpretations of some of the codes. We'll be using this same format in a variety of programs later in this chapter.

Notice that we've placed more than one statement on the same line in this program:

```
printf("Function key 1\n"); break;
```

It is generally easier to read (and debug) a C program when only one statement per line is used, but in the `switch` construct, statements are often doubled up this way to save space and provide a cleaner format.

Now that we've introduced the extended keyboard codes, let's see how they're used in a typical situation: for cursor control.

Text-Window Functions

Classic C-language text output functions, such as `printf()` and `puts()`, allow you to display characters on the screen. However, these functions are based on the old teletype-oriented idea that each new line of text will be displayed directly below the last one. They don't allow you to control the position of text on the screen (except in rudimentary ways like tabbing along a line or issuing a bunch of linefeeds). Also, they don't allow you to take advantage of the capabilities of modern displays, such as using text in different colors.

To provide a more modern text display technology, Borland includes in Turbo C++ a group of library routines called the text-window functions. Among other capabilities, these functions allow you to control the cursor position, specify text and background colors, and define windows (rectangles) on the screen that act as boundaries for text output.

The text-window functions provide many of the advantages of a graphics display, such as color and the ability (using graphics characters) to draw simple shapes like boxes. Also, because the text-window functions operate entirely in character mode (addressing 25 times 80 or 2000 character positions), they're faster and easier to program than true graphics functions (which address—in a VGA display—640 times 480 or 307,200 pixels). We'll discuss graphics functions in Chapter 10, "Turbo C++ Graphics."

We should mention that a few computers have video adapters that aren't completely compatible with the IBM industry standard. If this is the case on your system, you may want to add another line to your program.

```
directvideo=0;    // use ROM BIOS routines for screen access
```

The `directvideo` variable determines whether the system writes directly to the video memory, which requires the display adapters to be completely IBM compatible, or whether it writes to the screen using ROM BIOS routines. The ROM BIOS approach works on almost all machines but is much slower. The default setting, `directvideo=1`, causes the system to use direct access to video memory, so if this approach works on your computer—which it probably will—you don't need to worry about setting this variable. If you have trouble, set it to 0.

Cursor Position

Our first example uses graphics characters to draw crude pictures on the screen. It demonstrates cursor control using the text-window functions. It also uses the extended codes described in the last section so that the four arrow keys can be used to move the cursor left, right, up, and down. (Don't forget to toggle the NumLock key to activate the arrow keys.)

```
// draw.c
// moves cursor on screen, leaves trail
#include <conio.h>        // for getch(), putch()
#define L_ARRO 75         // extended codes for arrow keys
#define R_ARRO 77
#define U_ARRO 72
#define D_ARRO 80
#define ACROSS 205        // horizontal line
#define UPDOWN 186        // vertical line

void main(void)
   {
   char ch;               // graphics character
   int x=40, y=12;        // screen coordinates (screen center)

   clrscr();              // clear screen
   gotoxy(x, y);          // set cursor in middle
   while ( getch() == 0 ) // quit if not extended code
      {
      switch( getch() )   // get extended code
         {
         case L_ARRO : x—; ch=ACROSS; break;  // go left
         case R_ARRO : x++; ch=ACROSS; break; // go right
         case U_ARRO : y—; ch=UPDOWN; break;  // go up
         case D_ARRO : y++; ch=UPDOWN; break; // go down
         } // end switch
      gotoxy(x, y);       // set cursor to new position
      putch(ch);          // print appropriate character
      } // end while
   } // end main()
```

The program begins by using the text-window function clrscr() to clear the screen. We'll emphasize the Turbo C++ text-window functions by summarizing them in boxes.

Clear Text Window
```
void clrscr(void);
```

This function takes no arguments; it merely clears the screen (actually the text window; more on this in a moment). Like all text-window functions, `clrscr()` requires you to #include the conio.h header file.

Next we use the text-window function `gotoxy()` to place the cursor in the center of the screen. This function takes as parameters the column and row (x and y) coordinates for the new cursor position. (As we'll see later, these coordinates are measured relative to the text window rather than the screen, but here they're the same.) On an 80 by 25 screen, the X coordinate ranges from 1 to 80, and the Y coordinate from 1 to 25.

```
void gotoxy(int x, int y);
       x        // x-coordinate of cursor (1 to 80)
       y        // y-coordinate of cursor (1 to 25)
```

The important part of draw.c is a `switch` statement embedded in a `while` loop. Within the loop we read the keyboard twice, looking for extended codes that represent the arrow keys. When we find one, we adjust the cursor coordinates x and y and also set the character to be printed: a vertical line for the Up and Down Arrow keys and a horizontal line for the Left and Right Arrow keys. The `putch()` function is used to draw these characters. It is analogous to `getch()` except that it outputs a character rather than reading one. The result of playing with the program is shown in Figure 8.2.

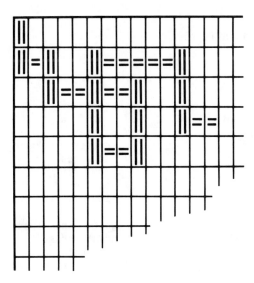

Figure 8.2. Session with draw.c.

Windows

A major purpose of the Turbo C++ text-window functions is to permit the use of windows. A window (in this context, at least) is simply a rectangular area of the screen that forms a boundary for video output. You've probably seen similar windows used in graphical interfaces such as Microsoft Windows and the Macintosh, although these are graphics-based rather than character-based windows. Turbo C++ itself uses character-based windows in its IDE; there is typically an Edit window and a Message window on the screen at the same time.

The text-window functions make it easy to manipulate text in a window instead of in the entire screen. For instance, if you're typing a line of text into a window, the cursor will be confined by the left and right edges of the window, rather than by the edges of the screen as it normally is.

Here's a short program that demonstrates a window and introduces several text-window functions. It sets up a window, and then repeatedly writes a word into the window until the window is full. Additional words cause the window contents to scroll upward.

```
// window.c
// tests text-window functions
#include <conio.h>               // for text-window functions
#include <dos.h>                 // for delay()
#define LEFT    10               // define window
#define TOP      8
#define RIGHT   52
#define BOT     21
#define HEIGHT (BOT-TOP+1)

void main(void)
   {
   int j;

   window(LEFT, TOP, RIGHT, BOT);   // specify window
   textcolor(RED);                  // set text color
   textbackground(GREEN);           // set text background
   for(j=0; j<100; j++)             // 100 words
      {
      cputs("Greetings ");          // print word
      delay(100);                   // slow down the loop
      }
   gotoxy(15, 8);                   // go to window center
   cputs("   THE  END   ");         // print phrase
   gotoxy(1, HEIGHT);               // cursor to bottom line
   getch();                         // wait for key press
   }
```

The window() function defines an area of the screen as the text window, using the left and right columns and the top and bottom rows as parameters.

Define Text Window
```
void window( int left, int top, int right, int bottom );
        left       // coordinates of window
        top        // on 80x25 screen,
        right      // range is from 1 to 80
        bottom     // and 1 to 25
```

If you use appropriate text output functions, such as cputs(), all the text you output will be confined inside the last text window you define with window(). Note that the default text window dimensions are the screen itself (1, 1, 80, 25), so if you don't use window() at all, you can write to the entire screen.

Assuming you have a color display, the next two functions, textcolor() and textbackground(), set the color of the characters to red and each character's background color to green. The symbols RED and GREEN are defined in the file conio.h, so there is no need to define them in the program. There are 16 text colors and 8 background colors. Following are the colors and their numeric equivalents.

Number	Name	Foreground	Background
0	BLACK	X	X
1	BLUE	X	X
2	GREEN	X	X
3	CYAN	X	X
4	RED	X	X
5	MAGENTA	X	X
6	BROWN	X	X
7	LIGHTGRAY	X	X
8	DARKGRAY	X	
9	LIGHTBLUE	X	
10	LIGHTGREEN	X	
11	LIGHTCYAN	X	
12	LIGHTRED	X	
13	LIGHTMAGENTA	X	
14	YELLOW	X	
15	WHITE	X	

The functions used to specify these colors take only one parameter—the color itself. Either the name or the numerical equivalent can be used.

Set Text Color
```
void textcolor(int color);
color    // from 0 to 15, numbers or constants
```

Set Background Color
```
void textbackground(int color);
        color        // from 0 to 7, numbers or constants
```

The textcolor() function can specify the blinking attribute in addition to the color if the number 128 is added to the numeric color value or if the constant BLINK is added to the color constant, as in RED+BLINK.

Note that the graphics functions examined so far return type void. Some graphics functions return an error code if they can't perform their mission, but these don't. If you give these functions an incorrect value, the operation isn't carried out, but your program has no way to discover this.

The cputs() function displays a string at the current cursor position.

Display String In Text Window
```
int cputs(const char *str);
str      // string to be displayed
// return value is last character printed
```

Once the colors are specified, the program writes the word Greetings 100 times. Because a window has been defined, the cputs() function automatically starts at the top of the window rather than at the top of the screen. This function is similar to puts() but works with text windows. It starts each line at the left edge of the window and wraps to the next line when it reaches the right edge. When it reaches the bottom of the window, it scrolls the contents of the window upward.

The delay caused by the delay() function, which pauses the program the number of milliseconds given it as a parameter, makes this action easier to see as the program runs. The delay() function requires the dos.h header file. The output of the program is shown in Figure 8.3.

Note that coordinates for gotoxy() are measured relative to the current text window. Thus the (15, 8) used in the program means 15 columns from the left edge of the window and 8 rows down from the top of the window. This is roughly the middle of the window. Once situated there, the program uses cputs() to write the phrase THE END.

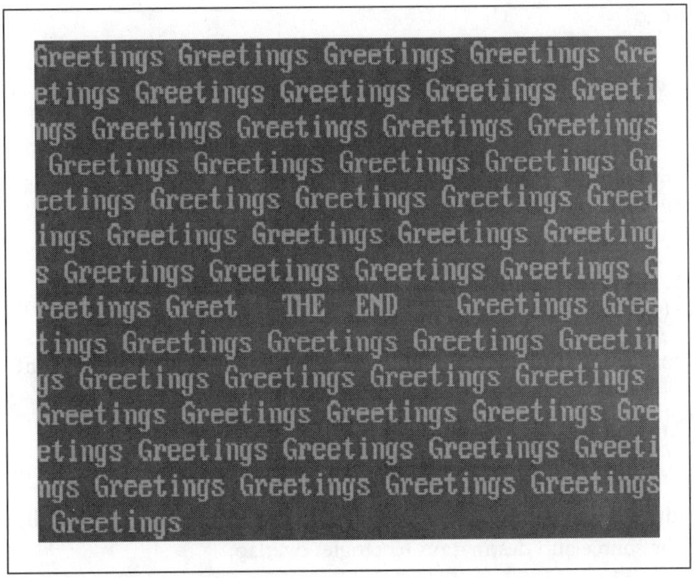

Figure 8.3. Output of the window.c program.

If we left the cursor in the middle of the window when the program terminated, the DOS prompt might overwrite part of the window, so the last statement in the program moves the cursor to the bottom of the window. What's the coordinate of the bottom of the window? It isn't BOT (21) used to define the window, because this is measured from the top of the screen. Rather it's the height of the window, which is BOT-TOP+1. Confusion between window and screen coordinates is a common source of errors in character-graphics programs.

Moving Text

Another text-window function, movetext(), copies a rectangular area of text from one part of the screen to another. The next example program creates a window, fills it with text, and then moves it to another location using this function.

```
// movetext.c
// moves text to memory and back
#include <conio.h>              // for text-window functions
#include <dos.h>                // for delay()
#define LEFT        26          // define window
#define TOP          7
#define RIGHT       65
#define BOT         20
#define DESLEFT      1          // destination NW corner
#define DESTOP       1
#define NUMCOLORS   16          // number of text colors
```

```
void main(void)
   {
   int j;

   textbackground(BLACK);              // clear screen to black
   clrscr();
   window(LEFT, TOP, RIGHT, BOT);      // specify window
   textbackground(GREEN);             // clear window to green
   for(j=0; j<98; j++)                 // display 98 words
      {
      textcolor(j % NUMCOLORS);        // change color every word
      cputs("Greetings ");             // print word
      }
   delay(3000);                        // delay for dramatic effect
                                       // move window
   movetext(LEFT, TOP, RIGHT, BOT, DESLEFT, DESTOP);
   getch();                            // wait for keypress
   }
```

The output of the program is shown in Figure 8.4. The move is successfully completed even though the source and destination rectangles overlap.

The movetext() function operates on absolute screen coordinates, not window coordinates. The function returns a 0 value if the operation wasn't successful, although we don't make use of that feature in this program. This error return can be caused by using coordinates outside the window area. We don't check for the function's return value in the example, but a serious graphics program should do this. The program could then alert the user or take whatever steps are appropriate.

Copy Text Rectangle to Different Screen Location
```
int movetext(int left, int top, int right, int bottom,
             int leftDest, topDest )
left        // coordinates of rectangle to be moved
top
right
bottom
leftDest    // upper-left corner of destination
topDest
```

You might use movetext() to move a text-filled window around on the screen when the user wants to reposition it.

The clrscr() function clears the current text window and fills it with the background color previously set with textbackground(). It also places the cursor in the upper-left corner.

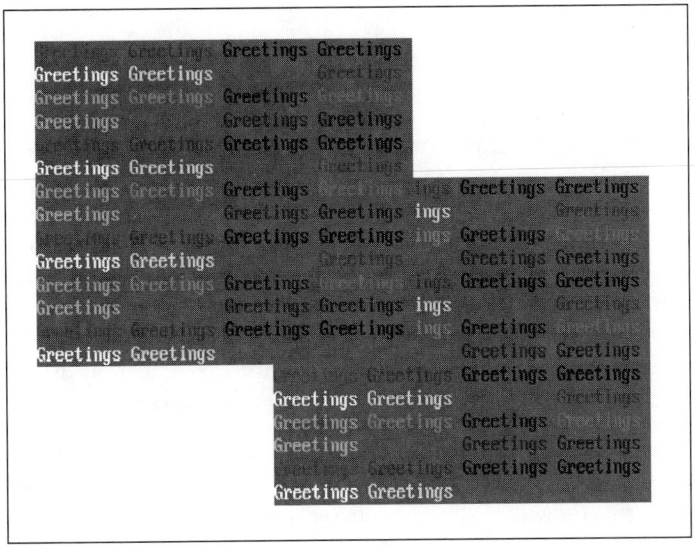

Figure 8.4. Output of the movetext.c program.

Saving and Restoring Screen Text

The text in a text window can be saved in memory and later restored to the same or a different location on the screen. This is useful in a variety of circumstances. You may want to put a small window containing a message on top of existing text on the screen and later remove it, restoring the existing text to its previous state. You may also have noticed how some applications, including Turbo C++ itself, save the existing screen before they begin and restore it when the user exits. Our next example does the same thing, using the functions gettext() and puttext().

```c
// savetext.c
// demonstrates saving and restoring screen text
#include <conio.h>            // needed for text-window functions
#define LEFT    1             // define entire screen
#define TOP     1
#define RIGHT   80
#define BOT     25
int buff[80][25];            // buffer for screen contents

void main(void)
   {
   int x, y, j;

   getch();                  // hold old screen until key press
   gettext(LEFT, TOP, RIGHT, BOT, buff);  // save old screen
   x = wherex();             // save old cursor position
   y = wherey();
```

275

```
clrscr();                    // clear screen
for( j=0; j<300; j++ )       // fill screen with text
   cputs("Turbo C++  ");
getch();                     // hold new image until key press

puttext(LEFT, TOP, RIGHT, BOT, buff);  // restore old screen
gotoxy(x, y-1);              // restore cursor position
getch();                     // hold old image until key press
}
```

This program first saves the contents of the entire screen to a memory buffer buff, using gettext(). The buffer requires two bytes for every screen character, so we use an integer data type, placing one character in each integer array element. We use a two-dimensional array, with the width and height of the entire screen as array dimensions. (A one-dimensional array 80 by 25, or 2000 integers, works just as well.)

The function takes as arguments the screen coordinates of the area to be saved and the address in memory to store it.

Copy Text from Screen to Memory
```
int gettext(int left, int top, int right, int bottom, void* addr);
left      // coordinates of rectangle to be copied
top
right
bottom
addr;     // address of buffer to hold text
```

The puttext() function is similar to gettext(), except that it moves text from memory back to the screen.

Copy Text from Memory to Screen
```
int puttext(int left, int top, int right, int bottom, void* addr);
left;     // coordinates of rectangle to be copied
top;
right;
bottom;
addr;     // address of buffer holding text
```

The type void *, used for the address of the data buffer, specifies a pointer of any kind of data. Thus your buffer can be of type char, or, if you prefer, of type int.

The program also saves the location of the cursor and, before exiting, restores it to its original position with gotoxy(). The cursor location is obtained with the functions wherex() and wherey(). These record the x and y coordinates of the cursor.

Returns Horizontal Cursor Position
```
int wherex(void)     // returns column number (1 to 80)
```

Returns Vertical Cursor Position
```
int wherey(void)     // returns row number (1 to 25)
```

The type void here means there are no arguments to these functions.

When the program runs, it fills the entire screen with the words Turbo C++. When the user presses a key, the program restores the previously saved screen contents using puttext() and exits. Restoring the old screen contents when terminating lends a professional effect to any program.

Drawing a Box with Characters

When displaying text you'll find many occasions to draw boxes. Boxes can be used to surround text for emphasis or to create graphic elements like dialog boxes and menus. (Later in this chapter, we'll see an example in which a box is used to create a menu.) Boxes in such contexts are usually created by drawing a line around the box with graphics characters.

Drawing such a box isn't trivial in character mode, because separate graphics characters must be used for each of the four corners and for the horizontal and vertical lines that make up the border of the box. Our next example shows how this is accomplished.

```
// linebox.c
// draws a box with a single line around it
#include <conio.h>              // for text-window functions

void main(void)
    {                           // box location and size
    int left=10, top=5, width=20, height=7;
    int j;                      // loop variable
    char string[81];            // utility string

    textbackground(BLACK);      // clear entire screen to black
    clrscr();
                                // define box-size window
```

```
window(left, top, left+width-1, top+height-1);
textbackground(GREEN);        // clear window to green
clrscr();
textcolor(RED);               // red outline on green

// add line so chars on bottom line won't cause scroll
window(left, top, left+width-1, top+height);

// draw top and bottom lines, with corners
for(j=1; j<width-1; j++)      // make string of
    string[j] = '\xC4';       //     horizontal characters
string[width] = '\0';         // end the string
string[0] = '\xDA';           // insert upper-left corner
string[width-1] = '\xBF';     // insert upper-right corner
gotoxy(1, 1);                 // display top line
cputs(string);
string[0] = '\xC0';           // insert lower-left corner
string[width-1] = '\xD9';     // insert lower-right corner
gotoxy(1, height);            // display bottom line
cputs(string);

// draw vertical lines on left and right
for(j=2; j<height; j++)       // for each row
    {
    gotoxy(1, j);             // on the left end,
    putch('\xB3');            // draw vertical character
    gotoxy(width, j);         // on the right end,
    putch('\xB3');            // draw vertical character
    }
}   // end main()
```

We first clear the area of the box using the window(), textbackground(), and clrscr() functions to define a window the size of the box and clear it to solid green. Then we prepare a string consisting of the characters for the top corners and horizontal line segments. This string is displayed on the top row of the box. A similar string but with different corners is displayed on the bottom row. Finally, in a for loop, we insert the character for the vertical line segments on the left and right side of the box.

Because you can't draw characters on a window's last line without scrolling the contents of the window, we make the window one row larger than the box before drawing characters in it.

Note that the putch() function, like getch() and getche(), works with text windows. All the functions that use the conio.h header file are aware of text windows and will confine their output to the window. Functions with other header files are clueless about text windows.

A Mini-Editor

Let's put the functions we've learned about so far, and some new ones, into a small application. With this program you can type text into a window and perform various editing functions.

The text you type wraps at the right edge of the window. If you type past the bottom of the window, the text scrolls upward. You can position the cursor anywhere in the window with the arrow keys.

The program introduces several new text-window functions. A new line can be inserted in a window at the current cursor position using `insline()`, and an existing line can be deleted using `delline()`. In this program, the Ins and Del keys are used to insert and delete lines.

Insert Text Line in Window
```
void insline(void)
```

Delete Text Line in Window
```
void delline(void)
```

Two other new functions used in the program are `highvideo()` and `lowvideo()`. The first sets the text to intensified, and the second restores it to normal. These options can be selected using the Alt H and Alt L key combinations.

Change to Intensified Text
```
void highvideo(void)
```

Change to Normal Text
```
void lowvideo(void)
```

We've also used the `gettext()` and `puttext()` functions to create an undo feature for our editor. Before a line is either inserted or deleted, the program saves the contents of the screen. Then, if the user decides that the insertion or deletion is a mistake, pressing the Alt U key combination restores the previous state of the screen.

Finally, if you're using a color display, you can change the text color by pressing the Alt C key combination followed by a single digit representing the color. (This gives you the first 9 of 15 colors.) Text typed after the selection will be in the new color.

Here's the listing:

```c
// ezedit.c
// mini editor works in window
#include <conio.h>              // needed for text-window functions
#define LEFT    10             // left side of window
#define TOP      8             // top of window
#define RIGHT   50             // right side of window
#define BOT     21             // bottom of window
#define WIDTH   (RIGHT-LEFT+1) // width of window
#define HEIGHT  (BOT-TOP+1)    // height of window
#define TRUE     1
#define ESC     27             // escape key
#define L_ARRO 75              // cursor control keys
#define R_ARRO 77
#define U_ARRO 72
#define D_ARRO 80
#define INS     82             // other extended code keys
#define DEL     83
#define ALT_H   35
#define ALT_L   38
#define ALT_C   46
#define ALT_U   22
int buff [WIDTH] [HEIGHT];     // buffer for undo

void main(void)
    {
    int x, y;
    char key;

    textbackground(BLACK);              // clear screen to black
    clrscr();
    window( LEFT, TOP, RIGHT, BOT );    // define window
    textbackground(BLUE);               // clear window to blue
    clrscr();
    x = 1; y = 1;                       // position cursor

    while( (key=getch()) != ESC )       // if [Esc], exit loop
        {
        if(key == 0)                    // if extended code,
            {
            switch(getch())             // read second character
                {
                case L_ARRO:            // move cursor left
                    if(x > 1)
                        gotoxy(-x, y);
                    break;
```

```
            case R_ARRO:              // move cursor right
               if(x < WIDTH)
                  gotoxy(++x, y);
               break;
            case U_ARRO:              // move cursor up
               if(y > 1)
                  gotoxy(x, —y);
               break;
            case D_ARRO:              // move cursor down
               if(y < HEIGHT)
                  gotoxy(x, ++y);
               break;
            case INS:                 // insert new line
               gettext( LEFT, TOP, RIGHT, BOT, buff );
               insline();
               break;
            case DEL:                 // delete line
               gettext( LEFT, TOP, RIGHT, BOT, buff );
               delline();
               break;
            case ALT_H:               // intensified text
               highvideo();
               break;
            case ALT_L:               // normal text
               lowvideo();
               break;
            case ALT_C:               // change text color
               textcolor( getch()-'0' );
               break;
            case ALT_U:               // undo: restore window
               puttext( LEFT, TOP, RIGHT, BOT, buff );
               break;
            }  // end switch
         }  // end if
      else                         // not extended code
         {
         putch(key);               // print normal char
         x = wherex();             // update cursor
         y = wherey();
         }  // end else
      }  // end while
   }  // end main()
```

If the user presses a key with an extended code, the program uses a switch statement to figure out what the code is and takes action accordingly. However, because the program defines a window, all the screen output is confined to the window. The coordinates x and y measure the cursor's position relative to the window edges.

If a normal character (not an extended code) is pressed, the putch() function will display it. This function confines its text display to inside the window, but in so doing, it will move the cursor either one character to the right or to the beginning of the next line.

To make sure it keeps track of the cursor's location, the program reads its coordinates after every use of putch(), using the wherex() and wherey() functions.

A Menu-Selection Example

You've probably been intrigued by the graphic user interface (GUI) used by Turbo C++ and many other programs. It employs pull-down menus, dialog boxes, and windows to create a user interface that is much easier and more intuitive than older programs that require you to type obscure commands.

Our next example models part of such a GUI: a pull-down menu. When it's first started, the program displays a menu with five items: Open, Close, Save, Print, and Quit. By operating the Up Arrow and Down Arrow keys, the user can cause any of these items to be highlighted (displayed in a different color). If the user presses the Enter key while a particular item is highlighted, an action corresponding to that item will be performed. In this program the action for four of the items is the same: the name of the item selected is printed on the bottom line of the screen. Of course in a real application, more substantive actions would follow from the menu selections. The fifth item, Quit, behaves just as it does in more serious programs; selecting it causes the program to terminate.

This program is somewhat more complicated than those we've seen before. To make it conceptually easier to follow, we've divided it into several functions. In main() a switch statement routes program control to different routines, depending on what key was pressed by the user. An external variable vpos keeps track of what menu item is currently selected. Program statements like

```
vpos = (vpos>0) ? —vpos : MAX_ITEMS-1;
```

decrement and increment vpos if the user presses the Up Arrow or Down Arrow keys. This statement is executed when the user presses the Up Arrow key. If vpos isn't 0, it's decremented; if it's 0 (the topmost item is selected), vpos is set to the bottom item. Thus the menu "wraps around," a convenience for the user.

The display_menu() function displays the menu—which consists of a box and the menu items—and highlights one of the items. It calls draw_box() to draw a box bordered by a single line. The draw_box() function uses the same code as in the earlier linebox.c example. The get_code() function analyzes the key pressed by the user, and the menu_action() function carries out the action when the user selects an item. The menu item names are stored in an array of strings called menu_item.

Figure 8.5 shows how the top part of the screen looks with the Save item selected. Except for Quit, menu selections are displayed on line 25.

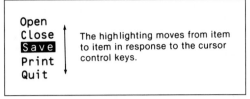

Figure 8.5. Operation of the menu.c program.

Here's the listing:

```c
// menu.c
// creates a drop-down menu
// uses extended codes and text-window functions

#include <conio.h>         // for text-window functions
#include <string.h>        // for strcmp(), etc.
#include <process.h>       // for exit()

#define TRUE          1
#define U_ARRO       72    // Up-arrow key
#define D_ARRO       80    // Down-arrow key
#define MENU_WIDTH   10    // width of menu
#define MAX_ITEMS     5    // number of menu items

char *menu_item[MAX_ITEMS] =      // menu item names
      { "Open", "Close", "Save", "Print", "Quit"};

void display_menu(void);          // prototypes
void draw_box(int left, int top, int width, int height);
char get_code(void);
void menu_action(char *item_name);

int vpos;    // position of active item on menu (0 at top)

// main()
// gets keypress from user, changes selected item, takes action
int main(void)
   {
   textbackground(BLUE);          // clear screen to blue
   clrscr();
   _setcursortype(_NOCURSOR);     // remove cursor

   while(TRUE)                    // cycle forever
      {
      display_menu();             // display the menu
      switch ( get_code() )       // get keypress from user
         {
         case U_ARRO:             // move highlight up
            vpos = (vpos>0) ? —vpos : MAX_ITEMS-1;
            break;
```

```
                    case D_ARRO:              // move highlight down
                        vpos = (vpos<MAX_ITEMS-1) ? ++vpos : 0;
                        break;
                    case '\r':                // perform menu action
                        menu_action( menu_item[vpos] );  // arg is item name
                        break;
                    }  // end switch
                }  // end while
            }  // end main()

// display_menu()
// displays box and menu items, highlights active item
void display_menu()
    {
    int j;

    textbackground(WHITE);                    // black on white
    textcolor(BLACK);
    draw_box(1, 2, MENU_WIDTH, MAX_ITEMS+2);  // draw the box

    for(j=0; j<MAX_ITEMS; j++)                // for each menu item
        {
        if(j==vpos)                           // if active item,
            textbackground(GREEN);            // green background
        gotoxy(3, j+3);                       // display item name
        cputs( menu_item[j] );
        textbackground(WHITE);                // restore background
        }
    }  // end display_menu()

// draw_box()
// draws a box with a single line around it
void draw_box(int left, int top, int width, int height)
    {
    int j;
    char string[81];                // utility string
                                    // define box-size window
    window(left, top, left+width-1, top+height-1);
    clrscr();                       // clear window to background color
    // now add line so chars on bottom line won't cause scroll
    window(left, top, left+width-1, top+height);

    // draw top and bottom lines, with corners
    for(j=1; j<width-1; j++)        // make string of
        string[j] = '\xC4';         //     horizontal characters
    string[width] = '\0';           // end the string
    string[0] = '\xDA';             // insert upper-left corner
    string[width-1] = '\xBF';       // insert upper-right corner
    gotoxy(1, 1);                   // display top line
    cputs(string);
    string[0] = '\xC0';             // insert lower-left corner
    string[width-1] = '\xD9';       // insert lower-right corner
```

```
   gotoxy(1, height);          // display bottom line
   cputs(string);

   // draw vertical lines on left and right
   for(j=2; j<height; j++)     // for each row
      {
      gotoxy(1, j);            // on the left end,
      putch('\xB3');           // draw vertical character
      gotoxy(width, j);        // on the right end,
      putch('\xB3');           // draw vertical character
      }
   window(1, 1, 80, 25);       // restore window to full screen
   }  // end draw_box()

// get_code()
// gets key press from user, returns extended code
char get_code(void)
   {
   char key;

   if( (key=getch()) == 0 )    // if extended code,
      return( getch() );       // return the code
   else if ( key == '\r' )     // if [Enter],
      return(key);             // return it
   else                        // if anything else,
      return(0);               // return 0
   }  // end get_code()

// menu_action()
// takes action, depending on name of menu item
void menu_action(char *item_name)
   {
   gotoxy(1,25);                              // lower-left
   clreol();                                  // clear line
   if( strcmp(item_name,      "Open") == 0 )
      cputs("Open");
   else if( strcmp(item_name, "Close") == 0 )
      cputs("Close");
   else if( strcmp(item_name, "Save") == 0 )
      cputs("Save");
   else if( strcmp(item_name, "Print") == 0 )
      cputs("Print");
   else if( strcmp(item_name, "Quit") == 0 )
      {
      _setcursortype(_NORMALCURSOR);  // restore cursor
      exit(0);                        // exit to DOS
      }
   }  // end menu_action
```

The only new text-window functions in this program are _setcursortype(), which can remove the cursor or change it to a solid block, and clreol(), which clears the current line of text.

```
Change or Remove Cursor
void _setcursortype(int cursor_type)
cursor_type    // type of cursor — can be one of
               // _NOCURSOR (turns off cursor)
               // _SOLIDCURSOR (block cursor)
               // _NORMALCURSOR (normal underline cursor)
```

Don't forget the underline before the function name and the constants.

```
Clear to End of Line
void clreol(void)
```

The *exit()* Function

Notice the use of the C library exit() function in menu.c. This function immediately terminates the program and passes control back to the calling entity, in this case the MS-DOS operating system or Turbo C++. It doesn't matter how deeply you're nested within functions; exit() still terminates the entire program.

If an argument is placed in the parentheses of the exit() function, that argument is returned to the operating system, where it is available to the ERRORLEVEL subcommand in the batch file processor. That is, you can put such commands as

```
IF ERRORLEVEL 1 GOTO ERR1
```

in a batch file to sample the value placed by the program in the exit() function. This gives the batch file the chance to change its operation depending on the results of the program.

A return value of 0 for exit() ordinarily indicates a normal termination, but a non-zero value may be used as an error code. Notice that the return type of main() is changed to int to reflect the fact that a value is being returned via exit(1). When this is true, main() should also terminate with return(0) for a normal return, unless there is no normal return. (This is the case in menu.c because there's no way but exit() out of the endless loop.)

We'll use the menu.c program as the basis for a larger application in Chapter 14, "Application Example." There you'll see how several menus are used together to provide a more complete character-based GUI.

Text Input with *cgets()*

The text-window functions include an improved form of gets() called cgets(), for reading text input from the user. Besides being "window aware," `cgets()` also gives the programmer control over the maximum number of characters the user can input. This prevents the user from overflowing the input buffer.

Of course there's a price for everything, and for `cgets()`, the programmer has to work a little harder to set everything up. Here's an outline of the process, assuming that the maximum number of characters we expect the user to type is 25:

```
char *ptr;              // for return value from cgets()
char buffer[28];        // string + 2-byte count + '\0'
buffer[0] = 26;         // 2 bytes less than buffer size
ptr = cgets(buffer);    // get input from user
```

You first need to create a buffer that is three bytes longer than the maximum length of the string. Then you fill in the first two bytes with the length of the string including the terminating /0 character. Finally you call the function. The user's input is stored in the buffer, but after (in this case) 25 keypresses, no more characters are displayed. The return value of cgets() is a pointer that points to the string typed, which starts at buffer[2].

To demonstrate `cgets()`, we'll show a short program that creates a colored window on the screen and displays a prompt in the window, requesting the user to type a name. The function cgets() is then used to receive the name. Here's the listing:

```
// cgets.c
// demonstrates cgets() function
#include <conio.h>          // for text-window functions

void main(void)
   {
   char *ptr;               // pointer for cgets() return
   char buffer[28];         // buffer for text input
                            // (first two bytes are char count)
   textbackground(BLACK);   // clear screen to black
   clrscr();
   window(21, 6, 64, 18);   // define a window
   textbackground(GREEN);   // clear it to green
   clrscr();
   gotoxy(2, 6);            // display prompt at left of window
   cputs("\nEnter your name: ");
   buffer[0] = 26;          // allows 25 input chars (plus '\0')
   ptr = cgets(buffer);     // get user input following prompt
   window(1, 1, 80, 25);    // restore full screen window
   gotoxy(1, 25);           // echo input at bottom of screen
   cprintf("String %s has %d characters", ptr, buffer[1]);
   }
```

The name entered is then displayed at the bottom of the screen, along with the length of the string typed, which is stored in the first two bytes of buffer, replacing the maximum length we placed there originally.

The function used to display this data is cprintf(), which acts like printf() but is "text window aware," confining its input to the current window and using the current text and background colors.

Other Text-Window Functions

We've covered almost all the text-window functions. Others are textattr(), which sets both text and background colors at the same time; and normvideo(), which restores the previous intensity, whether high or low. Another function, gettextinfo(), reads several kinds of information: the video mode, the window position and dimensions, the foreground and background colors, and the cursor position.

The textmode() function changes from one text mode to another. It takes one of the following values as an argument:

Value	Mnemonic	Change to
−1	LASTMODE	previous text mode
0	BW40	black and white, 40 columns
1	C40	color, 40 columns
2	BW80	black and white, 80 columns
3	C80	color, 80 columns
7	MONO	monochrome, 80 columns
64	C4350	EGA 43-line or VGA 50-line

This function should be used only to switch between text modes and not from graphics to text mode.

Note that the Turbo C++ text-window functions don't permit multiple windows to be active at the same time. Functions like cputs() relate only to the last window defined. However, you can create the effect of multiple windows by defining one window and writing to it, and then defining another window and writing to it.

Command-Line Arguments

You've used application programs (including Turbo C++ itself) in which, when you invoke the program from the operating system, you can type not only the name of the program but various other items as well, such as the name of a file the application is to work on. A typical example might be

```
C>wordproc letter.txt
```

where wordproc is an application program and letter.txt is a file this application will open and process. Here the string "letter.txt" is used as a command-line argument: an argument that appears on the command line following the C> prompt.

Use of multiple arguments in the command line is clearly a helpful feature, so how can we access these arguments from within the application?

Here's another question: Will we ever find anything besides void to put inside the parentheses of the main() function?

As you may have guessed, the answers to these seemingly unrelated questions are in fact two sides of a coin. By putting the right things inside the parentheses of main(), we can allow our program to read command-line arguments to its heart's content. C automatically adds to all C programs the capability to read these arguments. As programmers, all we need to do is make use of it.

Demonstrating Command-Line Arguments

The following program shows the rudiments of programming command-line arguments:

```
// comline.c
// demonstrates command line arguments
#include <stdio.h>                       // for printf()

void main( int argc, char *argv[] )
   {
   int j;

   printf("\nNumber of arguments is %d\n", argc);
   for(j=0; j<argc; j++)
      printf("Argument number %d is %s\n", j, argv[j] );
   }
```

Here's a sample run with the program, in which we simply type the words one, two, and three as command-line arguments following the program name. It's easiest to use the program from DOS, so get out of Turbo C++ with the Alt X key combination and type the following at the DOS prompt (you can also use the Arguments item in the IDE Run menu):

```
C>comline one two three
```

The program will respond with

```
Number of arguments is 4
Argument number  0 is C:\TCPROGS\CHAP8\COMLINE.EXE
Argument number  1 is one
Argument number  2 is two
Argument number  3 is three
```

The two arguments used in the parentheses following main() are argc and argv. The variable argc is the total number of command-line arguments typed; in this case, 4 (the pathname of the program is counted as the first argument).

> The arguments in main(argc, argv) are the number of command-line arguments and an array of pointers to the individual arguments.

The variable *argv[] represents an array of pointers to strings, where each string holds one command-line argument. The strings can be accessed by referring to them as argv[1], argv[2], and so on (or in array notation, *(argv+1), *(argv+2), etc.). The first string, argv[0], is the full pathname of the program.

The names argc (for argument count) and argv (for argument values) are traditionally used in these roles, but any other name would work just as well (although you might confuse tradition-bound C programmers).

Using Command-Line Arguments

Let's put command-line arguments to work in a quasi-useful situation. The following program allows the user to clear the output screen to one of several colors: black, blue, green, red, or white. The color is specified as a command-line argument when the program is invoked; for example

```
C>clrcolor blue
```

paints the screen blue. Again, this is most conveniently done from the DOS prompt, but you can also invoke clrcolor.c from the Turbo C++ IDE if you specify the color argument in the Arguments selection from the Run menu.

```c
// clrcolor.c

// sets screen to color provided by user on command line
#include <stdio.h>              // for printf()
#include <conio.h>              // for text window
#include <process.h>           // for exit()
#include <string.h>            // for strcmp()

int main( int argc, char *argv[] )
    {
    int code;           // color code for textbackground()

    if(argc != 2)
        { printf("\nFormat: clrcolor color"); exit(1); }
    if( strcmp(argv[1], "black")==0 )
        code=0;
    else if (strcmp(argv[1], "blue")==0 )
        code=1;
    else if (strcmp(argv[1], "green")==0 )
        code=2;
    else if (strcmp(argv[1], "red")==0 )
        code=4;
    else if (strcmp(argv[1], "white")==0 )
        code=7;
    else
        { printf("\nNot a supported color"); exit(1); }
    textbackground(code);
    clrscr();
    return(0);
    }
```

It's normal to check at the beginning of the program that the user has typed the correct number of command-line arguments. If the value of argc is incorrect, the user probably doesn't understand how the program is to be used and should be reminded with a short message. It's also good to check that the argument has a correct value. This program does both these things.

Command-line arguments are most commonly used to supply filenames to applications that deal with disk files. We'll see examples of this in Chapter 11, "Files."

Redirection

Speaking of files, the MS-DOS operating system incorporates a powerful feature that allows a program to read and write files, even when this capability hasn't been built into the program. This is done through a process called *redirection.* Like command-line arguments, redirection lies in the gray area between C and MS-DOS.

Redirection provides an easy way to save the results of a program; its use is vaguely similar to that of the PrtScr key (Ctrl PrtSc on older keyboards) to save program output to the printer, except that the results can be sent to a disk file. This is often a more convenient and flexible approach than providing a separate function in the program to write to the disk. Similarly, redirection can be used to read information from a disk file directly into a program.

Ordinarily, a program derives its input from the *standard input device,* which is assumed to be the keyboard, and sends its output to the *standard output device,* which is assumed to be the display screen. In other words, DOS makes certain assumptions about where input should come from and where output should go. Redirection enables us to change these assumptions.

> Output can be redirected to a file instead of the screen. Input can be redirected to come from a file instead of the keyboard.

Redirecting Output

Let's see how we might redirect the output of a program to go, not to the screen, but to a file instead. We'll start by considering this simple program:

```
// mirror.c
// echoes typing to the screen
#include <stdio.h>      // for putchar()
#include <conio.h>      // for getch()

void main(void)
   {
   int ch=0;
```

```
while( (ch=getch()) != '\r' )   // get char from standard input
    putchar(ch);                // send char to standard output
putchar('\r');
}
```

The putchar function outputs one character to the standard output device. Ordinarily, when we run this program, putchar() will cause whatever we type to be printed on the screen, until the Enter key is pressed, at which point the program will terminate, as shown in this sample run:

```
C>mirror
All's well that ends well.
C>
```

Note that the programs in this section on redirection should be run directly from the DOS prompt, not from Turbo C++'s IDE.

Now let's see what happens when we invoke the program from DOS in a different way, using redirection.

```
C>mirror >file.txt

C>
```

Now when we call the program and type the same phrase, All's well that ends well., nothing appears on the screen! Where did our typing go? We've caused it to be redirected to the file called file.txt. Can we prove that this has actually happened? Yes, by using the DOS command TYPE.

```
C>type file.txt
All's well that ends well.
```

There's the result of our typing, sitting in the file. The redirection operator, which is the greater-than symbol (>), causes any output intended for the screen to be written to the file whose name follows the operator.

The data to be redirected to a file doesn't need to be typed by a user at the keyboard; the program itself can generate it. Any output normally sent to the screen can be redirected to a disk file. As an example, we could invoke the simple oneline.c program from the first chapter of this book, and redirect its output to a file.

```
C>oneline >file.txt
C>type file.txt
I charge thee, speak!
```

When we examine file.txt with TYPE, we see that the output of oneline.c has been written to the file. This can be a useful capability any time you want to capture the output of a program in a file, rather than displaying it on the screen.

DOS predefines a number of filenames for its own use. One of these names is PRN, which stands for the printer. Output can be redirected to the printer by using this filename. For example, if you invoke the mirror.c program this way:

```
C>mirror >PRN
```

anything you type will be printed on the printer when you press the Enter key.

Redirecting Input

We can also redirect input to a program so that, instead of reading characters from the keyboard, the program reads them from a file. Fortunately we can demonstrate this with the same program, mirror.c, that we used to demonstrate redirection of output. This is because the program both accepts input from the keyboard and outputs it to the screen.

To redirect the input, we need to have a file containing something to be printed. We'll assume we've placed the message The greatest of these is charity in the file called file.txt using the Turbo C++ editor or redirecting the output of mirror.c. (Make sure to include Enter at the end.) Then we use the less-than sign (<) before the filename.

```
C>mirror <file.txt
The greatest of these is charity.
C>
```

The phrase is printed on the screen with no further effort on our part. Using redirection, we've made our mirror.c program perform the work of the DOS TYPE command.

Figure 8.6 shows how redirected input and output look compared with normal input and output.

Both Ways at Once

Redirection of input and output can be used together; a program's input can come from one file via redirection, while at the same time its output is being redirected to another file. In DOS nomenclature, we can say the program acts as a *filter*.

To demonstrate this process, we'll use a slightly fancier example than before. Instead of simply storing and retrieving files in their original form, we'll develop a pair of programs, one to code a message and another to decode it.

Here's the program that does the coding:

```
// code.c
// encodes file
// to be used with redirection
#include <stdio.h>      // for putchar()
#include <conio.h>      // for getch()

void main(void)
   {
   char ch;

   while( (ch=getch()) != '\r' )  // get char from standard input
      putchar(ch+1);              // code and send to std output
   putchar('\r');
   }
```

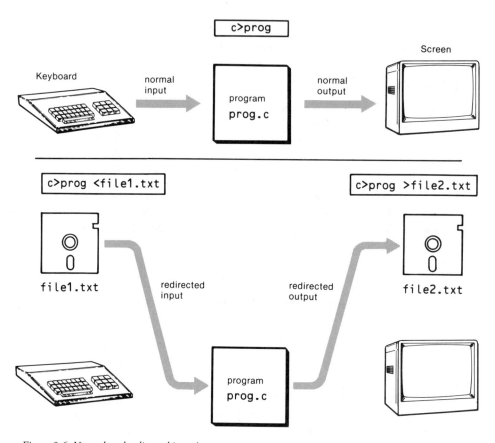

Figure 8.6. Normal and redirected input/output.

This program reads a character, either from the keyboard or—using redirection—from a file, and outputs it in coded form, either to the screen or to another file. The cipher is rudimentary; it consists of adding 1 to the ASCII code for the character. Of course any 10-year-old could break this code, but if you're interested, you can probably think of ways to make it tougher.

Notice that we don't encode the '/r' character: that's why we leave the writing of this character outside the loop. We need it to be in uncoded form to terminate the message.

Let's assume you've generated a file, called file1.txt, which contains the message you wish to code. You can create this file using either the mirror.c program with redirection (although it's hard to use because the characters aren't echoed to the screen) or by using the Turbo C++ editor. If you use the editor, make sure to end the file with Enter. We can verify what's in the file this way:

```
C>type file1.txt
Meet me at the hollow tree.
```

To code this file, we redirect our input from file1.txt, to code.c and also redirect the output to a different file, file2.txt, like this:

```
C>code <file1.txt >file2.txt
```

Data will be read from file1.txt, coded, and written to file2.txt. Having done this, we can use TYPE to see what the coded file looks like.

```
C>type file2.txt
Nffu!nf!bu!uif!ipmmpx!usff/
```

To decode the file, we use a program that looks very much like code.c:

```
// decode.c
// decodes file
// to be used with redirection
#include <stdio.h>      // for putchar()
#include <conio.h>      // for getch()

void main(void)
   {
   char ch;

   while( (ch=getch()) != '\r' )  // get char from standard input
      putchar(ch-1);              // decode and send to std out
   putchar('\r');
   }
```

This program subtracts 1 from the value of each character, thus reversing the coding process. We'll write the decoded results to file3.txt. Here's how we apply the program, again using double redirection, to our coded file:

```
C>decode <file2.txt >file3.txt
```

Finally, to prove that both the coding and decoding have worked correctly, we print the file containing the decoded message.

```
C>type file3.txt
Meet me at the hollow tree.
```

A point to note about redirection: the output file is erased before it's written to, so don't try to send output to the same file from which you're receiving input.

The programs in this section use the '\r' character to signal end-of-file. In more general-purpose programs, you may want to use −1 or the '\x1A' character for this purpose.

Redirection can be a powerful tool for developing utility programs to examine or alter data in files.

Redirection is used to establish a relationship between a program and a file. Another DOS operator can be used to relate two programs directly so that the output of one is fed directly into another, with no files involved. This is called *piping* and uses the bar character (¦). We won't pursue this topic, but you can read about it in the DOS documentation.

Summary

You now can read the codes of the extended character set so that your program can tell when such keys as the function and cursor-control keys are pressed. You've also learned how to use the Turbo C++ text-window functions for confining text output to a window, changing text and background colors, controlling the cursor, clearing the screen, and other purposes.

You know how your program can interpret command-line arguments (words typed following a program name at the C> prompt), and you've seen how the input and output of a program can be redirected to come from and be sent to disk files, using the DOS redirection operators (<) and (>).

In the next chapter we'll look into structures, an important aspect of the C language.

Questions

1. The purpose of the extended keyboard codes is to

    a. Read foreign language characters
    b. Read letter keys typed with Alt and Ctrl
    c. Read the function and cursor control keys
    d. Read graphics characters

2. How many extended codes are there (including codes that aren't used)?

3. How many bytes are used to represent an extended keyboard code?

4. True or false: extended keyboard codes represent only single keys such as F1.

5. Which of the following is the extended code for the F1 key?

    a. 97
    b. 1 78
    c. '\xDB'
    d. 0 59

6. True or false: you can draw circles and ellipses with Turbo C++ text-window functions.

7. A text window is a screen area in which

    a. Colors can be confined
    b. Text can be confined
    c. Graphics can be confined
    d. Both text and graphics can be confined

8. To use Turbo C++ text-window functions, the file _____ must be #included in your program.

9. The function gotoxy() places the following item at x, y:

    a. The current position (CP)
    b. The text about to be written
    c. The next line to be drawn
    d. The cursor

10. Each character saved in memory by savetext() requires _____ bytes of storage.

11. The textbackground() function changes the background color

    a. Whenever it's executed
    b. Only when the screen is cleared
    c. Only when text is displayed
    d. When text is displayed or the screen is cleared

12. True or false: the putch() and getche() functions are text-window aware; that is, they always confine their output to the text window.

13. The statement gotoxy(wherex()+1, wherey()); has the effect of

    _____.

14. True or false: the exit() function causes an exit from a function.

15. The clreol() function

    a. Clears from the cursor to the end of the line
    b. Clears the line containing the cursor
    c. Clears the line given as an argument
    d. Clears all the lines

16. True or false: the _setcursortype() function can make the cursor disappear altogether.

17. Command-line arguments are

    a. Something that happens in the military
    b. Additional items following the C> prompt and a program name on the command line
    c. The arguments argc and argv
    d. The arguments argv[0], argv[1], and so forth

18. True or false: the window() function draws a rectangular-shaped window on the screen.

19. Redirection is

    a. Sending the output of a program somewhere besides the screen
    b. Getting a program from somewhere besides an .exe file
    c. Getting input to a program from somewhere besides the keyboard
    d. Changing the definition of the standard input and output devices

20. Write a DOS command that will cause a program called prog1 to take its input from a file called f1.c and send its output to a file called f2.c.

Exercises

1. Write a program that will enable the user to type a phrase, echoing characters to the screen. If the user presses the Left Arrow key (not the Backspace), the program should erase the character to the left of the cursor so that the whole phrase can be erased one character at a time. Use extended keyboard codes and text-window cursor control.

2. Write a program that uses a command-line argument to perform decimal to hexadecimal conversion; that is, the decimal number will be typed on the command line, following the program name.

   ```
   C>decihex 128
   Hex=80
   C>
   ```

   Use unsigned integers, so the program can convert values between 0 and 65535. Hint: use the %x format specifier in printf().

3. Write a program that will read a C source code file using redirection and determine whether the file contains the same number of left and right braces. This program can then be used to check for mismatched braces before compiling. Its operation should look like this in cases where there are unequal numbers of braces:

   ```
   C>braces <prog.c
   Mismatched braces
   C>
   ```

   Use getchar() to read the characters and terminate on the EOF character defined in the STDIO.H header file.

Structures

- Structures
- Nested structures
- Arrays of structures
- Structures and pointers
- Unions

In this chapter we explore C's most versatile device for representing data: the structure. There's quite a lot to know about structures, including how to declare them, define them, access their members, and initialize them. We'll also see how structures can be used in arrays and as function arguments. At the end of the chapter we'll describe a close cousin of the structure: the union.

Structure Basics

We have seen how simple variables can hold one piece of information at a time and how arrays can hold a number of pieces of information of the same data type. These two data storage mechanisms can handle a great variety of situations, but we often want to operate on data items of different types together as a unit. In this case, neither the variable nor the array is adequate.

For example, suppose you want a program to store data concerning an employee in an organization. You might want to store the employee's name (a character array), department number (an integer), salary (a floating point number), and so forth. Perhaps you also have other employees, and you want your program to deal with them as elements of an array.

Even a multidimensional array won't solve this problem, because all the elements of an array must be of the same data type. You could use several different arrays—a character array for names, a floating point array for salaries, and so on—but this is an unwieldy approach that obscures the fact that you're dealing with a group of characteristics relating to a single entity: the employee.

To solve this sort of problem, C provides a special data type: the structure. A structure consists of a number of data items—which need not be of the same type—grouped together. In our example, a structure would consist of the employee's name, department number, salary, and any other pertinent information. The structure could hold as many of these items as we want. Figure 9.1 shows the differences among simple variables, arrays, and structures.

Pascal programmers will recognize a C structure as similar to a record.

Structures are useful, not only because they can hold different types of variables, but also because they can form the basis for more complex constructions, such as linked lists. We'll provide an example of this later on.

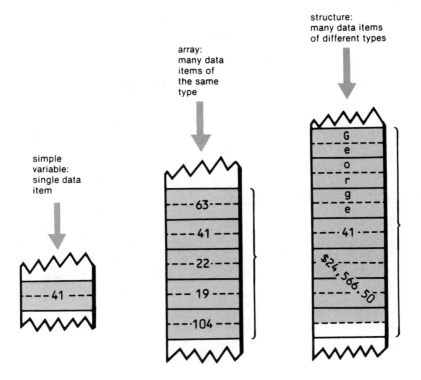

Figure 9.1. Simple variables, arrays, and structures.

A Simple Structure

Here's a program that uses a simple structure containing two data items: an integer variable num and a character variable ch. The data items in a structure are called *members*.

```
// struct.c
// demonstrates structures
#include <stdio.h>   // for printf()

void main(void)
   {
   struct easy         // declares data type 'struct easy'
      {
      int num;         // structure member
      char ch;         // structure member
      };

   struct easy ez1;    // defines 'ez1' to be
                       //    of type 'struct easy'

   ez1.num = 3;        // gives values to members of 'ez1'
```

```
    ez1.ch = 'Z';
                        // gets values from members of 'ez1'
    printf("\nez1.num=%d, ez1.ch=%c", ez1.num, ez1.ch );
    }
```

When run, this program will generate the following output:

```
ez1.num=2, ez1.ch=Z
```

This program demonstrates the three fundamental aspects of using structures: declaring the structure type, defining structure variables, and accessing members of the structure. We'll look at these three operations in turn.

Declaring a Structure Type

The fundamental data types used in C, such as int and float, are predefined by the compiler. Thus, when you use an int variable, you know it will always consist of two bytes (at least in Turbo C) and that the compiler will interpret the contents of these two bytes in a certain way. This isn't true of structures. Because a structure may contain any number of members of different types, the programmer must tell the compiler what a particular structure is going to look like before using variables of that type.

In the example program, the following statement declares the structure type:

```
struct easy
    {
    int num;
    char ch;
    };
```

This statement declares a new data type called struct easy. Each variable of this type will consist of two members: an integer variable called num and a character variable called ch. Note that this statement doesn't define any variables, so it isn't setting aside any storage in memory. It just tells the compiler what the data type struct easy looks like, conveying the plan for the structure. Figure 9.2 shows the format of a structure type declaration.

The keyword struct introduces the statement. The name easy is called the tag. It names the kind of structure being defined. Note that the tag isn't a variable name, because we aren't defining a variable; it's a *type* name. The members of the structure are surrounded by braces, and the entire statement is terminated by a semicolon.

A structure is a data type whose format is defined by the programmer.

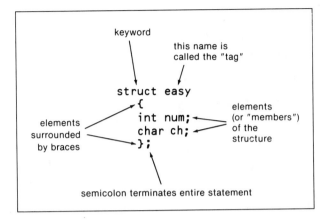

Figure 9.2. Format of a structure type declaration.

Defining Structure Variables

Once we've declared our new data type, we can define one or more variables to be of that type. In our program, we define a variable ez1 to be of type struct easy.

```
struct easy ez1;
```

This statement does set aside space in memory. It establishes enough space to hold all the items in the structure: in this case, three bytes: two for the integer and one for the character. (In some situations the compiler may allocate more bytes so that the next variable in memory will come out on an even address.) The variable definition struct easy ez1; performs a function similar to such variable definitions as float salary; and int count; it tells the compiler to set aside storage for a variable of a specific type and gives a name to the variable. Figure 9.3 shows what the structure variable ez1 looks like, first grouped together conceptually and then as the members of the structure would look in memory.

Accessing Structure Members

Now how do we refer to individual members of the structure? In arrays, we can access individual elements with a subscript: array[7]. Structures use a different approach: the *dot operator* (.), which is also called the *membership operator*. Here's how we would refer to the num part of the ez1 structure:

```
ez1.num
```

The variable name preceding the dot is the structure name; the name following is the specific member of the structure. Thus the statements

```
ez1.num = 2;
```

```
ez1.ch = 'Z';
```

give a value of 2 to the num member of the structure ez1 and a value of 'Z' to the ch member. Similarly, the statement

```
printf("ez1.num=%d, ez1.ch=%c\n", ez1.num, ez1.ch );
```

causes the values of these two member variables to be printed.

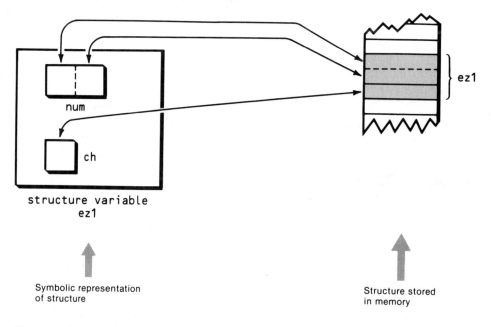

Figure 9.3. Structure ez1 *stored in memory*

The dot operator (.) connects a structure variable name with a member of the structure.

The dot operator provides a powerful and clear way to specify members of a structure. An expression like employee.salary is more comprehensible than employee[27].

Multiple Structure Variables of the Same Type

Just as there can be more than one int or float variable in a program, there also can be any number of variables of a given structure type. In the following program, for example, there are two variables, ez1 and ez2, both of type struct easy:

```
// struct2.c
// demonstrates structures
// uses two structure variables
#include <stdio.h>    // for printf()

void main(void)
    {
    struct easy        // declares data type 'struct easy'
       {
       int num;
       char ch;
       };

    struct easy ez1;   // defines 'ez1' and 'ez2' to be
    struct easy ez2;   //   of type 'struct easy'

    ez1.num = 3;       // give values to members of 'ez1'
    ez1.ch = 'Z';
    ez2.num = 4;       // give values to members of 'ez2'
    ez2.ch = 'Y';
                       // get values of all members
    printf("\nez1.num=%d, ez1.ch=%c", ez1.num, ez1.ch );
    printf("\nez2.num=%d, ez2.ch=%c", ez2.num, ez2.ch );
    }
```

Notice how the members of the two different structures are accessed: ez1.num gets num from the structure ez1, while ez2.num gets it from ez2.

Combining Declarations

You can combine in one statement the declaration of the structure type and the definition of structure variables. As an example, the easy2.c program can be rewritten like this:

```
// struct2a.c
// demonstrates structures
// combines declaration and definition
#include <stdio.h>    // for printf()

void main(void)
    {
    struct easy        // declares data type 'struct easy'
       {               // defines 'ez1' and 'ez2' to be
       int num;        //   of type 'struct easy'
       char ch;
       } ez1, ez2;

    ez1.num = 3;       // reference members of 'ez1'
    ez1.ch = 'Z';
    ez2.num = 4;       // reference members of 'ez2'
    ez2.ch = 'Y';
    printf("\nez1.num=%d, ez1.ch=%c", ez1.num, ez1.ch );
    printf("\nez2.num=%d, ez2.ch=%c", ez2.num, ez2.ch );
    }
```

305

The effect is the same as that provided by the separate statements, but the format is more compact (though perhaps less clear).

Entering Data into Structures

Let's examine a slightly more realistic programming example that involves placing data into structures and reading it out again. This will be the first version of a program that will evolve throughout the chapter. Our goal, which will require several intermediate steps, is to develop a simple database program that will demonstrate one of the most useful ways data can be organized in C: as an array of structures.

In the following program, we construct a database for a typical employee category: the secret agent. If you're setting up a clandestine operation in a foreign country, the program will be right up your (dark) alley. If your needs are more pedestrian, you'll find the program is easily adaptable to other sorts of personnel.

In this program, the database stores two items of information about each secret agent: a name, represented by a character array, and a code number, represented by an integer. This information is entered into the program by the user and is then printed again by the program. In this version of the program, there is space to store the data for only two agents; in later versions we'll show how to expand the program's capacity.

Here's the program:

```
// twoagent.c
// stores and retrieves data for two secret agents
#include <stdio.h>                    // for printf(), gets()

void main(void)
    {
    struct personnel                  // declare data structure
        {
        char name [30];               // name
        int agnumb;                   // code number
        };
    struct personnel agent1;          // define a struct variable
    struct personnel agent2;          // define another one
    char numstr[81];                  // for number input

    printf("\nAgent 1.\nEnter name: ");        // get first name
    gets(agent1.name);
    printf("Enter agent number (3 digits): "); // get number
    gets(numstr);
    agent1.agnumb = atoi(numstr);

    printf("\nAgent 2.\nEnter name: ");        // get 2nd name
    gets(agent2.name);
    printf("Enter agent number (3 digits): "); // get number
    gets(numstr);
    agent2.agnumb = atoi(numstr);
```

```
    printf("\nList of agents:\n" );
    printf("   Name: %s\n", agent1.name);        // display first
    printf("       Agent number: %03d\n", agent1.agnumb);
    printf("   Name: %s\n", agent2.name);        // display second
    printf("       Agent number: %03d\n", agent2.agnumb);
    }
```

We declared a structure type called personnel, which will be used as the model for the structure variables that hold the data for the two agents. The structure variables agent1 and agent2 are then defined to be of type struct personnel.

Data is then placed into the appropriate structure members using the statements

```
gets(agent1.name);
```

and

```
gets(numstr);
agent1.agnumb = atoi(numstr);
```

These statements are similar to those that we would use for simple variables, but the dot operator indicates that we're dealing with structure members.

We have used the gets() and atoi() combination, described in Chapter 8, to avoid a problem with scanf() and the keyboard buffer.

The four printf() statements print the contents of our small database.

Here's a sample run:

```
Agent 1.
Enter name: Harrison Tweedbury
Enter agent number (3 digits): 102

Agent 2.
Enter name: James Bond
Enter agent number (3 digits): 007

List of agents:
    Name: Harrison Tweedbury
    Agent number: 102
    Name: James Bond
    Agent number: 007
```

Notice that we can print leading zeros: this is accomplished by preceding the field width in the printf() statement with a zero: %03d.

Figure 9.4 shows how the structure variable agent1 looks symbolically and how it looks stored in memory.

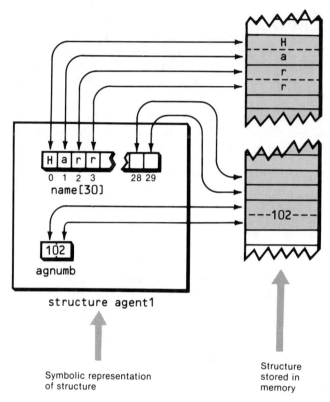

Figure 9.4. Structure agent1 stored in memory.

Let's look at some other structure operations that will be useful later on: initializing structures, passing their values in assignment statements, and using them as arguments to functions.

Initializing Structures

Like simple variables and arrays, structure variables can be initialized—given specific values—at the beginning of a program. The format used is quite similar to that used to initialize arrays.

Here's an example, using a modified version of our twoagent.c program. In this case the data on the two agents is contained in initialization statements within the program, rather than being input by the user:

```
// initage.c
// demonstrates initialization of structures
#include <stdio.h>                    // for printf()
```

```
struct personnel                 // declares structure
   {
   char name [30];               // name
   int agnumb;                   // code number
   };

struct personnel agent1 =        // initializes struct variable
   { "Harrison Tweedbury", 012 };

struct personnel agent2 =        // initializes another one
   { "James Bond", 007 };

void main(void)
   {
   printf("\nList of agents:\n" );
   printf("   Name: %s\n", agent1.name);      // first agent
   printf("        Agent number: %03d\n", agent1.agnumb);
   printf("   Name: %s\n", agent2.name);      // second agent
   printf("        Agent number: %03d\n", agent2.agnumb);
   }
```

Here, after the usual declaration of the structure type, the two structure variables are defined and initialized at the same time. As with array initialization, the equal sign is used, followed by braces enclosing a list of values, with the values separated by commas.

When this program is executed, it will generate output similar to that of our previous example.

Assignment Statements Used with Structures

In the original version of C defined by Kernighan and Ritchie, it was impossible to assign the values of one structure variable to another variable using a simple assignment statement. In ANSI-compatible versions of C, including Turbo C++, this is possible. That is, if agent1 and agent2 are structure variables of the same type, the following statement can be used:

```
agent2 = agent1;
```

The value of one structure variable can be assigned to another structure variable of the same type.

This is an important capability, so let's look at an example of its use. In this modification of our secret agent program, information is obtained from the user about one agent and is then assigned to a second structure variable, using an assignment statement.

```
// twins.c
// demonstrates assignment of structures
```

```
#include <stdio.h>                    // for printf(), gets()

void main(void)
    {
    struct personnel                  // declare data structure
        {
        char name [30];               // name
        int agnumb;                   // code number
        };

    struct personnel agent1;          // define a struct variable
    struct personnel agent2;          // define another one

    printf("\nAgent 1.\nEnter name: ");   // get first name
    gets(agent1.name);
    printf("Enter agent number (3 digits): "); // get number
    scanf("%d", &agent1.agnumb);

    agent2 = agent1;                  // assigns one structure
                                      // to another!
    printf("\nList of agents:\n" );
    printf("   Name: %s\n", agent1.name);     // first agent
    printf("       Agent number: %03d\n", agent1.agnumb);
    printf("   Name: %s\n", agent2.name);     // second agent
    printf("       Agent number: %03d\n", agent2.agnumb);
    }
```

When we run this program, data on two agents will be printed as before, but it will be exactly the same data for both agents.

This is a rather amazing capability when you think about it: when you assign one structure to another, all the values in the structure are actually being assigned, all at once, to the corresponding structure members. Only two values are assigned in this example, but there could be far more. Simple assignment statements can't be used this way for arrays, which must be moved element by element.

Nested Structures

Just as there can be arrays of arrays, there can also be structures that contain other structures. This can be a powerful way to create complex data types.

For a simple example, imagine that our secret agents are sent out as a team, consisting of one "chief" and one "indian." The following program creates a structure with the tag team. This structure consists of two other structures of type personnel.

```
// team.c
// demonstrates nested structures
#include <stdio.h>                    // for printf()

struct personnel                      // declares structure
    {
    char name [30];                   // name
```

```
    int agnumb;              // code number
    };

struct team                  // declares structure
    {                        // whose members are
    struct personnel chief;  // themselves structures
    struct personnel indian;
    };

struct team team1 =          // defines and
    { { "Harrison Tweedbury", 012 },   // initiailizes
      { "James Bond",         007 } };  // struct 'team1'

void main(void)
    {
    printf("\nChief:\n" );
    printf("    Name: %s\n", team1.chief.name);
    printf("        Agent number: %03d\n", team1.chief.agnumb);
    printf("Indian:\n" );
    printf("    Name: %s\n", team1.indian.name);
    printf("        Agent number: %03d\n", team1.indian.agnumb);
    }
```

Figure 9.5 shows the arrangement of nested structures.

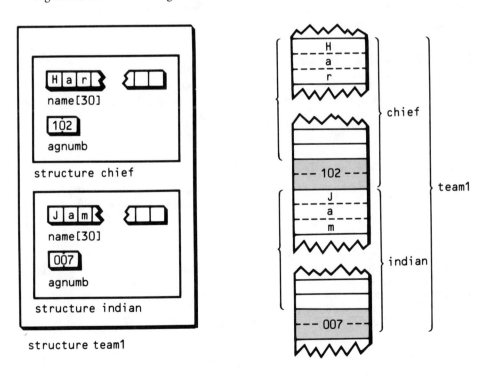

Figure 9.5. Structure team1 *stored in memory.*

Let's look at some details in this program.

First, we've defined a structure variable team1, which is of type team, and initialized it to the values shown. As when multidimensional arrays are initialized, nested braces are used to initialize structures within structures.

Second, notice the method we used to access the members of a structure that is part of another structure. Here the dot operator is used twice, as in the expression

```
team1.chief.name
```

This refers to element name in the structure chief in the structure team1.

Of course, the nesting process need not stop at this level; we can nest a structure within a structure within a structure. Such constructions give rise to variable names that can be surprisingly self-descriptive, for instance,

```
triumph.1962.engine.carb.bolt.large
```

Structures and Other Program Elements

So far we've concentrated on structures used by themselves. Now we'll examine how structures interact with other program features. We'll see how to pass structures as arguments to functions and return structure values from them, how to arrange structures in arrays, and how pointers can be used to access structure members.

Structures and Functions

Structure variables can be used as return values from functions and passed to functions as arguments, just as simple variables can. This is a powerful feature that greatly simplifies the use of structures and thus the writing of well-constructed modular programs that use structures. We'll show a fairly short example and then a longer one.

Passing and Returning Agent Data

Let's rewrite our twoagent.c program to incorporate two functions. The newname() function will obtain data about an agent from the user, and the list() function will display the data. Here's the program:

```
// passtwo.c
// stores two agents
// demonstrates passing structures to functions
#include <stdio.h>              // for printf(), etc.
#include <stdlib.h>             // for atoi()

struct personnel               // declare data structure
   {
   char name[30];              // agent name
   int agnumb;                 // agent number
   };
```

```
struct personnel newname(void);   // function prototypes
void list(struct personnel);      // (using struct personnel)

void main(void)
    {
    struct personnel agent1;    // define structure variable
    struct personnel agent2;    // define another one

    agent1 = newname();         // get data for first agent
    agent2 = newname();         // get data for 2nd agent
    list(agent1);               // print data for first agent
    list(agent2);               // print data for 2nd agent
    }

// newname()
// puts a new agent in the database
struct personnel newname()
    {
    char numstr[81];            // for number
    struct personnel agent;     // new structure

    printf("\nNew agent\nEnter name: ");        // get name
    gets(agent.name);
    printf("Enter agent number (3 digits): "); // get number
    gets(numstr);
    agent.agnumb = atoi(numstr);
    return(agent);                              // return struct
    }

// list()
// prints data on one agent
void list(struct personnel age)    // struct passed from main()
    {
    printf("\nAgent: \n");
    printf("   Name: %s\n", age.name);
    printf("   Agent number: %03d\n", age.agnumb);
    }
```

Because both functions, as well as the main program, need to know how the structure type personnel is declared, this declaration is made global by placing it outside of all functions, before main(). The functions main(), newname(), and list() define their own local structure variables, called agent1 and agent2, agent, and age; to be of this type.

Returning Structure Values

The function newname() is called from the main program to obtain information from the user about the two agents. This function places the information in the local structure variable agent and returns the value of this variable to the main program using a return statement, just as if it were returning a simple variable. The function newname() itself must be declared to be of type struct personnel, because it returns a value of this type.

Passing Structures As Arguments

The main program assigns the values returned from newname() to the structure variables agent1 and agent2. Then main() calls the function list() to print the values in agent1 and agent2, passing the values of these two structures to the function as arguments. Each time it's called, list() assigns one of these values to a local structure variable age and accesses the individual members of this structure to print the values.

A Text Box Example

If you're familiar with Microsoft Windows or the Macintosh, you know about dialog boxes. The Turbo C++ IDE uses them, too. Dialog boxes are fixed-size windows that appear on the screen to display information and get input from the user. Our next example creates a visual element similar to a dialog box, except that it does nothing but display text; it can't obtain user input. We'll call it a *text box.*

In our program, a structure called textbox includes the data necessary to define a text box. There are coordinates left and top, dimensions width and height, and the strings title and message. In main(), two text boxes are defined to be of type textbox: aboutbox and errorbox. The chief purpose of main() is to call the make_textbox() function twice: once with aboutbox as an argument and once with errorbox. The make_textbox() function displays the text box by calling draw_box() to draw a box outline on the screen, displaying the title in the center of the top line of the box and finally displaying the text in the center of the box. Figure 9.6 shows the first text box.

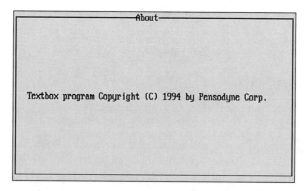

Figure 9.6. Output of the textbox.c program.

The program looks long, but you're already familiar with the draw_box() function from Chapter 8. Here's the listing:

```
// textbox.c
// models 'textbox' — dialog-type box containing text
#include <conio.h>        // for text display functions
#include <string.h>       // for strlen()
```

```
#define TITLE_LENGTH  20  // maximum length of textbox title
#define TEXT_LENGTH   80  // maximum length of textbox text
                          // prototypes
void make_textbox(struct textbox);
void draw_box(int left, int top, int width, int height);

// textbox structure declaration
struct textbox
    {
    int left;                   // left
    int top;                    // top
    int width;                  // width
    int height;                 // height
    char title[TITLE_LENGTH+1]; // title
    char text[TEXT_LENGTH+1];   // text
    };

void main(void)
    {
    // definition of 'aboutbox' textbox
    struct textbox aboutbox = { 10, 3, 62, 15, "About",
        "Textbox program Copyright (C) 1994 by Pensodyne Corp." };

    // definition of 'errorbox' textbox
    struct textbox errorbox = { 20, 7, 40, 9, "Danger",
                                "Press Eject Key Immediately!" };

    _setcursortype(_NOCURSOR); // remove cursor
    textbackground(BLACK);     // clear screen to black
    clrscr();
    make_textbox(aboutbox);    // display about textbox
    getch();                   // wait for key press

    textbackground(BLACK);     // clear screen to black
    clrscr();
    make_textbox(errorbox);    // display error textbox
    getch();                   // wait for key press
    _setcursortype(_NORMALCURSOR);  // restore cursor
    }

// make_textbox()
// draws textbox with title and text
void make_textbox(struct textbox box)
    {
    textbackground(BLUE);
    textcolor(WHITE);
    // draw the box outline
    draw_box(box.left, box.top, box.width, box.height);

    // go to center of top line and display the title
    gotoxy(box.left+(box.width-strlen(box.title))/2-1, box.top);
    cputs(box.title);
```

```
        // go to center of box and display the text
        gotoxy(box.left+(box.width-strlen(box.text))/2-1,
                                    box.top+(box.height-1)/2);
        cputs(box.text);
        }  // end make_textbox()

// draw_box()
// draws a box with a single line around it
void draw_box(int left, int top, int width, int height)
    {
    int j;
    char string[81];             // utility string
                                 // define box-size window
    window(left, top, left+width-1, top+height-1);
    clrscr();                    // clear window to background color
    // now add line so chars on bottom line won't cause scroll
    window(left, top, left+width-1, top+height);
    // draw top and bottom lines, with corners
    for(j=1; j<width-1; j++)     // make string of
        string[j] = '\xC4';      //     horizontal characters
    string[width] = '\0';        // end the string
    string[0] = '\xDA';          // insert upper-left corner
    string[width-1] = '\xBF';    // insert upper-right corner
    gotoxy(1, 1);                // display top line
    cputs(string);
    string[0] = '\xC0';          // insert lower-left corner
    string[width-1] = '\xD9';    // insert lower-right corner
    gotoxy(1, height);           // display bottom line
    cputs(string);
    // draw vertical lines on left and right
    for(j=2; j<height; j++)      // for each row
        {
        gotoxy(1, j);            // on the left end,
        putch('\xB3');           // draw vertical character
        gotoxy(width, j);        // on the right end,
        putch('\xB3');           // draw vertical character
        }
    window(1, 1, 80, 25);        // restore window to full screen
    }  // end draw_box()
```

The make_textbox() function takes a variable of type struct textbox as an argument.

```
make_textbox(aboutbox);    // display about textbox
```

and

```
make_textbox(errorbox);    // display error textbox
```

The make_textbox() function uses the parameter box, of type struct textbox, to represent its copy of the argument. The function then accesses the members of the textbox with expressions such as box.left and box.height, in such statements as

```
draw_box(box.left, box.top, box.width, box.height);
```

The function goes to some trouble to ensure that the title is automatically centered on the top border and that the text is centered both vertically and horizontally.

```
// go to center of top line and display the title
gotoxy(box.left+(box.width-strlen(box.title))/2-1, box.top);
cputs(box.title);
// go to center of box and display the text
gotoxy(box.left+(box.width-strlen(box.text))/2-1,
                              box.top+(box.height-1)/2);
cputs(box.text);
```

Notice that, as with simple variables, you can't change the values of any variables in the calling program's copy of the structure. In other words, make_textbox() can't modify the contents of textbox or errorbox in main(). For that we would need to pass a pointer to the function. We'll see what that entails later in this chapter.

Arrays of Structures

We now know enough to realize our goal, mentioned earlier in this chapter, of creating an array of structures. Each structure will represent the data for one secret agent. This is a more ambitious program. We've provided a simple user interface, consisting of a choice of two single-letter selections. If the user types an e, the program will allow information on one agent to be entered. If the user types an l, the program will list all the agents in the database.

We've also added an additional item of information: the agent's height (a floating point variable), just to prove that structures can have more than two members. Here's the listing:

```
// agent.c
// maintains list of agents in memory
#include <stdio.h>            // for printf()
#include <conio.h>            // for getche()
#include <stdlib.h>           // for atof()
#define TRUE 1

void newname(void);          // prototypes
void listall(void);

struct personnel             // declare data structure
    {
    char name [30];          // name
    int agnumb;              // code number
    float height;            // height in inches
    };
struct personnel agent[50];  // array of 50 structures
int n = 0;                   // number of agents listed

void main(void)
    {
    char ch;
```

```
        while ( TRUE )
           {
           printf("\nType 'e' to enter new agent,"); // print
           printf("\n  'l' to list all agents,");     // selections
           printf("\n  'q' to quit: ");
           ch = getche();                             // get choice
           switch (ch)
              {
              case 'e':                    // enter new name
                 newname(); break;
              case 'l':                    // list entire file
                 listall(); break;
              case 'q':
                 exit(0);
              default:                     // user mistake
                 puts("\nEnter only selections listed");
              } // end switch
           } // end while
        } // end main()

// newname()
// puts a new agent in the database
void newname(void)
   {
   char numstr[81];                          // for number

   printf("\nRecord %d.\nEnter name: ", n+1); // get name
   gets(agent[n].name);
   printf("Enter agent number (3 digits): "); // get number
   gets(numstr);
   agent[n].agnumb = atoi(numstr);
   printf("Enter height in inches: ");        // get height
   gets(numstr);
   agent[n++].height = atof(numstr);   // convert to float
   } // end newname()

// listall()
// lists all agents and data
void listall(void)
   {
   int j;
   if (n < 1)                            // check for empty list
      printf("\nEmpty list.\n");
   for (j=0; j < n; j++)                 // print list
      {
      printf("\nRecord number %d\n", j+1);
      printf("  Name: %s\n", agent[j].name);
      printf("  Agent number: %03d\n", agent[j].agnumb);
      printf("  Height: %4.2f\n", agent[j].height);
      }
   } // end listall()
```

Here's a sample run:

```
Type 'e' to enter new agent
    'l' to list all agents: e
Record 1.
Enter name: Harrison Tweedbury
Enter agent number (3 digits): 102
Enter height in inches: 70.5

Type 'e' to enter new agent
    'l' to list all agents: e
Record 2.
Enter name: Ursula Zimbowski
Enter agent number (3 digits): 303
Enter height in inches: 63.25

Type 'e' to enter new agent
    'l' to list all agents: e
Record 3.
Enter name: James Bond
Enter agent number (3 digits): 007
Enter height in inches: 74.3

Type 'e' to enter new agent
    'l' to list all agents: l

Record number 1
    Name: Harrison Tweedbury
    Agent number: 102
    Height: 70.50

Record number 2
    Name: Ursula Zimbowski
    Agent number: 303
    Height: 63.25

Record number 3
    Name: James Bond
    Agent number: 007
    Height: 74.30
```

Following this interaction we could then have continued by adding more agents, or listing the agents again, as the spirit moved us.

Defining an Array of Structures

Notice how the array of structures is defined.

```
struct personnel agent[50];
```

This statement provides space in memory for 50 structures of type personnel. This structure type is declared by the statement

```
struct personnel                    /* declare data structure */
    {
    char name [30];                 /* name */
    int agnumb;                     /* code number */
    float height;                   /* height in inches */
    };
```

Figure 9.7 shows conceptually what this array of structures looks like.

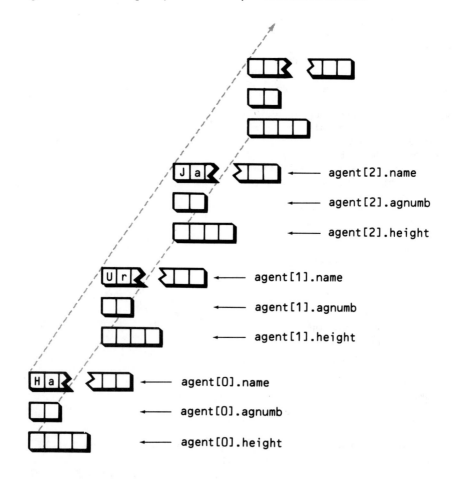

Figure 9.7. Array of structures.

For simplicity, we've defined the array of structures as a global variable so that all the functions in the program can access it. You could also make it a variable local to main(), as we'll see later.

Accessing Members of Array of Structures

Individual members of a structure in our array of structures are accessed by referring to the structure variable name agent, followed by a subscript, followed by the dot operator, and ending with the structure element desired, as in this example:

```
agent[n].name
```

The balance of the program uses constructions we've discussed before.

> The expression agent[n].name refers to element name of the nth structure in an array of structures of type agent.

The overall scheme of this program can be applied to a wide variety of situations for storing data about particular entities. It could, for example, be used for inventory control, where each structure variable contained data about a particular item, such as the stock number, price, and number of items available. Or it could be used for a budgeting program, where each structure contained information about a budget category, such as name of the category, the budgeted amount, and the amount spent to date.

About the only thing lacking to make this program a useful database application is a way to store the data as a disk file, a topic we'll explore in Chapter 11, "Files."

Pointers and Structures

Pointers used with simple variables (like type int and char) provide increased power: the ability to do things in your program that are difficult or impossible any other way. The same is true of pointers used with structures. We'll look first at the basic syntax, and then show some examples of pointers to structures in more complex programs.

Syntax of Pointers to Structures

Here's an important question when dealing with pointers to structures: if a pointer points to a structure, can you use the pointer to access the structure members? Well, of course the answer is yes, because in C you can do anything you want. The next example shows the syntax.

```
// ptrstr.c
// demonstrates pointers to structures
#include <stdio.h>    // for printf()

void main(void)
    {
    struct xx           // declare structure type
        {
        int num1;
```

```
        char ch1;
        };
struct xx xx1;      // define structure variable
struct xx *ptr;     // define pointer to structure

ptr = &xx1;         // assign address of struct to ptr
ptr->num1 = 303;    // refer to members of structure
ptr->ch1 = 'Q';
printf("\nptr->num1=%d", ptr->num1 );
printf("\nptr->ch1=%c",  ptr->ch1 );
}
```

Here we've declared a structure xx and defined a structure variable xx1 of type struct xx. You've seen this before, but the next step is new: we define a variable of type *pointer to structure xx* in the statement,

```
struct xx *ptr;
```

Next we assign the address of the structure variable xx1 to ptr using the line

```
ptr = &xx1;
```

Thus, if the structure xx1 happened to be located at address 1000, the number 1000 would be placed in the variable ptr.

Now, let's see how to refer to the members of the structure using the pointer instead of the structure name itself. As you already know, if we know the name of a given structure variable, we can access its members using this name and the dot operator. For instance, in the example above, the expression xx.num1 refers to the element num1 in the structure xx. What is the analogous construction using ptr instead of xx? We can't use ptr.num1 because ptr isn't a structure but a pointer to a structure, and the dot operator requires a structure on the left side.

A literal approach would be to use the expression (*ptr).num1. Because we know that ptr points to xx1, it follows that *ptr is the contents of xx1. Substituting this in the expression xx1.num1, therefore, gives us (*ptr).num1. (The parentheses are needed around *ptr because the dot operator has higher priority than the indirection operator.) However, this is an unwieldy expression, so C provides a simpler approach, the two-part operator -> is used. The two-part operator is a combination of the minus and less-than signs and is called the *arrow operator,* as in the expression ptr->num1. This has exactly the same effect as (*ptr).num1.

> The . operator connects a structure with a member of the structure; the -> operator connects a pointer with a member of the structure.

In the ptrstr.c program example above, we've used this construction to assign values to the members of the structure, as in the expression

```
ptr->num1 = 303;
```

Similar constructions are used to read those values back out again with `printf()` statements.

Pointers to Structures as Function Arguments

One of the most common uses for pointers to structures is as function arguments. They're used for the same reason as pointers to simple variables: so that values can be passed back from the function to the calling program. In the case of structures, it's the values of the structure members that are passed back. We may want to return values for all or only some of the structure members, but in any case, we pass back the values of all the members at once by passing back the entire structure.

Note that there is a key difference between using an array name and a structure name as a function argument. Values can be passed back to the array using the array name, because the name itself represents an address. However, a structure name isn't an address, and only a copy of the structure is created in the function. If values are to be passed back to the calling routine, a pointer to the original structure must be used.

Our first example, agentptr.c, is a modification of the agent.c program from earlier in this chapter. In that program an array of structures was used to store agent records. This array of structures was defined as a global variable. The present agentptr.c example uses a similar array of structures, but it's defined as a local variable in `main()`. This affects how the various functions in the program access the data. In agent.c all functions could access the data directly, because it was global. Now in agentptr.c, `main()` must pass individual structures, or the entire array, as arguments to functions that it calls.

```
// agentptr.c
// maintains list of agents in memory

#include <stdio.h>              // for printf()
#include <conio.h>              // for getche()
#include <stdlib.h>             // for atof()
#define TRUE 1

struct personnel               // declare data structure
   char name[30];              // name
   int agnumb;                 // code number
   float height;               // height in inches
   };
                               // prototypes
void newname(int n, struct personnel *ptragent);
void listall(int n, struct personnel agentarr[]);

void main(void)
   {
   struct personnel agentarr[50];  // array of 50 structures
   struct personnel *ptragent;     // pointer to structure
   int n = 0;                      // number of agents listed
```

```
              char ch;

          while( TRUE )
             {
             printf("\nType 'e' to enter new agent,"); // print
             printf("\n  'l' to list all agents,");    // selections
             printf("\n  'q' to quit: ");
             ch = getche();                            // get choice
             switch (ch)
                {
                case 'e':                        // enter new name
                   ptragent = &agentarr[n];      // ptr to empty struct
                   newname(n, ptragent );
                   n++;
                   break;
                case 'l':                        // list entire file
                   listall(n, agentarr);
                   break;
                case 'q':
                   exit(0);
                default:                         // user mistake
                   puts("\nEnter only selections listed");
                } // end switch
             } // end while
          } // end main()

// newname()
// puts a new agent in the database
void newname(int num, struct personnel *ptrag)
   {
   char numstr[81];                                 // for number

   printf("\nRecord %d.\nEnter name: ", num+1); // get name
   gets(ptrag->name);
   printf("Enter agent number (3 digits): ");    // get number
   gets(numstr);
   ptrag->agnumb = atoi(numstr);
   printf("Enter height in inches: ");           // get height
   gets(numstr);
   ptrag->height = atof(numstr);                 // convert to float
   } // end newname()

// listall()
// lists all agents and data
void listall(int num, struct personnel agentarr[])
   {
   int j;
   if (num < 1)                              // check for empty list
      printf("\nEmpty list.\n");
   for (j=0; j < num; j++)                   // print list
      {
      printf("\nRecord number %d\n", j+1);
```

```
     printf("   Name: %s\n", agentarr[j].name);
     printf("   Agent number: %03d\n", agentarr[j].agnumb);
     printf("   Height: %4.2f\n", agentarr[j].height);
     }
 }  // end listall()
```

For the listall() function, main passes the entire array of structures. Because an array is being passed and because listall() doesn't need to modify any of the structures in main() anyway, no pointers are necessary. For the newname() function, however, main() wants the function to pass back an entire structure with the data that has been filled in by the user. Thus main() uses a pointer to a structure as an argument. Using this pointer, newname() fills in the members of the structure with the data provided by the user.

In main(), we first declare the array of 50 structures and then a pointer to a structure.

```
struct personnel agentarr[50];   // array of 50 structures
struct personnel *ptragent;      // pointer to structure
```

To call the newname() function, we must first assign to a pointer the address of the structure we want the user to fill with data. This is the nth element of the array, which is the first empty array element.

```
ptragent = &agentarr[n];   // ptr to empty struct
newname(n, ptragent );
```

The pointer is the second argument to the function; the first is the number of agents (filled-in elements) already entered into the array. Both listall() and newname() need to know this number, which, for consistency, we've made a local variable along with the array of structures.

In the newname() function, the parameter ptrag stores the value of the pointer passed to it. The members of the structure are accessed using this variable and the -> operator.

```
gets(ptrag->name);
```

This statement obtains the name from the user and puts it in the name member of the structure pointed to by ptrag, which is agentarr[n]. In most other ways agentptr.c is similar to agent.c

A Dialog Box Example

Using a pointer to a structure as a function argument is an important concept, so let's look at another example that uses this construction. This program is an extension of the textbox.c example earlier in this chapter, in which a colored, bordered box displayed a line of text. However, the present example, dialbox.c, allows the user to type a string into an input field. Such a dialog box is often used in GUIs to obtain filenames and other text data from the user.

The program creates two dialog boxes, the first of which is shown in Figure 9.8.

Figure 9.8. Output of the dialbox.c program.

In this program the dialog box is modeled by a structure called `dialbox`. The members of this structure are the coordinates and dimensions of the dialog box, a title, a prompt (such as `Enter file name: `), and an empty array to store the user's input (such as `AGENTS.DAT`).

In `main()` the function `make_dialog()` is called twice, once for each of two dialogs. The dialogs, of type `struct dialbox`, are called `filedial` and `namedial`.

When we return from the `make_dialog()` function, we want to have access to whatever the user typed into the input field. We'll do this by passing a pointer to a `struct dialbox` as an argument to the function. When the function gets the text input from the user, it can then use the pointer to insert the text into the `input` member of the calling program's original copy of the structure.

```
// dialbox.c
// models 'dialbox' -- dialog with text and input field
#include <conio.h>          // for text display functions
#include <string.h>         // for strlen()
#define TITLE_LENGTH  20    // maximum length of title
#define PROMPT_LENGTH 40    // maximum length of text
#define MAX_LENGTH    40    // maximum length of input buffer
                            // prototypes
void make_dialbox(struct dialbox *dbox);
void draw_box(int left, int top, int width, int height);

// dialbox structure declaration
struct dialbox
    {
    int left;                       // left edge of box
    int top;                        // top edge of box
    int width;                      // width of box
    int height;                     // height of box
    int inlength;                   // length of input field
    char title[TITLE_LENGTH+1];     // title
    char prompt[PROMPT_LENGTH+1];   // prompt
    char input[MAX_LENGTH+1];       // input buffer
    };


void main(void)
    {
    // definition of 'filedial' dialbox
```

```
      struct dialbox filedial = { 10, 3, 42, 5, 21, "Open File",
                               "Enter file name: "};

   // definition of 'namedial' dialbox
   struct dialbox namedial = { 15, 3, 50, 9, 21, "Agent Name",
              "Enter surname of agent: "};

   textbackground(BLACK);     // clear screen to black
   clrscr();
   make_dialbox(&filedial);   // make file dialbox

   textbackground(BLACK);     // clear screen to black
   clrscr();
   make_dialbox(&namedial);   // make name dialbox

   gotoxy(1, 25);                 // display data on bottom line
   cprintf("File is %s, name is %s",
                       filedial.input, namedial.input);
   }

// make_dialbox()
// draws dialbox with title and prompt, gets input from user
void make_dialbox(struct dialbox *pb)
   {
   char *ptr;                 // for cgets() return
   char buffer[MAX_LENGTH+3]; // for cgets() input
   int vcenter;               // vertical center of window
   int instart;               // x-coordinate of input field

   textbackground(BLUE);
   textcolor(WHITE);
   // draw the box outline
   draw_box(pb->left, pb->top, pb->width, pb->height);

   // go to center of top line and display the title
   gotoxy(pb->left+(pb->width-strlen(pb->title))/2-1, pb->top);
   cputs(pb->title);

   // go to left of box and display the prompt
   vcenter = pb->top + (pb->height-1)/2;
   gotoxy(pb->left+2, vcenter);
   cputs(pb->prompt);

   // display the input field in a different color
   instart = pb->left + strlen(pb->prompt) + 2;
   gotoxy(instart, vcenter); // go to start of input field

   memset(pb->input, ' ',  MAX_LENGTH ); // fill with blanks
   pb->input[pb->inlength] = '\0';        // terminate string
   textbackground(GREEN);                 // set field color
   cputs(pb->input);                      // display field
```

```
                    // get input from user
                    gotoxy(instart, vcenter);      // start of input field
                    buffer[0] = pb->inlength + 1;  // set up buffer count
                    ptr = cgets(buffer);           // get input
                    strcpy(pb->input, ptr);        // copy input to dialog box
                    }  // end make_dialbox()

// draw_box()
// draws a box with a single line around it
void draw_box(int left, int top, int width, int height)
    {
    int j;
    char string[81];                // utility string
                                    // define box-size window
    window(left, top, left+width-1, top+height-1);
    clrscr();                       // clear window to background color
    // now add line so that chars on bottom line won't cause scroll
    window(left, top, left+width-1, top+height);
    // draw top and bottom lines, with corners
    for(j=1; j<width-1; j++)        // make string of
        string[j] = '\xC4';         //    horizontal characters
    string[width] = '\0';           // end the string
    string[0] = '\xDA';             // insert upper-left corner
    string[width-1] = '\xBF';       // insert upper-right corner
    gotoxy(1, 1);                   // display top line
    cputs(string);
    string[0] = '\xC0';             // insert lower-left corner
    string[width-1] = '\xD9';       // insert lower-right corner
    gotoxy(1, height);              // display bottom line
    cputs(string);
    // draw vertical lines on left and right
    for(j=2; j<height; j++)         // for each row
        {
        gotoxy(1, j);               // on the left end,
        putch('\xB3');              // draw vertical character
        gotoxy(width, j);           // on the right end,
        putch('\xB3');              // draw vertical character
        }
    window(1, 1, 80, 25);           // restore window to full screen
    }  // end draw_box()
```

As you can see from the declaration of struct dialbox, the members of the structure are the left and top coordinates of the dialog box, its width and height, the maximum length allowed for the user's input, a title, a prompt, and an array to store the user's input. Here's how one of the two dialog boxes is defined:

```
struct dialbox filedial = { 10, 3, 42, 5, 21, "Open File",
                            "Enter file name: "};
```

To display this dialog box and get the user input to it, main() calls the make_dialog() function using the address of this dialbox structure as an argument, like this:

```
make_dialbox(&filedial);    // make file dialbox
```

In the `make_dialog()` function we access the structure representing the dialog using the pointer `pb`. For instance, here's how we draw a box around the dialog:

```
draw_box(pb->left, pb->top, pb->width, pb->height);
```

Here `pb->left` represents the `left` member of the dialog pointed to by `pb`, and so on. Similar statements display the title and prompt and draw the input field in a contrasting color.

We use the `cgets()` function to get the input from the user. This requires setting up a buffer to receive the input; we call this buffer `buffer`. We fill in its first two bytes with the length of the input field, plus one for the terminating `\0`. A pointer `ptr` points to the actual input string, which we then copy into the input member of the structure.

```
buffer[0] = pb->inlength + 1;   // set up buffer count
ptr = cgets(buffer);            // get input
strcpy(pb->input, ptr);         // copy input to dialog box
```

The function `memset()` in this program is used to set the input field to all blanks. This creates a green rectangle for the user to type text into.

```
memset(pb->input, ' ',  MAX_LENGTH ); // fill with blanks
```

This function fills in an area of memory with a byte value. The first argument is the address of the area to be filled, the second is the character to be filled in, and the third is the number of characters to fill in.

This concludes our discussion of what we might call "real" structures. However, there is another entity in C that is very much like a structure: the union.

Unions

Unions have the same relationship to structures that you might have to a distant cousin who resembled you but turned out to be smuggling contraband in a third-world country; they may look the same, but they are engaged in different enterprises.

Both structures and unions are used to group a number of different variables together, but while a structure enables us to treat as a unit a number of different variables stored at different places in memory, a union enables us to treat the same space in memory as a number of different variables. That is, a union is a way for a section of memory to be accessed as a variable of one type on one occasion and as a different variable of a different type on another occasion.

You might wonder why it would ever be necessary to do such a thing. We'll examine a practical application in Chapter 15, "Hardware-Oriented C." For now, let's look at a simple example.

```
// union.c
// demonstrates unions
```

```
#include <stdio.h>          // for printf()

void main(void)
   {
   union intflo               // declare union of type 'intflo'
      {
      int intnum;          //     integer member
      float fltnum;        //      floating point member
      } unex;              // define 'unex' to be type intflo
   printf("sizeof(union intflo)=%d\n", sizeof(union intflo) );
   unex.intnum = 734;
   printf("unex.intnum=%d\n", unex.intnum );
   unex.fltnum = 867.43;
   printf("unex.fltnum=%.2f\n", unex.fltnum );
   }
```

As you can see, we declare a union type (intflo) and a union variable (unex) in much the same way we declare structure types and variables. However, the similarity ends there, as we can see from the output of the program.

```
sizeof(union inflo)=4
unex.intnum=734
unex.fltnum=867.43
```

Although the union holds a floating point number (fltnum) and an integer (intnum), its size is only four bytes. Thus, it's big enough to hold one element or the other but not both at the same time. In the program we first give a value to the variable unex.intnum and then print it. Then we give a value to unex.fltnum and print it. We can't give values to these two variables at the same time, because they occupy the same space in memory; if we assigned unex.intnum a value, and then tried to read out a value of unex.fltnum, we'd get nonsense because the program would try to interpret an integer as a floating point number. Figure 9.9 shows a conceptual view of the union intflo and its relationship to memory.

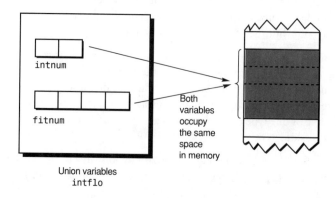

Figure 9.9. Union variable intflo stored in memory.

Why use unions? One reason is to use a single variable name to pass data of different types. We could rewrite the C library function sqrt(), for example, so that instead of requiring an argument of type double, it would accept any data type. A union could be used in the function to store the incoming data; any data type would be acceptable. The union might look like this:

```
union number
    {
    double dnum;
    float fnum;
    long lnum;
    int inum;
    char cnum;
    };
```

In this way the same function would serve for all data types. (The function would need to examine the data in the union to determine which type it was or it would need to be told the type via a second parameter.) Another use for unions is to give the same data different names and treat it as different types, depending on the needs of the function using it.

> A union provides a way to look at the same data in several different ways.

Summary

In this chapter we've covered the use of structures, which allow us to combine several variables of different types into a single entity. We've seen how to use structures as function arguments and return values, and also as array elements. We saw several examples of pointers to structures used as function arguments. Finally we examined unions, which allow one area of memory to be treated in several different ways.

Questions

1. Array elements must all be of the _____ _____, whereas structure members can be of _____ _____.

2. True or false: an appropriate use for a structure is to store a list of prices.

3. The purpose of declaring a structure type is to

   a. Set aside the appropriate amount of memory
   b. Define the format of the structure
   c. Specify a list of structure members
   d. Declare a new data type

4. Write a statement that declares a structure type consisting of two members: a string of 10 characters and an integer.

5. How many structure variables of a given type can you use in a program?

   a. One
   b. None
   c. As many as you like
   d. As many as there are members in the structure

6. Before you can access a member of a structure, you must

   a. Declare the structure _____,
   b. Define a structure _____,
   c. Give the item in step b a _____.

7. Write a statement that will define a structure variable `car` to be of structure type `vehicle`.

8. Assume the following statements have been made:

```
struct body
    {
    int arms;
    int legs;
    };
struct body jim;
```

   Write an assignment statement that will set the number of arms in `jim`'s body equal to 2.

9. Is it possible to declare a structure type and define a structure variable in the same statement? If so, rewrite the example in question 8 to use this approach.

10. Assuming that `struct1` and `struct2` are structure variables of the same type, is the following statement possible?

```
struct1 = struct2;
```

11. Given the statement

```
xxx.yyy.zzz = 5;
```

    which of the following are true?

    a. Structure `zzz` is nested within structure `yyy`.
    b. Structure `yyy` is nested within structure `xxx`.
    c. Structure `xxx` is nested within structure `yyy`.
    d. Structure `xxx` is nested within structure `zzz`.

12. Write a statement that declares a structure of type `partners` containing two structures of type `body`.

13. True or false: it's possible to pass a structure to a function in the same way a simple variable is passed.

14. Write a statement that defines a pointer to type `struct book`.

15. If `temp` is a member of the structure `weather`, and the statement

    ```
    addweath = &weather;
    ```

    has been executed, which of the following represents `temp`?

    a. weather.temp
    b. (*weather).temp
    c. addweath.temp
    d. addweath->temp

16. Assume this structure is declared:

    ```
    struct blech
        {
        int i;
        float f;
        };
    ```

    Write a complete function called `blorg` that takes no /arguments and returns a structure of type `bleck` with values 3 and 7.25.

17. Imagine an array called `multi`. Its elements are structures of type `cyclops`. Which is the correct expression for the `greep` member of the seventh element of the array?

    a. `multi.cyclops.greep[7]`
    b. `multi.cyclops[7].greep`
    c. `multi.greep[7]`
    d. `multi[7].greep`

18. True or false: a pointer to a structure may be useful for passing values back from a function.

19. Assume you pass the address of a structure called `alpha` of type `beta` to a function called `gamma()`, which takes a single parameter called `delta` and returns no value. Write the prototype for `gamma()`.

20. True or false: in a union you can store three different values of different data types at the same place in memory at the same time.

Exercises

1. Write a short program that will

    a. Set up a structure to hold a date (the structure will consist of three integer values, for the month, day, and year)
    b. Assign values to the members of the structure
    c. Print the values in the format 12/31/88

2. Modify the program of exercise 1 so that the date is printed by a function. Pass the structure as an argument to the function.

3. Modify the program of exercise 2 to include a function to obtain a date from the user. Use a pointer to a structure as the argument to the function so that the date can be passed back.

Turbo C++ Graphics

- Initializing the graphics system
- Rectangles, ellipses, and polygons
- Filling and patterns
- Bit images and animation
- Adding text to graphics

The ability to draw pictures—in color and in a fraction of a second—is one of the most fascinating capabilities of modern computers. Graphics can be used in almost any computer program. Bar and pie charts can help make sense of the numbers produced in spreadsheet or database programs. Most games rely heavily on graphics. The user interface to many programs uses graphics, and of course, entire operating systems—such as Microsoft Windows, OS/2, and the Macintosh—use graphic user interfaces. The chances are that the program you're writing can profit from graphics, too.

In this chapter we'll explore the library functions that Turbo C++ makes available for graphics. In Chapter 15, "Hardware-Oriented C," we'll examine other techniques for creating graphics, but the Turbo C++ graphics functions are the most convenient. They allow you to draw graphics elements like circles, rectangles, and lines; fill shapes with patterns and use a variety of text fonts in different sizes; control the color of text and graphics elements; and much more.

There are close to 100 graphics functions, so we can't demonstrate them all in this chapter. However, we will cover the majority, concentrating on the most important.

In general we'll show short, easy-to-follow examples of each function as it's introduced. At the end of the chapter, several more ambitious examples demonstrate some of the effects possible with Turbo C++ graphics. These include a presentation-quality bar-graph generator, a hypnotic kinetic painting, and a program that generates the extraordinary images of the Mandelbrot set.

To run the example programs you'll need a graphics adapter board and a graphics display monitor; a character-only display won't work. A VGA system is preferable, but most of the examples will work, perhaps with some modification, with EGA as well. Although some examples can be modified to work with CGA, others can't, so we don't recommend a CGA display for this chapter.

Preparing for Graphics Functions

Before you can use Turbo C++ graphics functions in your program you must take three preliminary steps. You must tell the Turbo C++ linker you plan to use graphics functions, you must include a header file in your program, and you must execute the `initgraph()` function.

Tell the Linker You're Doing Graphics

Perhaps the easiest thing to forget when writing a graphics program is telling the Turbo C++ linker that you plan to use graphics functions. You need to do this because the code for the graphics functions is in a different file than that used for normal C functions. This file is called graphics.lib, and it must be linked into your program.

Fortunately, the Turbo C++ IDE makes this simple. Select Linker from the Options menu and select the Libraries submenu. Then click the Graphics Library checkbox. (The Standard Runtime box should already be checked, but the other boxes should not be.)

The graphics.h Header File

All the Turbo C++ graphics functions require the graphics.h header file to be included in the program. This file contains prototypes for these functions. Because many graphics functions use constants instead of numbers to specify such values as colors, patterns, and fonts, the graphics.h file also contains definitions for these constants. You won't get far in Turbo C++ graphics programming if you don't include this file.

Initializing with *initgraph()*

Before any of the graphics functions can be used, the graphics system must be initialized, using the function initgraph(). This function loads a graphics driver (probably called egavga.bgi) from the disk and changes the display to the appropriate graphics mode. It is thus the first graphics function to be executed in a program.

A related function, closegraph(), shuts down the graphics system and returns the display to its previous mode. This function should be executed just before your program terminates.

A Simple Example

Our first example uses initgraph() to initialize the system, and then draws a circle and a line. Notice that it includes the header file graphics.h, that initgraph() is executed first, and that closegraph() comes last. Don't forget to tell the linker we'll be using graphics functions. Here's the listing:

```c
// circline.c
// draws circle and line using auto detect
#include <graphics.h>          // for graphics functions
#include <conio.h>             // for getch()

void main(void)
   {
   int driver, mode;           // graphics driver and mode
   int x1=0, y1=0;             // one end of line
   int x2=199, y2=199;         // other end of line
   int xC=100, yC=100;         // center of circle
   int radius=90;              // radius of circle

   driver = DETECT;            // autodetect
   // ('mode' doesn't need a value)
                               // initialize graphics
   initgraph(&driver, &mode, "c:\\tc\\bgi");
```

```
line(x1, y1, x2, y2);        // draw line
circle(xC, yC, radius);      // draw circle

getch();                     // keep picture until keypress
closegraph();                // shut down graphics system
}
```

The *initgraph()* Function

The initgraph() function is of type void far, and takes three arguments of type int far *. These are the addresses where the graphics driver will be specified, the address where the mode will be specified, and the address of a string holding the pathname to the file containing the graphics driver.

Don't worry about the modifier far in these data types. It's used in many Turbo C++ graphics functions. We'll examine what this, and its counterpart near, mean in Chapter 12, "Memory." In the meantime you can ignore it.

Initialize Graphics System

```
void far initgraph(int far *addrDriver,
                   int far *addrMode,
                   int far *addrPath);
addrDriver    // address of driver number
addrMode      // address of mode number
addrPath      // string containing driver path
```

In most of our examples we'll set the driver variable to the constant DETECT. This will cause the graphics system to automatically select the graphics mode with the highest resolution. If you have a standard VGA system, it will select a resolution of 640 by 480 with 16 colors. (That is, the display will consist of 480 horizontal lines, each with 640 colored dots called pixels.) If you have an EGA system, a resolution of 640 by 350, with 16 colors, will be selected.

Actually a pixel is more complicated than just a colored dot. In a color display, a pixel is composed of a red dot, a green dot, and a blue dot. Illuminating these three dots in different proportions produces pixels of different colors. The three colored dots may form a triangle, giving a pixel a triangular shape, although you can't see this without a magnifying glass. For most purposes you can think of pixels as colored dots.

When DETECT is used, the mode variable need not be specified. (We'll see how to use values for driver other than DETECT in a moment.)

The third argument to initgraph() is the pathname for the graphics driver. If you're using EGA or VGA graphics, the driver is the egavga.bgi file. If you're using CGA graphics it's cga.bgi. Other graphics adapters, such as Hercules and IBM 8514, use different files. In the current version of Turbo C++, these driver files are located in the subdirectory \TC\ BGI\, so this is the pathname used in the third argument to `initgraph()`.

If you're using Borland C++, change the line that invokes `initgraph()` to

```
initgraph(&driver, &mode, "c:\\borlandc\\bgi");
```

because the whole system is installed in a different directory.

Remember that in C the backslash is used as an escape character, so it must be doubled when used in an argument string. (You can substitute a forward slash (/), which MS-DOS interprets as a backslash; a forward slash does not need to be doubled.)

Because the graphics driver is a separate file, your program must be able to access it to run. Thus your program cannot run as a stand-alone application on computers that don't have Turbo C++ installed. The final section of this chapter, "Creating Stand-Alone Executables," shows how to circumvent this problem.

Lines and Circles

Once the circline.c program has initialized the graphics system, it draws a circle with a line through it, as shown in Figure 10.1.

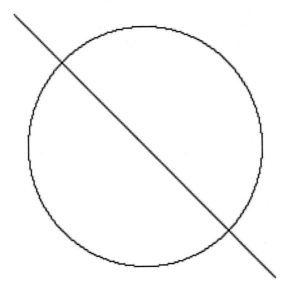

Figure 10.1. Output of circline.c program.

The function that draws the line, `line()`, requires four parameters: the x and y coordinates of the start of the line, and the x and y coordinates of the end.

Draw Line Between Two Locations

```
void far line(int x1, int y1, int x2, int y2);
x1    // coordinates of one end of line
y1
x2    // coordinates of other end of line
y2
```

All these coordinates are expressed in pixels, measured from x=0 y=0 at the upper-left corner of the screen. The arguments to the functions are of type int (as are the majority of arguments to graphics functions).

The circle function requires the x and y coordinates of the center of the circle and the circle's radius.

Draw Circle

```
void far circle(int xC, int yC, int radius );
xC          // center of circle (pixels)
yC
radius;     // radius of circle
```

Holding the Picture

In text-mode (non-graphics) programs you can use the Alt F5 key combination to flip back and forth between the IDE and the output screen. This doesn't work in graphics programs, because once the display system has been changed from graphics back to text mode, the picture is lost. Thus in a graphics program you must inspect the output before the program terminates. To make this possible, we put the statement

```
getch();
```

near the end of the program. The program output will remain on the screen until the user presses a key.

Closing Down the System

At the end of the program you should always execute the statement

```
closegraph();
```

This restores the original text mode. Failure to do this doesn't cause a problem when executing from the IDE, but if you fail to execute closegraph() in a program you're executing from DOS, you may lose your cursor or end up with the wrong size characters. The `closegraph()` function also deallocates the memory used by the graphics system.

Closes Graphics System

```
void far closegraph(void);
```

Specifying Driver and Mode

Sometimes you want to set the graphics system to a specific graphics mode that isn't the highest resolution of the system. For example, you might have a program designed to run in EGA even when it finds itself in a VGA system. To specify a particular mode, you can use various constants for the `driver` and `mode` values in `initgraph()`. Table 10.1 shows the choices for the driver.

Table 10.1. Driver values for `initgraph()`.

Value	Constant	Comment
0	DETECT	System detects highest graphics mode
1	CGA	Normal CGA
2	MCGA	
3	EGA	Normal EGA
4	EGA64	64K memory on EGA board
5	EGAMONO	No color
6	IBM8514	
7	HERCMONO	Hercules
8	ATT400	
9	VGA	Normal VGA
10	PC3270	

The symbolic constants shown in Table 10.1 are defined in the graphics.h header file, so you can use either the constant or the value it represents as an argument. However, the constant makes it much clearer what your program is doing: VGA is clearer than 9, for example.

For each value of driver there are several choices for the mode constant. The modes for the CGA, EGA, and VGA drivers are shown in Table 10.2.

Table 10.2 Driver modes for CGA, EGA, and VGA.

Driver	Value	Constant	Resolution	Palette/Colors
CGA	0	CGAC0	320x200	palette 0, 4 colors
	1	CGAC1	320x200	palette 1, 4 colors
	2	CGAC2	320x200	palette 2, 4 colors
	3	CGAC3	320x200	palette 3, 4 colors
	4	CGAHI	640x200	2 colors
EGA	0	EGALO	640x200	16 colors
	1	EGAHI	640x350	16 colors
VGA	0	VGALO	640x200	16 colors
	1	VGAMED	640x350	16 colors
	2	VGAHI	640x480	16 colors

The first four CGA modes have the same resolution and four colors, but the set of colors (palette) is different for each mode. Here's how to specify palette 0:

```
driver = CGA;
mode = CGAC0;
```

For EGA you would normally set mode to EGAHI, which provides the best resolution:

```
driver = EGA;
mode = EGAHI;
```

Notice that, for a given program, the size of the picture is related to the resolution specified by the values of driver and mode. For example, if your normal system is VGA, but you specify EGAHI in the circline.c program, the picture will appear taller on the screen because there are only 350, instead of 480, horizontal lines in this EGA mode, so the picture will occupy a larger proportion of the screen. The picture will be larger still in any of the CGA modes, which have only 200 lines of vertical resolution.

Incidentally, when you're playing with graphics programs, you may, even if you're careful to use closegraph(), inadvertently alter the DOS graphics mode. When this happens you can usually restore DOS to normal by entering

```
C>mode co80
```

at the DOS prompt. The DOS MODE command changes graphics modes (among other duties) and the co80 sets the system to 80-column color, which is usually what you want for running (say) Turbo C++.

Errors

If some functions—such as initgraph()—fail, they cause an error code to be generated in the graphics system. This error code can be queried with the function graphresult().

Returns Error Code

```
int far graphresult(void);
```

The following example demonstrates the use of this function:

```c
// error.c
// checks results of initgraph()
#include <graphics.h>          // for graphics functions
#include <stdio.h>             // for printf()
#include <conio.h>             // for getch()
#include <process.h>          // for exit()

int main(void)
    {
    int driver, mode, error;
    char *errptr;             // pointer to error message

    driver = DETECT;          // autodetect
                              // bad path name
    initgraph(&driver, &mode, "c:\\not\\here");

    error = graphresult();    // check for error
    if(error != grOk)
        {
        errptr = grapherrormsg(error);  // get message ptr
        printf("\nError %d\n%s", error, errptr);
        exit(1);                        // return error code
        }
    printf("\nGraphics OK");   // normal processing goes here
    getch();                   // keep display until keypress
    closegraph();              // shut down graphics system
    return(0);                 // return success code
    }
```

Graph result returns the error number. Once this number has been discovered, it can be used as an argument to the function grapherrormsg(), which returns a pointer to a standard message string that describes the error in terms a human may understand.

> **Returns Error Message String**
> ```
> char * far grapherrormsg(int error);
> error     // error code
> ```

The error.c program intentionally creates an error by using a pathname that does not contain the graphics driver. The program responds to this unfortunate mistake with the output

```
Error -3
Device driver file not found (EGAVGA.BGI)
```

A list of error messages can be found in the description of `graphresult()` in the Turbo C++ documentation. They include such problems as not finding the graphics driver, not having enough memory to load the graphics system, a specification for a graphics mode that isn't available on the system, and so on.

Most of the example programs in this chapter don't include the sort of error-checking code found in error.c. This makes the listings shorter and easier to understand. However, in a serious program, `graphresult()` should be employed whenever there is the slightest chance that a function might not work correctly. Examining the error code will make an application—and the program's user—aware of errors that might otherwise go undetected.

Getting System Information

When you use auto detection your program may find itself running in a variety of graphics modes. You may have written a program that works in VGA, for example, but someone else may load this program in an EGA system. In this case `initgraph()`—if the driver is set to DETECT—will be happy to run the program in EGA mode.

Several problems can arise when the program doesn't know in advance what mode it's going to be in. First, it may not be able to run at all, and second it may need to size its picture according to the screen dimensions.

Finding the Driver and Mode

If your program needs a certain minimum screen resolution, or a minimum number of colors to run, it will need a way to find what mode it's in before it gets started. The following program shows how this is accomplished:

```
// modetest.c
// tests graphics modes, drivers
#include <graphics.h>          // for graphics functions
#include <conio.h>             // for getch()
#include <stdio.h>             // for printf()
```

```
void main(void)
    {
    int driver, mode;
    char *drivername;
    char *modename;

    driver = DETECT;              // use highest available resolution
                                  // initialize graphics
    initgraph(&driver, &mode, "\\tc\\bgi");

    drivername = getdrivername();      // get driver name
    mode = getgraphmode();             // get mode number
    modename = getmodename(mode);      // get mode name
    printf("\nDriver=%s, Mode number=%d, Mode name=%s",
                                    drivername, mode, modename);
    getch();                    // keep picture until keypress
    closegraph();               // shut down graphics system
    }
```

This program uses three new functions to find the driver name (a string such as "EGAVGA" or "CGA"), the mode (a number such as 1) and the mode name (a string such as "640 x 350 EGA").

Returns Pointer to String Describing Graphics Driver

```
char * far getdrivername(void);
```

Returns Graph Mode Number

```
in far getgraphmode(void);
```

The mode name is derived from the mode number:

Returns Pointer to String Describing Graphics Mode

```
char * far getmodename(int mode_number);
mode number     // number returned by getgraphmode()
```

Here's the output of the modetest.c when the program runs on a standard VGA system:

```
Driver=EGAVGA, Mode number=2, Mode name=640 x 480 VGA
```

Using these functions, your program could find out what driver and mode are in use and—if the mode isn't sufficiently powerful—inform the user that it can't run.

Finding the Screen Size

If you're writing a program in which it's critical that a picture fit on the screen, you need to know how big the screen is before drawing. It won't do to tell the system to put a pixel on line number 479 if there are only 350 lines on the screen.

The next example shows how this is accomplished. This program draws a border around the entire screen. However, before drawing the border, the code checks to see how big the screen is. The border is sized accordingly. This program thus can work in any graphics mode.

```
// border.c
// draws border around screen
#include <graphics.h>          // for graphics functions
#include <conio.h>             // for getch()

void main(void)
    {
    int driver = DETECT;       // auto-detect driver
    int mode;                  // use best mode
    int maxx, maxy;            // size of screen in pixels
    int left, top, right, bot; // sides of rectangle

    initgraph(&driver, &mode, "c:\\tc\\bgi");
    maxx = getmaxx();          // get screen dimensions
    maxy = getmaxy();
    left = top = 0;            // set rectangle sides
    right = maxx;              //    to edges of screen
    bot = maxy;
    rectangle(left, top, right, bot);   // draw rectangle
    getch();
    closegraph();
    }
```

The getmaxx() and getmaxy() functions take no arguments and return the appropriate screen dimension in pixels.

Returns Maximum Horizontal Screen Coordinate

```
int far getmaxx(void);
```

Returns Maximum Vertical Screen Coordinate

```
int far getmaxy(void);
```

The border is drawn with the function `rectangle()`. It takes four arguments that specify, in pixels, the four edges of the rectangle to be drawn. As with other pixel-based graphics functions, the coordinate system starts at 0,0 in the upper-left corner.

Draw Rectangle

```
void far rectangle(int left, int top,
                   int right, int bottom);
left      // edges of rectangle
top
right
bottom
```

Line Width and Style

It's possible to vary the thickness of the lines used by the Turbo C++ graphics functions. This is done with the `setlinestyle()` function. The next example draws the same circle and line as did the circline.c program but uses thicker lines. Here's the listing:

```
// linetype.c
// draws circle and line with different line styles
#include <graphics.h>          // for graphics functions
#include <conio.h>             // for getch()
#define IGNORED  0

void main(void)
   {
   int driver, mode;           // graphics driver and mode
   int x1=0, y1=0;             // one end of line
   int x2=199, y2=199;         // the other end of line
   int xC=100, yC=100;         // center of circle
   int radius=90;              // radius of circle

   driver = DETECT;            // autodetect
                               // initialize graphics
   initgraph(&driver, &mode, "c:\\tc\\bgi");
                               // line pattern and thickness
   setlinestyle(DASHED_LINE, IGNORED, THICK_WIDTH);
   line(x1, y1, x2, y2);       // draw line
   circle(xC, yC, radius);     // draw circle
```

```
getch();
closegraph();
}
```

The result is shown in Figure 10.2.

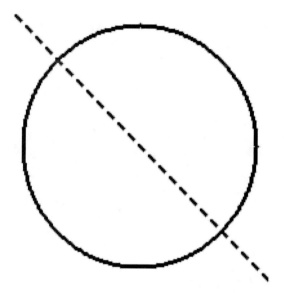

Figure 10.2. Output of the linetype.c program.

An interesting aspect of the output is that the straight line is dashed, but the circle is not. The `setlinestyle()` function includes a parameter to specify different kinds of dotted lines (the line *style*), but this parameter applies only to straight lines, not to circles or other curved lines.

Specify Line Width and Style

```
void far setlinestyle(int style, unsigned pattern, int thickness);
style           // solid, dotted, dashed, etc.
pattern         // user-defined pattern when style=4
thickness       // normal or thick
```

Here are the possible values for the `style` parameter.

Value	Constant
0	SOLID_LINE
1	DOTTED_LINE
2	CENTER_LINE
3	DASHED_LINE
4	USERBIT_LINE

A center line (used to indicate the center of objects in mechanical drawings) has a dot-dash, dot-dash pattern. If the USERBIT_LINE value is used for the style argument, the pattern argument defines a 16-bit value, where each bit specifies whether a corresponding dot on a line section will be on or off. For example, a hex value of 0xFF00 would turn on the first half of the section and turn off the second, thus creating long dashes. 0xF0F0 would make shorter dashes, and 0xF6F6 provides a dash-dot dash-dot effect. (See Appendix B, "Hexadecimal Numbering.")

The thickness parameter has two possible values

Value	Constant	Comment
1	NORM_WIDTH	1 pixel line width
3	THICK_WIDTH	3 pixels line width

The graphresult() function will return −11 if improper arguments are used for setlinestyle().

Color

It's easy to specify the color of lines, circles, and other graphics elements. This is done with the setcolor() function. The next program draws the same line and circle as in previous examples but colors the line green and the circle red.

```
// lincolor.c
// draws circle and line with different colors
#include <graphics.h>     // for graphics functions
#include <conio.h>        // for getch()
#define IGNORED  0

void main(void)
   {
   int driver, mode;      // graphics driver and mode
   int x1=0, y1=0;        // one end of line
   int x2=199, y2=199;    // the other end of line
   int xC=100, yC=100;    // center of circle
   int radius=90;         // radius of circle

   driver = DETECT;       // auto detect
                          // initialize graphics
```

```
initgraph( &driver, &mode, "c:\\tc\\bgi" );
                              // line pattern and thickness
setlinestyle(DASHED_LINE, IGNORED, THICK_WIDTH);

setcolor(GREEN);            // set color
line( x1, y1, x2, y2 );     // draw line
setcolor(RED);              // set color
circle( xC, yC, radius );   // draw circle
getch();
closegraph();
}
```

The setcolor() function takes only one argument: the color.

Specifies Color

```
void far setcolor(int color);
color    // color value for drawing operations
```

The colors that can be used depend on the graphics mode. If you're using standard VGA, you can access the same 16 colors used for text, as described in Chapter 8, "Keyboard and Cursor." These are

Number	Name
Dark Colors	
0	BLACK
1	BLUE
2	GREEN
3	CYAN
4	RED
5	MAGENTA
6	BROWN
7	LIGHTGRAY
Bright Colors	
8	DARKGRAY
9	LIGHTBLUE
10	LIGHTGREEN
11	LIGHTCYAN
12	LIGHTRED
13	LIGHTMAGENTA
14	YELLOW
15	WHITE

In EGA, surprisingly, these numbers and the corresponding constants are different (at least in theory).

Number	Name
Dark Colors	
0	EGA_BLACK
1	EGA_BLUE
2	EGA_GREEN
3	EGA_CYAN
4	EGA_RED
5	EGA_MAGENTA
20	EGA_BROWN
7	EGA_LIGHTGRAY
Light Colors	
56	EGA_DARKGRAY
57	EGA_LIGHTBLUE
58	EGA_LIGHTGREEN
59	EGA_LIGHTCYAN
60	EGA_LIGHTRED
61	EGA_LIGHTMAGENTA
62	EGA_YELLOW
63	EGA_WHITE

However, for most purposes you can use the VGA color constants for EGA as well.

If you're using CGA you can use only one palette of four colors at a time, selected by the mode variable to initgraph(). There are four palettes. Color 0 is BLACK in all of them. Here are the remaining three colors:

Palette	Color 1	Color 2	Color 3
CGAC0	CGA_LIGHTGREEN	CGA_LIGHTRED	CGA_YELLOW
CGAC1	CGA_LIGHTCYAN	CGA_LIGHTMAGENTA	CGA_WHITE
CGAC2	CGA_GREEN	CGA_RED	CGA_BROWN
CGAC3	CGA_CYAN	CGA_MAGENTA	CGA_LIGHTGRAY

Ellipses and Polygons

In addition to lines, circles, and rectangles, which we've encountered already, Turbo C++ also provides functions to create ellipses and polygons.

Here's a program that generates a series of nested ellipses:

```
// ellipse.c
// draws nested ellipses
#include <graphics.h>            // for graphics functions
#include <conio.h>               // for getch()

void main(void)
   {
   int driver, mode;            // graphics driver and mode
   int xE=150, yE=100;          // center of ellipse
   int xRad=150, yRad;          // radii of ellipse
   int stAngle=0, endAngle=360; // arc start and end angles

   driver = DETECT;             // autodetect
                                // initialize graphics
   initgraph( &driver, &mode, "c:\\tc\\bgi" );

                                // draw ellipses
   for( yRad=0; yRad<100; yRad+=10 )      // step thru y radii
      ellipse( xE, yE, stAngle, endAngle, xRad, yRad );
   getch();
   closegraph();
   }
```

An ellipse has two radii, one in the x direction and one in the y direction. In this example, we vary the y radius so that 10 ellipses are drawn. The effect looks something like a watermelon, as shown in Figure 10.3.

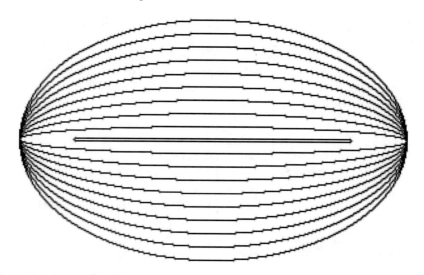

Figure 10.3. Output of the ellipse.c program.

The `ellipse()` function takes six arguments:

Draws Ellipse

```
void far ellipse(int xE, int yE, int stAngle,
                 int endAngle, int xRad, int yRad);
xE              // center of ellipse
yE
stAngle;        // starting and ending angles
endAngle
xRad            // radii of ellipse
yRad
```

The center of the ellipse corresponds to our intuitive idea of the center; it's not one of the focii used in geometry. If you want to draw only part of the ellipse—an elliptical arc—the starting and ending angles can specify this arc. The angles are measured starting with 0 degrees at the 3 o'clock position and increase counterclockwise, as they do on the coordinate plane.

The x and y radii correspond to the semimajor and semiminor axes used in geometry.

Polygons are figures consisting of an arbitrary number of straight line segments. Examples are triangles, rectangles, parallelograms, pentagons (five-sided figures), and so forth. Actually, in Turbo C++ any collection of line segments is considered a polygon. The lines don't need to form a closed figure, and they can cross over each other.

In Turbo C++ the coordinates of these lines are placed on a list, and the function `drawpoly()` then creates the polygon from the list.

Here's an example that uses polygons to create the effect of a three-dimensional box. The front of the box consists of a rectangle, but the top and right side of the box are polygons, as shown in Figure 10.4.

The `drawpoly()` function takes only two parameters. The first is the number of points to connect with lines, and the second is the address of a list containing the points to connect.

The list of points is an array of integer values, with two values—the x coordinate first and then y—for each point. The `number` variable is the number of points, not the number of integers (because there are two integers per point).

Draws Polygon

```
void far drawpoly(int number, int far *addrList);
number          // number of points
addrList        // address of list of points
```

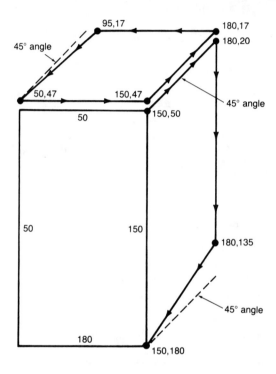

Figure 10.4. Output of the poly.c program.

To form a complete four-sided polygon, five points must be specified; the first point must be repeated at the end of the list, because that's where the last line segment ends. We use five points for the top polygon. We've also moved the top polygon up three pixels to provide visual separation between it and the rest of the box. For the polygon on the right we specify only four points. This creates three lines. The missing line corresponds with the right hand line of the rectangle, so it doesn't need to be drawn.

In theory the top and side would be parallelograms (both pairs of sides equal), but to make the perspective convincing the lines that appear to go toward the back of the picture must converge on an imaginary single point (the *vanishing point*). The necessary change in angle of these lines is shown in the figure. The figure also uses arrows to show the order in which the points are placed on the lists. Here's the listing:

```
// poly.c
// draws polygons
#include <graphics.h>          // for graphics functions
#include <conio.h>             // for getch()

#define LEFT   50              // coordinates for rectangle
#define TOP    50
#define RIGHT 150
#define BOT    180
                              // coordinates for polygons
int rightpara[] = { 150,50, 180,20, 180,135, 150,180 };
int toppara[] = { 50,47, 150,47, 180,17, 95,17, 50,47 };

void main(void)
   {
   int driver, mode;         // graphics driver and mode

   driver = DETECT;          // auto detect
                             // initialize graphics
   initgraph(&driver, &mode, "c:\\tc\\bgi");
                             // draw rectangle
   rectangle(LEFT, TOP, RIGHT, BOT);
   drawpoly(4, rightpara);   // draw right polygon
   drawpoly(5, toppara);     // draw top polygon

   getch();
   closegraph();
   }
```

Filling and Patterns

Turbo C++ can fill the outlines of graphics shapes with color by using several functions.
One of the most useful is fillpoly(). This function is similar to drawpoly() in that it
draws a polygon. However, it goes further by filling the inside of the polygon with the
current fill pattern and fill color.

Draws and Fills Polygon

```
void far fillpoly(int number, int far *addrList);
number          // number of points
addrList        // address of list of points
```

The current fill pattern and fill color are established by another function,
setfillstyle().

Set Fill Pattern and Color

```
void far setfillstyle(int pattern, int color);
pattern     // pattern constant
color       // color constant
```

The pattern variable can be one of the following, as is defined in graphics.h:

Name	Number	Result
EMPTY_FILL	0	Solid background
SOLID_FILL	1	Solid color
LINE_FILL	2	Horizontal lines
LTSLASH_FILL	3	///// Thin lines
SLASH_FILL	4	///// Thick lines
BKSLASH_FILL	5	\\\\\ Thick lines
LTBKSLASH_FILL	6	\\\\\ Thin lines
HATCH_FILL	7	Light hatch
XHATCH_FILL	8	Heavy cross-hatch
INTERLEAVE_FILL	9	Interleaved lines
WIDE_DOT_FILL	10	Wide-spaced dots
CLOSE_DOT_FILL	11	Close-spaced dots
USER_FILL	12	User-defined pattern

We won't demonstrate the process, but you can also create custom patterns by specifying the pattern with another function, setfillpattern(), and setting the pattern argument in setfillstyle() to USER_FILL.

The color is selected from the same list as it was for setcolor(). (Invalid input to the function results in an error code of –11 being returned to graphresult().)

Here's an example program that draws the same three-dimensional box as drawpoly.c and then fills the front of the box with one color and pattern and the top and side with a different color and pattern, as shown in Figure 10.5.

```
// fillpoly.c
// draws polygons, fills them with color
#include <graphics.h>
#include <conio.h>
                                    // front rectangle
int rect[] = { 50,50, 150,50, 150,180, 50,180, 50,50 };
                                    // side (fourth edge on rect)
int sidepara[] = { 150,50, 180,20, 180,135, 150,180 };
                                    // top (raised 3 pixels)
int toppara[] = { 50,47, 150,47, 180,17, 95,17, 50,47 };

void main(void)
```

```
{
int driver, mode;              // graphics driver and mode
driver = DETECT;               // auto detect
                               // initialize graphics
initgraph(&driver, &mode, "c:\\tc\\bgi");
                               // set fill for rectangle
setfillstyle(CLOSE_DOT_FILL, YELLOW);
fillpoly(5, rect);             // draw front rectangle
                               // set fill for side and top
setfillstyle(SOLID_FILL, RED);
fillpoly(4, sidepara);         // draw right polygon
fillpoly(5, toppara);          // draw top polygon

getch();
closegraph();
}
```

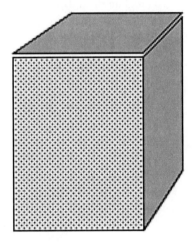

Figure 10.5. Output of the fillpoly.c program.

We use fillpoly() to draw and fill the front rectangle as well as the top and side polygons.

Another approach to filling areas is the floodfill() function. The advantage of this function is that it fills any arbitrary area, whether it's a polygon, a circle, an ellipse, or a series of unrelated lines or dots. (If you're using CGA, be careful; floodfill() doesn't always work correctly.)

Fill Any Bounded Area

```
void far floodfill(int x, int y, int border);
x           // x coordinate for fill start
y           // y coordinate for fill start
border      // color of border (fill stops here)
```

The floodfill() function needs to know the point where the fill begins. This point is called the *seed point*. The fill spreads outward from the seed point until it encounters a boundary that has the color specified in the border parameter. The area either outside or inside a shape can be filled, depending on where the seed point is located. If you try to fill an area that isn't completely bounded, the fill will "escape" and cover the area outside as well as inside of the object. Here's a program that fills a circle.

```
// floodco.c
// fills circle with color using floodfill()
#include <graphics.h>            // for graphics functions
#include <conio.h>               // for getch()
#define XC       300             // center of circle
#define YC       175
#define RADIUS   150             // radius of circle

void main(void)
    {
int driver, mode;               // graphics driver and mode

    driver = DETECT;                // auto detect
                                    // initialize graphics
    initgraph(&driver, &mode, "c:\\tc\\bgi");
    setcolor(RED);                          // set line color
    circle(XC, YC, RADIUS);                 // draw circle
    setfillstyle(CLOSE_DOT_FILL, LIGHTBLUE);  // set fill pattern
    floodfill(XC, YC, RED);                 // fill circle
    getch();
    closegraph();
    }
```

The color used for fill may be the same or different from that used to outline the area. Note, however, that the color used in the border parameter to floodfill() must be the same as that used to draw the outline of the shape. In this case, the constant RED is used for both these arguments.

Graphs

Turbo C++ contains several functions that simplify the creation of graphs. These are bar(), bar3d(), and pieslice(). The first two are similar. Both draw a rectangle and fill it with the current color and fill pattern, thus creating a bar suitable for use in a bar graph. The difference is that bar3d() also draws lines to the right and (optionally) above the bar to provide a three-dimensional effect.

Draw Three-Dimensional Bar

```
void far bar3d(int left, int top, int right,
               int bottom, int topflag);
left       // coordinates of bar
top
right
bottom
depth      // "depth" of bar
topflag    // 0=no top on bar, !0=top
```

Our next example uses bar3d() to create a simple graph. The result is shown in Figure 10.6.

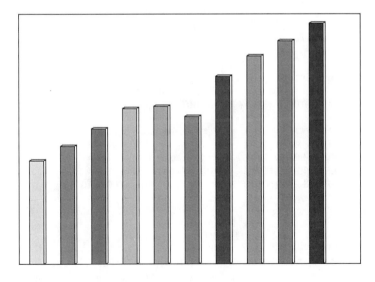

Figure 10.6. Output of the bargraph.c program.

The program could simply use 10 calls to bar3d(), each with different arguments. However, a program is easier to modify if it uses a loop to call the function repeatedly, changing the arguments each time to draw bars of different heights at different positions.

Using #define statements, we can make it easy to change the number of bars and their width, depth, separation, and other characteristics.

```c
// bargraph.c
// generates bar graph
#include <graphics.h>            // for graphics functions
#include <conio.h>              // for getch()
#define N        10             // number of values to graph
#define BWIDTH   20             // width of each bar
#define SEP      24             // separation between bars
#define DI      (BWIDTH+SEP)    // distance from bar to bar
#define SHFT     15             // between border and 1st bar
#define WIDTH  ( (N+1) * DI )   // width of chart
#define LEFT     5              // left side of graph
#define DEPTH    3              // depth of bar
#define TOPFLAG  1              // put 3-D top on bar
#define BOT      349            // bottom of graph
#define TOP      5              // top of graph
#define PPD (float)(BOT-TOP)/100   // pixels per data unit

void main(void)
    {
    int driver, mode, j;
                                // data to display
    int data[N] = { 41, 47, 54, 62, 63, 59,
                    75, 83, 89, 96  };
    driver = DETECT;            // auto detect
                                // initialize graphics
    initgraph(&driver, &mode, "\\tc\\bgi" );
                                // draw border
    rectangle(LEFT, TOP, LEFT+WIDTH, BOT);

    for(j=0; j<N; j++)          // draw bars
        {
        setfillstyle(SOLID_FILL, j+1);    // cycle colors
        bar3d( LEFT+SHFT+j*DI,         BOT-data[j]*PPD,
               LEFT+SHFT+j*DI+BWIDTH, BOT, DEPTH, TOPFLAG );
        }
    getch();
    closegraph();
    }
```

The program draws a border around the chart with rectangle(), then in a loop, repeatedly sets the color of the bar with setfillstyle() and draws the bar with bar3d(). (We use j+1, so the first color is 1 instead of 0 because black doesn't show up well.)

We'll see a more sophisticated bar graph later in this chapter when we've learned how to place text on a graphics image.

The function pieslice() draws an arc (a part of a circle). It also fills the arc with the current color and fill pattern. Like the ellipse, the angles of the arc are measured with 0 at the 3 o'clock position, running counterclockwise.

Draws and Fills Arc (for Pie Charts)

```
void far pieslice(int xP, int yP, int stAngle, int endAngle, radius )
xA          // center of slice
yA
stAngle     // starting and ending angles
endAngle
radius      // radius of slice
```

Repeated use of this function will generate a pie chart. Pie charts are typically used to show how a quantity is divided—how the federal budget is spent, for example.

Our demonstration program creates a pie chart from six data items. The angle occupied by each item is calculated by adding all the items together, and then dividing the value of each item by this total to find the fraction of the circle it occupies. The first slice begins at the 3 o'clock position, and each succeeding slice starts where the last one ended.

```
// pie.c
// generates pie chart
#include <graphics.h>        // for graphics functions
#include <conio.h>           // for getch()
#define N        6           // number of data items
#define RADIUS   170         // radius of pie
#define X        175         // center of pie
#define Y        175


void main(void)
    {
    int driver, mode, j;
    float dataSum, startAngle, endAngle, relAngle;
    int data[N] = { 11, 19, 44, 32, 15, 7, };  // data items

    driver = DETECT;             // auto detect
                                 // initialize graphics
    initgraph(&driver, &mode, "\\tc\\bgi" );
                                 // sum the data values
    for(j=0, dataSum=0; j<N; j++)
        dataSum += data[j];
    endAngle = 0;                // start at 3 o'clock angle
    for(j=0; j<N; j++)           // draw slices
        {
        startAngle = endAngle;   // start at end of last slice
        relAngle = 360 * (data[j] / dataSum); // calculate angle
        endAngle = startAngle + relAngle;     // find end angle
```

```
        setfillstyle(SOLID_FILL, j+1);        // set fill, color
                                              // draw one slice
        pieslice(X, Y, startAngle, endAngle, RADIUS);
        }
    getch();
    closegraph();
    }
```

As with the bar chart, we change the color for each slice to make the chart easier to read.

Viewports

Viewports provide a way to restrict to an arbitrary size the area of the screen used for drawing. They are somewhat like windows as defined in character functions. You can draw an image that would ordinarily occupy the entire screen, but if a viewport is in use, only part of the image will be visible. Note that viewports don't scale the image; the image isn't compressed to fit the viewport. Rather, the parts of the image that don't fit in the viewport simply aren't visible; the image is "clipped" at the edge of the viewport.

The following example is similar to the circline.c program from earlier in the chapter, except that a viewport is installed that is smaller than the image to be drawn. A rectangle is also drawn around the edge of the viewport so that its location is more obvious. Figure 10.7 shows the resulting screen image.

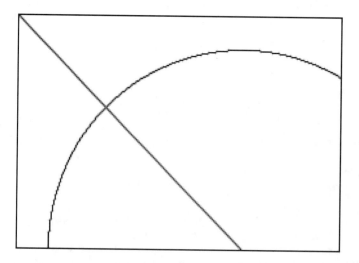

Figure 10.7. Output of the viewport.c program.

```
// viewport.c
// draws circle and line within viewport
```

```
#include <graphics.h>          // for graphics functions
#include <conio.h>             // for getch

void main(void)
   {
   int driver, mode;           // graphics driver and mode
   int left=0, top=0, right=250, bot=175;  // viewport
   int clip=1;                 // viewport clipping enabled
   int x1=0, y1=0;             // one end of line
   int x2=349, y2=349;         // other end of line
   int xC=175, yC=175;         // center of circle
   int radius=150;             // radius of circle

   driver = DETECT;            // auto detect
                               // initialize graphics
   initgraph(&driver, &mode, "c:\\tc\\bgi");
                               // set viewport dimensions
   setviewport(left, top, right, bot, clip);
                               // draw rectangle on viewport
   rectangle(left, top, right, bot);
   line(x1, y1, x2, y2);       // draw line
   circle(xC, yC, radius);     // draw circle
   getch();
   closegraph();
   }
```

The viewport is created with the setviewport() function.

The clipping parameter determines whether an image will be clipped (not displayed) beyond the boundaries of the viewport. Normally this is set to a non-zero value to provide clipping. (The graphresult() function will return −11 if invalid input is supplied to this function.)

Set Viewport Dimensions

```
void far setviewport(int left, int top, int right, int bottom,
                     int clip);
left      // dimensions of viewport
top
right
bot
clip      // 0=no clipping, !0=clipping
```

Viewports can be used in any situation where you want to restrict the area occupied by an image. In a program that produces both text and graphics, for example, the viewport can be used to place the graphics in one area, while the window() function confines the text to a different area. The size of the viewport and the text window can be controlled by the user, thus providing a capability like Microsoft Windows.

The function clearviewport() erases the image from the viewport, leaving the rest of the screen untouched, and getviewsettings() returns the dimensions and clipping status of the viewport.

Relative Drawing

So far the graphics functions we've seen have used absolute screen coordinates, relative to the upper-left corner of the screen. Several graphics functions use a relative coordinate system. In this system, drawing is done relative to a movable point called the *current position* or *CP*.

Lines are the only graphics element that can be drawn using the relative coordinate system. The program that follows includes a function, square() (which is part of the program—not a library function), whose purpose is to draw a box. This function uses the linerel() library function, which draws a line relative to the CP.

Draws Line from Current Position

```
void far linerel(int dx, int dy);
dx        // horizontal distance from CP
dy        // vertical distance from CP
```

The linerel() function draws the line and advances the CP to the end of the line.

Because the square() function isn't concerned with absolute coordinates, it can be used to draw a box anywhere on the screen. The program makes use of this fact to create a checkerboard, using repeated calls to square() and advancing the CP to the appropriate place with the library function moveto(), which moves the CP to an absolute position on the screen. (Actually this position isn't truly absolute: it is relative to the current viewport, if one is in use.)

Move Current Position

```
void far moveto(int x, int y);
x    // absolute (or viewport) position
y
```

Here's the example. The main part of the program consists of one loop nested inside another. The inner loop moves the CP across eight screen positions, calling square() to draw a square at each position. The outer loop moves the CP down through eight rows.

```
// checker.c
// draws checkerboard, demonstrates relative motion
#include <graphics.h>          // for graphics functions
#include <conio.h>             // for getch()
#define MAX    320             // size of board
#define GRID   40              // separation of grid points
#define SIDE   36              // size of square
void square(int side);        // prototype

void main(void)
   {
   int driver, mode;
   int x, y;
   driver = DETECT;            // auto detect
                              // initialize graphics
   initgraph(&driver, &mode, "c:\\tc\\bgi");
   for(y=0; y<MAX; y+=GRID)    // move down rows
     for(x=0; x<MAX; x+=GRID)  // move across columns
        {
        moveto(x, y);          // move current position
        square(SIDE);          // draw a square there
        }
   getch();
   closegraph();
   }

// square()
// function to make square
void square(int side)
   {
   linerel(side, 0);           // top, left to right
   linerel(0, side);           // right side, top to bottom
   linerel(-side, 0);          // bottom, right to left
   linerel(0, -side);          // left side, bottom to top
   }
```

Figure 10.8 shows the output of the program.

Many drawing activities are carried out more easily by using relative rather than absolute coordinates. Some systems (such as the *turtle graphics* approach in the Logo programming language) contain a more complete group of relative functions. However, the relative functions in Turbo C++ will be useful in situations where a simple line drawing is needed.

Related functions are lineto(), which draws a line from the CP to an absolute position x, y, and moverel(), which moves the CP relative to the old CP.

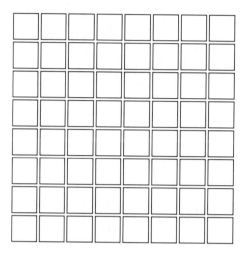

Figure 10.8. Output of the checker.c program.

The Aspect Ratio Problem

In some graphics modes, the pixels aren't square; each pixel is higher than it is wide. If you magnified a single pixel, it would look like a rectangle. The ratio of a pixel's height to its width is called its *aspect ratio*. A square pixel has an aspect ratio of 1.0.

The fact that pixels aren't square leads to some complexities in creating graphics images. When square pixels are used to create a circle, for instance, the circle can be 100 pixels high and 100 pixels wide, and it will look like a circle. However, when pixels have an aspect ratio that differs from 1.0, a 100-pixel by 100-pixel circle will look like an ellipse. If the pixels are too narrow for their height, the circle will also be too narrow for its height. Similarly, a 100-pixel by 100-pixel square will look like a tall but narrow rectangle.

The typical video screen has a width 4/3 (or 1.3333) times its height. To achieve square pixels there should be 1.3333 times as many pixels per line as there are horizontal lines. This is the case in VGA graphics, which has 640 pixels per line and 480 lines (640/480 = 1.3333). Thus in VGA the pixels are square, with an ideal aspect ratio of 1.0. If you never intend to use EGA or CGA graphics, that's all you need to know about aspect ratios, and you can skip the rest of this section.

However, EGA and CGA deviate from this ideal 1.0 ratio. The ratio in EGA is 1.8286 (640/350), and in CGA it is 1.6 (320/200). Other graphics standards have different ratios.

To compensate for the nonideal aspect ratio of a pixel, Turbo C++ takes liberties when drawing circles and arcs.

Our next example demonstrates this situation. It uses EGA 640 by 350 mode to draw two circles centered in a box. The box, created by rectangle(), is 200 pixels wide and 200 pixels high, but because the pixels aren't square in EGA, it appears to be higher than it is wide. The circles appear to be round, but because the box isn't square, they don't touch all four of its sides.

The first circle is created with `circle()` using a radius of 100. You would expect this circle to be 200 pixels high and 200 pixels wide. However, to make it look round, Turbo C++ makes it only 77 pixels from the center to the top (and from the center to the bottom), although it's a true 100 pixels from the center to the left or right. This is the inner circle shown in Figure 10.9.

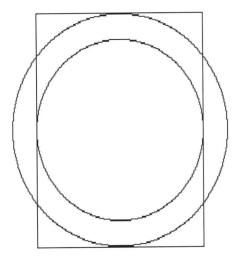

Figure 10.9. Output of the aspect.c program.

Note that this inner circle just touches the right and left sides of the box but doesn't come close to the top or bottom.

The outer circle just touches the top and bottom of the box, although it extends beyond the left and right sides. How do we create this circle? We need to know what *radius* to specify that will create a vertical radius of 100. Fortunately, the Turbo C++ function `getaspectratio()` provides this information. It returns two numbers from which the aspect ratio of the pixels can be derived. Using this aspect ratio we can calculate the appropriate radius.

Gets Pixel Aspect Ratio

```
void far getaspectratio(int far *addrXaspect,
                        int far *addrYaspect);
addrXaspect    // address of X part of ratio
addrYaspect    // address of Y part of ratio
```

The Y parameter received from getaspectratio() is always 10,000. Dividing by the X parameter, which is less than this (7750 for EGA or 8333 for CGA), gives the desired ratio. In our example, we use this approach to find the radius to use for the second circle. We use the reciprocal of the ratio, 1 divided by 0.775, or 1.29. Multiplying by the radius, 100, gives a value of 129 for the radius parameter to circle(). The resulting circle will just touch the top and bottom of the box. Here's the listing:

```c
// aspect.c
// shows use of getaspectratio()
#include <graphics.h>          // for graphics functions
#include <conio.h>             // for getch()
#define LEFT     100           // borders of rectangle
#define TOP        0
#define RIGHT    300
#define BOT      200
#define HEIGHT   (BOT-TOP)     // rectangle height and width
#define WIDTH    (RIGHT-LEFT)  //    (200 by 200)
#define XC       (LEFT+WIDTH/2) // center of circle
#define YC       (TOP+HEIGHT/2)

void main(void)
   {
   int driver, mode;
   int radius;                 // radius of circle
   int xAspect, yAspect;       // for getaspectratio()
   float ratio;                // aspect ratio

   driver = EGA;               // EGA
   mode = EGAHI;               // 640 x 350

   initgraph( &driver, &mode, "c:\\tc\\bgi" );
                               // draw rectangle
   rectangle(LEFT, TOP, RIGHT, BOT);
   radius = HEIGHT/2;          // 'naive' radius (100)
   circle(XC, YC, radius);     // draw circle

   getaspectratio(&xAspect, &yAspect);   // get aspect ratio
   ratio = (float)yAspect / (float)xAspect;   // calculate it
   radius = radius * ratio;    // find 'clever' radius (129)
   circle(XC, YC, radius);     // draw corrected circle
   getch();
   closegraph();
   }
```

If you revise this program to run in VGA 640 by 480 mode, the box will appear square, and you'll see only one circle, because both circles are drawn in exactly the same place. This circle will touch the box on all four sides. Square pixels certainly make things easier!

The aspect ratio problem also arises when drawing arcs. (An arc is a part of a circle, like an unfilled pie slice.) Suppose you wanted to create a box with rounded corners. It's natural to use quarter-circle arcs to connect the lines and create the corners. However, without special care, the arcs won't meet up correctly with the lines on the top and bottom of the box. Figure 10.10 shows what will happen.

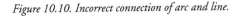

Figure 10.10. Incorrect connection of arc and line.

Our next program uses the `arc()` function to draw an arc connecting a vertical and a horizontal line.

> **Draws Arc**
>
> ```
> void far arc(int xA, int yA, int stAngle,
>              int endAngle, int radius);
> xA           // center of arc
> yA
> stAngle      // starting and ending angles
> endAngle
> radius       // radius of arc
> ```

This function must be given the coordinates of the center of the arc, the starting and ending angles (measured from the 3 o'clock position counterclockwise, in degrees), and the radius.

The program uses a new function, getarccoords(), to find out where the arc has actually been drawn.

Get Arc Coordinates

```
void far getarccoords(struct arccoordstype far *addrStr);
addrStr    // address of structure
```

This function fills in a structure whose address has been provided to it as an argument. The structure is defined in graphics.h as

```
struct arccoordstype
    {
    int x, y;
    int xstart, ystart, xend, yend;
    };
```

The x and y members of the structure are the center of the arc (which your program probably knows anyway), and xstart, ystart, xend, and yend are the actual coordinates of the starting and ending points of the arc. The program uses these coordinates to decide where to put the vertical and horizontal lines that connect to the arc, as shown in Figure 10.11.

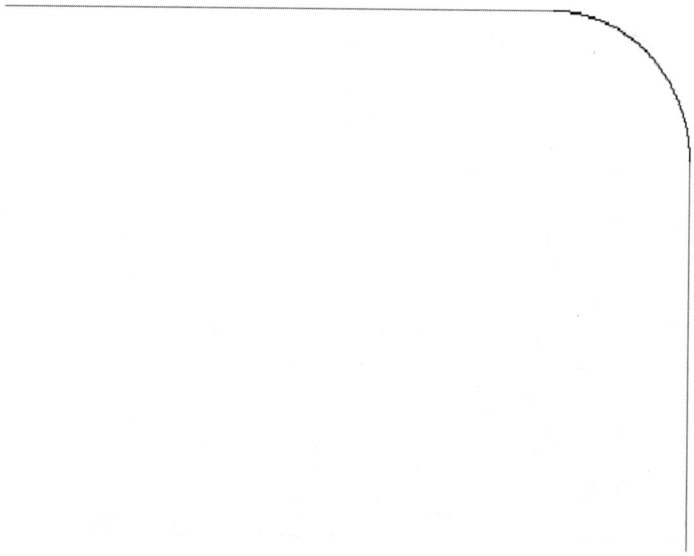

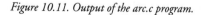

Figure 10.11. Output of the arc.c program.

```
// arc.c
// draws rounded corner, using arc
#include <graphics.h>          // for graphics functions
#include <conio.h>             // for getch()

void main(void)
    {
    int driver, mode;
    int L1x1, L1y1, L1x2, L1y2;   // horizontal line
    int L2x1, L2y1, L2x2, L2y2;   // vertical line
    int xA, yA, radius;           // for arc
    int stAngle, endAngle;        // arc start and end angles
    struct arccoordstype ai;      // structure for arc info

    driver = EGA;                 // EGA
    mode = EGAHI;                 // 640 x 350
                                  // initialize graphics
    initgraph(&driver, &mode, "c:\\tc\\bgi");

    xA = 400;    yA = 100;        // center of arc
    radius = 100;                 // radius of arc
    stAngle = 0; endAngle = 90;   // arc angles
    arc(xA, yA, stAngle, endAngle, radius);  // draw arc

    getarccoords(&ai);            // get arc coordinates
    L1x1 = 0;         L1y1 = ai.yend;   // horiz line
    L1x2 = ai.xend;   L1y2 = ai.yend;   //      along top
    L2x1 = ai.xstart; L2y1 = ai.ystart; // vert line
    L2x2 = ai.xstart; L2y2 = 300;       //      on right
    setcolor(GREEN);
    line(L1x1, L1y1, L1x2, L1y2);  // draw 1st line
    line(L2x1, L2y1, L2x2, L2y2);  // draw 2nd line
    getch();
    closegraph();
    }
```

Pixels

Individual pixels can be plotted using the putpixel() function. This is useful when graphing mathematical functions and in draw- or paint-type programs that enable the user to create complex images.

Places a Pixel on the Screen

```
void far putpixel(int x, int y, int color);
x        // coordinates of pixel
y
color   // color to make pixel
```

Our example program uses `putpixel()` to plot the `sin()` function.

```
// plot.c
// plots function, demonstrates putpixel()
#include <graphics.h>          // for graphics functions
#include <conio.h>             // for getch()
#include <math.h>              // for sin()

void main(void)
   {
   int driver, mode;          // graphics driver and mode
   double angle, sinofA;      // angle and sin of angle
   int x, y;                  // screen coordinates

   driver = DETECT;           // auto detect
                              // initialize graphics
   initgraph(&driver, &mode, "c:\\tc\\bgi");

   line(0, 100, 200, 100);    // line along x-axis
   for(x=0; x<200; x++)
      {
      angle = ((double)x / 200) * (2 * 3.14159265);
      sinofA = sin(angle);
      y = 100 - 100*sinofA;
      putpixel(x, y, YELLOW);
      }
   getch();
   closegraph();
   }
// angle 0.0,   1.6,   3.1,   4.7,   6.2
// sin   0.0    1.0    0.0   -1.0    0.0
// x     0      50     100    150    199
// y     100    200    100    0      96
```

The angle used as input to the `sin()` function is expressed in radians. (There are 2 times pi radians in a circle, so 1 radian is about 57 degrees.) We'll let the angle in our program vary from 0 to 360 degrees, which is from 0 to 2 times pi radians, or about 6.3 radians. On the screen, the x coordinate rises to 1.0 at about 1.6 radians, goes back to 0 at 3.1 radians, down to –1.0 at 4.7 radians, and is finally back to 0 at 6.3 radians. We plot the x axis (where y=0) at 100 pixels, and x varies between 0 and 199 pixels. Figure 10.12 shows the result.

Another function, `getpixel()`, can be used to find the color of a pixel at a particular point.

Bit Images and Animation

A rectangular area of the screen image can be stored in memory. However it was created—whether from lines, circles, or other elements—the image consists of pixels. Storing an image in memory means storing the color of each pixel in a known order. An image stored in memory can be written back to the screen in the same location or at a different location.

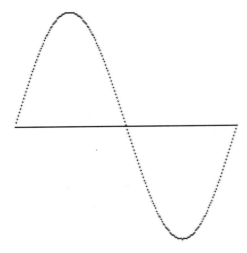

Figure 10.12. Output of the plot.c program.

Why would one want to save and restore graphics images? One use of this technique is in animation. In animation, an image moves on the screen. It may change its position, as in the image of a car moving from left to right, or the image may change its shape; for example, a coin spinning so that it appears first as a circle, then as an ellipse, and then—edge on—as a line.

In such cases the images must be drawn quickly to simulate continuous motion. However, drawing the image from scratch at each position may be too time-consuming. Drawing all the details of a car, for instance, may require many calls to graphics functions for headlights, doors, wheels, and so on. It is often faster to draw the image once, store it in memory, and then transfer the complete image back onto the screen in different places.

Our example program shows a ball bouncing within a rectangular box. Each time it hits the edge of the box, it bounces off in a new direction. Here's the listing:

```
// image.c
// bouncing ball created from bit image
#include <graphics.h>              // for graphics functions
#include <conio.h>                 // for kbhit()
#define LEFT      0                // boundary of rectangle
#define TOP       0
#define RIGHT   400
#define BOTTOM  349
#define RADIUS   20                // radius of ball

void main(void)
    {
    int driver, mode;             // for initgraph()
    int x, y, dx, dy, oldx, oldy; // ball coordinates
    unsigned char ballbuff[2000]; // buffer for ball image
```

```
    driver = DETECT;                    // auto detect
                                        // set graphics mode
    initgraph(&driver, &mode, "c:\\tc\\bgi");
                                        // draw boundary
    rectangle(LEFT, TOP, RIGHT, BOTTOM);

    x = LEFT + RADIUS + 10;             // create image of ball
    y = TOP  + RADIUS + 10;
    setcolor(LIGHTGREEN);
    setfillstyle(SOLID_FILL, LIGHTGREEN);
    circle(x, y, RADIUS);
    floodfill(x, y, LIGHTGREEN);
                                        // place image in memory
    getimage(x-RADIUS, y-RADIUS, x+RADIUS, y+RADIUS, ballbuff);
    dx = 2;                             // set speed of ball
    dy = 2;
    while ( !kbhit() )                  // exit on keypress
       {                                // memory image to screen
       putimage(x-RADIUS, y-RADIUS, ballbuff, COPY_PUT);
       oldx = x; oldy = y;             // remember where it was
       x += dx;  y += dy;              // move its coordinates
                                        // reflect it at edges
       if( x<=LEFT+RADIUS+2 || x>=RIGHT-RADIUS-2 )
          dx = -dx;
       if( y<=TOP+RADIUS+2 || y>=BOTTOM-RADIUS-2 )
          dy = -dy;
                                        // erase old image
       putimage(oldx-RADIUS, oldy-RADIUS, ballbuff, XOR_PUT);
       }
    closegraph();
}
```

The image of the ball is created with `circle()` and stored in memory with a function called `getimage()`.

Places Graphics Image in Memory

```
void far getimage(int left, int top,
                  int right, int bottom,
                  void far *addrBuff);
left       // coordinates of screen area to be saved
top
right
bottom
addrBuff   // address of memory buffer for image
```

How large an array do you need to hold the image? You can estimate it by assuming two bytes per pixel (in VGA graphics) plus several hundred bytes of overhead. You can also use the `imagesize()` function, which returns the memory required for an image whose coordinates are supplied as its four parameters. If you run your program once using this function and a `printf()` statement to display the size, you can see how large to make the storage array.

```
size = imagesize(x-RADIUS, y-RADIUS, x+RADIUS, y+RADIUS);
printf("size=%u", size);
```

However, a better way is to obtain memory dynamically, using the `malloc()` function. We'll find out how to do this in Chapter 12, "Memory."

Once the image is stored in memory, the program enters a loop in which the image is read back from memory to different places on the screen. This creates the illusion of a moving image. The image is restored to the screen using the function `putimage()`.

Restores Graphics Image from Memory to Screen

```
void far putimage(int left, int top, void far *addrBuff, int putop);
left        // location to place image
top
addrBuff    // address of memory buffer holding image
putop       // interaction between new and old pixels
```

This function is given the upper-left corner of the area where the image will go, the address in memory holding the image, and an operator value. The possible values for this operator, as defined in graphics.h, are

Value	Constant	Comment
0	COPY_PUT	Replaces old image with new
1	XOR_PUT	XOR old and new images
2	OR_PUT	OR old and new images
3	AND_PUT	AND old and new images
4	NOT_PUT	Replace with inverse of new image

The operator can be used to achieve different effects. Typically a new image is drawn with the operator set to COPY_PUT, and the old image is erased with it set to XOR_PUT. The effect of XORing one image with the same image is to erase it.

Text with Graphics

Turbo C++ makes available functions that will draw text characters in graphics mode. These functions can be used to mix text and graphics in the same image. They also make it possible to change text fonts and vary the size of text, much as if you were using a graphics-oriented operating system like Windows.

We should note that while you can use such text-mode functions as `printf()` in graphics mode, these functions don't really mix very well with graphics. They can't print in different colors, and you have no control over the font or character size. Also they erase a character-size shape behind each character, which may not be the effect you want. The specialized Turbo C++ functions are far more effective in graphics programs.

Writing in Different Fonts

A font is a set of characters in a particular style. The function `settextstyle()` is used to select different fonts and to specify the orientation (vertical or horizontal) and size of the type.

Specify Text Font, Orientation, Size

```
void far settextstyle(int font, int direction,
                      int charsize);
font        // which font to use
direction   // horizontal or vertical
charsize    // size of characters
```

There are currently eleven fonts available (although it's easy to add others to the system). They are

Value	Constant	File	Comment
0	DEFAULT_FONT	built in	Bit-mapped, 8x8
1	TRIPLEX_FONT	TRIP.CHR	Times-Roman style
2	SMALL_FONT	LITT.CHR	For small letters
3	SANS_SERIF_FONT	SANS.CHR	Heavy sans-serif
4	GOTHIC_FONT	GOTH.CHR	Gothic
5	SCRIPT_FONT	SCRI.CHR	Script
6	SIMPLEX_FONT	SIMP.CHR	Light sans-serif
7	TRIPLEX_SCR_FONT	TSCR.CHR	Italic
8	COMPLEX_FONT	LCOM.CHR	Heavy Times Roman
9	EUROPEAN_FONT	EURO.CHR	Square letters
10	BOLD_FONT	BOLD.CHR	Thick letters

The DEFAULT_FONT is a bit-mapped font. This means that the characters are defined using bit patterns. Bit-mapped characters expand into exact replicas of their normal-size versions; each pixel is enlarged. Using this font in larger sizes therefore produces letters made up of blocks—the "computer look."

The other fonts are *stroked* fonts. These are created from a number of lines and arcs, or strokes. When these characters are expanded they maintain their clean, detailed look; the pixels don't expand into blocks as in the bit-mapped font. These are the preferred fonts for most graphics applications.

The disadvantage of stroked fonts is that they require more storage space. For this reason, the stroked fonts are kept in separate files with the extension .chr, as shown in the table, and loaded into memory only when needed. To use the stroked fonts, the file for each font must be available in a directory where the system can find it (in the /TC/BGI directory, for example).

Loading these files at runtime takes time and also means that an application must consist of multiple files. To avoid these problems, it is possible to link the .chr files with your application. We discuss this in the last section of this chapter.

The direction argument to settextstyle() can have one of two values.

Value	Constant	Comment
0	HORIZ_DIR	From left to right
1	VERT_DIR	From bottom to top

Horizontal is the default. When VERT_DIR is used, the message is written from bottom to top; it looks the same as the horizontal text but is rotated 90 degrees.

When the charsize argument is 1, the characters are the smallest size. A value of 2 doubles the size, 3 triples it, and so on. There are no fractional sizes; if smaller type is needed, use the SMALL_FONT, which starts out with smaller characters than the other fonts, or use setusercharsize(), to be described soon.

Our example program generates all the fonts. The output from the program is shown in Figure 10.13.

```
// stroke.c
// tests stroked characters
#include <graphics.h>       // for graphics functions
#include <conio.h>          // for getch()

void main(void)
   {
   int driver, mode;
   int fontsize;

   driver = DETECT;              // auto detect
                   // initialize graphics
   initgraph(&driver, &mode, "\\tc\\bgi");
```

```
      fontsize = 6;
      settextstyle(GOTHIC_FONT, HORIZ_DIR, fontsize);
      outtext("Gothic  ");

      settextstyle(TRIPLEX_FONT, HORIZ_DIR, fontsize);
      outtext("Triplex");

      moveto(0, 70);
      settextstyle(SMALL_FONT, HORIZ_DIR, fontsize);
      outtext("Small   ");

      settextstyle(SANS_SERIF_FONT, HORIZ_DIR, fontsize);
      outtext("Sans_serif");

      moveto(0, 140);
      settextstyle(DEFAULT_FONT, HORIZ_DIR, fontsize);
      outtext("Default");

      moveto(400, 0);
      settextstyle(TRIPLEX_FONT, VERT_DIR, fontsize);
      outtext("Triplex");

      fontsize = 4;
      moveto(0, 210);
      settextstyle(BOLD_FONT, HORIZ_DIR, fontsize);
      outtext("Bold  ");
      settextstyle(SIMPLEX_FONT, HORIZ_DIR, fontsize);
      outtext("Simplex  ");
      settextstyle(TRIPLEX_SCR_FONT, HORIZ_DIR, fontsize);
      outtext("Triplex_Scr");

      moveto(0, 280);
      settextstyle(SCRIPT_FONT, HORIZ_DIR, fontsize);
      outtext("Script  ");
      settextstyle(COMPLEX_FONT, HORIZ_DIR, fontsize);
      outtext("Complex  ");
      settextstyle(EUROPEAN_FONT, HORIZ_DIR, fontsize);
      outtext("European");

      getch();
      closegraph();
      }
```

The text is placed at the current position (CP), so the function moveto() is used to move the CP to the desired place on the screen prior to printing. The text is written to the screen with the outtext() function, which takes as its only argument the string to be displayed.

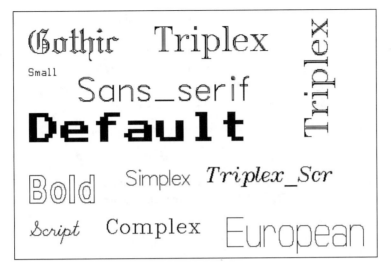

Figure 10.13. Output of the stroke.c program.

Display Text in Graphics Mode

```
void far outtext(char far *addrString);
addrString    // address of string to be displayed
```

The `outtext()` function displays the string using the font, orientation, and size specified by `settextstyle()`.

Another function, `outtextxy()`, is similar to `outtext()`, but displays text at a particular location rather than at the current CP.

Justifying and Sizing Text

The term *justification* means (at least in Turbo C++) how a text string will be placed relative to the CP. A text string is normally placed so that the CP is at its upper-left corner. This can be altered using the `settextjustify()` function.

Set Text Justification (Position Relative to CP)

```
void far settextjustify(int horiz, int vert);
horiz  // horizontal justification constant
vert   // vertical justification constant
```

The horizontal justification constant can have one of three values.

Value	Constant	Description
0	LEFT_TEXT	CP at left of text (default)
1	CENTER_TEXT	CP in horizontal center of text
2	RIGHT_TEXT	CP at right of text

The vertical justification constant is similar to the horizontal.

Value	Constant	Description
0	BOTTOM_TEXT	CP at bottom of text
1	CENTER_TEXT	CP in vertical center of text
2	TOP_TEXT	CP at top of text (default)

Our example program prints messages on a grid of lines so that the effect of different justifications can be seen, as shown in Figure 10.14.

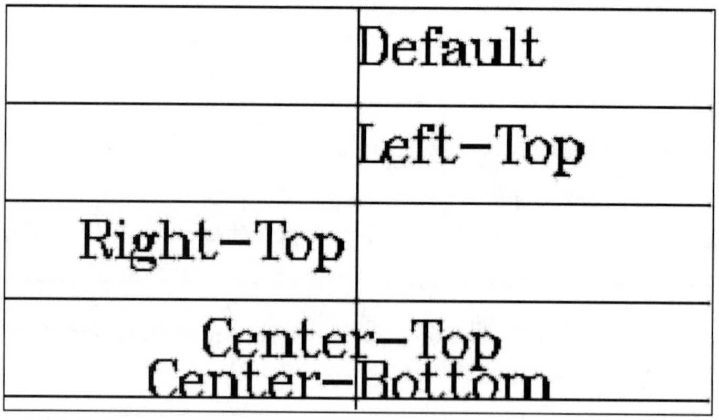

Figure 10.14. Output of the justify.c program.

```
// justify.c
// demonstrates justification
#include <graphics.h>      // for graphics functions
#include <conio.h>         // for getch()
#define CL        150      // center line
#define LEAD       40      // vertical space between lines
#define FONT_SIZE   3

void main(void)
    {
    int driver, mode, j;
```

```
driver = DETECT;          // auto detect
                          // initialize graphics
initgraph(&driver, &mode, "\\tc\\bgi" );

settextstyle(TRIPLEX_FONT, HORIZ_DIR, FONT_SIZE);
line(CL, 0, CL, 200);
for(j=0; j<LEAD*5; j+=LEAD)
   line(0, j, 300, j);

moveto(CL, 0);
outtext("Default");

moveto(CL, LEAD);
settextjustify(LEFT_TEXT, TOP_TEXT);
outtext("Left-Top");

moveto(CL, LEAD*2);
settextjustify(RIGHT_TEXT, TOP_TEXT);
outtext("Right-Top");

moveto(CL, LEAD*3);
settextjustify(CENTER_TEXT, TOP_TEXT);
outtext("Center-Top");

moveto(CL, LEAD*4);
settextjustify(CENTER_TEXT, BOTTOM_TEXT);
outtext("Center-Bottom");

getch();
closegraph();
}
```

The size and also the proportions of stroked characters can be varied with the setusercharsize() function.

This function provides two factors for the width of the character and two factors for the height. Each pair of factors forms a fraction that is multiplied by the normal size of the character. For instance, if multx is 3 and divx is 2, the resulting characters will be 3/2 times as wide as normal.

When setusercharsize() is used, the settextstyle() function should previously have set the charsize variable to USER_CHAR_SIZE, or 0. This is equivalent to a character size of 4, and permits setusercharsize() to scale the characters.

Change Character Size and Proportions

```
void far setusercharsize(int multx, int divx,
                         int multy, int divy);
multx    // multiplies width of character
```

```
divx      // divides width of character
multy     // multiplies height of character
divy      // divides height of character
```

The example program generates text in a variety of sizes, as shown in Figure 10.15.

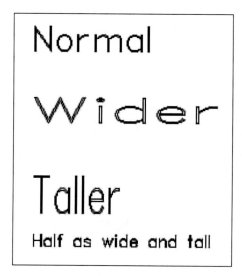

Figure 10.15. Output of the charsize.c program.

```
// charsize.c
// uses different character sizes
#include <graphics.h>              // for graphics functions
#include <conio.h>                 // for getch()

void main(void)
    {
    int driver, mode;
    int multx, divx, multy, divy;   // factors for text size

    driver = DETECT;                // auto detect
                                    // initialize graphics
    initgraph(&driver, &mode, "\\tc\\bgi" );

    settextstyle(SANS_SERIF_FONT, HORIZ_DIR, USER_CHAR_SIZE);
    outtext("Normal");

    moveto(0, 60);                  // twice as wide
    multx=2; divx=1; multy=1; divy=1;
```

```
setusercharsize(multx, divx, multy, divy);
outtext("Wider");

moveto(0, 120);                    // 3/2 as tall
multx=1; divx=1; multy=3; divy=2;
setusercharsize(multx, divx, multy, divy);
outtext("Taller");

moveto(0, 180);                    // half size
multx=1; divx=2; multy=1; divy=2;
setusercharsize(multx, divx, multy, divy);
outtext("Half as wide and tall");
getch();
closegraph();
}
```

An Annotated Bar Graph

Let's put together what we've learned about text and graphics to create an annotated bar chart. This example is an enhancement of the bargraph.c program shown earlier. Tick marks have been added, the horizontal axis is labeled with the 12 months of the year, and the vertical axis is labeled with numbers. In addition, the graph sports a title. The result is shown in Figure 10.16.

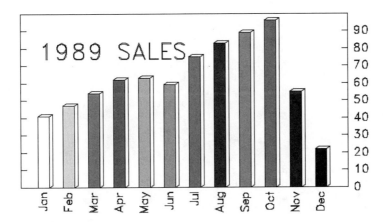

Figure 10.16. Output of the bartest.c program.

As in bargraph.c, bartext.c can be easily modified by changing the #define directives at the start of the program.

```
// bartext.c
// generates bar graph with text, title, etc.
#include <graphics.h>          // for graphics functions
#include <conio.h>             // for getch()
#include <stdlib.h>            // for itoa()
```

```
#define N        12          // number of values to graph
#define BWIDTH   20          // width of each bar
#define SEP      24          // separation between bars
#define SHFT     30          // between border and 1st bar
#define LEFT     5           // left side of graph
#define DEPTH    6           // depth of bar
#define TOPFLAG  1           // put 3-D top on bar
#define BOT      300         // bottom of graph
#define TOP      5           // top of graph
#define TICKS    10          // number of tick marks
#define TWIDTH   10          // width of tick marks
#define MAXDATA 100          // maximum data units
#define XTITLE   40          // location of title
#define YTITLE   40
#define FONT     SANS_SERIF_FONT  // font for labels
#define DI       (BWIDTH+SEP)     // distance from bar to bar
#define WIDTH    ( (N+1) * DI )   // width of chart
                                  // pixels between ticks
#define PBT ( (float)(BOT-TOP ) / TICKS )
                                  // pixels per data unit
#define PPD ( (float)(BOT-TOP) / MAXDATA )
void main(void)
    {
    int driver, mode, j;
    char string[40];
                                  // data to display
    int data[N] = { 41, 47, 54, 62, 63, 59,
                75, 83, 89, 96, 55, 22 };
    char months[12][4] =
            { "Jan", "Feb", "Mar", "Apr", "May", "Jun",
              "Jul", "Aug", "Sep", "Oct", "Nov", "Dec"  };

    driver = DETECT;              // auto detect
    initgraph(&driver, &mode, "\\tc\\bgi");
                                  // draw border
    rectangle(LEFT, TOP, LEFT+WIDTH, BOT);
                                  // draw title
    setusercharsize(4, 3, 4, 3);
    settextstyle(FONT, HORIZ_DIR, 0);
    moveto(XTITLE, YTITLE);
    outtext("1989 SALES");

    setusercharsize(2, 3, 2, 3);
    settextstyle(FONT, HORIZ_DIR, 0);
    for(j=0; j<TICKS; j++)        // draw ticks and numbers
        {
        line( LEFT,               BOT-j*PBT,        // left tick
              LEFT+TWIDTH,        BOT-j*PBT );
        line( LEFT+WIDTH-TWIDTH,  BOT-j*PBT,        // right tick
              LEFT+WIDTH,         BOT-j*PBT );
        moveto( LEFT+WIDTH+SEP/2,  BOT-j*PBT-PBT/2 );
        itoa(j*(MAXDATA/TICKS), string, 10);        // number
```

```
    outtext( string );
    }
settextstyle(FONT, VERT_DIR, 0);
for(j=0; j<N; j++)              // draw bars and months
    {
    setfillstyle(SOLID_FILL, j);
    bar3d( LEFT+SHFT+j*DI,         BOT-data[j]*PPD,  // bar
           LEFT+SHFT+j*DI+BWIDTH, BOT, DEPTH, TOPFLAG );
    moveto(LEFT+SEP+j*DI, BOT+5);                    // month
    outtext( months[j] );
    }
getch();
closegraph();
}
```

A different number of data items can be graphed by changing the constant N and the values in the arrays data[ ] and months[ ]. The data items graphed here lie in the range from 0 to 100. Different ranges of data can be graphed by changing the MAXDATA constant.

Dazzling Graphics Effects

The two programs in this final section don't introduce any new Turbo C++ graphics functions, but they do show how these functions can be used to create interesting graphics effects. The first program is short and simple, but creates a dazzling and hypnotic kinetic pattern. The second program generates the Mandelbrot set. This mathematical construct can produce some of the most astonishing displays seen on a computer screen.

Bouncing Lines

This program works on a simple principle. Two points bounce around inside a rectangle, as the ball did in the image.c program. At each position a line is drawn between the two points. The resulting series of lines is displayed. The color of the line changes every few hundred iterations, resulting in colored shapes drawn on top of each other. Surprisingly, the shapes produced appear to be curved and to move like waves in an ever-changing kaleidoscopic pattern.

Because the effect of this program depends so much on color and the rapid changing of the design, a figure can't do it justice. A rough idea can be gained from Figure 10.17.

```
// liner.c
// bouncing line creates abstract patterns
#include <graphics.h>          // for graphics functions
#include <conio.h>             // for kbhit()
#define LEFT      0            // screen borders
#define TOP       0
#define LINES    200           // lines per color change
#define MAXCOLOR 15            // maximum color value
```

```
void main(void)
    {
    int driver, mode;
    int right, bottom;                // screen size
    int x1, y1;                       // one end of line
    int x2, y2;                       // other end of line
    int dx1, dy1, dx2, dy2;           // increments to move points
    int count=0;                      // how many lines drawn
    int color=0;                      // color being used

    driver = DETECT;                  // auto detect
    initgraph(&driver, &mode, "c:\\tc\\bgi");
    right = getmaxx();                // get size of screen
    bottom = getmaxy();
    x1 = x2 = y1 = y2 = 10;           // start points
    dx1 = dy1 = 2;                    // point 1: 2 pixels per cycle
    dx2 = dy2 = 3;                    // point 2: 3 pixels per cycle
    while ( !kbhit() )                // terminate on keypress
        {
        line(x1, y1, x2, y2);         // draw line
        x1 += dx1;   y1 += dy1;       // move points
        x2 += dx2;   y2 += dy2;
        if(x1<=LEFT ¦¦ x1>=right)     // if points are
            dx1 = -dx1;               //    off the screen,
        if(y1<=TOP ¦¦ y1>=bottom)     //    reverse direction
            dy1 = -dy1;
        if(x2<=LEFT ¦¦ x2>=right)
            dx2 = -dx2;
        if(y2<=TOP ¦¦ y2>=bottom)
            dy2 = -dy2;
        if(++count > LINES)           // every LINES lines,
            {                         // change color
            setcolor(color);         // MAXCOLOR colors
            color = (color >= MAXCOLOR)  ?  0  :  ++color;
            count = 0;
            }
        }  // end while
    closegraph();
    }  // end main()
```

This program will run until a key pressed. If you think it goes too fast, you might try inserting a delay() function in the loop. You can also achieve different effects by altering the LINES constant and dx1 and related variables.

The Mandelbrot Program

In the past few years a mathematical construct called the *Mandelbrot set* has emerged as one of the most fascinating—and beautiful—objects in mathematics. The set consists of those points on a two-dimensional plane that satisfy certain characteristics. The set consists of those points on a two-dimensional plane that satisfy certain characteristics. The boundary of the set, which occupies the area between about –2 and +0.5 on the x axis and +1.25 and –1.25 on the y axis is astonishingly complex. Looked at in its entirety, the boundary consists of several rounded shapes with other rounded shapes attached to them, and strange lightning-like filaments radiating from them. If one then "zooms in" on small areas of this boundary, details can be seen—more rounded shapes, fern-like curlicues, and spirals. It turns out that the boundary is a *fractal*. Each time you zoom in to a smaller area, more details and more astonishing shapes are revealed. There is no end to how far you can zoom in. It is quite easy to zoom down to a detail never before seen by human eyes.

Figure 10.17. Output of the liner.c program.

The mandel.c program shown here enables you to explore the Mandelbrot set. You can view the complete set, or by changing parameters in the program, zoom in for more detailed views.

The program contains two nested loops. The outer one steps down from line to line, and the inner one steps across from pixel to pixel on each line. At each pixel location the program calculates whether the point corresponding to that screen location is a member of the Mandelbrot set. If it is, the pixel is drawn as black. If not, the pixel is colored. How are the colors chosen? This has to do with how the set is defined. Before we get into that, here's the listing:

```
// mandel.c
// generates the mandelbrot set
#include <graphics.h>          // for graphics functions
#include <conio.h>             // for kbhit(), getch()
#include <process.h>           // for exit()
#define XMAX 400               // change these to change size
#define YMAX 250               //    of picture
#define MAXCOUNT 16            // number of iterations
```

```
void main(void)
    {
    int x, y;                       // location of pixel on screen
    float xscale, yscale;           // distance between pixels
    float left, top;                // location of top left corner
    float xside, yside;             // length of sides
    float zx, zy;                   // real and imag parts of z
    float cx, cy;                   // real and imag parts of c
    float tempx;                    // briefly holds zx
    int count;                      // number of iterations
    int driver, mode;               // graphics driver and mode

    left = -2.0;                    // coordinates for entire
    top = 1.25;                     //     mandelbrot set
    xside = 2.5;                    //     change to see details
    yside = -2.5;                   //     of set
    xscale = xside / XMAX;          // set scale factors
    yscale = yside / YMAX;
    driver = DETECT;                // auto detect
    initgraph(&driver, &mode, "\\tc\\bgi" );  // initialize
    rectangle( 0, 0, XMAX+1, YMAX+1 );  // border

    for(y=1; y<=YMAX; y++)          // for each pixel column
        {
        for(x=1; x<=XMAX; x++)      // for each pixel row
            {
            cx = x*xscale+left;     // set c to pixel location
            cy = y*yscale+top;
            zx = zy = 0;            // set z = 0
            count = 0;              // reset count
                                    // size of z < 2
            while( zx*zx+zy*zy<4 && count<MAXCOUNT )
                {
                tempx = zx*zx - zy*zy + cx;  // set z = z*z + c
                zy = 2*zx*zy + cy;
                zx = tempx;
                count++;            // another iteration
                }
            putpixel(x, y, count); // color is count

            if( kbhit() )           // to abort program
                exit(0);            // before picture finished
            }  // end for(x)
        }  // end for(y)
    getch();
    closegraph();
    }  // end main()
```

As shown, the program generates a picture 400 pixels wide and 250 pixels high. If your computer draws the picture too slowly, you can make this screen area smaller, say 100 by 100 pixels, by changing XMAX and YMAX, or you might want to see more detail and not care about speed. In that case, make the drawing area the size of your screen.

The output of the program is shown in Figure 10.18. Unfortunately, the figure can't do justice to the intricate colored image produced by the program.

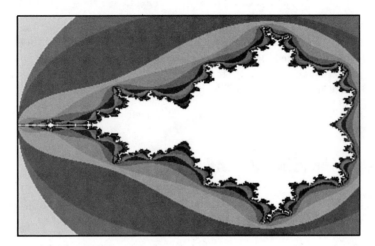

Figure 10.18. Output of the mandel.c program.

A description of the algorithm used to generate the Mandelbrot set is beyond the scope of this book. Roughly, a point is in the set if a certain iterated calculation performed on it doesn't escape to infinity. If the calculation does escape to infinity, the point is outside the set, and the speed with which it escapes determines the color of the pixel at that point. Refer to the Mathematical Recreations column in Scientific American for August, 1985, and November, 1987, for a very lucid presentation. (These articles are reprinted in *The Armchair Universe* by A. K. Dewdney, W. H. Freeman Company, 1988.)

Almost any spot on the boundary provides an interesting place to zoom in and start exploring the details of the Mandelbrot set. For instance, try the following settings:

```
left = -1.5;
top = -0.2;
xside = 0.25;
yside = 0.4;
```

Creating Stand-Alone Executables

The example programs in this chapter have required that the appropriate BGI file, such as EGAVGA.BGI, be installed in a known directory in the system, a directory specified by an argument to the initgraph() function. If fonts are used, the font file, such as GOTH.CHR, also must be available in the same directory.

Although this approach is convenient for a C development environment, it isn't so satisfactory for applications destined for release to the outside world. Users like to load as few files as possible and don't want to worry about directory structures. It would be nice if there were a way to link the .BGI and .CHR files with the program file, creating a single complete .EXE file. Fortunately, this is possible, although there are several steps involved.

First, the .BGI and .CHR files must be converted to .OBJ files. Second, new graphics functions are used in the program to register the public names of these .OBJ files. Finally, a project file must be created that contains the names of the various program components. The use of project files is an advanced topic. However, if you read the relevant sections in Chapter 13, "Advanced Topics," you'll be ready for the following discussion.

As an example, let's create a self-contained .EXE file from the bartext.c example described earlier.

Converting the .BGI and .CHR Files

The first step is to convert any .BGI or .CHR files used by the program into .OBJ files that the linker can deal with. The BGIOBJ utility, located in the \tc\bgi directory, is used for this purpose.

Our example program uses the EGAVGA.BGI file as a graphics driver and the SANS.CHR file to supply the sans serif font for adding captions to the graph. Move to \tc\bgi and enter the following command (don't use the file extension):

```
C>bgiobj egavga
```

The utility will tell you that EGAVGA.OBJ has been created. It will also tell you the public name of this file: _EGAVGA_driver. Now enter

```
C>bgiobj sans
```

This creates SANS.OBJ and gives it a public name of _sansserif_font. These public names will be used in the next step.

After typing the program, move the object files you just created, BGAVGA.OBJ and SANS.OBJ, from \tc\bgi to the directory where you're developing your program. It's easiest for the linker if all the files you're going to need are in the same directory.

Registering the Public Names

The program must be modified to tell the graphics system that the .BGI and .CHR files are linked to the program. Here's the modified program:

```
// baralone.c
// generates bar graph as a standalone executable
#include <graphics.h>          // for graphics functions
#include <conio.h>             // for getch()
#include <stdlib.h>            // for itoa()
#define N       12             // number of values to graph
#define BWIDTH  20             // width of each bar
#define SEP     24             // separation between bars
#define SHFT    30             // between border and 1st bar
```

```
#define LEFT      5             // left side of graph
#define DEPTH     6             // depth of bar
#define TOPFLAG   1             // put 3-D top on bar
#define BOT      300            // bottom of graph
#define TOP       5             // top of graph
#define TICKS    10             // number of tick marks
#define TWIDTH   10             // width of tick marks
#define MAXDATA 100             // maximum data units
#define XTITLE   40             // location of title
#define YTITLE   40
#define FONT    SANS_SERIF_FONT // font for labels
#define DI      (BWIDTH+SEP)    // distance from bar to bar
#define WIDTH   ( (N+1) * DI )  // width of chart
                                // pixels between ticks
#define PBT ( (float)(BOT-TOP ) / TICKS )
                                // pixels per data unit
#define PPD ( (float)(BOT-TOP) / MAXDATA )
void main(void)
   {
   int driver, mode, j;
   char string[40];
                                       // data to display
   int data[N] = { 41, 47, 54, 62, 63, 59,
                75, 83, 89, 96, 55, 22 };
   char months[12][4] =
           { "Jan", "Feb", "Mar", "Apr", "May", "Jun",
             "Jul", "Aug", "Sep", "Oct", "Nov", "Dec"  };

   registerbgidriver(EGAVGA_driver);  // register driver
   registerbgifont(sansserif_font);   // and font

   driver = DETECT;                    // auto detect
   initgraph(&driver, &mode, "" );     // NOTE: null pathname

                             // draw border
   rectangle(LEFT, TOP, LEFT+WIDTH, BOT);
                             // draw title
   setusercharsize(4, 3, 4, 3);
   settextstyle(FONT, HORIZ_DIR, 0);
   moveto(XTITLE, YTITLE);
   outtext("1989 SALES");

   setusercharsize(2, 3, 2, 3);
   settextstyle(FONT, HORIZ_DIR, 0);
   for(j=0; j<TICKS; j++)      // draw ticks and numbers
      {
      line( LEFT,               BOT-j*PBT,      // left tick
            LEFT+TWIDTH,        BOT-j*PBT );
      line( LEFT+WIDTH-TWIDTH, BOT-j*PBT,      // right tick
            LEFT+WIDTH,         BOT-j*PBT );
      moveto(LEFT+WIDTH+SEP/2,  BOT-j*PBT-PBT/2);
      itoa(j*(MAXDATA/TICKS), string, 10);      // number
      outtext(string);
```

```
        }
    settextstyle(FONT, VERT_DIR, 0);
    for(j=0; j<N; j++)              // draw bars and months
        {
        setfillstyle(SOLID_FILL, j);
        bar3d( LEFT+SHFT+j*DI,          BOT-data[j]*PPD,  // bar
               LEFT+SHFT+j*DI+BWIDTH, BOT, DEPTH, TOPFLAG );
        moveto(LEFT+SEP+j*DI, BOT+5);                    // month
        outtext( months[j] );
        }
    getch();
    closegraph();
    }
```

The important new lines from this program are

```
registerbgidriver(EGAVGA_driver);  // register driver
registerbgifont(sansserif_font);   // register font
- - - - - - - - -
initgraph(&driver, &mode, "");     // pathname is null
```

The registerbgidriver() and registerbgifont() functions register the driver and font, and the initgraph() function is modified to have a null string as the driver path.

Creating the Project File

To learn how to create project files, read Chapter 13, "Advanced Topics," on larger programs. Create a project file called baralone.prj and add the following files to it:

```
BARALONE.C
EGAVGA.OBJ
SANS.OBJ
```

After the project list is complete, select the Make .EXE File command from the Compile menu. Turbo C++ will generate the baralone.exe file. This is a completely stand-alone file, which can be loaded into any machine and executed. Using a similar technique, you can change any graphics program into a stand-alone application.

Disadvantages of the Turbo C++ Graphics Functions

You should be aware of several potential disadvantages of using the Turbo C++ graphics functions. First, these functions are specific to the Borland family of C/C++ compilers. If you want to recompile your source code using, for example, the Microsoft compiler, you'll need to change all the calls to the Borland functions to their equivalents in the Microsoft compiler.

Second, using the Turbo C++ graphics functions may not provide the ultimate in performance. If you want to squeeze out the last few percentage points of speed in your graphics displays, you may want to examine the approach to graphics described in Chapter 15, "Hardware-Oriented C." That chapter shows how to directly access the graphics display memory, which is potentially the fastest approach to graphics programming.

Summary

This chapter focused on the graphics functions built into Turbo C++. With these functions you can draw lines, circles, ellipses, rectangles, points, and polygons. You can draw in different colors, fill closed shapes with color and patterns, and vary the width and pattern of lines.

To use the graphics functions you must alert the linker so that it can combine the graphics.lib file with your program. You must also #include the file graphics.h and use the initgraph() function to tell the graphics system where to find a graphics driver such as egavga.bgi. This driver can be linked dynamically to the program at runtime, or it can be permanently combined with the program.

Special functions exist to write text in graphics mode, so graphs and drawings can be labeled. These functions normally use stroke fonts, which require a font file to be available to the system. Like graphics drivers, font files can be linked to the application dynamically or permanently at link time.

Questions

1. What files must be available to your program if you want to draw lines and circles?

2. In Turbo C++ graphics, the graphics mode determines
   a. How many pixels the screen can hold
   b. Whether you can draw text on the screen
   c. How many colors can be displayed
   d. The aspect ratio of the pixels

3. True or false: the same video driver works for all display modes.

4. Graphics is initialized with the _____ function.

5. Errors in graphics functions like initgraph() can be determined by
   a. Examining the function's parameters
   b. Examining the return value of the function
   c. Calling the function graphresult()()
   d. Hoping for a sudden inspiration

6. True or false: a Turbo C++ library function can select the highest resolution graphics mode available with the attached equipment.

7. Dashed circles can be drawn using the function _____.

8. In Turbo C++ the angles for arcs, pie slices, and parts of ellipses are measured starting at

   a. 0 degrees
   b. The 12 o'clock position
   c. The 3 o'clock position
   d. 180 degrees

9. A viewport is a screen area in which

   a. Colors can be confined
   b. Text drawn with `outtext()` can be confined
   c. Graphics can be confined
   d. Text drawn with `printf()` can be confined

10. Functions that perform relative line drawing do so relative to

    a. The cursor position
    b. The last text written
    c. The last relative line drawn
    d. The current position

11. Square pixels

    a. Have an aspect ratio of 1.0
    b. Have the same height and width
    c. Cause no distortion of images
    d. Are often really triangular

12. There are _____ colors in VGAHI mode.

13. The actual code for the Turbo C++ graphics functions is in

    a. The IDE
    b. The graphics.lib file
    c. The graphics.h file
    d. The linker

14. To find out how wide your screen is, use the _____ function.

15. The `settextstyle()` function sets the

    a. Font
    b. Color
    c. Orientation
    d. Character size

16. True or false: a circle with a radius of 100 stays the same size no matter what graphics mode is selected by `initgraph()`.

17. When filling a closed figure with `floodfill()`, which of the following must be the same color?

   a. The last parameter to `floodfill()` and the last parameter to `setfillstyle()`
   b. The outline of the figure and the last parameter to `setfillstyle()`
   c. The parameter to `setcolor()` and last parameter to `setfillstyle()`
   d. The last parameter to `floodfill()` and the outline of the figure

18. True or false: you must specify the ending point of a closed figure drawn with `drawpoly()`.

19. You can draw bar charts with the _____ function, pie charts with the _____ function, and scatter graphs (isolated points) with the _____ function.

20. The `getimage()` function

   a. Retrieves an image stored by `putimage()`
   b. Places a bit-mapped graphics image in memory
   c. Handles instructions for drawing an image
   d. Automatically creates different views

Exercises

1. Create a program that draws a color chart. That is, the program should color each of 16 squares a different color.

2. Write a program that allows the user to draw on the screen using the cursor keys. At each position the program should draw a dot so that patterns of vertical and horizontal lines can be created.

3. Produce a program that creates the animated image of a coin rotating about its vertical axis, as if it were spinning on a table top. The graphics functions `getimage()` and `putimage()` are appropriate.

Files

- Standard file I/O
- Character, string, and formatted I/O
- Block I/O
- Binary and text modes
- System-level I/O
- Standard files and redirection

Most programs need to read and write data to disk-based storage systems. Word processors need to store text files, spreadsheets need to store the contents of cells, and databases need to store records. In this chapter we explore the facilities that C makes available for input and output (I/O) to a disk system.

Disk I/O operations are performed on entities called files. A *file* is a collection of bytes that is given a name. In most microcomputer systems, files are used as a unit of storage primarily on floppy-disk and fixed-disk data storage systems (although they can be used with other devices as well, such as CD-ROM players, RAM-disk storage, tape backup systems, and other computers). The major use of the MS-DOS or PC DOS operating system is to handle files: to manage their storage on the disk, load them into memory, list them, delete them, and so forth.

A C-language program can read and write files in a variety of ways. In fact, sorting all the options out can prove rather confusing, so in the first section of this chapter we'll discuss the various categories of disk I/O. Then we'll examine the individual techniques.

Types of Disk I/O

A group of objects can be divided into categories in more than one way. For instance, automobiles can be categorized as foreign or domestic; cheap or expensive; four, six, or eight cylinders; and so on. A car will fit into more than one category at the same time; it might be a cheap foreign car with four cylinders, for example. Similarly, the various ways file I/O can be performed in C form a number of overlapping categories. In this section we'll give a brief overview of the most important of these categories—a view of the forest before we examine the trees.

Standard I/O Versus System I/O

Probably the broadest division in C file I/O is between standard I/O (often called stream I/O), and system-level (or low-level I/O). Each of these is a more or less complete system for performing disk I/O. Each has functions for reading and writing files and performing other necessary tasks, and each provides variations in the way reading and writing can be performed. In many ways these two systems are similar, and in fact, most I/O tasks can be handled by either system. There are, however, important differences between the two.

Standard I/O, as the name implies, is the most common way of performing I/O in C programs. It has a wider range of commands and in many respects is easier to use than system I/O. Standard I/O conceals from the user some of the details of file I/O operations, such as buffering, and it automatically performs data conversion (we'll see what this means later). If there were only one system available for disk I/O in C, standard I/O probably would be it.

System I/O provides fewer ways to handle data than standard I/O, and it can be considered a more primitive system. The techniques it employs are much like those used by the operating system. The programmer must set up, and keep track of, the buffer used to transfer data, and the system does not perform any format translations. Thus, in some ways, system I/O is harder to program than standard I/O. Because it is more closely related to the operating system, however, it is often more efficient, both in terms of speed of operation and the amount of memory used by the program.

Character, String, Formatted, and Record I/O

The standard I/O package makes available four different ways of reading and writing data. (System-level I/O, by contrast, only uses one of these ways.) Happily, three of these four ways of transferring data correspond closely to methods you've already learned for reading data from the keyboard and writing it to the display.

First, data can be read or written one character at a time. This is analogous to how such functions as putchar() and getche() read data from the keyboard and write it to the screen.

Second, data can be read or written as strings, as such functions as gets() and puts() do with the keyboard and display.

Third, data can be read or written in a format analogous to that generated by printf() and scanf() functions: as a collection of values that may be mixed characters, strings, floating point, and integer numbers.

And fourth, data may be read or written in a new format called a *record,* or *block.* This is a fixed-length group of data and is commonly used to store a succession of similar data items, such as array elements or structures.

In the section on standard I/O, we'll look at each of these ways to transfer data. Figure 11.1 shows the relationship of standard and system I/O to these four categories and the functions used to read and write data for each one.

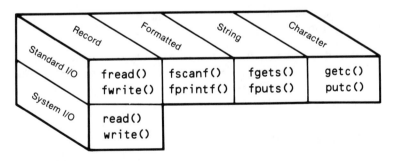

Figure 11.1. Categories of disk I/O.

Text Versus Binary

Another way to categorize file I/O operations is according to whether files are opened in text or binary mode. Which of these two modes is used to open the file determines how various details of file management are handled; how newlines are stored, for example, and how end-of-file is indicated. The reason that these two modes exist is historical: UNIX systems (on which C was first developed) do things one way, and MS-DOS does them another. The two modes are, as we'll see, an attempt to reconcile the standards of the two operating systems.

Just to confuse matters, there is a second distinction between text and binary: the format used for storing numbers on the disk. In text format, numbers are stored as strings of characters, but in binary format they're stored as they are in memory: two bytes for an integer, four for floating point, and so on, as we learned in Chapter 2, "C Building Blocks." Some file I/O functions store numbers as text; others store them as binary.

> Text versus binary mode is concerned with newline and EOF translation. Text versus binary format is concerned with number representation.

These two formats arise, not from different operating system standards (as with text versus binary modes), but because different formats work more conveniently in different situations. We'll have more to say about both these text-versus-binary distinctions later on.

At this point we'll narrow our focus from an overview of I/O categories to the details of the various techniques.

Standard Input/Output

Standard I/O is probably the easier to program and understand, so we'll start with it, leaving system-level I/O for later in the chapter.

Of the four kinds of standard I/O, we'll explore the first three in this section: character I/O, string I/O, and formatted I/O. (We'll save record I/O for a later section.) We'll initially look at these three approaches using text mode; later we'll see what differences occur when binary mode is used.

Character Input/Output

Our first example program will take characters typed at the keyboard and, one at a time, write them to a disk file. We'll list the program and show what it does, then dissect it line by line. Here's the listing:

```
// writec.c
// writes one character at a time to a file
```

```
#include <stdio.h>              // for standard I/O
#include <conio.h>              // for getche()

void main(void)
    {
    FILE *fptr;                 // ptr to FILE
    char ch;

    fptr = fopen("textfile.txt","w"); // open file, set fptr
    while( (ch=getche()) != '\r' )    // get character
        putc(ch,fptr);          // write it to file
    fclose(fptr);               // close file
    }
```

In this chapter you're going to be using many DOS commands and many programs that take command-line arguments. You'll find it convenient to get in the habit of executing all the examples from the DOS shell (select it from the File menu).

The writec.c program sits there and waits for you to type a line of text. When you've finished, press the Return key to terminate the program. Here's a sample run (with a phrase from the nineteenth-century poet William Blake):

```
C>writec
Tiger, tiger, burning bright / In the forests of the night
C>
```

What you've typed will be written to a file called textfile.txt. To see that the file has in fact been created, you can use the DOS TYPE function, which will display the contents of the file.

```
C>type textfile.txt
Tiger, tiger, burning bright / In the forests of the night
C>
```

Now that we know what the program does, let's look at how it does it.

Opening a File

Before we can write a file to a disk, or read it, we must open it. Opening a file establishes an understanding between our program and the operating system about which file we're going to access and how we're going to do it. We provide the operating system with the name of the file and other information, such as whether we plan to read or write to it. Communication areas are then set up between the file and our program. One of these areas is a C structure that holds information about the file.

This structure, which is defined to be of type struct FILE, is our contact point. When we make a request to open a file, what we receive back (if the request is granted) is a pointer to a particular FILE structure. Each file we open will have its own FILE structure, with a pointer to it. Figure 11.2 shows this process.

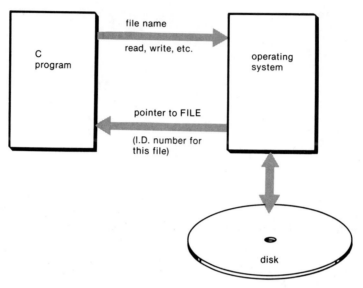

Figure 11.2. Opening a file.

The FILE structure contains information about the file being used, such as its current size and the location of its data buffers. The FILE structure is declared in the header file stdio.h (for *standard I/O*). You need to include this file with your program whenever you use standard I/O (but not system-level I/O). In addition to defining the FILE structure, stdio.h also defines a variety of other identifiers and variables that are useful in file-oriented programs. We'll come across some of them later.

In the writec.c program we first declare a variable of type `pointer-to-FILE`, in the statement

```
FILE *fptr;
```

Then, we open the file with the statement

```
fptr = fopen("textfile.txt","w");
```

This tells the operating system to open a file called textfile.txt. (We could also have specified a complete MS-DOS pathname, such as \samples\jan\textfile.txt.) This statement also indicates, via the `"w"`, that we'll be writing to the file. The `fopen()` function returns a pointer to the FILE structure for our file, which we store in the variable `fptr`.

The one-letter string `"w"` (note that it is a string and not a character; hence the double- and not single-quotes) is called a type. The `"w"` is but one of several types we can specify when we open a file. Here are the other possibilities:

`"r"`	Open for reading. The file must already exist.
`"w"`	Open for writing. If the file exists its contents will be overwritten. If it doesn't exist it will be created.
`"a"`	Open for append. Material will be added to the end of an existing file, or a new file will be created.
`"r+"`	Open for both reading and writing. The file must already exist.
`"w+"`	Open for both reading and writing. If the file exists its contents are overwritten.
`"a+"`	Open for both reading and appending. If the file doesn't exist it will be created.

In this section we'll be concerned mostly with the `"r"` and `"w"` types.

Writing to a File

Once we've established a line of communication with a particular file by opening it, we can write to it. In the writec.c program we do this one character at a time, using the statement

```
putc(ch,fptr);
```

The `putc()` function is similar to the `putch()` and `putchar()` functions. However, these functions always write to the console (unless redirection is employed), while `putc()` writes to a file. What file? The file whose FILE structure is pointed to by the variable `fptr`, which we obtained when we opened the file. This pointer has become our key to the file; we no longer refer to the file by name, but by the address stored in `fptr`.

The writing process continues in the `while` loop; each time the `putc()` function is executed, another character is written to the file. When the user presses the Return key, the loop terminates.

Closing the File

When we've finished writing to the file we need to close it. This is carried out with the statement

```
fclose(fptr);
```

Again we tell the system what file we mean by referring to the address stored in `fptr`.

Closing the file has several effects. First, any characters remaining in the buffer are written to the disk. What buffer? We haven't said much about a buffer before, because it is invisible to the programmer when using standard I/O. However, a buffer is necessary even if it's invisible. Consider, for example, how inefficient it would be to actually access the disk just to write one character. It takes a while for the disk system to position the head correctly and wait for the right sector of the track to come around. On a floppy disk system the motor actually has to start the disk from a standstill every time the disk is accessed. If you typed several characters rapidly and each one required a completely separate disk access, some of the characters probably would be lost. This is where the buffer comes in.

When you send a character off to a file with putc(), the character is actually stored in a buffer—an area of memory—rather than being written immediately to the disk. When the buffer is full, its contents are written to the disk all at once, or if the program knows the last character has been received, it forces the buffer to be written to the disk by closing the file. A major advantage of using standard I/O (as opposed to system I/O) is that these activities take place automatically; the programmer doesn't need to worry about them. Figure 11.3 shows this "invisible" buffer.

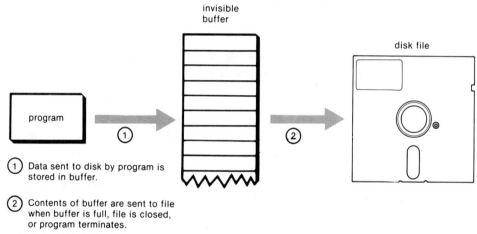

Figure 11.3. Invisible buffer.

Another reason to close the file is to free the communications areas used by that particular file so that they are available for other files. These areas include the FILE structure and the buffer itself.

Reading from a File

If we can write to a file, we should be able to read from one. Here's a program that does just that, using the function getc():

```
// readc.c
// reads one character at a time from a file
#include <stdio.h>                    // for standard I/O

void main(void)
    {
    FILE *fptr;                       // ptr to FILE
    int ch;
```

```
   fptr = fopen("textfile.txt","r"); // open file, set fptr
   while( (ch=getc(fptr)) != EOF )   // get char from file
      printf("%c", ch);              // print it
   fclose(fptr);                     // close file
   }
```

As you can see, this program is quite similar to writec.c. The pointer to FILE is declared the same way, and the file is opened and closed in the same way. The getc() function reads one character from the file textfile.txt; this function is the complement of the putc() function. (When you try this program, make sure that the file has already been created by writec.c.)

End-of-File

A major difference between this program and writec.c is that readc.c must be concerned with knowing when it has read the last character in the file. It does this by looking for an end-of-file (EOF) signal from the operating system. If it tries to read a character and reads the EOF signal instead, it knows it's come to the end of the file.

What does EOF consist of? It's important to understand that it isn't a character. It's actually an integer value, sent to the program by the operating system and defined in the stdio.h file to have a value of −1. No character with this value is stored in the file on the disk. Rather, when the operating system realizes that the last character in a file has been sent, it transmits the EOF signal. (We'll have more to say about how the operating system knows where the file ends when we look at binary mode files later on.)

> The EOF signal sent by the operating system to a C program is not a character, but an integer with a value of −1.

Our program goes along reading characters and printing them, looking for a value of −1 or EOF. When it finds this value, the program terminates. We use an integer variable to hold the character being read so that we can interpret the EOF signal as the integer −1. What difference does it make? If we used a variable of type char, the character with the ASCII code 255 decimal (FF hex) would be interpreted as an EOF. We want to be able to use all the character codes from 0 to 255—all possible 8-bit combinations, that is; so by using an integer variable we ensure that only a 16-bit value of −1, which isn't the same as any of our character codes, will signal EOF.

Trouble Opening the File

The two programs we've presented so far have a potential flaw; if the file specified in the fopen() function can't be opened, the programs won't run. Why couldn't a file be opened? If you're trying to open a file for writing, it's probably because there's no more space on the disk. If for reading, it's much more common that a file can't be opened; you can't read it if it hasn't been created yet.

Thus it's important for any program that accesses disk files to check whether a file has been opened successfully before trying to read or write to the file. If the file cannot be opened, the fopen() function returns a value of 0 (defined as NULL in stdio.h). Because in C this isn't considered a valid address, the program infers that the file couldn't be opened.

Here's a variation of readc.c that handles this situation:

```
// operror.c
// reads one character at a time from a file
// checks for fopen() error
#include <stdio.h>                    // for standard I/O
#include <stdlib.h>                   // for exit()

int main(void)                        // returns type int
   {
   FILE *fptr;                        // ptr to FILE
   char ch;

                                      // non-existent file
   if( (fptr=fopen("badfile.txt","r"))==NULL )   // open file
      {
      printf("\nCan't open file badfile.txt.");
      exit(1);                        // error return value
      }
   while( (ch=getc(fptr)) != EOF )    // get char from file
      printf("%c", ch);               // print it
   fclose(fptr);                      // close file
   return(0);                         // normal return value
   }
```

Here the fopen() function is enclosed in an if statement. If the function returns NULL, an explanatory message is printed and the exit() is executed, causing the program to terminate immediately and avoiding the embarrassment of trying to read from a nonexistent file. We ensure that the file is non-existent by changing its name to badfile.txt.

Because we use the exit() function to return a value, we also use return for a normal program termination, returning a value of 0 rather than 1, which indicates an error. Also, the data type of main() is changed from void to int.

Counting Characters

The capability of reading and writing to files on a character-by-character basis has many useful applications. For example, here's a variation on our readc.c program that counts the characters in a file:

```
// charcntf.c
// counts characters in a file
#include <stdio.h>                    // for standard I/O
#include <stdlib.h>                   // for exit()

int main( int argc, char *argv[] )
   {
   FILE *fptr;
   int count=0;

   if(argc != 2)                      // check number of args
      { printf("\nFormat: C>charcntf filename"); exit(1); }
   if( (fptr=fopen(argv[1], "r")) == NULL)  // open file
      { printf("\nCan't open file %s.", argv[1]); exit(1); }
   while( getc(fptr) != EOF )         // get char from file
      count++;                        // count it
   fclose(fptr);                      // close file
   printf("\nFile %s contains %d characters.", argv[1], count);
   return(0);
   }
```

In this program we've used a command-line argument to obtain the name of the file to be examined, rather than writing it into the fopen() statement. We start by checking the number of arguments; if there are two, the second one, argv[1], is the name of the file. For compactness, we've also placed the two statements following the if on one line.

The program opens the file, checking to make sure it can be opened, and cycles through a loop, reading one character at a time and incrementing the variable count each time a character is read.

If you try the charcnt.c program on files whose length you've checked with a different program—say the DOS DIR command—you may find that the results don't quite agree. The reason for this has to do with the difference between text and binary mode files. We'll explore this further in the section on string I/O.

Counting Words

It's easy to modify our character-counting program to count words. This can be a useful utility for writers or anyone else who needs to know how many words an article, chapter, or composition comprises. Here's the program:

```
// wordcntf.c
// counts words in a file
#include <stdio.h>                    // for standard I/O
#include <stdlib.h>                   // for exit()

int main( int argc, char *argv[] )
   {
   FILE *fptr;
   char ch;
   int white=1;                       // whitespace flag
   int count=0;                       // word count
```

407

```
    if(argc != 2)                          // check number of args
        { printf("\nFormat: C>wordcntf filename"); exit(1); }
    if( (fptr=fopen(argv[1], "r")) == NULL)  // open file
        { printf("\nCan't open file %s.", argv[1]); exit(1); }

    while( (ch=getc(fptr)) != EOF )        // get char from file
        {
        switch(ch)
            {
            case ' ':                      // if space, tab, or
            case '\t':                     // newline, set flag
            case '\n':
                white++; break;
            default:                       // non-whitespace, and
                if(white) { white=0; count++; }  // flag set,
            }                                    // count word
        }
    fclose(fptr);                          // close file
    printf("\nFile %s contains %d words.", argv[1], count);
    return(0);
    }
```

What we really count in this program is the change from whitespace characters (spaces, newlines, and tabs) to actual (non-whitespace) characters. In other words, if there's a string of spaces or carriage returns, the program reads them, waiting patiently for the first actual character. It counts this transition as a word. Then it reads actual characters until another whitespace character appears. A *flag* variable keeps track of whether the program is in the middle of a word or in the middle of whitespace; the variable white is 1 in the middle of whitespace and 0 in the middle of a word. Figure 11.4 shows the operation of the program.

This program may not work accurately with files produced by some word processing programs—such as WordStar in document mode—which use nonstandard characters for spaces and carriage returns. However, it will work with standard ASCII files.

The wordcntf.c program shows the versatility of character I/O in C. For many purposes, character I/O is just what's needed. However, in other situations, different functions may be more efficient, for instance, in reading and writing whole strings of characters at one time, which is our next topic.

String (Line) Input/Output

Reading and writing strings of characters from and to files is almost as easy as reading and writing individual characters. Here's a program that writes strings to a file, using the string I/O function fputs().

```
// writes.c
// writes lines typed at keyboard, to file
#include <stdio.h>                     // for fopen(), etc.
#include <string.h>                    // for strlen()
```

```
void main(void)
   {
   FILE *fptr;                       // declare ptr to FILE
   char string[81];                  // storage for strings

   fptr = fopen("user.txt", "w");    // open file
   while(strlen( gets(string) ) > 0) // get string from keybd
      {
      fputs(string, fptr);           // write string to file
      fputs("\n", fptr);             // write newline to file
      }
   fclose(fptr);                     // close file
   }
```

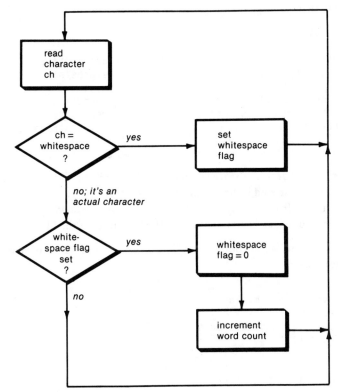

Figure 11.4. Operation of the wordcntf.c program.

The user types a series of strings, terminating each by pressing Return. To terminate the entire program, the user presses Return at the beginning of a line. This creates a string of zero length, which the program recognizes as the signal to close the file and exit.

We've set up a character array to store the string; the `fputs()` function then writes the contents of the array to the disk. Since `fputs()` does not automatically add a newline character to the end of the line, we must do this explicitly to make it easier to read the string back from the file.

Note that—for simplicity—in this and the next program we have not included a test for an error condition on opening the file, as we did in previous examples. This test should be included in any serious program.

Here's a program that reads strings from a disk file:

```
// reads.c
// reads strings from file
#include <stdio.h>                       // for standard I/O

void main(void)
   {
   FILE *fptr;                           // ptr to FILE
   char string[81];                      // stores strings

   fptr = fopen("user.txt", "r");        // open file
   while( fgets(string, 80, fptr) != NULL ) // read string
      printf("%s", string);              // print string
   fclose(fptr);                         // close file
   }
```

The function `fgets()` takes three parameters. The first is the address where the string will be stored, and the second is the maximum length of the string. This parameter keeps the `fgets()` function from reading in too long a string and overflowing the array. The third parameter, as usual, is the pointer to the FILE structure for the file.

Here's a sample run (again courtesy of William Blake), showing the operation of both writes.c and reads.c:

```
C>writes
I told my love, I told my love,
I told her all my heart,
Trembling, cold, in ghastly fears,
Ah! she did depart!

C>reads
I told my love, I told my love,
I told her all my heart,
Trembling, cold, in ghastly fears,
Ah! she did depart!
```

The Newline Problem

Earlier we mentioned that our charcntf.c program might not always return the same results as other character-counting programs, such as the DOS DIR command. Now that we can write a file containing several strings, let's investigate this further.

Here's what happens when we try to verify the length of the four-line William Blake excerpt shown above:

```
C>dir user.txt
TEXTFILE TXT      116  10-27-87    2:36a

C>charcntf user.txt
File textfile.txt contains 112 characters.
```

Using DIR we find 116 characters in the textfile.txt file, whereas using our homemade charcntf.c program we find 112.

This discrepancy occurs because of the difference in the way C and MS-DOS represent the end of a line. In C the end of a line is signaled by a single character: the newline character, '\n' (ASCII value 10 decimal). In DOS, on the other hand, the end of a line is marked by two characters, the carriage return (ASCII 13 decimal), and the linefeed (which is the same as the C newline: ASCII 10 decimal).

> The end of a line of text is represented by a single character in C (the newline), but by two characters in MS-DOS files (carriage return and linefeed).

When your program writes a C text file to disk, Turbo C causes all the newlines to be translated into the carriage return plus linefeed (CR/LF) combination. When your program reads in a text file, the CR/LF combination is translated back into a single newline character. Thus, DOS-oriented programs such as DIR will count two characters at each end of line, while C-oriented programs, such as charcntf.c, will count one. In our example there are four lines, so there is a discrepancy of four characters.

As we'll see later, binary mode files handle this translation differently from text files.

Reproducing the DOS TYPE Command

As a practical use for string I/O, we can reproduce the DOS TYPE command, as demonstrated in this example:

```
// type2.c
// reads strings from file
#include <stdio.h>                    // for standard I/O
#include <stdlib.h>                   // for exit()

int main( int argc, char *argv[] )
   {
   FILE *fptr;
   char string[81];

   if(argc != 2)
      { printf("Format: C>type2 filename"); exit(1); }
```

```
if( (fptr=fopen(argv[1], "r")) == NULL)    // open file
    { printf("Can't open file %s.", argv[1]); exit(1); }
while( fgets(string, 80, fptr) != NULL )  // read string
    printf("%s",string);                    // print string
fclose(fptr);                               // close file
return(0);
}
```

This program takes the content of a text file and displays it on the screen, just as the DOS TYPE command does. The advantage of using a homemade command is that you can customize it; you could, for example, add line numbers to your printout or interpret certain characters differently.

Printer Output

There are several ways to send output to the printer. In this section we'll look at two approaches that use standard I/O. The first approach uses standard file handles, and the second uses standard file names.

Standard File Handles

We've seen several examples of obtaining file pointers that refer to files. Handles are similar to file pointers. MS-DOS predefines five standard handles that refer to devices rather than files. These handles are accessed using names defined to be of type *FILE in the stdio.h file. They are

Number	Handle	Device
0	"stdin"	Standard input (keyboard, unless redirected)
1	"stdout"	Standard output (screen, unless redirected)
2	"stderr"	Standard error (screen)
3	"stdaux"	Auxiliary device
4	"stdprn"	Printer

The standard input and output normally refer to the keyboard and screen, but they can be redirected (we discussed redirection in Chapter 8, "Keyboard and Cursor"). Standard error, which is where errors are normally reported, always refers to the screen. The auxiliary device can be assigned when the system is set up; it is often used for a serial device. The standard printer handle is what we want for printing.

Because these standard handles are opened by the system, we don't need to open them before using them. Our example program sends the contents of a text file to the printer, using an approach similar to the reads.c and writes.c examples. It opens the file to be read in the usual way, but the printer isn't opened. To write to the printer, `fputs()` is used with a filename of stdprn.

```
// print2.c
// prints file on printer -- uses standard handle
```

```
#include <stdio.h>                          // for standard I/O
#include <stdlib.h>                         // for exit()

int main( int argc, char *argv[] )
   {
   FILE *fptr;
   char string[81];

   if(argc != 2)                            // check args
      { printf("\nFormat: print2 filename"); exit(1); }
   if( (fptr=fopen(argv[1], "r")) == NULL)  // open file
      { printf("\nCan't open file %s.", argv[1]); exit(1); }
   while( fgets(string, 80, fptr) != NULL ) // read string
      {
      fputs(string, stdprn);                // send to printer
      putc('\r', stdprn);                   // with return
      }
   fclose(fptr);                            // close file
   return(0);
   }
```

We'll see an example later in this chapter where, with system-level I/O, you use predefined handle numbers rather than names for standard devices.

You may want to eject the page automatically after printing. If so, insert the following statement after the while loop:

```
fputc('\x0C', stdprn);
```

The character with the ASCII code of 0C hex (12 decimal) is the form feed, which causes the printer to eject the page.

Standard File Names

You can also refer to devices by names rather than handles. These names are used very much like filenames. For instance, you probably know that you can create short text files by typing

```
C>copy con readme.txt
This is a short text file.
^Z
```

The CON filename refers to the console, which is the keyboard or screen, depending on whether input or output is intended. Similarly, the standard auxiliary device can be called AUX, and the standard printer can be called PRN.

Here's an example that uses the PRN filename to access the printer. Because this is a name and not a handle, the device must be opened before it is used.

```
// print3.c
// prints file on printer -- uses standard file name
```

```
#include <stdio.h>                          // for standard I/O
#include <stdlib.h>                         // for exit()

int main( int argc, char *argv[] )
    {
    FILE *fptr1, *fptr2;
    char string[81];

    if(argc != 2)                           // check args
        { printf("Format: C>print3 filename"); exit(1); }
    if( (fptr1=fopen(argv[1], "r")) == NULL)    // open file
        { printf("Can't open file %s.", argv[1]); exit(1); }
    if( (fptr2=fopen("PRN", "w")) == NULL)      // open printer
        { printf("Can't access printer."); exit(1); }
    while( fgets(string, 80, fptr1) != NULL )   // read string
        fputs(string,fptr2);                    // send to printer
    fclose(fptr1); fclose(fptr2);               // close files
    return(0);
    }
```

This approach is advantageous if you use more than one printer. The name LPT1 is (usually) a synonym for PRN, but if you have additional printers, you can send output to them using the filenames LPT2, LPT3, and so on.

Formatted Input/Output

So far we have dealt with reading and writing only characters and text. How about numbers? To see how we can handle numerical data, let's take a leaf from our secret agent dossier in Chapter 9, "Structures." We'll use the same three items we used there to record the data for an agent: name (a string), code number (an integer), and height (a floating point number). Then we'll write these items to a disk file.

This program reads the data from the keyboard, and then writes it to our agent.txt file. Here's the listing:

```
// writef.c
// writes formatted data to file
#include <stdio.h>                  // for standard I/O
#include <string.h>                 // for strlen()

void main(void)
    {
    FILE *fptr;                     // declare ptr to FILE
    char name[40];                  // agent's name
    int code;                       // code number
    float height;                   // agent's height

    fptr = fopen("agent.txt", "w"); // open file
    do {
        printf("Type name, code number, and height: ");
        scanf("%s %d %f", name, &code, &height);
```

```
        fprintf(fptr, "%s %d %f", name, code, height);
        }
    while(strlen(name) > 1);              // no name given?
    fclose(fptr);                         // close file
    }
```

The key to this program is the `fprintf()` function, which writes the values of the three variables to the file. This function is similar to `printf()`, except that a FILE pointer is included as the first argument. As in `printf()`, we can format the data in a variety of ways; in fact, all the format conventions of `printf()` operate with `fprintf()` as well.

For simplicity this program requires the user to indicate that input is complete by typing a one-letter agent name followed by dummy numbers; this avoids using extra program statements to check whether the user is done, but it's not particularly user-friendly. Here's some sample input:

```
C>writef
Type name, code number, and height: Bond 007 74.5
Type name, code number, and height: Salsbury 009 72.25
Type name, code number, and height: Fleming 999 69.75
Type name, code number, and height: x 0 0
```

This information is now in the agent.txt file. We can look at it there with the DOS TYPE command—or with type2.c. When we use these programs all the output will be on the same line, because there are no newlines in the data. To format the output more conveniently, we can write a program specifically to read agent.txt.

```
// readf.c
// reads formatted data from file
#include <stdio.h>                        // for standard I/O

void main(void)
    {
    FILE *fptr;                           // declare ptr to FILE
    char name[40];                        // agent's name
    int code;                             // code number
    float height;                         // agent's height

    fptr = fopen("agent.txt", "r");       // open file
    while( fscanf(fptr, "%s %d %f", name, &code, &height) != EOF )
        printf("%s %03d %.2f\n", name, code, height);
    fclose(fptr);                         // close file
    }
```

This program uses the `fscanf()` function to read the data from the disk. This function is similar to `scanf()`, except that, as with `fprintf()`, a pointer to FILE is included as the first argument.

We can now display the data in a more readable format, using `printf()`.

```
C>readf
Bond 007 74.50
```

```
Salsbury 009 72.25
Fleming 999 69.75
x 000 0.00
```

Of course, we can use similar techniques with fprintf() and fscanf() for other sorts of formatted data: any combination of characters, strings, integers, and floating point numbers.

Number Storage in Text Format

It's important to understand how numerical data is stored on the disk by fprintf(). Text and characters are stored one character per byte, as we would expect. Are numbers stored as they are in memory, two bytes for an integer, four bytes for floating point, and so on? No. They are stored as strings of characters. Thus, the integer 999 is stored in two bytes of memory but requires three bytes in a disk file, one for each 9 character. The floating point number 69.75 requires four bytes when stored in memory but five when stored on the disk: one for each digit and one for the decimal point. Numbers with more digits require even more disk space. Figure 11.5 shows how this looks.

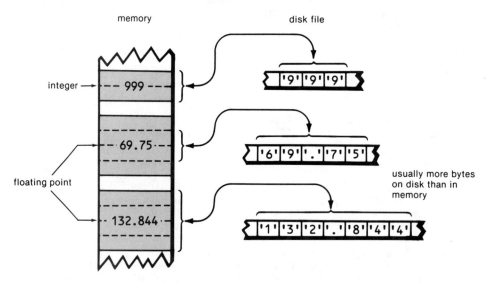

Figure 11.5. Storage of numbers in text format.

Using formatted I/O numbers with more than a few significant digits requires substantially more space on the disk than they do in memory. Thus, if a large amount of numerical data is to be stored in a disk file, using text format can be inefficient. The solution is to use a function that stores numbers in binary format. We'll explore this option in the section on record I/O.

We've now described three methods in standard I/O for reading and writing data. These three methods write data in text format. The fourth method, record I/O, writes data in binary format. When writing data in binary format it is often desirable to use binary mode, so we'll investigate the differences between binary and text modes before discussing record I/O.

Binary Mode and Text Mode

As we noted at the beginning of this chapter, the distinction between text and binary can be applied to two different areas of disk I/O. On the one hand, there is the question of how numbers are stored; this is the distinction between text versus binary format. On the other hand, we can talk about how files are opened and the format interpretations this leads to; this can be called text versus binary mode. It's this second distinction we want to examine in this section.

The need for two different modes arose from incompatibilities between C and the MS-DOS operating system. C originated on UNIX systems and used UNIX file conventions. MS-DOS, which evolved separately from UNIX, has its own, somewhat different, conventions. When C was ported over to the MS-DOS operating system, compiler-writers had to resolve these incompatibilities. Borland's solution (but not that of all C compiler-writers on the PC) was to have two modes. One, the text mode, made files look to C programs as if they were UNIX files. The other, binary mode, made files look more like MS-DOS files.

> Text mode imitates UNIX files. Binary mode imitates MS-DOS files.

There are two main areas where text and binary mode files are different: the handling of newlines and the representation of end-of-file. We'll explore these two areas here.

Text Versus Binary Mode: Newlines

We've already seen that, in text mode, a newline character is translated into the carriage return-linefeed (CR/LF) combination before being written to the disk. Likewise, the CR/LF on the disk is translated back into a newline when the file is read by the C program. However, if a file is opened in binary mode, as opposed to text mode, these translations won't take place.

As an example, let's revise our charcntf.c program to open a file in binary mode and see what effect this has on the number of characters counted in the file. As you may recall, charcnt.c counted fewer characters in a file than did the DOS command DIR, because DIR counted each end-of-line as two characters, whereas charcnt.c counted it as one. Perhaps we can eliminate this discrepancy. Here's the listing:

```
// charcnt2.c
// counts characters in a file opened as binary
#include <stdio.h>                    // for standard I/O
#include <stdlib.h>                   // for exit()

int main( int argc, char *argv[] )
    {
    FILE *fptr;
    int count=0;

    if(argc != 2)                     // check number of args
        { printf("Format: C>charcnt2 filename"); exit(1); }
    if( (fptr=fopen(argv[1],"rb")) == NULL)  // open file
        { printf("Can't open file %s.", argv[1]); exit(1); }
    while( getc(fptr) != EOF )         // get char from file
        count++;                      // count it
    fclose(fptr);                     // close file
    printf("File %s contains %d characters.", argv[1], count);
    return(0);
    }
```

There is only one difference between this program and the original charcntf.c; we have introduced the letter "b" as part of the type string, following the "r".

```
fptr=fopen(argv[1], "rb")
```

The "b" means that the file should be opened in binary mode. (In earlier programs we could have used a "t" to specify text mode, but because this is the default for character I/O, this isn't normally necessary.)

Now if we apply charcnt2.c to our earlier example of the William Blake poem, we'll get the same character count we got using the DOS DIR command—116 characters; with the text mode charcntf.c we got 112 characters:

```
C>charcnt2 user.txt
File user.txt contains 116 characters.

C>charcntf user.txt
File user.txt contains 112 characters.
```

There are four carriage return-linefeed combinations in the file. Each counts as one character in the text mode program charcntf.c but as two characters in the binary mode program charcnt2.c; hence the difference of four characters. In binary mode the translation of the CR/LF pair into a newline does not take place: the binary charcnt2.c program reads each CR/LF as two characters, just as it's stored in the file.

Text Versus Binary Mode: End-of-File

The second difference between text and binary modes is in the way end-of-file is detected. Both systems actually keep track of the total length of the file and will signal an EOF when this length has been reached. In text mode, however, a special character, 1A hex

(26 decimal), inserted after the last character in the file, is also used to indicate EOF. (This character can be generated from the keyboard by pressing the Ctrl z key combination and often is written ^Z.) If this character is encountered at any point in the file, the read function will return the EOF signal (–1) to the program.

This convention arose in the days of CP/M, when all files consisted of blocks of a certain minimum length. To indicate that a file ended in the middle of a block, the ^Z character was used, and its use has carried over into MS-DOS.

There is a moral to be derived from the text-mode conversion of 1A hex to EOF. If a file stores numbers in binary format, it's important that binary mode be used in reading the file back, because one of the numbers might well be the number 1A hex (26 decimal). If this number were detected while we were reading a file in text mode, reading would be terminated (prematurely) at that point.

Also, when writing in binary format, we don't want numbers that happen to have the value 10 decimal to be interpreted as newlines and expanded into CR/LFs. Thus, both in reading and writing binary format numbers, we should use binary mode when accessing the file.

Figure 11.6 shows the differences between text and binary modes.

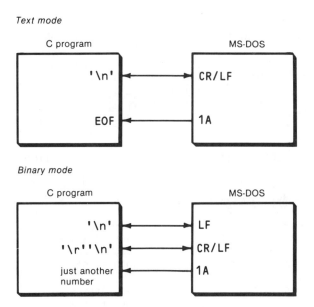

Figure 11.6. Text and binary modes.

Binary Dump Program

Before leaving the subject of binary versus text modes, let's look at a program that uses binary mode to investigate files. This program looks at a file byte by byte in binary mode and displays what it finds there. The display consists of two parts: the hexadecimal code for each character and—if the character is displayable—the character itself. This program provides a sort of x-ray of a disk file. It is modeled after the "dump" function in the DEBUG utility in MS-DOS.

Here's the listing:

```c
// bindump.c
// does binary dump of disk file
// each line is ten ASCII codes followed by ten characters
#include <stdio.h>                    // for standard I/O
#include <stdlib.h>                   // for exit()
#define LENGTH 10                     // length of display line
#define TRUE    1
#define FALSE   0

int main( int argc, char *argv[] )
    {
    FILE *fileptr;                    // pointer to file
    int ch;
    int j, not_eof;
    unsigned char string[LENGTH+1];   // buffer for chars

    if(argc != 2)                     // check arguments
       { printf("Format: C>bindump filename"); exit(1); }
    if( (fileptr=fopen(argv[1],"rb"))==NULL )   // binary read
       { printf("Can't open file %s", argv[1]); exit(1); }
    not_eof = TRUE;                   // not EOF flag
    do
       {
       for(j=0; j<LENGTH; j++)        // chars in one line
          {
          if( (ch=getc(fileptr)) == EOF )  // read character
             not_eof = FALSE;         // clear flag on EOF
          printf("%3x ", ch);         // print ASCII code
          if (ch > 31)
             *(string+j) = ch;        // save printing char
          else                        // use period for
             *(string+j) = '.';       // non-printing char
          }
       *(string+j) = '\0';            // end string
       printf("   %s\n", string);     // print string
       }
    while(not_eof == TRUE);           // quit on EOF
    fclose(fileptr);                  // close file
    return(0);
    }
```

To use this program, you type the name of the program followed by the name of the file to be investigated. If the file is too big to fit on one screen, scrolling can be paused with the Ctrl s key combination.

Earlier we wrote a William Blake poem to the file user.txt. Let's see what happens when we apply bindump.c to that file.

```
C>bindump user.txt
49  20  74  6f  6c  64  20  6d  79  20    I told my
6c  6f  76  65  2c  20  49  20  74  6f    love, I to
6c  64  20  6d  79  20  6c  6f  76  65    ld my love
2c   d   a  49  20  74  6f  6c  64  20    ,..I told
68  65  72  20  61  6c  6c  20  6d  79    her all my
20  68  65  61  72  74  2c   d   a  54     heart,..T
72  65  6d  62  6c  69  6e  67  2c  20    rembling,
63  6f  6c  64  2c  20  69  6e  20  67    cold, in g
68  61  73  74  6c  79  20  66  65  61    hastly fea
72  73  2c   d   a  41  68  21  20  73    rs,..Ah! s
68  65  20  64  69  64  20  64  65  70    he did dep
61  72  74  21   d   a ffff ffff ffff ffff    art!..~~~~
```

In each row the numbers correspond to the characters printed on the right: 49 hex is I, 20 is a space, 74 is t, and so on. Notice that the CR/LF combination is represented as D hex followed by A hex. If we had opened the file in text mode, we would have seen only the A's. Also, if the program encounters the number 1A hex, it will print it just like any other number; it won't be interpreted as EOF, as it would have been in text mode.

At the end of the file, the program starts to read real EOFs, which are printed as ffff hex. The program reads until the end of a line, even if it has found an EOF, so the rest of the line is filled out with ffff. With a modest increase in complexity, the program could be rewritten to terminate on the first EOF. Also, if you prefer decimal to hexadecimal output, changing the format specifier in the printf() statement will do the trick.

> Ordinarily, binary mode is used for binary format data and text mode for text format data, although there are exceptions.

Now that we know something about binary mode, let's investigate the fourth method of performing standard I/O: record I/O.

Record Input/Output

Earlier we saw how numbers can be stored using the formatted I/O functions fscanf() and fprintf(). However, we also saw that storing numbers in the format provided by these functions can take up a lot of disk space, because each digit is stored as a character. Formatted I/O presents another problem; there is no direct way to read and write complex data types such as arrays and structures. Arrays can be handled, although inefficiently, by writing each array element one at a time. Structures must also be written piecemeal.

In standard I/O, one answer to these problems is record I/O, sometimes called block I/O. Record I/O writes numbers to disk files in binary (or "untranslated") format so that integers are stored in two bytes, floating point numbers in four bytes, and so on, for the other numerical types—the same format used to store numbers in memory. Record I/O also permits writing any amount of data at once; the process isn't limited to a single character or string or to the few values that can be placed in a fprintf() or fscanf() function. Arrays, structures, structures of arrays, and other data constructions can be written with a single statement.

Writing Structures with *fwrite()*

Taking the structure used for secret agent data in Chapter 9, "Structures," we'll devise a pair of programs to read and write such structures directly. The first one, listed here, will write a file consisting of a number of agent records, each one consisting of the structure agent defined in the program.

```
// writer.c
// writes agent's records to file
#include <stdio.h>                    // for standard I/O
#include <stdlib.h>                   // for exit(), atof(), etc.
#include <conio.h>                    // for getche()

int main(void)
    {
    struct                            // define structure
        {
        char name[40];                // name
        int agnumb;                   // code number
        double height;                // height
        } agent;

    char numstr[81];                  // for numbers
    FILE *fptr;                       // file pointer

    if( (fptr=fopen("agents.rec","wb"))==NULL )  // open file
        { printf("\nCan't open file agents.rec"); exit(1); }
    do
        {
        printf("\nEnter name: ");     // get name
        gets(agent.name);
        printf("Enter number: ");     // get number
        gets(numstr);
        agent.agnumb = atoi(numstr);
        printf("Enter height: ");     // get height
        gets(numstr);
        agent.height = atof(numstr);
```

```
                                        // write struct to file
      fwrite(&agent, sizeof(agent), 1, fptr);
      printf("Add another agent (y/n)? ");
      }
   while(getche()=='y');
   fclose(fptr);                        // close file
   return(0);
   }
```

This program will accept input concerning name, number, and height of each agent and then will write the data to a disk file called agents.rec. Any number of agents can be entered. Here's a sample interaction:

```
C>writer
Enter name: Holmes, Sherlock
Enter number: 010
Enter height: 73.75
Add another agent (y/n)? y
Enter name: Bond, James
Enter number: 007
Enter height: 74.5
Add another agent (y/n)? n
```

Most of this program should be familiar to you from Chapter 9 and from earlier examples in this chapter. Note, however, that the agents.rec file is opened in binary mode.

The information obtained from the user at the keyboard is placed in the structure agent. Then the following statement writes the structure to the file:

```
fwrite(&agent, sizeof(agent), 1, fptr);
```

The first argument of this function is the address of the structure to be written. The second argument is the size of the structure. Instead of counting bytes, we let the program do it for us by using the sizeof() function. The third argument is the number of such structures we want to write at one time. If we had an array of structures, for example, we might want to write the entire array at once. This number could then be adjusted accordingly, as we'll see shortly. In this case, however, we want to write only one structure at a time. The last argument is the pointer to the file we want to write to.

Try using the bindump.c program to examine the file agents.txt generated with writer.c. You'll see that the numbers, because they're in binary format, are all represented by funny-looking symbols. Only the names are unchanged.

Reading Structures with *fread()*

To read the structure written by writer.c, we can concoct another program, similar to writer.c.

```
// readr.c
// reads agent's records from file
```

```
#include <stdio.h>                       // for standard I/O
#include <stdlib.h>                      // for exit()

int main(void)
   {
   struct
      {
      char name[40];                     // name
      int agnumb;                        // code number
      double height;                     // height
      } agent;

   FILE *fptr;

   if( (fptr=fopen("agents.rec","rb"))==NULL )
      { printf("Can't open file agents.rec"); exit(1); }
   while( fread(&agent,sizeof(agent),1,fptr)==1 )
      {                                  // read file
      printf("\nName: %s\n", agent.name);       // print name
      printf("Number: %03d\n", agent.agnumb);   // print number
      printf("Height: %.2lf\n", agent.height);  // print height
      }
   fclose(fptr);                         // close file
   return(0);
   }
```

The heart of this program is the expression

```
fread(&agent,sizeof(agent),1,fptr)
```

which causes data read from the disk to be placed in the structure agent; the format is the same as fwrite(). The fread() function returns the number of items read. Ordinarily this should correspond to the third argument, the number of items we asked for—in this case, 1. If we've reached the end of the file, however, the number will be smaller—in this case, 0. By testing for this situation, we know when to stop reading.

The fread() function places the data from the file into the structure; to display it, we access the structure members with printf() in the usual way. Here's how it looks:

```
C>readr

Holmes, Sherlock
010
73.75

Bond, James
007
74.50
```

In record I/O, numerical data is stored in binary mode. This means that an integer always occupies two bytes, a floating point number always occupies four bytes, and so on. Figure 11.7 shows the relationship of data stored in memory and on the disk in binary format. As you can see, record I/O, because it makes use of binary format, is more efficient for the storage of numerical data than functions that use text format, such as fprintf().

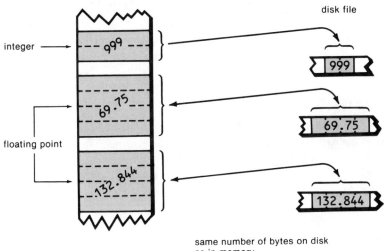

Figure 11.7. Storage of numbers in binary format.

Because data is stored in binary format, it's important to open the file in binary mode. If it were opened in text mode, and should the number 26 decimal be used in the file (as an agent number, for instance), the program would interpret it as an EOF and stop reading the file at that point. We also want to suppress the conversion of newlines to CR/LFs.

Arrays and Record Input/Output

The fwrite() and fread() functions need not be restricted to writing and reading structures. We can use them to work with other data as well. For example, suppose we wanted to store an integer array of 10 elements in a disk file. We could write the 10 items one at a time using fprintf(), but it is more efficient to take the following approach:

```
// warray.c */
// writes array to file */
#include <stdio.h>              // for standard I/O
#include <stdlib.h>             // for exit()

int table[10] = { 1, 2, 3, 4, 5, 6, 7, 8, 9, 10 };

void main(void)
   {
   FILE *fptr;                  // file pointer */
```

```
if( (fptr=fopen("table.rec","w"))==NULL )  // open file */
   { printf("Can't open file agents.rec"); exit(1); }
fwrite(table, sizeof(table), 1, fptr);     // write array */
fclose(fptr);                        // close file
}
```

This program doesn't accomplish anything useful, but it does demonstrate that the writing of an array to the disk is similar to the writing of a structure. (We'll soon see an example of writing an array of structures.)

A Database Example

For a more ambitious example of record I/O at work, we'll add disk reading and writing capability to our agent.c program from Chapter 9, "Structures." The resulting program will allow data for up to 50 agents to be entered into an array of structures in memory. Then a single command will write the entire array to disk thus saving the database for future access. Another command reads the array back in again.

Here's the listing:

```
// agentr.c
// maintains list of agents in file
#include <stdio.h>              // for standard I/O
#include <stdlib.h>             // for exit()
#include <conio.h>              // for getche()
#define TRUE 1
void listall(void);            // prototypes
void newname(void);
void rfile(void);
void wfile(void);

struct personnel                     // define data structure
   {
   char name [40];             // name
   int agnumb;                 // code number
   double height;              // height in inches
   };

struct personnel agent[50];    // array of 50 structures
int n = 0;                     // number of agents listed
char numstr[40];               // number input string

void main(void)
   {
   while(TRUE)                  // cycle until user chooses 'q'
      {
      printf("\n'e' enter new agent\n'l' list all agents");
      printf("\n'w' write file\n'r' read file\n'q' exit: ");
      switch ( getche() )
         {
         case 'e': newname(); break;
         case 'l': listall(); break;
```

```
         case 'w': wfile();     break;
         case 'r': rfile();     break;
         case 'q': exit(0);     break;
         default:                          // user mistake
            puts("\nEnter only selections listed");
         }  // end switch
      }  // end while
   }  // end main()

// newname()
// puts a new agent in the database
void newname(void)
   {
   printf("\nRecord %d.\nEnter name: ", n+1); // get name
   gets(agent[n].name);
   printf("Enter agent number (3 digits): "); // get number
   gets(numstr);
   agent[n].agnumb = atoi(numstr);
   printf("Enter height in inches: ");        // get height
   gets(numstr);
   agent[n++].height = atof(numstr);
   }

// listall()
// lists all agents and data
void listall(void)
   {
   int j;

   if(n < 1)                              // check for empty list
      printf("\nEmpty list.\n");
   for(j=0; j < n; j++)                   // print list
      {
      printf("\nRecord number %d\n", j+1);
      printf("   Name: %s\n", agent[j].name);
      printf("   Agent number: %03d\n", agent[j].agnumb);
      printf("   Height: %4.2lf\n", agent[j].height);
      }
   }

// wfile()
// writes array of structures to file
void wfile(void)
   {
   FILE *fptr;

   if(n < 1)
      { printf("\nCan't write empty list.\n"); return; }
   if( (fptr=fopen("agents.rec","wb"))==NULL )
      printf("\nCan't open file agents.rec\n");
   else
      {
```

```
        fwrite(agent, sizeof(agent[0]), n, fptr);
        fclose(fptr);
        printf("\nFile of %d records written.\n", n);
        }
    }

// rfile()
// reads records from file into array
void rfile(void)
    {
    FILE *fptr;

    if( (fptr=fopen("agents.rec","rb"))==NULL )
        printf("\nCan't open file agents.rec\n");
    else
        {
        while( fread(&agent[n],sizeof(agent[n]),1,fptr)==1 )
            n++;                        // count records
        fclose(fptr);
        printf("\nFile read. Total agents is now %d.\n", n);
        }
    }
```

Using this program, we can enter a number of secret agents, using the 'e' option.

```
C>agentr

'e' enter new agent
'l' list all agents
'w' write file
'r' read file: e
Record 1.
Enter name: Mike Hammer
Enter agent number (3 digits): 004
Enter height in inches: 74.25
```

We can continue this process for as many names as we want. Once we've entered the names, we write them to disk with the 'w' option. Then we can quit the program, turn off the computer, whatever; it doesn't matter if the array in memory is destroyed. When we run the program again, we can read the list back in from the disk. The following sequence shows that there is nothing in the list until we read the file; then we can list the contents.

```
C>agentr

'e' enter new agent
'l' list all agents
'w' write file
'r' read file: l
Empty list.

'e' enter new agent
'l' list all agents
```

```
'w' write file
'r' read file: r
File read. Total agents is now 3.

'e' enter new agent
'l' list all agents
'w' write file
'r' read file: l

Record number 1
    Name: Mike Hammer
    Agent number: 004
    Height: 74.25

Record number 2
    Name: Lew Archer
    Agent number: 026
    Height: 71.50

Record number 3
    Name: Sam Spade
    Agent number: 492
    Height: 71.75
```

The new capabilities of this program are in the functions wfile() and rfile(). In wfile() the statement

```
fwrite(agent, sizeof(agent[0]), n, fptr);
```

causes the entire array of n structures to be written to disk at once. The address of the data is at agent; the size of one record is sizeof(agent[0]), which is the size of the first record; the number of such records is n; and the file pointer is fptr.

When the function rfile() reads the data back in, it must do so one record—that is, one structure—at a time, because it doesn't know in advance how many agents are in the database. Thus, the expression

```
fread(&agent[n],sizeof(agent[n]),1,fptr)
```

is embedded in a while loop, which waits for the fread() function to report that no bytes were read, indicating end-of-file. This expression causes the data in the structure to be stored at address &agent[n] and to have the size of agent[n]. It causes one such structure to be read at a time, from the file pointed to by fptr.

> The fread() and fwrite() functions work with any kind of data, including arrays and structures, and store numbers in binary format.

This program, although it deals with secret agents, could serve as a skeleton for all sorts of database applications, from recipes and stamp collecting to employee records and inventory control.

Random Access

So far all our file reading and writing has been sequential. That is, when writing a file we've taken a group of items—whether characters, strings, or more complex structures—and placed them on the disk one at a time. Likewise, when reading, we've started at the beginning of the file and gone on until we came to the end.

It's also possible to access files *randomly*. This means directly accessing a particular data item, even though it may be in the middle of the file.

The following program allows random access of the file agents.rec, created with the agentr.c program above.

```c
// randr.c
// reads one agent's record from file
#include <stdio.h>        // for standard I/O
#include <process.h>      // for exit()

int main(void)
    {
    struct
        {
        char name[40];                        // name
        int agnumb;                           // code number
        double height;                        // height
        } agent;

    FILE *fptr;
    int recno;                                // record number
    long int offset;                          // note: type long
                                              // open file
    if( (fptr=fopen("agents.rec","rb"))==NULL )
        { printf("\nCan't open file agents.rec"); exit(1); }

    printf("\nEnter record number: ");        // get record num
    scanf("%d", &recno);
    offset = (recno-1) * sizeof(agent);       // find offset
    if(fseek(fptr, offset, 0) != 0)           // go there
        { printf("\nCan't move pointer there."); exit(1); }

    fread(&agent,sizeof(agent),1,fptr);       // read record
    printf("Name: %s\n", agent.name);         // print name
    printf("Number: %03d\n", agent.agnumb);   // print number
    printf("Height: %.2lf\n", agent.height);  // print height
    fclose(fptr);                             // close file
    return(0);
    }
```

And here—assuming the same database exists that we created with the agentr.c program earlier—is what it looks like if we use randr.c to ask for the second record in the file:

```
C>randr
Enter record number: 2

Name: Lew Archer
Number: 026
Height: 71.50
```

File Pointers

To understand how this program works, you need to be familiar with the concept of file pointers. A *file pointer* is a pointer to a particular byte in a file. The functions we've examined in this chapter made use of the file pointer: each time we wrote something to a file, the file pointer moved to the end of that something—whether character, string, structure, or whatever—so that writing would continue at that point with the next write function.

When we closed a file and then reopened it, the file pointer was set back to the beginning of the file so that if we then read from the file, we would start at the beginning. If we had opened a file for append (using the "a" type option), the file pointer would have been placed at the end of an existing file before we began writing.

> The file pointer points to the byte in the file where the next access will take place. The fseek() function lets us move this pointer.

The function fseek() gives us control over the file pointer. Thus, to access a record in the middle of a file, we use this function to move the file pointer to that record. In the preceding program the file pointer is set to the desired value in the expression:

```
if(fseek(fptr, offset, 0) != 0)
```

The first argument of the fseek() function is the pointer to the FILE structure for this file. (As you know, this also is referred to as a *file pointer,* but it is something quite different from the file pointer that indicates where we are in the file. We have to trust to context to indicate which file pointer we mean.)

The second argument in fseek() is called the *offset.* This is the number of bytes from a particular place to start reading. Often this place is the beginning of the file; that's the case here. (We'll see other possibilities in a moment.) In our program the offset is calculated by multiplying the size of one record—the structure agent—by the number of the record we want to access. In the example we access the second record, but the program thinks of this as record number 1 (because the first record is 0), so the multiplication will be by 1. It is essential that the offset be a long integer.

431

The last argument of the `fseek()` function is called the *mode*. There are three possible mode numbers, and they determine where the offset will be measured from.

Mode	Offset Is Measured From
0	Beginning of file
1	Current position of file pointer
2	End of file

Once the file pointer has been set, we read the contents of the record at that point into the structure `agent` and display its contents.

For simplicity we've demonstrated random access to the agents.rec file as a separate program, but it easily could be incorporated into agentr.c as a function, becoming another option for the user.

Another function, `ftell()`, returns the position of the file pointer in the file. You can use it to tell the file size by setting the file pointer to the end of the file with `fseek()` and then reading its position:

```
fseek(fptr, 0, 2);          // set pointer to 0 bytes from end
file_size = ftell(fptr);    // pointer position is file size
```

Error Conditions

In most cases, if a file can be opened, it can be read from or written to. There are situations, however, when this is not the case. A hardware problem might occur while either reading or writing is taking place, a write operation might run out of disk space, or some other problem might occur.

In our programs so far, we have assumed that no such read or write errors occur. In some situations, however, such as programs where data integrity is critical, it may be desirable to check explicitly for errors.

Most standard I/O functions don't have an explicit error return. For example, if `putc()` returns an EOF, this might indicate either a true end-of-file or an error; if `fgets()` returns a NULL value, this might indicate either an EOF or an error, and so forth.

To determine whether an error has occurred we can use the function `ferror()`. This function takes one argument: the file pointer (to FILE). It returns a value of 0 if no error has occurred and a nonzero (TRUE) value if there is an error. This function should be reset by closing the file after it has been used.

Another function is also useful in conjunction with `ferror()`. This one is called `perror()`. It takes a string supplied by the program as an argument; this string is usually an error message indicating where in the program the error occurred. The function prints the program's error message and then goes on to display a system-error message.

Here's how we could rewrite the earlier writef.c program to incorporate these two error-handling functions:

```c
// recerror.c
// writes formatted data to file
// includes error-handling functions
#include <stdio.h>               // for standard I/O
#include <stdlib.h>              // for exit()
#include <string.h>             // for strlen()

int main(void)
    {
    FILE *fptr;                 // declare ptr to FILE
    char name[40];              // agent's name
    int code;                   // code number
    float height;              // agent's height
                                // open file
    if( (fptr=fopen("agent.txt","w"))==NULL )
        { printf("\nCan't open textfile.txt"); exit(1); }
    do {
        printf("\nType name, code number, and height: ");
        scanf("%s %d %f", name, &code, &height);
        fprintf(fptr, "%s %d %f", name, code, height);
        if( ferror(fptr) )       // check for error
            {
            perror("\nWrite error");    // write message
            fclose(fptr);               // close file
            exit(1);
            }
        } while(strlen(name) > 1);     // no name given?
    fclose(fptr);                       // close file
    return(0);
    }
```

In the event that, for example, there is a disk error, ferror() will return a nonzero value and perror() will display the following message:

```
Write error: Bad data
```

The first part of this message is supplied by the program and the second part, from the colon on, is supplied by the system.

Explicit error messages of this type can be informative both for the user and for the programmer during development.

We've completed our exploration of standard I/O, so we're ready to move on to the second type of C-language input/output: system-level I/O.

System-Level Input/Output

System-level (sometimes called low-level) I/O parallels the methods used by MS-DOS for reading and writing files. In system-level I/O, data can't be written as individual characters, or as strings, or as formatted data, as is possible using standard I/O. There is only one way data can be written: as a buffer full of bytes.

Writing a buffer full of data resembles record I/O in the standard I/O package. However, unlike standard I/O, the programmer must set up the buffer for the data, place the appropriate values in it before writing, and take them out after reading. Figure 11.8 shows that the buffer in system I/O is part of the program rather than being invisible as in standard I/O.

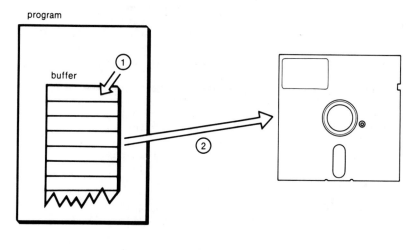

1   data is placed in the buffer by the program

2   **write( )** function sends contents of buffer to disk file

Figure 11.8. Visible buffer.

There are advantages to system-level I/O. Because it parallels the methods that MS-DOS uses to write to the disk, system-level I/O is more efficient than standard I/O. The amount of code used by the C library routines is less than with standard I/O, so programs can be smaller. Finally, because there are fewer layers of routines to go through, system I/O can also operate faster. Actually, because it's the more basic system, system I/O routines are used by many compiler writers to create the standard I/O package.

Reading Files in System I/O

Our first example is a program that reads a file from the disk and displays it on the screen. We've seen several examples of how this operation is carried out in standard I/O, so this program will point out the differences between the two approaches.

As an example of the program's operation, we'll use it to display its own source file.

```
c>sysread sysread.c
// sysread.c
// reads and displays file
#include <io.h>                       // for system I/O
#include <fcntl.h>                    // for oflags
#include <stdio.h>                    // for printf()
#include <stdlib.h>                   // for exit()
#include <conio.h>                    // for putch()
#define BUFFSIZE 512                  // buffer size
char buff[BUFFSIZE];                  // buffer

int main( int argc, char *argv[] )
   {
   int inhandle, bytes, j;
   if(argc != 2)                      // check arguments
      { printf("Format: C>sysread filename"); exit(1); }
                                      // open file
   if( (inhandle = open(argv[1], O_RDONLY | O_BINARY)) < 0)
      { printf("Can't open file %s.", argv[1]); exit(1); }
                                      // read one buffer
   while( (bytes = read(inhandle,buff,BUFFSIZE)) > 0)
      for(j=0; j<bytes; j++)          // print buffer
         putch(buff[j]);
   close(inhandle);                   // close file
   return(0);
   }
```

Setting Up the Buffer

The first difference you'll notice in this program is that we declare a character buffer with the statements:

```
#define BUFFSIZE 512
char buff[BUFFSIZE];
```

This is the buffer in which the data read from the disk will be placed. The size of this buffer is important for efficient operation. Depending on the operating system, buffers of certain sizes are handled more efficiently than others. In MS-DOS, the optimum buffer size is a multiple of 512 bytes. As we'll see later, the absolute size of the buffer is also important. In some cases a large buffer is more efficient, so multiples of 512, such as 2048 or 4096, should be used.

Opening the File

As in standard I/O, we must open the file before we can access it. This is done in the expression

```
if( (inhandle = open(argv[1], O_RDONLY | O_BINARY)) < 0)
```

We open the file for the same reason we did in standard I/O: to establish communications with the operating system about the file. We tell the system the name of the file we want to open—in this case, the name placed in the command-line array argv[1] by the user. We also indicate whether we want to read or write to the file and whether we want the file opened in binary or text mode. However, the method used to indicate this information is different in system I/O. Each characteristic is indicated by a constant called an *oflag*. A list of oflags is shown in Table 11.1.

Table 11.1. System-level Oflags.

Oflag	Meaning
O_APPEND	Place file pointer at end of file
O_CREAT	Create a new file for writing (has no effect if file already exists)
O_RDONLY	Open a new file for reading only
O_RDWR	Open file for both reading and writing
O_TRUNC	Open and truncate existing file to 0 length
O_WRONLY	Open file for writing only
O_BINARY	Open file in binary mode
O_TEXT	Open file in text mode

Some of the possibilities listed in Table 11.1 are mutually exclusive: you can't open a file for read-only and read-write at the same time, for example.

The prototypes of the system I/O functions are in the header file io.h, so this file must be #included when system-level I/O is used.

In our sysread.c program we open a file using the oflags O_RDONLY and O_BINARY. We'll see examples of other oflags in use as we go along. The oflags are defined in the file fcntl.h, so this file must be #included in programs using system I/O. (Note, though, that the stdio.h file, which was necessary in standard I/O, is not necessary for system I/O.)

When two or more oflags are used together, they are combined using the bitwise OR operator (|).

File Handles

Instead of returning a pointer, as fopen() did in standard I/O, open() returns an integer value called a *file handle*. This is a number assigned to a particular file, which is used thereafter to refer to the file.

If open() returns a value of –1 rather than a valid file handle (which must be greater than 0), an error has occurred. (We can find out more about the error by using another function, as we'll see in the next example.)

> The system-level function open() returns a file handle, which isn't a pointer, but simply a reference number to identify a file.

Reading the File into the Buffer

The following statement reads the file—or as much of it as will fit—into the buffer:

```
bytes = read(inhandle,buff,BUFFSIZE)
```

The read() function takes three arguments. The first is the file handle. The second is the address of the buffer—in this case, the variable buff. The third argument is the maximum number of bytes we want to read. In this case we'll allow the function to fill the entire buffer, but in some situations reading fewer bytes might be desirable. Reading more bytes than the buffer can hold is not, of course, recommended.

The read() function returns the number of bytes actually read. This is an important number, because it may well be less than the buffer size, and we'll need to know just how full the buffer is before we can do anything with its contents. We assign this number to the variable bytes.

Once the buffer is full we can display it. We do this with a for loop running from 0 to bytes, printing one character at a time.

Closing the File

No surprises here: we use the close() function to close the file. This releases the communications areas and the file handle for use by other files.

Error Messages

As with standard I/O, it's possible in system I/O to query the system about what went wrong in the event that an error condition is encountered when an open( ) or other file operation is attempted. A return value of –1 indicates an error, and the type of error can be determined with the function perror( ). This function, as we saw earlier, uses as its argument an error message from the program and, when executed, prints not only the program's message, but also the system-error message.

Here's a modification of sysread.c that incorporates this function to check for errors on opening the file:

```
// syserror.c
// reads and displays file, uses perror() to display errors
#include <io.h>                          // for system I/O
#include <fcntl.h>                       // for oflags
#include <stdio.h>                       // for printf(), perror()
#include <stdlib.h>                      // for exit()
#include <conio.h>                       // for putch()
#define BUFFSIZE 512                     // buffer size
char buff[BUFFSIZE];                     // buffer

int main( int argc, char *argv[] )
    {
    int inhandle, bytes, j;

    if(argc != 2)                        // check arguments
        { printf("\nFormat: C>syserror filename"); exit(1); }
                                         // open file
    if( (inhandle = open(argv[1], O_RDONLY | O_BINARY)) < 0)
        { perror("\nCan't open input file"); exit(1); }
                                         // read one buffer
    while( (bytes = read(inhandle,buff,BUFFSIZE)) > 0)
        for(j=0; j<bytes; j++)           // print buffer
            putch(buff[j]);
    close(inhandle);                     // close file
    return(0);
    }
```

Here's a sample of the program's operation when the user attempts to operate on a nonexistent file:

```
C>syserror nofile.xxx
Can't open input file: No such file or directory
```

The first part of the message is the program's, the second comes from the system.

This technique can be used to provide information about read and write errors as well as errors in opening a file.

Buffer Operations

Putting the contents of a file in a buffer has certain advantages; we can perform various operations on the contents of the buffer without having to access the file again. There are several functions that can speed up operations on buffered data, as our next example demonstrates. This program searches a text file for a word or phrase typed by the user.

```
// search.c
// searches file for phrase
#include <io.h>                          // for system I/O
#include <fcntl.h>                       // for oflags
```

```
#include <stdio.h>                    // for printf()
#include <string.h>                   // for memchr()
#include <process.h>                  // for exit()
#define BUFFSIZE 1024                 // buffer size

char buff[BUFFSIZE];                  // buffer
void search(char *, int);             // prototype

int main( int argc, char *argv[] )
   {
   int inhandle, bytes;

   if(argc != 3)                      // check arguments
      { printf("\nFormat: C>search filename phrase"); exit(1); }
                                      // open file
   if( (inhandle = open(argv[1], O_RDONLY )) < 0)
      { printf("\nCan't open file %s.", argv[1]); exit(1); }
                                      // read file
   while( (bytes = read(inhandle,buff,BUFFSIZE)) > 0)
      search(argv[2],bytes);          // search for phrase
   close(inhandle);                   // close file
   printf("\nPhrase not found");
   return(0);
   }

// search()
// searches buffer for phrase
void search(char *phrase, int buflen)
   {
   char *ptr, *p;

   ptr = buff;
   while( (ptr=memchr(ptr,phrase[0],buflen)) != NULL)
      if( memcmp(ptr,phrase,strlen(phrase)) == 0)  // if match
         {
         printf("First occurrence of phrase:\n");
         for(p=ptr-100; p<ptr+100; p++)            // display it
            putchar(*p);
         exit(0);
         }
      else                                         // otherwise,
         ptr++;                                     // next char
   }  // end search()
```

This program requires the user to type two arguments on the command line (in addition to the program name): the name of the file to be searched and the phrase to be searched for. The program then finds the first occurrence of this phrase. To show where the phrase is in the file, the characters on each side of the phrase are printed so that it can be seen in context.

Here's an example of the program searching the manuscript version of Chapter 9 of this book for the word *aside:*

```
C>search chp9.ms aside
First occurrence of phrase:

list of prices.
3. The purpose of declaring a structure type is to
      a. set aside the appropriate amount of memory
      b. define the format of the structure
      c. specify
```

The main part of this program is similar to sysread.c. One difference is that the file has been opened in text mode. This is the default when no mode is specified, and we didn't include the O_BINARY oflag. This means that CR/LFs will be translated into newlines when we read the file.

This program could be improved—at the expense of making it more complicated—by making sure it doesn't read outside the buffer.

Buffer Manipulation Functions

The function search(), called by the main program, makes use of several buffer manipulation functions. The first such function is memchr(). This function searches a buffer for a specific character. In our example, the expression

```
ptr=memchr(ptr,phrase[0],buflen)
```

shows the three arguments necessary for memchr(). The first is the address of the buffer. Here we've assigned the address to the pointer variable ptr. The second argument is the character to be searched for—in this case, the first character of the phrase typed by the user, argv[2]. This is passed to the function search() and stored in the variable phrase. The third parameter is the length of the buffer to be searched.

The memchr() function returns a NULL if the character isn't found; otherwise it returns a pointer to the character in the buffer. Here it assigns the pointer to the variable ptr.

The search() function then enters an if statement to see whether the character actually marks the beginning of the sought-after phrase. This comparison is handled by the function memcmp() in the expression

```
if( memcmp(ptr,phrase,strlen(phrase)) == 0)
```

This function also takes three arguments: a pointer to the place in the buffer where the comparison should begin, the address of the phrase to be compared, and the length of the phrase. The function then compares the phrase with the characters in the buffer; if they match, it returns 0.

If a match is found, the search() function prints the characters on both sides of the match and exits. Otherwise, the process is repeated until memchr() can no longer find the character in the file.

The buffer manipulation functions require that the string.h (or mem.h) file be #included with the program.

Writing Files in System I/O

Writing a file in system I/O is somewhat more complicated than reading a file. As an example, let's look at a program that copies one file to another; that is, it imitates the DOS COPY command.

To use this function, the user types the name of the source file (which should already exist) and the destination file (which will be created) on the command line.

```
C>copy2 source.txt dest.txt
```

Because the files are opened in binary, any file can be copied, whether a text file or a binary file such as an executable program.

Here's the listing:

```
// copy2.c
// copies one file to another
#include <io.h>                        // for system I/O
#include <fcntl.h>                     // for oflags
#include <sys/stat.h>                  // for sflags
#include <stdio.h>                     // for printf()
#include <stdlib.h>                    // for exit()
#define BUFFSIZE 4096                  // buffer size

char buff[BUFFSIZE];                   // buffer

int main( int argc, char *argv[] )
   {
   int inhandle, outhandle, bytes;

   if(argc != 3)                       // check arguments
      { printf("\nFormat: C>copy2 infile outfile"); exit(1); }
                                       // open files
   if( (inhandle = open(argv[1], O_RDWR | O_BINARY)) < 0)
      {printf("\nCan't open infile %s.", argv[1]); exit(1); }
   if( (outhandle = open(argv[2],
        O_CREAT | O_WRONLY | O_BINARY, S_IWRITE)) < 0)
      { printf("\nCan't open outfile %s.", argv[2]); exit(1); }
                                       // copy file
   while( (bytes = read(inhandle,buff,BUFFSIZE)) > 0)
      write(outhandle,buff,bytes);
   close(inhandle);                    // close files
   close(outhandle);
   return(0);
   }
```

Two files are opened. One is the source file, whose handle is assigned to the variable inhandle. The other is the destination file, whose handle will be in outhandle. The expression that opens the source file should look familiar from previous examples. The one that opens the destination file, though, has some unfamiliar features.

```
if( (outhandle = open(argv[2],
     O_CREAT ¦ O_WRONLY ¦ O_BINARY, S_IWRITE)) < 0)
```

This expression is so large it must be written on two lines. To create a nonexistent file, we use the O_CREAT oflag. We want to write and not read to this file, so we also use O_WRONLY. We also want to use binary mode, so we use O_BINARY.

Whenever the O_CREAT oflag is used, another variable must be added to the open() function to indicate the read/write status of the file to be created. These options are called the *permiss* (for *permission*) arguments. There are three possibilities.

Permiss	Meaning
S_IWRITE	Writing permitted
S_IREAD	Reading permitted
S_IREAD I S_IWRITE	Reading and writing permitted

If the permiss flags are to be recognized, the file sys/stat.h must be #included with the source file for this program, along with fcntl.h.

The write() function is similar in format to read(). Like read(), it takes three arguments: the handle of the file to be written to, the address of the buffer, and the number of bytes to be written.

To copy the file, we use both the read() and write() functions in a while loop. The read() function returns the number of bytes actually read; this is assigned to the variable bytes. This value will be equal to the buffer size until the end of the file, when the buffer probably will be only partially full. The variable bytes therefore is used to tell the write() function how many bytes to write from the buffer to the destination file.

Notice that we've used a larger buffer size in this program than in previous examples. The larger the buffer, the fewer disk accesses the program must make, so increasing the size of the buffer significantly speeds up the operation of the program. With a buffer size of 4096, an 80K file is copied twice as fast as with a buffer size of 512. You can experiment with buffer size to see what works best in your particular application.

When large buffers are used they must be made global variables; otherwise stack overflow occurs.

Writing to the Printer in System I/O

You can write to the printer easily using system level I/O functions. As we saw earlier, there are five predefined file handles. The file handle argument supplied to write() is a number (unlike the handles used in standard I/O), so we use the numbers from 0 to 4 to select one of the predefined handles. The number for the printer is 4.

Here's a program that prints the contents of a file whose name is typed on the command line by the user.

```
// print4.c
// prints file to printer -- using standard file number
#include <io.h>                    // for system I/O
#include <fcntl.h>                 // for oflags
#include <stdio.h>                 // for printf()
#include <stdlib.h>                // for exit()
#define BUFFSIZE 4096              // buffer size

char buff[BUFFSIZE];               // buffer

int main( int argc, char *argv[] )
   {
   int inhandle, bytes;

   if(argc != 2)                             // check arguments
      { printf("\nFormat: C>print4 sourcefile"); exit(1); }
                                             // open input file
   if( (inhandle = open(argv[1], O_RDWR | O_BINARY)) < 0 )
      { printf("\nCan't open file %s.", argv[1]); exit(1); }
                                             // send file to printer
   while( (bytes = read(inhandle, buff, BUFFSIZE)) > 0)
      write(4, buff, bytes);                 // standard handle is 4
   close(inhandle);                          // close file
   return(0);
   }
```

This program is similar to the print2.c example shown before. No file needs to be opened for the printer, because we already know the handle number.

Redirection

In Chapter 8, "Keyboard and Cursor," we discussed redirection: the capability built into DOS and the C runtime system to redirect output that would normally go to the screen to a disk file and to take input that would normally come from the keyboard from a disk file.

It is also possible to modify disk-oriented programs, such as those in this chapter, so that they make use of redirection. This can be helpful if the programs are to be used, UNIX-style, in such a way that they act as filters, taking input from one program via redirection, modifying it, and passing it on to another program, again via redirection. (For more on filters and the related subject of pipes, see your DOS manual or the other books listed in the bibliography.)

Let's see how we would modify the copy2.c program to use redirection. Essentially we rewrite the program so that its input, instead of coming from a file, comes from the keyboard, and its output, instead of going to a file, goes to the display. Then, when the program is used, redirection can be employed to specify that input should again come from a file and that output should also go to a file (or be piped to another program).

The simplest way to invoke this new version of the program would be

```
C>copy3 <source.ext >dest.ext
```

where source.ext is the file we want to copy and dest.ext is the destination file. However, if we wanted to copy the output of another program, say prog1, and send the copied file to a third program, say prog2, we could write

```
C>prog1 ¦ copy3 ¦ prog2
```

A fringe benefit of using redirection is that the programming is somewhat simplified. Here's the modified version of copy2.c:

```
// copy3.c
// copies one file to another
// uses redirection; format is C>copy3 <source.xxx >dest.xxx
#include <io.h>                    // for system I/O
#include <fcntl.h>                 // for oflags
#define inhandle 0                 // stdin file
#define outhandle 1                // stdout file
#define BUFFSIZE 4096              // buffer size

char buff[BUFFSIZE];               // buffer

void main(void)
    {
    int bytes;

    setmode(inhandle, O_BINARY);   // set file mode
    setmode(outhandle, O_BINARY);  //    to binary
                                   // copy file
    while( (bytes = read(inhandle,buff,BUFFSIZE)) > 0)
        write(outhandle,buff,bytes);
    }
```

We use the predefined handle numbers 0 and 1 for standard input and output, so we don't need to open any files.

Because we don't open files, we can't use the open() function to specify which mode—text or binary—we want the file to be in. However, there is another way to do this: the setmode() function. setmode() can take one of two arguments: O_TEXT and O_BINARY. You'll recognize these from our discussion of the open() function; they're defined in the file fcntl.h.

The actual reading and writing of the files is done the same way in this program as in copy2.c.

When to Use What

Because of the multiplicity of functions available for file access in C, it's sometimes hard to know which method to use.

Standard I/O is probably most valuable where it's natural to handle data as characters, strings, or formatted `printf()` style. System I/O is more natural in situations where blocks of data, such as arrays, are to be handled. In many cases, standard I/O is simpler to program, but system I/O usually generates more efficient code, both in terms of speed and the size of the executable file.

It's important not to mix standard and system-level I/O. If a file has been opened with `fopen()`, don't try to use `read()` or `write()` with it, and vice versa. Thus, although system-level I/O usually would be used for reading blocks of data, for compatibility, `fread()` and `fwrite()` might be used if the file is already being used by other standard I/O functions.

Text mode usually is used with files containing text, and binary mode is used for files that may contain numbers other than ASCII codes. This avoids translation problems that would corrupt numerical data. However, as in the bindump.c program, it's occasionally useful to use binary mode on text files.

Summary

The subject of file input/output in Turbo C is a rich and complex one. In this chapter we've only covered the highlights, but you probably have enough of a head start to finish the exploration of files on your own.

We've shown that there are two main families of file-handling functions: standard I/O and system-level I/O. Standard I/O can deal with data in a larger variety of ways, but system I/O is generally the more efficient. In standard I/O we showed examples of the four ways to handle data: as characters, as strings, as formatted data in the style of `printf()`, and as fixed-length records or blocks. We saw that the first three of these ways store data—whether text or numbers—as ASCII characters. The fourth way, record I/O, causes numerical data to be stored in binary format.

We also explored the difference between text and binary modes (not to be confused with text and binary formats). In text modes C newlines are translated into the MS-DOS CR/LF pair, and the character 1A indicates an EOF; in binary mode neither of these is true.

We finished the chapter with a look at system-level I/O. This family of commands requires that the programmer set up a buffer for the data and use only one system for reading and writing; data is always considered to consist of a block of bytes. Buffer manipulation functions can help with operations on the data in the buffer.

Questions

1. The two main systems of I/O available in C are _____ I/O and _____ I/O.

2. A file must be opened so that

   a. The program knows how to access the file
   b. The operating system knows what file to access
   c. The operating system knows if the file should be read from or written to
   d. Communications areas are established for communicating with the file

3. A file opened with `fopen()` will thereafter be referred to by its _____ .

4. The function `fopen()` can specify which of the following?

   a. The file may be opened for appending
   b. The file may be opened in binary mode
   c. The file may be given read-only status
   d. Numbers in the file will be written in binary format

5. In standard I/O the function used to close a file is _____.

6. When reading one character at a time, which of the following functions is appropriate?

   a. `fread()`
   b. `read()`
   c. `fgets()`
   d. `getc()`

7. True or false: closing a file after writing to it is optional.

8. Text and binary mode have to do with

   a. The way numbers are stored on the disk
   b. The way numbers are stored in memory
   c. The way newlines are handled
   d. The way EOFs are handled

9. To examine every single byte of a file, is text or binary mode more suitable?

10. Which of the following are valid parts of standard input/output?

    a. Record I/O
    b. Structure I/O
    c. Character I/O
    d. Array I/O
    e. String I/O
    f. Formatted I/O

11. When writing numbers to disk, the file should usually be opened in _____ mode.

12. To write a small number of mixed string and integer variables to a file, the appropriate function is

    a. `fputs()`
    b. `fgets()`
    c. `fprintf()`
    d. `fwrite()`

13. True or false: because files must be read sequentially, there is no way to read data from the middle of a file without starting at the beginning.

14. Whenever a file is open, a number indicates at what position in the file the next access will be made. This number is called the

    a. Read/write status (type int)
    b. File handle (type int)
    c. File pointer (type pointer to char)
    d. File pointer (type long int)
    e. File handle (type long int)

15. To write a block of data to a file in standard I/O, the appropriate function is

    _____.

16. The offset is the number of _____ from a certain point in a file.

17. The function `fseek()`

    a. Finds a given word or phrase in a file
    b. Finds the correct file
    c. Helps access records in the middle of a file
    d. Moves the file pointer to the desired location

18. A file opened by `open()` will thereafter be referred to by its file _____.

19. Which of the following describes system I/O?

    a. Closer to DOS methods
    b. Slower
    c. More data formats
    d. Smaller executable programs

20. In system-level I/O, the function used to read from a file is _____.

21. When a predefined file handle is used, text or binary mode may be specified using the _____ function.

22. Which of the following functions will search a block of data for a specific character?

    a. `search()`
    b. `strchr()`
    c. `memchr()`
    d. `buffcmp()`

23. True or false: a system-level file can be opened for reading and writing at the same time.

24. An oflag can

    a. Signal when a file is unreadable
    b. Specify if a file should be read or written
    c. Signal when EOF is detected
    d. Specify binary mode

25. If O_CREAT is used, the _____ argument must be added to indicate the read/write protection mode for the file.

26. If data is to be treated in large blocks, the _____ I/O system is usually more appropriate.

27. The advantage of using redirection is that the input to a program may then come from

    a. The keyboard
    b. Pipes
    c. Filters
    d. Other programs

28. Write a DOS command to use indirection to read input data from the file file1.txt to the program encrypt, and then write the output of this program to the file file2.txt.

29. If a system-level program employs redirection, it should

    a. Use standard file handles for keyboard and display
    b. Open files in binary mode
    c. Set binary mode using the `setmode()` function
    d. Use the `redir()` function

30. True or false: there is only one right way to do things in the world of C files.

Exercises

1. Write a program that will read a C source file and verify that the number of right and left braces in the file are equal. Use a command-line argument for the name of the file and the getc() function to read in the file.

2. Sometimes it is desirable to store a group of strings of different lengths in the same file. It is also desirable sometimes to access these strings randomly—that is, to read only the desired one, without starting at the beginning of a file. To do this, the offset of each string can be placed in a table. To compile the table of offsets, one can use the function ftell(), which returns the current offset, taking only the file pointer (fptr) as an argument.

   Write a program that uses string I/O, enabling the user to type a group of phrases and that tells the user the offset of each phrase typed, like this:

   ```
   C>writedex
   Open the pod bay doors, Hal.
   Offset=0

   Klingons attacking!
   Offset=29

   Your fuel is dangerously low.
   Offset=49

   Unknown craft approaching at warp factor 7.
   Offset=79
   ```

3. Write a function that can be added to the agentr.c program so that an agent's record can be deleted from the database. The file is first read in, the deletion is made in memory, and then the revised list of agents is written out to the file.

Memory

- Storage classes
- Dynamic memory allocation
- Linked lists
- Far and huge pointers
- Memory models

The philosophers say that we are no more than the sum of our memories. If this is true of humans, it's even more true of computer programs. A computer's memory stores not only the variable and constant data a program works with, but the program itself.

What entity actually installs these program elements in memory? So far we haven't thought too much about this process. The example programs haven't needed too much data, and the variables were handled in a relatively simple way. In these circumstances it turns out that the compiler, working with MS-DOS, makes all the decisions about memory allocation.

However, there are times when you need to take control of the allocation process yourself, so that your program can allocate memory as it runs. A variety of situations require dynamic memory allocation.

You may not know how much memory you'll need in advance or you may need a lot of memory or you may need to store data in a more complicated arrangement than an array.

Allocating memory while the program is running is called *dynamic memory allocation*. In this chapter we'll explore dynamic allocation and some of its complexities. First, however, we'll lay the groundwork by reviewing the concept of storage classes, which we've touched on in previous chapters. This will make it clearer what the compiler does when *it* allocates memory.

Storage Classes

Every C variable possesses an attribute called its *storage class*. The storage class defines two characteristics of the variable: its lifetime and its visibility (or scope). We've mentioned these characteristics before; now let's take a closer look.

First, why are storage classes necessary? The answer is that, by using variables with the appropriate lifetime and visibility, we can write programs that use memory more efficiently, run faster, and are less prone to programming errors. Correct use of storage classes is especially important in large programs.

Lifetime

The *lifetime* of a variable is the length of time it retains whatever value it has been given. In terms of their lifetimes, variables can be divided into two categories: short-lived automatic variables and longer-lived static and external variables. We'll look at these cases in turn.

Lifetime of Automatic Variables

Automatic variables are the most commonly used in C; the majority of the variables we've used so far have been of this class. In a program's source file, automatic variables are written inside the braces that serve as delimiters for a function. They are created (that is, memory space is allocated to them) when the function containing them is called, and destroyed (their memory space is "deallocated") when the function terminates. In the following function,

```
func()
    {
    int alpha;
    auto int beta;
    register int gamma;
    }
```

all three variables are created when the function func() is called and disappear when it has finished and control returns to the calling function. Such variables are called *automatic* because they're created and destroyed automatically.

Automatic variables are stored on the stack, an area of memory that expands and shrinks to accommodate the variables stored.

> Variables of type auto and register are created when the function containing them is called, and they are destroyed when control returns to the calling program.

The variable alpha is automatic by default, while beta has been made automatic explicitly, using the auto keyword. The effect is exactly the same, but this keyword is sometimes used to avoid confusion.

The gamma variable is a special kind of automatic variable called a register variable. In theory the compiler will attempt to assign it to one of the CPU registers rather than keeping it on the stack. In early compilers this could lead to faster operation if often-accessed variables (such as loop variables) were given the register class. Now, however, most compilers, including Turbo C++, are so good at optimizing code that the use of the register class is seldom necessary.

Lifetime of Static and External Variables

If we want a variable to retain its value after the function that defines it is terminated, we have several choices. First, the variable can be defined to be of type static, as shown in this example:

```
func()
    {
    static int delta;
    }
```

A static variable is known only to the function in which it is defined, but, unlike automatic variables, it doesn't disappear when the function terminates. Instead it keeps its location in memory and therefore its value. In the preceding example, even after the function func() has terminated, delta will retain the value it was given in the function.

If program control returns to the function again, the value of delta will be there for the function to use. For example, a static variable might be used in a function that increments a count each time it's called. The variable holding the count would be made static, so it wouldn't lose its value each time the function returned.

Another way to ensure that a variable retains its value throughout the course of a program is to make it external, as we've mentioned in earlier chapters. This is done by placing the variable outside of any function, as zeta is in this example:

```
int zeta;
main()
    {
    }

func()
    {
    }
```

Note that it's the placement of the variable, not a keyword, that makes it external. Like static variables, external variables exist for the life of the program. The difference between them has to do with their visibility, which we'll examine in the next section.

> Variables of type external, static, and external static exist for the life of a program.

Reasons for Different Lifetimes

Why do some variables have longer lifetimes than others? The advantage of eliminating a variable when the function containing it terminates is that the memory space used for the variable can be freed and made available for other variables. Depending on the program, a considerable saving in memory can result, thus permitting more data to fit in memory. This is a good reason for using automatic variables whenever possible.

Visibility

The visibility (or scope) of a variable refers to which parts of a program will be able to recognize it. There are more distinctions involved in visibility than there are in lifetime: a variable may be visible in a block, a function, a file, a group of files, or an entire program. In this section we'll examine these possibilities in more detail.

Visibility of Automatic and Static Variables

An automatic variable is only recognized within the function in which it is defined; therefore, it's sometimes called a local variable. For instance, in this example:

```
main()
   {
   }
func()
   {
   int eta;
   }
```

the variable eta is recognized only in the function func(), not in main(). In fact, we could have another variable called eta in main(); the two would be completely different.

The same is true of static variables (unless they're external, a possibility we'll examine later). They're visible only in the function where they're defined.

Blocks

The visibility of automatic and static variables can be restricted even further; they can be defined inside a block. A *block* is a section of code set off by braces. Here's an example of a block within a function:

```
main()
   {
   int epsilon;
      {
      int pi;
      }
   }
```

In this example the variable pi is visible only within the inner set of braces, while epsilon is visible throughout the function main(). The braces used to group statements in an if or while construction form blocks; variables defined within such blocks won't be visible outside the block.

It isn't common practice in C to define variables within blocks, but in some complicated functions it can provide increased flexibility. Two variables with the same name could be used in the same function, for example.

Visibility of External Variables

To create a variable that is visible to more than one function, we must make it external. As noted in the discussion of lifetime, this means defining the variable outside of any function. Thus, in the example

```
int theta;
main()
   {
   }
```

```
func()
    {
    }
```

the variable `theta` will be visible to both `main()` and `func()` or to any functions placed after the definition of `theta` in this file.

An external variable (unless it is declared elsewhere) is visible only to those functions that follow it in the file. If we rearranged our example like this:

```
main()
    {
    }

int theta;

func()
    {
    }
```

the variable `theta` will be visible to the function `func()`, but it will be invisible to `main()`.

In Chapter 13, "Advanced Topics," we will discuss how separate files, each containing part of a program, can be compiled separately and linked together to create a final program. As we will see there, it's possible for an external variable to be visible in files other than the one in which it's defined, provided it's declared with the keyword `extern`.

Summary of Storage Classes

Table 12.1 summarizes the lifetime and visibility of the storage classes we've discussed so far. (We'll extend this list slightly when we discuss multifile programs in the next chapter.)

Table 12.1. Storage classes.

Keyword	Where Declared	Lifetime	Visibility
auto (or none)	Within function	Function	Function
register	Within function	Function	Function
static	Within function	Program	Function
(none)	External	Program	Program

The first two storage classes shown in the table are local: those defined within a function. Their visibility is confined to that function, and their lifetime are also the same as that of the function. (The keyword `auto` is normally not necessary, as it's the default.) The third class, using the keyword `static`, is visible only within the function but has a lifetime of the program. These first three variable types also can be defined within a block (a pair of braces). In that case, they will be visible only within the block.

Variables of the last class, which requires no keyword, are defined external to any function. They're visible to all functions from the point of definition onward, and their lifetime is the life of the program.

The Data Segment

Computers that run the MS-DOS operating system and use Intel 80x86 microprocessors divide memory into entities called *segments*. A segment has a maximum size of 65,536 bytes. In small memory-model programs (which we've used so far in this book), all variables, no matter what their storage class, fit into a single segment. Figure 12.1 shows how this data segment is organized.

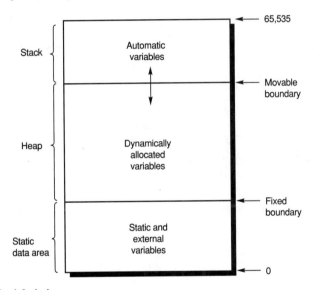

Figure 12.1. The default data segment.

The Stack

The stack, which is used for automatic variables, starts at the top of the data segment and grows downward. When you call a function, its automatic variables (as well as its arguments and return address) are created and placed on the stack and the stack expands. When the function returns, its variables are destroyed and the stack shrinks. The more automatic variables a function has, the more stack space it uses. Also, if many functions call each other at the same time, more stack space is used. Thus you never know in advance how large the stack will be. However, it seldom exceeds a few thousand bytes.

(Recursive functions, which call themselves over and over, are an exception; they may require a larger stack.)

The Static Data Area

External and static variables are stored in the *static data area* at the bottom of the data segment. This area is just large enough to hold all such variables defined in the program. Because external and static variables have a lifetime equal to the program, the size of the static data area is fixed at compile time and doesn't change when the program runs.

The Near Heap

The space between the static area and the stack is called the *near heap* or *local heap.* (There is also a *far heap,* as we'll see later, but you can ignore that possibility for the moment.) The near heap can be allocated by the program as it runs. This is called *dynamic memory allocation.*

The size of the near heap depends on the size of the static data area and the size of the stack. If you have only a few static and automatic variables, the heap can be almost as large as the entire data segment: perhaps 60,000 bytes. The next section describes how to access the near heap.

Dynamic Memory Allocation

Suppose you want to read a large file into memory from the disk. Perhaps it contains information about a certain number of people. When you first design the program, however, you have no way of knowing how many people are involved and thus how large the file may be. If you don't know how large the file is, how do you allocate memory to hold it?

One solution is to define an array that's large enough to hold the largest possible file. Unfortunately there are serious disadvantages to this approach. A really large array may fit in memory in one computer but not in another that has other programs already loaded. Also, if the array won't fit, you won't even be able to load the program, because the array is part of the program, or you may size the array a little smaller, but the disk file is a little larger than you thought, so it won't fit in the array. Another possibility is that the file is much smaller than you thought, so your program wastes a lot of memory that could be used by other programs or by other parts of your program.

A better solution is to let the program allocate memory after it has started to run. It can examine the disk file, see how large it is, allocate just the right amount of memory, and then read the file into the newly allocated area. With this approach, no memory is wasted. If there's enough memory available for that particular disk file, the program can load it. Otherwise it can tell the user that the file is too big to fit in memory.

What does allocation really mean? It means asking the operating system (MS-DOS) for a certain amount of memory. Why do we need to ask? Why not just take it? We could pick some address and use indirection to store data there. The problem, if we do that, is that there might be something else there: another program, part of our program, or part of the operating system. Only MS-DOS keeps track of where everything is. If we ask it for memory, it can tell us whether the amount of memory we want is available, and if so, where it's located. If we don't ask first, we may crash the system.

Allocating memory for disk files is just one example of dynamic memory allocation offering a better solution. In this section we'll examine several situations where dynamic memory allocation is helpful. We'll start off by exploring the C library functions used for dynamic memory allocation.

Allocation Using *malloc()*

In practice, dynamic memory allocation means calling a function that returns a pointer to the memory you can use. An argument to the function specifies how much memory you want, and the function interacts with the operating system to find a contiguous block of memory of that size. This memory is located in the near heap. If the memory allocation function is successful, you can use the pointer it returns to reference any part of the memory block.

In C, the workhorse memory allocation function is `malloc()`. Its prototype can be found in either stdlib.h or alloc.h, so you must include one of these files in your listing. Here's a simple example that demonstrates this function:

```
// ezmem.c
// allocates memory using malloc()
#include <alloc.h>              // for malloc()

void main(void)
    {
    unsigned mem_ints = 20000;    // number of ints to store
    unsigned mem_bytes;           // bytes of memory needed

    int *ptr;                     // pointer to start of memory
    unsigned j;                   // loop counter

    mem_bytes = mem_ints * sizeof(int);  // find bytes needed

    ptr = malloc(mem_bytes);      // get memory

    for(j=0; j<mem_ints; j++)     // fill memory with data
        ptr[j] = j;

    free(ptr);                    // free memory
    }  // end main()
```

How Much Memory?

Here we want to allocate enough memory for 20,000 integers, and we need to communicate this information to malloc(). However, malloc() needs to be told how many *bytes* of memory are necessary, not how many data items. This is a common source of confusion. Thus if we want to store 20,000 integers, and each integer takes 2 bytes, we must ask for 40,000 bytes of memory. (We assume we're running on a platform, such as MS-DOS, where an integer does take two bytes. On other platforms this may not always be the case.) Thus the argument we must give malloc() is 40,000. The first executable statement in the program uses the sizeof operator to calculate the number of bytes necessary to store 20,000 integers.

The type of the argument to malloc() is specified to be size_t, which is defined as unsigned (really unsigned int). A variable of this size enables you to specify, in theory, any amount of memory up to 65,535 bytes. In practice you can't get that much, because the static data area at the bottom of your data segment, and the stack at the top, require some space. We'll see in a moment how your program can tell how much memory is available.

Data Pointer

The malloc() function returns a pointer to a block of memory of the size specified. This pointer must be of the same data type as the data you want to access. In this particular example, we want to store data of type int, so the pointer is type pointer-to-int, or int*.

> The data type of the pointer returned from malloc() must agree with the type of the data to be stored.

The malloc() function returns type void*, a pointer to anything. Many programmers use an explicit cast to convert this type to the actual type of the pointer.

```
ptr = (int *)malloc(mem_bytes);
```

However, this isn't necessary, as the compiler will perform the cast for you.

Accessing the Memory

We can use either pointer notation or array notation to access the memory obtained with malloc(). The program example shows the array approach, ptr[j], but the pointer approach, *(ptr+j), works just as well. Either way you're treating the memory like an array of the requested size. Each value of j accesses a different integer.

This example fills up the memory block with integers in ascending order:

```
for(j=0; j<mem_ints; j++)
    ptr[j] = j;
```

This isn't too useful, but it does demonstrate how the memory is accessed.

Freeing the Memory

Once you've finished using the memory you obtained dynamically, it's a good idea to tell the system you don't need it any more. This makes it available to other functions in your program or to other programs in memory. The function that frees the memory is called, appropriately, free(). It takes as an argument the pointer obtained from malloc().

Measuring Memory

You can use a function called coreleft() to find how much memory is available on the heap. (The name harkens back to the days when computer memories consisted of thousands of tiny magnetic doughnuts called *cores*.) This function takes no arguments and returns a value of type unsigned. Our next example demonstrates its use.

```
// coreleft.c
// displays amount of memory available
#include <stdio.h>              // for printf()
#include <alloc.h>              // for malloc(), coreleft()

void main(void)
    {
    unsigned mem_doubles = 7000;   // number of doubles to store
    unsigned mem_bytes;            // bytes needed per segment
    double *ptr;                   // pointer to memory

    printf("\nBefore allocation, %u bytes available\n",
                                             coreleft() );
    mem_bytes = mem_doubles * sizeof(double);  // calculate bytes
    printf("Allocating %u bytes\n", mem_bytes);
    ptr = malloc(mem_bytes);       // get memory

    printf("After allocation, %u bytes available\n", coreleft() );
    free(ptr);                     // free memory
    }  // end main()
```

In this program we assume we're going to be storing data of type double (rather than int, as in the last program). The pointer ptr is defined accordingly.

Here's some typical output from the program, assuming there is enough space left on the heap:

```
Before allocation, 62560 bytes available
Allocating 56000 bytes
After allocation, 6560 bytes available
```

In this example 62,560 bytes are available when we begin. Each variable of type double takes 8 bytes, so if we ask for space for 7000 variables we'll need 56,000 bytes. This is probably available in most computer systems.

If we had requested too much memory, the program would not have worked, but we would have had no way to know that. This isn't too satisfactory a situation, so let's see how to correct it.

Handling Errors

It's quite possible that you won't be able to obtain the memory you ask for. The static data area and the stack may be too large, or other functions may have already allocated too much of the near heap. If malloc() can't find the memory requested, it returns NULL (defined as 0). Our next example shows how to make use of this fact.

```c
// memerr.c
// allocates memory using malloc(), checks for error return
#include <stdio.h>              // for printf()
#include <stdlib.h>            // for malloc() and exit()

int main(void)
    {
    unsigned mem_ints;          // number of ints to store
    unsigned mem_bytes;         // bytes of memory needed

    int *ptr;                   // pointer to start of memory
    unsigned j;                 // loop counter

    printf("\nEnter number of integers to store: ");
    scanf("%u", &mem_ints);
    mem_bytes = mem_ints * sizeof(int);   // calculate bytes

    ptr = malloc(mem_bytes);    // get memory
    if(ptr==NULL)               // error return from malloc()
        {
        printf("Can't allocate memory");
        exit(1);
        }
    for(j=0; j<mem_ints; j++)    // fill memory with data
        ptr[j] = j;
    for(j=0; j<mem_ints; j++)    // check the data
        if( ptr[j] != j )
            {
            printf("Memory error: j=%u, ptr[j]=%u", j, ptr[j] );
            exit(1);
            }
    free(ptr);                   // free memory
    printf("Memory test successful");
    return(0);
    } // end main()
```

In this example we let the user specify how many integers need to be stored in memory. Here's a typical interaction with the program:

```
Enter number of integers to store: 20000
Memory test successful
```

If you use too high a number, you trigger the error return from `malloc()`.

```
Enter number of integers to store: 32000
Can't allocate memory
```

Notice that you shouldn't even attempt to enter a number greater than 32,767, because twice this (plus 1) is 65,535, the largest number you can store in type `unsigned`, which is the data type of `mem_bytes`.

We have also included a section of code that verifies that the memory stored is correct. If you have successfully allocated the memory, this check should always work.

Save the Pointer

In some situations you may want to obtain a memory address from `malloc()` in a function, and then retain this pointer value between calls to the function. When this is the case, don't forget to make the pointer static or external. If the pointer is an automatic variable then when the function returns, the address value will be lost, and you'll lose your only connection to the data stored in that block of memory. The data will still be there, but you won't know where it is. (You also won't be able to free the memory.)

Allocation Using *realloc()*

What happens if you allocated some memory, and you later realize that you need more? Or not as much? You can change the amount of memory you've allocated with a function called `realloc()`. This function keeps the contents of a memory block intact while changing its size. It takes two arguments: the pointer to the memory previously obtained, and the new size desired.

In our next example we invite the user to enter some integers. We start off by allocating enough room for 5 integers (10 bytes). If the user enters a sixth integer, the program allocates space for another 5 integers. It informs the user of each allocation.

```
// realloc.c
// reallocates memory using realloc()
#include <stdio.h>              // for printf()
#include <stdlib.h>            // for realloc() and exit()
#define CHUNK 10               // bytes of additional memory

void main(void)
   {
   int *ptr = NULL;            // pointer to memory
   int n = 0;                  // number of data items stored
```

```
        int total_bytes = 0;            // total bytes allocated
        int j;                          // loop variable

        printf("\n");
        do
            {
            if(n*sizeof(int) >= total_bytes)    // if no more memory,
                {
                ptr = realloc(ptr, CHUNK);      // get another chunk
                if(ptr==NULL)
                    { printf("\nCan't reallocate memory"); exit(1); }
                total_bytes += CHUNK;
                printf("Total bytes allocated = %d\n", total_bytes );
                }
            printf("Enter a number: ");         // get data from user
            scanf( "%d", &ptr[n] );             // store in memory
            }
        while(ptr[n++] != 0);                   // user enters 0

        for(j=0; j<n-1; j++)                    // display the data
            printf("%7d ", ptr[j]);
        free(ptr);                              // free memory
        }
```

Here's some sample interaction with the program:

```
Total bytes allocated = 10
32
89
47
84
61
Total bytes allocated = 20
93
38
78
35
28
Total bytes allocated = 30
42
75
0
32    89    47    84    61    93    38    78    35    28
42    75
```

The user enters 0 to terminate the input. The program then displays the numbers already entered to verify that they've been successfully stored.

If realloc() is called with a pointer value of NULL as the first argument, it operates the same as malloc(). In this example, the first time realloc() is called, ptr is NULL, so it operates like malloc() and obtains the first chunk of 10 bytes. On subsequent calls, realloc() expands this block by 10 bytes without destroying the data in the block.

Dynamic Allocation for Secret Agents

Let's see how dynamic memory allocation might be used in a more realistic programming situation. We'll modify the agentr.c program from Chapter 11, "Files," so that it uses dynamic memory allocation instead of a fixed-size array. This is a longish program, but if you followed the earlier agentr.c example you won't have much trouble with it.

```c
// agalloc.c
// maintains list of agents in file, allocates memory
#include <stdio.h>              // for standard I/O
#include <stdlib.h>             // for exit()
#include <conio.h>              // for getche()
#define TRUE 1
void listall(void);            // prototypes
void newname(void);
void rfile(void);
void wfile(void);

struct personnel               // declare data structure
    {
    char name [40];            // name
    int agnumb;                // code number
    float height;              // height in inches
    };
struct personnel *agptr = NULL;  // pointer to memory for agents
int n = 0;                       // number of agents listed

void main(void)
    {
    while(TRUE)                 // cycle until user chooses 'q'
        {
        printf("\n'e' enter new agent\n'l' list all agents");
        printf("\n'w' write file\n'r' read file\n'q' exit: ");
        switch ( getche() )
            {
            case 'e': newname(); break;
            case 'l': listall(); break;
            case 'w': wfile();   break;
            case 'r': rfile();   break;
            case 'q': exit(0);   break;
            default:                // user mistake
                puts("\nEnter only selections listed");
            }  // end switch
        }  // end while
    }  // end main()

// newname()
// puts a new agent in the database
void newname(void)
    {
    char numstr[40];                // number input string
                                    // get more memory for new agent
```

```
        agptr = realloc( agptr, (n+1)*sizeof(struct personel) );
        if(agptr==NULL)
            { printf("\Can't reallocate memory"); return; }
        printf("\nRecord %d.\nEnter name: ", n+1); // get name
        gets(agptr[n].name);
        printf("Enter agent number (3 digits): "); // get number
        gets(numstr);
        agptr[n].agnumb = atoi(numstr);
        printf("Enter height in inches: ");          // get height
        gets(numstr);
        agptr[n++].height = atof(numstr);
        }

// listall()
// lists all agents and data
void listall(void)
    {
    int j;

    if(n < 1)                              // check for empty list
        printf("\nEmpty list.\n");
    for(j=0; j < n; j++)                   // print list
        {
        printf("\nRecord number %d\n", j+1);
        printf("   Name: %s\n", agptr[j].name);
        printf("   Agent number: %03d\n", agptr[j].agnumb);
        printf("   Height: %4.2f\n", agptr[j].height);
        }
    }

// wfile()
// writes agent structures from memory buffer to file
void wfile(void)
    {
    FILE *fptr;

    if(n < 1)
        { printf("\nCan't write empty list.\n"); return; }
    if( (fptr=fopen("agents.rec","wb"))==NULL )
        { printf("\nCan't open file agents.rec\n"); return; }
                          // write all the records at once
    if( fwrite(agptr, sizeof(struct personnel), n, fptr) != n )
        { printf("\nCan't write file\n"); fclose(fptr); return; }
    fclose(fptr);
    printf("\nFile of %d records written.\n", n);
    }

// rfile()
// reads records from file into memory buffer
void rfile(void)
    {
    FILE *fptr;
```

```
    long int file_size;   // size of file in bytes

    if( (fptr=fopen("agents.rec","rb"))==NULL )
       { printf("\nCan't open file agents.rec\n"); return; }
    fseek(fptr, 0, SEEK_END);     // put file ptr at end of file
    file_size = ftell(fptr);      // file size is file pointer
    fseek(fptr, 0, SEEK_SET);     // return file ptr to start
                          // allocate memory for entire file
    if( (agptr=malloc((size_t)file_size)) == NULL )
       { printf("\nAllocation error"); fclose(fptr); return; }
                          // calculate n from file size
    n = (int)file_size / sizeof(struct personnel);
                          // read entire file
    if( fread(agptr, sizeof(struct personnel), n, fptr) != n )
       { printf("\nCan't read file"); fclose(fptr); return; }

    fclose(fptr);
    printf("\nFile read. Total agents is now %d.\n", n);
    }
```

Instead of an array of type struct personnel, we declare a pointer to this type. Then in the newname() function we use realloc() to obtain memory for one (or for one additional) structure. The data entered by the user is placed in this structure.

The rfile() function is executed when the user presses r to read a file from disk into memory. This function first figures out how large the file is by using fseek() to move the pointer to the end of the file and ftell() to find the pointer location. (When you do this don't forget to restore the file pointer to the beginning of the file with fseek() before attempting to read it.) The program then uses malloc() to obtain memory for a file of exactly this size and reads the entire file with one call to fread().

The listall() and wfile() functions, which don't involve memory allocation, operate just the same as their counterparts in agentr.c.

From the user's perspective the agalloc.c program operates identically to the agentr.c program. Behind the scenes, however, it's handling memory much more efficiently, allocating only as much memory as it needs.

Obtaining Memory for Graphics Images

Here's another situation where dynamic memory allocation is almost essential. In the image.c program in Chapter 10, "Turbo C Graphics," we fudged a bit and defined an array that we guessed would be large enough to hold the image of the ball. But guessing is a bad approach. It's better to let the program find out exactly how big the image is and allocate just that amount of memory. The following example shows how it's done. (Don't forget to turn on the graphics library by invoking the Options/Linker/Libraries menu option and checking the Graphics Library box. Also, change "c:\\tc\\bgi" to "c:\\borlandc\\bgi" in the call to initgraph() if you're using Borland C++)

```
// imagaloc.c
// bouncing ball created from bit image
// bit image stored in dynamically allocated memory
#include <graphics.h>              // for graphics functions
#include <conio.h>                 // for kbhit()
#include <stdlib.h>                // for malloc() and exit()
#include <stdio.h>                 // for printf()
#define LEFT      0                // boundary of rectangle
#define TOP       0
#define RIGHT    400
#define BOTTOM   349
#define RADIUS   20                // radius of ball

void main(void)
   {
   int driver, mode;              // for initgraph()
   int x, y, dx, dy, oldx, oldy;  // ball coordinates
   unsigned char *ptrball;        // pointer to ball image
   unsigned size;                 // size of image of ball

   driver = DETECT;               // auto detect
                                  // set graphics mode
   initgraph(&driver, &mode, "c:\\tc\\bgi");
                                  // draw boundary
   rectangle(LEFT, TOP, RIGHT, BOTTOM);

   x = LEFT + RADIUS + 10;        // create image of ball
   y = TOP  + RADIUS + 10;
   setcolor(LIGHTGREEN);
   setfillstyle(SOLID_FILL, LIGHTGREEN);
   circle(x, y, RADIUS);
   floodfill(x, y, LIGHTGREEN);
                                  // find size of ball image
   size = imagesize(x-RADIUS, y-RADIUS, x+RADIUS, y+RADIUS);
   ptrball = malloc(size);        // allocate memory
   if(ptrball==NULL)
      { printf("\nCan't get memory"); closegraph(); exit(1); }
                                  // place image in memory
   getimage(x-RADIUS, y-RADIUS, x+RADIUS, y+RADIUS, ptrball);
   dx = 2;                        // set speed of ball
   dy = 2;
   while ( !kbhit() )             // exit on keypress
      {                          // memory image to screen
      putimage(x-RADIUS, y-RADIUS, ptrball, COPY_PUT);
      oldx = x; oldy = y;         // remember where it was
      x += dx;   y += dy;         // move its coordinates
                                  // reflect it at edges
      if( x<=LEFT+RADIUS+2 || x>=RIGHT-RADIUS-2 )
         dx = -dx;
      if( y<=TOP+RADIUS+2 || y>=BOTTOM-RADIUS-2 )
         dy = -dy;
```

```
                                    // erase old image
      putimage(oldx-RADIUS, oldy-RADIUS, ptrball, XOR_PUT);
      }
   free(ptrball);                    // free memory
   closegraph();
   }
```

Instead of an array, we define a pointer to type `unsigned char`: `ptrball`. (Remember that this type can refer to numerical bytes, not just characters.) Then we use the `imagesize()` function, which returns the number of bytes necessary to store an image, where the dimensions of the image are given as arguments to the function.

We use the size returned from `imagesize()` as the argument to `malloc()` to obtain the correct amount of memory. The return value from `malloc()` is assigned to `ptrball`, which is then used to store and read back the image, as in the previous version of the program.

Linked Lists

So far we've used dynamic memory allocation to store data in arrays (or at least in blocks of memory obtained with `malloc()` that we treat as arrays). However, there are other ways to store data. Perhaps the most common of these alternatives is the *linked list* (sometimes simply called a *list*).

What's wrong with an array as a storage arrangement? Imagine that you have a large array of structures stored in memory. Let's assume that each such structure stores the data for one employee in a company, such as name, social security number, and so on. Now suppose you want to delete one of the structures (perhaps the employee has quit). Say there are 2,000 such structures, and you want to delete number 50. Since arrays don't operate well with empty elements, you must now eliminate the deleted data by copying number 51 into the space formerly occupied by 50, 52 into 51, 53 into 52, and so on up to 2,000. All this copying is time-consuming and slows down the operation of the program.

The same problem arises for insertions if the elements of the array are stored in order (say alphabetically by the last names of the employees). When this is the case you must move a great many elements every time you insert a new structure, since all the elements above the one to be inserted must be moved up. Thus the array has some serious speed limitations for both insertion and deletion.

The Linked List to the Rescue

The linked list solves these problems by permitting insertion and deletion without moving any of the exiting structures. It consists of structures related to one another by pointers rather than by being members of an array. To demonstrate this construction, we'll rewrite the agent.c and agentptr.c programs from Chapter 9, "Structures," to store data as a linked list.

In a linked list, each link, or member of the list, is a structure (just as each element in the array in agent.c was a structure). However—this is the secret—each structure on the list contains a pointer to the next structure. That's what establishes the connection between the links. The pointer in the last structure on the list doesn't point to anything, so we give it the value NULL. Figure 12.2 shows how this looks.

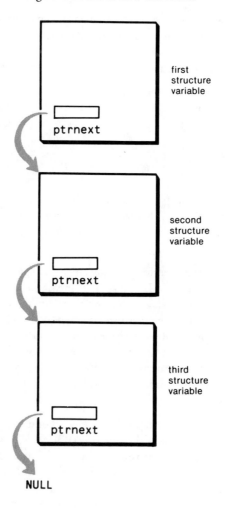

Figure 12.2. Linked list.

Here's the listing for the program. In many ways it's similar to the earlier agent.c program that used an array of structures, but the differences are significant and will require some explanation.

```
// agelink.c
// maintains list of agents
// uses linked list
#include <stdio.h>              // for printf()
#include <conio.h>             // for getche()
#include <stdlib.h>           // for atof()
#define TRUE 1
void newname(void);           // prototypes
void listall(void);

struct prs                    // declare data structure
    {
    char name [30];           // agent's name
    int agnumb;               // agent's number
    float height;             // height in inches
    struct prs *ptrnext;      // ptr to next structure
    };

struct prs *ptrfirst = NULL;  // pointer to first link

void main(void)
    {
    char ch;

    while(TRUE)
       {
       printf("\nType 'e' to enter new agent"); // print
       printf("\n  'l' to list all agents,");   // options
       printf("\n  'q' to quit: ");
       ch = getche();                    // get choice
       switch(ch)
          {
          case 'e':                      // enter new name
             newname(); break;
          case 'l':                      // list entire file
             listall(); break;
          case 'q':                      // exit program
             exit(0);
          default:                       // user mistake
             puts("\nEnter only selections listed");
          } // end switch
       } // end while
    } // end main

// newname()
// puts a new agent in the database
void newname(void)
    {
    struct prs *ptrthis;                 // utility pointer
    char numstr[81];                     // for numbers
```

```
    ptrthis =  malloc( sizeof(struct prs) );   // get memory space
    if(ptrthis==NULL)
       {printf("Allocation error"); return; }
    ptrthis->ptrnext = ptrfirst;         // connects to old first
    ptrfirst = ptrthis;                  // this becomes new first

    printf("\nEnter name: ");            // get name
    gets(ptrthis->name);
    printf("Enter number: ");            // get number
    gets(numstr);
    ptrthis->agnumb = atoi(numstr);
    printf("Enter height: ");            // get height
    gets(numstr);
    ptrthis->height = atof(numstr);
    }

// listall()
// lists all agents and data
void listall(void)
    {
    struct prs *ptrthis;                 // utility list pointer

    if (ptrfirst == NULL )               // if empty list
       { printf("\nEmpty list.\n"); return; }  //    return
    ptrthis = ptrfirst;                  // start at first item
    do
       {                                 // print contents
       printf("\nName: %s\n", ptrthis->name );
       printf("Number: %03d\n", ptrthis->agnumb );
       printf("Height: %4.2f\n", ptrthis->height );
       ptrthis = ptrthis->ptrnext;       // move to next item
       }
    while(ptrthis != NULL);              // quit on null ptr
    }
```

For the user, the program works in much the same way as the agent.c program, with one notable exception. Here's the sample interaction with the program:

```
Type 'e' to enter new agent
   'l' to list all agents
   'q' to quit: e
Enter name: George Smiley
Enter number: 999
Enter height: 64.3

Type 'e' to enter new agent
   'l' to list all agents
   'q' to quit: e
Enter name: James Bond
Enter number: 007
Enter height: 74.25
```

```
Type 'e' to enter new agent
   'l' to list all agents
   'q' to quit: e
Enter name: Mata Hari
Enter number: 121
Enter height: 58.75

Type 'e' to enter new agent
   'l' to list all agents
   'q' to quit: l
Name: Mata Hari
Number: 121
Height: 58.75

Name: James Bond
Number: 007
Height: 74.25

Name: George Smiley
Number: 999
Height: 64.30

Type 'e' to enter new agent
   'l' to list all agents
   'q' to quit: q
```

Notice that the agent's information is displayed in the opposite order it is entered. The last agent entered is the first agent on the list. This arrangement makes the programming easier (although it may be a little disconcerting for the user).

The challenging part of understanding this program is following what happens to the pointers. As we've noted, the basic idea is that each structure variable contains a pointer to the next structure on the list. We name these pointer members ptrnext, since they point to the next structure. Figure 12.3 shows how this looks, assuming that the first structure is assigned the address 3000.

In addition to the ptrnext variable contained in each structure, two other pointers are necessary to the operation of the list. One of these, ptrfirst, is a global variable used to hold the address of the first structure in the list. This is a key address, since it's how the program finds the list. At the beginning of the program when the pointer is defined, it is set to NULL by the statement

```
struct prs *ptrfirst = NULL;
```

The NULL value implies that the list is empty. As soon as the first agent is added to the list, this pointer will point to the new structure. Each time an agent is added, this value will change, since each new agent is added at the beginning of the list.

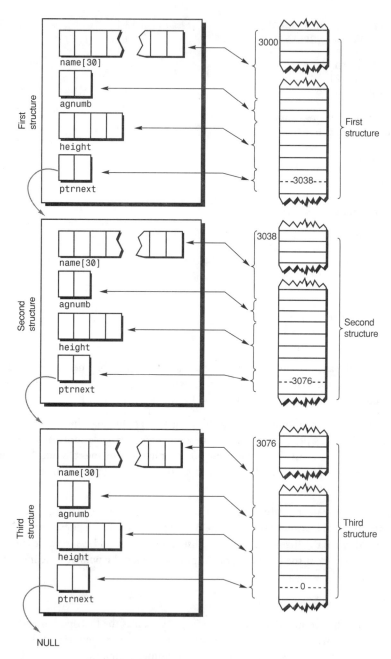

Figure 12.3. Structures in the agelink.c program.

Another pointer, `ptrthis`, is a utility pointer, defined locally in each function that needs it. It's used to point to each structure in turn or to hold the address of a newly-allocated memory block.

Adding an Agent to the List

If the user wants to add an agent to the database, the program calls the function `newname()`. This function first uses `malloc()` to get a pointer to a memory space big enough for the new structure (38 bytes as it turns out). This address is assigned to a pointer called `ptrthis`. The trick now is to link the new structure pointed to by `ptr this` with the rest of the list.

As the user enters data for a new agent, the structure containing the new data is placed at the beginning of the list. (This may seem backward, but it simplifies the programming, since it's easier to find the beginning of the list than the end.) To link this new structure into the list we need to do two things:

Change `ptrfirst` so that it points to the new structure.

Set the `ptrnext` member of the new structure so that it points to the structure previously first on the list.

Figure 12.4 shows how this looks.

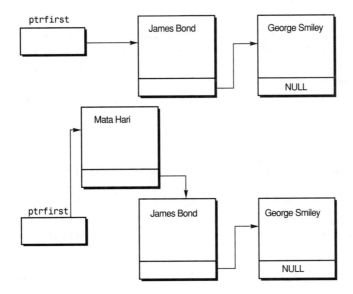

Figure 12.4. Adding an item to a list.

In the program we do the second of these actions first, since we want to assign the old value of `ptrfirst` before changing it.

```
ptrthis->ptrnext = ptrfirst;
```

Then `ptrfirst` is set to point to the new structure.

```
ptrfirst = ptrthis;
```

Once the links are set up, the user can fill in the data for the various members of the new structure, `ptrthis->name`, `ptrthis->agnumb`, and so on, as was done in the agentptr.c example.

Displaying the Data on the List

The list of agents is displayed with the function `listall()`. This function first makes sure the list isn't empty by checking whether `ptrfirst` is NULL. If not, it sets the temporary pointer `ptrthis` to `ptrfirst` (the address of the first link in the list) and enters a `do while` loop. In the loop it displays the elements of the structure pointed to by `ptrthis`. Then it moves `ptrthis` to the next link, the address of which is stored in `ptrthis->ptrnext`. To see whether to exit from the loop, it checks this new value of `ptrthis` and (because the `ptrnext` of the last structure has nothing to point to) terminates when it's NULL.

Freeing Memory

We have neglected something important in the agelink.c program: we haven't freed the memory allocated for the links. Failing to free memory when you're done with it is rather bad programming practice, but in this case it involves following the chain from link to link and freeing each one separately, a complexity we wished to avoid. In agelink.c failing to free memory doesn't cause much of a problem, because the amount of memory is small and is, in any case, freed when the program terminates.

Deleting an Item From a Linked List

We've said that deleting items quickly is one reason for the use of linked lists, so let's see how to delete an item. Our next example is derived from agelink.c but adds another function, `delink()`, which is executed when the user presses d. This function prompts the user for the name of the agent to be deleted. The program then follows the chain of pointers to the item with this name (the value of the `name` member) and deletes it.

To delete the selected structure, we need only reroute the pointer that points to it. Say the structure to be deleted is B. Then the `ptrnext` pointer in the preceding structure, A, is changed to point to C rather than B. When we've done this, link B is no longer part of the list, and we can free its memory with `free()`. Figure 12.5 shows how this looks.

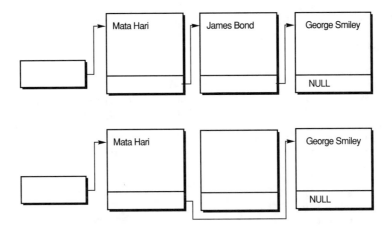

Figure 12.5. Deleting an item from a list.

The program is similar to aglink.c, except that the delink() function has been added and the switch statement in main() has been expanded to accommodate it.

We've also added a function, memexit(), which is called when the user presses q to terminate the program. This function follows the chain from link to link, using free() to free the memory for each link in turn. When it's done, it executes exit(). This solves the problem, just mentioned, of failing to delete allocated memory.

```
// delink.c
// maintains list of agents, allows deletion of link
// uses linked list
#include <stdio.h>              // for printf()
#include <conio.h>             // for getche()
#include <stdlib.h>            // for atof()
#include <string.h>           // for strcmp()
#define TRUE 1
void newname(void);           // prototypes
void listall(void);
void delink(void);
void memexit(void);


struct prs                    // declare data structure
   {
   char name[30];             // agent's name
   int agnumb;                // agent's number
   float height;              // height in inches
   struct prs *ptrnext;       // ptr to next structure
   };

struct prs *ptrfirst = NULL;  // pointer to first link
```

```
void main(void)
    {
    char ch;

    while(TRUE)
        {
        printf("\nType 'e' to enter new agent"); // print
        printf("\n  'l' to list all agents,");   // options
        printf("\n  'd' to delete an agent,");
        printf("\n  'q' to quit: ");
        ch = getche();                     // get choice
        switch(ch)
            {
            case 'e':                      // enter new name
                newname(); break;
            case 'l':                      // list entire file
                listall(); break;
            case 'd':                      // delete link
                delink(); break;
            case 'q':                      // exit program
                memexit(); break;
            default:                       // user mistake
                puts("\nEnter only selections listed");
            }  // end switch
        }  // end while
    }  // end main

// newname()
// puts a new agent in the database
void newname(void)
    {
    struct prs *ptrthis;               // utility pointer
    char numstr[81];                   // for numbers
                                       // get memory space
    ptrthis =  malloc( sizeof(struct prs) );
    if(ptrthis==NULL)
        {printf("Allocation error"); return; }
    ptrthis->ptrnext = ptrfirst;       // connects to old first
    ptrfirst = ptrthis;                // this becomes new first

    printf("\nEnter name: ");          // get name
    gets(ptrthis->name);
    printf("Enter number: ");          // get number
    gets(numstr);
    ptrthis->agnumb = atoi(numstr);
    printf("Enter height: ");          // get height
    gets(numstr);
    ptrthis->height = atof(numstr);
    }
```

```
// listall()
// lists all agents and data
void listall(void)
    {
    struct prs *ptrthis;                // utility pointer

    if (ptrfirst == NULL )              // if empty list
        { printf("\nEmpty list.\n"); return; }  //   return
    ptrthis = ptrfirst;                 // start at first item
    do
        {                               // print contents
        printf("\nName: %s\n", ptrthis->name );
        printf("Number: %03d\n", ptrthis->agnumb );
        printf("Height: %4.2lf\n", ptrthis->height );
        ptrthis = ptrthis->ptrnext;     // move to next item
        }
    while(ptrthis != NULL);             // quit on null ptr
    }

// delink()
// delete entry in agent file
void delink(void)
    {
    struct prs *ptrthis;                // utility pointer
    struct prs *ptrlast;                // ptr to previous link
    char delname[81];                   // for name to delete

    if (ptrfirst == NULL)               // if empty list
        { printf("\nEmpty list.\n"); return; }  //   return
    printf("\nEnter name to be deleted: ");
    gets(delname);
    ptrthis = ptrfirst;                 // start at first item
    do
        {                               // if names match
        if( strcmp(ptrthis->name, delname)==0 )
            {
            if(ptrthis==ptrfirst)              // if first item
                ptrfirst = ptrthis->ptrnext;  // reset ptrfirst
            else                              // otherwise, reset
                ptrlast->ptrnext = ptrthis->ptrnext;  // last ptr
                // (ignore warning about ptrlast definition)
            free(ptrthis);                    // free link's memory
            return;                           // we're done
            }
        ptrlast = ptrthis;              // remember last ptr
        ptrthis = ptrthis->ptrnext;     // move to next item
        }
    while(ptrthis != NULL);            // NULL is end of list
    printf("No such name on list\n");
    }
```

```
// memexit()
// free all memory and exit
void memexit(void)
   {
   struct prs *ptrthis, *ptrfree;      // utility pointers

   if (ptrfirst == NULL )              // if empty list
      exit(0);                         //    exit program
   ptrthis = ptrfirst;                 // start at first item
   do
      {
      ptrfree = ptrthis;               // remember pointer
      ptrthis = ptrthis->ptrnext;      // get ptr to next item
      free(ptrfree);                   // free this item
      }
   while(ptrthis != NULL);             // quit on null ptr
   exit(0);                            // exit program
   }
```

The delink() function starts at the first item on the list and checks the name with strcmp() in a do while loop. If there's no match, it remembers the address of the link it just looked at by setting ptrlast to ptrthis. It then sets ptrthis to the next item, ptrthis->ptrnext, and loops again.

If there's a match, it checks whether the item is the first one in the list. If it is, it sets ptrfirst to the next item, stored in ptrthis->ptrnext. If it isn't the first item, it sets the pointer in the previous item, ptrlast->ptrnext, to the address of the next item, ptrthis->ptrnext. After a match, the memory used by the item is freed and the function returns.

Linked List Refinements

Many refinements can be made to the approach to linked lists we've shown here. Perhaps most obviously, you might want to store each new item at the end of the list rather than the beginning. To do this you would need to follow the chain of pointers to the end (as the listall() function does) and insert the new item following the last one.

As you can see from the delink() function in delink.c, it's easy to search through linked lists for a particular name or other data item. The search program follows the chain of pointers and checks each structure to see whether it contains the desired item. You can then access the data for that item or insert or delete an item at that point.

Sometimes a pointer to the last item, as well as to the first, is stored. Having this pointer available avoids having to read through the entire list to add a new item to the end; the program can go directly to the last item. Lists also can be linked backward as well as forward, with ptrnext and ptrlast members of each structure. This is called a doubly-linked list.

The linked list is built on the idea of a structure that contains a pointer to other similar structures. Pointers to structures can be used for many configurations other than the linked list. For example, there is the tree structure, where each element points to two or more elements, each of which points to other elements, and so on. We'll leave these topics to other books.

> Many complex data organizations can be built on the idea of a structure containing a pointer to other structures.

Far and Huge Pointers

Earlier in this chapter we said that all the data used by a program—static, automatic, and the near heap—is contained in a single segment of 65,536 bytes. This may seem like a lot of bytes, but you can use it up in no time. Imagine that you're storing an array of structures, each of which represents an employee in a company. With a first and last name, address, job description, and other data, such a structure could easily exceed 300 bytes. You can fit only 200 or so such structures in a segment. If your company has more than 200 employees, you're out of luck.

Fortunately, you can use more than one segment to store data. However, doing this requires learning some new techniques. The first approach we'll look at is the use of far pointers and the closely related huge pointers. Another approach, which we'll examine in the last section of this chapter, involves memory models.

Architecture of Intel Microprocessors

The need for far pointers arises from the architecture of the Intel 8086 microprocessor chip used in the earliest MS-DOS computers. MS-DOS has been written to accommodate the limitations of this chip ever since, even though later versions of the chip (the 80286, 80386, 80486, Pentium, and so on) are more sophisticated.

Registers

As we've seen, each byte in a computer's memory has a unique number called its *address*. To access a memory location, the microprocessor must put a number representing its address into something called an *address register*. A register is a little like a variable in that it can hold different numerical values. However, it isn't stored in memory; it's a separate hardware device. Unfortunately, because of technical limitations back in the days of the 8086, registers were only 16 bits wide. With 16 bits you can store numbers from 0 to 65,535. Thus with one register you can access only 65,536 bytes (64K) of memory.

So far in this book, the example programs have always used this single-register approach to accessing memory. The total amount of data in a program was therefore limited to one 64K segment: the default data segment described earlier. Let's review how such addresses look in your program.

Near Pointers

When you define a pointer, as in the statement

```
int *ptr;    // a near pointer to int
```

the pointer variable occupies two bytes, or 16 bits, of memory. To access a memory location using a pointer, the compiler arranges for the 16-bit address value stored in the pointer variable to be transferred into an address register. That's what happens when your program executes a statement like

```
avalue = *ptr;   // get a value from memory
```

The address value in ptr is placed in the 16-bit address register, and the value at this memory address is retrieved from memory and assigned to avalue. Thus this pointer can address any byte within a 64K segment. Such pointers are called *near pointers*. They are the default in the small memory model, which is the default in Turbo C++ and what we've been using all along.

More Than One Segment

Even though registers are limited to 16 bits, the microprocessor is capable of accessing memory outside of a program's default data segment. However, it must work a little harder. To access additional segments, the microprocessor must use two registers rather than one. Roughly speaking, the first register is used to specify the address of a particular segment, while the second specifies the address of the data within the segment; this is called the *offset.*

To load these two address registers—segment and offset—you need an address value 32 bits wide rather than 16. You can tell the compiler to create a 32-bit pointer variable to hold such an address by using the keyword far in a pointer definition:

```
int far *farptr1;      // a far pointer to int
```

If you then reference a memory address using this pointer, as in

```
*farptr1 = 300;
```

the compiler will use a 32-bit address and be able to access data in many different segments.

> Near pointers hold 16-bit values that can address only a single segment. Far pointers hold 32-bit values that can address multiple segments.

The Usual Complications

You might think that, with two address registers providing a total of 32 bits of address space, it would be possible to address 65,536 times 65,536, or 4,294,967,296 bytes. This is 4 gigabytes, or 4,096 megabytes; certainly plenty for most programs. However, when the 8086 chip was designed, a total of 1 megabyte of memory was considered adequate, so essentially only 4 bits of the segment register are used, providing 20 bits of address space. (Actually the contents of the segment register are shifted left 4 bits and added to the offset register, so all the bits are used. However, all but 4 are redundant.) Using 20 bits permits addressing 1,048,576 decimal bytes, or 1 megabyte. In MS-DOS, however, less than 640K bytes are available for the user's program; the rest is used by the hardware. Thus arises the infamous 640K memory barrier.

(This barrier can be breached in several ways, such as protected mode programming and expanded memory, but these techniques are beyond the scope of this book. Anyway, you can do a great deal in 640K.)

The Far Heap

The memory above the default data segment, all the way to the end of the 640K limit, is called the *far heap*. This is shown in Figure 12.6.

If there isn't too much other stuff in memory, your program is small, and you have the full 640K of memory (or more) installed in your system, then the far heap may contain somewhat more than 500,000 bytes.

How do we obtain memory from the far heap? As with the near heap, we can allocate it dynamically. There are two approaches, depending on whether an individual memory object (such as an array) is larger than a 64K segment. If an individual item can fit entirely within a segment, we can access it with far pointers. However, if it's larger than a segment, we must use huge pointers. We'll cover far pointers and huge pointers in turn.

Allocation with Far Pointers

Our next example shows the mechanics of obtaining memory from the far heap, using far pointers. The key library function is `farmalloc()`. It's similar to `malloc()` but takes an argument of type `unsigned long` rather than `unsigned` and returns a far pointer rather than a near one.

Incidentally, you should run all programs that use the far heap directly from DOS rather than from Turbo C++'s IDE. The far heap space allocated by Turbo C++ can hold only a few thousand bytes, not enough for most purposes. To run under DOS, you can use the DOS shell, available from the File menu, or you can exit from Turbo C++ altogether. This second approach provides somewhat more far heap space.

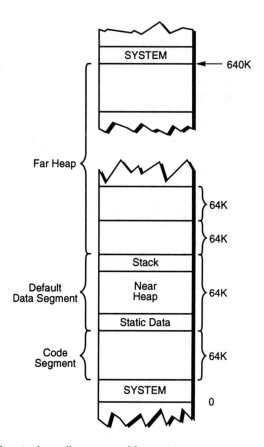

Figure 12.6. The far heap in the small memory model.

Our next example program shows the basics of allocating memory from the far heap.

```
// ezfar.c
// allocates memory using farmalloc()
// (run from DOS, not the IDE)
#include <stdio.h>              // for printf()
#include <alloc.h>             // for farmalloc()
#include <stdlib.h>            // for exit()

int main(void)
    {
    unsigned long mem_doubles;    // number of doubles to store
    unsigned long mem_bytes;      // bytes of memory needed
    unsigned j;                   // loop variable (note: not long)
    double far *ptr;              // pointer to memory block (far)
```

```
mem_doubles = 8000;              // 8000 * 8 = 64000
mem_bytes = mem_doubles * sizeof(double);   // calculate bytes

ptr = farmalloc(mem_bytes);   // get far memory
if(ptr==NULL)                 // error return
   { printf("\nCan't allocate block"); exit(1); }

for(j=0; j<mem_doubles; j++) // fill memory with data
   ptr[j] = (double)j;       // data is j (0.0 to 7999.0)

farfree(ptr);               // free memory
return(0);
}  // end main()
```

This program allocates space for 8000 variables of type double, each of which takes 8 bytes. This is 64,000 bytes, or almost all of a segment.

Note that the pointer to the memory is type far, and that the argument to farmalloc() is type unsigned long. Otherwise things work much as they do when obtaining near memory.

When the program is finished with memory obtained with farmalloc(), it should return it to the operating system by executing farfree().

Limitation of Far Pointers

Although farmalloc() can allocate a block as large as all of available memory, you can't use far pointers to access a memory object (like an array) that is larger than one segment. Why is this? The problem is that far pointers don't handle the addresses correctly if the object crosses the boundary from one segment to another.

For example, suppose you've set your far pointer to point to the last byte in a segment, say byte number 65,535 in segment 1. Now you increment the pointer, hoping it will point to byte number 0 in segment 2. Unfortunately, far pointers aren't smart enough to do this. They simply "wrap around" to the same segment, pointing to byte 0 of segment 1 again. They can point to any byte in any segment, but they can't make the transition from one segment to another. To solve this problem, we'll need huge pointers, discussed in the next section.

We should note that farmalloc() and similar functions that operate on the far heap aren't ANSI standard, but are specific to the Turbo C++ compiler. Other compilers may use other names for similar functions. (For example, the equivalent to farmalloc() in Microsoft C is the _fmalloc() function.)

Multiple Memory Objects on the Far Heap

Although far pointers can't access a single memory object larger than a segment, they can access as many objects as will fit in the far heap, provided each object is smaller than a segment. For example, if there are 500,000 bytes of memory available, there's room for

500,000 divided by 65,536, or 7 full-sized segments. Segments don't need to be a full 64K. You could also allocate 15 segments of 32,768 bytes, 25 segments of 20,000 bytes, and so forth.

Our next example stores several large segments. It asks the user how many variables of type double should be stored in each segment. The maximum size you can request is 8,191 (65,536 divided by 8 bytes, the size of a variable of type double, minus 1). The program calculates the resulting segment size, and figures out how many segments of this size can fit in the far heap. It then places a different memory object, an array of type double, in each one.

The program uses an array of far pointers to point to the different segments. The farmalloc() function is called to allocate memory for each object, and its return value is assigned to one of the pointers. Each segment is filled with data, and the data is then checked for accuracy.

```c
// farmem.c
// allocates multiple segments using farmalloc()
// (run from DOS, not the IDE)
#include <stdio.h>               // for printf()
#include <alloc.h>              // for farmalloc()
#include <stdlib.h>            // for exit()
#define MAX_SEGS 1000          // maximum number of segments

int main(void)
    {
    unsigned long doubles_seg;    // doubles to store per segment
    unsigned long total_mem;      // bytes of memory available
    unsigned long bytes_seg;      // bytes needed per segment

    double far *ptr[MAX_SEGS];    // array of pointers to segments
    unsigned j;                   // counts variables
    int num_segs;                 // number of segments
    int k;                        // counts segments

    total_mem = farcoreleft();    // memory available
    printf("\nThere are %lu bytes on far heap", total_mem);
    printf("\nEnter number of doubles to store ");
    printf("per segment (8191 max): ");
    scanf("%lu", &doubles_seg);
    bytes_seg = doubles_seg * sizeof(double);  // calculate bytes
    num_segs = (int)(total_mem / bytes_seg);   // calculate segs
    printf("\n%d segments of %lu bytes\n", num_segs, bytes_seg);

    for(k=0; k<num_segs; k++)              // for each segment,
        {
        ptr[k] = farmalloc(bytes_seg);    // get memory for seg k
        if(ptr[k]==NULL)                  // error return
            { printf("Can't allocate segment %d", k); exit(1); }
        printf("After seg %d, mem = %lu\n", k, farcoreleft() );
```

```
    for(j=0; j<doubles_seg; j++)      // for each segment,
        ptr[k][j] = (double)(j+k);    // fill memory with j+k
    }  // end for(k)

for(k=0; k<num_segs; k++)             // for each segment,
    for(j=0; j<doubles_seg; j++)      // check the data
        if( ptr[k][j] != (double)(j+k) )
            { printf("Error in seg %d: j=%u", k, j); exit(1); }

for(k=0; k<num_segs; k++)             // for each segment,
    farfree(ptr[k]);                  // free memory

printf("Memory test successful");
return(0);
}  // end main()
```

The farcoreleft() function operates like coreleft(), except that it returns the memory remaining in the far heap rather than the near heap. Before terminating, the program frees all the objects with farfree(). Here's some sample output:

```
There are 458128 bytes on the far heap
Enter number of doubles to store per segment (8191 max): 8000
7 segments of 64000 bytes
After seg 0, mem = 394112
After seg 1, mem = 330096
After seg 2, mem = 266080
After seg 3, mem = 202064
After seg 4, mem = 138048
After seg 5, mem = 74032
After seg 6, mem = 10016
Memory test successful
```

We invoked the program from the Turbo C++ DOS shell, and it starts off with 458,128 bytes. We entered 8000 as the number of variables of type double to store in each of the segments. That's 64,000 bytes per segment, so the far heap can hold 7 segments of this size.

The program uses farcoreleft() to tell you how much memory is left after allocating each object. Notice, however, the figures reported by the program for the memory remaining after each segment is allocated. If you subtract each figure from the preceding one, you'll see that each segment allocated actually reduces the amount of memory by 64,016 bytes. The extra 16 bytes is the overhead imposed by each memory object. The moral here is don't use a great number of small memory objects, because the overhead would be excessively large.

If you enter a smaller number of variables to store per segment, the number of segments will increase. For example, if you specify 2000 variables per segment, the program reports that it can cram in 28 segments of 16000 bytes each. Warning: if you make the number of variables too small, the number of segments becomes so large that the 16 bytes-per-segment overhead becomes significant and the program's calculations fail. To correct this you could add 16 to the `bytes_seg` variable when calculating the number of segments.

Compiler Warning

The compiler will try to save you from yourself if you attempt to use far pointers to access objects larger than one segment. You might think you could perform such access using an array index of type `unsigned long` instead of type `unsigned`, so it could point at more than 65,536 variables, like this:

```
double far *ptr;      // far pointer
unsigned long j;      // don't use type long with far pointers
. . . . .
ptr[j] = 300;         // compiler warning here
```

However, the compiler knows you shouldn't use a far pointer (`ptr`) with an index (`j`) that can have a value greater than 65,536. It issues a warning, `Conversion may lose significant digits`. Remember that `ptr[j]` really means `*(ptr+j)`. The warning occurs because you're trying to add a long (4 byte) value of `j` to a short (2-byte) value of `ptr`.

Far Arrays

Although it isn't as common as dynamic allocation, you can use far memory to store variables allocated at compile time as well as those allocated dynamically. All you need to do is place the keyword `far` in their definitions:

```
char far chararr1[64000L];   // allocate three large arrays
char far chararr2[64000L];   // in the far heap
char far chararr3[64000L];
```

References to these arrays will look like any other array references:

```
chararr1[j] = 12;
```

Of course you need to know the size of the arrays at compile time, so this isn't as flexible an approach as dynamic allocation.

Disadvantage of Far Pointers

Of course there's no free lunch, so there's a drawback to using far—as opposed to near— pointers. Because address calculations must be made on 32-bit values rather than 16-bit values, it takes somewhat longer to access a memory variable with far pointers. Also, since the machine-language instructions to manipulate far pointers are larger than those for near pointers, your program code will be slightly larger as well. However, if you need the extra data space this is a small price to pay.

Allocation with Huge Pointers

If you need to create a memory object, such as an array, that is larger than one segment, you'll need to access it with a huge pointer. This is a common situation when accessing memory. For instance, when you read a large disk file, you probably want to store it in a single continuous array rather than a number of segment-sized memory objects. Our next example shows how such huge memory objects are created and accessed.

```c
// hugemem.c
// allocates memory using farmalloc() with huge pointers
// (run from DOS, not the IDE)
#include <stdio.h>              // for printf()
#include <alloc.h>             // for farmalloc()
#include <stdlib.h>            // for exit()

int main(void)
   {
   unsigned long mem_doubles;    // number of doubles to store
   unsigned long mem_bytes;      // bytes of memory needed

   double huge *ptr;             // pointer to start of memory
   unsigned long j;              // loop counter (note: long)

   printf("Far heap bytes available = %lu", farcoreleft() );
   printf(", or %lu doubles", farcoreleft()/sizeof(double) );
   printf("\nEnter number of doubles to store in one object: ");
   scanf("%lu", &mem_doubles);
   mem_bytes = mem_doubles * sizeof(double);  // calculate bytes

   ptr = farmalloc(mem_bytes);  // get memory
   if(ptr==NULL)                // error return from farmalloc()
      { printf("Can't allocate memory"); exit(1); }
   printf("Far heap after allocation = %lu", farcoreleft());

   for(j=0; j<mem_doubles; j++)    // fill memory with j
      ptr[j] = (double)j;

   for(j=0; j<mem_doubles; j++)    // check the data
      if( ptr[j] != (double)j)
         {
         printf("\nMemory error: j=%lu, ptr[j]=%lf", j, ptr[j] );
         exit(1);
         }
   farfree(ptr);                    // free memory
   printf("\nMemory test successful");
   return(0);
   }  // end main()
```

Again, run this program from DOS or the DOS shell rather than the IDE. Otherwise you'll have little memory available. Here's some sample output:

```
Far heap bytes available = 457024, or 57128 doubles
```

```
Enter number of doubles to store in one object: 55000
Far heap after allocation = 17008
Memory test successful
```

The programming is comparatively easy. With huge pointers you use `farmalloc()` to obtain a memory object that's as large as you want, up to the limit of available memory. Then you access the individual variables as elements of an array. This is the same approach as with far pointers, except that the array is really—well, huge. You can stop worrying about individual segments; no tricky finagling is necessary.

You can use an array index of type `unsigned long` (indeed you must if you want to access all of memory):

```
double huge *ptr;      // huge pointer
unsigned long j;       // unsigned long is OK with huge
. . . . .
ptr[j] = 300;          // no compiler warning
```

Disadvantage of Huge Pointers

It's even slower to access memory with huge pointers than far pointers, because each access must check to see whether a segment boundary has been crossed and alter the segment register accordingly. This extra register manipulation takes time.

Reallocating Memory for Secret Agents

Let's put what we know about huge pointers to work in a program that allocates memory for secret agents. It is frequently the case in database programs that you allocate a large block of memory, as when you read the contents of a file into memory, and then reallocate this block to add small amounts of additional data (each time you add a new secret agent to the database, for example). We'll use the `farrealloc()` function for this reallocation. It's analogous to `realloc()` but operates on the far heap.

In our example we "artificially" generate data for 2000 secret agents. That is, the program concocts it and places it in memory. This saves you having to invent and enter this data but makes the data rather dull. Each agent's name is the string `"Agent"` followed by a number, as in `"Agent1027"`. (The agents have four-digit serial numbers because there are too many agents for three digits). The agents' heights vary from 68 inches to 72 inches, with the actual height calculated from the serial number (Agent0027 has a height of 68.27 inches, for example). It takes 100,000 bytes of memory for 2,000 agents, since the `personnel` structure occupies 50 bytes.

Once the program has generated this data, it allows the user to display the data for any one agent by typing d followed by the agent number or to add the data for a new agent by typing e. New data is added at the end of the array.

```
// aghuge.c
// creates agent records accessible by huge pointers
// (run from DOS, not the IDE)
```

```
#include <stdio.h>              // for printf()
#include <stdlib.h>             // for exit(), itoa()
#include <conio.h>              // for getche()
#include <alloc.h>              // for faralloc(), etc.
#include <mem.h>                // for _fmemcpy()
#include <string.h>             // for strcpy(), strcat()
#define TRUE 1
void agdisp(void);             // prototypes
void newname(void);

struct personnel                  // declare data structure
    {
    char name[40];             // name
    int agnumb;                // code number
    float height;              // height in inches
    char padding[18];          // make structure 64 bytes long
    }anagent;                  // define utility struct

struct personnel huge *agptr = NULL;  // pointer to memory
unsigned long n;                      // number of agents listed

void main(void)
    {
    char utilstr[40];          // utility string
    int j;                     // loop counter for agents

    n = 2000;                  // start with 2000 agents
                               // allocate memory for them
    agptr = farmalloc( n * sizeof(struct personnel) );
    if(agptr==NULL)            // error return from farmalloc()
        { printf("Can't allocate memory"); exit(1); }

    // generate data for n agents (record 0 is ignored)
    printf("Generating %d agent records", n-1);
    for(j=0; j<n; j++)
        {                          // create data for agent j
        strcpy(anagent.name, "Agent");
        strcat(anagent.name, itoa(j, utilstr, 10) );
        anagent.agnumb = j;
        anagent.height = 68.0+(float)(j%800)/100.0;   // 68" to 76"
                               // copy data into far memory
        _fmemcpy( agptr+j, &anagent, sizeof(struct personnel) );
        }

    while(TRUE)                // cycle until user chooses 'q'
        {
        printf("\n'e' enter new agent\n'd' display an agent");
        printf("\n'q' exit: ");
        switch ( getche() )
            {
            case 'e': newname(); break;
            case 'd': agdisp();  break;
```

```
        case 'q': exit(0);    break;
        default:                      // user mistake
            puts("\nEnter only selections listed");
        } // end switch
    } // end while
} // end main()

// newname()
// puts a new agent in the database
void newname(void)
    {
    char utilstr[40];              // utility string
    struct personnel huge *agptr2;   // temporary pointer

                                    // get more memory for new agent
    agptr2 = farrealloc( agptr, (n+1)*sizeof(struct personnel) );
    if(agptr2==NULL)
        { printf("\nCan't reallocate memory"); return; }
    agptr = agptr2;                // save new value
    printf("\nRecord %d.\nEnter name: ", n);   // get name
    gets(utilstr);
    _fmemcpy(agptr[n].name, utilstr, strlen(utilstr)+1 );
    printf("Enter agent number (4 digits): "); // get number
    gets(utilstr);
    agptr[n].agnumb = atoi(utilstr);
    printf("Enter height in inches: ");        // get height
    gets(utilstr);
    agptr[n++].height = atof(utilstr);
    }

// agdisp()
// display agent's data whose number is entered by user
void agdisp(void)
    {
    int j;                        // record number
    char utilstr[40];             // utility string

    printf("\nEnter agent number to display (1 to %d): ", n-1);
    j = atoi( gets(utilstr) );              // get number from user

    if(j > n-1)                            // check for wrong number
        { printf("Only %d agents in memory\n", n-1); return; }
    printf("\nRecord number %d\n", j);
    printf("   Name: %Fs\n", agptr[j].name);  // note 'F'
    printf("   Agent number: %04d\n", agptr[j].agnumb);
    printf("   Height: %4.2f\n", agptr[j].height);
    }
```

Output of aghuge.c

Human beings like to see the first item in a list numbered 1 rather than 0, so we don't count Agent0000 when we report the total number of agents. When the program starts, the user is told there are 1999 agents in memory. The user can enter new data for agents 2000 and up.

Here's a session with the program, in which we ask to see the last agent on the list, then enter a new agent, and then ask to see the new agent's record.

```
Generating 1999 agent records
'e' enter new agent
'd' display an agent
'q' exit: d
Enter agent number to display (1 to 1999): 1999

Record number 1999
   Name: Agent1999
   Agent number: 1999
   Height: 71.99

'e' enter new agent
'd' display an agent
'q' exit: e
Record 2000.
Enter name: James Bondski
Enter agent number (4 digits): 2000
Enter height in inches: 75.00

'e' enter new agent
'd' display an agent
'q' exit: d
Enter agent number to display (1 to 2000): 2000

Record number 2000
   Name: James Bondski
   Agent number: 2000
   Height: 75,00
```

(Be careful not to use duplicate numbers, or the program subsequently finds only the first agent with this number.)

Far Versions of Memory Manipulation Routines

Notice that you can't use ordinary string functions like strcpy() to manipulate far memory. These functions (unless you use a different memory model, as we'll soon see) only operate with near pointers. However, some string functions have far versions. These start with an underscore (to show that they're not ANSI compatible functions) and the letter f. For instance, _fstrlen() finds the length of a string accessed with a far pointer (as strlen() does with a near pointer). However, there is no far version of strcpy().

In Chapter 6, "Arrays and Strings," we mentioned the existence of functions that manipulate non-string data in memory. Some of these functions have variations specifically designed to work with far pointers. In the aghuge.c program we use the _fmemcpy() function to copy data from a near structure to far memory. This is a far version of memcpy(), which can be used to copy data between near blocks of memory. The _fmemcpy function takes three arguments, as shown by its prototype:

```
void far *far_fmemcpy(void far *dest, const void far *src, size_t n);
```

where size_t is unsigned.

Watch the Segment Boundary

The far versions of the library functions work with far pointers but not huge pointers. Thus, because far pointers can't cross segment boundaries, it's important that whatever program element these functions address doesn't cross a segment boundary either. We've ensured that this is the case by sizing the personel structure so that it divides evenly into a 65,536-byte segment. To do that, we padded it from 46 bytes to 64 bytes. All the powers of 2 (4, 8, 16, 32 and so on) divide evenly into 65,536.

Although it may waste some memory, you will usually want to size any structures that are elements of a huge array the same way: their size should divide evenly into a 65,536-byte segment.

Save the Old Pointer

Note that, when we reallocate memory in newname(), we save the value returned from farrealloc() in a temporary pointer, agptr2. This ensures that, if the reallocation fails, we won't lose the value of the existing pointer and all the data it points to. After we've checked to be sure agptr2 is valid (not NULL), we can assign its value to agptr.

Initializing Allocated Memory

There are variations to the memory allocation functions that may be useful in some situations. For example, the functions calloc() and farcalloc() operate like malloc() and farmalloc(), but initialize memory to all zeros as they allocate it. Instead of using one argument representing the number of bytes to store, these functions take two arguments: the number of data items to store and the size of the items. The following statement obtains far memory for 2000 structures of type personel:

```
farcalloc( 2000, sizeof(struct personel) );
```

It's often convenient (and sometimes safer) to initialize memory to all zeros, and these functions also save you the trouble of calculating the number of bytes to allocate for a certain number of objects of a certain size. Many programmers use them instead of malloc() and farmalloc().

Summary of Memory Allocation Approaches

Let's summarize the various approaches to addressing memory with different kinds of pointers.

With near pointers you use the `malloc()` function, or a variation like `calloc()` or `realloc()`, to allocate memory. These functions return near pointers to the memory on the near heap. Memory obtained this way is limited to that remaining in the default data segment after other program variables have been allocated, so it's always less than 64K (sometimes much less). Variables used for address arithmetic with near pointers can be no larger than `unsigned int`. Use `free()` to deallocate the memory when you're done with it. Near pointers provide the fastest way to access memory.

With far pointers you use the `farmalloc()` function, or a variation like `farcalloc()` or `farrealloc()`. These functions return a far pointer to memory on the far heap. The far heap consists of all the memory in the computer not being used for something else, but the size of each individual memory object (such as an array) must be less than one segment. Use `farfree()` to free memory. Memory access with far pointers is slower than with near pointers.

With huge pointers you use `farmalloc()` and its variations, but the address value returned is a huge pointer. Individual memory objects can be larger than one segment; in fact, they can be as large as available memory. However, individual elements of such an object (variables in an array) shouldn't cross segment boundaries. Memory access with huge pointers is the slowest of all.

Memory Models

So far the programs in this book have been designed to be compiled with the small memory model. This model, the default in Turbo C++, assumes there is only one 64K segment for all a program's data (the default data segment) and another single 64K segment for all a program's code.

We've seen how, using the `far` and `huge` keywords, it's possible to access memory outside the default data segment. However, there's another approach to accessing more memory: using different memory models.

Memory models allow the compiler to make different assumptions about how much data and how much code will be in the program. Turbo C++ specifies six possible memory models: tiny, small, compact, medium, large, and huge. Figure 12.7 shows the possibilities.

If the code for your program fits inside one 64K segment and the data fits inside another, you can use the small memory model. If the code for your program is larger than 64K, but the data fits inside 64K, you should use the medium model. If the code is less than 64K but the data is larger, the compact model is appropriate. If both code and data require more than 64K, the large model is necessary.

The tiny memory model is used in special cases where the amount of memory available for code and data together is limited to 64K. It is rare today for a PC's memory to have only 64K, so this model is seldom used. It can be used to generate a kind of executable file called a .com file, which is in some ways simpler than a .exe file, but is used only in special circumstances.

The huge model is provided for the case of single data items, usually arrays, that are each larger than 64K.

Model	Total Segments	Code Segments	Data Segments	Segments for One Data Item
tiny	1	(1 shared)		1
small	2	1	1	1
medium	many	many	1	1
compact	many	1	many	1
large	many	many	many	1
huge	many	many	many	many

Figure 12.7. Memory Models.

Changing the Default

The choice of memory model determines the default type of any pointers you define in your program. In the small and medium memory models, near pointers are the default, since it's assumed only one segment will be used for all data. In these models, if we want to define far pointers to access far memory, you must explicitly use the keyword far, as we've already seen.

On the other hand, if you're using the compact or large memory models, the default is far pointers, because these models assume there will be too much data to fit in a single segment. In these models, if you want to define a near pointer, you must explicitly insert the keyword near.

Finally, if you want huge pointers to be the default, you can compile with the huge model.

Far Versions of Library Functions

Different memory models also use different versions of many of the C-language library functions. Specifically, most functions that use pointers for arguments or return values have different versions. When the small and medium models are used, the linker automatically provides library functions that use near pointers. When the compact, large, or huge models are used, the linker provides functions that use far pointers.

These differing versions of library functions are invisible to the programmer. Both use the same prototype in the header file. However, the prototype is interpreted differently depending on the memory model, and the actual code for the function is different.

Compiling with the Compact Memory Model

Let's look at a program example designed to be compiled with the compact memory model. This model assumes multiple data segments but only one code segment.

To compile with the compact model, select Compiler from the Options menu, select the Code Generation submenu, and click the Compact button in the Model box. (Don't forget to switch back to the small model when you're done.)

```
// compact.c
// compile with the compact memory model
// run from DOS, not the IDE
#include <stdio.h>              // for printf()
#include <alloc.h>             // for farmalloc()
#include <stdlib.h>            // for exit()
#include <mem.h>              // for _fmemcpy()
#include <string.h>           // for strcpy(), strcmp()
#define SIZE 30000            // bytes to allocate

int main(void)
   {
   char *ptr1;         // pointer to memory block 1
   char *ptr2;         // pointer to memory block 2
   unsigned j;         // loop counter

   ptr1 = farmalloc(SIZE);      // allocate block 1
      if(ptr1==NULL)
         { printf("Can't allocate memory 1"); exit(1); }

   ptr2 = farmalloc(SIZE);      // allocate block 2
      if(ptr2==NULL)
         { printf("Can't allocate memory 2"); exit(1); }

   for(j=0; j<SIZE; j++)        // fill block 1 with data
      ptr1[j] = j%128;

   _fmemcpy(ptr2, ptr1, SIZE);  // copy block 1 to block 2

   for(j=0; j<SIZE; j++)        // check data in block 2
      if( ptr1[j] != ptr2[j] )
         printf("Error: j=%d", j);
   printf("\nBuffer test successful");

   strcpy(ptr1, "Cats");        // copy string to block 1
```

```
strcpy(ptr2, ptr1);          // copy block 1 to block 2
if( strcmp(ptr2, "Cats") != 0 )  // check block 2
    printf("\nString copied incorrectly");
else
    printf("\nString test successful: string is %s", ptr2);
farfree(ptr1);               // free memory
farfree(ptr2);
return(0);
} // end main()
```

In this program we allocate two blocks of far memory. Note that we must use farmalloc(), because the memory is far. The pointers ptr1 and ptr2 aren't explicitly defined to be of type far (which is the type farmalloc() returns); instead they're automatically compiled as far because we're compiling under the compact model.

The program inserts data in the first block of memory and copies it to the second block with _fmemcpy(). It then checks to be sure the second block holds the same data as the first. Next the program copies the string "Cats" to block 1 using strcpy(), copies the contents of block 1 to block 2, and finally, using strcmp(), checks that the string in block 2 is the same one we started with. Note that the compiler doesn't complain, even though we're using far pointers with functions that normally take near pointers. Because we're using the compact model, the compiler automatically substitutes versions of these functions that take far pointers.

Note that some functions, like memcpy() and strcat(), have far versions with different names (_fmemcpy() and _fstrcat()). Others, like strcpy(), use the same name for near and far versions. Online help or a reference book (see the bibliography) will tell you which functions have different names for their far versions.

Functions like malloc() and farmalloc() may seem like different versions of the same function, but they actually do different things: malloc() obtains memory from the near heap, no matter which memory model you use, while farmalloc() obtains it from the far heap. There are two different versions of malloc(), depending on the memory model, and two different versions of farmalloc().

Memory Access for Program Code

We've seen how to use different memory models when a program's data is larger than one 64K segment. A program's code can also be larger than 64K. When this is the case, we must again use a different memory model, since the small model only supports one segment's worth of code.

The medium model allows multiple code segments, but restricts data to one segment. The large model allows multiple code and multiple data segments, and the huge model allows multiple code and multiple data segments and in addition permits huge data objects.

Thus if your program has grown too large for one code segment, you'll need to use either the medium, large, or huge memory models, depending on the size of your data. In these models the compiler generates program code that includes 32-bit addresses, rather than 16, for machine-language instructions like jumps and branches. Of course there's the usual tradeoff: these instructions execute more slowly and increase the program's size.

Fine Tuning

We've already seen that, when using the small memory model, it's possible to use the far keyword when a variable is outside the normal data segment. Similarly, if we use the compact or large models, we can declare a near data type to refer to variables that we know are in the near heap. This can reduce the time needed to access these variables.

By combining memory models and near and far storage types in different ways, it's possible to achieve just the right compromise between execution speed, data storage capacity, and program size.

Summary

We started this chapter by reviewing the various storage classes generated by the compiler: automatic, external, static, and so on. Each of these storage classes can be characterized by its lifetime and visibility.

Next we discussed how to use malloc() to allocate memory at runtime, rather than compile time. We saw how this technique can be used in various situations, such as obtaining memory for disk files, for graphics images, and for linked lists. We also saw how the realloc() function can change the size of a previously-allocated memory block.

If you need to store data that occupies more than a segment, you can allocate memory with farmalloc() and access data placed in this memory with far pointers (for individual objects smaller than a segment) or huge pointers (for objects larger than a segment).

Memory models provide a way to change the default values for the maximum sizes of your code and data. The small and medium models assume only one data segment. In these models near pointers, and library functions that use near pointers, are the default. The compact, large, and huge models assume multiple data segments. Far pointers, and library functions that use far pointers, are the default. The huge memory model assumes huge pointers. The medium, large, and huge memory models also permit more than one segment of program code.

Questions

1. The storage class of a variable is related to
   a. The amount of memory space the variable occupies
   b. The data type of the variable
   c. The time the variable will occupy a space in memory
   d. What parts of the program can "see" the function

2. External variables are stored in an area of memory called the _____.

3. For a variable to be visible in many functions, it must have the storage class

    a. External
    b. Static
    c. Automatic
    d. Register

4. An automatic variable is one that is automatically c_____ and d_____.

5. A static (nonexternal) variable can be seen only within

    a. A block
    b. A function
    c. A file
    d. Many files

6. True or false: an external variable is always visible throughout the file in which it's defined.

7. Automatic variables are stored in an area of memory called the _____.

8. Dynamic memory allocation is useful because

    a. Dynamic variables have a longer lifetime
    b. You can use exactly as much memory as you need
    c. Data retains its value when a function returns
    d. You can move data around in memory while the program is running

9. The primary function for allocating memory from the near heap is _____.

10. True or false: the near heap can be up to 65,536 bytes long.

11. The pointer that is assigned the value returned from `malloc()` should always be

    a. Type `void *`
    b. A pointer to the type of data being stored
    c. Type `void far *`
    d. Static or external

12. To make a dynamically-allocated near memory block larger or smaller, you can use the function _____.

13. True or false: you can access any size memory object with far pointers.

14. Far pointers point to memory objects

    a. In the near heap
    b. On the stack
    c. Beyond the default data segment
    d. With addresses higher than 640K

15. The far heap occupies

    a. No more than one segment
    b. The default data segment
    c. As many segments as will fit
    d. All the memory in the computer not used for something else

16. Using different memory models is useful when a program or data becomes too

    _____.

17. The medium memory model permits

    a. More than one code segment
    b. More than one data segment
    c. Only one code segment
    d. Only one data segment

18. Memory models are necessary because of the

    a. Stack-based architecture of the microprocessor
    b. Segmentation of memory
    c. Large size of the data or code in some programs
    d. Need to keep programmers guessing

19. True or false: different memory models can be selected from within the IDE.

20. The disadvantage of using a memory model that is larger than necessary is that

    a. Simple data types cannot be used
    b. The program will be larger than necessary
    c. Program files are harder to link
    d. Program instructions take longer to execute

Exercises

1. Write a program that uses dynamic memory allocation on the near heap to obtain enough memory to hold 2,000 variables of type `float`. Fill the memory with data and check that it has been stored correctly. Also check that the memory allocation function has returned a valid pointer. Don't forget to free the memory when you're done.

2. Write a program that prompts the user to enter strings, and then uses dynamic memory allocation to obtain just enough near memory to store each string, no matter what its length is (don't forget the '\0'). When the user enters a string of zero length, terminate the input part of the program and display all the strings. Store the pointers to the strings in an array. (For extra credit you could obtain memory dynamically for the pointers as well.

3. Blend together the aglink.c program and the agalloc.c program so that data is stored on memory in the form of a linked list (as in aglink.c), but in addition the program allows the user to write the data to a disk file and read it back in again (as in agalloc.c). You'll need to read and write each agent's data with a separate function call, because the structures aren't stored continuously in memory. Don't worry if the reading and writing process changes the order of the data. For extra credit, free all memory when the program exits and free any old memory if the program reads in a new file.

Advanced Topics

- Multifile programs
- Enumerated data types
- typedef
- Type conversion and casting
- Conditional compilation

When discussing any complex subject (which is probably a fair description of C), some topics inevitably fail to group themselves naturally into a single easily specified category. This chapter is meant to deal with some of these topics. It's divided into three relatively unconnected sections.

In the first section we'll discuss multifile programs, one of C's major advantages in large programming projects. Next we'll cover a potpourri of topics connected with variables: the enumerated data type, `typedef`, type conversion and casting, and complex declarations. The third section covers conditional compilation, identifiers and naming classes, and `goto` statements.

Multifile Programs

So far in this book our programs have consisted of a single file. We have written, compiled, and linked this one file to create an executable program. The program might have had several functions in it, but they were all treated as a single entity for the purpose of compilation. However, it is possible to break a program apart into separate files, each file consisting of one or more functions. These files can be compiled separately and then linked together to form the executable program.

Let's examine some simple examples of this process; then we'll discuss why we might want to use separate compilation.

Here's a complete C source file, called mainprog.c.

```c
// mainprog.c
// main program to test separate compilation
#include <stdio.h>        // for printf(), scanf()
int formula(int, int);    // prototype

void main(void)
    {
    int a, b, ans;

    printf("Type two integers: ");
    scanf("%d%d", &a, &b);
    ans = formula(a,b);
    printf("The sum of the squares is %d.", ans);
    }
```

This is a variation of a program from Chapter 5, "Functions," multifun.c, which calculated the sum of the squares of two numbers. However, part of the multifun.c program is missing here. We'll see where it went in a moment.

Type in this source file with the Turbo C++ editor and save it as mainprog.c. You can compile this file with no problem, but you can't link it. Why not? If you try it, the linker displays the error message

```
undefined symbol _formula() in module mainprog.c
```

The linker doesn't know what to do when it encounters the reference to the function `formula()` in the next-to-last statement of the listing.

```
ans = formula(a,b);
```

We're going to solve this problem by providing this function but in a separate file. Type in and save the following file, giving it the name formula.c. Remember that you can have two or more files open at the same time in the IDE, in separate windows. It's convenient to keep both mainprog.c and formula.c available this way.

```
// formula.c
// function returns sum of squares of arguments
int formula(int x, int y)
   {
   return( x*x + y*y );
   }
```

The formula.c file contains, as you can see, the missing function, `formula()`.

How do we turn these two source files—mainprog.c and formula.c—into a complete program? We use a hitherto unexamined capability of Turbo C++.

Using Turbo C++'s Project Feature

Turbo C++ uses something called a *project* to compile multiple source files into a single program. Operations pertaining to projects are carried out from the Project menu in the IDE.

At the heart of the project is a file with the .PRJ extension. This file contains the names of all the files that will be combined into a single program. Turbo C++ will use this file as a guide to creating the program.

You don't need to type the list of files into the .PRJ file list yourself. Turbo C++ creates it automatically. However, you must tell Turbo C++ what files to put on the list. Here's how to do it.

Open a Project

To begin, you must have created all the source (.C) files for the project. (There may also be already compiled files, such as .LIB or .OBJ files, such as when you make stand-alone graphics programs.) Make sure all these files are in the current directory. Now call up Turbo C++ and select Open Project from the Project menu. (It's simplest if you don't have any windows open on the screen.) Type the name of the project file into the Open Project File box, giving it the .PRJ file extension; for example, sumsqr.prj. The name you use for the .PRJ file will also be given to the .EXE file that will be the end result of the process; in this example, sumsqr.exe.

Press the Enter key when you've typed the project filename. The Open Project File box will disappear, and a window called Project: SUMSQR (or whatever name you gave the project file) will appear at the bottom of the screen. This window will show the files used in the project, but it's blank until you add the files to the list.

Adding Files to the Project

To add a file to the project list, press the Insert key (or select Add Item from the Project menu). A box called `Add to Project List` appears. In the Name box, type the names of the files you want to add to the project (mainprog.c and formula.c in this example), pressing the Enter key after each one. Another possibility is to enter *.C in the Name box to display all the .C files, select each one with the mouse, and click the Add button.

As each program is added to the project list, you'll see it appear in the Project window. If you must add .LIB or .OBJ files (as when creating stand-alone graphics programs), type them into the Name field too. If you make a mistake and add the wrong file to the list, you can delete it by clicking its name in the Project window and then selecting Delete Item from the Project menu.

When the project list is complete, press the Done button In the `Add to Project List` box to tell Turbo C++ the project is complete. This makes the Add to Project List box go away. You'll be back in the main IDE window.

Compiling, Linking, and Running

To compile and link the source files into an executable program, choose Make from the Compile menu (or press the F9 key). You'll see Turbo C++ compiling the various files—mainprog.c and formula.c in our example—and linking the resulting .obj files together into sumsqr.exe. You can run the resulting program in the usual way, either from Turbo C++ (select Run from the Run menu) or by exiting to DOS and invoking sumsqr.exe directly. Here's some sample output:

```
Type two integers: 3 4
The sum of the squares is 25
```

Modifying the Source Files

If you now make a change in one of your source files, you can rebuild your whole project quickly. First, if the project isn't open, open it by selecting Open Project from the Project menu and then double-clicking the appropriate project file (such as sumsqr.prj) in the File list of the Open Project File box. Now you can simply select Make from the Compile menu, and Turbo C++ will rebuild your project, creating a new executable program.

Note how convenient Turbo C++'s multiwindow capability is when working with multiple source files. You can keep a window open on each of several source files at the same time, so you can see, for example, whether the arguments you're passing to a function in a different file are what the function expects to receive. Try this with mainprog.c and formula.c, for example. Simply select Open from the File menu to open a second file.

Compile First

Another approach to using Project is to compile (but not link) each source file as you create it, using Compile in the Compile menu. When you're debugging, this may be a more efficient method, as it lets you correct errors on each file separately. When all the source files compile correctly into object files, you can select Make from the Compile menu to link the object files into the final executable file. This happens automatically when Make is invoked: source files that have already been compiled won't be compiled again (unless they've been changed since the last compile).

The Linking Process

How does the linker connect the call to formula() in mainprog.c, with this function in formula.c? When it sees the reference to formula() in mainprog.obj, it looks for this function in all of the other files being linked; in this case, there is only one: formula.c. Finding the function in this file, it makes the appropriate connection. The result is an executable file called sumsqr.exe, which contains both functions main() and formula(), almost as if you had typed them into the same file. Figure 13.1 shows this process.

Closing a Project

To close the currently open project, select Close Project from the Project menu. This removes from the screen all the files involved in the project.

Note that if you don't close the project (perhaps you simply close all the source file windows until you have a blank screen), then the project remains open. This can be disconcerting if you then open a different source file and attempt to compile, link, and run it by selecting Run from the Run menu. In this case it's the project that will run, not the source file you just opened.

Advantages of Multifile Programs

Now that we've shown how to generate a single .exe file from two source files, what have we accomplished? With a program this small, not much, but when programs start to get larger, with many functions and hundreds or thousands of lines of code, then breaking them up into separately compiled files starts to have some real advantages. Why?

One reason is that compile time is proportional to the size of the file being compiled, and usually, a programmer is only working on one part of a program at a time. To minimize compile time, a programmer compiles only those parts of a program that have been changed since the last compilation. The parts of the program that are already working and debugged aren't recompiled; they form a group of permanent object files. Each time a new version of the current file—the part of the program that is currently being written and debugged—is compiled, it can be linked with the previously compiled files. Using this approach, only a small part of the program need be compiled at any one time; the rest already exists in the form of .obj files.

If several programmers are working on a project, they can share previously developed object files. Because a module need not be recompiled after it is developed and debugged, there is less chance that it will be inadvertently modified or that two programmers will be using different versions of the same function.

A more important reason for using multifile programs is that it enables you to write well-structured, modular programs. We'll return to this topic in a moment. First we'll look at how functions in separately compiled files share data.

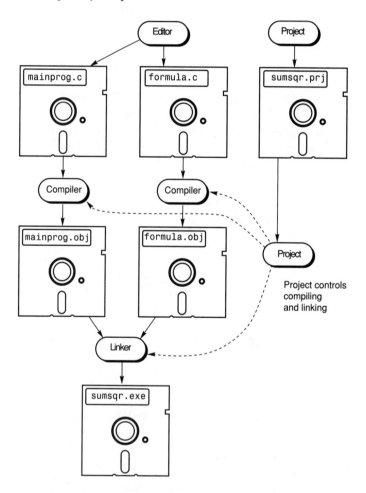

Figure 13.1. Separate compilation of functions.

External Variables and Separately Compiled Files

In our example, in which mainprog() and formula() were linked, two numbers were passed from mainprog() to formula() using arguments, and the result from formula() was returned to mainprog() with a return statement. This kind of data communication between separately compiled functions is easy to implement. It requires no special statement in either function, but suppose we wanted functions in separately compiled files to have access to the same external variable?

A function in file B can access an external variable defined in file A, provided that file B declares the variable using the keyword extern.

Define and Declare

What do we mean by *declare?* Let's pause briefly to make sure we understand the distinction between define and declare. When a variable is defined, it is given a data type (int or whatever) and a name. Also—this is the key point—memory is set aside for it; it is given physical existence. Defining variables is what we have done so far in this book.

However, a variable can also be declared, which specifies the name and type of the variable, but does not set aside any memory. A declaration is simply an announcement that a variable with a particular name and type exists. A variable can be defined only once, but it can be declared many times.

To show how this works, we'll rewrite the mainpro.c and formula.c files this way:

```
// mainpro2.c
// main program to test separate compilation
#include <stdio.h>   // for printf() and scanf()
int formula(void);   // prototype

int a, b;            // definition of external variables

void main(void)
    {
    int ans;

    printf("Type two integers: ");
    scanf("%d%d", &a, &b);
    ans = formula();
    printf("The sum of the squares is %d.", ans);
    }
```

This is similar to the mainprog.c file shown earlier, except that we've moved the variables a and b, which hold the two integers entered by the user, to a position outside the function, making them external variables. Now when mainpro2.c calls formula2, it no longer needs to pass any arguments.

Here's the revised formula.c file:

```
// formula2.c
// function returns sum of squares of arguments
```

```
// uses global variables for input

int formula(void)
    {
    extern int a, b;        // declaration of external variables

    return( a*a + b*b );
    }
```

Here you can see that we no longer need to declare any variables as formal arguments to the function but that we do declare the two variables a and b to be of type extern int. What does this mean?

The *extern* Keyword

As we saw in Chapter 12, "Memory," an external variable is visible in the file in which it's defined, from the point of the definition onward. But for an external variable to be visible in a file other than the one in which it's defined, it must be declared using the extern keyword. This keyword tells the compiler: "Somewhere in another file we've defined this variable. Don't worry that it isn't defined in this file but leave a message for the linker about it." When the linker gets this message from the compiler, it looks for the definition of the variable in all the other files. When the linker finds the definition, it makes the appropriate connections. In this example that means that references to a and b in the formula2.c file will be correctly linked to the definitions of a and b in the mainpro2.c file. Figure 13.2 shows an external variable declared in two different files.

To combine these two files, create a project file called sumsqr2.prj, whose contents are mainpro2.c and formula2.c. Then make your project as described above.

Figure 13.3 shows how the extern keyword is used to extend the visibility of external variables to a second file in a variety of ways. The visibility of automatic and other external variables is shown for comparison.

Storage Classes Revisited

Now that we're familiar with multifile programs, we can extend the discussion of storage classes presented in the last chapter. As we've seen, external variables are normally only visible in the file in which they're defined, but by using the keyword extern, they can be made visible in other files.

A variation on the external storage class is static external. This class uses the keyword static, but the variables are defined outside of any function. This class provides a way of hiding variables from other files. Why would you want to do that? One reason is that you might want to use a common variable name, like buffer, in a file you were writing, but you were afraid that someone else might use the same name in another file, causing conflict when the files were linked. Making your external variable static solves this problem by hiding the name within your file.

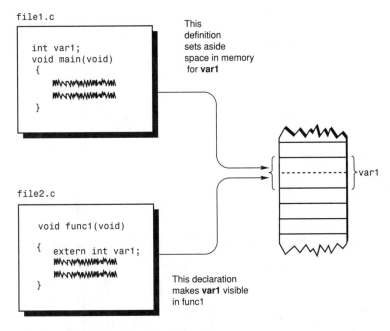

Figure 13.2. External variable declared in different files.

Table 13.1 summarizes the lifetime and visibility of all the storage classes; it's an extension of the table in the last chapter.

Table 13.1. Storage classes.

Keyword	Where Declared	Lifetime	Visibility
auto (or none)	Within function	Function	Function
register	Within function	Function	Function
static	Within function	Program	Function
(none)	External (defined)	Program	One file
extern	External (declared)	Program	Another file
static	External	Program	One file only

By using the correct storage class for each variable, the programmer can economize on memory requirements by restricting the lifetime of the variables and can help maintain a modular, well-structured program by allowing only those files and functions that need it access to a program's variables. The number of ways to vary the visibility and lifetime of variables is an important reason for C's popularity with developers of large programs and systems.

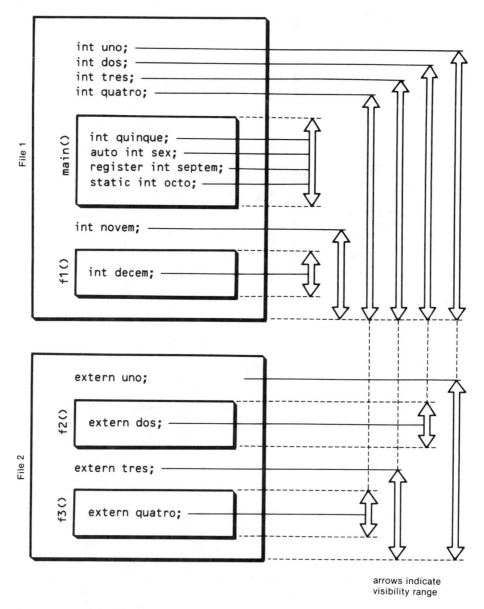

Figure 13.3. Visibility of variables.

Multifile Programs and Program Design

Perhaps the most important reason for using separate compilation is that it helps you to write well-structured, modular programs. Let's examine the relation of C to modular programming.

> Dividing a program into separately compiled files helps to organize it.

The Modular Approach

You probably know that it isn't considered good programming practice to write a large program as a single unit. Instead, the program should be broken down into smaller, easily understood parts. A C program usually consists of a main() function which calls several other functions to carry out the important tasks of the program. Each of these functions in turn calls other functions, and so on, until the functions being called are so simple that they need not make further calls.

Each function should carry out a single, clearly defined task. At the upper level, a function might calculate a payroll, for example. This function might call another function to calculate withholding tax. This function might call still another function to look up tax rates in a table. The important points are these: first, the role of a function should be clearly defined; and second, the function shouldn't be too large. Some programmers use a rule of thumb that no function should exceed one page in length, but of course many functions should be smaller.

How does separate compilation fit into modular programming? Using separate files gives us a different size building block to use when constructing programs. A program can be broken down into files and each file can be further broken down into functions, as shown in Figure 13.4.

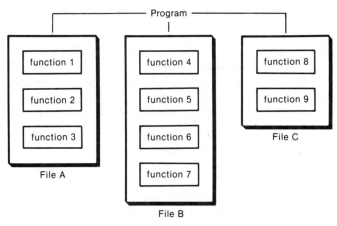

Figure 13.4. Separate compilation and modular programming.

As we've seen, it's possible to restrict variables, not only to one function but to one file as well. This ability to hide data from parts of the program is another aid to modular programming, since it is important that the variables in one part of a program not have access to variables in another part unless it is absolutely necessary.

Top-Down Design

C provides the tools for designing well-structured programs, but it's up to the programmer to use them effectively.

Any large program should be planned in considerable detail before a single line of code is written. Each function should be specified. The specification should include the purpose of the function, the arguments to be passed to it and returned by it, and the functions it will call. Most programmers recommend a "top down" approach. This means specifying the most general functions first and working down to the specific functions that perform low-level tasks, such as putting a character on the screen. In some situations, however, low-level functions must be planned concurrently with the higher-level ones.

Data storage should also be thoroughly specified before code is written. Special care must be given to large data items such as arrays and structures. External variables should be used only when absolutely necessary. As we have noted, external variables are vulnerable to being altered inadvertently by functions that shouldn't be accessing them. Care should be given to the naming of external variables so that their names don't conflict with other variables. Long, descriptive names are better than short ones. For instance, the external variable names a and b, used earlier in this chapter, wouldn't be appropriate in a large program; it would be too easy to confuse them with other variables. Names like SystemTemperature and GlobalErrorStatus are better. Automatic variables should be given meaningful names as well, but it's less critical.

The programmer must decide how to divide the program into different files. Major sections of the program, or those to be worked on by different programmers, might be placed in different files. A group of routines that can be used with other programs as well as the one under development might be placed in a library file to facilitate its use in different situations.

If a program is thoroughly specified before the code is written, it is possible to write almost any individual function before those functions that it calls, and that call it, are written. Dummy functions can supply it with data, so it can be tested and debugged independently from the other parts of the program. Once all the functions have been tested and shown to work independently, it's far more likely that they will work together in the final program.

Advanced Variables

Although we have been using variables all along in this book, there's still more to learn. Nothing we're going to say about variables in this section is essential to writing C programs, but the techniques can help simplify your programs and make them easier to understand. They're also used by many programmers, so you should be familiar with them.

The Enumerated Data Type

The enumerated type gives you the opportunity to invent your own data type and specify what values it can take on. This can help make listings more readable, which can be an advantage when a program gets complicated or when more than one programmer will be working on it. Using enumerated types can also help reduce programming errors.

Example of an Enumerated Type

Let's invent a data type called `birds` that has as its possible values `sparrow`, `robin`, `eagle`, and `egret`. Don't confuse these values with variable names; `sparrow`, for instance, has the same relationship to the variable `birds` that the value 12 has to an integer variable.

The keyword `enum` is used to specify an enumerated data type. The format of the `enum` definition is similar to that of a structure. Here's how the preceding example would be implemented:

```
enum birds                      // declare data type
   {
   sparrow,                     // specify values
   robin,
   eagle,
   egret
   };

enum birds thisbird, thatbird;     // define variables
```

The first statement declares the data type itself—type `enum birds`—and specifies its possible values, which are called *enumerators*. The second statement defines one or more variables—`thisbird` and `thatbird`—to be of this type. Now we can give values to these variables.

```
thisbird = sparrow;
thatbird = egret;
```

We can't use values that aren't in the original declaration. The expression

```
thisbird = magpie;
```

would cause an error.

Internally, the compiler treats enumerated variables as integers. Each value on the list of permissible values corresponds to an integer, starting with 0. Thus, in the birds example, `sparrow` is stored as 0, `robin` as 1, `eagle` as 2, and `egret` as 3.

The programmer can override this way of assigning numbers by initializing the enumerators to different integer values, as shown in this example:

```
enum birds                          // declare data type
   {
   sparrow = 10,                    // specify and
   robin = 20,                      // initialize values
   eagle = 30,
   egret = 40
   };
enum birds thisbird, thatbird;    // define variables
```

In some compilers, the following expressions are illegal, but they work in Turbo C++.

```
thisbird = 1;
num = eagle;
thisbird = 2*sparrow;
if(thisbird<thatbird)
if(thisbird<eagle)
magpie++;
```

In other words, you can treat enumerated variables much as if they were integers.

Using the Enumerated Data Type

Enumerated variables are usually used to clarify the operation of a program. For instance, if we need to use a group of employee categories in a payroll program, it makes the listing easier to read if we use values like management and clerical rather than integer values like 0 and 2.

Here's a short example that makes use of enumerated variables and also points out one of their weaknesses. (This approach would ordinarily be part of a larger program.)

```
// enums.c
// demonstrates enumerated variables
#include <stdio.h>             // for printf()
#include <string.h>            // for strcpy()

void main(void)
   {                           // declare new type and values
   enum empcats {management, research, clerical, sales};

   struct                      // declare structure
      {
      char name[30];
      float salary;
      enum empcats category;   // use new type for member
      } employee;

   strcpy(employee.name, "Benjamin Franklin");
   employee.salary = 118.50;
   employee.category = research;    // assign value to member

   printf("Name = %s\n", employee.name);
   printf("Salary = %6.2f\n", employee.salary);
   printf("Category = %d\n", employee.category);  // print it
```

```
if(employee.category==clerical)   // with relational operator
   printf("Employee category is clerical.\n");
else
   printf("Employee category is not clerical.\n");
}
```

We first declare the type enum empcats (for *employee categories*) and specify four possible values: management, research, clerical, and sales. A variable of type enum empcats, called category, is then defined in a structure. The structure, employee, has three variables containing employee information.

The program first assigns values to the variables in the structure. The expression

```
employee.category = research;
```

assigns the value research to the employee.category variable, which is of type enum empcats. This is much more informative to anyone reading the listing than a statement like

```
employee.category = 1;
```

The next part of the program shows the weakness of using enum variables: there is no way to use the enum values directly in input and output functions such as printf() and scanf(). Here's the output of the program:

```
C>enums
Name = Benjamin Franklin
Salary = 118.50
Category = 1
Employee category is not clerical.
```

The printf() function isn't sophisticated enough to perform the translation; the category is displayed as 1, not as research. Of course we could write a routine to display the correct enumerated values, using a table or a switch statement, but that would decrease the clarity of the program.

Even with this limitation, however, there are many situations in which enumerated data types are a useful addition to the C language.

Renaming Data Types with *typedef*

Let's look at another technique which, in some situations, can help clarify the source code for a C program. This is the typedef declaration, whose purpose is to redefine the name of an existing variable type. It can result in clearer programs because the name of a type can be shortened and made more meaningful.

For example, consider the following statement in which the type unsigned char is redefined to be of type byte:

```
typedef unsigned char byte;
```

Now we can declare variables of type `unsigned char` by writing

```
byte var1, var2;
```

instead of

```
unsigned char var1, var2;
```

Our assumption here is that `var1` and `var2` will be used in a context in which declaring them to be of type `byte` is more meaningful than declaring them to be of type `unsigned char`. This is often the case with programs that deal directly with the hardware, as we'll see in Chapter 15, "Hardware-Oriented C." Using the name `byte` suggests to anyone reading the program that the variables are used in one-byte registers.

> The `typedef` declaration causes the compiler to recognize a different name for a variable type.

While the increase in readability is probably not great in this example, it can be significant when the name of a particular type is long and unwieldy, as it often is with structure declarations.

For example, suppose we have the following structure declaration:

```
struct personnel        // define data structure
    {
    char name[30];      // agent name
    int agnumb;         // agent number
    };
```

Using `typedef`, we could declare a new name for the type `struct personnel`.

```
typedef struct personnel AGENT;   // new name for this type
```

Subsequent references to `struct personnel` can now be replaced with AGENT throughout the program, for example,

```
AGENT agent1;                // declare structure variable
AGENT agent2;                // declare another one
```

Actually, there's a shortcut way to do this. Rather than declaring the structure in one statement and `typedef`ing it to another name in a separate statement, you can combine them.

```
typedef struct personnel
    {
    char name[30];     // agent name
    int agnumb;        // agent number
    } AGENT;
```

This has the same effect.

The typedef declaration looks something like the #define directive, but it actually works in a different way. Using #define causes the preprocessor to perform a simple substitution of one phrase for another throughout the program. Using typedef, on the other hand, causes the compiler to actually recognize a new name for a specific type. This can make a difference when pointers are involved, as the following statement demonstrates:

```
typedef struct personnel *PTRAGENT;
```

This statement defines PTRAGENT to be a synonym for the data type pointer to struct personnel. Now we can use the declaration

```
PTRAGENT agent1, agent2;
```

which is equivalent to

```
struct personnel *agent1, *agent2;
```

A #define directive couldn't have been used in this situation, since the asterisks are repeated for each variable.

By reducing the length and apparent complexity of data types, typedef can help clarify source listings. It's commonly used, and the larger and more complex the program, the more likely you are to find it.

Type Conversion and Casting

You have probably noticed by this time that it's possible to mix data types in C expressions. Thus the following program will elicit no error message from the compiler (as a similar construction would in Pascal, for instance):

```
void main(void)
   {
   int intnum = 2;          // integer type
   float fltnum = 3.3;      // floating point type
   double ans;              // double precision type
   ans = intnum + fltnum;   // mixed expression is legal
   }
```

Although this works, there are dangers involved in mixing types. That's why some languages make such mixing illegal, but the philosophy in C is that it's better to give the programmer the freedom to mix types, which often leads to simpler code, than to try to keep the programmer out of trouble by flagging type mismatches as an error. Of course, with the freedom to mix data types comes the responsibility to make sure that such mixing isn't the result of a mistake, such as assuming a variable is of one type when it really is of another.

When data types are mixed in an expression, the compiler converts the variables to compatible types before carrying out the intended operation. In these conversions, variables of lower rank are converted to the rank of the higher-ranking operand. The ranking corresponds roughly to how many bytes each type occupies in memory. This is shown in Figure 13.5.

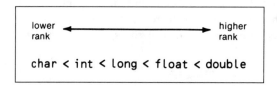

lower   ⟵————————————⟶   higher
rank   rank

`char < int < long < float < double`

Figure 13.5. Ranking of data types.

As an example, consider the following program fragment:

```
char ch;
int intnum;
long longnum;
float fltnum;
double doubnum;
int answer;
```

```
answer = (ch * intnum) +  (ch * longnum) + (fltnum * doubnum);
```

Before each operator is applied to the appropriate pair of variables, the variable with the lower rank is converted to the rank of the higher-ranking variable. This process is shown in Figure 13.6.

Promotion, or moving from a lower rank to a higher rank, usually doesn't cause problems. Demotion, however, can easily result in a loss of precision or even yield a completely incorrect result. Table 13.2 details what happens when demotion occurs.

Table 13.2. Data type demotion.

Demotion	Result
`int` to `char`	Low-order byte used
`long` to `char`	Low-order byte used
`float` to `char`	`float` converted to `long` and low-order byte used
`double` to `char`	`double` converted to `float`, `float` to `long`, and low-order byte used
`long` to `int`	Low-order word (two bytes) used
`float` to `int`	`float` converted to `long` and low-order word used

Demotion	Result
double to int	double converted to float, float to long, and low-order word used
float to long	Truncate at decimal point; if result is too large for long, it's undefined
double to long	Truncate at decimal point; if result is toolarge for long, it's undefined

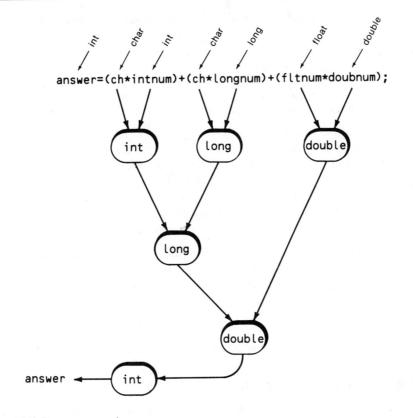

Figure 13.6. Data type conversion.

Generally, if a number is too large to fit into the type to which it is being demoted, its value will be corrupted. Some loss of precision can even occur in the promotion of long to float, although these two types both use four bytes.

The moral is, avoid type conversions unless there's a good reason for them and be especially careful when demoting a variable, because you may lose data. The compiler will warn you about this.

Typecasting

We've used typecasting before from time to time. Let's review the process. Typecasting provides a way to force a variable to be of a particular type. This overrides the normal type conversions we just described. The mechanism for typecasting is to precede the variable by the desired type, enclosed in parentheses. For example, in this statement

```
answer = (int)fltnum;
```

the typecast will cause the value of fltnum to be converted to an integer value before being assigned to answer, no matter what type fltnum is.

A common use for typecasting is in arithmetic expressions. Consider the following code fragment:

```
float flans;
int intvar1 = 6, intvar2 = 4;

flans = intvar1 / intvar2;                  // flans = 1.000000
flans = (float)intvar1 / (float)intvar2;    // flans = 1.500000
```

In the first assignment statement, the variable flans will be assigned the value 1.000000, an incorrect result. In the second it will be assigned a correct value of 1.500000. In the first statement integer division is used. The result is then converted to float, but the fractional part of the operation has been lost. In the second, the casts force floating point division to be used, which results in a correct answer of type float, which is then assigned to flans. Actually you only need to cast one of the operands, since the other will be promoted from int to float before the division is carried out.

Another use for typecasting is to ensure that a value passed to a function is of the type the function is expecting. For instance, suppose we have a variable intnum of type int and we want to take its square root. However, the square root function requires a variable of type long. We could use the expression

```
sqroot( (long)intnum )
```

and the effect would be to pass a variable of type long to the function.

The Addresses of Functions

Sooner or later in your study of C you'll run into a situation in which you use a pointer to a function to refer to the function. For example, you might want to place the addresses of a group of related functions in a table and jump to the appropriate function using its address. How do you execute a function whose name you don't know but whose address you do?

It turns out that the address of a function is the function name itself, without the parentheses. This is similar to using an array name without the brackets to denote the address of the array.

Here's a short example program that demonstrates assigning a function address to a pointer and then executing the function by referring to the pointer, rather than the function name.

```
// funcaddr.c
// shows use of function addresses
#include <stdio.h>          // for printf()
int func(int, int);         // prototype for function

void main(void)
   {
   int ans;
   int (*fptr)(int, int);   // declare pointer to function

   fptr = func;             // put function address in pointer
   ans = (*fptr)(3, 5);     // call function using pointer
   printf("ans=%d\n", ans);
   }

int func(int a1, int a2)    // function definition
   {
   return(a1 + a2);         // returns sum of arguments
   }
```

The function is very simple: it returns the sum of the two arguments passed to it. However, the definition of the pointer to the function isn't so simple.

```
int (*fptr)(int, int);  // declare pointer to function
```

This declaration is read "fptr is a pointer to a function taking two arguments of type int and returning type int." We'll discuss how such declarations are unraveled in the next section. Also note the statement that assigns the address of the function func to the pointer.

```
fptr = func;            // put function address in pointer
```

Now when we call (execute) the function, we refer to the contents of the pointer, *(fptr); we don't need to refer to the actual function name at all.

```
ans = (*fptr)(3, 5);    // call function using pointer
```

We pass the arguments in parentheses, just as if (*fptr) were a function name.

Unraveling Complex C Definitions

The declaration of the pointer fptr in the funcaddr.c program may not be immediately obvious. Earlier we said that C definitions (or declarations) can be unraveled by working from right to left. It's true that the data type (and possibly the storage class and other modifiers) on the left are the last elements to be translated, but that's only part of the story. Let's see how complex C definitions can be understood.

Suppose you have a definition like this:

```
int *aptr[];
```

How do you know whether this is a pointer to an array or an array of pointers? It turns out that C definitions use strict precedence rules, in fact the same precedence rules as those used for C operators. Here's what you need to know: brackets [], denoting arrays, and parentheses (), denoting functions, have a higher priority than the indirection operator *.

The previous expression therefore is interpreted as "aptr is an array of pointers to int." You translate "array" first because it has a higher priority than *, meaning "pointer to."

As with other C operators, parentheses can be used to override the normal precedence. Thus the declaration

```
int (*agptr)[];
```

means "aptr is a pointer to an array of int." You translate what's inside the parentheses first.

The situation is similar for pointers to functions. The definition

```
void *func();
```

means "func is a function returning a pointer to void." Again, the parentheses denoting a function have higher priority than the indirection operator. For example,

```
void (*func)();
```

means "func is a pointer to a function returning type void." This is the usage in the funcaddr.c program.

Things can get more complicated, but the same rules apply. Start with the variable name, check for parentheses and brackets to see whether it's a function or array, then check for asterisks to see whether it's a pointer. However, always interpret things inside parentheses first.

How about

```
int **arr[];
```

Here, arr is an array of pointers to pointers to int. On the other hand, in

```
int *(*func)();
```

func is a pointer to a function returning a pointer to int.

One more,

```
float *(*arr[])();
```

means arr is an array of pointers to functions returning pointers to float.

With these rules you should be able to decipher most C definitions.

Miscellaneous Topics

Finally we come to a group of topics so unrelated to each other that all we can do is call them *miscellaneous*. No matter how unrelated they are, however, they're useful members of your bag of programmer's tricks.

Conditional Compilation

A situation may arise where it is useful to compile parts of a source file under some circumstances but not others. For example, suppose you want to measure the speed of a section of your program. You insert statements that will print start and stop messages at the beginning and end of the crucial section of code. This way, you can time the execution of the code with a stopwatch (assuming the program is slow enough). However, you only want these messages to be printed when you're testing the program, not when it's running normally.

> The directive #ifdef, along with other directives, permits sections of a program to be compiled in some circumstances but not others.

You could simply insert statements to print the start and stop messages each time you wanted to test the program and then remove them and recompile the program when testing was completed. However, if there are a lot of such messages in a program, or they're complex, this could be inconvenient. A better way is to use a combination of preprocessor directives: #define, #ifdef, and #endif. With this system, you can keep your test statements in the listing at all times, but activate them only when you wish—by changing one #define statement at the beginning of the program. You'll still need to recompile your program to activate or deactivate the test mode, but the rewriting of code is minimized.

Here's an example:

```
// define.c
// demonstrates #ifdef, #else, #endif
#include <stdio.h>                  // for printf()
#define TIMER                       // remove if no test

void main(void)
   {
   int j, k;

   #ifdef TIMER                     // executed only if
      printf("Starting test\n");    // TIMER is defined
   #endif

   for(j=0; j<3000; j++)            // main part of program
```

```
        for(k=0; k<3000; k++)          //     lengthy loop
          ;

    #ifdef TIMER                        // executed only if
        printf("Ending test\n");        //    timer is defined
    #else                               // executed only if
        printf("Done\n");               //    timer is not defined
    #endif
    }
```

In this program we want to test how long a timing loop, consisting of two nested for loops, takes to execute. We insert a statement to print Starting test at the beginning of the loop and another to print Ending test at the end of the loop. By enclosing these statements in the #ifdef #endef combination, we ensure that they will be executed only if the directive #define TIMER is executed. If the program is compiled and executed as shown above, it will print

```
C>define
Starting test
Ending test
```

with a delay of several seconds between the two messages. (You may need to change the loop limits if your computer runs too fast or too slow.) If we remove the #define TIMER directive, or make it into a comment like this,

```
// #define TIMER
```

our "test" statements won't be executed. The program will run but without the test messages, printing only Done at the end.

The *#ifdef* and *#endif* Directives

The #ifdef TIMER directive tells the compiler to compile the statements that follow it only if TIMER is #defined. The #endif indicates that this conditional part of the compilation is over and that the compiler can go back to the normal mode of compiling all statements. Thus, #define acts as a switch, and #ifdef and #endif act as delimiters for the section of code switched by #define.

The *#else* Directive

In the define.c program, if TIMER isn't defined, another message (Done) will be printed when the loop is over. This is arranged with the #else directive. It fulfills a role analogous to the else in a normal C if...else statement: whatever follows it is compiled only when the matching #define directive has not been executed.

Alternative Syntax

Instead of the `#ifdef` directive, you may see

```
#if defined(TIMER)
```

which has the same effect but is a more clumsy construction.

Other Uses for Conditional Compilation

There are many other circumstances in which conditional compilation might prove useful. Any sort of debugging statements can be compiled conditionally, say when a constant DEBUG is defined. That means you can leave debugging statements in a production version of your program.

Another handy technique is temporarily to incapacitate part of a program by surrounding it with an `#ifdef` `#endif` pair. This can help to isolate an offending section of code during the debugging process.

You might need two versions of a program: one to run under MS-DOS, for example, and one to run in Microsoft Windows. Instead of creating two complete source files, you could group those statements in the program that varied from one version to another and enclose them by appropriate `#ifdef`, `#else`, and `#endif` statements. Then, inserting a single statement at the beginning of the program, such as

```
#define WINDOWS
```

would convert the program from the MS-DOS version to the Windows version.

The *#ifndef* Directive

The reverse of the `#ifdef` directive is `#ifndef`, which tells the compiler to compile the code that follows it only if a constant is not defined. You'll find this directive used frequently in the Turbo C++ include files to avoid including another file more than once. Here's the idea:

```
#ifndef NULL
#include <null.h>
#endif
```

The constant NULL may be needed in several include files (stdio.h and stdlib.h, for example). It could be defined in both files, but suppose the programmer includes both files in his program? It's bad form to `#define` something more than once, so NULL is defined in the _null.h file, and any file that wants to use this definition includes this file conditionally; if NULL is already defined, the file isn't included, thus avoiding multiple definitions.

The *#undef* Directive

Another related preprocessor directive is `#undef`, which cancels the action of a previous `#define` directive. For example, if at some point in your program you insert the directive

```
#define TEST
```

and later in the program you insert

```
#undef TEST
```

then at this point TEST will no longer be defined. You can use this directive to make conditional compilation specific to certain sections of the program.

Another use for #undef is to "turn off" macros that you have previously defined with a #define directive. This might be useful in a large and complex program where the same name is used for different macros in different parts of the program, and you want to avoid the possibility of conflict. Turning off a macro with #undef makes your macro a "local" macro, known only in a limited section of the program.

Labels and the *goto* Statement

We have deliberately put off a discussion of the goto statement until this late date in the book. There is seldom a legitimate reason for goto, and its use is one of the leading reasons that programs become unreliable, unreadable, and hard to debug. Yet many programmers (especially those accustomed to BASIC) find goto seductive. In a difficult programming situation it seems so easy to throw in a goto to get where you want to go. Almost always, however, there is a more elegant construction using an if or switch statement or a loop. Such constructions are far easier to understand than goto statements. A goto statement can cause control to end up almost anywhere in the program, for reasons that are often hard to unravel.

We trust that, by getting this far without using a goto, we have provided proof that, at least in most cases, its use can be avoided. If you turned to this page from the index, desperate to use a goto, try hard to employ another approach.

For completeness, however, here's how goto is used. Consider the following program fragment:

```
- - -
if(temp > max)
  goto scramble;             // goto label
- - -
scramble:                    // note colon after label
  printf("Emergency! Meltdown imminent");
- - -
```

The goto statement transfers control to the label scramble, causing the printf() statement to be executed immediately after the goto. The goto must specify a label, and the label must exist or a compiler error will result. Because the compiler doesn't care about whitespace, the label, which must be followed by a colon, can be on a separate line or on the same line as another statement.

```
scramble: printf("Emergency!");
```

Labels are used only with `goto` statements. Other statements on the same line as a label will operate as if the label didn't exist.

Identifiers and Naming Classes

So far we've named variables and functions without saying too much about what the restrictions are on such names. In this section we'll mention these restrictions and then go on to show how the same name can be used, under some circumstances, for different elements in a program.

The name given to variables, functions, and various other programming elements is *identifiers*. Allowable characters in identifiers are the letters from A to Z (in both upper- and lowercase), the digits from 0 to 9, and the underscore character (_). The identifier must begin with a letter or an underscore. C distinguishes between upper- and lowercase, so the compiler will treat

`BigVar`

as a different variable than

`bigvar`

Identifiers can have any number of characters but only the first 32 will be recognized by the Turbo C++ compiler. (It isn't clear why anyone would want to use more than 32 characters anyway. For those of us who wrote programs in early versions of BASIC, which only recognized variable names of 2 characters, 32 is the ultimate in luxury.)

As in most computer languages, identifiers in C can't be the same as certain keywords used in the language itself. Fortunately, there are fewer keywords in C than in many languages. In Turbo C++ these keywords fall into two classes. Common keywords used for defining data include `auto`, `char`, `const`, `double`, `enum`, `extern`, `far`, `float`, `huge`, `int`, `long`, `near`, `register`, `short`, `signed`, `static`, `struct`, `typedef`, `union`, `unsigned`, `void`, and `volatile`. Those used for program control include `asm`, `break`, `case`, `cdecl`, `continue`, `default`, `do`, `else`, `for`, `goto`, `if`, `interrupt`, `pascal`, `return`, `sizeof`, `switch`, and `while`. There are a few others; a complete list can be found in the *Turbo C++ User's Guide*.

Naming Classes

The various program elements named with identifiers, such as functions and variables, are divided into categories called *naming classes*. Within a naming class, each item must have a distinct identifier. (In other words, you can't have two variables with the same name.) However, you can use the same name for different elements if the elements are in different naming classes. The five naming classes are described next.

1. Variables and Functions

A variable can't have the same name as a function in which it is visible. A function's formal parameters also fall into this naming class, so they can't have the same name as any of the variables used in the function. (However, as we mentioned in the discussion of storage classes, several variables within a function can have the same name if they're in separate blocks.) Enumeration constants are also part of this naming class; you can't use the same name for an enumeration constant and for a variable (unless they have different visibilities).

2. Tags

As you may recall, structures, unions, and classes of enumeration variables are named with a tag. For instance, in the structure definition

```
struct ex1
    {
    int intnum;
    float fltnum;
    } svar1;
```

the identifier ex1 is the tag, while svar1 is a variable name. Tags form their own naming class.

3. Members

Members of structures and unions, such as intnum and fltnum in our example, form a separate naming class. They must be distinct from other members of the same structure or union, but they can be the same as other identifiers in the program.

In the following example the identifier apple is used in three different places. Because each use is a different naming class, the compiler will find this perfectly acceptable.

```
struct apple        // 'apple' names a tag
    {
    int apple;      // 'apple' names a member
    float pear;     // can't use 'apple' here
    } apple;        // 'apple' names a variable
```

Of course, using the same name for different program elements may be confusing to humans, even if the compiler can handle it. Use discretion when taking advantage of this capability.

4. Statement Labels

Statement labels (used with goto) form a distinct naming class. Within a function, statement labels must all have distinct names, but these can be the same as those of variables or members of other naming classes.

5. *typedef* Names

The names of types defined with typedef are treated by the compiler as if they were keywords. Thus, once a name has been defined in a typedef statement, no other program elements, no matter what naming class they're in, can use the same identifier.

Of course, none of the rules about naming classes alter the rules about visibility. If the visibility of two program elements is different, then they can have the same identifier, even if they're in the same naming class (for example, two automatic variables in different functions).

Summary

In this chapter we've covered a variety of more or less unrelated topics. We examined separate compilation of program files and discussed how external variables can be shared between such files using the extern keyword. Separate compilation can speed up program development and help with good program design.

We examined enumerated data types, which permit the programmer to define a new data type and a set of values for it; and typedef, which lets the programmer give a new name to an existing data type. We've also seen how variables are converted automatically from one type to another and how this conversion can be overridden with typecasting. We examined conditional compilation, which uses (among others) the #define, #ifdef, #else, and #endif preprocessor directives to permit selective compiling of various parts of a source file.

We looked at labels and their use with the goto statement. Finally we examined the conventions used for naming variables and other elements in C programs and saw how these names or identifiers apply to different categories of program elements called *naming classes*.

Questions

1. Separate compilation of source files can be advantageous because

    a. It speeds compilation, since not all files need be recompiled
    b. It allows automatic variables defined in multiple files
    c. It speeds the linking process
    d. It allows a large program to be broken up into more manageable pieces

2. For a variable to be visible in a file other than the one where it's defined, it must be
   _____ using the _____ keyword.

3. A variable definition differs from a declaration in that

    a. The declaration sets aside storage space

    b. The declaration specifies the name and type of the variable

    c. The definition sets aside storage space

    d. The definition specifies the name and type of the variable

4. True or false: the keyword `static` applied to an external variable causes the variable to have the lifetime of the program rather than the function.

5. A statement labeling a variable with the `extern` keyword causes the variable to be visible within

    a. A block

    b. A function

    c. A file

    d. Many files

6. True or false: an enumerated data type uses names for variable values.

7. To restrict the visibility of a variable to one file, it must be of type _____ _____.

8. In an enumerated data type, the programmer can define

    a. Whether the new type will be integer or floating point

    b. The number of bytes used by variables of the new type

    c. The values of the new type

    d. Many types of the same storage class

9. If `fish` has already been defined as an enumerated data type, what statement will define the variable `gamefish` to be of this type?

10. The `typedef` declaration is used to

    a. Declare a new data type

    b. Perform a #define-style substitution of one identifier for another

    c. Define a new data type

    d. Give a new name to a data type

11. Identifiers are the _____ given to variables and other elements in a program.

12. A naming class is

    a. A category of variables of the same data type

    b. A lecture describing how to name variables

    c. A category in which identifiers must be distinct

    d. The category of functions and variables

13. True or false: the same identifier can be used for a structure and a member of that

structure.

14. The rank of a variable in data conversions is roughly indicated by the number of _____ of _____ used by the character.

15. A typecast is used to
    a. Force a value to be of a particular data type
    b. Define a new data type
    c. Rename an old data type
    d. Make a copy of a variable type

16. True or false: you can use parentheses to override the precedence of the operators in a variable definition.

17. Conditional compilation
    a. Checks what microprocessor you're using before compiling
    b. Uses C-language assignment statements
    c. Can be used to compile parts of a program but not others
    d. Depends on whether a constant is #defined or not

18. Write a statement that causes program control to go immediately to a program line labeled george.

19. The goto statement should be used
    a. Routinely
    b. Seldom
    c. Never
    d. To exit from the program

20. Identifiers in Turbo C++ can have up to _____ characters in their names.

Exercises

Due to the many small topics discussed in this chapter, there are no exercises.

Application Example

- Multiple source code files
- Header files for definitions
- File management
- Graphic user interface (GUI)
- Self-documenting code

It's one thing to understand the various elements of C syntax, but it's quite another to put this knowledge to work in a serious program. This chapter presents a real, working application so that you can see how all the pieces fit together.

This application, called PHONE, is a "phone book" or "address book" program. It lets the user create a database consisting of the names, addresses, and phone numbers of a large number of people. The database is stored in a disk file. New data can be added, deleted, or edited, and the database can be searched for particular names. It's easy to modify the program to store any kind of data you want, such as lists of movies in your cassette library, coins in your coin collection, sales contacts, recipes, or whatever.

PHONE runs in character mode. It makes extensive use of the text-mode Turbo C graphics functions. To run it you'll need a DOS system, preferably with a color monitor. A mouse isn't necessary.

The Graphic User Interface

PHONE uses a character-mode graphic user interface (GUI). That is, the program uses pull-down menus and dialog boxes to communicate with the user, much as Turbo C++ itself does. We call this part of the program the MiniGui. It's like a junior version of an operating environment like Microsoft Windows. Of course it isn't nearly as sophisticated as Windows, but it's compact and easy to learn, both for the user and the programmer. To keep the listing as short as possible we've restrained our natural desire to add more features to the GUI. It's a stripped down user interface, but if you want to add a feature or change the way it works, you need only modify the source code and recompile.

The application is constructed in such a way that it's easy to extract the MiniGui and use it in your own applications. Perhaps you have an old-style application, in which the user and the program communicate by typing at each other, like this:

```
Type 'N' to open a new file,
    'O' to open an existing file, or 'E' to exit: O
Enter the name of the file to be opened: SAMPLE.DAT
Enter the starting number of the entries to be displayed: 25
```

and so on. Using the MiniGui, you can transform such a program into a modern-looking application where the user chooses what to do from a menu and imparts information to the program using dialog boxes. This approach is far more user friendly, because it works the same way as Windows and many other character-based applications that imitate the Windows interface.

Using the Application

When you first start the PHONE application, you'll see the screen shown in Figure 14.1.

There's a menu bar at the top of the screen with the menu names File, Entry, and Search. There's also an information bar at the bottom of the screen. This bar tells you what to do next. Here it says `[Alt]+[First letter] activates menu`. That means you can select one of the menus by pressing the Alt key and the first letter of the menu name. Almost everything that happens in the program is the result of the user making a menu selection.

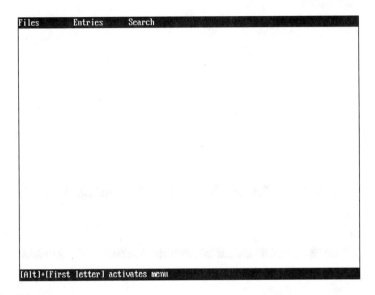

Figure 14.1. The screen on startup.

Managing Menus

Select the File menu by pressing the Alt and F key combination. You'll see the menu shown in Figure 14.2.

Initially the top item, New, is highlighted. You can move the highlight up and down the menu with the Up Arrow and Down Arrow keys. You can also move to other menus with the Left Arrow and Right Arrow keys. To execute the menu item that's selected (that is, highlighted), press the Enter key. To make the menus go away, press the Esc key.

Creating a New File

To begin, you must create a file in which to store your data. Select New from the File menu. (We can abbreviate this File/New.) A dialog box appears on the screen. Into the green text field in this box, type the name of the file you want to create, as shown in Figure 14.3.

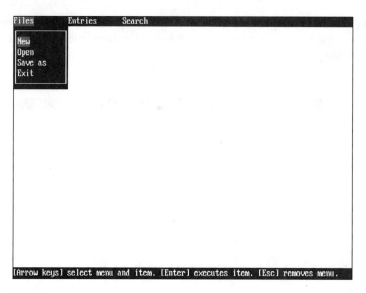

Figure 14.2. The File menu.

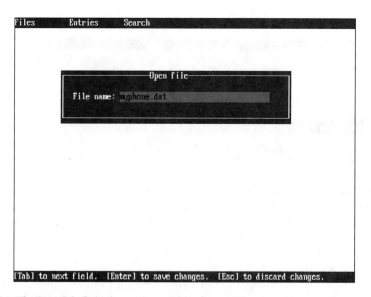

Figure 14.3. The Open File dialog box.

Use any name and extension you want. Press the Enter key when you're done. A message box appears that says Use Entries/Add to add entries. This is a reminder that to add information to the database, you need to select the Add item from the Entries menu, as we'll describe next. To make the message box go away, press the Enter key (actually any other key will work).

Entering Names and Numbers

Once a file has been created, you can add names, addresses, and telephone numbers to it. Select Add from the Entries menu, which is shown in Figure 14.4.

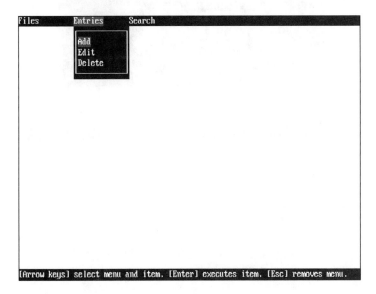

Figure 14.4. The Entries menu.

A dialog box will appear. Type the data into the appropriate fields. You can backspace over mistakes. Use the Tab key to move to the next field. The Enter Data dialog box, with the fields filled in with a sample entry, is shown in Figure 14.5.

When you're done filling in all the fields, press the Enter key. If you decide you don't want to save the information you've entered, press the Esc key. The information line at the bottom of the screen will remind you of these options whenever a dialog box is on the screen.

The information you type into the Enter Data dialog box is called an *entry*. It corresponds to one card in your Rolodex. When it's written to the disk it will be a *record*. You can leave out any part of the information in the entry except the last name. However, the last name is necessary because it's used to position the entry alphabetically in the screen display.

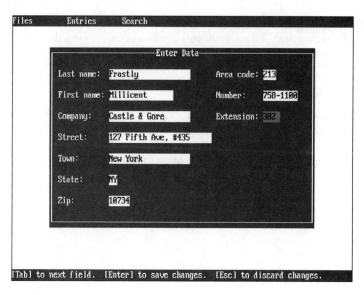

Figure 14.5. The Enter Data dialog box.

The Screen Display

When you've typed data into the Enter Data dialog box and pressed the Enter key, the dialog box will disappear and you'll see the name and telephone number (but not the address) displayed on the screen. Figure 14.6 shows the screen display when many entries have been made.

Last names are on the left, followed by first names and the area code, phone number, and extension (if any). The entries are arranged alphabetically by last name. This order is obtained automatically: whenever you create a new entry, the program inserts it at the correct location in the file.

One of the entries in the screen display (initially the top line) is highlighted. The Up Arrow and Down Arrow keys move the highlight up and down one line, and the PgUp and PgDn keys move the display up and down one screen. If you press the Enter key, the information for the highlighted entry will be displayed in the Enter Data dialog box, shown in Figure 14.5, where it can be edited. This allows you to change the information in any entry. You can bring up this same dialog box for the highlighted entry by selecting Edit from the Entries menu. You can delete the selected entry by selecting Delete from the Entries menu.

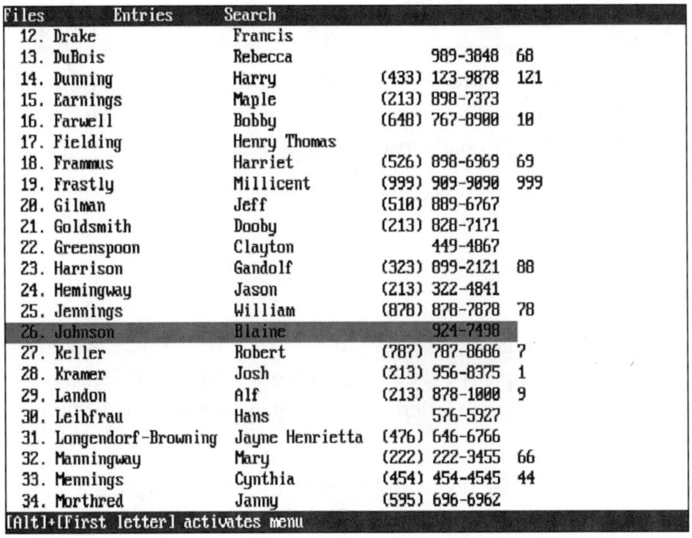

```
Files       Entries      Search
   12. Drake             Francis
   13. DuBois            Rebecca                     989-3848   68
   14. Dunning           Harry            (433) 123-9878   121
   15. Earnings          Maple            (213) 898-7373
   16. Farwell           Bobby            (648) 767-8988   18
   17. Fielding          Henry Thomas
   18. Frammus           Harriet          (526) 898-6969   69
   19. Frastly           Millicent        (999) 989-9098   999
   20. Gilman            Jeff             (510) 889-6767
   21. Goldsmith         Dooby            (213) 828-7171
   22. Greenspoon        Clayton                     449-4867
   23. Harrison          Gandolf          (323) 899-2121   88
   24. Hemingway         Jason            (213) 322-4841
   25. Jennings          William          (878) 878-7878   78
   26. Johnson           Blaine                      924-7498
   27. Keller            Robert           (787) 787-8686   7
   28. Kramer            Josh             (213) 956-8375   1
   29. Landon            Alf              (213) 878-1088   9
   30. Leibfrau          Hans                        576-5927
   31. Longendorf-Browning  Jayne Henrietta  (476) 646-6766
   32. Manningway        Mary             (222) 222-3455   66
   33. Mennings          Cynthia          (454) 454-4545   44
   34. Morthred          Janny            (595) 696-6962
[Alt]+[First letter] activates menu
```

Figure 14.6. The screen display.

Searching

You can search for entries by last name, first name, or company name by selecting the appropriate item from the Search menu, which is shown in Figure 14.7.

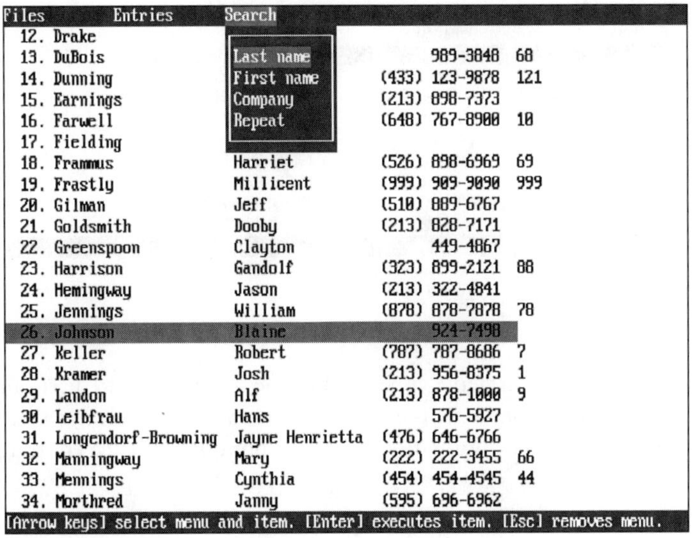

```
Files       Entries      Search
   12. Drake
   13. DuBois         ┌───────────┐        989-3848   68
   14. Dunning        │ Last name │ (433) 123-9878   121
   15. Earnings       │ First name│ (213) 898-7373
   16. Farwell        │ Company   │ (648) 767-8988   18
   17. Fielding       │ Repeat    │
   18. Frammus        └───────────┘Harriet    (526) 898-6969   69
   19. Frastly           Millicent        (999) 989-9098   999
   20. Gilman            Jeff             (510) 889-6767
   21. Goldsmith         Dooby            (213) 828-7171
   22. Greenspoon        Clayton                     449-4867
   23. Harrison          Gandolf          (323) 899-2121   88
   24. Hemingway         Jason            (213) 322-4841
   25. Jennings          William          (878) 878-7878   78
   26. Johnson           Blaine                      924-7498
   27. Keller            Robert           (787) 787-8686   7
   28. Kramer            Josh             (213) 956-8375   1
   29. Landon            Alf              (213) 878-1088   9
   30. Leibfrau          Hans                        576-5927
   31. Longendorf-Browning  Jayne Henrietta  (476) 646-6766
   32. Manningway        Mary             (222) 222-3455   66
   33. Mennings          Cynthia          (454) 454-4545   44
   34. Morthred          Janny            (595) 696-6962
[Arrow keys] select menu and item. [Enter] executes item. [Esc] removes menu.
```

Figure 14.7. The Search menu.

Selecting one of these items brings up a dialog box into which you can type the text to be searched for. If the text is found, its entry is highlighted in the screen display. If you want to search for a second occurrence of the same string, select Repeat from the Search menu. If there's no match, a message box informs you of that fact. (Searching for the last name provides a quick way to find an entry in a long file.)

You don't need to enter a complete name; the search will succeed even if you enter part of a name.

Message Boxes

There are two kinds of message boxes: OK and Yes/No. The OK box is used simply to tell the user something. An example is the box that appears with the message No records to search if you try to search for text when no file is open. Pressing the Enter key (or any key) makes an OK box go away.

A Yes/No box gives the user a choice. An example is shown in Figure 14.8.

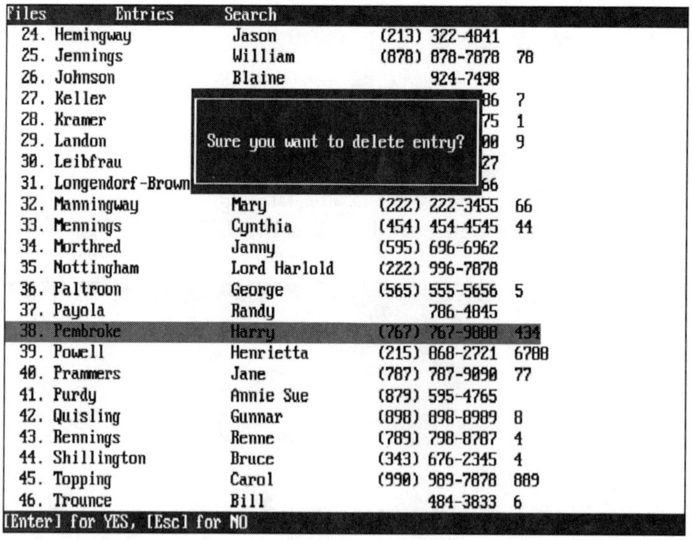

```
Files          Entries       Search
   24. Hemingway      Jason           (213) 322-4841
   25. Jennings       William         (878) 878-7878    78
   26. Johnson        Blaine          924-7498
   27. Keller                                         86  7
   28. Kramer                                         75  1
   29. Landon         Sure you want to delete entry?  88  9
   30. Leibfrau                                       27
   31. Longendorf-Brown                               66
   32. Manningway     Mary            (222) 222-3455   66
   33. Mennings       Cynthia         (454) 454-4545   44
   34. Morthred       Janny           (595) 696-6962
   35. Nottingham     Lord Harlold    (222) 996-7878
   36. Paltroon       George          (565) 555-5656   5
   37. Payola         Randy           786-4845
   38. Pembroke       Harry           (767) 767-9888  434
   39. Powell         Henrietta       (215) 868-2721  6788
   40. Prammers       Jane            (787) 787-9898   77
   41. Purdy          Annie Sue       (879) 595-4765
   42. Quisling       Gunnar          (898) 898-8989   8
   43. Rennings       Renne           (789) 798-8787   4
   44. Shillington    Bruce           (343) 676-2345   4
   45. Topping        Carol           (990) 989-7878  889
   46. Trounce        Bill            484-3833   6
[Enter] for YES, [Esc] for NO
```

Figure 14.8. A Yes/No message box.

The message shown in this figure appears when the user is about to delete an entry. Having to answer the question in the box decreases the chances of deleting a name by mistake. As can be seen in the information line at the bottom of the screen, you press the Enter key for yes and the Esc key for no. Message boxes are easy to program; invoking one requires only a single line of code.

Disk File Used for Storage

Various approaches can be used to store the data in a program such as PHONE. For example, all the data on a disk file could be read into memory when a file was opened and written back to disk when the file was closed. This would make some operations, like searching, faster, because the disk wouldn't need to be accessed. However, the memory in DOS is limited to 640K, minus however much is used by the application itself, other programs, DOS, TSRs, and so on. Each record in PHONE requires 128 bytes, so you would be limited to fewer (perhaps many fewer) than about 400 entries if the entire file were stored in memory. (Using extended or expanded memory is another possibility, but the techniques involved are rather complex and beyond the scope of this book.)

Another problem with storing large amounts of data in memory is that a data object larger than one segment requires far or huge pointers. Many C library functions use only near pointers and cannot address large objects. For example, you can't read or write more than 64K from a disk file with a single function call. The result is a lot of copying of data from near to far storage areas and back again. This gets complicated.

In PHONE we take a different approach. No data is stored in memory; it's all kept in the disk file. When you add an entry, it's written to the file immediately, and when you delete an entry, it's deleted from the disk immediately. Every time you change the screen display, new records are read from disk and displayed. A file is opened when you select New or Open and closed when you exit from the program, open a new file, or save a file under a different name (by selecting Save as).

With this disk-based approach the amount of data you can store in a file is limited only by the amount of unused space on your hard disk. Also, the programming is simplified considerably. The potential disadvantage is that certain operations, like deleting a record from a large file, may run more slowly than they would have with the all-data-in-memory approach.

Organization of the Application Files

As we've noted in earlier chapters, a large application is usually divided into several files. In PHONE there are two source files: minigui.c and phone.c. The minigui.c file handles all the aspects of the MiniGui. It creates drop-down menus and dialog boxes and handles all user input. The phone.c file handles the data: it reads and writes to the disk and displays a screen-full of entries. To obtain input from the user, it calls routines in minigui.c.

In many situations a software developer buys a library of user-interface functions from a third-party developer and combines these with custom-written code to produce a finished program. You might think of minigui.c as representing the third-party user-interface library, which can be adapted to many different programs, and phone.c as the custom code for a specific application.

The application part of the program, phone.c, needs to know some of the same definitions used in minigui.c, such as the declarations for menus and dialog boxes; so one header file, called minigui.h, is included in both minigui.c and phone.h. This second header file, phone.h, is used for items that only phone.c needs to know and is included only in phone.c. Figure 14.9 shows the arrangement of these files.

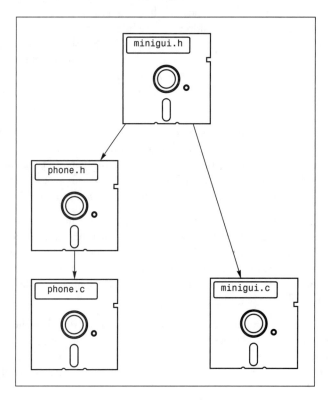

Figure 14.9. File arrangement.

Because there is more than one source file, you'll need to use Borland's Project feature to build the program. Simply add the two source files, phone.c and minigui.c, to the project as described in Chapter 13.

Major Functions

A brief introduction to some of the functions in phone.c will help you find your way around the program.

The main() function is located in phone.c, and of course this is where control is transferred when the program starts. However, main() does only one thing: it calls make_menus() in the minigui.c file. It passes as arguments a description of the menu arrangement in the form of several arrays, which are defined in phone.h.

The make_menus() function is the key to the operation of the MiniGui. It creates and displays the menu system and waits for the user to select a menu item. It monitors the arrow keys so that it knows what menu and what item are selected, and maintains two global variables, hpos (the menu number) and vpos (the item number), to record this information.

Once a menu item is selected, make_menus() calls a function in phone.c, menu_action(), which decides what action to take. The make_menus() function receives other kinds of user input as well. In addition to selecting a menu item, the user may press the Enter key to edit a particular entry in the address list or keys like Up Arrow and PgUp to view different entries on the display.

The make_menus() function can be in one of two states: menus active or not active. This determines how keystrokes are interpreted. For example, if menus are active (dropped down and displayed), pressing the Enter key causes the activity associated with the highlighted menu item to be executed. If menus are not active, pressing the Enter key causes the highlighted data entry to be displayed in a dialog box, where it can be edited. A flag in this function, menus_active, keeps track of the state.

In addition to menu_action(), the make_menus() function calls several other functions to carry out various requests from the user. These functions are all in the phone.c file, because they are more closely connected with the data than with the GUI. There are four such functions.

- menu_action() is called when the user selects a menu item. It calls a specific function to carry out the action associated with the item.

- enter_action() is called when the user presses the Enter key (and menus aren't active). It carries out a single, specific action; in phone.c it brings up the Enter Data dialog box.

- display_data() may be called at any time to display or redisplay data. This happens when, for example, a menu has temporarily hidden part of the display and is then removed.

- adjust_display() is called when the user presses the Up Arrow, PgUp, Down Arrow, or PgDn keys. It changes the display by reading one or more new records from the open file.

These functions are called *callback functions* because they're located in the application but called from the MiniGui, which you can think of as a small operating system. This is the reverse of the usual situation in DOS, where applications call functions in the operating system, hence the name.

As we've seen, when the user selects a menu item, make_menus() calls the menu_action(_) function in the phone.c file, using the item name as an argument. The menu_action() function then calls an appropriate function in phone.c to carry out the action. These functions are

- `new_file()` creates a new file.

- `open_file()` opens an existing file.

- `save_as()` saves a file under a different name.

- `exit_prog()` causes PHONE to terminate.

- `add_data()` adds an entry to the file.

- `edit_data()` edits an existing entry.

- `delete_data()` deletes an entry.

- `search_text()` finds a specified text string.

The `enter_action()` function, called by `make_menus()` when menus aren't active and the user presses the Enter key, also calls `edit_data()`. (As you have seen, this is equivalent to selecting the Entries/Edit menu item for the highlighted data record.)

All these functions in phone.c may call functions in minigui.c to carry out specific GUI-related tasks. The most common functions in MiniGui called from phone.c are `make_dialog()` to get user input from a dialog box, `make_message()` to tell the user something or to get a yes/no answer to a question, `erase_screen()`, which erases all but the menu bar and the information bar, and `gui_exit()`, which is called to clean up the screen and exit the program. Figure 14.10 summarizes the relationships among these various functions.

Not shown on this diagram are several functions used internally by phone.c and minigui.c. Here are the internal functions in phone.c:

- `delete_rec()` deletes a record from the disk file.

- `insert_rec()` inserts a new record into the disk file.

- `insert_display()` reads data from the disk file to insert into the display.

Internal functions in minigui.c mostly display particular aspects of the GUI (such as menus) and receive input from the user. They are

- `clear_dialog()` clears the entry fields in a dialog box.

- `display_bar()` displays the menu bar at the top of the screen.

- `display_info()` displays the information line at the bottom of the screen.

- `display_menu()` displays a drop-down menu.

- `draw_box()` draws a box surrounded by a line; it's used for menus, dialog boxes, and message boxes.

- `draw_field()` draws a text field (a line of colored blanks) into which the user can enter data.

- get_code() reads the keystroke typed by the user and does a little translating so that the keystroke can be more easily interpreted by other routines.

- get_field() gets the input the user typed into a text field.

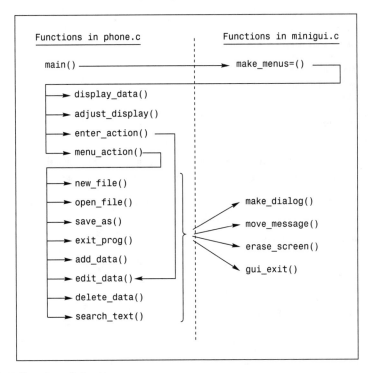

Figure 14.10. Function relationships.

Data Structures

The data is stored in the disk file as a series of structures of type record. This is the important data storage structure in the program. Here's its declaration from the phone.h file:

```
struct record
    {
    char lastname[MAXLAST+1];
    char firstname[MAXFIRST+1];
    char company[MAXCO+1];
    char street[MAXST+1];
    char town[MAXTOWN+1];
    char state[MAXSTATE+1];
    char zip[MAXZIP+1];
    char areacode[MAXAREA+1];
```

```
char phone[MAXPHONE+1];
char ext[MAXEXT+1];
};
```

The #defines necessary for the array dimensions are also in phone.h.

```
#define MAXLAST   19
#define MAXFIRST  15
#define MAXCO     19
#define MAXST     24
#define MAXTOWN   19
#define MAXSTATE   2
#define MAXZIP     5
#define MAXAREA    3
#define MAXPHONE   8
#define MAXEXT     4
```

All the members of this structure are strings. The #defines specify the length of each string. The strings are made one character longer to hold the terminating \0.

An array of record structures, called screen, is used to hold the information placed on the screen by the display_data() function.

```
struct record screen[MAX_LINES];
```

Each element of the array represents one line on the screen. Thus

```
screen[3]
```

is the entry on the fourth line (since the first element is 0), and

```
screen[3].lastname
```

is the name (like *Smith*) displayed on that line. As the user presses Up Arrow and similar keys, the contents of the screen array changes as a new set of records is read in from the disk.

Using MiniGui For Other Programs

You can use the MiniGui part of the program to add a visual interface to any character-based program. To do this, you start with the minigui.c and minigui.h files. Then you create a file to hold your application; let's say it's called myapp.c. You'll probably also want a header file, myapp.h, for your definitions and includes. Make sure to #include minigui.h in this file, since you'll need access to various definitions from it.

Menus

Next you need to create the menu structure for your program. This takes five statements. You need to specify the number of drop-down menus, the names of the menus (File,

Search, and so on), the ASCII codes produced when the first letter of the menu name is typed with the Alt key pressed, the names of the menu items, and the number of items on each menu. Here's how that looks in the PHONE example:

```
//////////////////////////////////////////////////////////////
// constants and definitions for menu structure
//////////////////////////////////////////////////////////////
#define NUM_MENUS 3    // number of menus

                // menu names
char *menu_name[NUM_MENUS] = { "Files", "Entries", "Search" };

                // ASCII codes for [Alt]+[First-letter]
int menu_name_alt[NUM_MENUS] = { 33, 18, 31 };  // Alt-F, etc.

                // menu item names
char *menu_item[NUM_MENUS][MAX_ITEMS] =  {
    { "New", "Open", "Save as", "Exit"},
    { "Add", "Edit", "Delete" },
    { "Last name", "First name", "Company", "Repeat" } };

                // number of items per menu
int num_items[NUM_MENUS] = { 4, 3, 4 };
```

Then, to display the menus, you call the make_menus() function with these variables as arguments:

```
make_menus(NUM_MENUS, menu_name, menu_name_alt,
           menu_items, num_items);
```

Callback Functions

You must install certain functions in your application so that the MiniGui can call them. These are the four callback functions mentioned earlier: menu_action(), enter_action(), display_data(), and adjust_display(). You can see how these functions work and how to integrate them into your program by studying the listings.

Message Boxes

You don't need to define any structures or arrays to create a message box. The first parameter to the function make_message() is the type, which can be OK or YES_NO; and the second parameter is the string to be displayed. The return value is True if the user pressed the Enter key for yes, or False if the user pressed the Esc key for no.

Dialog Boxes

To create a dialog box, you must define a structure and an array. The structure, of type dialog, specifies the dialog box location, dimensions, and title. The array holds a number of structures of type `text_field`, each of which specifies the dimensions and location of a text input field. The `dialog` and `text_field` structures are defined in minigui.h; that's one reason it must be included in your application file. All the locations are measured in rows and columns starting at (1,1) in the upper-right corner of the screen. Here are the declarations for `dialog` and `text_field`:

```
// dialog box structure needed by application as well as minigui
struct dialog              // dialog box
    {
    int left;              // top of dialog
    int top;               // left of dialog
    int width;             // width of dialog
    int height;            // height of dialog
    char title[TITLE_LENGTH+1];  // dialog title
    int number_fields;     // number of fields
    };

// text field structure needed by application as well as minigui
struct text_field
    {
    int xp;                // starting position of prompt
    int yp;
    char prompt[PROMPT_LENGTH+1];  // prompt string
    int size;              // length of input area
    int xi;                // starting position of input area
    char input[FIELD_LENGTH+1];    // input area
    };
```

Here are the definitions needed for the Enter Data dialog box, which is the most complicated one in the program, with 10 entry fields. These definitions are found in the phone.h file.

```
/////////////////////////////////////////////////////////////
// constants and definitions for entrydialog dialog box
/////////////////////////////////////////////////////////////
#define ENTRY_FIELDS 10     // number of fields in entry box
#define MAXLAST   19        // length of fields in entry box
#define MAXFIRST  15
#define MAXCO     19
#define MAXST     24
#define MAXTOWN   19
#define MAXSTATE  2
#define MAXZIP    5
#define MAXAREA   3
#define MAXPHONE  8
#define MAXEXT    4

// dialog dimensions for entrydialog
struct dialog entrydialog = { 10, 4, 62, 17,
                              "Enter Data", ENTRY_FIELDS };
```

```
// entry fields for entrydialog
struct text_field entryfields[ENTRY_FIELDS] =
    { { 12, 6,   "Last name:",   MAXLAST,  24 },
      { 12, 8,   "First name:",  MAXFIRST, 24 },
      { 12, 10,  "Company:",     MAXCO,    24 },
      { 12, 12,  "Street:",      MAXST,    24 },
      { 12, 14,  "Town:",        MAXTOWN,  24 },
      { 12, 16,  "State:",       MAXSTATE, 24 },
      { 12, 18,  "Zip:",         MAXZIP,   24 },
      { 49, 6,   "Area code:",   MAXAREA,  60 },
      { 49, 8,   "Number:",      MAXPHONE, 60 },
      { 49, 10,  "Extension:",   MAXEXT,   60 }  };
```

You can adapt these definitions to create any size dialog and any arrangement of text fields you like. You'll need to figure out the dimensions and location of the dialog box and each text field, which takes a little trial and error, but this isn't too hard in a character-based system.

To create a dialog box, you simply call make_dialog(), using the appropriate dialog structure and array of text field structures as arguments. When this function returns, the text fields, such as

entryfields[3].input

will have been filled in by the user. Your program can then use this data as necessary.

Listing Format

The balance of this chapter is devoted to the actual program listings. A long program can be rather intimidating, especially if you didn't write it yourself. Take it slow. Go through the listing, identifying the different functions. You won't understand it all immediately, but with a little study it will start to make sense.

Notice how these listings look. Most companies and software-development organizations specify various aspects of how source files should be formatted. This makes it easier for one programmer to read the work of other programmers.

In particular, each function is preceded by a comment section that describes the function's purpose and other details of its operation. In our listings we include four parts in this comment section: the function declarator (name, arguments and return type), the function's purpose, inputs to the function, and outputs from it. Most organizations use a variation of these items. Some use a more detailed pseudo-code description of a function's operation; others add a revision history for the function, including who wrote and modified it. Ideally the text in the comment area should give the reader a good idea what the function does and how it interacts with the rest of the application.

Within each file, the functions are arranged alphabetically. This makes it easier to find the function you're looking for. Other arrangements are sometimes used (such as putting the important functions first), but the alphabetical approach is the most common for large programs.

The phone.h File

This file contains includes, definitions, and prototypes that are used in phone.c. In addition there are definitions of the menu system and all the dialog boxes used in the program. These definitions will be used as arguments to make_menus() and make_dialog(). The declaration for the record structure also goes in this file, because all file-related activities take place in phone.c.

```
///////////////////////////////////////////////////////////////
// FILE:     phone.h
// PURPOSE: Provides header files, function prototypes, and
//          definitions of menus and dialog boxes
//          needed by the phone.c file
///////////////////////////////////////////////////////////////

// header files for phone.c
#include <stdio.h>       // for sprintf(), etc.
#include <stdlib.h>      // for min(), etc.
#include <fcntl.h>       // for open()
#include <sys\stat.h>    // for open()
#include <io.h>          // for chsize()
#include "minigui.h"     // for dialog and text_field defs

// prototypes for functions in phone.c
void add_data(void);
void delete_data(void);
void delete_rec(int rec_num);
void edit_data(void);
void exit_prog(void);
void insert_display(int locat, int num_recs, int rec_number);
void insert_rec(struct record *prec);
void new_file(void);
void open_file(void);
void save_as(void);
void search_text(int);

///////////////////////////////////////////////////////////////
// constants and definitions for menu structure
///////////////////////////////////////////////////////////////
#define NUM_MENUS 3    // number of menus

                       // menu names
char *menu_name[NUM_MENUS] = { "Files", "Entries", "Search" };

                       // ASCII codes for [Alt]+[First-letter]
int menu_name_alt[NUM_MENUS] = { 33, 18, 31 };
```

```
                        // menu item names
char *menu_item[NUM_MENUS][MAX_ITEMS] =  {
        { "New", "Open", "Save as", "Exit"},
        { "Add", "Edit", "Delete" },
        { "Last name", "First name", "Company", "Repeat" } };

                        // number of items per menu
int num_items[NUM_MENUS] = { 4, 3, 4 };

////////////////////////////////////////////////////////////////
// constants and definitions for entrydialog dialog box
////////////////////////////////////////////////////////////////
#define ENTRY_FIELDS 10     // number of fields in entry box
#define MAXLAST   19        // length of fields in entry box
#define MAXFIRST 15
#define MAXCO     19
#define MAXST     24
#define MAXTOWN   19
#define MAXSTATE   2
#define MAXZIP     5
#define MAXAREA    3
#define MAXPHONE   8
#define MAXEXT     4

// dialog dimensions for entrydialog
struct dialog entrydialog = { 10, 4, 62, 17,
                                "Enter Data", ENTRY_FIELDS };
// entry fields for entrydialog
struct text_field entryfields[ENTRY_FIELDS] =
        { { 12, 6,  "Last name:",  MAXLAST, 24 },
          { 12, 8,  "First name:", MAXFIRST, 24 },
          { 12, 10, "Company:",    MAXCO,    24 },
          { 12, 12, "Street:",     MAXST,    24 },
          { 12, 14, "Town:",       MAXTOWN,  24 },
          { 12, 16, "State:",      MAXSTATE, 24 },
          { 12, 18, "Zip:",        MAXZIP,   24 },
          { 49, 6,  "Area code:",  MAXAREA,  60 },
          { 49, 8,  "Number:",     MAXPHONE, 60 },
          { 49, 10, "Extension:",  MAXEXT,   60 }
        };

////////////////////////////////////////////////////////////////
// constants and definitions for open dialog box
////////////////////////////////////////////////////////////////
#define OPEN_FIELDS 1     // number of fields in open box
#define MAXOPEN 34        // length of field in open box

// dialog dimensions for opendialog
struct dialog opendialog = { 12, 6, 54, 5,
                                "Open file", OPEN_FIELDS };
// entry fields for opendialog
struct text_field openfields[OPEN_FIELDS] =
                { { 15, 8,  "File name:",  MAXOPEN+1, 26 }, };
```

```
///////////////////////////////////////////////////////////////
// constants and definitions for Save As dialog box
///////////////////////////////////////////////////////////////
#define SAVEAS_FIELDS 1        // number of fields in saveas box
#define MAXSAVEAS 34           // length of field in saveas box

// dialog dimensions for saveas box
struct dialog saveasdialog = { 12, 6, 54, 5,
                              "Save file as", SAVEAS_FIELDS };
// entry fields for saveas dialog
struct text_field saveasfields[SAVEAS_FIELDS] =
                { { 15, 8,  "File name:",  MAXSAVEAS+1, 26 }, };


///////////////////////////////////////////////////////////////
// constants and definitions for Search dialog box
///////////////////////////////////////////////////////////////
#define SEARCH_AGAIN   -1      // search type codes
#define SEARCH_FIRST   1       // first name
#define SEARCH_LAST    2       // last name
#define SEARCH_COMPANY 3       // company name
#define SEARCH_FIELDS  1       // number of fields in search box
#define MAXSEARCH      24      // length of field in search box

// dialog dimensions for searchdialog
struct dialog searchdialog = { 23, 6, 34, 5,
                              "Search for", SEARCH_FIELDS };
// entry fields for searchdialog
struct text_field searchfields[SAVEAS_FIELDS] =
                { { 25, 8,  "Text:",  MAXSEARCH, 31 }, };


///////////////////////////////////////////////////////////////
// structure for one record to be stored in file
///////////////////////////////////////////////////////////////
#define RECSIZE sizeof(struct record)
#define TOP     -1        // insertion points for new recs
#define BOTTOM -2
// a record contains 128 bytes
struct record
    {
    char lastname[MAXLAST+1];
    char firstname[MAXFIRST+1];
    char company[MAXCO+1];
    char street[MAXST+1];
    char town[MAXTOWN+1];
    char state[MAXSTATE+1];
    char zip[MAXZIP+1];
    char areacode[MAXAREA+1];
    char phone[MAXPHONE+1];
    char ext[MAXEXT+1];
    };

/////////////// end of phone.h file ///////////////////////////
```

The phone.c File

Functions in this file carry out the real work of the program, such as opening a data file, getting data from the user and adding a record to the file, and displaying data on the screen. As we noted, these functions are mostly called from the menu_action() and enter_action() functions, which are in turn called from the make_menus() function in minigui.c. Some functions in phone.c, such as insert_rec() and delete_rec(), are called internally.

Some important global variables keep track of the program's state.

● total_records is the number of records (entries) in the open file.

● top_record is the number of the record that appears at the top of the screen display.

● select_rec is the number of the record that is highlighted (selected) on the screen display.

● file_name is a string that holds the name of the current open file.

● file_open is True if a file is open, False otherwise.

We've already mentioned screen, which is an array of structures of type record for holding the records to be displayed. The comments in the listing explain other aspects of the program, including function arguments and local variables.

```c
///////////////////////////////////////////////////////////////
// FILE:     phone.c
// PURPOSE: Creates and manages address list.
//          Calls functions in minigui.c file for user interface.
//          Handles file activities and screen display.
///////////////////////////////////////////////////////////////

#include "phone.h"          // for menu and dialog defs

// global variables
struct record screen[MAX_LINES]; // for screen display
int total_records = 0;      // number of records in memory
int top_record = 0;         // record at top of screen
int select_rec = 0;         // highlighted record
FILE *fptr;                 // master file pointer
char file_name[MAX_COLS];   // name of open file
int file_open = FALSE;      // TRUE if file is open

///////////////////////////////////////////////////////////////
// FUNCTION: void main(void)
// PURPOSE:  Program entry point
//           Calls MINIGUI to display menus and wait for user
```

```
//              to select menu item
// INPUTS:   none
// OUTPUTS:  none
////////////////////////////////////////////////////////////////
void main(void)
    {
    // give control to minigui, send it menu details
    make_menus(NUM_MENUS, menu_name, menu_name_alt,
             menu_item, num_items);
    }


////////////////////////////////////////////////////////////////
// FUNCTION: void add_data(void)
// PURPOSE:  Gets data from user for one record (entry)
// INPUTS:   Calls 'entrydialog' to get user input
// OUPUTS:   Calls insert_rec to insert record in file in
//           alphabetical position by last name
////////////////////////////////////////////////////////////////
void add_data(void)
    {
    struct record a_rec;  // temporary record for data entry

    if( !file_open )     // file not open
        {
        make_message(OK, "No file open.  Use New or Open.");
        return;
        }
                        // clear dialog text fields
    clear_dialog(entrydialog, entryfields);
                        // do dialog box
    if( !make_dialog(entrydialog, ENTRY_FIELDS, entryfields) )
        return;         // user pressed [Esc]

    // move data from dialog into utility record
    memset(&a_rec, '\0', RECSIZE);
    strncpy(a_rec.lastname,  entryfields[0].input, MAXLAST);
    strncpy(a_rec.firstname, entryfields[1].input, MAXFIRST);
    strncpy(a_rec.company,   entryfields[2].input, MAXCO);
    strncpy(a_rec.street,    entryfields[3].input, MAXST);
    strncpy(a_rec.town,      entryfields[4].input, MAXTOWN);
    strncpy(a_rec.state,     entryfields[5].input, MAXSTATE);
    strncpy(a_rec.zip,       entryfields[6].input, MAXZIP);
    strncpy(a_rec.areacode,  entryfields[7].input, MAXAREA);
    strncpy(a_rec.phone,     entryfields[8].input, MAXPHONE);
    strncpy(a_rec.ext,       entryfields[9].input, MAXEXT);

    insert_rec(&a_rec); // insert record alphabetically into file
    display_data();
    return;
    }  // end add_data()
```

```
/////////////////////////////////////////////////////////////
// FUNCTION:   void adjust_display(char key)
// PURPOSE:    Changes which entries are displayed, and which
//             entry is highlighted on screen
//             Note: this function is called from MINIGUI
// INPUTS:     Argument 'key' is code of key pressed by user
//             (Can be UpArrow, DnArrow, PgUp, PgDn)
// OUTPUTS:    Calls insert_display() to add records to display
//             Changes top_record and select_rec
/////////////////////////////////////////////////////////////
void adjust_display(char key)
    {
    int num_recs;

    switch(key)
        {
        case U_ARRO:            // move selection up one line
           if(select_rec == top_record && top_record > 0)
              {
              --top_record; --select_rec;
              insert_display(TOP, 1, select_rec);
              }
           else if(select_rec > 0 && select_rec > top_record)
              --select_rec;
           break;

        case D_ARRO:            // move selection down one line
           if(select_rec == top_record+MAX_LINES-1 &&
              select_rec < total_records-1)
              {
              ++top_record; ++select_rec;
              insert_display(BOTTOM, 1, select_rec);
              }
           else if(select_rec < total_records-1 &&
                   select_rec < top_record+MAX_LINES-1)
              ++select_rec;
           break;

        case PGUP:              // move display down one screen
           if(total_records<=MAX_LINES || top_record<=MAX_LINES)
              top_record = select_rec = 0;
           else  // room to move up
              top_record = select_rec = top_record-MAX_LINES;
           num_recs = min(total_records, MAX_LINES);
           insert_display(TOP, num_recs, top_record);
           break;

        case PGDN:              // move display up one screen
           if(total_records <= MAX_LINES)
              top_record = 0;
           else if(top_record >= total_records - 2*MAX_LINES)
```

```
              top_record =  total_records-MAX_LINES;
          else
              top_record = top_record+MAX_LINES;
          select_rec = min(total_records-1, top_record+MAX_LINES-1);
          insert_display(TOP, min(total_records, MAX_LINES),
                          top_record);
          break;
      }  // end switch
   }  // end adjust_display

////////////////////////////////////////////////////////////////
// FUNCTION:   void delete_data(void)
// PURPOSE:    Deletes record from file and display
// INPUTS:     Record number to be deleted is 'select_rec'
// OUTPUTS:    Calls delete_record() to delete record from file,
//             then refills 'screen' using new file data
////////////////////////////////////////////////////////////////
void delete_data(void)
   {
   int num_recs;

   if( total_records == 0 )
      { make_message(OK, "No records to delete"); return; }
   if( !make_message(YES_NO, "Sure you want to delete entry?") )
      return;
   delete_rec(select_rec);          // delete from file

   // redisplay screen
   memset( screen, '\0', RECSIZE );  // clear screen
   if(total_records > 0)             // if any records left
      {
      // read file into screen, starting at top_record
      fseek(fptr, top_record*RECSIZE, SEEK_SET);
      num_recs = min(total_records-top_record, MAX_LINES);
      if( fread(screen, RECSIZE,
               num_recs, fptr) != num_recs )
         { make_message(OK, "Can't read record"); return; }
      }
   display_data();
   }

////////////////////////////////////////////////////////////////
// FUNCTION: void delete_rec(int rec_num)
// PURPOSE:  Deletes record from file
// INPUTS:   Argument 'rec_num' -- record number to delete
// OUTPUTS:  Records are rearranged to write over deleted record
//           and file is shortened by one record
////////////////////////////////////////////////////////////////
void delete_rec(int rec_num)
   {
   int j;
   struct record a_rec;
```

```
    int handle;

    if(rec_num==total_records-1)      // if at last record
       --select_rec;                  // select previous rec
    else  // not at last record, must move records
       {
       for(j=rec_num; j<total_records-1; j++)
          {
          fseek(fptr, (j+1)*RECSIZE, SEEK_SET); // read at j+1
          if( fread(&a_rec, RECSIZE, 1, fptr) != 1)
             { make_message(OK, "Can't read file"); return; }
          fseek(fptr, j*RECSIZE, SEEK_SET);      // write at j
          if( fwrite(&a_rec, RECSIZE, 1, fptr) != 1 )
             { make_message(OK, "Can't write file"); return; }
          }  // end for
       }  // end else not at last record

    // reduce file size by one record
    --total_records;
    fclose(fptr);   // switch from stream I/O to handle I/O
    handle = open(file_name, O_WRONLY, O_BINARY);
    chsize(handle, RECSIZE*total_records);  // change size
    close(handle);  // switch back to stream I/O
    if( (fptr=fopen(file_name, "r+b")) == NULL )
       { make_message(OK, "Can't open file"); return; }
    }

/////////////////////////////////////////////////////////////
// FUNCTION:  void display_data(void)
// PURPOSE:   Displays names and phone numbers
//            Note: this function may be called from MINIGUI
// INPUTS:    Data comes from 'screen' array of structures
// OUTPUTS:   The entries are displayed on the screen
/////////////////////////////////////////////////////////////
void display_data(void)
   {
   char format_str[MAX_COLS];
   char print_str[MAX_COLS];
   int j;                 // loop index
   int n;                 // record number of each line

   erase_screen();        // clean the screen
   if(total_records==0)   // if no records, no display
      return;

   // display the lines of data that will fit on the screen
   textcolor(WHITE);
   textbackground(BLUE);
   n = top_record;              // start with top

   // display one line for each rec, names and numbers only
   for(j=0; j<MAX_LINES && n<total_records; j++)
```

```
    {
    if( strlen(screen[j].areacode) == 0 )   // no area code
       strcpy(format_str, "%4d. %-20s %-16s  %3s   %8s   %s");
    else                                      // area code
       strcpy(format_str, "%4d. %-20s %-16s (%3s) %8s   %s");
    sprintf(print_str, format_str,
            n+1, screen[j].lastname, screen[j].firstname,
                 screen[j].areacode, screen[j].phone,
                 screen[j].ext);
    gotoxy(1, j+2);
    if(n++ == select_rec)        // if it's selected record
       {
       textbackground(GREEN);
       cputs(print_str);          // highlight it
       textbackground(BLUE);
       }
    else                          // otherwise it's a
       cputs(print_str);          // normal record
    }  // end for
  }  // end display_data()

//////////////////////////////////////////////////////////////////
// FUNCTION: void edit_data(void)
// PURPOSE:  Allows user to edit (or simply view) one record
//               by pressing [Enter] when line is highlighted
//               or selecting Edit from Entry menu
// INPUTS:   The record number to edit is 'select_rec'
//               Old data from 'screen' is copied into dialog
//               Calls MINIGUI w/ entrydialog to get data from user
// OUTPUTS:  The edited record is written to 'screen' and file
//////////////////////////////////////////////////////////////////
void edit_data(void)
  {
  char old_name[MAX_COLS];
  int j;

  if(total_records==0)
     { make_message(OK, "No data to edit"); return; }

  j = select_rec - top_record; // record number in screen

                       // move data from screen into dialog
  strncpy(entryfields[0].input, screen[j].lastname, MAXLAST);
  strncpy(entryfields[1].input, screen[j].firstname, MAXFIRST);
  strncpy(entryfields[2].input, screen[j].company, MAXCO);
  strncpy(entryfields[3].input, screen[j].street, MAXST);
  strncpy(entryfields[4].input, screen[j].town, MAXTOWN);
  strncpy(entryfields[5].input, screen[j].state, MAXSTATE);
  strncpy(entryfields[6].input, screen[j].zip, MAXZIP);
  strncpy(entryfields[7].input, screen[j].areacode, MAXAREA);
  strncpy(entryfields[8].input, screen[j].phone, MAXPHONE);
  strncpy(entryfields[9].input, screen[j].ext, MAXEXT);
```

```
                    // save old last name
    strncpy(old_name, screen[j].lastname, MAXLAST);
                        // do dialog box
    if( !make_dialog(entrydialog, ENTRY_FIELDS, entryfields) )
        return;         // user pushed [Esc]

                        // move data from dialog into screen
    memset( &screen[j], '\0', RECSIZE );  // clear screen
    strncpy(screen[j].lastname,  entryfields[0].input, MAXLAST);
    strncpy(screen[j].firstname, entryfields[1].input, MAXFIRST);
    strncpy(screen[j].company,   entryfields[2].input, MAXCO);
    strncpy(screen[j].street,    entryfields[3].input, MAXST);
    strncpy(screen[j].town,      entryfields[4].input, MAXTOWN);
    strncpy(screen[j].state,     entryfields[5].input, MAXSTATE);
    strncpy(screen[j].zip,       entryfields[6].input, MAXZIP);
    strncpy(screen[j].areacode,  entryfields[7].input, MAXAREA);
    strncpy(screen[j].phone,     entryfields[8].input, MAXPHONE);
    strncpy(screen[j].ext,       entryfields[9].input, MAXEXT);

    // if last name has not changed, rewrite in same place
    if( strcmp(old_name, screen[j].lastname) == 0 )
        {               // write record from screen /to file
        fseek(fptr, (long)select_rec*RECSIZE, SEEK_SET);
        if( fwrite(&screen[j], RECSIZE, 1, fptr) != 1 )
            { make_message(OK, "Can't write record"); return; }
        }
    else  // last name is changed, so reinsert record
        {
        delete_rec(select_rec);  // delete selected record
        insert_rec(&screen[j]);  // insert record from screen
        }
    display_data();             // redisplay screen data
    } // end edit_data()

////////////////////////////////////////////////////////////
// FUNCTION: void enter_action(void)
// PURPOSE:  Causes user pressing [Enter] to initiate editing
// INPUTS:   Called from MINIGUI when user presses [Enter]
//           (if menus are not active)
// OUTPUTS:  Calls enter_data so user can edit selected record
////////////////////////////////////////////////////////////
void enter_action(void)
    {
    edit_data();     // edit the selected record
    }


////////////////////////////////////////////////////////////
// FUNCTION: void exit_prog(void)
// PURPOSE:  Exit procedure for application
// INPUTS:   none
// OUTPUTS:  Calls gui_exit in MINIGUI to clean up display,
//           closes data file
////////////////////////////////////////////////////////////
```

```
void exit_prog(void)
   {
   if(file_open)
      fclose(fptr);      // close the file
   gui_exit();           // call exit routine in minigui
   }

/////////////////////////////////////////////////////////////////////
// FUNCTION: void insert_display(int location, int num_recs,
//                                 int rec_number)
// PURPOSE:  Read records from disk, insert in screen display
//           Can read one record or many records
// INPUTS:   Argument 'location' is place in display for
//               insertion: can be TOP or BOTTOM (if 1 record)
//           Argument 'num_recs' is how many records to read
//           Argument 'rec_number' is record number in file
//               to start reading from
// OUTPUTS:  Array of structures 'screen' is filled with data
//           (Does not actually display the data)
/////////////////////////////////////////////////////////////////////
void insert_display(int location, int num_recs, int rec_number)
   {
   struct record *locptr;

   if(num_recs==1)  // move one line up or down
      {
      if(location==TOP)
         {                                // move data down
         memmove(&screen[1], &screen[0],
               RECSIZE*(MAX_LINES-1));
         locptr = &screen[0];        // insert at top
         }
      else  // location is BOTTOM
         {                                // move data up
         memmove(&screen[0], &screen[1],
               RECSIZE*(MAX_LINES-1));
         locptr = &screen[MAX_LINES-1]; // insert at bottom
         }                                // move file pntr to record
      }  // end if (one line move)
   else  // multi-line move, so read in all new data from disk
      {
      memset( screen, '\0', sizeof(screen) );
      locptr = &screen[0];
      }
   fseek(fptr, rec_number*RECSIZE, SEEK_SET);
   if( fread( locptr, RECSIZE, num_recs, fptr) != num_recs)
      { make_message(OK, "Can't read record"); return; }
   }  // end insert_display()
```

```
/////////////////////////////////////////////////////////////////
// FUNCTION: void insert_rec(struct record *prec)
// PURPOSE:  Inserts record into disk file, choosing location
//           so last names are ordered alphabetically
// INPUTS:   Argument 'prec' is pointer to record to be inserted
// OUTPUTS:  Record is inserted into file, file size increases
//           Also reads new data from file into 'screen' array
//           and displays data with new record at top of screen
/////////////////////////////////////////////////////////////////
void insert_rec(struct record *prec)
   {
   int j, rec_num;
   struct record a_rec;

   // find rec_num, the place to insert new record
   if(total_records == 0)  // if no records yet,
      rec_num = 0;         // insert at start of file
   else  // many records
      {
      // find place to insert new record in file
      fseek(fptr, 0L, SEEK_SET);        // go to beginning
      for(j=0; j<total_records; j++)    // for each record
         {
         // read record
         if( fread( &a_rec, RECSIZE, 1, fptr) != 1 )
            { make_message(OK, "Can't read record"); return; }

         // compare last names in record and dialog
         if( stricmp(a_rec.lastname, prec->lastname) > 0 )
            break;  // leave loop when record is larger
         }
      rec_num = j;
      }  // end else many records

   // now that we know insertion point, do actual insertion
   if(rec_num==total_records)      // if at last record
      {
      fseek(fptr, 0L, SEEK_END);  // go to end, write record
      if( fwrite(prec, RECSIZE, 1, fptr) != 1 )
         { make_message(OK, "Can't write file"); return; }
      }
   else  // not at last record, must move later records forward
      {
      for(j=total_records; j>rec_num; j--)      // move recs
         {
         fseek(fptr, (j-1)*RECSIZE, SEEK_SET); // read at j-1
         if( fread(&a_rec, RECSIZE, 1, fptr) != 1)
            { make_message(OK, "Can't read file"); return; }
         fseek(fptr, j*RECSIZE, SEEK_SET);      // write at j
         if( fwrite(&a_rec, RECSIZE, 1, fptr) != 1 )
            { make_message(OK, "Can't write file"); return; }
         }
```

```
        // write new record at rec_num
        fseek(fptr, rec_num*RECSIZE, SEEK_SET);
        if( fwrite(prec, RECSIZE, 1, fptr) != 1 )
            { make_message(OK, "Can't write file"); return; }
        }  // end else not at last record

    // set select_rec and top_record and display data
    select_rec = rec_num;        // inserted record is selected
    // if insertion point is off screen, move to top of screen
    if(j<top_record || j-top_record >= MAX_LINES)
        top_record = rec_num;

    // read file into screen, starting at top_record
    memset(screen, '\0', RECSIZE);
    fseek(fptr, top_record*RECSIZE, SEEK_SET);
    rec_num = min(total_records+1-top_record, MAX_LINES);
    if( fread(screen, RECSIZE, rec_num, fptr) != rec_num )
        { make_message(OK, "Can't read record"); return; }
    ++total_records;      // one more record in file
    }  // end insert_rec

////////////////////////////////////////////////////////////////
// FUNCTION: void menu_action(char *item_name)
// PURPOSE:  Translates menu selections into action
// INPUTS:   Called by MINIGUI in response to user making
//           menu selection
//           Argument 'item_name' is name of selection
// OUTPUTS:  Calls appropriate routine in phone.c to
//           perform action
////////////////////////////////////////////////////////////////
void menu_action(char *item_name)
    {
    if( strcmp(item_name,      "New") == 0 )
        new_file();
    else if( strcmp(item_name, "Open") == 0 )
        open_file();
    else if( strcmp(item_name, "Save as") == 0 )
        save_as();
    else if( strcmp(item_name, "Exit") == 0 )
        exit_prog();
    else if( strcmp(item_name, "Add") == 0 )
        add_data();
    else if( strcmp(item_name, "Edit") == 0 )
        edit_data();
    else if( strcmp(item_name, "Delete") == 0 )
        delete_data();
    else if( strcmp(item_name, "Last name") == 0 )
        search_text(SEARCH_LAST);
    else if( strcmp(item_name, "First name") == 0 )
        search_text(SEARCH_FIRST);
    else if( strcmp(item_name, "Company") == 0 )
        search_text(SEARCH_COMPANY);
```

```
      else if( strcmp(item_name, "Repeat") == 0 )
        search_text(SEARCH_AGAIN);
      }

///////////////////////////////////////////////////////////////
// FUNCTION: void new_file(void)
// PURPOSE:  Opens new (non-existent) file
// INPUTS:   Closes any open file
//           Gets new file name from user with 'opendialog'
// OUTPUTS:  File is opened for reading and writing
///////////////////////////////////////////////////////////////
void new_file(void)
   {
   if(file_open)                              // if file open
      {
      fclose(fptr);                           // close it
      memset( screen, '\0', sizeof(screen) ); // erase 'screen'
      total_records = 0;                      // reset
      top_record = select_rec = 0;
      erase_screen();
      }
   if( !make_dialog(opendialog,  // get file name from user
              OPEN_FIELDS, openfields) )
      return;                     // user pressed [Esc]
   // warn user if file exists
   if( (fptr=fopen(openfields[0].input, "rb")) != NULL )

      {
      make_message(OK,
            "File aleady exists.  Use Open for existing file");
      fclose(fptr);
      return;
      }
   strcpy(file_name, openfields[0].input);  // save name
   // create a new file for reading and writing
   if( (fptr=fopen(file_name, "w+b")) == NULL )
      { make_message(OK, "Can't open file"); return; }
   file_open = TRUE;
   make_message(OK, "Use Entries/Add to add entries");
   }

///////////////////////////////////////////////////////////////
// FUNCTION: void open_file(void)
// PURPOSE:  Opens existing file
// INPUTS:   Closes any open file
//           Gets new file name from user with 'opendialog'
// OUTPUTS:  File is opened for reading and writing
//           Data is read into 'screen' array for later display
///////////////////////////////////////////////////////////////
void open_file(void)
   {
   long file_size;      // size of file in bytes
   int num_recs;        // size of file in records
```

```
        if( !make_dialog(opendialog,  // get file name from user
                OPEN_FIELDS, openfields) )
            return;             // user pressed [Esc]

        if(file_open)          // if file already open
            {
            fclose(fptr);       // close it and clear screen memory
            memset( screen, '\0', sizeof(screen) );
            erase_screen();    // erase screen and reset
            total_records = top_record = select_rec = 0;
            }
        // open existing file for reading and writing
        if( (fptr=fopen(openfields[0].input, "r+b"))==NULL )
            { make_message(OK, "Can't open file"); return; }
        file_open = TRUE;
        fseek(fptr, 0L, SEEK_END);      // move file pntr to end
        file_size = ftell(fptr);        // current offset is size
        if(file_size % RECSIZE != 0)  // one of "our" files?
            { make_message(OK, "Invalid format"); return; }
        total_records = (int)(file_size / RECSIZE);
        fseek(fptr, 0L, SEEK_SET);      // restore ptr to start
        strcpy(file_name, openfields[0].input);  // save name
        num_recs = min(total_records, MAX_LINES);
        memset( screen, 0, sizeof(screen) );
        if( fread(screen, RECSIZE,      // read file into screen
                num_recs, fptr) != num_recs  )
            { make_message(OK, "Can't read record"); return; }
        }  // end open_file()

//////////////////////////////////////////////////////////////////
// FUNCTION: void save_as(void)
// PURPOSE:  Copies current file to a new one
// INPUTS:   Gets new file name from user with 'saveasdialog'
// OUTPUTS:  Opens new file, copies old file to new one,
//           closes old file. New file becomes current file.
//////////////////////////////////////////////////////////////////
void save_as(void)
    {
    FILE *fptr2;         // file pointer
    struct record a_rec; // temporary storage
    int j;               // loop counter

    if( !file_open )     // if no file open
        { make_message(OK, "No open file to save"); return; }

    if( !make_dialog(saveasdialog,  // get file name from user
                SAVEAS_FIELDS, saveasfields) )
        return;
                                // create new file
    if( (fptr2=fopen(saveasfields[0].input, "w+b"))==NULL )
        { make_message(OK, "Can't open file"); return; }
    fseek(fptr, 0L, SEEK_SET);       // beginning of old file
```

```
   // write records from old file to new file
   for(j=0; j< total_records; j++)
      {
      fread(&a_rec, RECSIZE, 1, fptr);
      fwrite(&a_rec, RECSIZE, 1, fptr2);
      }
   fclose(fptr);     // close the old file
   fptr = fptr2;     // use its pointer variable for new file
   strcpy(file_name, saveasfields[0].input);  // save name
   }  // end save_as()

//////////////////////////////////////////////////////////////
// FUNCTION: void search_text(int search_type)
// PURPOSE:  Searches file records for text string
// INPUTS:   Argument 'search_type' specifies field to search;
//           it depends on which menu item was selected. (Values
//           are SEARCH_FIRST for first name, etc.)
//           Gets text to be searched for from 'searchdialog'
// OUTPUTS:  Searches for specified string in specified field
//           in disk file. Changes display and highlights
//           record, if text found.
//////////////////////////////////////////////////////////////
void search_text(int search_type)
   {
   char source[MAX_COLS];      // string to be searched
   struct record a_rec;        // temporary record
   int j;                      // loop counter
   int start_rec;              // remember last find
   int num_recs;               // how many to put in display
   static int old_type;        // old search type
   static char target[MAX_COLS];  // for target string

   if(total_records==0)        // if no data
      { make_message(OK, "No records to search"); return; }

   if(search_type==SEARCH_AGAIN)  // "Search again"
      {
      if( !old_type )          // if old_type never set
         { make_message(OK, "No previous search"); return; }
      start_rec = select_rec+1;    // start from selected rec
      search_type = old_type;      // use old type and target
      }
   else  // not search again, so do dialog
      {
      if( !make_dialog(searchdialog,  // get text from user
                  SEARCH_FIELDS, searchfields) )
         return;  // 0 return from make_dialog: user hit [Esc]
      strcpy(target, searchfields[0].input);  // save text
      start_rec = 0;  // start at first record
      old_type = search_type;  // save search type
      }  // end else do dialog
```

```
        fseek(fptr, start_rec*RECSIZE, SEEK_SET);
        for(j=start_rec; j<total_records; j++)  // for each record
            {
            fread(&a_rec, RECSIZE, 1, fptr);
            if(search_type==SEARCH_FIRST)        // "First name"
                strcpy(source, a_rec.firstname);
            else if(search_type==SEARCH_LAST)    // "Last name"
                strcpy(source, a_rec.lastname);
            else if(search_type==SEARCH_COMPANY) // "Company"
                strcpy(source, a_rec.company);

            // compare names in record and search dialog
            strupr(source); strupr(target);      // all upper case
            if( strstr(source, target) )         // if found,
                {
                select_rec = j;   // set selected record
                top_record = j;   // set top record on screen
                memset( screen, '\0', sizeof(screen) );
                num_recs = min(total_records-top_record, MAX_LINES);
                fseek(fptr, top_record*RECSIZE, SEEK_SET);
                if( fread(screen, RECSIZE, num_recs, fptr) != num_recs )
                    { make_message(OK, "Can't read record"); return; }
                return;              // we're done
                } // end if strcmp
            }  // end for j
        make_message(OK, "Can't find text");  // fell thru loop
        }  // end search_text()

///////////////// end of phone.c file ///////////////////////////
```

The minigui.h File

The minigui.h file contains all the includes, definitions, structure declarations, and prototypes for minigui.c. Many of these items, notably the dialog and text_field structures and the functions adjust_display(), display_data(), enter_action() and menu_action(), are also used by phone.c, so minigui.h must be included not only in minigui.c, but in phone.h as well.

```
///////////////////////////////////////////////////////////////
// FILE:    minigui.h
// PURPOSE: Provides header files, function prototypes, and
//          declarations needed by both MINGUI and the
//          application
///////////////////////////////////////////////////////////////

// include files used by minigui.c (and application)
#include <conio.h>          // for text display functions
#include <string.h>         // for strcpy(), etc.
#include <mem.h>            // for memset(), etc.
```

```
#include <dos.h>          // for sound(), etc.
#include <process.h>      // for exit()

// defines used by minigui.c (and sometimes by application)
#define TRUE           1
#define FALSE          0
#define L_ARRO        75  // Left-arrow key
#define R_ARRO        77  // Right-arrow key
#define U_ARRO        72  // Up-arrow key
#define D_ARRO        80  // Down-arrow key
#define PGUP          73  // PageUp key
#define PGDN          81  // PageDown key

#define ESCAPE        27  // Escape key
#define MAX_COLS      80  // width of screen in chars
#define MAX_ROWS      25  // height of screen in chars
#define MAX_LINES     23  // height of display area
#define MENU_WIDTH    13  // width of menu
#define TITLE_LENGTH  20  // maximum length of dialog title
#define FIELD_LENGTH  80  // maximum length of text field
#define PROMPT_LENGTH 80  // maximum length of prompt field
#define MAX_ITEMS     10  // maximum items per menu
#define OK             0  // message box type: OK
#define YES_NO         1  // message box type: yes-or-no

// dialog box structure needed by application as well as minigui
struct dialog                // dialog box
   {
   int left;                 // left of dialog
   int top;                  // top of dialog
   int width;                // width of dialog
   int height;               // height of dialog
   char title[TITLE_LENGTH+1]; // dialog title
   int number_fields;        // number of fields
   };

// text field structure needed by application as well as minigui
struct text_field
   {
   int xp;                   // starting position of prompt
   int yp;
   char prompt[PROMPT_LENGTH+1];  // prompt string
   int size;                 // length of input area
   int xi;                   // starting position of input area
   char input[FIELD_LENGTH+1];    // input area
   };

// prototypes for functions used by application
void adjust_display(char key);
void display_data(void);
void enter_action(void);
```

```
void menu_action(char *item_name);

// prototypes for functions by MINIGUI
void clear_dialog(struct dialog, struct text_field *);
void display_bar(int num_menus, char **menu_name);
void display_info(char* info_string);
void display_menu(char *[][MAX_ITEMS], int *num_items);
void draw_box(int left, int top, int width, int height);
void draw_field(int x, int y, int num_blanks,
                int color, char *oldtext);
char get_code(void);
char get_field(struct text_field *);
void erase_screen(void);
void gui_exit(void);
int make_dialog(struct dialog, int num_fields,
                struct text_field *);
void make_menus(int num_menus, char **menu_name,
                int *menu_name_alt,
                char *menu_item[][MAX_ITEMS], int *num_items);
int make_message(int type, char *message);

//////////////////// end of minigui.h file ////////////////////////
```

The minigui.c File

Here is where the interaction with the user takes place. The make_menu() function translates the user's keystrokes into menu selections, make_dialog() displays dialog boxes and gets the input typed into their text fields, and message_box() displays brief messages to the user or gets the answers to yes-or-no questions. Other functions act in a supporting role for these activities.

Global variables in this file keep track of what menu and what item on that menu are currently selected:

- hpos is the number of the active (selected) menu, starting with 0 on the left.

- vpos is the number of the selected item, starting with 0 on the top.

The functions that actually receive input from the user are get_field(), which applies when the user is typing into a text field in a dialog box, and get_code(), which applies on other occasions. The get_code() function cares mostly about extended-code characters like the arrow keys, while get_field() mostly listens for normal characters the user is typing into a text field.

```
//////////////////////////////////////////////////////////////
// FILE:    minigui.c
// PURPOSE: Provides user interface, including menus and dialogs
//////////////////////////////////////////////////////////////
```

```
#include "minigui.h"       // common declarations

// global variables
int menus_active;          // TRUE if menus are displayed
int hpos = 0;              // column of active menu (0...n)
int vpos = 0;              // row of active item (0...n)
char string[MAX_COLS+1];   // utility string

// strings for bottom "info" line
char *active_info =
"Arrow keys select menu and item. [Enter] executes item. \
[Esc] removes menu.";

char *inactive_info =
"[Alt]+[First letter] activates menu";

char *dialog_info =
"[Tab] to next field.  [Enter] to save changes.  \
[Esc] to discard changes.";


char *ok_info = "[Enter] to remove message";

char *yes_no_info = "[Enter] for YES, [Esc] for NO";

////////////////////////////////////////////////////////////
// FUNCTION: void clear_dialog(struct dialog dia,
//                            struct text_field fields[] )
// PURPOSE:  Clears all entry fields in dialog, so user has
//               a "clean slate"
// INPUTS:   Argument 'dia' is the dialog box
//           Argument fields is the array of entry fields
// OUTPUTS:  Empty entry fields
////////////////////////////////////////////////////////////
void clear_dialog(struct dialog dia,
                  struct text_field fields[] )
   {
   int j;

   // zero each text input field in the dialog
   for(j=0; j<dia.number_fields; j++)
     memset( fields[j].input, '\0', fields[j].size );
   }  // end clear_dialog()

////////////////////////////////////////////////////////////
// FUNCTION: void display_bar(int num_menus, char **menu_name)
// PURPOSE:  Displays menu bar with menu names
// INPUTS:   Argument 'num_menus' is the number of menus
//           Argument 'menu_name' is array of menu names
// OUTPUTS:  Displays menu bar at top of screen with menu
//               names, selected menu is highlighted
////////////////////////////////////////////////////////////
```

```
void display_bar(int num_menus, char **menu_name)
    {
    int j;

    textbackground(WHITE);              // black on white
    textcolor(BLACK);
    gotoxy(1,1);                        // top row
    clreol();                           // clear the line
    for(j=0; j<num_menus; j++)          // for each menu name
        {
        gotoxy( 1+(j*MENU_WIDTH), 1);   // where to write
        if(j==hpos && menus_active)     // if this menu active,
            textbackground(GREEN);      // change background
        cputs(menu_name[j]);            // write the name
        textbackground(WHITE);          // restore background
        }
    }  // end display_bar()

////////////////////////////////////////////////////////////////
// FUNCTION: void display_info(char *info_string)
// PURPOSE:  Displays info text at bottom of screen
// INPUTS:   Argument 'info_string' is the string to display
// OUTPUTS:  Info line on bottom row of screen
////////////////////////////////////////////////////////////////
void display_info(char *info_string)
    {
    textbackground(WHITE);  // red on white
    textcolor(RED);
    gotoxy(1, MAX_ROWS);    // bottom left corner
    clreol();               // clear line
    cputs(info_string);     // display string
    }  // end display_info()

////////////////////////////////////////////////////////////////
// FUNCTION: void display_menu(char *menu_item[][MAX_ITEMS],
//                             int *num_items)
// PURPOSE:  Displays a drop-down menu
// INPUTS:   Called when user selects a menu
//           Argument 'menu_item' is the array of items
//           Argument 'num_items' is array of the number
//              of items in each menu
// OUTPUTS:  Displays menu with menu items, selected item
//              is highlighted
////////////////////////////////////////////////////////////////
void display_menu(char *menu_item[][MAX_ITEMS], int *num_items)
    {
    int j;
                                        // draw the box
```

```
      draw_box((hpos*MENU_WIDTH)+1, 2,
              MENU_WIDTH, 2+num_items[hpos]);
      textbackground(WHITE);              // black on white
      textcolor(BLACK);
      for(j=0; j<num_items[hpos]; j++)    // for each menu item
         {
         if(j==vpos)                      // if active item,
            textbackground(GREEN);        // green background
         gotoxy(2+(hpos*MENU_WIDTH), j+3); // display menu item
         cputs( menu_item[hpos][j] );
         textbackground(WHITE);           // restore background
         }
   }  // end display_menu()

//////////////////////////////////////////////////////////////
// FUNCTION: void draw_box(int left, int top,
//                         int width, int height)
// PURPOSE:  Draws a box on the screen, using the supplied
//              dimensions.
// INPUTS:   Arguments 'left' and 'top' are the coordinates of
//              the upper left corner of the box
//           Arguments 'width' and 'height' are the dimensions
//              of the box
//           Minimum size is width=2, height=2 (no room inside)
// OUTPUTS:  Character-mode single-line box, black line
//              surrounding white rectangle.
//////////////////////////////////////////////////////////////
void draw_box(int left, int top, int width, int height)
   {
   int j;

   textbackground(WHITE);        // black on white
   textcolor(BLACK);

   // top and bottom lines, with corners
   for(j=1; j<width-1; j++)      // make string of
      string[j] = '\xC4';        // horizontal characters
   string[width] = '\0';         // end the string
   string[0] = '\xDA';           // upper left corner
   string[width-1] = '\xBF';     // upper right corner
   gotoxy(left, top);            // display top row
   cputs(string);
   string[0] = '\xC0';           // lower left corner
   string[width-1] = '\xD9';     // lower right corner
   gotoxy(left, top+height-1);   // display bottom row
   cputs(string);

   // horizontal and vertical lines, and interior
   for(j=1; j<width-1; j++)      // middle of line: blanks
      string[j] = '\x20';        // space character
   string[0] = '\xB3';           // left edge: vertical char
```

```
    string[width-1] = '\xB3';      // right edge: vertical char

    for(j=1; j<height-1; j++)      // for each row
        {
        gotoxy(left, top+j);       // draw the row
        cputs(string);
        }
    }   // end draw_box()

//////////////////////////////////////////////////////////////////
// FUNCTION: void draw_field(int x, int y, int num_blanks,
//                              int color, char* oldtext)
// PURPOSE:  Displays text on colored background
// INPUTS:   Arguments 'x' and 'y' are starting column and row
//           Argument 'num_blanks' is length of field
//           Argument 'color' is color of field
//           Argument 'oldtext' is text to be placed in field
// OUTPUTS:  Single line of colored blanks; may contain text
//////////////////////////////////////////////////////////////////
void draw_field(int x, int y, int num_blanks,
                int color, char* oldtext)
    {
    gotoxy(x, y);                 // go to start of field
    strcpy(string, oldtext);      // fill with any existing text

    memset(string+strlen(oldtext), ' ',   // fill rest of field
            num_blanks-strlen(oldtext) ); // with blanks
    string[num_blanks] = '\0';            // terminate string
    textcolor(WHITE); textbackground(color);  // set colors
    cputs(string);                            // display field
    }   // end draw_field()

//////////////////////////////////////////////////////////////////
// FUNCTION: void erase_screen(void)
// PURPOSE:  Erase display area of screen
// INPUTS:   none
// OUTPUTS:  Screen is erased, except for menu bar and info line
//////////////////////////////////////////////////////////////////
void erase_screen(void)
    {
    textbackground(BLUE);
    window(1, 2, MAX_COLS, MAX_ROWS-1); // change window size
    clrscr();                           // clear smaller window
    window(1, 1, MAX_COLS, MAX_ROWS);   // restore entire window
    }   // end erase_screen()

//////////////////////////////////////////////////////////////////
// FUNCTION: char get_code(void)
// PURPOSE:  Gets keystroke from user
// INPUTS:   User presses key
// OUTPUTS:  Returns keystrokes "digested" for user interface
//////////////////////////////////////////////////////////////////
char get_code(void)
```

```
   {
   char key;

   if( (key=getch()) == 0 )   // if extended code,
       return( getch() );      // return the code
   else if ( key == '\r' )     // if [Enter],
       return(key);            // return it
   else if (key == ESCAPE)     // if [Escape],
       return(key);            // return it
   else                        // if anything else,
       { sound(2000); delay(100); nosound(); } // beep
   return(0);                  // return 0
   }  // end get_code()

//////////////////////////////////////////////////////////////
// FUNCTION: char get_field(struct text_field *ptf)
// PURPOSE:  Handles text typed into text field by user
// INPUTS:   Argument 'ptf' is pointer to text field.
// OUTPUTS:  Text field is highlighted. Displays text typed by
//           user in the field, stores text in ptf->input.
//           Returns code for [Tab], [Enter], or [Esc]
//////////////////////////////////////////////////////////////
char get_field(struct text_field *ptf)
   {
   char ch;
   int first_time = TRUE;
   int n = 0;  // number of chars read

   draw_field(ptf->xi, ptf->yp,    // color the input area green
             ptf->size, GREEN, ptf->input);
   gotoxy(ptf->xi, ptf->yp);
   textcolor(WHITE);
   textbackground(GREEN);
   _setcursortype(_NORMALCURSOR); // turn on the cursor
   while(TRUE)
      {
      ch = getch();                 // get char from user
      if(ch=='\r' || ch=='\t' || ch==ESCAPE)     // user done
         {                          // color input area blue
         draw_field( ptf->xi, ptf->yp,
                     ptf->size, BLUE, ptf->input);
         gotoxy(ptf->xi, ptf->yp);
         textbackground(BLUE);
         textcolor(WHITE);
         cputs(ptf->input);         // display input member
         _setcursortype(_NOCURSOR); // turn off the cursor
         return(ch);
         }
      // if first character and field not empty
      if( first_time && strcmp(ptf->input, "") != 0)
         {
         strcpy(ptf->input, "");    // empty the field
```

```
            draw_field( ptf->xi, ptf->yp,
                        ptf->size, GREEN, ptf->input);
            gotoxy(ptf->xi, ptf->yp);
            }
        first_time = FALSE;              // but never again
        if(ch=='\b')  // if it's a backspace
            {
            if(n > 0)
                {
                gotoxy( wherex()-1, wherey() );  // cursor left
                putch(' ');           // space over last character
                gotoxy( wherex()-1, wherey() );  // left again
                ptf->input[ -n] = '\0';          // shorten input
                }
            else  // at left margin
                { sound(2000); delay(100); nosound(); } // beep
            }
        else if(ch=='\0')  // if it's extended character
            getch();               // eat the rest of it
        else                   // it's a normal character
            {
            if( n < ptf->size )  // if we still have room
                {
                putch(ch);  // display the character
                ptf->input[n++] = ch;  // add char to input
                ptf->input[n] = '\0';  // terminate input string
                }
            else  // at right margin
                { sound(2000); delay(100); nosound(); }  // beep
            }
        }  // end while
    }  // end get_field()

//////////////////////////////////////////////////////////////////
// FUNCTION: void gui_exit(void)
// PURPOSE:  Cleans up the screen display and exits
// INPUTS:   none
// OUTPUTS:  Restores normal display colors, clears screen,
//           exits to DOS
//////////////////////////////////////////////////////////////////
void gui_exit(void)
    {
    textcolor(WHITE);               // reset to normal
    textbackground(BLACK);          // colors
    _setcursortype(_NORMALCURSOR);  // restore cursor
    clrscr();                       // clear screen
    exit(0);                        // exit from program
    }  // end gui_exit()

//////////////////////////////////////////////////////////////////
// FUNCTION: int make_dialog(struct dialog dia, int num_fields,
//                           struct text_fields[] )
// PURPOSE:  Draw dialog box, interact with dialog user
```

```
// INPUTS:    Argument 'dai' is structure of type dialog
//            Argument 'num_fields' is the number of entry
//            fields in the dialog box.
//            Argument 'fields' is an array of structures
//            of type text_field, containing the text fields
// OUTPUTS:   Accepts typed input, displays it in appropriate

//            text field. Moves to next field on [Tab]
//            Returns TRUE if user terminates with [Enter]
//            (decides to make changes), or FALSE if user
//            terminates with [Esc] (discards changes).
/////////////////////////////////////////////////////////////
int make_dialog(struct dialog dia, int num_fields,
                struct text_field fields[] )
    {
    int n = 0;      // number of the field with keyboard focus
    char ch;
    int j;
    struct text_field *ptf;

    // draw the box outline and the title
    draw_box(dia.left, dia.top, dia.width, dia.height);
    gotoxy( dia.left+(dia.width-strlen(dia.title))/2-1, dia.top);
    textcolor(BLACK);
    textbackground(WHITE);
    cputs(dia.title);

    display_info(dialog_info);  // dialog info on bottom line

    // draw prompts, text fields in blue
    for(j=0; j<dia.number_fields; j++)  // for each text field
        {
        gotoxy( fields[j].xp, fields[j].yp );  // draw prompt
        textcolor(BLACK);
        textbackground(WHITE);
        cputs( fields[j].prompt );
                                        // draw input area
        draw_field( fields[j].xi, fields[j].yp,
                fields[j].size, BLUE, fields[j].input);
        }

    while(TRUE)             // user fills in fields[n].input
        {
        ptf = &fields[n];       // ptr to field
        ch = get_field(ptf);    // highlight field, get data
        switch(ch)
            {

            case ESCAPE:    // user pressed [Esc], don't save data
                display_data();
                return(FALSE);      // exit dialog box, no new data
```

```
              case '\t':      // user pressed [Tab], move to next field
                 n = (n < num_fields-1) ? ++n : 0;
                 break;

              case '\r':      // user pressed [Enter], save data
                 display_data();
                 // if nothing in first field, assume no data
                 if( strlen(fields[0].input)==0 )
                    return(FALSE); // exit dialog box, no new data
                 return(TRUE);      // exit dialog box, new data
           }  // end switch
        }  // end while
     }  // end make_dialog()


//////////////////////////////////////////////////////////////////
// FUNCTION: void make_menus(int num_menus, char **menu_name,
//                int *menu_name_alt, char *menu_item[][],
//                int *num_items)
// PURPOSE:  Starts MINIGUI system, displays menus, waits for
//                user to press keys.
//                This function gets all user key presses
// INPUTS:   Argument 'num_menus' is number of drop-down menus
//                Argument 'menu_name' is array of menu names
//                Argument 'menu_name_alt' is array of ASCII codes
//                   for [Alt] plus [first letter] of each menu name
//                Argument 'menu_item' is a 2-D array of menu
//                   item names
//                Argument 'num_items' is an array holding the
//                   number of items on each menu
//                All activities are initiated by the user selecting
//                   a menu item
// OUTPUTS:  Displays menu selected by user, highlights menu
//                and item. Handles keys pressed by user to
//                communicate with user interface. Calls
//                menu_action in application to carry out actions
//////////////////////////////////////////////////////////////////
void make_menus(int num_menus, char **menu_name,
                int *menu_name_alt, char *menu_item[][MAX_ITEMS],
                int *num_items)
   {
   int j;
   int extcode;                       // extended key code

   textbackground(BLUE);              // clear screen
   _setcursortype(_NOCURSOR);         // remove cursor
   clrscr();
   menus_active = FALSE;
   display_bar(num_menus, menu_name);  // display menu bar


   while(TRUE)                        // wait for user key presses
      {
      if(menus_active)
         {
```

```
        display_info(active_info); // info on bottom line
        switch ( get_code() )      // act on key pressed
            {
            case L_ARRO:              // display menu to left
                vpos = 0;
                hpos = (hpos>0) ? --hpos : num_menus-1;
                display_bar(num_menus, menu_name);
                display_data();
                display_menu(menu_item, num_items);
                break;

            case R_ARRO:              // display menu to right
                vpos = 0;
                hpos = (hpos<num_menus-1) ? ++hpos : 0;
                display_bar(num_menus, menu_name);
                display_data();
                display_menu(menu_item, num_items);
                break;

            case U_ARRO:              // move highlight up
                vpos = (vpos>0) ? --vpos : num_items[hpos]-1;
                display_menu(menu_item, num_items);
                break;

            case D_ARRO:              // move highlight down
                vpos = (vpos<num_items[hpos]-1) ? ++vpos : 0;
                display_menu(menu_item, num_items);
                break;

            case '\r':                // perform action
                menus_active = FALSE;
                display_bar(num_menus, menu_name);
                display_data();
                // call menu_action() -- argument is item name
                menu_action( menu_item[hpos][vpos] );
                vpos = 0;             // next time start at top
                display_data();       // display data
                break;

            case ESCAPE:              // user types [Esc]
                vpos = 0;             // next time start at top
                menus_active = FALSE;
                display_data();      // display data
                display_bar(num_menus, menu_name);
                break;
            } // end switch
        } // end if (menus active)

    else  // menus are not active
        {
        display_info(inactive_info); // info on bottom line
        extcode = get_code();        // get user key
```

```
              switch(extcode)                    // take action
                 {
                 case '\r':      // display manipulation keys
                    enter_action();
                    break;
                 case PGUP:
                 case PGDN:
                 case U_ARRO:
                 case D_ARRO:
                    adjust_display(extcode);    // send key code
                    display_data();
                    break;

                 // it's probably a menu selection
                 default:
                    for(j=0; j<num_menus; j++)  // check each menu

                       // is key [Alt]+[letter] code for menu?
                       if( extcode==menu_name_alt[j] )
                          {                        // if so, it's a
                          menus_active = TRUE;   // menu selection
                          hpos = j;               // set menu number
                          display_data();
                          display_bar(num_menus, menu_name);
                          display_menu(menu_item, num_items);
                          }
                    break;  // end default (menu selection)
                 } // end switch
              } // end else (menus not active)
           } // end while
        } // end make_menus()

/////////////////////////////////////////////////////////////////
// FUNCTION: int make_message(int type, char *message)
// PURPOSE:  Draw message box, interact with user
// INPUTS:   Argument 'type' is OK or YES_NO, depending on
//           which option is offered to the user
//           Argument 'message' is the text of the message
//           to be displayed
// OUTPUTS:  Draws box with message, awaits user response,
//           which can be [Enter] for an OK box,
//           or [Enter]or [Esc] for YES_NO box.
//           Returns TRUE for [Enter], FALSE for [Esc]
/////////////////////////////////////////////////////////////////
int make_message(int type, char *message)
   {
   int top = 5, height = 5;     // all boxes have same height
   int left, width;
   char ch;

   width = strlen(message) + 4;         // width based on text
   left = (MAX_COLS - width) / 2;       // left side ditto
   draw_box(left, top, width, height);  // display box
```

```
    gotoxy(left+2, height+2);
    textcolor(BLACK);
    textbackground(WHITE);
    cputs(message);                    // display message
    if(type==OK)
        display_info(ok_info);         // put dialog info
    else  // type is YES_NO            // on bottom line
        display_info(yes_no_info);
    ch = get_code();                   // get user response
    display_data();
    // return TRUE if user pressed [Enter], FALSE for [Esc]
    return (ch=='\r') ? TRUE : FALSE;
    }  // end make_message()

//////////////// end of mingui.c file ////////////////////////////
```

Summary

It may take a while to understand in detail how the PHONE application works, but the reward for your time is an understanding of how a full-scale application is constructed and how the various pieces fit together.

You should be aware that, large as it is, this is still not quite a commercial application. If it were, we would pay more attention to such issues as error checking and making sure the user typed the expected input. However, this would increase the size of the listing and make it more difficult to understand.

Questions

1. A graphic user interface (GUI) is advantageous because

    a. It uses graphics instead of characters.
    b. The user doesn't need to remember commands.
    c. All possible user actions are listed in dialog boxes.
    d. It makes the program run faster.

2. In the application in this chapter, minigui.c file handles the _____ while the phone.c program handles the actual _____.

3. True or false: in this application a message box is a place where the program stores temporary data.

4. You can think of the MiniGui part of the program (minigui.c and minigui.h) as

    a. A program module concerned with files
    b. Being useful for many different applications

c. A program module concerned with data

d. A separate product a software developer might purchase

5. Constants that must be known to both minigui.c and phone.c are kept in the file
_____.

6. When it isn't doing anything else, the program is executing instructions in the
_____ function.

7. A callback function is one that

a. Is located in minigui.c but called by phone.c

b. Is located in phone.c but called by minigui.c

c. Is located in the operating system but called by phone.c

d. Is located in the operating system but called by minigui.c

8. The definitions (not declarations) for dialog boxes are located in the
_____ file.

9. A database in this application is

a. Stored entirely in memory, once the file is opened

b. Stored on the disk, except for what's being displayed

c. Stored partly in memory, once the file is opened

d. Always in up-to-date form on the disk

10. In this application dialog boxes allow only _____ input.

Exercises

There are no formal exercises in this chapter (that is, no answers). However, here are some suggestions for extending the program:

1. Add a Help menu that calls up descriptions of how the program works. You could include an About item that provides information about the program.

2. Add a Print item to the File menu. This should print the contents of the database.

3. Add code that validates the data typed in. For instance, make sure that phone numbers have the correct number of digits and that names aren't too long.

4. Add the GUI part of the program (minigui.h and minigui.c) to another program, such as the agentr.c program from Chapter 11, to give it a modern interface.

5. If you want a challenge, you might try extending the MiniGui part of the program to include resizable, scrollable windows. Hint: use the Turbo C++ window() function.

Hardware-
Oriented C

- The bitwise operators
- Direct-access character display
- System memory
- The ROM BIOS
- Direct-access color graphics
- Input/output ports

In previous chapters we showed example programs that used library functions to interact with hardware. However, a major advantage of the C language is that it can be used to deal directly with hardware. Unlike many languages (such as BASIC), C provides bit-level operators and other amenities that make hardware-related activities easy.

Why would you want to interact directly with hardware? Often you can obtain dramatic improvements in program performance: your programs run faster or require less memory. You can also perform some operations that are impossible with library functions. Finally, learning the techniques necessary for handling hardware will extend your skill as a C programmer.

Of course this chapter isn't a definitive treatment of PC hardware; that would require several large books. Our intention is to introduce some of the main topics, whet your appetite for more, and give you a chance to practice some of your C programming skills. To learn more about PC hardware, consult the books listed in the bibliography.

In this chapter we'll focus on three aspects of direct hardware access: the character display, the read-only-memory basic input/output system (ROM BIOS), and the color graphics display. Getting the maximum utility out of direct hardware access requires an understanding of the C bitwise operators, which permit individual bits to be accessed and manipulated. Accordingly, we'll start this chapter with a discussion of these operators.

This chapter requires some understanding of the hexadecimal and binary numbering systems. If these topics are unfamiliar to you, you should read Appendix B, "Hexadecimal Numbering," before continuing.

Bit Twiddling

So far we've thought of variables as containing numbers or characters. We haven't attempted to look within these variables to see how they're constructed out of individual bits and how these bits can be manipulated. Being able to operate on the bit level, however, can be vital if a program must interact directly with hardware. Although programming languages are data-oriented, hardware tends to be bit-oriented; that is, a hardware device often requires input and output in the form of individual bits.

The Bitwise AND (&) Operator

As you probably know, C variables are composed of bytes, and each byte contains eight bits. A bit can have only two possible values, 0 or 1. The C bitwise operators actually operate on normal C integer and character variables (not floating point), but they treat the contents of the variable as consisting of individual bits rather than as a single number. There are six bitwise operators, summarized in the following list:

Operation	Operator
AND	&
Inclusive OR	¦
Exclusive OR (XOR)	^
Right-shift	>>
Left-shift	<<
Complement	~

Because the operators affect individual bits, it's important to know how to refer to the bits in a character or integer. The bits are numbered from right to left, as shown in Figure 15.1.

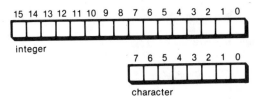

Figure 15.1. Bit numbering.

We'll start by looking at the bitwise AND operator. This operator is represented by the ampersand (&). Don't confuse this *bitwise* operator with the *logical* AND operator—represented by two ampersands (&&)—which was introduced in Chapter 3, "Loops."

The bitwise AND operator takes two operands, which must be of the same data type. The idea is that the two operands are compared on a bit-by-bit basis. If bit 0 of the first operand is a one and bit 0 of the second operand is also a one, then bit 0 of the answer is a one; otherwise it's zero. This rule can be summarized as shown in Figure 15.2.

> The bitwise operators AND, OR, and XOR operate on a pair of operand bits to yield a result bit. The process is applied to each bit position in turn.

The rule is applied to all the bits of a data item in turn. Unlike operations involving normal arithmetic—such as addition—each pair of corresponding bits is completely independent; there is no carry from one column to another. Figure 15.3 shows an example of two variables of type char being bitwise ANDed together.

A good way to become familiar with the logical operators is to write a program that allows experimentation with different inputs to see what results are produced by particular operators. The most convenient format for input and output is hexadecimal, because each hex digit corresponds to exactly four bits. Here's a simple program that uses hexadecimal character variables to permit testing of the AND operator:

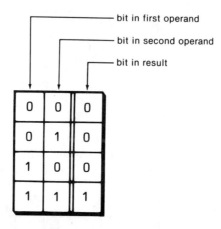

Figure 15.2. Rules for combining bits using AND (&) operator.

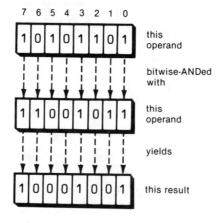

Figure 15.3. Example of bitwise AND.

```
// andtest.c
// demonstrates bitwise AND operator
#include <stdio.h>                    // for printf(), scanf()

void main(void)
    {
    unsigned int x1=0xFF, x2=0xFF;  // ensure they're not 0

    while( x1 != 0 || x2 != 0 )      // terminate on 0,0
        {
        printf("\nEnter two hex numbers (ff or less): ");
        scanf("%x %x", &x1, &x2);
        printf("%02x & %02x = %02x\n", x1, x2, x1 & x2 );
        }
    }
```

This program uses the (&) operator in the expression

```
x1 & x2
```

to find the appropriate answer, which is then displayed by the `printf()` statement.

Here are some examples of the AND operator at work using the program:

```
Enter two hex numbers (ff or less): 1 0
01 & 00 = 00
```

and (with the prompt line and user input not shown):

```
00 & 01 = 00
```

```
01 & 01 = 01
```

For a more advanced example, here are the two hex digits c and 7 ANDed together:

```
0c & 07 = 04
```

The expansion of these hex digits into bits is shown in Figure 15.4.

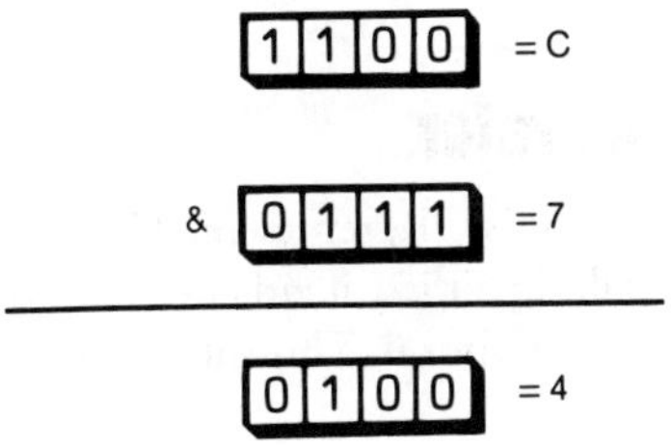

Figure 15.4. Two hex digits ANDed together.

The bitwise AND operator is often used to test whether a particular bit in a data item is set to 0 or 1. The testing process works because 0 ANDed with either 0 or 1 is still 0, while 1 ANDed with a bit is whatever the bit is. For example, to test if bit 3 of a character variable `ch` is 0 or 1, the following statement can be used:

```
bit3 = ch & 0x08;
```

Figure 15.5 shows this process in operation. Here if bit 3 of `ch` is 1, the variable `bit3` will be assigned the value 1, otherwise 0 will be assigned.

We'll see an example of the bitwise AND used for testing bits in the program hextobin.c, coming up soon.

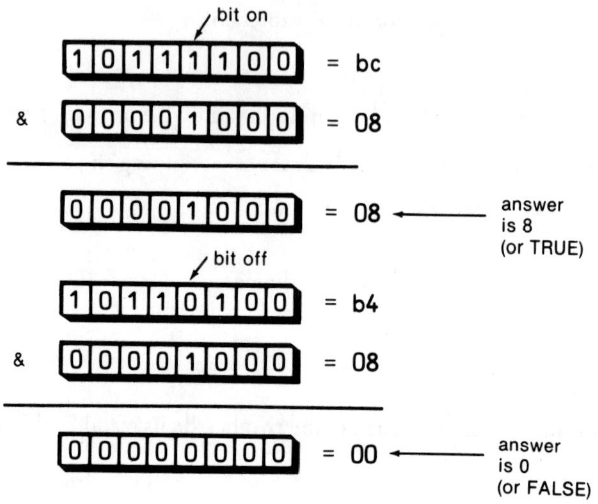

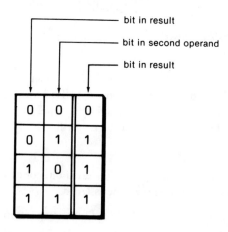

Figure 15.5. Bitwise AND used for test.

The Bitwise OR (¦) Operator

Another important bitwise operator is OR, represented by the vertical bar (¦). When two bits are ORed together, the resulting bit is 1 if either or both of the two operand bits is 1. If neither of the two bits is 1, the result is 0. This rule is shown in Figure 15.6.

Figure 15.6. Rules for combining bits using OR (¦) operator.

Here's a program that demonstrates the OR operator:

```
// ortest.c
// demonstrates bitwise OR operator
#include <stdio.h>                    // for printf(), scanf()

void main(void)
    {
    unsigned int x1=0xFF, x2=0xFF;   // ensure they're not 0

    while( x1 != 0 || x2 != 0 )      // terminate on 0,0
        {
        printf("\nEnter two hex numbers (ff or less): ");
        scanf("%x %x", &x1, &x2);
        printf("%02x | %02x = %02x\n", x1, x2, x1 | x2 );
        }
    }
```

And here's some sample output (without the prompt lines):

```
00 | 01 = 01
01 | 00 = 01
01 | 01 = 01
0c | 07 = 0f
ad | cb = ef
```

If you're hazy about these results—or those in the last section on AND—you should verify that they're correct by expanding them into their binary form, performing the OR operation on each pair of corresponding bits and translating them back into hexadecimal.

The bitwise OR operator is often used to combine bits from different variables into a single variable. For example, suppose we had two character variables, ch1 and ch2, and suppose bits 0 through 3 of ch1 contained a value we wanted, while bits 4 through 7 of ch2 were the ones we wanted. Assuming the unwanted part of both variables was set to all 0s, we could then combine the two with the statement

```
ans = ch1 | ch2;
```

Figure 15.7 shows how this works, assuming that ch1 is 0x07 and ch2 is 0xd0.

The Bitwise Right-Shift (>>) Operator

In addition to bitwise operators that operate on two variables, there are several bitwise operators that operate on a single variable. An example is the right-shift operator, represented by two greater-than symbols (>>). This operator moves each bit in the operand to the right. The number of places the bits are moved is determined by the number following the operand. Thus, the expression

```
ch >> 3
```

causes all the bits in ch to be shifted right three places. Figure 15.8 shows an example of the hex value 72 being shifted right two places. Note that shifting right one bit is the same as dividing the operand by 2.

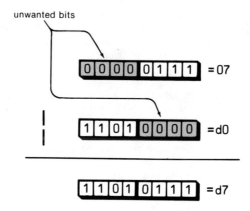

Figure 15.7. Bitwise OR operator used to combine values.

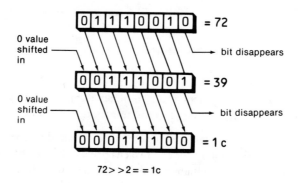

Figure 15.8. Example of right-shift operator.

Here's a program that demonstrates the right-shift operator:

```
// shiftest.c
// demonstrates bitwise right-shift operator
#include <stdio.h>                    // for printf(), scanf()

void main(void)
   {
   unsigned int x=0xFF, bits;        // ensure x not 0

   while( x != 0 )                    // terminate on x=0
      {
      printf("\nEnter hex number (ff or less) and number of bits ");
      printf("\nto shift (8 or less; example 'cc 3'): ");
      scanf("%x %d", &x, &bits);
      printf("%02x >> %d = %02x\n", x, bits, x >> bits );
      }
   }
```

Here's some sample output:

```
Enter hex number (ff or less) and number of bits
to shift (8 or less; example 'cc 3'): 80 1
80 >> 1 = 40
```

Here are some other examples:

```
80 >> 2 = 20
80 >> 7 = 01
f0 >> 4 = 0f
```

Again, if this isn't clear, translate the hex numbers into binary, shift them by hand, and translate back into hex to verify that the results are correct.

In the examples so far, zeros are inserted into the leftmost bit. This is because the data type being shifted is unsigned char. However, this may not be the case if the data type is char, which is assumed to be signed, with the leftmost bit being the sign bit. If the leftmost bit of a type char variable starts out equal to 1, the number is considered negative. To maintain the sign of the number when it is right-shifted, 1s are inserted in the leftmost bit. Thus the following statement will be true:

```
80 >> 2 == e0
```

> If the sign bit is set in a signed operand, right-shifts will cause 1s to be shifted in from the left.

Hexadecimal to Binary Conversion

We've mentioned several times that you might want to perform hex to binary conversions to verify our results. It would be nice if you could get the computer to do this. As we've seen in the past, it's easy to perform conversion to and from hexadecimal in C by using the %x type specifier in printf() and scanf() functions. However, there is no corresponding specifier for binary, so let's write a program to carry out this conversion for us.

Here's the program:

```
// hextobin.c
// converts hex number to binary
#include <stdio.h>                    // for printf(), scanf()

void main(void)
    {
    int j, num=0xFF, bit;
    unsigned int mask;

    while(num != 0)                    // terminate on 0
        {
```

```
        mask = 0x8000;                    // 1000000 binary
        printf("\nEnter number: ");
        scanf("%x", &num);
        printf("Binary of %04x is:   ", num);
        for(j=0; j<16; j++)               // for each bit
            {
            bit = (mask & num) ? 1 : 0;   // bit is 1 or 0
            printf("%d ", bit);           // print bit
            if(j==7)                      // print dash between
                printf("-- ");            //     bytes
            mask >>= 1;                   // shift mask to right
            }  // end for
        }  // end while
    }  // end main()
```

Here's some sample interaction:

```
Enter number: 1
Binary of 0001 is:  0 0 0 0 0 0 0 0--0 0 0 0 0 0 0 1
Enter number: 80
Binary of 0080 is:  0 0 0 0 0 0 0 0--1 0 0 0 0 0 0 0
Enter number: 100
Binary of 0100 is:  0 0 0 0 0 0 0 1--0 0 0 0 0 0 0 0
Enter number: f00
Binary of 0f00 is:  0 0 0 0 1 1 1 1--0 0 0 0 0 0 0 0
Enter number: f0f0
Binary of f0f0 is:  1 1 1 1 0 0 0 0--1 1 1 1 0 0 0 0
```

This program uses a for loop to go from left to right through all 16 bits of an integer variable. The heart of the operation is contained in two statements that use bitwise operators.

```
bit = (mask & num) ? 1 : 0;
```

and

```
mask >>= 1;
```

In the first statement we make use of a mask. This is a variable that starts out with a single bit in the leftmost position. The mask is then ANDed with the number that we want to express in binary, the variable num. If the result is nonzero (true), we know the corresponding bit in num is 1; otherwise it's 0. The conditional statement assigns the value 1 to the variable bit if the bit being tested in num is 1, and 0 otherwise.

The right-shift statement then shifts the mask one bit to the right, and the process is repeated for the next bit. The first time through the loop the mask will be 1000000000000000 binary, the second time through it will be 0100000000000000, and so forth. Eventually all 16 bits will be printed.

Other Logical Operators

There are six bitwise operators in all, of which we've looked at three. We'll briefly review the remaining three and then show a six-function bitwise calculator that, if you type it in and compile it, will enable you to experiment with and learn more about the bitwise operators.

The Bitwise XOR (^) Operator

The ordinary bitwise OR operator, ($|$) discussed earlier, returns a value of 1 when either bit, or both bits, in the operand is 1. The bitwise exclusive OR, or XOR operator, by contrast, returns a value of 1 when either bit, but *not* both bits, is 1. This operator is represented by the caret (^). Figure 15.9 shows the rules for this operator.

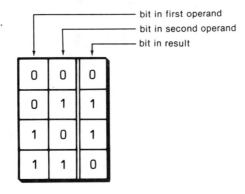

Figure 15.9. Rules for combining bits using XOR operator.

The XOR operator can be useful for *toggling* a bit, that is, switching it back and forth between 0 and 1. This is true because a 1 XORed with 1 is 0, while a 1 XORed with a 0 is 1.

> An XOR operation applied twice to particular bits in an operand yields the original operand.

For instance, to toggle bit 3 in a variable ch of type char, we could use the statement

```
ch = ch ^ 0x08;
```

Figure 15.10 shows how repeated application of this operation toggles bit 3 back and forth while leaving the other bits unchanged. The variable ch is assumed to start with the value 0xBC. We'll see an example of a bit being toggled to produce a useful result later on in the chapter.

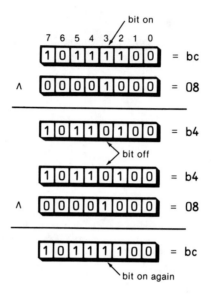

Figure 15.10. Bitwise XOR operator used as toggle.

The Bitwise Left-Shift Operator (<<)

The left-shift operator is, as you might guess, similar to the right-shift operator, except that bits are shifted left instead of right. The value of the bits inserted on the right is always 0, regardless of the sign or data type of the operand.

The Bitwise Complement Operator (~)

The bitwise complement operator (~) acts on a single operand; it takes every bit in the operand and makes it 1 if it was a 0 and 0 if it was a 1. For example, the following equalities are true:

```
~03 == fc
~ffff == 0
~cc == 33
~88 == 77
```

Complementing a number twice always returns the original number.

The Bitwise Calculator

Let's put all the bitwise operators into one program. This program acts as a bitwise calculator into which we type any suitable operand and a bitwise operator. It then displays the result. It's a useful program for exploring and learning about all the bitwise operations.

```
// bitcalc.c
// performs bitwise calculations
```

```
#include <stdio.h>                    // for printf(), scanf()
void pbin(int);                       // prototypes
void pline(void);

void main(void)
   {
   char op[10];
   unsigned int x1=0xFF, x2=0xFF;

   while( x1 != 0 ¦¦ x2 != 0 )  // terminate on 0 op 0
      {
      printf("\n\nEnter expression (example 'ff00 & 1111'): ");
      scanf("%x %s %x", &x1, op, &x2);
      printf("\n");
      switch( op[0] )
         {
         case '&':
            pbin(x1); printf("& (and)\n"); pbin(x2);
            pline(); pbin(x1 & x2);
            break;
         case '¦':
            pbin(x1); printf("¦ (incl or)\n"); pbin(x2);
            pline(); pbin(x1 ¦ x2);
            break;
         case '^':
            pbin(x1); printf("^ (excl or)\n"); pbin(x2);
            pline(); pbin(x1 ^ x2);
            break;
         case '>':
            pbin(x1); printf(">> "); printf("%d\n", x2);
            pline(); pbin(x1 >> x2);
            break;
         case '<':
            pbin(x1); printf("<< "); printf("%d\n", x2);
            pline(); pbin(x1 << x2);
            break;
         case '~':
            pbin(x1); printf("~ (complement)\n");
            pline(); pbin(~x1);
            break;
         default: printf("Not valid operator.\n");
         }  // end switch
      }  // end while
   }  // end main()

// pbin
// prints number in hex and binary
void pbin(int num)
   {
   unsigned int mask;
   int j, bit;
   mask = 0x8000;                        // one-bit mask
```

```
    printf("%04x  ", num);              // print in hex
    for(j=0; j<16; j++)                 // for each bit in num
        {
        bit = (mask & num) ? 1 : 0;     // bit is 1 or 0
        printf("%d ", bit);             // print bit
        if(j==7)                        // print dash between
            printf("-- ");              //     bytes
        mask >>= 1;                     // shift mask to right
        }
    printf("\n");
    }  // end pbin()

// pline()
void pline(void)
    {
    printf("----------------------------------------\n");
    }
```

As you can see, this program consists mostly of a large switch statement containing all the bitwise operations. The user types an operand, a bitwise operator, and another operand. The program displays the result. One anomaly is in the complement operator, which takes only one operand but requires a second operand to be typed after the operator (~) to satisfy the variable list in the scanf() statement (any number will do). Also note that typing the one-character symbols '<' or '>' invoke the two-character operands << and >>. This is potentially misleading but simplifies the programming.

Here are some examples of interaction with the program. For brevity, the initial prompt is only shown in the first example:

```
Enter expression (example 'ff00 & 1111'): f0f0 | 3333
f0f0  1 1 1 1 0 0 0 0--1 1 1 1 0 0 0 0
| (incl or)
3333  0 0 1 1 0 0 1 1--0 0 1 1 0 0 1 1
----------------------------------------
f3f3  1 1 1 1 0 0 1 1--1 1 1 1 0 0 1 1

f0f0  1 1 1 1 0 0 0 0--1 1 1 1 0 0 0 0
<< 2
----------------------------------------
c3c0  1 1 0 0 0 0 1 1--1 1 0 0 0 0 0 0

f0f0  1 1 1 1 0 0 0 0--1 1 1 1 0 0 0 0
^ (excl or)
3333  0 0 1 1 0 0 1 1--0 0 1 1 0 0 1 1
----------------------------------------
c3c3  1 1 0 0 0 0 1 1--1 1 0 0 0 0 1 1

f0f0  1 1 1 1 0 0 0 0--1 1 1 1 0 0 0 0
~ (complement)
----------------------------------------
0f0f  0 0 0 0 1 1 1 1--0 0 0 0 1 1 1 1
```

This program makes use of the routine from the hextobin.c program, transformed into the function pbin(), to display binary versions of the operands and results.

Now that you know how to manipulate bits, we're ready to explore memory-mapped graphics and see what role bit manipulation plays in influencing the display.

Direct-Access Character Display

The character display places characters, as opposed to graphics, on the screen. When you see the DOS prompt,

```
C>
```

you're looking at a character display. The screen is divided into 80 columns and 25 rows of characters. (Some displays may have a different arrangement.) The character display operates whether you have a monochrome character display or a graphics display adapter.

This section focuses on manipulating the character display using direct memory access. In past chapters we've explored a variety of techniques to place characters on the screen, but all these techniques have made use of C library functions. The new approach can yield much faster and more versatile results.

Display Memory

When you attach a video monitor to your PC you must also install in the computer a printed circuit board called a *graphics adapter*. This board has on it the circuitry necessary to convey information from the computer to the display. What does this hardware consist of, and how can we access it from our programs?

Communication between the adapter and the computer takes place using a special section of memory as a sort of common ground. This section of memory is physically located on the adapter board and can be accessed both by the microprocessor and by the display screen. The microprocessor can insert values into this memory and read them out just as it can with ordinary random-access memory (RAM). However, whatever characters are placed in the display memory also appear automatically on the screen.

The normal character display consists of 25 lines of 80 characters each, for a total of 2,000 characters. Each of these characters is associated with a particular address in the display memory. Two bytes in the memory are used for each character: one to hold the extended ASCII character code, a value from 0 to 255 (0 to FF in hexadecimal), and one to hold the attribute. (We'll investigate the details of the attribute byte later in this chapter.) Thus 4,000 bytes of memory are needed to represent the 2,000 characters on the screen.

When we call a C library routine to display a character, it calls a routine in ROM BIOS. The ROM BIOS routine puts the character on the screen by placing the values for the character's extended code and attribute byte in the appropriate address in the adapter's memory. However, we can take a shortcut. If our program inserts values for these bytes directly into memory, we can save a lot of time, because (among other reasons) we eliminate the overhead of calling one routine that calls another routine.

Hexadecimal Memory Addresses

The display memory occupies certain fixed addresses. We need to use the numerical values of these addresses in our program, so we can use pointers to access the memory contents. However, representing these numbers isn't quite as straightforward as it could be. Let's learn how to represent fixed memory addresses in C.

All the normal (base) memory in an MS-DOS computer, whether RAM used for programs or system memory devoted to hardware, occupies 1 megabyte and has absolute addresses ranging from 0 to 1,048,575 decimal. When discussing memory, it's convenient to use the hexadecimal numbering system to represent addresses. Each hex digit runs from 0 to F (0 to 15 decimal) for a total of 16 possible values per digit. 1,048,575 decimal equals 16*16*16*16*16, or FFFFF hex. Thus addresses up to one megabyte therefore can be expressed by exactly five hexadecimal digits, from 00000 to FFFFF.

What is the absolute memory address of the character display memory? That depends whether you're using an old-fashioned monochrome character-only display or a graphics display. For the character display the addresses start at B0000 (hex) and go up to B0F9F (F9F hex is 3999 decimal). In a graphics display, which is probably used in the majority of systems, the addresses start at B8000 and go up to B8F9F.

We'll assume you have a graphics display. If you're using a character display you should translate references to address B8000 in the text to address B0000. Figure 15.11 shows the relationship between this memory and the display, assuming a color graphics display is used.

We need 20-bit numbers, represented by 5 hex digits, to represent absolute memory addresses. If there were 20-bit registers in the 8086 family of computers, that would be the end of the problem. We would put the appropriate 5-digit hex number in the register and access any byte in memory. However, as we noted in Chapter 12, "Memory," the address registers in the 8086 and its descendants are only 16 bits wide. Thus we can't address memory using a single register. Instead we must put part of the number in one register and the other part in another register.

This is why the segment/offset approach is used. Memory is thought of as being divided into a certain number of segments, each of which can hold up to 65,536 bytes. A segment register holds the address of a segment, which can run from 0 to 65,535, or 0000 to FFFF hex; and an offset register holds the offset within a segment, also ranging from 0 to FFFF hex.

How does the memory-addressing hardware combine the contents of the segment and offset registers to yield an absolute address? Here's the story: the segment register is shifted left four bits (one hex digit) and then added to the offset address. Figure 15.12 shows how this looks for a byte in the middle of the display memory.

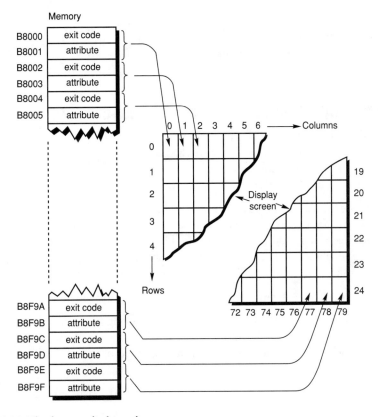

Figure 15.11: The character display and memory.

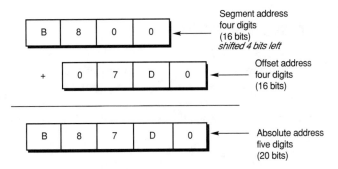

Figure 15.12. Combining segment and offset addresses.

In Figure 15.12 the segment address, B800, is shifted left four bits and then added to the offset address, 07D0. The result is the absolute memory address, B87D0.

> In the microprocessor the absolute address is obtained by shifting the segment address left four bits and then adding the offset address.

Representing Segment-Offset Addresses in C

In C, hexadecimal numbers can occupy either two bytes (16-bit integers) or four bytes (32-bit long integers). In either case a hexadecimal constant is specified by preceding the number with 0x (the digit 0 and the letter x). An example of a 16-bit hex constant is 0xAB12, and a 32-bit constant might be 0xABCD1234.

Because the segment that holds the display memory isn't part of our program's default data segment, we must use 32-bit far pointers to address it. A 32-bit hex constant, representing the memory address, is assigned to this far pointer. What does this constant look like? You might think that you would use the absolute address. Thus to set a pointer to the address shown in the figure, B87D0, you would use the statement

```
farptr = 0xB87D0;    // not how to represent absolute B87D0
```

However, this isn't how it's done. Instead, C makes use of the same segment-offset combination as the hardware. The 32-bit (eight hex digits) representation consists of the four digits of the segment address followed by the four digits of the offset address. Thus the statement

```
farptr = 0xB80007D0;    // correct representation of absolute B87D0
```

shows the correct way to represent absolute address B87D0: as B800 (the segment address) followed by 07D0 (the offset address).

Filling the Screen with a Character

Let's see how to fill the screen with 2,000 copies of a single character. To show how rapid this approach is, compared with using such C library routines as putch, we'll make it possible to change all the characters in the display at once by pressing a key. Each time the user presses a new key, the entire screen is filled, almost instantaneously, with the new character. The program terminates when the user presses the Enter key. Here's the listing:

```
// dfill.c
// uses direct memory access to fill screen
#include <stdio.h>                    // for printf()
```

```
#include <conio.h>              // for getch()
#define LENGTH 2000             // number of characters

void main(void)
    {
    int far *farptr;            // pointer to video memory
    int position;               // character position
    char ch;

    printf("Type character to start, type again to change");
    farptr = (int far *) 0xB8000000L;   // (B0000000 for mono)
    while( (ch=getch()) != '\r' )       // terminate on [Enter]
       for(position=0; position<LENGTH; position++)
           *(farptr + position) = ch ¦ 0x0700;
    }
```

Remember that if you're using a monochrome character-only monitor for text display, you should use the constant 0xB0000000 instead of 0xB8000000. This is true of all programs in this chapter that directly address the character display memory; if you're using a character display, change the address.

This program uses a simple for loop, running from 0 to 2,000, to fill in all the memory addresses in the character memory. The statement that does the job is

```
*(farptr + position) = ch ¦ 0x0700;
```

This statement references each address in turn by adding the number position, which runs from 0 to 1999, to the starting address of video memory, which we set farptr to before the loop.

On the right side of this assignment statement the variable ch is the character we want to place in memory; it was obtained from the keyboard. The constant 0x0700 is the attribute byte, shifted left one byte to place it on the left side of the two-byte (integer) quantity. This constant, 0x07, is the *normal* attribute; that is, the one that creates nonblinking, nonbold, white-on-black text. We'll see why soon.

Cycling through the loop 2,000 times inserts 2,000 integers in memory; the high byte of the integer is the extended character code and the low byte is the attribute.

Another statement that requires explanation is

```
farptr = (int far *)0xB8000000L;
```

Why do we need to typecast the hex representation of the memory address? The constant 0xB8000000 and the variable farptr are of different types: the constant looks like a long integer, while farptr is a far pointer to int. To avoid a warning from the compiler, we force the constant to be a far pointer to int.

Let's make a small change to the program.

```
// dfill2.c
// uses direct memory access to fill screen
```

```
#include <stdio.h>              // for printf()
#include <conio.h>              // for getche()
#define ROMAX 25               // number of screen rows
#define COMAX 80               // number of screen columns

void main(void)
   {
   int far *farptr;
   int col, row;
   char ch;

   printf("Type character to start, type again to change");
   farptr = (int far *)0xB8000000L;
   while( (ch=getche()) != '\r' )
      for(row=0; row<ROMAX; row++)
         for(col=0; col<COMAX; col++)
            *(farptr + row*COMAX + col) = (int)ch | 0x0700;
   }
```

In future programs, we'll make use of functions that accept as input the row and column number of a character and then display the character on the screen at the appropriate place using direct memory access. The dfill2.c program shows how it's done. In the last line, the variables row and col represent the row and column number of the character to be inserted. The corresponding memory address is found by multiplying the row number by the number of columns in a row, and then adding the result and the column number to the starting address of the character memory in farptr. Because we're now imagining the screen as a two-dimensional entity of rows and columns (rather than a one-dimensional group of memory addresses), we use two nested loops to insert the characters.

Speed Comparison

To get an idea of the speed advantage provided by direct memory access using far pointers, we'll rewrite dfill2.c to use the putch() library function. Here's the listing:

```
// cfill.c
// uses putch() to fill screen
#include <stdio.h>              // for printf()
#include <conio.h>              // for getch()
#define ROMAX 25
#define COMAX 80

void main(void)
   {
   int col, row;
   char ch;

   printf("Type character to start, type again to change");
   while( (ch=getch()) != '\r' )
      for(row=0; row<ROMAX; row++)
```

```
        for(col=0; col<COMAX; col++)
            printf("%c", ch);
    }
```

This program also fills the screen with a single character, but, at least on our system, it takes about 20 times longer than dfill2.c. Unless your display is very fast you'll see a noticeable delay when you press a key during a run of this program.

The Attribute Byte

As we've noted before, the location in the graphics memory corresponding to a single character position on the screen consists of two bytes: one to hold the extended code of the character, the other to hold its attribute. In Chapter 8, "Keyboard and Cursor," we discussed the attributes: underline, intensified, blinking, and reverse video. How do these relate to the attribute byte?

Figure 15.13 shows how the attribute byte is divided into sections. Two of these sections consist of a single bit. Bit 3 controls intensity, and bit 7 controls blinking. If one of these bits is set to 1, the corresponding attribute (blinking or intensified) is turned on; when the bit is set to 0, the attribute is off.

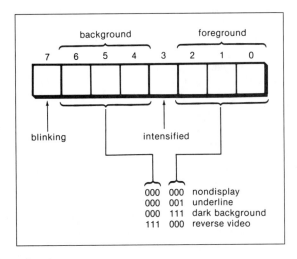

Figure 15.13. The attribute byte.

The two other sections of the attribute byte consist of three bits each. Bits 0, 1, and 2 make up the *foreground color,* and bits 4, 5, and 6 make up the *background color.* (In a monochrome character-only system there is no color, but the same attribute-byte format is used in the color character display.) There are three choices for the monochrome display foreground color: black, white (or green or amber, depending on your monitor), and underline. The underline attribute is treated as a color for some reason. For the background there are only two color choices: black or white. Figure 15.13 shows the four meaningful ways these "colors can be combined, yielding nondisplay (invisible), underline, normal video (white on black), and reverse video (black on white).

Here's a revision of our dfill2.c program that fills the screen with characters all having the blinking attribute. Pressing the Enter key (or any key) starts the screen blinking, and pressing it again terminates the program. Before exiting, the program sets all the attribute bytes back to normal. The operating system doesn't reset them automatically when the program terminates, so you must either get the program to do it or manually use the DOS command CLS, which does reset them.

```
// dfill3.c
// fills screen using blinking attribute
#include <stdio.h>                      // for printf()
#include <conio.h>                      // for getch()
#define ROMAX 25
#define COMAX 80
void main(void)
    {
    int far *farptr;
    int col, row;
    char ch;

    farptr = (int far *) 0xB8000000L;
    ch = 'X';
    printf("\nType [Enter] to start, type again to exit");
    getch();
    for(row=0; row<ROMAX; row++)
       for(col=0; col<COMAX; col++)                    // set to
          *(farptr + row*COMAX + col) = ch | 0x8700;   // blinking
    getch();
    for(row=0; row<ROMAX; row++)
       for(col=0; col<COMAX; col++)                    // set to
          *(farptr + row*COMAX + col) = ch | 0x0700;   // normal
    }
```

In the last program we used the attribute 07, which is 00000111 in binary. That is, the three bits of the foreground color are set to 1s, but everything else is a 0. To turn on blinking, we want to set bit 7 to 1, so we use the hex number 87, which is 10000111 in binary. This byte is then in effect shifted left eight bits, as described earlier, so it's on the left side of the integer that will be placed in memory.

The Attribute Fill Program

To get a better idea of the attributes and how they interact, enter and compile the following program. This is a variation of dfill.c, but it includes a switch statement that permits different attributes to be selected when the screen is filled. In addition to demonstrating the attribute byte, this program also provides a demonstration of the bitwise operators at work.

```
// attrfill.c
// allows user to change all attributes
#include <stdio.h>                        // for printf()
#include <conio.h>                        // for getch()
#define ROMAX 25
#define COMAX 80
void fill(char, char);    // prototype

void main(void)
    {
    char ch, attr;

    printf("Type 'n' for normal,\n");
    printf("     'u' for underlined,\n");
    printf("     'i' for intensified,\n");
    printf("     'b' for blinking,\n");
    printf("     'r' for reverse video,\n");
    while( (ch=getch()) != '\r' )
        {
        switch (ch)
            {
            case 'n':
                attr = 0x07;       // set to normal
                break;             // 0000 0111
            case 'u':
                attr = attr & 0x88; // set to underline
                attr = attr | 0x01; // x000 x001
                break;
            case 'i':
                attr = attr ^ 0x08; // toggle intensified
                break;             // xxxx Txxx
            case 'b':
                attr = attr ^ 0x80; // toggle blinking
                break;             // Txxx xxxx
            case 'r':
                attr = attr & 0x88; // set to reverse
                attr = attr | 0x70; // x111 x000
                break;
            }
        fill(ch,attr);
        }
    }

// fill()
// fills screen with character 'ch', attribute 'attr'
void fill(char ch, char attr)
    {
    int far *farptr;
    int col, row;

    farptr = (int far *) 0xB8000000L;
    for(row=0; row<ROMAX; row++)
```

```
        for(col=0; col<COMAX; col++)
            *(farptr + row*COMAX + col) = ch | (attr << 8);
    }
```

When the screen is filled, using the `fill()` function, the variable `attr` is used for the attribute byte rather than a constant as before. This value of `attr` is set by the various options in the `switch` statement.

Different options are handled in differing ways. Typing `'n'` for normal always resets `attr` to 07 hex, which provides the standard attribute. The two one-bit attributes, blinking and intensified, can be toggled on and off, using the bitwise XOR operator on the appropriate bit. Reverse video and underline are set by masking off only the "color attributes and resetting them without disturbing the one-bit attributes. On color displays pressing `'u'` for underline actually causes the characters to be colored rather than underlined. Press the Enter key to exit the program.

In previous programs we placed the attribute in an integer: 0x0700. Here we use a character for the attribute, so we need to shift it left one byte before combining it with the character `ch`. We do this using the left-shift (`<<`) operator in the last statement in `fill()`.

A style note: for clarity we've written the bitwise operations as separate statements. To achieve compactness, however, we could have combined them so that, for example, these lines

```
attr = attr & 0x88;   // set to underline
attr = attr | 0x01;   // x000 x001
```

would become

```
attr = (attr & 0x88) | 0x01;
```

Bit Fields

In the attrfill.c program we accessed individual bits and groups of bits using the bitwise operators. We can take an entirely different approach to accessing bits: the use of bit fields. A *bit field* is a special kind of structure. Each of the members of such a structure occupies a certain number of bits. The number of bits each member occupies is specified following a colon in the structure declaration. The members of the structure then are packed into an unsigned integer. The members must all be of type `unsigned int`. Here's an example of a bit-field declaration:

```
struct
    {
    unsigned int twobits  : 2;   // bits 0 and 1
    unsigned int sixbits  : 6;   // bits 2 through 7
    unsigned int againsix : 6;   // bits 8 through 13
    unsigned int onebit   : 1;   // bit 14
    unsigned int extrabit : 1;   // bit 15
    } sample;
```

Figure 15.14 shows how the integer represented by this structure looks.

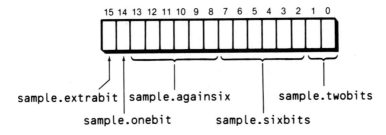

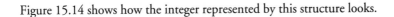

Figure 15.14. Bit fields.

Accessing the members of a field requires the same format as accessing members of other structures: the dot operator is used to connect the name of the structure variable with the name of the member, as in these examples:

```
sample.twobits = 3;
sample.sixbits = 63;
sample.onebit = 1;
```

Note that you can't give a field element a value that exceeds its capacity; a one-bit field can have only two values, 0 and 1, and a six-bit field can have values from 0 up to 63. Thus the values assigned in the sample are all maximums.

The following version of the attrfill.c program uses bit fields to access the various parts of the attribute byte:

```
// attrf2.c
// allows user to change all attributes
// bitfields represent attribute byte
#include <stdio.h>                    // for printf()
#include <conio.h>                    // for getch()
#define ROMAX 25
#define COMAX 80
void fill(char, unsigned int);

void main(void)
   {
   struct bits                    // bit fields
      {
      unsigned int foregnd : 3;    // bits 0, 1, 2
      unsigned int intense : 1;    // bit 3
      unsigned int backgnd : 3;    // bits 4, 5, 6
      unsigned int blinker : 1;    // bit 7
      } b1;                        // define struct variable

   union                          // declare union
      {                           // of
```

```
        unsigned int attr;          // unsigned int and
        struct bits b1;             // bitfield
        } u1;                       // define union variable

   char ch;

   printf("Type 'n' for normal,\n");
   printf("     'u' for underlined,\n");
   printf("     'i' for intensified,\n");
   printf("     'b' for blinking,\n");
   printf("     'r' for reverse video,\n");
   while( (ch=getch()) != '\r')   // terminate on [Enter]
      {
      switch (ch)
         {
         case 'n':                  // set to normal
            u1.b1.blinker = 0;
            u1.b1.backgnd = 0;
            u1.b1.intense = 0;
            u1.b1.foregnd = 7;
            break;
         case 'u':                  // set to underline
            u1.b1.foregnd = 1;
            break;
         case 'i':                  // toggle intensity
            u1.b1.intense = (u1.b1.intense==1) ? 0 : 1;
            break;
         case 'b':                  // toggle blinking
            u1.b1.blinker = (u1.b1.blinker==1) ? 0 : 1;
            break;
         case 'r':                  // set to reverse
            u1.b1.foregnd = 0;
            u1.b1.backgnd = 7;
            break;
         }  // end switch
      fill(ch, u1.attr);
      }  // end while
   }  // end main()

// fill()
// fills screen with character 'ch', attribute 'attr'
void fill(char ch, unsigned int attr)
   {
   int far *farptr;
   int col, row;

   farptr = (int far *) 0xB8000000L;
   for(row=0; row<ROMAX; row++)
      for(col=0; col<COMAX; col++)
         *(farptr + row*COMAX + col) = ch | (attr << 8);
   }
```

Because the attributes must be accessed both as bit fields and as an integer, a union is used so that they can be referred to in either way. (When you compile this program, ignore the warning about b1 being declared but never used; the compiler is confused about this.)

To set foreground and background colors, the appropriate fields are assigned the desired values. To toggle the blinking and intensity attributes, the conditional operator is used to assign values to the appropriate bits.

> Bit fields provide an organized approach to accessing individual bits and groups of bits.

Using fields probably gives a cleaner-looking approach, but the bitwise operators, which closely mirror the underlying assembly language instructions, are faster.

System Memory

Now that you know how to access absolute memory addresses, we can introduce another feature of the MS-DOS system: system memory. This is an area in lower memory that holds various kinds of information about the system. As an example of such information, we'll look at the equipment list word and the memory size word.

The *equipment list word* is a two-byte area at absolute address 410 hex that contains information about the equipment connected to the computer. When the computer is first turned on, the ROM BIOS Startup Routine examines the computer's various connectors to see what peripherals are connected, and then sets the bits in this word accordingly.

The equipment list word can be useful in two ways. First, a program often needs to know whether a certain piece of equipment is present. There's no use trying to print on the serial printer, for instance, if one isn't hooked up to the system. Second, it's sometimes necessary to alter the settings in the equipment list word.

Figure 15.15 shows the layout of the equipment list word. To access the word, we use a far pointer, as we did with character display memory. In this case, however, the pointer will point to segment 0000, offset address 0410 (hex), which is represented in C as 00000410 hex, or simply 0x410.

To examine the individual bits and groups of bits in the word, we'll use the bitwise operators (we could also have used fields). In general, we'll shift the equipment list word to the right, to put the bits we want on the right of the word, and then we'll mask any unwanted bits on the left with the bitwise AND operator.

In addition to the equipment list word, we also read a word that contains the size of installed memory in Kbytes. The *memory size word* is located at absolute address 413 hex, so to access it we need to reset the variable farptr to point to this new address.

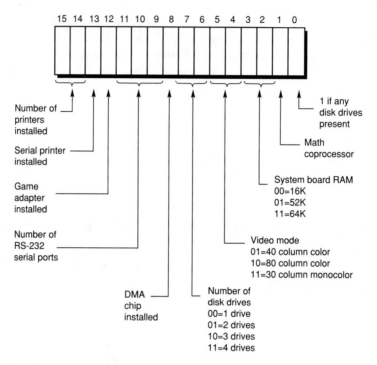

Figure 15.15. The equipment list word.

Here's the listing:

```
// eqlist.c
// lists equipment attached to computer
#include <stdio.h>          // for printf()
#define EQLIST 0x410        // location of equipment list word
#define MEMSIZ 0x413        // location of memory size word
void main(void)
    {
    int far *farptr;
    unsigned int eq, data;

    farptr = (int far *)EQLIST;
    eq = *(farptr);
    data = eq >> 14;                     // printers
    printf("Number of printers is %d.\n", data);
    if(eq & 0x2000)                      // serial printer
        printf("Serial printer is present.\n");
    data = (eq >> 9) & 7;                // serial ports
    printf("Number of serial ports is %d.\n", data);
    if(eq & 1)                           // diskette drives
        {
```

```
        data = (eq >> 6) & 3;
        printf("Number of diskette drives is %d.\n", data+1);
        }
    else
        printf("No diskette drives attached.\n");
    data = (eq >> 4) & 3;                    // video mode
    switch (data)
        {
        case 1: printf("Video is 40 column color.\n"); break;
        case 2: printf("Video is 80 column color.\n"); break;
        case 3: printf("Video is 80 column monochrome.\n");
        }
    if(eq & 2)
        printf("Math coprocessor");
    else
        printf("No math coprocessor");
    farptr = (int far *)MEMSIZ;
    printf("Memory is %d Kbytes.\n", *(farptr) );
    }
```

Here's a sample run for a particular installation:

```
Number of printers is 1.
Number of serial ports is 1.
Number of diskette drives is 2.
Video is 80 column color.
No math coprocessor.
Memory is 640 Kbytes.
```

The memory reported is conventional memory; it will say 640 no matter how much additional memory you may have installed.

You should be aware that Turbo C++ provides functions for reading the equipment list word and the memory size directly. These are `biosequip()`, which returns the equipment list word, and `biosmemory()`, which returns the memory size word. These are slightly easier to use, because you don't need to remember any absolute addresses. However, they aren't as educational as accessing memory directly.

There's a variety of useful words and bytes stored in the data area from 400 to 600 hex. To learn more about this area, you can consult one of the books referred to in Appendix C, "Bibliography."

The ROM BIOS

MS-DOS computers come with a set of routines built into the hardware. Collectively these are called the read-only-memory basic input/output system, or more commonly the ROM BIOS. Although these routines are built into hardware, they can be called as if they were functions in a normal program. C programs can use them to perform a variety of input/output activities. In this section we'll explore the ROM BIOS and see how it can be accessed from C.

As the name implies, the BIOS routines mostly handle input/output operations. Some of the routines duplicate Turbo C++ library functions. However, the ROM BIOS routines are often faster or more flexible than performing the same activity with a C library function, and some activities have no equivalent C function. Using a ROM BIOS routine rather than a Turbo C++ library function also makes your program more portable: the source code can be compiled by compilers other than Turbo C++, which don't use the Turbo C++ library functions.

The largest category of ROM BIOS routines deals with the video display. Available routines include setting the video mode, controlling the cursor size and position, reading and writing characters, and placing pixels on the graphics screen. There are also ROM routines for other input/output devices, including the diskette drives, the serial port, joysticks, user-defined devices, the keyboard, and the printer.

The ROM BIOS routines are written in assembly language and were designed to be called by assembly language programs. As a consequence, calling them from C isn't as simple as calling C library functions. C compilers designed for the PC generally provide a method to access these routines, but using this method requires at least some understanding of the architecture of the microprocessor chip that powers the computer. This chip can be the 8086, 80286, 80386, 80486, Pentium, and so on, depending on the particular machine. For our discussion we'll assume that these chips all operate in the same way.

Microprocessor Architecture for C Programmers

As you know, when you call a C function from a C program, you can pass values using arguments placed in the parentheses following the function name, as in the expression strcat(s1, s2). These values (in this example the addresses of strings) are placed on the stack (see Chapter 12, "Memory") where the function can find and operate on them.

Registers

When we use C to call a BIOS routine, the process is somewhat different. Instead of values being placed in an area of memory, they're placed in hardware devices called *registers*. We've already mentioned address registers, but other registers perform arithmetic and many other operations. Here we're concerned only with using registers as locations for passing arguments to the BIOS.

There are a number of registers in the microprocessor; the ones we'll be most concerned with are shown in Figure 15.16. As you can see, each of these four registers, AX, BX, CX, and DX, consist of two bytes. (Either upper- or lowercase may be used for register names, so they can be called ax, bx, cx, and dx as well.) In some ways the registers are like integer variables in C. They can hold two bytes of data, and we can put whatever values we like into them, just as we can assign whatever value we want to a variable. Unlike C variables, however, the registers are fixed; they're always there, and they always have the same names. They can be thought of as special-purpose permanent variables.

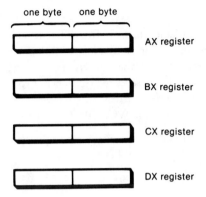

Figure 15.16. The main 8086 registers.

The Dual Role of the Registers

Another difference between C variables and registers is that registers can be accessed in two different ways: either as four two-byte registers or as eight one-byte registers, as shown in Figure 15.17.

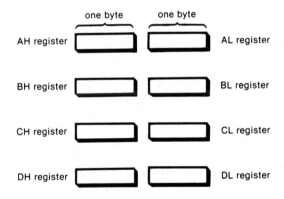

Figure 15.17. Registers as one-byte storage.

In the one-byte interpretation, each register is split into a high half (AH, BH, CH, and DH) and a low half (AL, BL, CL, DL). Although the register is the same physical object whether used as one two-byte device or two one-byte devices, the rest of the hardware in the chip interprets them differently, and so each must be accessed differently by the software.

A Union of Structures

The idea of using the same variable storage in two different ways should sound familiar; it is similar to our description of a union in Chapter 9, "Structures." In fact, a union is the mechanism used to communicate with the registers. Two structures are defined in the dos.h header file: WORDREGS represents the registers as two-byte devices, and BYTEREGS represents them as one-byte devices. (In assembly language a two-byte piece of data is called a *word*, hence the name WORDREGS, for *word registers*.)

A union, REGS, then causes these structures to occupy the same location in memory. Here's how this looks in the dos.h header file:

```
struct WORDREGS          // registers as 16-bit words
    {
    unsigned int ax;
    unsigned int bx;
    unsigned int cx;
    unsigned int dx;
    unsigned int si;
    unsigned int di;
    unsigned int flags;
    };

struct BYTEREGS          // registers as 8-bit bytes
    {
    unsigned char al, ah;
    unsigned char bl, bh;
    unsigned char cl, ch;
    unsigned char dl, dh;
    };

union REGS               // either bytes or words
    {
    struct WORDREGS x;
    struct BYTEREGS h;
    };
```

The first structure, whose tag is WORDREGS, consists of all the registers in their two-byte interpretation. The data type used is `unsigned int`, because the numbers stored in the registers aren't considered to be signed.

WORDREGS declares the four two-byte registers we discussed: the AX, BX, CX, and DX registers. It also declares several registers we didn't mention: the SI, DI, and FLAGS registers. We don't need these registers in the ROM calls we use, but they must appear in the structure, because the `int86` function is expecting them. BYTEREGS declares the eight one-byte registers: AL, AH, BL, BH, CL, CH, DL, DH.

The union REGS creates a set of variables that can be looked at either as four two-byte registers or as eight one-byte registers. The WORDREGS structure is given the variable name x (because all the two-byte registers end in this letter), and the BYTEREGS structure is given the name h (because the high half of the registers end in this letter). The union variable declared to be of type REGS is called `regs`.

Thus to access a register we use the dot operator twice.

`regs.x.bx`

means the BX register, and

`regs.h.cl`

refers to the CL register.

Before we put all this to work in an example, we need to explore one other idea.

Interrupt Numbers

The ROM BIOS routines are accessed through interrupts. We need not concern ourselves with exactly how interrupts work; for our purposes an interrupt can be thought of as a group of functions. Each such group has its own interrupt number. For instance, all the routines that deal with the video display use interrupt number 10 (hex), and all those that deal with the disk drive use number 13 (hex). Thus, in order to call a ROM BIOS routine, we must first know its interrupt number.

> An interrupt provides access to a group of ROM BIOS routines.

To specify a routine within one of these groups, we place a value in the one-byte AH register. Various other registers may also hold values, depending on the specific function called.

The *int86()* Function

The mechanism used to access a ROM BIOS routine is a C library function called `int86()`. The int stands for *interrupt* and the *86* refers to the 80x86 family of chips. This function takes the interrupt number and two union variables as arguments. The first union represents the values in the registers being sent to the ROM routine, and the second represents the values in the registers being returned from the ROM routine to the C program. Figure 15.18 shows the format of this function. Notice that the function actually requires the addresses of the unions, not the unions themselves (in the same way `scanf()` requires the addresses of numerical variables).

Now, we're ready for an actual example of a program that accesses the ROM BIOS.

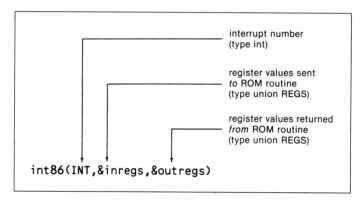

Figure 15.18. Format of the `int86()` *function.*

Finding the Memory Size

One of the routines built into the ROM BIOS returns the size of conventional RAM. (This is the third way to find this value: we've already seen how to read absolute address 0x413 and call the `biosmemory()` function.) The data required for this ROM BIOS routine is summarized in the following box. We'll use similar boxes for other ROM BIOS routines as we go along.

ROM BIOS routine	Memory Size
Interrupt 12 hex	Memory size
Input registers	None
Output registers	AX=memory size in Kbytes

Here there are only two pertinent items of data about the routine: we invoke it by calling interrupt 12 hex, and the memory size is read from the AX register. No other registers are used. (Other ROM BIOS routines will use additional registers for input and output values.) Here's the program:

```
// memsize.c
// uses ROM BIOS routine to find memory size
#include <stdio.h>              // for printf()
#include <dos.h>               // for int86(), REGS
#define VIDEO 0x12             // BIOS interrupt number

void main(void)
   {
   union REGS regs;            // regs to be type union REGS
   unsigned int size;
```

```
int86(VIDEO, &regs, &regs); // call video interrupt
size = regs.x.ax;           // get value from AX register
printf("Memory size is %u Kbytes", size );
}
```

Here's the output generated on a particular machine:

```
Memory size is 640 Kbytes
```

In this program, we don't need to send any values to the routine, so nothing is placed in any of the registers before we call `int86()`. Interrupt number 12 (hex) is unusual in this respect; most interrupt numbers require more information, as we'll see. Because one argument isn't used, we can use the same union variable, regs, for both the outgoing and incoming values.

```
int86(MEM, &regs, &regs);
```

On the return from `int86()` the memory size has been placed in the AX register, which we access in the expression

```
size = regs.x.ax
```

The data type of `size` agrees with that of `regs.x.ax` because they're both unsigned integers.

Setting the Cursor Size

Let's look at an example that requires us to send values to a ROM BIOS routine rather than just reading them back. This program will call a routine that changes the size of the cursor, so let's first examine how the cursor is created.

If you're using a VGA graphics display, the cursor can potentially consist of 14 lines, numbered from 0 to 13, as shown in Figure 15.19. (The same is true for a monochrome character-only display, but for CGA and EGA, there are only 8 lines, numbered from 0 to 7).

The default cursor, the one you're most used to seeing, uses only two of these lines 12 and 13 at the bottom of the character position (7 and 8 in EGA and monochrome). To redefine the size of the cursor, we call the BIOS routine at interrupt 10 (hex), with the AH register containing 1.

ROM BIOS routine	Set Cursor Size
Interrupt 10 hex	Video
Input registers	AH=01
	CH=starting scan line (0 to 13 dec)
	CL=ending scan line (0 to 13 dec)
Output registers	None

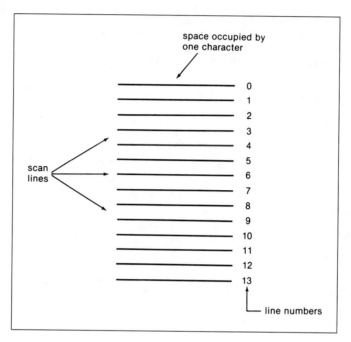

Figure 15.19. Cursor line numbering.

We also place the starting cursor line number in the CH register and the ending line number in the CL register. Here's the program:

```
// setcur.c
// sets cursor size
#include <dos.h>            // for int86(), REGS
#define CURSIZE 1           // "set cursor size" service
#define VIDEO 0x10          // video BIOS interrupt number

void main( int argc, char *argv[] )
   {
   union REGS regs;
   int start, end;
   if (argc != 3)
      {
      printf("Example usage: C>setcur 12 13");
      exit();
      }
   start = atoi( argv[1] );   // string to integer
   end = atoi( argv[2] );
   regs.h.ch = (char)start;   // starting line number
   regs.h.cl = (char)end;     // ending line number
```

```
    regs.h.ah = CURSIZE;        // service number
    int86(VIDEO, &regs, &regs); // call video interrupt
    }
```

In this example we make use of command-line arguments (described in Chapter 8, "Keyboard and Cursor") to get the starting and ending cursor lines numbers from the user. To cause the cursor to fill the entire character block, we would type

```
C>setcur 0 13
```

(Do this from DOS, not Turbo C++'s IDE.) To return to the normal cursor, we would type

```
C>setcur 12 13
```

You can make a thinner-than-normal cursor with 13 13 and a thicker cursor with 11 13. You can move the cursor to the top of the box with 0 1 and make it thinner and thicker with 0 0 and 0 2.

Making the Cursor Disappear

You can make the cursor vanish if you set bit 5, in the byte placed in the CH register, to 1, as shown in Figure 15.20. To do this we place the hex number 20 in the CH register; hex 20 is 00100000 in binary.

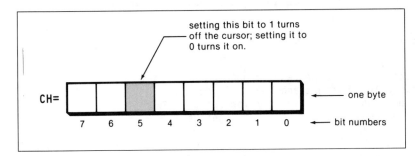

Figure 15.20. The cursor on/off bit.

The following program accomplishes the task:

```
// curoff.c
// turns cursor off
#include <dos.h>       // declares REGS
#define CURSIZE 1      // "set cursor size" service
#define VIDEO 0x10     // video BIOS interrupt number
#define STOPBIT 0x20   // this bit turns cursor off

void main(void)
    {
```

```
    union REGS regs;
    regs.h.ah = CURSIZE;         // service number
    regs.h.ch = STOPBIT;         // turns cursor off
    int86(VIDEO, &regs, &regs);  // call video interrupt
    }
```

This program is similar to setcur.c, except that we don't need to put anything into the CL register. When you run it, the cursor will vanish (which can be unnerving).

To turn the cursor back on, use the setcur.c program. Because it sends a value in CH that includes a 0 value for bit 5, the cursor will reappear no matter which values you use for the starting and stopping lines (provided they're between 0 and 13). Of course, as we already saw in Chapter 10, "Turbo C++ Graphics," you can also turn the cursor on and off with the setcursortype() Turbo C++ library function. However, it isn't as versatile as the Set Cursor Size ROM BIOS routine.

One-Line Word Processor

Let's put what we know about direct access to character memory together with ROM BIOS routines to create a simple word processing program—one that is so simple it operates on only a single line of text. It allows the user to type a line of characters and to move the cursor back and forth along the line, and it permits insertion and deletion. By pressing the Alt u key combination you can cause any subsequent text you type to be underlined, and by pressing the Alt r key combination you can cause it to appear in reverse video.

Here's the listing:

```
// wordrev.c
// rudimentary word-processing program
// with delete, insert and reverse video
#include <dos.h>              // for int86(), REGS
#include <conio.h>            // for getche()

#define COMAX   80            // max number of columns
#define R_ARRO  77            // right arrow
#define L_ARRO  75            // left arrow
#define BK_SPC   8            // backspace
#define ALT_N   49            // [Alt] and [n] key combo
#define ALT_U   22            // [Alt] and [u] key combo
#define ALT_R   19            // [Alt] and [r] key combo
#define VIDEO  0x10           // video ROM BIOS service
#define NORMAL 0x07           // normal attribute
#define UNDER  0x01           // underline attribute
#define REVERSE 0x70          // reverse video

void cursor(void);           // prototypes
void insert(char, char);
void delete(void);
void clear(void);
```

```
int col=0;                   // cursor position
int length=0;                // length of phrase
int far *farptr;             // pointer to video memory

void main(void)
    {
    char ch, attr=NORMAL;

    farptr = (int far *)0xB8000000L;
    clear();                         // clear screen
    cursor();                        // position cursor
    while( (ch=getch()) != '\r' )    // exit on [Enter]
        {
        if ( ch == 0 )               // if char is 0
            {
            ch = getch();            // read extended code
            switch(ch)
                {
                case R_ARRO: if(col<length) ++col; break;
                case L_ARRO: if(col>0)      --col; break;
                case ALT_U: attr = UNDER;   break;
                case ALT_R: attr = REVERSE; break;
                case ALT_N: attr = NORMAL;  break;
                }
            }
        else
            switch(ch)
                {
                case BK_SPC:
                    if(length>0) delete(); break;
                default:
                    if(length<COMAX) insert(ch,attr);
                }
        cursor();
        }
    }  // end main()

// cursor()
// move cursor to row=0, col
void cursor(void)
    {
    union REGS regs;

    regs.h.ah = 2;               // 'set cursor pos' service
    regs.h.dl = col;             // column varies
    regs.h.dh = 0;               // always top row
    regs.h.bh = 0;               // page zero
    int86(VIDEO, &regs, &regs);  // call video interrupt
    }

// insert()
// inserts character at cursor position
```

```
void insert(char ch, char attr)
   {
   int j;

   for(j=length; j>col; j--)              // shift chars right
      *(farptr + j) = *(farptr + j - 1); //   to make room
   *(farptr + col) = ch | (attr<<8);      // insert char
   ++length;                              // increment count
   ++col;                                 // move cursor right
   }

// delete()
// deletes character at position one left of cursor
void delete(void)
   {
   int j;

   for(j=col; j<=length; j++)             // shift chars left
      *(farptr + j - 1) = *(farptr + j);
   --length;                              // decrement count
   --col;                                 // move cursor left
   }

// clear()
// clears character screen by inserting 0 at every location
void clear(void)
   {
   int j;

   for(j=0; j<2000; j++)                  // fill screen memory
      *(farptr + j) = 0x0700;             // with 0's (attr=07)
   }
```

Almost everything in this program should already be familiar to you. The program first clears the screen, using a routine that fills the display memory with zeros; this is the same approach we used to fill the screen with a character in dfill.c. Then the cursor is moved to the beginning of the single line (the top line of the screen) using the set cursor position video ROM BIOS service.

ROM BIOS routine	Position Cursor
Interrupt 10 hex	Video
Input registers	AH=02
	DH=row number
	DL=column number
	BH=page number (usually 0)
Output registers	None

The switch statement approach to deciphering the cursor keys was used in Chapter 8, "Keyboard and Cursor." Pressing the appropriate cursor key increments or decrements the variable col, which indicates the column the cursor is on. A call to the cursor() function moves the cursor to this column.

If the character typed isn't an extended character (namely a cursor key) it is inserted into the display at column col using the insert() subroutine, which should be familiar from the preceding discussion of far pointers. The col variable is incremented when a character is inserted so that the next character will be typed just to its right.

Pressing the Alt U key combination starts underlining; pressing the Alt R key combination starts reverse video. Pressing the Alt N key combination restores the normal attribute.

To insert a character, the user simply moves the cursor to the desired spot and starts typing. The characters to the right will be shifted further right to make room. To delete, the user presses the Backspace key; this deletes the character to the left of the cursor. Any characters to the right will be shifted left to fill the space.

The insert() function uses a for loop with direct memory access and a far pointer to shift one space to the right all the characters that are to the right of the cursor. This shifting process must start at the right-hand end of the existing phrase; if the shifting were to start on the left, the leftmost character would overwrite the character next to it before it could be shifted. When all the characters have been shifted out of the way, the character typed by the user is inserted at the cursor position. Figure 15.21 shows this process.

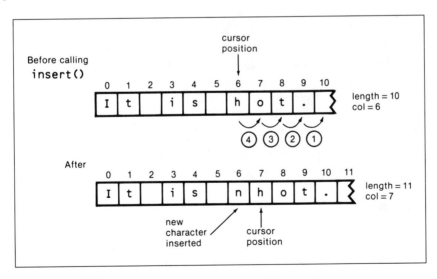

Figure 15.21. The insert() *function.*

Deletion is carried out in a similar way; all the characters to the right of the cursor are shifted left one space; the leftmost character writes over the character to be deleted. In this case the shifting starts on the left-hand end.

Using Interrupts to Call DOS

In addition to the routines built into the ROM BIOS, there are a number of routines in the MS-DOS operating system that can be called by a C program. In general, these DOS call routines are less useful for the C programmer. Many of them deal with disk input/output, which is already handled very well by normal C library functions, and we won't explore them in this book. However, the method of accessing these DOS interrupt routines is similar to that for accessing the ROM BIOS routines.

Direct-Access Graphics

In the first section of this chapter we saw how to directly access the memory that controls the character display. In the character memory each byte (actually each pair of bytes) represented a character. The graphics display memory can be directly accessed in a similar way. However, in the graphics memory each byte (or part of a byte, or group of bytes, depending on the mode) represents a pixel on the screen rather than a character.

By using direct access to the graphics memory you can generate all the same image elements you can using the Turbo C++ graphics functions. In fact, some of those functions use direct access themselves. However, in many cases you can speed up graphics displays dramatically by using the direct access approach. Learning this approach will also teach you a great deal about how the graphics display works.

To run the programs in this chapter you'll need a graphics adapter and a graphics display monitor; a character-only system won't work. We'll assume that you're using a VGA graphics system. If you're still using an older CGA or EGA system, we suggest you update it immediately. VGA provides a superior display and in some ways is easier to program as well. However, if you have only an EGA display, you can adapt the programs we describe in the section on VGA mode 18 to run in EGA mode 13.

To execute a graphics program, you need to know how to switch into a graphics mode. So before we start putting pixels on the screen, we'll discuss graphics modes.

Display Modes

Just as an artist can choose from a variety of media when creating a picture (oils, etching, or watercolors), so a PC graphics programmer can choose from a variety of different *modes,* or formats. Each mode provides a different combination of graphics characteristics. These characteristics include the resolution, the number of possible colors, whether text or graphics are to be displayed, and other elements. Different modes require different hardware (monitors and adapter boards) and different programming approaches.

Table 15.1 summarizes the available modes and the graphics characteristics of each one. We'll explain the elements of this table in the following sections.

Table 15.1. Graphics modes.

Mode (dec)	Colors	Resolution	Adapter	Monitor	Minimum Memory	Pages	Starting Address.
0 text	16 gray	40x25*	CGA	CD	2K	8 (16K)	B8000.
1 text	16	40x25*	CGA	CD	2K	8 (16K)	B8000.
2 text	16 gray	80x25*	CGA	CD	4K	4 (16K)	B8000.
3 text	16	80x25*	CGA	CD	4K	4 (16K)	B8000.
4 grph	4	320x200	CGA	CD	16K	1 (16K)	B8000.
5 grph	4 gray	320x200	CGA	CD	16K	1 (16K)	B8000.
6 grph	2 (B&W)	640x200	CGA	CD	16K	1 (16K)	B8000.
7 text	2 (B&W)	80x25*	MA	MD	4K	1 (4K)	B0000.
**							
13 grph	16	320x200	EGA	ECD	32K	2 (64K)	A0000.
14 grph	16	640x200	EGA	ECD	64K	1 (64K)	A0000.
15 grph	2 (B&W)	640x350	EGA	ECD	64K	1 (64K)	A0000.
16 grph	16	640x350	EGA	ECD	128K	1(128K)	A0000.
17 grph	2 (B&W)	640x480	VGA	VD	256K	4(256K)	A0000.
18 grph	16	640x480	VGA	VD	256K	1(256K)	A0000.
19 grph	256	320x200	VGA	VD	256K	4(256K)	A0000

* Characters. Other resolutions in pixels.

** Modes 8, 9, and 10 were for the PC jr. Modes 11 and 12 are used internally by the EGA board.

grph	= Graphics	MA	= Monochrome Adapter
MD	= Monochrome Display	CGA	= Color Graphics Adapter
CD	= Color Display	EGA	= Enhanced Graphics Adapter
ECD	= Enhanced Color Display	VGA	= Video Graphics Array
VD	= VGA Display		

Other mode numbers are used for higher graphics standards, such as Super VGA (SVGA) and XGA, but these standards lack the wide acceptance of the VGA and may require special drivers. Accordingly we'll stick with VGA, which is a more or less universal standard.

Resolution

As we noted in Chapter 10, "Turbo C++ Graphics," graphics images on a computer screen are composed of tiny dots called *pixels*. The number of pixels on the screen determines the resolution, and each graphics mode uses a particular resolution. For example, mode 19 uses a resolution of 200 rows, each 320 pixels across. This is abbreviated 320 by 200, or 320x200. Higher resolution means a sharper, clearer picture, with less pronounced *jaggies*—the stairstep effect on diagonal lines. On the other hand, higher resolution means more pixels to process and is therefore slower.

Each pixel can appear in a variety of different colors (assuming the correct mode is set and the correct hardware is available). The arrangement of pixels on the screen is shown in Figure 15.22.

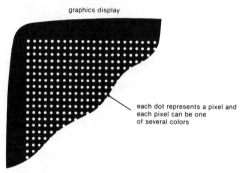

graphics display

each dot represents a pixel and each pixel can be one of several colors

Figure 15.22. Graphic images are made from pixels.

Text or Graphics

Some modes are character modes; they exist only to place text on the screen. Modes 0, 1, 2, and 3 are character modes for color (or grayscale) screens. Mode 7 is for a character-only monochrome display. A typical color display system uses mode 3 to display characters. That's probably the mode that MS-DOS and Turbo C++ use in your system.

All the other modes are for displaying graphics. The graphics modes can display text as well but often in a crude form and without the cursor.

Color

Some graphics modes provide more colors than others. Several modes provide only two colors: black and white (or perhaps black and green or amber, depending on your monitor). Other modes provide 4, 16, or 256 colors.

The Display Adapter

A display adapter is necessary to display graphics on a PC computer. In many computers the display adapter is a printed circuit board that plugs into one of the slots inside the computer. On other computers the adapter is built into the computer. There are different display adapters corresponding to the four graphics standards listed in Table 15.1: monochrome (text only), CGA, EGA, and VGA. The original IBM PC was released with a text-only monochrome adapter. A CGA adapter was an option. It displayed only the CGA modes: 0 through 6. Later, EGA-capable adapters were introduced that could display additional modes, from 13 through 16, as well as the CGA modes. More recently VGA adapters appeared that can display modes from 17 to 19, as well as the CGA and EGA modes. More advanced adapters (such as SVGA) can usually display all the CGA, EGA, and VGA modes.

> The greater the resolution of a graphics system, and the more colors, the more memory is required on the graphics adapter.

Display Memory

Like the character display, the graphics display uses memory to hold the data being displayed. This random access memory is similar to normal RAM, except that data placed in it causes an immediate change in the picture on the screen.

Different display adapters come with different amounts of memory. The text-only monochrome adapter has only 4K, enough for two bytes for each of 2,000 characters (80 columns times 25 rows). The CGA has more memory, 16K, which is enough for 640 by 200 pixels if only two colors are used. In this case, each bit in memory corresponds to one pixel. The figure 16K is derived from the total number of pixels: 640 times 200 is 128,000 pixels. Because each pixel corresponds to one bit, we can divide by 8 bits per byte to arrive at 16,000 bytes (this is actually slightly less than 16K, which is 16,384 bytes).

If the resolution is cut in half, to 320 by 200, we can now use two bits for each pixel, and two bits can represent four colors. This is another mode available on the CGA.

EGA adapters originally came with 64K of memory, which allowed 16 colors with a resolution of 640 by 200. Later 256K became the standard, which made possible additional pages, as is described next. VGA comes with at least 256K of memory, which provides 640 by 480 resolution with 16 colors or 320 by 200 with 256 colors.

Pages

When enough graphics memory is available in the adapter, it's possible to keep several screens of data in the memory at the same time. Thus, on the EGA board, mode 13 (320 by 200, 16 colors) requires only 32K, but at least 64K is available. The extra memory can be used to hold a second screen image. By switching from one page to another, rapid changes can be made to the image on the screen.

Starting Address

As with other parts of RAM, a memory location in a graphics adapter is identified by its address. We've already learned that the character memory for color graphics systems starts at absolute address B8000 and that for text-only monochrome systems starts at B0000. The graphics memory in the CGA modes starts at B8000, and in the EGA and VGA modes it starts at A0000.

Setting the Mode

If you're using a color graphics display, when you first turn on your computer you'll probably boot up in mode 3, a text mode. This mode doesn't permit you to do graphics. In this section we're going to explore two VGA-specific graphics modes: 18 and 19. Before we can display pictures in these modes, however, we need to switch the display adapter from the character mode to the graphics mode. We saw how to do that using Turbo C++ graphics functions in Chapter 10, "Turbo C++ Graphics," but there's a more direct way.

The ROM BIOS Set Mode Command

To select the mode, we make use of a ROM BIOS routine called Set Video Mode. This involves putting 0 in the AH register, the desired mode number in the AL register, and executing an interrupt number 10 (hex).

ROM BIOS routine	Set Video Mode
Interrupt 10 hex	Video
Input registers	AH=0
	AL=mode number
Output registers	None

The setmode.c Program

Here's the program that lets us switch graphics modes. It reads a command-line argument to know which mode we want. Thus, to switch to mode 19, we would type

```
C>setmode 19
```

from the DOS prompt. Here's the program:

```
// setmode.c
// sets graphics mode to value supplied
#include <stdio.h>       // for printf()
#include <process.h>     // for exit()
#include <stdlib.h>      // for atoi()
#include <dos.h>         // for REGS
#define SETMODE 0        // "set video mode" service
#define VIDEO 0x10       // video BIOS interrupt number

void main( int argc, char *argv[] )
   {
   union REGS regs;
   int mode;

   if (argc != 2)
      { printf("Example usage: setmode 7"); exit(1); }

   mode = atoi( argv[1] );      // string to integer
   regs.h.al = (char)mode;      // mode number in AL register
   regs.h.ah = SETMODE;         // service # in AH register
   int86(VIDEO, &regs, &regs);  // call video interrupt
   }
```

Don't use this program within Turbo C's IDE. Run it directly from DOS or from a DOS shell invoked from the IDE.

After you've switched to a graphics mode, The C> prompt should appear (looking somewhat different), but you won't see the flashing cursor; that's because the graphics modes don't support the cursor. Want to restore the cursor? Switch back to mode 3; that restores the prompt with the cursor.

You can call the Set Mode ROM routine to switch modes from within a more complex program. We handle mode switching in a separate program to make the listings simpler and to make it clearer what's going on. Notice that switching modes clears the screen. This can be a useful (though slow) way to clear the screen, either by using setmode.c or from within a program.

VGA Mode 19: 256 Colors

VGA offers all the modes of CGA and EGA graphics, as well as three new modes: 17, 18, and 19. Mode 17 is a black and white mode; we won't cover it here. Mode 18 provides the same 16 colors as EGA but with higher resolution, and mode 19 permits the simultaneous display of 256 colors. Mode 19 is the easiest to program, so we'll look at it first. Then we'll explore mode 18.

Display Memory Organization

VGA mode 19 can display 256 colors simultaneously, with a resolution of 320 by 200. It is conceptually the simplest of the graphics modes. There are 64,000 pixels on the screen (320 times 200). Each pixel is represented by one byte in memory. The pixels are mapped into memory in the most straightforward way, starting with the upper-left pixel and scanning line by line down the screen. This is much the same as the arrangement in the character display, except that in mode 19 each byte represents a pixel instead of two bytes representing a character.

The value in the byte that corresponds to a particular pixel determines the color of the pixel. A byte has eight bits, so each pixel can have up to 2^8, or 256 colors.

Drawing a Line of Pixels

Our first example is a simple one: it draws a single line of red pixels across the screen. However, it demonstrates many of the techniques for using mode 19. Here's the listing:

```
// vredline.c
// draws a red line across the screen -- use VGA mode 19
#define MAXX 320        // horizontal resolution
#define MAXY 200        // vertical resolution

void main(void)
    {
    char far *farptr;       // pointer to video memory
    int x, y;               // pixel coordinates (0-319, 0-199)
    unsigned char color;    // color value (0-255)

    farptr = (char far *) 0xA0000000L;  // set ptr to VGA memory
    color = 12;                         // red
    y = MAXY / 2;                       // middle of screen
    for(x=0; x<MAXX; x++)               // cycle across the line
        *(farptr + y*MAXX + x) = color; // set the pixel
    }
```

To run this program, first change to mode 19.

```
C>setmode 19
C>vredline
```

Follow this same approach with the rest of the programs in this chapter: change the mode, and then run the program. As we did with the character display, we set a far pointer to char, called farptr, to point to the beginning of display memory. In this mode the memory starts at A0000 hex.

We set the y coordinate to the center of the screen and x to the leftmost column. Then we cycle along a horizontal line, incrementing the x coordinate and inserting a red pixel at each location. The address of the pixel is the address of the beginning of the VGA memory (farptr), plus the length of each row times the particular row number (y*MAXX), plus the column number (x).

The byte at all locations is assigned the same number, 12. This produces a red color. The next program will show you how to tell which value produces which color.

Colors in Mode 19

Every possible value we can give a variable of type unsigned char corresponds to a unique color in mode 19. How do we find out which color goes with which number? The next program solves this problem by displaying all 256 colors.

```
// vcolors.c
// draws 256 different colored squares -- use VGA mode 19
#include <conio.h>       // for getch()
#define MAXX 320         // horizontal pixels
#define MAXY 192         // vert pixels (divisible by 16)
#define PPBX (MAXX/16)   // pixels per color box, horizontal
#define PPBY (MAXY/16)   // pixels per color box, vertical

void main(void)
   {
   char far *farptr;     // pointer to video memory
   int x, y;             // pixel coordinates (0-319, 0-191)
   int row, col;         // color box coordinates (0-15)
   unsigned char color;  // color of box (0-255)

   farptr = (char far *)0xA0000000L;    // set ptr to VGA memory
   for(y=0; y<MAXY; y++)                 // cycle down
      for(x=0; x<MAXX; x++)              // cycle across
         {
         col = x/PPBX;                   // find box coords
         row = y/PPBY;
         color = col + row*16;           // calculate color
         *(farptr + y*MAXX + x) = color; // set the pixel
         }
   getch();
   }
```

The vcolors.c program generates a color chart consisting of 16 rows and 16 columns, as shown in Figure 15.23.

Each color box is 20 pixels wide and 12 pixels high, and there are 256 boxes on the screen, in a 16 by 16 matrix. The program keeps track of two sets of coordinates: x and y specify the pixel location, and col and row specify the color box location. For each pixel location the program calculates the box location and colors the pixel accordingly. (There are faster ways to do this, but they complicate the program.)

The first row of boxes displays the 16 EGA colors, the second row is a gray scale, and subsequent rows contain a variety of color blends. By counting the rows and columns you can match each color with its number, starting with 0 for black in the upper-left corner ending with 255 in the lower-right corner.

Figure 15.23. Output of the vcolors.c program.

Animation in Mode 19

Let's liven things up with a little animation using mode 19. We'll draw a more or less round ball and have it move around the screen. Every time it hits the edge of the screen, it reflects or "bounces" at a 45-degree angle like a ball on a pool table, so it ends up traversing a complicated pattern, as shown in Figure 15.24.

This program uses a new technique, a bit-mapped pattern, to represent the ball. A bitmapped image can be drawn quickly. In this program we draw the image, wait briefly, erase it, and then draw the same image again in a slightly different place. A while loop in main() takes care of this process, as well as sensing when the ball has reached the edge of the screen and reversing its direction when it does. The actual drawing of the ball is handled by the function drawball().

```
// vbounce.c
// draws bouncing ball -- use VGA mode 19
#include <conio.h>                      // for kbhit()
#include <dos.h>                        // for delay()
#define MAXX 320
#define MAXY 200
#define RED   12
#define BLACK  0
void drawball(int, int, unsigned char);      // prototype

unsigned char far *farptr;              // to hold screen address
```

```
void main(void)
   {
   int x=10, y=10;              // starting point
   int dx=1, dy=1;              // increments
                                // set to screen address
   farptr = (unsigned char far *)0xA0000000L;
   while( kbhit()==0 )          // cycle until keypress
      {
      x += dx;  y += dy;        // increment location
      if(x<0 || x>MAXX-15)      // if at left or right,
         dx *= -1;              //     reverse direction
      if(y<0 || y>MAXY-15)      // if at top or bottom,
         dy *= -1;              //     reverse direction
      drawball(x, y, RED);      // draw ball at x, y
      delay(5);                 // slow things down
      drawball(x, y, BLACK);    // erase ball
      } // end while
   } // end main()

// drawball()
// draws ball, radius 16 pixels. Upper-left corner at col, row.
void drawball(int col, int row, unsigned char color)
   {
   unsigned mask;
   unsigned x, y, dotpat;
                                // picture of ball
   unsigned ball[16] = { 0x07E0, 0x1FF8, 0x3FFC, 0x7FFE,
                         0x7FFE, 0xFFFF, 0xFFFF, 0xFFFF,
                         0xFFFF, 0xFFFF, 0xFFFF, 0x7FFE,
                         0x7FFE, 0x3FFC, 0x1FF8, 0x07E0 };
   for(y=0; y<16; y++)          // for each of 16 rows
      {
      dotpat = ball[y];         // pattern for this row
      mask = 0x8000;            // one-bit mask on left
      for(x=0; x<16; x++)       // for each of 16 columns
         {
         if(mask & dotpat)      // if part of pattern
           *(farptr + (y+row)*MAXX + x+col) = color;  // set the pixel
         mask >>= 1;            // move mask right
         } // end for x
      } // end for y
   } // end drawball()
```

The pattern of the ball is stored as an array of integers in the function drawball(). The value of each integer is represented as a hexadecimal constant, which makes it easier to see the pattern of the bits. Each integer has 16 bits, and there are 16 integers, so the array ball can define a rectangular object of 16 by 16 pixels. The relationship between the hex numbers and the pattern is shown in Figure 15.25.

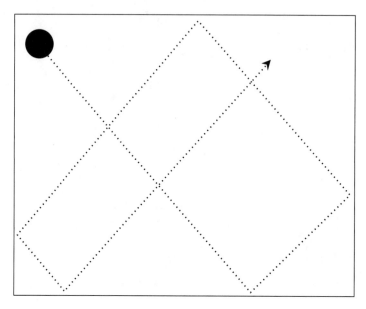

Figure 15.24. Bouncing ball.

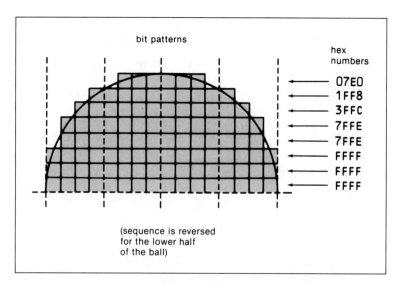

Figure 15.25. Hex numbers representing ball.

Each hex digit is represented by four squares; the dotted lines in the figure divide the pattern into hex digits. You can translate each hex digit into binary bits (hex 7 is 0111 binary). Then each bit represents a square, with 0 being a white square and 1 being a black square. For example, the first row, representing the top of the ball, is 07E0 hex, which is 0000,0111,1110,0000 binary.

The drawball() function uses a for loop to go through each of the 16 integers in turn. For each number, an inner for loop uses a one-bit mask to test each bit of the pattern word. If the bit is on, a dot is written to the screen using the far pointer. If it's not on, no bit is drawn. The result is the image of a ball.

To move the ball, the main program draws it, then erases it, then calculates the new location and draws it again. When the ball comes too close to the edge of the screen, which is checked for by the if statements, the signs of dy and dx—the increments by which the x and y coordinates of the ball are increased—are reversed, thus reversing the ball's direction of motion.

Of course other patterns could be used here as well— spaceships, running men, icons representing disks or files, or whatever. The size of the pattern could also be changed: an array of type char, with only 64 pixels, could be drawn faster than the present 256-pixel pattern.

VGA Mode 18: High Resolution

VGA mode 18 provides 640 by 480 resolution, using 16 colors. It uses a different and much more complex approach to putting pixels on the screen than we saw with mode 19. To program in this mode you'll need to learn a good bit about the internal structure of the VGA graphics adapter.

If you have only an EGA display, you'll be happy to know that EGA mode 13 is similar to VGA mode 18. The main difference is in resolution, which in EGA is 320 by 200, instead of 640 by 480. You can easily adapt the example programs to run in mode 13 by changing the resolution, given as the constants MAXX and MAXY, to 320 and 200.

Bit Planes

In mode 18 the hardware thinks of each of four primary colors as occupying a separate area of memory. Memory is divided into four sections, or *planes,* one for red, one for green, one for blue, and one for intensified. In any given plane, each bit represents one pixel, so eight blue pixels are packed into a byte in the blue plane, eight red pixels into a byte in the red plane, and so on. Figure 15.26 shows how this looks.

By selecting bits in the four different color planes, any of 16 colors can be created. These are the same 16 colors already listed for EGA graphics in Chapter 10, "Turbo C++ Graphics." The following list shows how each color is created by turning on bits in the four color planes.

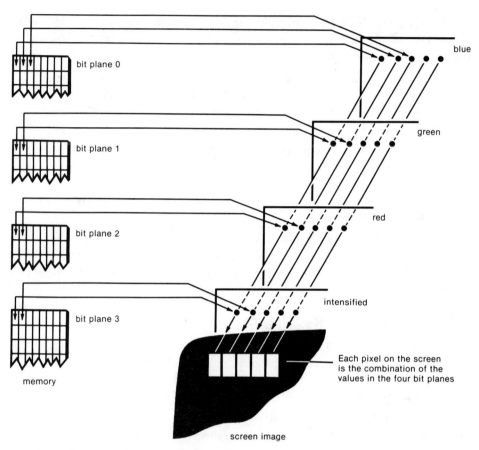

Each pixel on the screen
is the combination of the
values in the four bit planes

Figure 15.26. Bit planes and pixels.

Color	Dec	Hex	Intense Plane 3	Red 2	Green 1	Blue 0
Black	0	00				
Blue	1	01	-	-	-	X
Green	2	02	-	-	X	-
Cyan	3	03	-	-	X	X
Red	4	04	-	X	-	-
Magenta	5	05	-	X	-	X
Brown	6	06	-	X	X	-
White	7	07	-	X	X	X
Gray	8	08	X	-	-	-
Light blue	9	09	X	-	-	X

Color	Dec	Hex	Intense Plane 3	Red 2	Green 1	Blue 0
Light green	10	0A	X	-	X	-
Light cyan	11	0B	X	-	X	X
Light red	12	0C	X	X	-	-
Light magenta	13	0D	X	X	-	X
Yellow	14	0E	X	X	X	-
Bright white	15	0F	X	X	X	X

If you're only going to work with, say, blue pixels, you can do all your work in bit plane 0. However, to create most colors, you'll need to work in several bit planes at the same time. For instance, to set a pixel to light cyan, you'll need to set the appropriate bit in plane 0 (blue), in plane 1 (green), and in plane 3 (intensified).

Now you might suppose that each of the four bit planes would occupy a different address space (range of addresses) in memory so that accessing a particular byte in a particular bit plane would simply be a matter of figuring out the appropriate address. However, the designers of VGA and EGA were more devious than that. Why? Suppose the bit planes were in separate address spaces (perhaps A0000, A2000, A4000, and A6000). Then, to put a light cyan pixel on the screen, you would need to put a bit in three different places in memory; this would require three separate write operations (using far pointers). Not very efficient.

Instead—hold onto your hat—all four bit planes occupy the same address space. They all start at address A0000 hex. In the case of mode 18, with 640 times 480—or 307,200—pixels, the amount of memory needed is 307,200 divided by 8 pixels per byte, which is 38,400 (dec) or 9600 (hex) bytes. So all four bit planes start at A0000 and run up to A9600.

All four mode-18 bit planes occupy the same memory address space.

If all the bit planes are in the same place in memory, how can we specify that we want to turn on a pixel in only one color—blue, for example? It looks as if to turn on one bit, we end up turning on four bits, one in each bit plane, at the same time. How can we select only the bit planes we want? To answer this question, we must know how to program something called the map mask register.

The Map Mask Register

The VGA display adapter contains a custom integrated circuit chip called the *sequencer*. This device contains several registers, including the map mask register. By placing an appropriate value in the lower four bits of the map mask register, we can specify which of the four bit planes we want to write to. We can specify one plane or a group of planes. Figure 15.27 shows the map mask register in relation to the bit planes.

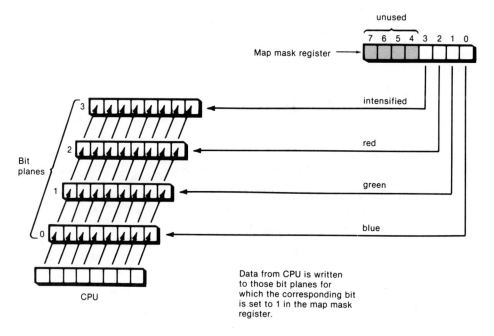

Figure 15.27. The map mask register.

For a pixel to be set to a particular color, the bits in the correct bit planes must be turned on. For this to happen, the bit must be set to 1 in the byte sent from the CPU, and the bit in the map mask register at the position corresponding to the desired color must also be set to 1. Figure 15.28 shows a single bit being set to the color red. We could turn on several different bits at once and several different bit planes could be activated as well so that the pixels could be colored with composite colors.

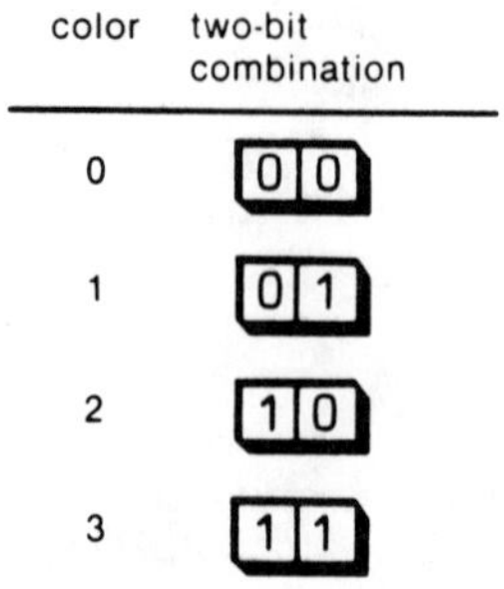

color	two-bit combination
0	0 0
1	0 1
2	1 0
3	1 1

Figure 15.28. Turning on red bit at bit position 3.

How do we go about putting values into the map mask register? To answer this question, we need to know how to use C to communicate with a generalized set of I/O devices called *ports*.

Input/Output Ports

So far in this book we've learned a variety of approaches for communicating with I/O devices. C library functions are the easiest but give the least control and performance. ROM BIOS routines are faster and give more control. Sometimes however, we need an even closer connection between our program and the hardware. At the most fundamental level, hardware on the IBM is accessed through the medium of input/output ports.

A port is an eight-bit register. It can be accessed by software, but it is also physically connected to a hardware device; in fact, it is usually built into a hardware device. The PC can have 65,536 ports connected to it; they're numbered from 0 to FFFF hex. However, only a small fraction of these addresses are actually used.

The ROM BIOS uses ports to communicate with almost all I/O devices. Usually we can use a ROM BIOS routine to access a device, so we don't need to know how the program accesses the ports. For some devices, though, there are no ROM BIOS routines available to our program. One example of this is the PC's speaker; if we want our computer to make noise (other than a simple beep), we must use ports. Another instance where we need to directly access ports is in programming various graphics modes, including mode 18.

How do we access a port using the C language? Turbo C++ provides two functions for this purpose: outportb(), which writes a byte to a port, and inportb(), which reads a byte from a port. The statement

```
result = inportb(portno);
```

reads the byte from the port with the address portno. The variable portno must be an unsigned integer between 0 and FFFF hex, and the function returns an integer value (although only the lower byte contains information).

Similarly, the C statement

```
outportb(portno, value);
```

causes the information in value to be written to the port with the address portno. Here portno is an unsigned integer, as before, and value is also an integer, though it can't have a value greater than FF (hex).

Thus, to output a value to an I/O port, all we need to know is the address of the port and the value to be sent to it; then we use outportb().

Writing to the Map Mask Register

At this point we know almost everything necessary to put the appropriate bit plane value in the map mask register. However, there is one added complexity. There are several registers associated with the sequencer (a clocking mode register, a character map select register, a memory mode register, and so on) in addition to the one we want, the map mask register. To simplify the hardware, all these registers use the same port address: 3C5 hex. Therefore, we need to be able to specify which of these registers we want to access through the port. This is done with yet another register in the sequencer; this one is called the *address register,* and its address is 3C4 hex. First we put an index number in the address register to tell it which register we want to refer to; for the map mask register, the index is 2. Then we put a number, representing the bit plane we want to reference, into 3C5.

> Accessing a register in the VGA generally requires writing to two ports: one to select the register and one to send it a value.

Writing Bytes to Mode-18 Memory

Now, finally, we're ready to write colors to the screen using VGA mode 18. The following program places 16 horizontal stripes on the screen, each one with a different color. Use setmode to set the mode to 18 before running the program.

```
// v8stripe.c
// horizontal stripes -- use mode 18 (640x480)
#include <dos.h>                    // for outportb()
#define MAXX 640                    // columns
#define MAXY 480                    // rows
#define MAXB (MAXX/8)               // bytes in a y
void main(void)
   {
   char far *farptr;               // pointer to VGA memory
   int y, x;
   unsigned char color;

   farptr = (char far *)0xA0000000L;  // set ptr to VGA mem
   for(y=0; y<MAXY; y++)           // move down one row
      {
      color = (y/30) & 0x0f;       // color change every 30 rows
      outportb(0x3C4,2);           // set color to write
      outportb(0x3C5,color);       //    in map mask register
      for (x=0; x<MAXB; x++)       // move across one column
         *(farptr + y*MAXB + x ) = 0xff; // set 8 pixels
      }
   }
```

The output is 16 horizontal stripes in different colors. Figure 15.29 shows how this looks.

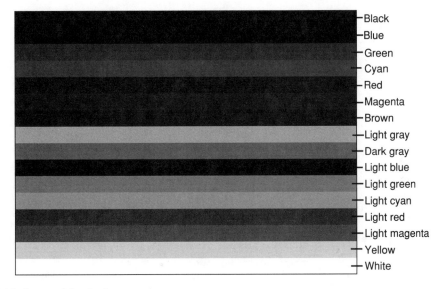

Figure 15.29. Output of the v8stripe.c program.

Because eight pixels are set with each memory access, it's a fast program. A program that used the Turbo C++ library `putpixel()` to accomplish the same thing would run many times more slowly.

Writing Bits to Mode-18 Memory

It isn't necessary to display whole bytes (8 pixels) at a time; we can also turn on individual bits. The following program draws 20 vertical lines on the screen. Each line is two pixels wide, so in the appropriate bytes, two bits are set to 1, and the remaining six are set to 0. Here's the listing:

```
// v8lines.c
// draws vertical lines -- use mode 18 (640x480)
#include <dos.h>                // for outportb()
#define MAXR 480               // rows
#define MAXC 640               // columns
#define PIX  8                 // pixels per byte
#define MAXB (MAXC/PIX)        // bytes in a row

void main(void)
   {
   char far *farptr;
   int row, col, addr;
   unsigned char color;

   farptr = (char far *)0xA0000000L;  // set ptr to VGA mem
```

```
// vertical lines, each two pixels wide
for(col=0; col<MAXC; col+=16)      // space vertical lines
   {                               //   every 16 pixels
   color = col/16;                 // change color every line
   outportb(0x3C4,2);              // set color to write
   outportb(0x3C5,color);          //   in map mask register
   for(row=0; row<MAXR; row++)     // draw one vertical line
      {
      addr = row*MAXB + col/PIX;    // calculate address
      *(farptr+addr) = 0xC0;    // send bits 7, 6 only
      }
   }
}
```

The output of this program is shown in Figure 15.30.

For simplicity, the lines are separated by 16 pixels, or two bytes. Thus, the leftmost two bits (numbers 7 and 6) of every other byte are set to the appropriate color, using the statement

```
*(farptr+addr) = 0xC0;
```

As before, the color is selected with the map mask register.

For some simple operations, the technique used in v8stripe.c and v8lines.c will suffice. However, when we try to use this technique in a more complicated situation, such as drawing one color on top of another, we run into trouble. To see the problem, clear the graphics screen (using the setmode.c program), run v8stripe.c and then, without clearing the screen, run v8lines.c.

```
C>setmode 18
C>v8stripe
C>v8lines
```

The vertical stripes will be drawn over the horizontal stripes. This is a rigorous test of a graphics system; if there is any inadequacy in the approach used, it will show up when one color is written on top of another. As it turns out, there is a problem; where a line crosses a stripe, in most cases there is an area to the right of the line where the stripe's color is changed or set to black, as shown in Figure 15.31.

The problem is that when a byte is written to a certain address on a given bit plane, those bits that are set to 1 are turned on, and those that are set to 0 are turned off. When we run v8stripe.c, therefore, the two leftmost bits in the byte being written to are set to the appropriate color, but the remaining six bits are turned off, causing a loss of that color in the six pixels to the right of each line. Fortunately there is a way to protect bits from being changed.

> Changing selected bits in a byte in the VGA bit planes requires protecting those bits that won't be changed.

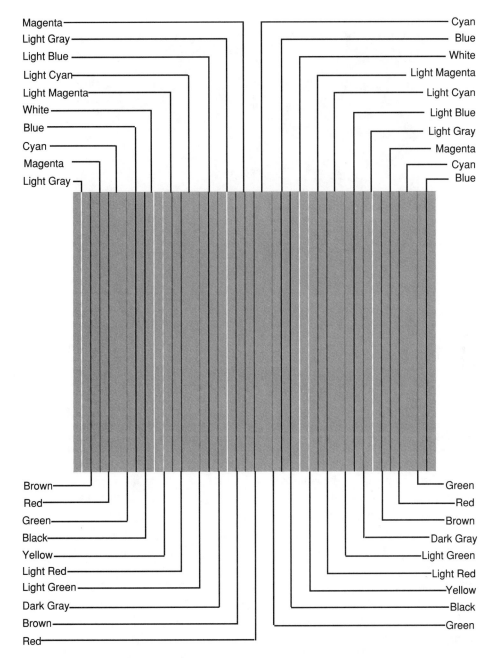

Figure 15.30. Output of the v8lines.c program.

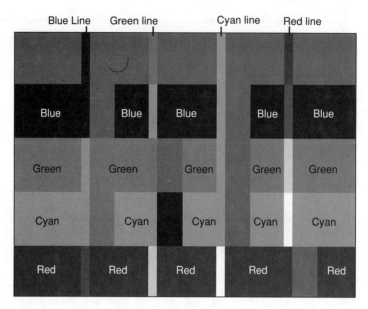

Figure 15.31. Incorrect interaction of stripes and lines.

The Bit Mask Register

We know that the map mask register can specify which bit planes are to be accessed when a byte is written to the mode 18 memory. In this case, those bit planes for which a bit is set to 1 in the map mask register can be written to, but those for which the bit is set to 0 will be unaffected by a write.

In a similar way it's possible to specify which bits in a byte (in all four bit planes) can be written to and which will be immune to change. The mechanism for this is the bit mask register. Figure 15.32 shows the relation of this register to the bit planes. To write to a certain bit in a particular bit plane, the corresponding bits in both the map mask register and the bit mask register must be set to 1.

When the VGA is first powered up, the bit mask register is set to all 1s, so all the bits can be written to. To protect a bit from being written to, we change the corresponding bit in the bit mask register to 0. Like the map mask register, the bit mask register is accessed using I/O ports. And, again like the map mask register, it requires that an index number be sent to a different port before the register itself can be accessed. Here's what the necessary program statements look like:

```
outportb(0x3CE,8);      // select the bit mask register
outportb(0x3CF,0xC0);   // specify bits to be changed
```

The bit mask register is part of a chip called the graphics controller register. To select the bit mask register, an 8 is sent to port 0x3CE. Then the desired bit configuration is sent to port 0x3CF.

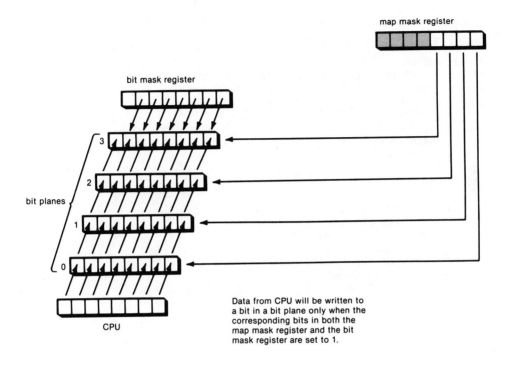

map mask register

bit mask register

3

2

bit planes

1

0

CPU

Data from CPU will be written to
a bit in a bit plane only when the
corresponding bits in both the
map mask register and the bit
mask register are set to 1.

Figure 15.32. The bit mask register.

Clearing the Background Pixels

Another potential problem involves the interaction that takes place when we write one
color over another one. In most cases we don't want the foreground color (the lines in
v8lines.c, for example) to blend with the background (the stripes from v8stripe.c). We
want the foreground to be unaffected by the background so that a red line, for example, is
red no matter what color stripe it crosses. To ensure this happens we need to clear the line
to black before drawing it in the desired color. We do this by setting the color in the map
mask register to bright white, or 15 decimal (0xF), which activates all four bit planes, and
then writing a 0x00 at the desired address. This removes the underlying color. If we
wanted to blend the colors we could omit this step or modify it in various ways.

The v8cross.c Program

Now that we know how to prevent certain bits from being altered when we write to a byte
in the mode-18 memory, we can solve the problem uncovered when we attempted to write
vertical lines on top of horizontal stripes. The following program combines the earlier
v8stripe.c and v8lines.c programs. The stripes part of the program is the same, but the
line-drawing routine has been altered so that all but the leftmost two bits of each byte
being written to are rendered immune to change. This is done by setting the rightmost six
bits to 0 in the bit mask register. The appropriate constant is 0xC0, which is 1100,0000 in

binary. We've also added the instructions to clear all the bit planes before writing the desired color. Here's the listing:

```c
// v8cross.c
// horizontal stripes, vertical lines -- use mode 18 (640x480)
#include <dos.h>                  // for outportb()
#define MAXX 640                  // columns
#define MAXY 480                  // rows
#define PIX  8                    // pixels per byte
#define MAXB (MAXX/PIX)           // bytes in a row
#define WHITE 15

void main(void)
    {
    char far *farptr;
    int y, x, addr;
    unsigned char color, temp;

    farptr = (char far *)0xA0000000L;  // set ptr to VGA mem
    // horizontal stripes
    for(y=0; y<MAXY; y++)              // draw rows of pixels
        {
        color = (y/12) & 0x0f;         // color change every 12 rows
        outportb(0x3C4, 2);            // set color to write
        outportb(0x3C5, color);        //     in map mask register
        for (x=0; x<MAXB; x++)
            *(farptr + y*MAXB + x ) = 0xff; // set 8 pixls
        }
// vertical lines, each four pixels wide
    outportb(0x3CE, 8);                // select bit mask reg
    outportb(0x3CF, 0xC0);             // change bits 7 and 6 only
    for(x=0; x<MAXX; x+=16)            // space vertical lines
        {                             //     every 16 pixels
        color = x/16;                  // change color every line
        for(y=0; y<MAXY; y++)          // draw one vertical line
            {
            addr = y*MAXB + x/PIX;      // calculate address
            temp = *(farptr+addr);      // read byte into latches
            outportb(0x3C4, 2);         // set color to bright white
            outportb(0x3C5, WHITE);     //     in map mask register
            *(farptr+addr) = 0x00;      // put 0 in every bit
            outportb(0x3C5, color);     //     set color in MMP
            *(farptr+addr) = 0xFF;      // put 1 in every bit
            } // end for y
        } // end for x                 // restore settings
    outportb(0x3CE, 8);                // select bit mask reg
    outportb(0x3CF, 0xFF);             // restore 'all bits' mode
    }
```

There's another important addition to this program, one that demonstrates how the bit mask register is used. Before writing the 0xC0 byte, the program reads the contents of the existing byte from VGA memory. However, the contents of this read, placed in temp, are never used. (This elicits a warning from the compiler, which you can ignore.) What then is the purpose of the read? To understand why reading is necessary before writing, you need to know about another set of VGA registers called the *latch registers*.

The Latch Registers

Our earlier diagrams of the bit planes simplified the situation; they showed data from the CPU going directly into the bit planes in VGA memory. Actually, there is another element in the data path between the CPU and the VGA memory: the latch registers. There is one latch register for each bit plane. When a byte is written by the CPU to the VGA, it actually goes to the latch registers first, then into memory. When it's read from memory, it goes to the latch registers on it's way to the CPU. This arrangement is shown in Figure 15.33.

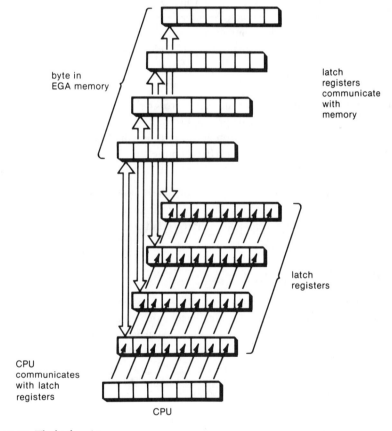

Figure 15.33. The latch registers.

The latch registers are important in the functioning of the bit mask register. Here's the sequence of events when a byte is written by the CPU to VGA memory. First, the byte arrives at the latch registers. (If some of the bit positions have been made immune to change by the bit mask register, though, the bits from the CPU will be blocked at these positions before they can get to the latch registers.) Finally, the contents of the latch registers are written into the VGA memory.

> The latch registers are an intermediate storage area between the CPU and the VGA memory.

The bits in the latch registers that don't receive CPU data are sent to memory as well. To ensure that these bits don't alter the data in memory, we read the data from memory into the latch registers before doing a write. Then when the write is performed, the new bits from the CPU are placed in the latches, the old bits remain as they were read from memory, and finally the complete contents of the latch registers are written back into memory. This process is shown in Figure 15.34. The figure shows only one of the four bit planes. However, a read or write operation transfers data between all four latch registers and all four bit planes simultaneously.

There is another detail to notice about the v8cross.c program; it's necessary to restore the bit mask register to all 1s when the program is finished. If this isn't done, only two bits in each byte can be written to by other programs accessing the VGA (including the operating system). This produces strange effects on the screen, to say the least, so it's important for every program that uses the bit mask register to restore it before exiting.

The v8cross.c program generates a much more pleasing picture on the screen than did the execution of v8stripe.c followed by v8lines.c. The lines no longer cause the unwritten pixels on their right to be destroyed, and the foreground and background colors no longer blend together.

A Dot-Writing Function

Let's put together everything we've learned about VGA mode 18 graphics to create a function that writes a dot to the screen. We'll invoke this function putpixel() from a simple program that draws two diagonal lines on the screen.

```
// v8dots.c
// uses putpoint() function to draw dots -- use mode 18 (640x480)
#include <dos.h>                    // for outportb()
#define MAXR 480                    // rows
#define MAXC 640                    // columns
#define PIX  8                      // pixels per byte
#define MAXB (MAXC/PIX)             // bytes in a row
#define CYAN   3
#define RED    4
#define WHITE 15
                                    // prototype
void putpixel(int x, int y, unsigned char color);
                                    // set ptr to VGA mem
```

```
char far *farptr = (char far *)0xA0000000L;

void main(void)
    {
    int col, row;

    // two diagonal lines, each 1 pixel wide
    for(row=0; row<MAXR; row++)    // for every row
        {
        col = row;                  // make lines diagonal
        putpixel(col, row, CYAN);      // top-left to bottom-right
        putpixel(MAXR-col, row, RED);  // top-right to bottom-left
        }
    outportb(0x3CE, 8);            // select bit mask reg
    outportb(0x3CF, 0xFF);         // restore 'all bits' mode
    }

// putpixel()
// draws pixel on screen at x, y, in specified color
void putpixel(int x, int y, unsigned char color)
    {
    int position;                 // pixel position (0 to 7)
    unsigned char onebit = 0x80;  // 1000,0000 binary
    unsigned addr;                // offset address
    unsigned char temp;           // for reading into latches
    position = x % 8;             // position of bit in byte
    onebit = onebit >> position;  // make byte with one bit set
    outportb(0x3CE, 8);           // select bit mask reg
    outportb(0x3CF, onebit);      // change one bit only
    addr = y*MAXB + x/PIX;        // calculate address
    temp = *(farptr+addr);        // read byte into latches
    outportb(0x3C4, 2);           // set color to bright white
    outportb(0x3C5, WHITE);       //   in map mask register
    *(farptr+addr) = 0x00;        // put 0 in every bit
    outportb(0x3C5, color);       //   set color in MMP
    *(farptr+addr) = 0xFF;        // put 1 in every bit
    }
```

The putpixel() function is called with the x and y coordinates of the pixel to be written, and its color. The only thing in this function you haven't seen in v8cross.c is the calculation needed to set an arbitrary pixel. The bit position of the pixel within its byte is found in the statement

```
position = x % 8;
```

This results in a value from 7 on the left of the byte to 0 on the right. We then start with a single bit, 0x80, and shift it left position times to install it at the correct position in the byte onebyte. Finally we send this byte to the bit mask register so that only this one bit will be affected when we later write colors to memory.

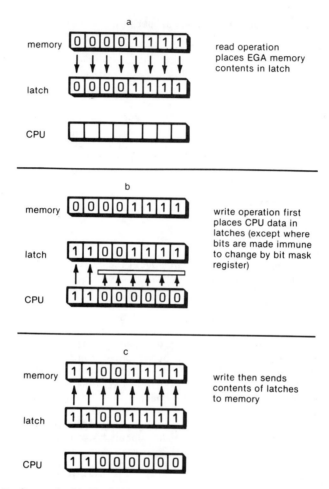

Figure 15.34. Reading sets latch registers before writing.

With the techniques shown in this chapter you can handle direct color access to the VGA high-resolution screen. Of course we've only scratched the surface of direct-access graphics programming. The books listed in the bibliography cover this topic in more detail.

Summary

This chapter has introduced a variety of hardware-related situations. We started by introducing the bitwise C operators, which permit manipulation of individual bits in variables. We then saw how to directly address the character display memory, in which two bytes in memory correspond to one character on the screen. Next we investigated the ROM BIOS, a set of routines hardwired into the computer, that permit interaction with various I/O devices. We used a ROM BIOS routine to change the graphics mode in the last section of the chapter, which showed how to program the VGA graphics modes 18 and 19. Along the way we picked up other techniques, such as how to access areas in low memory that contain information about the system, such as the equipment list word, and how to program I/O ports, which is the most direct connection our program can have with the hardware.

Questions

1. Express the following hexadecimal values in binary:

   a. 0x01
   b. 0xf8
   c. 0x1234
   d. 0xfc0a

2. Numbers are represented internally in the computer as

   a. Decimal
   b. Binary
   c. Hexadecimal
   d. None of the above

3. Which of the following will be true if bit 5 of the character variable ch is a 1?

   a. (ch & 8)
   b. (ch & 10)
   c. (ch & 20)
   d. (ch & 40)

4. The bitwise OR operator is often used to _____ bits from different variables.

5. If num is of type int, what does (num >> 8) evaluate to when num has the value 0xf000?

   a. 0x000f
   b. 0x00f0
   c. 0xff00
   d. 0xfff0

6. The bitwise AND operator is often used to _____ a particular bit in a variable.

7. Before being added to the offset address, the value in the segment register is

   a. Shifted left four bits
   b. Multiplied by 0x10
   c. Converted to decimal
   d. Complemented

8. Suppose the segment address is A100 (hex) and the offset address is 1234 (hex). The resulting absolute address, expressed as a C `far` pointer constant, is

    a. 0xA1234

    b. 0xA234

    c. 0xA2234

    d. 0xA1001234

9. In the character display, every two _____ in memory correspond to a _____ on the screen.

10. The attribute byte is located

    a. In low memory

    b. At the beginning of each segment

    c. After each character

    d. In the display memory

11. The intensity and blinking attributes are controlled by individual _____ in the attribute byte, while the foreground and background "colors" are controlled by _____.

12. Bit fields provide a way to

    a. Access individual bits

    b. Simplify access to arrays of data

    c. Access groups of bits

    d. Modify bits

13. Which of the following is necessary for direct access to the display memory?

    a. Setting a pointer to the start of display memory

    b. Calculating how far into the memory a pixel is

    c. Using the indirection operator to access a byte

    d. Providing color information to the graphics adapter

14. True or false: low system memory can be accessed using far pointers.

15. One important advantage of direct memory access for text and graphics displays is _____.

16. One bit plane holds

    a. The information about a single color

    b. The even-numbered rows

    c. The color values for certain pixels

    d. The bits in certain positions in a byte

17. True or false: writing can take place to only one bit plane at a time.

18. To send information to a register in the VGA controller, one must use

    a. Direct memory access
    b. A Turbo C++ library function
    c. A port
    d. A ROM BIOS routine

19. The map mask register is used to tell the VGA what _____ pixels we want to write.

20. Which of the following statements is appropriate for sending a value to a port?

    a. outportb(portno, value);
    b. value = inportb(portno);
    c. *(portno) = value;
    d. port(number, value);

21. In VGA mode 19 how many pixels are there per byte?

22. In VGA mode 18 how many pixels are there per byte?

23. What is the correct bit plane number for the color cyan?

    a. 0
    b. 1
    c. 2
    d. 3

24. The bit mask register is used to select which _____ will be written to.

25. The latch registers serve as an intermediate storage area between

    a. VGA memory and the bit map register
    b. The CPU and the map mask register
    c. The map mask register and the CPU
    d. VGA memory and the CPU

Exercises

1. Write a program that resembles ortest.c but that allows the user to play with the XOR bitwise operator rather than the OR bitwise operator.

2. Write a program that will allow the user to type a binary number (up to 16 1s and 0s) and that then will convert this number into both hexadecimal and decimal.

3. The draw.c program from Chapter 8 draws lines on the screen in response to the user pressing the cursor keys. Modify this program so that, instead of library functions, it uses direct access to the character display memory. Note: when the character being placed on the screen is one of the extended character set (such as the cursor keys), a problem may arise because the character will be interpreted as being negative. Use bitwise operators to remove the offending bits.

4. Modify the vbounce.c program in this chapter to work with VGA mode 18, rather than mode 19.

Appendixes

Reference

This appendix provides a reference for some of the more fundamental constructions in the C programming language. Our goal is not to cover the entire language; the manuals that accompany your compiler perform that task. Rather, we want to present, in an easily accessible format, those aspects of the language that will be most useful for readers of this book.

Wherever possible we've used examples, as this is the quickest and most easily grasped way to communicate particular formats. For more detailed explanations, see the relevant sections of the book. Note that the examples only demonstrate format; they are not intended as working programs. Also, they are not intended to cover all possible situations, only the most general ones.

A. Control Constructions

In the following examples, the word `statement` represents any suitable program statement.

1. Structure of Simple C Program

```
void main(void)
    {
    statement;
    statement;
    }
```

2. The *for* Loop

```
for(j=0; j<10; j++)      // single-statement loop
    statement;

for(j=0; j<10; j++)      // multistatement loop
    {
    statement;
    statement;
    }

// multiple initialization and increments
for(j=0, other=0; j<20; j++, other++)
    statement;
```

3. The *while* Loop

```
while (ch != 'X')        // single-statement loop
    statement;

while (y < 10)           // multistatement loop
    {
    statement;
    statement;
```

```
    }
while (getche() != 'X')        // function used as variable
    statement;

while ((ch=getche()) != 'X')   // assignment statement used
    statement;                 // as variable
```

4. The *do while* Loop

```
do                             // single-statement loop
    statement;
while (ch != 'X');

do                             // multistatement loop
    {
    statement;
    statement;
    }
while (x <= 42);
```

5. The *if* and *if...else* Statements

```
if(x==42)          // single statement if
    statememt;

if(x < 19)         // multistatement if
    {
    statement;
    statement;
    }

if(ch=='a')        // if-else
    statement;
else
    statement;

if(x < 10)         // nested ifs
    if(y > 5)
        statement;

if(ch=='a')        // "else-if" construct
    statement;
else if(ch=='b')
    statement;
else if(ch=='c')
    statement;

if(x > 5)          // else paired with second of two ifs
    if(y < 10)
        statement;
    else
```

```
        statement;

if(x > 5)          // else paired with first of two ifs
    {              // (braces are necessary)
    if(y < 10)
        statement;
    }
else
    statement;
```

6. The *break* Statement

```
while(ch != "X")
    {
    statement;
    if( count>MAX )
        break;          // causes exit from loop
    statement;
    }
```

7. The *continue* Statement

```
while(ch != 'X')
    {
    if(ch==SPACE)
        continue;  // skip other loop statements,
    statement;     //    go to start of loop
    statement;
    }
```

8. The *switch* Statement

```
switch (j)              // integer switch
    {
    case 1:
        printf("j is 1");
        break;
    case 2:
        printf("j is 2");
        statement;
        break;
    default;
        printf("j is anything else");
    }

switch (ch)             // character switch
    {
    case 'a':
    case 'b':
        printf("ch is 'a' or 'b'.");
        break;
```

```
    case 'c':
        printf("ch is 'c'.");
    }
```

B. Function Formats

1. Simple Function

```
void fun1(void);            // prototype
void main(void)             // define main
    {
    puts("\nMain program.")
    fun1();         // call function
    }

void fun1(void)     // define function
    {
    puts("\nFunction.");   // body of function
    }
```

2. Returning a Value from a Function

```
int always7(void);  // prototype
void main(void)     // define main
    {
    printf("Value returned is %d.", always7() );
    }

int always7(void)   // define function
    {
    return(7);      // return statement
    }
```

3. Passing Arguments to a Function

```
void sum(int, int);      // prototype
void main(void)
    {
    int x=2, y=3;        // pass any number of values
    printf("Sum of x and y is %d.", sum(x,y) );
    }

void sum(int xf, int xy)  // declare function with arguments
    {
    return(xf+yf);       // return only one value
    }
```

4. Passing Arguments Using Pointers

```
void sumarray(int *);                       // prototype
void main(void)
    {
    static int list[3] = { 25, 36, 42 };    // declare array
    printf("Sum = %d.", sumarray(list) );   // pass it to func
    }

void sumarray(int *ptr)                     // define func
    {
    return( *(ptr) + *(ptr+1) + *(ptr+2) ); // elements of array
    }
```

C. Data Constructions

1. Arrays

```
void main(void)         // defining arrays
    {
    int list[3];        // one-dimensional array; 3 items
    char table[4][3];   // 2-dimen array, 4 rows, 3 columns
    list[2] = 333;      // referring to array elements
    table[1][3] = 'c';
    }

// initializing arrays
int lista[3] = { 23, 34, 45 };  // initialize as external var
void main(void)
    {
    int listb[2][3] =           // initialize as static var
    { { 2, 4, 6 },
    { 3, 5, 7 } };
    }
```

2. Strings

```
char name[30];                    // string is char array
char salute[] = "Greetings!";     // initialize string
char *salute = "Greetings!";      // initialize string
puts(salute);                     // refer to string
salute[2]=='e'                    // character in string
char names[3][30] =               // array of strings
            { "Katrina", "Sam", "Rodney" };
char *names[30] =                 // array of strings
            { "Nancy", "Robert", "Laurie" };
puts(&names[2][0]);               // ref to string in array
```

3. Pointers

```
// initializing pointers
int *ptr;                       // pointer to int (or int array)
char *charptr;                  // pointer to char (or char array)
//other variables used in example below
int numb;                       // integer variable
int table[3] = {5, 6, 7};       // array
// using pointers
ptr = &numb;                    // assign address to pointer
*ptr = 8;                       // assign 8 to numb
prt=table;                      // assign array address to pointer
printf("%d", *ptr );            // print first element of array
printf("%d", *(ptr+1) );        // print second element of array
```

4. Structures

```
struct employee            // declare structure of type employee
    {
    int empno;             // three members in this structure
    float  salary;
    char name[40];
    };
struct employee clerks;    // define clerks to be variable of
                           //     type struct employee
struct employee staff;     // define other variables
                           // reference elements of structure
printf("Clerk's employee number is %d", clerks.empno );
printf("Clerk's salary is %f", clerks.salary );

// shorthand way to define a structure variable
struct                     // no need to name structure type
    {
    int empno;
    float  salary;
    char name[40];
    } clerks;              // define clerk var of type struct
```

5. Unions

```
union intflo        // declare union
    {               // memory location can be referred to
    int intnum;     // as either float or int
    float fltnum;
    } unionex;      // define union variable
unionex.intnum;     // reference to two-byte int
unionex.fltnum;     // reference to four-byte float
```

D. Operators

1. Arithmetic Operators

Symbol	Operator	Example
+	Addition	a+b
-	Subtraction	a-b
*	Multiplication	a*b
/	Division	a/b
%	Remainder	a%b

2. Increment and Decrement Operators

Symbol	Operator	Example
++	Increment	a++ or ++a
—	Decrement	a— or —a

3. Relational Operators

Symbol	Operator	Example
<	Less than	a<b
>	Greater than	a>b
<=	Less than or equal	a<=b
>=	Greater than or equal	a>=b
==	Equal	a==b
!=	Not equal	a!=b

4. Logical Operators

Symbol	Operator	Example
&&	AND	a<b && c>d
>>	OR	a<b ¦¦ c>d
c>d. !	NOT	!(a<b)

5. Bitwise Operators

Symbol	Operator	Example
&	AND	a & b
¦	Inclusive OR	a ¦ b
^	Exclusive OR	a ^ b
~	Complement	~a
>>	Right shift	a >> 2
<<	Left shift	b << 3

6. Assignment Operators

Symbol	Operator	Example
=	Equal	a = b
+=	Addition	a += b (same as a=a+b)
-=	Subtraction	a -= b (same as a=a-b)
*=	Multiplication	a *= b (same as a=a*b)
/=	Division	a /= b (same as a=a/b)
%=	Remainder	a %= b (same as a=a%b)
&=	Bitwise AND	a &= b (same as a=a&b)
¦=	Bitwise inclusive OR	a ¦= b (same as a=a¦>b)
^=	Bitwise exclusive OR	a ^= b (same as a=a^b)
<<=	Left shift	a <<= 2 (same as a=a<<2)
>>=	Right shift	a >>= 3 (same as a=a>>3)

7. Conditional Operator

```
result = (expression) ? value1 : value2;     max = (a>b) ? a : b;
```

8. Precedence and Associativity of Operators

Operators	Type	Associativity
() [] . ->	Groups, membership	Left to right
- ~ ! * &	Unary	Right to left
++ -- sizeof casts	Unary	Right to left
* / %	Multiplicative	Left to right
+ -	Additive	Left to right
<< >>	Shift	Left to right
< > <= >=	Relational	Left to right

continues

Operators	Type	Associativity
== !=	Equality	Left to right
&	Bitwise AND	Left to right
^	Bitwise excl OR	Left to right
¦	Bitwise incl OR	Left to right
&&	Logical AND	Left to right
¦¦	Logical OR	Left to right
? :	Conditional	Right to left
= *= /= %= += -=	Assignment	Right to left
<<= >>= &= ^= ¦=		
,	Comma (series)	Left to right

Hexadecimal Numbering

The hexadecimal numbering system is widely used on PC (and many other) computer systems. In essence, this is because hexadecimal is closer to the binary system than is decimal. Let's see why binary is important, and then see how it relates to hexadecimal.

The Binary System

A numbering system can be defined by how many distinct digits are available in the system. In the decimal system there are 10: the digits from 0 to 9. After using 10 digits in the one's column, the ten's column must be employed to express larger numbers, such as 10 and 11. In the binary system there are only 2 digits: 0 and 1. After using only 2 digits in the one's column, the next column over—the two's column—must be used. After two more numbers are counted, the four's column comes into play. Thus counting in binary looks like this: 0, 1, 10, 11, 100, 101, 110, 111, 1000, and so on.

Binary is a natural system for computers because the circuits used to store numbers can be in one of only two states: off or on. These two states can be represented by the binary digits 0 or 1. Two such circuits then represent the four binary numbers 00, 01, 10, and 11. Three such circuits can represent eight numbers (from 000 to 111), eight circuits can represent 256 numbers (from 00000000 to 11111111), and so on.

Binary is not convenient for humans, however, since it's hard to read long strings of 0s and 1s. Another system is needed, and as it turns out, hexadecimal is that more convenient system.

The Hexadecimal System

Hexadecimal (or hex) is a numbering system that uses 16 digits. Since there are only 10-digit symbols on most computers, letters are used for the remaining digits, so counting in hex looks like this: 0, 1, 2, 3, 4, 5, 6, 7, 8, 9, A, B, C, D, E, F, 10, 11, 12, and so on. You can count up to F (15 decimal) in the one's column before needing to use the next column.

To see why hexadecimal is more closely related to binary than is decimal, examine Table B-1.

Table B.1. Comparison of hexadecimal, binary, and decimal.

Decimal	Binary	Hexadecimal
0	0	0
1	1	1
2	10	2
3	11	3

Decimal	Binary	Hexadecimal
4	100	4
5	101	5
6	110	6
7	111	7
8	1000	8
9	1001	9
10	1010	A
11	1011	B
12	1100	C
13	1101	D
14	1110	E
15	1111	F
16	10000	10
17	10001	11
18	10010	12
255	11111111	FF
256	100000000	100
4095	111111111111	FFF
4096	1000000000000	1000
65535	1111111111111111	FFFF
65536	10000000000000000	10000

The key point to notice here is that one hexadecimal digit is exactly represented by four binary digits. When the shift is made from one to two hex digits (from F to 10 hex), a corresponding shift is made from four to five binary digits. Likewise, when the shift is made from two to three hex digits, the binary digits go from eight to nine. There is no such easy correspondence between binary and decimal: when the decimal digits shift from one to two (from 9 to 10), the binary digits remain at four, and when the binary digits go from three to four (from 111 to 1000), the decimal digits remain at one (going from 7 to 8).

Thus it is convenient to arrange binary digits into groups of four, and represent each group by a hexadecimal number. The binary number 1111001101111100, for example, can be divided into groups of four (1111 0011 0111 1100) and translated by sight into the hex number F37C.

Translating large numbers back and forth between decimal and hexadecimal is not easy, and is best left to a computer program. We show how this is done in Exercise 2 in Chapter 8 and in Chapter 15, "Hardware-oriented C."

Bibliography

There are hundreds of books available on various aspects of C. This bibliography covers only a few of those we like and find especially useful.

Barkakati, Nabajyoti, *The Waite Group's Turbo C Bible,* Howard W. Sams Company, 1989.

> An excellent reference to (almost) all the C library functions. Thorough descriptions, useful organization, and extensive program examples make this a useful book for any C programmer.

Feuer, Alan, *The C Puzzle Book,* Prentice Hall, 1982.

> Using this book will hone your programming ability to a fine edge. If you can answer all the questions it poses, you're ready for anything.

Gehani, Narain, *Advanced C: Food for the Educated Palate,* Computer Science Press, 1985.

> A literate exploration of some of the finer points of C. This book is fun to read after you've digested the fundamentals.

Holzner, Steven, *C Programming: The Accessible Guide to Professional Programming,* Brady Publishing, 1991.

> An intermediate-level book that starts with C fundamentals but also covers more advanced topics like graphics, memory management, the mouse, and assembly language.

Kernighan, Brian, and Dennis Ritchie, *The C Programming Language,* Second Edition, Prentice Hall, 1988.

> The first edition of this book, in 1978, defined the C language, at least for the UNIX-based systems on which C was originally developed. The watchword still is, "when in doubt, follow Kernighan and Ritchie." This is not a beginner's book, but it's useful and interesting, and it covers C thoroughly. Serious C programmers will want to own a copy. The second edition is ANSI-compatible.

Lafore, Robert, *Object-Oriented Programming in Turbo C++,* Waite Group Press, 1991.

> An easy entry-level look into the mysteries of object-oriented programming. Assumes no previous knowledge of C or anything else.

Waite, Mitchell, and Steven Prata, *New C Primer Plus,* Second Edition, Howard W. Sams & Co., 1993.

> A classic generic C tutorial (that is, not connected with any particular compiler or hardware platform), clearly written and easy to learn from, full of valuable insights about C.

Waite, Mitchell, Stephen Prata, and Wex Woolard, *Master C,* Waite Group Press, 1990.

   A disk-based approach to C for those who like interactive learning.

Williams, Al, *DOS 6: A Developer's Guide,* M & T Books, 1993.

   An advanced book dealing with direct access to display hardware, ROM BIOS, expanded memory, device drivers, and TSR programming. Clearly written, but you may need some assembly language.

ASCII
Chart

Table D-1. IBM Character Codes

DEC	HEX	Symbol	Key	Use in C
0	00	(NULL)	Ctrl 2	
1	01	☺	Ctr-A	
2	02	●	Ctrl B	
3	03	♥	Ctrl C	
4	04	♦	Ctrl D	
5	05	♣	Ctrl E	
6	06	♠	Ctrl F	
7	07	●	Ctrl G	Beep
8	08	▣	Backspace	Backspace
9	09	○	Tab	Tab
10	0A	■	Ctrl J	Linefeed (newline)
11	0B	♂	Ctrl K	Vertical Tab
12	0C	♀	Ctrl L	Form Feed
13	0D	♪	Enter	Carriage Return
14	0E	♫	Ctrl N	
15	0F	☼	Ctrl O	
16	10	▶	Ctrl P	
17	11	◀	Ctrl Q	
18	12	↕	Ctrl R	
19	13	‼	Ctrl S	
20	14	¶	Ctrl T	
21	15	§	Ctrl U	
22	16	▬	Ctrl V	
23	17	↨	Ctrl W	
24	18	↑	Ctrl X	
25	19	↓	Ctrl Y	
26	1A	→	Ctrl Z	
27	1B	←	Esc	Escape
28	1C	∟	Ctrl \	

Table D-1 (cont.)

DEC	HEX	Symbol	Key
29	1D	↔	Ctrl]
30	1E	▲	Ctrl 6
31	1F	▼	Ctrl -
32	20		SPACE BAR
33	21	!	!
34	22	"	"
35	23	#	#
36	24	$	$
37	25	%	%
38	26	&	&
39	27	'	'
40	28	(	(
41	29	)	)
42	2A	*	*
43	2B	+	+
44	2C	,	,
45	2D	—	—
46	2E	.	.
47	2F	/	/
48	30	0	0
49	31	1	1
50	32	2	2
51	33	3	3
52	34	4	4
53	35	5	5
54	36	6	6
55	37	7	7
56	38	8	8
57	39	9	9
58	3A	:	:
59	3B	;	;
60	3C	<	<
61	3D	=	=
62	3E	>	>
63	3F	?	?
64	40	@	@
65	41	A	A
66	42	B	B
67	43	C	C
68	44	D	D
69	45	E	E
70	46	F	F

Table D-1 (cont.)

DEC	HEX	Symbol	Key
71	47	G	G
72	48	H	H
73	49	I	I
74	4A	J	J
75	4B	K	K
76	4C	L	L
77	4D	M	M
78	4E	N	N
79	4F	O	O
80	50	P	P
81	51	Q	Q
82	52	R	R
83	53	S	S
84	54	T	T
85	55	U	U
86	56	V	V
87	57	W	W
88	58	X	X
89	59	Y	Y
90	5A	Z	Z
91	5B	[	[
92	5C	\	\
93	5D	]	]
94	5E	^	^
95	5F	_	_
96	60	`	`
97	61	a	a
98	62	b	b
99	63	c	c
100	64	d	d
101	65	e	e
102	66	f	f
103	67	g	g
104	68	h	h
105	69	i	i
106	6A	j	j
107	6B	k	k
108	6C	l	l
109	6D	m	m
110	6E	n	n
111	6F	o	o
112	70	p	p

Table D-1 (cont.)

DEC	HEX	Symbol	Key
113	71	q	q
114	72	r	r
115	73	s	s
116	74	t	t
117	75	u	u
118	76	v	v
119	77	w	w
120	78	x	x
121	79	y	y
122	7A	z	z
123	7B	{	{
124	7C	¦	¦
125	7D	}	}
126	7E	~	~
127	7F	Δ	Ctrl ←
128	80	Ç	Alt 128
129	81	ü	Alt 129
130	82	é	Alt 130
131	83	â	Alt 131
132	84	ä	Alt 132
133	85	à	Alt 133
134	86	å	Alt 134
135	87	ç	Alt 135
136	88	ê	Alt 136
137	89	ë	Alt 137
138	8A	è	Alt 138
139	8B	ï	Alt 139
140	8C	î	Alt 140
141	8D	ì	Alt 141
142	8E	Ä	Alt 142
143	8F	Å	Alt 143
144	90	É	Alt 144
145	91	æ	Alt 145
146	92	Æ	Alt 146
147	93	ô	Alt 147
148	94	ö	Alt 148
149	95	ò	Alt 149
150	96	û	Alt 150
151	97	ù	Alt 151
152	98	ÿ	Alt 152
153	99	Ö	Alt 153
154	9A	Ü	Alt 154

Table D-1 (cont.)

DEC	HEX	Symbol	Key
155	9B	¢	Alt 155
156	9C	£	Alt 156
157	9D	¥	Alt 157
158	9E	P_t	Alt 158
159	9F	ƒ	Alt 159
160	A0	á	Alt 160
161	A1	í	Alt 161
162	A2	ó	Alt 162
163	A3	ú	Alt 163
164	A4	ñ	Alt 164
165	A5	Ñ	Alt 165
166	A6	ª	Alt 166
167	A7	º	Alt 167
168	A8	¿	Alt 168
169	A9	⌐	Alt 169
170	AA	¬	Alt 170
171	AB	½	Alt 171
172	AC	¼	Alt 172
173	AD	¡	Alt 173
174	AE	«	Alt 174
175	AF	»	Alt 175
176	B0	░	Alt 176
177	B1	▒	Alt 177
178	B2	▓	Alt 178
179	B3	│	Alt 179
180	B4	┤	Alt 180
181	B5	╡	Alt 181
182	B6	╢	Alt 182
183	B7	╖	Alt 183
184	B8	╕	Alt 184
185	B9	╣	Alt 185
186	BA	║	Alt 186
187	BB	╗	Alt 187
188	BC	╝	Alt 188
189	BD	╜	Alt 189
190	BE	╛	Alt 190
191	BF	┐	Alt 191
192	C0	└	Alt 192
193	C1	┴	Alt 193
194	C2	┬	Alt 194
195	C3	├	Alt 195
196	C4	─	Alt 196

Table D-1 (cont.)

DEC	HEX	Symbol	Key
197	C5	┼	Alt 197
198	C6	╞	Alt 198
199	C7	╟	Alt 199
200	C8	╚	Alt 200
201	C9	╔	Alt 201
202	CA	╩	Alt 202
203	CB	╦	Alt 203
204	CC	╠	Alt 204
205	CD	═	Alt 205
206	CE	╬	Alt 206
207	CF	╧	Alt 207
208	D0	╨	Alt 208
209	D1	╤	Alt 209
210	D2	╥	Alt 210
211	D3	╙	Alt 211
212	D4	╘	Alt 212
213	D5	╒	Alt 213
214	D6	╓	Alt 214
215	D7	╫	Alt 215
216	D8	╪	Alt 216
217	D9	┘	Alt 217
218	DA	┌	Alt 218
219	DB	█	Alt 219
220	DC	▄	Alt 220
221	DD	▌	Alt 221
222	DE	▐	Alt 222
223	DF	▀	Alt 223
224	E0	α	Alt 224
225	E1	β	Alt 225
226	E2	Γ	Alt 226
227	E3	π	Alt 227
228	E4	Σ	Alt 228
229	E5	σ	Alt 229
230	E6	μ	Alt 230
231	E7	τ	Alt 231
232	E8	Φ	Alt 232
233	E9	Θ	Alt 233
234	EA	Ω	Alt 234
235	EB	δ	Alt 235
236	EC	∞	Alt 236
237	ED	φ	Alt 237
238	EE	ε	Alt 238

Table D-1 (cont.)

DEC	HEX	Symbol	Key
239	EF	∩	Alt 240
240	F0	≡	Alt 241
241	F1	±	Alt 242
242	F2	≥	Alt 243
243	F3	≤	Alt 244
244	F4	⌠	Alt 245
245	F5	⌡	Alt 246
246	F6	÷	Alt 246
247	F7	≈	Alt 247
248	F8	°	Alt 248
249	F9	•	Alt 249
250	FA	.	Alt 250
251	FB	√	Alt 251
252	FC	η	Alt 252
253	FD	²	Alt 253
254	FE	■	Alt 254
255	FF	(blank)	Alt 255

Those key sequences consisting of "Ctrl" are typed in by pressing the CTRL key, and while it is being held down, pressing the key indicated. These sequences are based on those defined for PC Personal Computer series keyboards. The key sequences may be defined differently on other keyboards.

IBM Extended ASCII characters can be displayed by pressing the Alt key and then typing the decimal code of the character on the keypad.

The Turbo C++ Editor

In this appendix we'll summarize the operation of the Turbo C++ editor. We don't cover all details of the editor; instead we provide enough quick and easy information for you to type in the programs in this book and perform a few other simple operations. For a complete list of features, see the Turbo C++ documentation and Turbo C++ Help (select Contents from the Help menu, and then double click Editor Commands).

We'll assume you've had experience with some kind of word processor. If you've used other Borland editors before—such as those for Turbo BASIC or Turbo Pascal—you'll find this one essentially the same. If you're familiar with the classic WordStar commands, you'll also feel right at home. However, the Turbo C++ editor is easy to learn, even without this experience.

Getting Started

The Turbo C++ editor is part of the integrated development environment (IDE). To call up this program, type tc at the DOS prompt.

Opening an Edit Window

After the IDE display appears, you must open an Edit window into which you can type your program. There are two approaches to this. First, you can type your program name as a command-line argument when you invoke Turbo C:

```
C>tc myprog.c
```

If myprog.c doesn't exist, a file will be created for it. If it exists already, the file will be opened. An Edit window will also be opened and labeled MYPROG.C.

If you're already in the IDE you can open an Edit window by selecting New from the File menu. This Edit window will be given the title NONAME00.C. If you want to open a file that already exists, select Open... from the File menu. A dialog window will appear. Type the name of the file in the Name field or select it from the list displayed. Note that only source files—those with the .C extension—are listed.

When you first start Turbo C++ it assumes you want to use the .CPP file extension (for the C++ language). Enter *.c into the Name field to list only files with the .C extension.

Making a Window Active

Before you can type into an Edit window it must be active. An active window has a double-line border, while an inactive window has a single-line border. If another window is active, you can cause your Edit window to be active by clicking it with the mouse or by pressing the F6 key, which cycles through all the open windows.

Exiting from the Editor

Before exiting from the IDE, you should close the Edit window containing the file you're working on. If you don't, this window will appear whenever you start the IDE, even if you're working on another program. To close the Edit window, click the square in the upper-left corner (the close box), select Close from the Window menu, or press the Alt F3 key combination.

To exit from the IDE, select Quit from the File menu or press the Alt X key combination. If you haven't saved the file you're working on, a dialog box will prompt you to do so.

Basic Editor Commands

The most important commands in any editor are those that move the cursor on the screen and insert and delete text. If you haven't used the editor before, you might want to type some sample text at this point so that you can experiment with these commands. The following summary shows some of the most common commands for the Turbo C++ editor.

Command	Action
Left Arrow	Move one character left
Right Arrow	Move one character right
Ctrl Left Arrow	Move one word left
Ctrl Right Arrow	Move one word right
Up Arrow	Move up one line
Down Arrow	Move down one line
Home	Go to start of line
End	Go to end of line
PgUp	Go up one screen
PgDn	Go down one screen
Backspace	Delete character to left of cursor
Del	Delete character at cursor position
Ins	Toggle insert mode on/off
Enter	Insert CR/LF, move to next line down

To insert text, move the cursor to the insertion point and start typing. The existing text will shift right to make room. If you want to type over existing text, toggle insert mode off by using the Ins key. To return to normal insertion mode, press the Ins key again.

The editor differs in several ways from an ordinary word processor. There is no word wrap. When you reach the end of the line, you keep typing, and the line scrolls left; you don't automatically drop down to the next line. You can type up to 249 characters on one line (although it's not clear why you would want to; usually you want the entire line to be visible on the screen). When you end one line and are ready to move down to the next line, press the Enter key.

In the Turbo C++ editor (unlike most word processors) you can move the cursor anywhere in the blank area at the right of a line or below the last line. This makes it easier to place material in columns (to line up comments, for example) without having to type a lot of spaces or tabs.

The Turbo C++ editor doesn't insert nonstandard control characters into the file, the way word processors like Microsoft Word and WordPerfect do. Such characters cannot be read by the Turbo C compiler.

Window Handling

Windows in Turbo C++ are areas for typing text or reading messages from the system. They have some surprisingly versatile features.

Scrolling

If your file has too many lines to fit in the window, or is too long, you can scroll its contents up and down or left and right with the mouse or with the cursor keys.

To scroll with the mouse, use the scroll bars on the right and bottom edges of the edit window. To scroll one line up or down, click the triangle-shaped arrows on the scroll bar. To scroll faster through the file, drag the scroll box—the highlighted box-in-a-box character situated on the scroll bar. (*Dragging* means to position the mouse pointer on an object, hold down the left mouse button, move the pointer, and release the button.) You can scroll one page at a time by clicking the shaded areas above and below the scroll box.

Resizing and Moving Windows

You can change the size of a window by dragging the lower-right corner. You can move a window by dragging the title bar—the double-line at the top of the window that contains the filename.

Opening Multiple Windows

Turbo C++ allows many Edit windows to appear on the screen at one time. This is a powerful feature. You can open windows on two files at the same time to compare them or to copy text from one to the other. (This is described in the section on block commands.) You can even open different windows on the same file, but at different places in the file. This enables you to do such things as looking at the call to a function and at the function itself at the same time or copying text from one part of a file to another.

To open a second Edit window, select Open... (or New) from the File menu, just as you would when opening the first Edit window. When you have several windows on the screen you may need to make them smaller, move them around, and scroll their contents, so you can see the relevant parts of all of them at the same time.

File Handling

Files are manipulated from the File menu. We've already discussed the Open... and New commands.

Saving Files

To save a file, select Save or Save as... from the File menu. These commands will save the file shown in the active window. Files in other windows won't be affected. The Save option saves the file under the name shown in the title bar. If you want to change the name, use the Save as... option. This invokes a dialog box containing a field into which you can type the new filename. The Save all option saves all open files.

Although the editor in the IDE is used primarily to edit C and C++ programs, it can be used to generate other kinds of text files. This is useful if you don't have a word processor program or if your word processor is too ponderous to use for short files. C programs must have the extension .C, but you can create files with any name and extension. You can create .BAT batch files, .CPP files for C++, .TXT text files, and so on. All you need to do is type them in and save them under the appropriate filename and extension.

Changing Directories

You can change the current directory by selecting the Change dir... option from the File menu. Once you've changed directories, Open will list the source files in the new directory. When you exit TC, you'll be in the new directory.

Printing

To send the contents of the active window to the printer, select Print from the File menu.

DOS Shell

You can call up a copy of DOS by selecting DOS shell from the File menu. In DOS you can delete or list files, change directories, and perform any other DOS command. To return to the IDE, enter the word `exit` at the DOS prompt.

Invoking the DOS shell is a useful way to position the cursor at the beginning of the line of the output screen.

Block Commands

You can select a block of text in an Edit window, and then move it to another place in the same window or to a different window. You can also perform other operations on selected text. We'll first see how to select a block of text; then we'll find out what you can do with it.

Selecting a Text Block

To select a block of text with the mouse, position the mouse pointer at the beginning of the block, hold down the left button, and drag the pointer to the end of the block. The selected block will be highlighted. To deselect the block, click anywhere.

To select a block from the keyboard, position the cursor at the beginning of the block, hold down the Shift key and use the cursor keys to move the cursor to the end of the block.

If you know the old WordStar-style commands, you can also use them to select blocks and carry out operations on them.

Cut, Copy, Paste, and Clear

Once a block is selected, you can perform various operations on it. These operations can be invoked from the Edit menu or by typing key combinations. They make use of an internal text buffer called the clipboard. The following list summarizes the possibilities.

Items on Edit menu	Shortcut keystrokes	Action
Cut	ShiftDel	Delete block and write it to clipboard
Copy	CtrlIns	Copy block to clipboard
Paste	ShiftIns	Insert block from clipboard at cursor
Clear	CtrlDel	Delete block; don't write to clipboard

To move a block of text, select it, and then select Cut or Copy. The text will be written to the clipboard, replacing whatever was there before. Then position the cursor where you want the block to go and select Paste. The block will be written at that location.

You can also copy text from the help file examples to the clipboard, using the Copy examples option in the Edit menu and from there paste this text to your listing.

Reading and Writing Blocks to Disk

Once you've selected a block, you can write it to disk. To do this you'll need to use a WordStar-key combination. Press the Ctrl and K keys at the same time, and then press the W key.

To read a file into a document at the cursor location, press the Ctrl K key combination and then the R key.

Search and Replace

You can search your text file for a string of up to 30 characters. To do this, select Find... from the Search menu, and type the string into the Text to Find field in the resulting dialog box. Options in the box let you specify the direction and origin of the search. Alternately, you can position the cursor on an instance of the word to be searched for, and then invoke Find... from the Search menu. The word will appear automatically in the Text to Find field.

Select Search Again from the Search menu to find the next instance of the same search string.

To do a search and replace operation, select Replace... from the Search menu. Type the text to find and the text to replace it with.

Other Commands

Here are some miscellaneous editor commands that you may find useful.

Restore Line

One of the most useful commands is Restore line in the Edit menu. This is a one-line *undo* feature. If the cursor is still on the line you have altered, this selection will restore the line to the state it was in when you first moved the cursor to it.

Matching Braces

When programs get complicated, you can lose track of which closing brace matches which opening brace. To sort things out, Turbo C++ provides a pair-matching facility. Position the cursor on the brace you want to match. Now, press the Ctrl Q key combination and type the open bracket key ([). The cursor will immediately jump to the brace that Turbo C++ thinks matches the one the cursor was on. If it jumps somewhere else, you've made a mistake somewhere. You can jump from a closing brace to an opening brace with the Ctrl Q] (the close bracket key).

The same keystrokes will find matching pairs of brackets and parentheses. In fact, it will find a match for double quotes ("), single quotes ('), angle brackets (< and >), and old-style comment symbols (/*) and (*/). For the comment symbols, make sure you place the cursor on the first of the two characters in the symbol: the (/) for an open comment, and the (*) for a close comment.

Jump to Last Cursor Position

To return to a previous cursor position, press the Ctrl Q key combination followed by the P key.

The Turbo C++
Debugger

One of the most useful features of Turbo C++ is the integration of debugging facilities into the IDE. In Chapter 1 we described how easy it is to correct syntax errors, but Turbo C++ goes far beyond this form of debugging. Using menu selections and function keys in the IDE, you can also single step through programs, watch variables change as the program runs, execute sections of the program at full speed and stop where you want, and change the value of variables in the middle of a program.

In this appendix we'll explain the major debugging features that Turbo C++ makes available. We'll use short program examples with obvious bugs. The bugs aren't very realistic, in that most beginners to C can spot them easily. However, our aim isn't to provide a play-by-play description of a search for a bug in a long and obscure program. Rather we want to familiarize you quickly with the tools Turbo C makes available for debugging (so you can apply them yourself to your own long and obscure programs).

The debugger doesn't work with the command-line version of Turbo C++, called TCC. You must be in the IDE.

Single Stepping

Even when your program compiles perfectly, it still may not work. Panic! What's the matter with it? Will you ever be able to find the problem?

Before you do anything, look through the listing carefully. Mentally review the program's operation, line by line. Often the mistake will be obvious, especially after a little thought. If the mistake is still obscure, you'll need some assistance. Fortunately, this assistance is close at hand.

One Step at a Time

The first thing the debugger can do for you is slow down the operation of the program. One trouble with finding errors is that a typical program executes in a few milliseconds, so all you can see is its final state. By invoking Turbo C++'s single-stepping capability, you can execute just one line of the program at a time. This way you can follow where the program is going.

Here's a small example program:

```c
// errelse.c
// demonstrates single stepping
#include <stdio.h>          // for printf()

void main(void)
    {
    int number, answer = -1;

    number = -50;            // test value
    if(number < 100)
```

```
    if(number > 0)
        answer = 1;
else
    answer = 0;
printf("answer is %d\n", answer );
}
```

Type the program and compile it in the usual way by selecting Make EXE File from the Compile menu.

Our intention in this program is that when number is between 0 and 100, answer will be 1, when number is 100 or greater, answer will be 0, and when number is less than 0, answer will retain its initialized value of –1. This is summarized in the following list:

Number	Answer
number<0	–1
0<number<100	1
number=>100	0

Unfortunately, when we run the program as shown with a test value of –50 for number, we find that answer is set to 0 at the end of the program instead of staying –1. What's wrong? (You may see the problem already but bear with us.)

Perhaps we can find where the problem is if we single step through the program. To do this, press the F7 key (or select Trace Into from the Run menu). Alternatively you can also press F8 (or select Step Over from the Run menu); this operates the same way as F7 unless functions are involved.

The first line of the program will be highlighted. This highlighted line is called the run bar. Press F7 again. The run bar will move to the next program line. The run bar appears on the line about to be executed. You can execute each line of the program in turn by pressing F7. Eventually you'll reach the first if statement:

```
if(num < 100)
```

This statement is true (because number is –50); so as we would expect, the run bar moves to the second if statement.

```
if(num > 0)
```

This is false. Because there's no else matched with the second if, we would expect the run bar to move to the printf() statement. But it doesn't! It goes to the line

```
answer = 0;
```

Now that we see where the program actually goes, the source of the bug should dawn on us: the else goes with the last if, not the first if as the indenting would lead us to believe. The else is executed when the second if statement is false, which leads to the erroneous result. We need to put braces around the second `if` or rewrite the program in some other way. We've successfully used the single stepping feature to track down a simple bug.

In this short example, single stepping may not be necessary to discover the bug, but in a more complex program, with multiple nested `if`s, loops, and functions, it's often an essential technique. Try single stepping through some programs containing loops and complex `if` statements.

Pressing the F7 or F8 keys for the first time starts a debugging session. During debugging, the IDE is in a somewhat different state than it is normally. For example, the Call Stack option in the Debug menu, which is normally not selectable, becomes selectable during a debugging session. If the .EXE or .OBJ versions of the program don't exist or aren't up to date when you press the F7 key, the system will recompile and relink your program.

Resetting the Debugger

Suppose you've single stepped part way through a program and want to start over at the beginning. How do you place the run bar back at the top of the listing? You can reset the debugging process and initialize the run bar by selecting the Program Reset option from the Run menu.

Watches

Single stepping is usually used with other features of the debugger. The most useful of these is the watch (or watch expression). This is a sort of magic microscope that lets you see how the value of a variable changes as the program runs.

Here's another short program. This one is intended to calculate the factorial of a number entered by the user. It's similar to the factor.c program in Chapter 3, but uses a `for` loop instead of a `while` loop.

```c
// errloop.c
// doesn't calculate factorials
// demonstates watchpoints
#include <stdio.h>                    // for printf(), scanf()

void main(void)
    {
    long number, j, answer;

    printf("Enter number: ");
    scanf("%D", &number );
    answer = 1;
    for( j=0; j<number; j++ )
       answer = answer * j;
    printf("Factorial of %ld = %ld\n", number, answer);
    }
```

Unfortunately, no matter what number we enter when we run this program, it always prints the same result.

```
Factorial of 5 is 0
```

The factorial of 5 should be 120. Can we find the problem with the debugger? Single stepping by itself isn't much help, as the program seems to go around the loop the correct number of times (5 in this case). Let's see whether Watches can cast more light on the problem.

We'll assume that you've typed in the program and successfully compiled it. Position the cursor on the name number in the variable definition. Select Watches from the Debug menu, and select Add Watch from the resulting submenu (or use the Ctrl F7 shortcut key combination). You'll see number in the Watch expression field in the resulting dialog box. Click Ok or press the Enter key. You'll see a new window, the Watch window, open at the bottom of the screen. (You may need to make the Edit window smaller to see it.) This window will contain the line

```
number: undefined symbol 'number'
```

The variable is undefined because we haven't yet executed the statement that defines it.

Repeat this process for j and answer. Similar lines for these variables will appear in the Watch window.

Now, make the Edit window active, and then single step through the program, using the F7 key. You'll see the run bar move down through the listing as before. You'll also see the values of the variables change in the Watch window. (You may need to resize the Edit window to bring the Watch window into view.) When you execute the program line where the variables are defined, the Watch window will change to something like this:

```
number: -43234244
j: 72319873
answer: 930986876
```

The variables are defined, but have garbage values because they haven't yet been initialized. When you execute the scanf() statement, the output screen will appear. Enter a small number, like 5. Continue single stepping through the program. In the Watch window you'll see number acquire the value 5, and answer the value 1. When you enter the loop, j becomes 0.

When you execute the loop, you'll see that the run bar highlights the line with the for statement only on the first time through the loop. After that, only the single statement in the loop body,

```
answer = answer * j;
```

is executed when you press the F7 key, so the run bar doesn't appear to move from this line. However, the program is going around the loop. You can tell this because the values in the Watch window change.

Can you figure out what the bug is? The variable answer is initialized to 1, but on the first cycle through the loop, it becomes 0, as you can see in the Watch window. From then on it remains 0, because anything times 0 is still 0. Why did it become 0? As we can also see in the Watch window, j is 0 the first time through the loop, and the program multiplies j by answer. The bug is that we start j at 0 instead of 1. To fix this, we must change j=0 to j=1 in the for loop, and j<number to j<=number. When we make these changes, the program works correctly.

If you no longer need to watch a particular variable, you can delete it from the Watch window. Click the variable name in the Watch window and then select Delete Watch from the Watches submenu of the Debug menu. You can also edit an existing Watch, or delete all Watches, using other options in this submenu.

Breakpoints

It often happens that you've debugged part of your program but must deal with a bug in another section and don't want to single-step through all the statements in the first part to get to the section with the bug. Conversely, you may have a loop with many iterations that would be tedious to single step through.

Here's an example. This program attempts to average the integers from 0 to 499.

```
// errbreak.c
// demonstrates breakpoints
#include <stdio.h>        // for printf()

void main(void)
    {
    int j, total=0, average;

    for( j=0; j<500; j++ )
        total += j;
    average = total / j;
    printf("average = %d\n", average );
    }
```

When we run the program, it says the average is –12. This doesn't look right; the average should be around 250. To figure out what's wrong, set up Watches for j, total, and average. Now try single stepping into the loop. Everything looks good for the first dozen or so cycles: j starts at 0 and is incremented each time, and total starts at 0 and is increased by whatever j is. We could go on stepping through the loop, but 500 iterations is too time-consuming. We want to stop the program, just after it has completed the entire loop so that we can check the variables at that point.

The way to do this is with a breakpoint. A *breakpoint* marks a statement where the program will stop. If you start the program it will execute all the statements up to the breakpoint, and then stop. Now you can use the Watch window to examine the state of the variables at that point.

Installing Breakpoints

To set a breakpoint, first position the cursor on the appropriate line; in this case

```
average = total / j;
```

Now select Toggle breakpoint from the Debug menu (or press the Ctrl F8 key combination). The line with the breakpoint will be highlighted (with a different color from the run bar).

To run the program down to the breakpoint, press the Ctrl F9 key combination or select Run from the Run menu. All the instructions in the loop will be executed, and the program will stop on the line with the breakpoint. Now look at the Watches. The `total` variable is –6322. A large negative number often results from the overflow of a positive number, so perhaps at this point we can guess that we've exceeded the capacity of signed integers. In fact, the actual total is 499 times 250, or 124,750, which is far larger than the 32,767 limit of type `int`. The cure is to use variables of type `long int`.

You can install as many breakpoints in a program as you want. This is useful if the program can take several different paths, depending on the result of `if` statements or other branching constructs. You can block all the paths with breakpoints, then see where it stops.

Removing Breakpoints

You can remove a single breakpoint by positioning the cursor on the line with the breakpoint and selecting Toggle breakpoint from the Debug menu (just as you did to install the breakpoint). The breakpoint highlight will vanish.

The Breakpoints Window

Calling up Breakpoints... from the Debug menu opens a window that gives you several other breakpoint options. When you call up this option, you'll see a list of all the currently set breakpoints, with their line numbers. Buttons allow you to select the options. Two of the most interesting are selected with the Edit button. This button allows you to set a pass count and a condition for each breakpoint.

The pass count modifies a breakpoint so that it doesn't stop the program flow the first time it's reached. It specifies how many times the program will pass this breakpoint before it stops. To set this option you must have already installed a breakpoint. In the errbreak.c example, delete existing breakpoints, and then place one on the line

```
total +=j;
```

Suppose we want to see what happens just before the end of the loop; we want to stop when j is 498. Call up Breakpoints... from the Debug menu. Click the Edit button. You'll see a dialog box with various fields. Type the number 498 into the Pass count field and press the Enter key. Click OK. Now when you run the program (resetting first if necessary) it will stop with j at 497, allowing you to single step through the final few cycles of the loop.

In a similar way, you can set a condition by entering it into the Condition field in the dialog box called up from the Edit button. A *condition* is an expression with a true or false value. In the current example, instead of using a pass count, you could use a condition of `total < 200`. This lets you stop the program when a variable reaches a certain value.

The Go To Cursor Option

If you only need to install one breakpoint, you can take a shortcut approach: the Go To Cursor option. Position the cursor on the line where you want the program to stop. Now run the program by selecting Go To Cursor from the Run menu or by pressing the F4 key. (Don't use the normal Run option or the Ctrl F9 key combination.) The effect is the same as if you had installed a breakpoint on the line with the cursor, but there is no breakpoint to remove later.

Function Debugging

When one function calls another, certain complexities arise in the debugging process. In this section we'll see how the Turbo C debugger handles these function-related situations.

Trace Into Versus Step Over

Suppose you're single stepping through the `main()` function, and it calls another function, say `func()`. Do you want to single step into `func()`, stepping through the lines of code that constitute the function, or do you want to step over it, treating it as a single line of code? The answer is, it depends: sometimes you want to go into (or trace into) a function, and sometimes you want to execute it as a single line of code, or step over it.

This is the purpose of the F7 and F8 keys. Both these keys provide single stepping, but the F7 key traces into any functions it encounters, while the F8 key steps over them. By selecting the appropriate key at each step, you can determine whether you trace into or step over a particular function.

For example, consider the following example program.

```
// errfunc.c
// demonstrates trace, step, call stack
void func1(void);        // prototypes
void func2(void);

void main(void)
    {
    func1();
    func1();
    }
```

```
void func1(void)
   {
   func2();
   }

void func2(void)
   {
   }
```

Try single stepping through this program with the F8 key. You'll see the run bar go from the line main() to the first func1() call, to the second func1() call, and then to the closing brace of main(). It never goes to the functions themselves.

Now reset the debugger with the Program Reset option, and use the F7 key to trace into the functions. The run bar goes to the first line of main(), then to the call to func1(), then to first line of func1() itself, then to the call to func2(), then to the first line of func2(), and so on. All the code in all the functions, no matter how deeply nested, will be traced into.

Even using the F7 key you can't trace into a Turbo C library routine such as printf(). For one thing the source file needs to be available for tracing to take place, and the source files for the library routines aren't included in the system. These routines are also presumably bug-free, so there is no need to debug them.

The Call Stack Option

When tracing into several levels of functions, it's easy to forget where you came from. You may know you're in a particular function, but you've forgotten which function called the function you're in.

Turbo C++ provides a handy way to see the whole chain of function calls that led to your present location in the program.

For instance, suppose you're single stepping through the errfunc.c program, using the F7 key to trace into every function. The main() function has called func1(), and func1() has called func2(). To see the function calls that have taken place up to this point, select the Call Stack... option from the Debug menu. The Call Stack list will look like this:

```
func2()
func1()
main()
```

It would be nice to watch new functions being added to and removed from the Call Stack list as you single stepped through a program, but this isn't possible. You can't leave the Call Stack list on the window as you single step. Call Stack is a snapshot, not a movie. However, it can remind you where you've come from if you get lost.

If a call to a function has arguments, the values of the arguments will also be shown on the Call Stack list.

Using the Call Stack window, you can cause the listing in the Edit window to scroll to a particular function. Select the function name from the Call Stack list and press the Enter key. The Call Stack window will vanish, and the Edit window will display that function, with the cursor marking the currently executing statement.

The Evaluate/Modify Window

You can use the Turbo C debugger to change the values of variables while a program is running. This can be useful if you've single stepped to a certain point and realize that a variable has an incorrect value, but want to see what would happen if you continued with the correct value. On the other hand, you might want to generate different values to test the operation of certain routines without actually inputting these values to the program.

The feature that makes it possible to change variable values is called the Evaluate/Modify window. You can call up this window by choosing the Evaluate/Modify option from the Debug menu, or by pressing the hot key combination Ctrl F4.

Evaluating Simple Variables

Let's try the Evaluation window with the faulty errloop.c example from earlier in this chapter.

Call up errloop.c, and set Watches for number, j, and answer, as described earlier. Now trace through the program with the F7 key, inputting the value 5 to the scanf(). Go slowly when you step into the for loop. The first time through the loop you'll see answer go to 0. This is the bug: once it's 0, this variable remains 0 no matter what it's multiplied by.

Suppose at this point we want to see whether the program would work correctly if answer started with the correct value. To change its value, select Evaluate/Modify from the Debug menu. You'll see a window with three fields: Expression, Result, and New Value.

The Expression field may already contain a word; it will repeat whatever word the cursor is resting on in the Edit window. If it does (and if it's the wrong word), backspace over it. Now type the name answer. When you press the Enter key you'll see the value of this variable (it should be 0) show up in the Result field.

To change the value, move the cursor down to the New Value field. Enter the new value: 1. You'll see the value of answer in the Result field change from 0 to 1.

When you leave the Evaluate window by pressing the Esc key you'll see the value of answer change in the Watch window as well.

Now you can continue single stepping through the program. This time answer will grow as expected, from 1 to 2 to 6 to 24. The program stops at this point—before it has calculated the correct value of 120—because we haven't changed the upper limit in the for loop from j<number to j<=number. However, we have seen that starting with a nonzero value of answer puts us on the right track.

Evaluating Expressions

You can use the Evaluate/Modify window to find the values of expressions as well as simple variables. In the previous example, single step the first few lines until the program gives answer the value 1. Now call up the Evaluate window, and type answer*3 into the Evaluate field. When you press the Enter key the Result field will show the value 3 (the result of 1*3). The entire expression has been evaluated.

You can use all sorts of expressions in the Evaluate field. They can involve one or more variable names and various operators. One common use for this feature is finding the values of array elements and the contents of pointers, such as list[2], *(ptr+7), or *(ptr+index).

The Evaluate window won't handle functions, like sin() or sqrt(), or anything created with a #define or typedef.

Inspecting Data

Another way to look at data is with the Inspect... option in the Debug menu. This is a more technical capability, best suited to looking at complex data such as structures, unions, arrays, arrays of structures, and so on. It shows you all the elements of such variables, displaying them in a window so that you can scroll through them if they are too large to see all at once.

To use this option, position the cursor on the variable you want to inspect. Select Inspect... from the Debug menu. The variable name should appear in the Inspect field in the resulting dialog box. If it doesn't, type it in. Press the Enter key and a window will appear containing the contents of the variable. If it's a structure or array, you may need to scroll the window to see all of it.

In this appendix we haven't covered all the debugging features, but what we've said should be enough to get you started debugging your programs and learning about the debugger's capabilities.

Answers to Questions and Exercises

Chapter 1—Answers to Questions

1. b

2. Compiled, linked, and executed

3. a and c are both correct

4. Automate

5. The parentheses following `main()` indicate that `main` is a function and provide a place to put arguments.

6. a and b

7. False: only the semicolon signals the end of a statement.

8. Here's what's wrong with the example:

   a. No parentheses following `main`
   b. Parentheses used instead of braces around body of program
   c. `print` used instead of `printf`
   d. No parentheses surrounding `printf()`'s argument
   e. No semicolon at the end of the statement
   f. Program statement not indented

9. On the left there is a string that will be printed; on the right is a series of constants (or variables) that will be placed in the string.

10. The output is

    ```
    one
    two
    three
    ```

Chapter 1—Suggested Answers to Exercises

Exercise 1

Here's one possibility, although there are others:

```
void main(void)
   {
   printf("\nMr. %s is %d,", "Green", 42);
   printf("\nMr. %s is %d.", "Brown", 48);
   }
```

Exercise 2

```
void main(void)
   {
   printf("\n%c, %c, and %c are all letters.", 'a', 'b', 'c');
   }
```

Chapter 2—Answers to Questions

1. a, b, and c are correct.

2. Character (char), integer (int), floating point (float), long integer (long), and double-precision floating point (double)

3. a, b, and d are correct; there is no type *double float*, except in ice-cream parlors. However, long float is the same as double.

4. True

5. Four

6. –32768 to 32767

7. d

8. False: it can hold numbers 65,536 times as large.

9. b and c are correct

10. '\x41' prints A and '\xE0' prints the Greek letter alpha

11. | | *Decimal* | *Exponential* |
    |---|---|---|
    | a. | 1,000,000 | 1.0e6 |
    | b. | 0.000,001 | 1.0e–6 |
    | c. | 199.95 | 1.9995e2 |
    | d. | –888.88 | –8.8888e2 |

12. | | *Exponential* | *Decimal* |
    |---|---|---|
    | a. | 1.5e6 | 1,500,000 |
    | b. | 1.5e–6 | 0.000,001,5 |
    | c. | 7.6543e3 | 7,654.3 |
    | d. | –7.6543e–3 | –0.007,654,3 |

13. There's no address operator preceding the years variable in the scanf() function.

14. d

15. True

16. a and c

17. `number++;`

18. `usa += calif;`

19. `'\t'` is the tab character, `'\r'` is the return character, which prints a carriage return (but no linefeed), and isn't to be confused with the newline character, `'\n'`, which prints both a carriage return and a linefeed.

20. d

21. False

22. b

23. a. False
    b. True (the ASCII codes are compared)
    c. False
    d. True

24. b

25. No. The old begin-comment symbol (`/*`) can't be used within an old-style comment.

Chapter 2—Suggested Answers to Exercises

Exercise 1

```
// age2.c
// calculates age in minutes
#include <stdio.h>

void main(void)
    {
    float years, minutes;

    printf("\nPlease type your age in years: ");
    scanf("%f", &years);
    minutes = years * 365 * 24 * 60;
    printf("You are %.1f minutes old.\n", minutes);
    }
```

Exercise 2

```
// square.c
// finds square of typed-in number
#include <stdio.h>

void main(void)
    {
    float square, number;

    printf("\nEnter number to be squared: ");
    scanf("%f", &number);
    square = number * number;
    printf("Square is %f", square);
    }
```

Exercise 3

```
// box2.c
// draws 4x4 box with graphics characters
#include <stdio.h>                    // for printf()

void main(void)
    {
    printf("\n\xC9\xCD\xCD\xBB");;    // top line
    printf("\n\xBA  \xBA");           // two spaces in the middle
    printf("\n\xBA  \xBA");           // ditto
    printf("\n\xC8\xCD\xCD\xBC");     // bottom line
    }
```

Chapter 3—Answers to Questions

1. Initialize, test, increment

2. d

3. Semicolon

4. b

5. Commas

6. a

7. False

8. b

9. Deeply

10. Value

11. a, b, c, and d are all correct.

12. True

13. b

14. b

15. False: it causes a return to the beginning of the loop.

Chapter 3—Suggested Answers to Exercises

Exercise 1

```c
// square2.c
// prints out the squares of the first 20 integers
#include <stdio.h>        // for printf()

void main(void)
    {
    int n;

    for(n=1; n<21; n++)
        printf("\nThe square of %2d is %3d", n, n*n);
    }
```

Exercise 2

```c
// charcnt3.c
// counts characters in a phrase typed in
// until period is typed
#include <stdio.h>      // for printf()
#include <conio.h>      // for getche()

void main(void)
    {
    int count=0;

    printf(')\nType a phrase (terminate with period):\n");
    while ( getche() != '.' )
        count++;
    printf("\nCharacter count is %d", count);
    }
```

Exercise 3

```c
// between.c
// tells how many letters between two letters
#include <stdio.h>        // for printf()
#include <conio.h>        // for getche()
```

```
void main(void)
   {
   char ch1 = 'a', ch2;

   while( ch1 != '\r' )
      {
      printf("\nType first character: ");
      ch1 = getche();
      printf("\nType second character: ");
      ch2 = getche();
      printf("\nThere are %d chars in between.", ch2-ch1-1);
      }
   }
```

Chapter 4—Answers to Questions

1. b and c are both correct.

2. Yes, except for the keyword then, which doesn't exist in C.

3. False

4. c

5. a—there is no conditional expression following else.

6. Yes: the compiler doesn't care if you put multiple statements on one line, although it is more difficult to read.

7. False

8. b

9. d

10. b

11. No: colons must be used after the case statements, and break statements are needed after the printf() statements.

12. False: break statements aren't used if two cases trigger the same set of statements.

13. No: variables, such as temp, can't be used in case expressions.

14. d

15. 0

Chapter 4—Suggested Answers to Exercises

Exercise 1

```
// speed.c
// prints appropriate responses to user's speed
#include <stdio.h>                    // for printf()

void main(void)
    {
    int speed;

    printf("\nPlease enter the speed you normally ");
    printf("travel in a 55 mph zone: ");
    scanf("%d", &speed);
    if(speed > 75)
        printf("I'm taking you to headquarters, buddy.");
    else
        if(speed > 55)
            printf("I'll let you off with a warning, this time.");
        else
            if(speed>45)
                printf("Have a good day, sir.");
            else
                printf("Can't you get the lead out, buddy?");
    }  // end main()
```

Exercise 2

```
// checker2.c
// draws a checkerboard on the screen
#include <stdio.h>                    // for printf()

void main(void)
    {
    int x, y, z;

    printf("\n\n");                    // start on new line
    for(y=1; y<=8; y++)                // stepping down screen
        for(z=1; z<=3; z++)            // 3 lines per square
            {
            for(x=1; x<=8; x++)        // stepping across screen
                if( (x+y) % 2 == 0 )   // even-numbered square?
                                       // print 6 rectangles
                    printf("\xDB\xDB\xDB\xDB\xDB\xDB");
                else
                    printf("      ");  // print 6 blank spaces
            if(y * z < 24)             // print newline,
                printf("\n");          // except on last line
            }  // end for z
    }  // end main()
```

Exercise 3

```
// linesX2.c
// prints four crossed lines on screen
#include <stdio.h>                    // for printf()

void main(void)
   {
   int x, y;

   printf("\n");                      // start on new line
   for(y=1; y<24; y++)                // step down screen
      {
      for(x=1; x<24; x++)             // step across screen
         if( x==y || x==24-y || x==12 || y==12 )
            printf("\xDB");           // print solid color
         else
            printf("\xB0");           // print gray
      printf("\n");                   // next line
      }
   } // end main()
```

Chapter 5—Answers to Questions

1. All except b are valid reasons for using functions. Functions don't run faster than inline code or macros.

2. True

3. No: the call to the function must be terminated with a semicolon.

4. False: you can return from a function by simply "falling through" the closing brace.

5. False: you can only return one data item with a function using return().

6. No: first, the declarator shouldn't be terminated with a semicolon. Second, the definition of the argument num should take place within the declarator. Third, the declarator should specify a return type of int.

7. a and c

8. False: functions commonly use local variables, which are accessible only to the function in which they're defined.

9. b and c, although we won't learn about c until the Chapter 7, "Pointers."

10. a, b, d, and e

11. No: the argument passed to the function is type int in the calling program but type float in the function.

12. a

13. Many

14. d

15. c

16. c

17. Substituted

18. No: you can't have spaces in the left-hand part of the statement (the identifier).

19. EXP is the identifier and 2.71828 is the text.

20. a and b are both correct.

21. a, b, and d

22. No: the macro expands into the incorrect

```
postage = rate*l + w + h
```

23. Inserted

24. b, c, and d

25. INCLUDE

Chapter 5—Suggested Answers to Exercises

Exercise 1

```c
// maximum.c
// prints largest of two numbers typed in
#include <stdio.h>       // for printf(), scanf()
int max(int, int);       // prototype

void main(void)
    {
    int num1, num2;

    printf("\nEnter two numbers: ");
    scanf("%d %d", &num1, &num2);
    printf("Largest one is %d.", max(num1,num2) );
    }

// max()
// returns largest of two integers
int max(int n1, int n2)
    {
    return( n1>n2 ? n1 : n2 );
    }
```

Exercise 2

```
//  times.c
//  calculates difference between two times
#include <stdio.h>          //for printf(), scanf()
float getsecs(void);        //prototype

 void main(void)
    {
    float secs1, secs2;      //declare variables

    printf("\nType first time (form 12:22:55): ");
    secs1 = getsecs();
    printf("Type second (later) time: ");
    secs2 = getsecs();
    printf("Difference is %.0f seconds.", secs2-secs1);
    }

//  getsecs()
//  gets time from kbd in hours-minutes-seconds format
//  returns time in seconds
float getsecs(void)
    {
    float hours, minutes, seconds;

    scanf("%f:%f:%f", &hours, &minutes, &seconds);
    return ( hours*60*60 + minutes*60 + seconds );
    }
```

Exercise 3

```
// timesM.c
// calculates difference between two times
// uses macro
#include <stdio.h>       // for printf(), scanf()
                         // macro
#define HMSTOSEC(hrs,mins,secs) (hrs*3600 + mins*60 + secs)

void main(void)
    {
    float secs1, secs2;
    float hours, minutes, seconds;

    printf("\nType first time (form 12:22:55): ");
    scanf("%f:%f:%f", &hours, &minutes, &seconds);
    secs1 = HMSTOSEC(hours, minutes, seconds);

    printf("Type second (later) time: ");
    scanf("%f:%f:%f", &hours, &minutes, &seconds);
    secs2 = HMSTOSEC(hours, minutes, seconds);

    printf("Difference is %.2f seconds.", secs2-secs1);
    }
```

713

Chapter 6—Answers to Questions

1. c

2. d

3. Type, name, size

4. No: brackets, not parentheses, are used in array declarations.

5. The fifth element

6. b

7. d

8. No: use `j<MAX`, and `&prices[j]`.

9. No: must use brackets following the name.

10. c

11. d

12. False

13. c and d

14. Sure

15. `array[1][0]`

16. Address

17. a

18. a and c, which are the same thing.

19. False: the function doesn't move the values stored in the array.

20. c, although some other choices aren't clearly false.

21. String, character.

22. c

23. Null `'\0'`.

24. `gets()`

25. 9 (space must be left for the `'\0'` character).

26. True

27. a

28. `&string[5]`

29. You can't use assignment statements with strings.

30. strlen(name)

Chapter 6—Suggested Answers to Exercises

Exercise 1

```
// temp2.c
// averages one week's temperatures
// prints them out along with average
#include <stdio.h>                    // for printf(), scanf()

void main(void)
   {
   int temper[7];              // array definition
   int day, sum;

   printf("\n");
   for (day=0; day<7; day++)     // put temps in array
      {
      printf("Enter temperature for day %d: ", day);
      scanf("%d", &temper[day]);
      }

   sum = 0;                    // calculate average
   for (day=0; day<7; day++)     // and print temperatures
      {
      printf("Temperature for day %d is %d.\n", day, temper[day]);
      sum += temper[day];
      }
   printf("Average is %d.", sum/7);
   }
```

Exercise 2

```
// fltemp3.c
// averages arbitrary number of temperatures
#include <stdio.h>                 // for printf(), scanf()
#define LIM 100

void main(void)
   {
   float temper[LIM];              // array definition
   float sum=0.0;
   int num, day=0;

   printf("\nEnter temperature for day 0: ");
   scanf("%f", &temper[0]);
```

```
while ( temper[day++] > 0 )      // put temps in array
   {
   printf("Enter temperature for day %d: ", day);
   scanf("%f", &temper[day]);
   }
num = day-1;                      // number of temps entered
for (day=0; day<num; day++)       // calculate average
   sum += temper[day];
printf("Average is %.1f", sum/num);
}
```

Exercise 3

```
// insert.c
// inserts a character into a string
#include <stdio.h>                // for printf(), etc.
#include <string.h>               // for strcpy()
void strins(char[], char, int);   // prototype

void main(void)
   {
   char charac;
   char string[81];
   int position;

   printf("\nType string [Return], character, position\n");
   gets(string);
   scanf("%c %d", &charac, &position);
   strins(string,charac,position);
   puts(string);
   }

// strins()
// inserts character into string
void strins(char str[], char ch, int n)
   {
   char scratch[81];              // temporary space

   strcpy( scratch, &str[n] );    // save 2nd half in scratch
   str[n] = ch;                   // insert character
   strcpy( &str[n+1], scratch );  // shift 2nd half right
   }
```

Chapter 7—Answers to Questions

1. b and c

2. a and c

3. True

4. False: we learned how to pass the addresses of arrays to functions in the last chapter.

5. False: when a value is passed to a function, the value itself (not its address) is stored in the function's memory space.

6. d

7. c

8. Addresses, declare, indirection

9. b

10. Both a and d will work (provided they are known to the function where the reference is made).

11. c

12. `*pointvar = *pointvar / 10;`

13. b and d

14. In the function's memory space

15. `ptrj = &j;`

16. No: it should be `scanf("%d", ptrx);`

17. a

18. No: you can't increment an address, which is a pointer constant.

19. Print the array elements: 4 5 6.

20. 2

21. Print the addresses of the array elements.

22. Print the array elements: 4 5 6.

23. Almost: the second creates a pointer as well as an array.

24. The same amount, different amounts

25. `"I come not to bury Caesar"`

    `I come not to bury Caesar`

    `to bury Caesar`

26. 13 bytes: 11 for the string plus null character and 2 for the pointer to the string.

27. False: every row of a two-dimensional array can be considered to be a one-dimensional array.

28. `arr7[1][1]`, `*(*(arr+1)+1)`

29. d

30. `*(*(arr7+x)+y)`

Chapter 7—Suggested Answers to Exercises

Exercise 1

```c
// zerovars.c
// tests function which zeros three variables
#include <stdio.h>              // for printf()
void zero(int *, int *, int *);  // prototype

void main(void)
   {
   int x=4, y=7, z=11;

   printf("\nx=%d, y=%d, z=%d.", x, y, z);
   zero( &x, &y, &z );
   printf("\nx=%d, y=%d, z=%d.", x, y, z);
   }

// zero()
// puts zero in three variables in calling program
void zero(int *px, int *py, int *pz)
   {
   *px = 0;
   *py = 0;
   *pz = 0;
   }
```

Exercise 2

```c
// zeroarr.c
// tests function to zero array elements
#include <stdio.h>              // for printf()
void zero(int *, int);         // prototype
#define SIZE 5                 // size of array

void main(void)
   {
   int array[SIZE] = { 3, 5, 7, 9, 11 };
   int j;

   printf("\n");
   for (j=0; j<SIZE; j++)          // print out array
      printf("%d  ", *(array+j) );
   zero(array, SIZE);              // call funct to insert 0s
   printf("\n");
   for (j=0; j<SIZE; j++)          // print out array
      printf("%d  ", *(array+j) );
   }

// zero()
```

```
// zeros out elements of array in calling program
void zero(int *ptr, int num)
    {
    int k;

    for(k=0; k<num; k++)
        *(ptr+k) = 0;
    }
```

Exercise 3

```
// zerostr.c
// tests function which puts null character in string
#include <stdio.h>            // for printf()
void zero(char *);            // prototype

void main(void)
    {
    char *phrase = "Don't test the river with both feet";

    printf("\nPhrase=%s.", phrase);
    zero(phrase);
    printf("\nPhrase=%s.", phrase);
    }

// zero()
// function to put null character at start of string
void zero(char *str)
    {
    *str = '\0';
    }
```

Chapter 8—Answers to Questions

1. b and c

2. 256

3. 2

4. False: key combinations such as Alt Z can be represented as well.

5. d

6. False

7. a and b

8. conio.h.

9. d

10. 2

11. d

12. True

13. Moves the cursor one character right

14. False: it causes an exit from the entire program.

15. a

16. True

17. b and d

18. False: it merely defines an area.

19. a, c, and d

20. C>prog1 <f1.c >f2.c

Chapter 8—Suggested Answers to Exercises

Exercise 1

```c
// backsp.c
// prints letters, backspaces with left arrow key
#include <stdio.h>                    // for printf()
#include <conio.h>                    // for text-window functions
#define L_ARRO 75                     // left arrow key

void main(void)
   {
   char key;

   printf("\n");
   while ( (key=getch()) != '\r' )   // read keyboard
      if( key == 0 )                 // if extended code,
         {
         if( getch() == L_ARRO )     // read second code
            {                        // if left arrow
            gotoxy( wherex()-1, wherey() );  // move cursor left
            printf(" ");             // print space over char
            gotoxy( wherex()-1, wherey() );  // move cursor left
            }
         }
      else
         putch(key);                 // not ext code, print char
   } // end main()
```

Exercise 2

```
// decihex.c
// translates decimal number into hexadecimal
// uses command-line arguments
#include <stdio.h>        // for printf()
#include <stdlib.h>       // for atoi()

void main( int argc, char *argv[] )
   {
   unsigned int num;

   if( argc != 2 )
      printf("Example usage: decihex 128");
   else
      {
      num = atoi( *(argv+1) );
      printf("Hex=%x", num );
      }
   }
```

Exercise 3

```
// braces.c
// checks numbers if right and left braces are equal
// uses redirection for input file
#include <stdio.h>        // for printf(), EOF (-1), getchar()

void main(void)
   {
   int left=0, right=0;
   char ch;

   while( (ch=getchar()) != EOF )    // (EOF defined as -1)
      {
      if( ch=='{' )
         left++;
      if( ch=='}' )
         right++;
      }
   if (left != right)
      printf("\nMismatched braces\n");
   else
      printf("\nBraces match\n");
   }
```

Chapter 9—Answers to Questions

1. Same type, different types

2. False: arrays are more appropriate for elements of the same type.

3. b, c, and d are all correct.

4.
```
struct xxx
      {
      char string[10];
      int num;
      };
```

5. c

6. Type, variable, value

7.
```
struct vehicle car;
```

8.
```
jim.arms = 2;
```

9.
```
struct body
      {
      int arms;
      int legs;
      }jim;
```

10. Yes, at least in modern compilers

11. a and b

12.
```
struct partners
      {
      struct body sandy;
      struct body pat;
      };
```

13. True (in modern compilers)

14.
```
struct book *ptrbook;
```

15. a and d. This expression will also work.

```
(*addweath).temp
```

16.
```
struct blech blorg(void)
      {
      struct blech ablech;
      ablech.i = 3;
      ablech.f = 7.25;
      return (ablech);
      }
```

17. d

18. True

19. void gamma(struct beta *delta);

20. False: you can store different values at the same place at different times.

Chapter 9—Suggested Answers to Exercises

Exercise 1

```
// date.c
// demonstrates structure to hold date
#include <stdio.h>      // for printf()

void main(void)
   {
   struct date
      {
      int month;
      int day;
      int year;
      };
   struct date today;

   today.month = 12;
   today.day = 31;
   today.year = 91;

   printf("\ndate is %d/%d/%d",
              today.month, today.day, today.year );
   }
```

Exercise 2

```
// date2.c
// demonstrates passing structure to function
#include <stdio.h>           // for printf()

struct date                  // structure definition
   {
   int month;                // structure members
   int day;
   int year;
   };

void prindate(struct date mmddyy);    // prototype (follows
                                      //     struct def)
void main(void)
   {
   struct date today;        // structure variable

   today.month = 12;         // give values to
```

```
    today.day = 31;        //    structure variables
    today.year = 91;
    prindate(today);       // print date from structure
    }

// prindate()
// prints date passed via structure
void prindate(struct date mmddyy)
    {
    printf("\ndate is %d/%d/%d",
              mmddyy.month, mmddyy.day, mmddyy.year );
    }
```

Exercise 3

```
// date3.c
// demonstrates passing pointer to structure
#include <stdio.h>         // for printf()
#include <stdlib.h>        // for atoi()

struct date                // structure definition
    {
    int month;             // structure members
    int day;
    int year;
    };
                           // prototypes
void prindate(struct date mmddyy);
void getdate(struct date *ptrd);

void main(void)
    {
    struct date adate;     // structure variable

    getdate(&adate);       // get date from user, store in adate
    prindate(adate);       // print date from adate
    }

// getdate()
// gets date from user
void getdate(struct date *ptrd)
    {
    char string[10];

    printf("\nEnter the month: ");
    ptrd->month = atoi( gets(string) );  // month
    printf("Enter the day: ");
    ptrd->day = atoi( gets(string) );    // day
    printf("Enter the year: ");
    ptrd->year = atoi( gets(string) );   // year
    }
```

```
// prindate()
// prints date passed via structure
void prindate(struct date mmddyy)
   {
   printf("\nDate is %d/%d/%d",
               mmddyy.month, mmddyy.day, mmddyy.year );
   }
```

Chapter 10—Answers to Questions

1. graphics.lib, a graphics driver like egabga.bgi, and graphics.h

2. a, c, and d

3. False

4. `initgraph()`

5. b and c

6. True

7. There is no such function.

8. a and c

9. a, b, and c

10. c and d

11. a, b, c, and d

12. 16

13. b

14. `getmaxx()`

15. a, c, and d

16. False

17. d

18. True

19. `bar()` or `bar3d()`, `pieslice()`, `putpixel()`

20. b

Chapter 10—Suggested Answers to Exercises

Exercise 1

```c
// trycolor.c
// creates color chart
#include <graphics.h>          // for graphics functions
#include <conio.h>             // for getch()
#define GRID    60             // separation of grid points
#define XMAX    (GRID * 8)     // size of board
#define YMAX    (GRID * 2)
#define SIDE    (GRID-4)       // size of square

void main(void)
    {
    int driver, mode;
    int x, y;
    int color = 0;
    driver = DETECT;                // auto detect
                                    // initialize graphics
    initgraph(&driver, &mode, "c:\\tc\\bgi");

    for(y=0; y<YMAX; y+=GRID)       // move down rows
       for(x=0; x<XMAX; x+=GRID)    // move across columns
          {
          moveto(x, y);             // move current position
          setcolor(WHITE);
          rectangle(x, y, x+SIDE, y+SIDE);
          setfillstyle(SOLID_FILL, color++);
          floodfill(x+1, y+1, WHITE);
          }
    getch();
    closegraph();
    }
```

Exercise 2

```c
// paint.c
// permits user to draw, using cursor
#include <graphics.h>          // for graphics functions
#include <conio.h>             // for getch()
#define ESC     27             // escape key
#define L_ARRO 75              // cursor control keys
#define R_ARRO 77
#define U_ARRO 72
#define D_ARRO 80

void main(void)
    {
    int driver= DETECT, mode;
```

```
int x, y, width, height;
char key;
                                    // initialize graphics
initgraph(&driver, &mode, "c:\\tc\\bgi");
width = getmaxx();                  // get screen dimensions
height = getmaxy();
x = width/2;                        // put dot in middle
y = height/2;
putpixel(x, y, WHITE);
while( (key=getch()) != ESC )       // if [Esc], exit loop
   {
   if( key == 0 )                   // if extended code,
      {
      switch( getch() )             // read second character
         {
         case L_ARRO:               // move cursor left
            if( x > 0 )
               --x;
            break;
         case R_ARRO:               // move cursor right
            if( x < width )
               ++x;
            break;
         case U_ARRO:               // move cursor up
            if( y > 0 )
               --y;
            break;
         case D_ARRO:               // move cursor down
            if( y < height )
               ++y;
            break;
         } // end switch
      putpixel(x, y, WHITE);        // draw dot
      } // end if
   } // end while
closegraph();                       // shut down graphics
}
```

Exercise 3

```
// coin.c
// displays a coin rotating about vertical axis
#include <graphics.h>              // for graphics functions
#include <dos.h>                   // for delay()
#include <conio.h>                 // for kbhit()
#define XC 160                     // center of ellipse
#define YC 100
#define RAD 30                     // vertical radius
#define N  8                       // number of views
#define DELAY 40                   // delay between views
```

```
void main(void)
   {
   int xRad;
   char buff[N][2000];                    // buffer for N images
   int j, mode;
   int driver = DETECT;
                                          // set graphics mode
   initgraph(&driver, &mode, "c:\\tc\\bgi" );

   for(j=0; j<N; j++)                     // make and store
      {                                   //    images of ellipses
      xRad = j * RAD / (N-1) ;            // find x radius
       if(j==0)  xRad = 1;                // vertical line
      cleardevice();                      // get rid of old images
      setcolor(WHITE);
      ellipse(XC, YC, 0, 360, xRad, RAD); // draw ellipse
      if(xRad>3)                          // if not a vertical line,
         {                                // color ellipse
         setfillstyle(SOLID_FILL, LIGHTGRAY);
         floodfill(XC, YC, WHITE);
         }
                                          // place image in memory
      getimage(XC-RAD, YC-RAD, XC+RAD, YC+RAD, buff[j]);
      }
   while( !kbhit() )                      // draw ellipses
      {                                   //    until keypress
      for(j=0; j<N; j++)                  // increasing width
         {                                // draw image
         putimage(XC-RAD, YC-RAD, buff[j], COPY_PUT);
         delay (DELAY);                   // delay, erase image
         putimage(XC-RAD, YC-RAD, buff[j], XOR_PUT);
         }
      for( j=N-1; j>0; j--)              // decreasing width
         {                                // draw image
         putimage(XC-RAD, YC-RAD, buff[j], COPY_PUT);
         delay(DELAY);                    // delay, erase image
         putimage(XC-RAD, YC-RAD, buff[j], XOR_PUT);
         }
      } // end while
   closegraph();
   }
```

Chapter 11—Answers to Questions

1. Standard I/O and system I/O

2. a, b, c, and d are all correct.

3. File pointer

4. a and b

5. `fclose()`

6. d

7. False: a file that is written to but not closed may lose data when the program is terminated.

8. c and d

9. Binary mode

10. a, c, e, and f

11. Binary, unless using formatted I/O

12. c

13. False

14. d (not to be confused with c)

15. `fwrite()`

16. Bytes

17. c and d

18. Handle

19. a and d

20. `read()`

21. `setmode()`

22. c

23. True

24. b and d

25. `permiss`

26. System-level

27. d

28. `C>encrypt <file1.txt >file2.txt`

29. a and c

30. False

Chapter 11—Suggested Answers to Exercises

Exercise 1

```c
// braces2.c
// checks if numbers of right and left braces are equal
#include <stdio.h>                       // for standard I/O
#include <stdlib.h>                      // for exit()

int main( int argc, char *argv[] )
   {
   FILE *fptr;
   int left=0, right=0;
   char ch;

   if( argc != 2)                        // check args
      { printf("Syntax: braces2 filename"); exit(1); }

   if( (fptr=fopen(argv[1], "r")) == NULL)  // open file
      { printf("Can't open file %s.", argv[1]); exit(1); }

   while( (ch=getc(fptr)) != EOF )       // get character
      {
      if( ch=='{' )  left++;             // count lefts
      if( ch=='}' )  right++;            // count rights
      }
   if (left != right)                    // check if equal
      printf("\nMismatched braces\n");
   else
      printf("\nBraces match.\n");
   fclose(fptr);                         // close file
   return(0);
   }
```

Exercise 2

```c
// writedex.c
// writes strings typed at keyboard, to file
// prints offset for each phrase
#include <stdio.h>                       // for standard I/O
#include <string.h>                      // for strlen()

void main(void)
   {
   FILE *fptr;                           // declare ptr to FILE
   char string[81];                      // storage for strings

   fptr = fopen("textfile.txt","w");     // open file
   while( strlen(gets(string)) > 0 )     // get string from keybd
      {
      printf("Offset=%ld\n\n", ftell(fptr) );  // print offset
```

```
        fputs(string, fptr);              // write string to file
        fputs("\n", fptr);               // write newline to file
        }
    fclose(fptr);                        // close file
    }
```

Exercise 3

```
// agentr2.c
// maintains list of agents in file
// permits deletion of one record
#include <stdio.h>            // for standard I/O
#include <conio.h>            // for getche(), etc.
#include <stdlib.h>           // for atof()
#define TRUE 1

void newname(void);          // prototypes
void listall(void);
void wfile(void);
void rfile(void);
void delrec(void);

struct personnel             // define data structure
    {
    char name [40];          // name
    int agnumb;              // code number
    float height;            // height in inches
    };

struct personnel agent[50];  // array of 50 structures
int n = 0;                    // number of agents listed

int main(void)
    {
    while (TRUE)
        {
        printf("\n'e' enter new agent\n'l' list all agents");
        printf("\n'w' write file\n'r' read file");
        printf("\n'd' delete record\n'q' quit: ");
        switch ( getche() )
            {
            case 'e': newname(); break;
            case 'l': listall(); break;
            case 'w': wfile();   break;
            case 'r': rfile();   break;
            case 'd': delrec();  break;
            case 'q': exit(0);   break;
            default:                          // user mistake
                puts("\nEnter only selections listed");
            } // end switch
        } // end while
    } // end main
```

```
// newname()
// puts a new agent in the database
void newname(void)
    {
    char numstr[81];              // temporary string storage

    printf("\nRecord %d.\nEnter name: ", n+1); // get name
    gets(agent[n].name);
    printf("Enter agent number (3 digits): "); // get number
    gets(numstr);
    agent[n].agnumb = atoi(numstr);
    printf("Enter height in inches: ");        // get height
    gets(numstr);
    agent[n++].height = (float)atof(numstr);
    }

// listall()
// lists all agents and data
void listall(void)
    {
    int j;
    if (n < 1)                            // check for empty list
        printf("\nEmpty list.\n");
    for (j=0; j < n; j++)                 // print list
        {
        printf("\nRecord number %d\n", j+1);
        printf("   Name: %s\n", agent[j].name);
        printf("   Agent number: %03d\n", agent[j].agnumb);
        printf("   Height: %4.2f\n", agent[j].height);
        }
    }

// wfile()
// writes array of structures to file
void wfile(void)
    {
    FILE *fptr;
    if(n < 1)
        { printf("\nCan't write empty list.\n"); return; }
    if( (fptr=fopen("agents.rec","wb"))==NULL )
        printf("\nCan't open file agents.rec\n");
    else
        {
        fwrite(agent, sizeof(agent[0]), n, fptr);
        fclose(fptr);
        printf("\nFile of %d records written.\n", n);
        }
    }

// rfile()
// reads records (structures) from file into array
void rfile(void)
    {
```

```
   FILE *fptr;
   if( (fptr=fopen("agents.rec","rb"))==NULL )
      printf("\nCan't open file agents.rec\n");
   else
      {
      while( fread(&agent[n],sizeof(agent[n]),1,fptr)==1 )
         n++;                    // count records
      fclose(fptr);
      printf("\nFile read. Total agents is now %d.\n", n);
      }
   }

// delrec()
// deletes selected structure (record) from memory
void delrec(void)
   {
   int recno, j;
   printf("\nEnter record number to be deleted: ");
   scanf("%d", &recno);
   if(recno<1 || recno>n)
      { printf("Invalid record number.\n"); return; }
   for (j=--recno; j<n-1; j++)   // write each structure
      agent[j] = agent[j+1];     //    over preceding one
   n--;                          // one less structure
   }
```

Chapter 12—Answers to Questions

1. c and d

2. Static data area

3. a

4. Created, destroyed

5. a or b

6. False: it is visible only from its declaration onward.

7. Stack

8. b

9. `malloc()` or `calloc()`

10. False: it must be somewhat smaller because the static data area and the stack take up some room.

11. b

12. `realloc()`

13. False: it must be smaller than 64K.

14. c

15. c and d

16. Large

17. a and d

18. b

19. True

20. b and d

Chapter 12—Suggested Answers to Exercises

Exercise 1

```
// memfloat.c
// allocates memory for 2000 floats, checks memory
#include <stdio.h>              // for printf()
#include <stdlib.h>             // for malloc() and exit()

int main(void)
   {
   unsigned mem_floats = 2000;  // number of floats to store
   unsigned mem_bytes;          // bytes of memory needed

   float *ptr;                  // pointer to start of memory
   unsigned j;                  // loop counter

   mem_bytes = mem_floats * sizeof(float);  // calculate bytes

   ptr = malloc(mem_bytes);     // get memory
   if(ptr==NULL)                // error return from malloc()
      { printf("Can't allocate memory"); exit(1); }
   for(j=0; j<mem_floats; j++)  // fill memory with data
      ptr[j] = (float)j;
   for(j=0; j<mem_floats; j++)  // check the data
      if( ptr[j] != (float)j)
         { printf("Memory error: j=%u", j); exit(1); }
   free(ptr);                   // free memory
   printf("Memory test successful");
   return(0);
   }  // end main()
```

Exercise 2

```
// alocname.c
// allocates space for strings typed in by user
```

```
#include <stdio.h>              // for printf()
#include <stdlib.h>             // for malloc() and exit()
#include <string.h>             // for strlen(), strcpy()
#define TRUE 1
#define MAX_STRINGS 100         // maximum number of strings


int main(void)
   {
   char *arrptr[MAX_STRINGS];   // array of pointers to strings
   int n = 0;                   // number of strings entered
   unsigned j;                  // loop index
   char inputstr[81];           // input string
   unsigned length;             // length of input string

   printf("\n");
   while(TRUE)
      {
      printf("Enter string %d: ", n);
      length = strlen( gets(inputstr) );  // get string
      if(length==0)                       // blank line means
         break;                           // no more input
      arrptr[n] = malloc(length+1);       // get memory for string
      if(arrptr[n]==NULL)
         { printf("Allocation error"); exit(1); }
      strcpy(arrptr[n++], inputstr);      // store string in heap
      }
   for(j=0; j<n; j++)                     // display all strings
      printf("\nString %u: %s", j, arrptr[j]);
   for(j=0; j<n; j++)                     // free all memory
      free( arrptr[j] );
   return 0;
   }
```

Exercise 3

```
// agfilink.c
// maintains list of agents
// uses linked list, reads and writes list to disk file
#include <stdio.h>             // for printf()
#include <conio.h>             // for getche()
#include <stdlib.h>            // for atof()
#define TRUE 1
void newname(void);           // prototypes
void listall(void);
void rfile(void);
void wfile(void);

struct prs                    // declare data structure
   {
   char name [30];            // agent's name
   int agnumb;                // agent's number
```

```
    float height;                    // agent's height in inches
    struct prs *ptrnext;             // pointer to next structure
    };
struct prs *ptrfirst;                // pointer to beginning of chain

void main(void)
    {
    ptrfirst = NULL;                             // no input yet
    while(TRUE)                                  // cycle until 'q' chosen
        {
        printf("\n'e' enter new agent\n'l' list all agents");
        printf("\n'w' write file\n'r' read file\n'q' exit: ");
        switch ( getche() )
            {
            case 'e': newname(); break;
            case 'l': listall(); break;
            case 'w': wfile();   break;
            case 'r': rfile();   break;
            case 'q': exit(0);   break;    // normal exit
            default:                       // user mistake
                puts("\nEnter only selections listed");
            }  // end switch
        }  // end while
    }  // end main

// newname()
// puts a new agent in the database
void newname(void)
    {
    struct prs *ptrthis;                 // utility list pointer
    char numstr[81];                     // for numbers
                                         // get memory space
    ptrthis =  malloc( sizeof(struct prs) );
    if(ptrthis==NULL)
        { printf("Allocation error"); return; }
    ptrthis->ptrnext = ptrfirst;         // connects to old first
    ptrfirst = ptrthis;                  // this becomes new first

    printf("\nEnter name: ");            // get name
    gets(ptrthis->name);
    printf("Enter number: ");            // get number
    gets(numstr);
    ptrthis->agnumb = atoi(numstr);
    printf("Enter height: ");            // get height
    gets(numstr);
    ptrthis->height = atof(numstr);
    }

// listall()
// lists all agents and data
void listall(void)
    {
    struct prs *ptrthis;                     // utility list pointer
```

```
   if (ptrfirst == NULL )                    // if empty list
      { printf("\nEmpty list.\n"); return; }  //   return
   ptrthis = ptrfirst;                       // start at first item
   do
      {                                       // print contents
      printf("\nName: %s\n", ptrthis->name );
      printf("Number: %03d\n", ptrthis->agnumb );
      printf("Height: %4.2f\n", ptrthis->height );
      ptrthis = ptrthis->ptrnext;            // move to next item
      }
   while(ptrthis != NULL);                    // quit on null ptr
   }

// wfile()
// writes linked list to file
void wfile(void)
   {
   FILE *fptr;
   struct prs *ptrthis;                       // utility list pointer

   if (ptrfirst == NULL )                    // if empty list
      { printf("\nEmpty list.\n"); return; }  //   return
   if( (fptr=fopen("agents.rec","wb")) == NULL )
      { printf("\nCan't open file agents.rec\n"); return; }

   ptrthis = ptrfirst;                       // start at first agent
   do
      {                                       // write one structure
      fwrite(ptrthis, sizeof(struct prs), 1, fptr);
      ptrthis = ptrthis->ptrnext;            // move to next agent
      }
   while(ptrthis != NULL);                    // quit on null ptr
   fclose(fptr);
   printf("\nFile written.\n");
   }

// rfile()
// reads records from file into array
void rfile(void)
   {
   struct prs *ptrthis;                       // utility list pointer
   FILE *fptr;
                                              // open the file
   if( (fptr=fopen("agents.rec","rb"))==NULL )
      printf("\nCan't open file agents.rec\n");
   ptrfirst = NULL;                          // start with empty list

   while(TRUE)
      {                                       // get memory space
      ptrthis = malloc( sizeof(struct prs) );
      if(ptrthis==NULL)
```

```
                { printf("Allocation error"); return; }
                                       // read record into it
        if( fread(ptrthis, sizeof(struct prs), 1, fptr) != 1 )
            {                          // if no record, EOF
            free(ptrthis);             // free unused block
            fclose(fptr);              // close file
            printf("\nFile read\n");   // we're done
            return;
            }
        ptrthis->ptrnext = ptrfirst;   // points to old first
        ptrfirst = ptrthis;            // this becomes new first
        }
    }
```

Chapter 13—Answers to Questions

1. a and d

2. Declared, `extern`

3. b, c and d

4. False: it causes it to be hidden from other files.

5. c

6. True

7. External static

8. c

9. `enum fish gamefish;`

10. d

11. Names

12. c

13. True

14. Bytes of memory, or number of bytes

15. a

16. True

17. c and d

18. `goto george;`

19. b or c

20. An unlimited number, but only the first 32 are recognized

Chapter 13—Suggested Answers to Exercises

Due to the many small topics discussed in this chapter, there are no exercises.

Chapter 14—Answers to Questions

1. b

2. User interface, data

3. False: it displays messages to the user.

4. b and d

5. minigui.h

6. `make_menus()`

7. b

8. phone.h

9. d

10. Text

Chapter 14—Suggested Answers to Exercises

Because this chapter is a description of an application rather than a tutorial, there are no exercises.

Chapter 15—Answers to Questions

1. 00000001, 11111000, 0001001000110100, 1111110000001010

2. b

3. c

4. combine

5. d, because the sign bit is shifted in on the left

6. test

7. a and b are equivalent, and both are correct.

8. d

9. bytes, character

10. c and d

11. bits, groups of bits

12. a, c, and d

13. a, b, c, and d

14. True

15. speed

16. a

17. False

18. b and c

19. color

20. a

21. 1

22. 8

23. None is correct: a single bit plane can't represent cyan.

24. bit

25. d

Chapter 15—Suggested Answers to Exercises

Exercise 1

```
// exortest.c
// demonstrates bitwise EXCLUSIVE OR operator
#include <stdio.h>                    // for printf(), scanf()
void main(void)
   {
   unsigned int x1=0xFF, x2=0xFF;

   while( x1 !=0 ¦¦ x2 != 0 )    // terminate on 0 0
      {
      printf("\nEnter two hex numbers (ff or less): ");
      scanf("%x %x", &x1, &x2);
      printf("%02x ^ %02x = %02x\n", x1, x2, x1 ^ x2 );
      }
   }
```

Exercise 2

```
// bintohex.c
// converts binary number typed by user to hex and decimal
```

```
#include <stdio.h>        // for printf()
#include <conio.h>        // for getche()

void main(void)
   {
   int count, ans=1;
   char ch;

   while( ans != 0 )       // terminate on 0
      {
      printf("Enter binary number: ");
      count=0; ans=0;
      while( count++ < 16 )
         {
         if( (ch=getche()) == '0' )
            ans <<= 1;
         else if( ch == '1')
            ans = (ans << 1) + 1;
         else if( ch == '\r' )
            break;
         else
            break;
         } // end while count
      printf("\n = %x (hex) = %u (dec)\n\n", ans, ans );
      } // end while ans
   } // end main()
```

Exercise 3

```
// ddraw.c
// moves cursor on screen,leaves trail
// uses direct display memory access
#include <conio.h>                 // for getch()
#define COMAX   80                 // max columns
#define ROMAX   25                 // max rows
#define L_ARRO  75                 // extended codes
#define R_ARRO  77
#define U_ARRO  72
#define D_ARRO   80
#define ACROSS 205                 // graphics characters
#define UPDOWN 186
#define BOX      177
void clear(void);                  // prototype
                                   // pointer to memory
unsigned far *farptr = (unsigned far *)0xB8000000L;

void main(void)
   {
   char ch;                        // keyboard character
   int col=40, row=12;             // screen position

   clear();                        // clear screen
                                   // start with char in center
```

741

```
      *(farptr + COMAX*row + col) = (UPDOWN & 0x00FF) ¦ 0x0700;
      while( (ch=getch()) == 0 )        // quit on any normal char
         {
         switch( getch() )              // read extended code
            {
            case R_ARRO: if(col<COMAX-1) ++col; ch=ACROSS; break;
            case L_ARRO: if(col>0)       --col; ch=ACROSS; break;
            case D_ARRO: if(row<ROMAX-1) ++row; ch=UPDOWN; break;
            case U_ARRO: if(row>0)       --row; ch=UPDOWN; break;
            default: ch=BOX;            // rectangle at corners
            }
         *(farptr + COMAX*row + col) = (ch & 0x00FF) ¦ 0x0700;
         } // end while
   } // end main()

// clear()
// clears screen using direct memory access
void clear(void)
   {
   int j;

   for(j=0; j<2000; j++)               // fill screen memory
      *(farptr + j) = 0x0700;          // with 0's (attr=07)
   }
```

Exercise 4

```
// v8bounce.c
// bouncing ball -- use mode 18 (640x480)
#include <conio.h>                     // for kbhit()
#include <dos.h>                       // for outportb()
#define MAXX 640                       // columns
#define MAXY 480                       // rows
#define PIX  8                         // pixels per byte
#define MAXB (MAXX/PIX)                // bytes in a row
#define CYAN 3
#define BLACK 0


                                       // prototypes
void drawball(int col, int row, unsigned char color);
void putpixel(int x, int y, unsigned char color);
                                       // set ptr to VGA mem
char far *farptr = (char far *)0xA0000000L;

void main(void)
   {
   int x=10, y=10;                     // starting point
   int dx=1, dy=1;                     // increments

   while( kbhit()==0 )                 // cycle until keypress
      {
```

```
        x += dx;  y += dy;              // increment location
        if(x<0 ¦¦ x>MAXX-15)           // if at left or right,
            dx *= -1;                   //    reverse direction
        if(y<0 ¦¦ y>MAXY-15)           // if at top or bottom,
            dy *= -1;                   //    reverse direction
        drawball(x, y, RED);            // draw ball at x, y
        drawball(x, y, BLACK);          // erase ball
        }  // end while
    outportb(0x3CE, 8);            // select bit mask reg
    outportb(0x3CF, 0xFF);         // restore 'all bits' mode
    }  // end main()

// drawball()
// draws ball, radius 16 pixels. Upper-left corner at col, row.
void drawball(int col, int row, unsigned char color)
    {
    unsigned mask;
    unsigned x, y, dotpat;
                                        // picture of ball
    unsigned ball[16] = { 0x07E0, 0x1FF8, 0x3FFC, 0x7FFE,
                          0x7FFE, 0xFFFF, 0xFFFF, 0xFFFF,
                          0xFFFF, 0xFFFF, 0xFFFF, 0x7FFE,
                          0x7FFE, 0x3FFC, 0x1FF8, 0x07E0 };
    for(y=0; y<16; y++)                 // for each of 16 rows
        {
        dotpat = ball[y];               // pattern for this row
        mask = 0x8000;                  // one-bit mask on left
        for(x=0; x<16; x++)             // for each of 16 columns
            {
            if(mask & dotpat)           // if part of pattern
                putpixel(x+col, y+row, color);  // draw the dot
            mask >>= 1;                 // move mask right
            }  // end for x
        }  // end for y
    }  // end drawball()

// putpoint()
// draws pixel on screen at x, y, in specified color
void putpixel(int x, int y, unsigned char color)
    {
    int position;                  // pixel position (0 to 7)
    unsigned char onebit = 0x80;   // 1000,0000 binary
    unsigned addr;                 // offset address
    unsigned char temp;            // for reading into latches

    position = x % 8;              // position of bit in byte
    onebit = onebit >> position;   // make byte with one bit set
    outportb(0x3CE, 8);            // select bit mask reg
    outportb(0x3CF, onebit);       // change one bit only

    addr = y*MAXB + x/PIX;         // calculate address
    temp = *(farptr+addr);         // read byte into latches
```

```
    outportb(0x3C4, 2);              // set color to bright white
    outportb(0x3C5, WHITE);         //   in map mask register
    *(farptr+addr) = 0x00;          // put 0 in every bit
    outportb(0x3C5, color);         //   set color in MMP
    *(farptr+addr) = 0xFF;          // put 1 in every bit
}
```

Index

N

O

Add to Your Sams Library Today with the Best Books for Programming, Operating Systems, and New Technologies

The easiest way to order is to pick up the phone and call
1-800-428-5331
between 9:00 a.m. and 5:00 p.m. EST.
For faster service please have your credit card available.

ISBN	Quantity	Description of Item	Unit Cost	Total Cost
0-672-30326-4		Absolute Beginner's Guide to Networking	$19.95	
0-672-30229-2		Turbo C++ for Windows Programming for Beginners (book/disk)	$39.95	
0-672-30280-2		Turbo C++ Programming 101 (book/disk)	$29.95	
0-672-30080-X		Moving from C to C++	$29.95	
0-672-30363-9		Your Borland C++ Consultant (book/disk)	$29.95	
0-672-30312-4		Mastering Windows Programming with Borland C++ 4.0 (book/disk)	$39.95	
0-672-30287-X		Tom Swan's Code Secrets (book/disk)	$39.95	
0-672-30292-6		Programming Windows Games with Borland C++ (book/disk)	$34.95	
		Shipping and Handling: See information below.		
		TOTAL		

❏ 3 ½" Disk

❏ 5 ¼" Disk

Shipping and Handling: $4.00 for the first book, and $1.75 for each additional book. Floppy disk: add $1.75 for shipping and handling. If you need to have it NOW, we can ship product to you in 24 hours for an additional charge of approximately $18.00, and you will receive your item overnight or in two days. Overseas shipping and handling: add $2.00 per book and $8.00 for up to three disks. Prices subject to change. Call for availability and pricing information on latest editions.

201 West 103rd Street, Indianapolis, IN 46290 USA

1-800-428-5331 — Orders   1-800-835-3202 — FAX   1-800-858-7674 — Customer Service

*The Waite Group's
C Programming
Using Turbo C++,
2nd Edition*

Waite Group Reader Feedback Card

Help Us Make A Better Book

To better serve our readers, we would like your opinion on the contents and quality of this book. Please fill out this card and return it to The Waite Group, 200 Tamal Plaza, Suite 101, Corte Madera, CA, 94925 (415) 924-2575.

Name _____

Company _____

Address _____

City _____

State _____ Zip _____ Phone _____

1. How would you rate the content of this book?

☐ Excellent   ☐ Fair
☐ Very Good   ☐ Below Average
☐ Good   ☐ Poor

2. What were the things you liked *most* about this book?

☐ Pace   ☐ Listings   ☐ Quizzes
☐ Content   ☐ Appendixes   ☐ Size
☐ Writing Style ☐ Design   ☐ Price
☐ Accuracy   ☐ Cover   ☐ Illustrations
☐ Examples   ☐ Index   ☐ Construction

3. Please explain the one thing you liked *most* about this book. _____
_____
_____

4. What were the things you liked *least* about this book?

☐ Pace   ☐ Listings   ☐ Quizzes
☐ Content   ☐ Appendixes   ☐ Size
☐ Writing Style ☐ Design   ☐ Price
☐ Accuracy   ☐ Cover   ☐ Illustrations
☐ Examples   ☐ Index   ☐ Construction

5. Please explain the one thing you liked *leasr* about this book. _____
_____
_____

6. How do you use this book? For work, recreation, look-up, self-training, classroom, etc?
_____
_____
_____

7. What would be a useful follow-up book to *C Programming Using Turbo C++ 2nd Edition* for you?
_____
_____

8. Where did you purchase this particular book?

☐ Book Chain   ☐ Direct
☐ Small Book Store ☐ Book Club
☐ Computer Store   ☐ School Book Store
☐ Other: _____
_____

9. Can you name another similar book you like better than this one, or one that is as good, and tell us why?
_____
_____
_____

10. How many Waite Group books do you own? _____

11. What are your favorite Waite Group books?
_____
_____

12. What topics or specific titles would you like to see The Waite Group develop?
_____
_____
_____

13. What programming languages do you know?
_____

14. Do you own an earlier edition of this book?
_____

15. Any other comments you have about this book or other Waite Group titles?
_____
_____
_____
_____
_____

16. ☐ Check here to receive a free Waite Group catalog.

Fold Here

- -

From:

The Waite Group, Inc.
200 Tamal Plaza, Suite 101
Corte Madera, CA 94925

Staple or tape here   22737

Installing the Companion Disk

The companion disk includes complete source code for the book's programming examples. Follow these steps to install the files to your hard drive:

Before you use the software included with this book, you need to install it to your computers hard drive.

> To install the files, you'll need at least 500K of free space on your hard drive.

1. From a DOS prompt, change to the drive that contains the installation disk. For example, if the disk is in drive B:, press B: and then press the Enter key.

2. Type

   ```
   INSTALL drive
   ```

   (where *drive* is the drive letter of your hard drive) and press the Enter key. For example, if your hard drive is drive C:, type INSTALL C: and press the Enter key.

This installs all the files to a directory called \CPROGRAM on your hard drive. The files are arranged by chapter in subdirectories. For example, you'll find the files for Chapter 16 in \CPROGRAM\CHAP16.